W9-BFC-574

Fundamentals of Software Engineering

Carlo Ghezzi
Politecnico di Milano, Milano, Italy

Mehdi Jazayeri
Hewlett-Packard Laboratories, Palo Alto, California and Pisa, Italy

Dino Mandrioli
Politecnico di Milano, Milano, Italy

PRENTICE HALL, Englewood Cliffs, NJ 07632

Library of Congress Cataloging-in-Publication Data

Ghezzi, Carlo.
    Fundamentals of software engineering / by Carlo Ghezzi, Mehdi
  Jazayeri, Dino Mandrioli.
      p.   cm.
    Includes bibliographical references and index.
    ISBN 0-13-820432-2
    1. Software engineering.   I. Jazayeri, Mehdi. II. Mandrioli,
  Dino. III. Title.
  QA76.758.G47 1991
  005.1--dc20   90-20198
                                                      CIP

Editorial/production supervision: Joe Scordato
Cover design: Bruce Kenselaar
Cover Art: Paolo Uccello (15th Century Florentine)
Manufacturing buyers: Linda Behrens and Patrice Fraccio
Acquisitions Editor: Marcia Horton

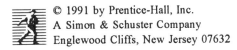

© 1991 by Prentice-Hall, Inc.
A Simon & Schuster Company
Englewood Cliffs, New Jersey 07632

Printed in the United States of America

10 9 8 7 6 5 4 3

ISBN-0-13-820432-2

TRADEMARK INFORMATION

Ada is a registered trademark of the U.S. Government, Ada
    Joint Program Office.

Eiffel is a trademark of Interactive Software Engineering, Inc.

Kee is a registered trademark of IntelliCorp, Inc.

Macintosh, MacDraw, QuickDraw, MacProject are registered
    trademarks of Apple Computer, Inc.

Software Through Pictures is a registered trademark of Interactive
    Development Environments, Inc.

STATEMATE is a registered trademark of i-Logix, Inc.

The teamwork logo, teamwork/SA, teamwork/SD, teamwork/
    ACCESS, teamwork/RT are registered trademarks; teamwork/
    IM, teamwork/ADA are trademarks of Cadre Technologies, Inc.

UNIX is a registered trademark of AT&T (Bell Laboratories).

X Window System is a trademark of the Massachusetts
    Institute of Technology.

Prentice-Hall International (UK) Limited, *London*
Prentice-Hall of Australia Pty. Limited, *Sydney*
Prentice-Hall Canada Inc., *Toronto*
Prentice-Hall Hispanoamericana, S.A., *Mexico*
Prentice-Hall of India Private Limited, *New Delhi*
Prentice-Hall of Japan, Inc., *Tokyo*
Simon & Schuster Asia Pte. Ltd., *Singapore*
Editora Prentice-Hall do Brasil, Ltda., *Rio de Janeiro*

Contents

Contents

We dedicate this book to our children:

Marta, Silvia, and Giacomo;
Darius and Ryan;
Leonardo and Laura;

who have lived cheerfully through the many revisions.

Preface

This is a textbook on **software engineering**. The theme underlying the book is the importance of rigor in the practice of software engineering. Traditional textbooks on the subject are based on the lifecycle model of software development–that is, requirements, specification, design, coding, maintenance–examining each phase in turn. In contrast, our presentation is based on important principles that can be applied independently of the lifecycle model and often in several phases of the lifecycle. Our emphasis is on identifying and applying fundamental principles that are applicable throughout the software lifecycle.

The general characteristics of the book are the following:

* *It deals with software engineering as opposed to programming.* Thus, we do not discuss any programming issues. For example, we omit any discussion of programming language constructs such as **goto**, loops, etc. We believe that the student of software engineering should have prior familiarity with these issues, which are more properly covered in textbooks on programming languages. On the other hand, we do discuss the issue of mapping software design constructs into specific programming languages. We concentrate on intermodule issues and assume as prerequisite the ability to program individual modules.

* *It emphasizes principles and techniques as opposed to specific tools (which may be used in examples).* Many companies are actively developing software engineering tools and environments today and we expect that better and more sophisticated tools will be invented as our knowledge of software engineering increases. Once the student understands the principles and techniques that the tool is based on, mastery of the tool will be easy. The principles and techniques are applicable across tools while mastering the use of any particular tool does not better prepare the student for the use of other tools. Further, use of tools without understanding their underlying principles is dangerous.

* *It presents engineering principles; it is not an engineering handbook.* Principles are general and are likely to remain applicable for many years while particular techniques will change due to technology, increased knowledge, etc. An engineering handbook may be consulted to learn *how* to apply a particular

technique: it contains a set of prescriptions. This book, on the other hand, aims to enable the reader to understand *why* a particular technique should be used and, just as important, why it should *not* be. Even though we do show how a particular technique can be used to implement a given principle, our primary emphasis is on the understanding of the *why* question.

This book embodies our beliefs in the use of fundamental principles and the importance of theory in the practice of engineering. We have used the material in this book in both university and professional courses on various aspects of software engineering.

AUDIENCE

This book is designed to be used as a textbook by students of software engineering either in a classroom or for self-study. Professional engineers and managers will find material here to convince them of the usefulness of modern practices of software engineering and the need to adopt them. It may be used by professionals who are willing to invest the time for serious study; it is not really appropriate for a cursory reading. In particular, wherever necessary, we have sacrificed breadth for depth. For the professional, the notes on further references will be especially helpful. An Instructor's Manual is available with ideas for course organizations and solutions to some of the exercises.

PREREQUISITES

The book is designed for junior, senior, or beginning-graduate level students in computer science. The reader must have had a course in data structures and should be fluent in one or more programming languages. We assume that the reader is already proficient in programming. Analytical reasoning, although not strictly necessary, will greatly enhance the ability of the reader to appreciate the deeper concepts of the book. This skill is developed by mathematics courses such as calculus, discrete mathematics, or–even better–theoretical computer science. "Mathematical maturity" is necessary for the student of any engineering discipline.

ORGANIZATION AND CONTENT

Software engineering is a large, multi-dimensional discipline. Organizing a textbook on the subject poses a challenge because a textbook should present material sequentially, but the many facets of software engineering are so interrelated that there is no optimal sequence of topics. We have organized this textbook based on the view that in software engineering:

- We are building a *product*: the software. ·
- We use a *process* to build that product; and
- We use *tools* in support of that process.

The book thus has three technical sections dealing in turn with the software product (Chapters 4 through 6), the software engineering process and management (Chapters 7 and 8), and the software engineering environment (Chapter 9). Chapters 1 through 3 form a general introduction to the field and the subsequent more technical sections of the book.

In Chapter 2, we discuss the many facets of software and common desirable characteristics for software. These characteristics impose constraints on the software builder and the process to be used. In Chapter 3, we present principles for building high-quality software. By studying principles rather than specific tools, the student gains knowledge that is independent of a particular technology and application environment. Because technology changes and environments evolve, the student should be armed with principles and techniques that can be utilized in different application areas. Chapters 4 through 8 present and discuss techniques for applying the principles of Chapter 3 to, respectively, design, specification, verification, engineering process, and engineering management. In Chapter 9, we discuss the use of computers themselves to help in the building of software. We postpone the discussion of any specific tools to this chapter.

While the material in the first two sections should withstand the passage of time, it is likely that the material in the third section will become outdated (we hope) because newer and better tools are being developed. Since programming languages are a fundamental tool of the software engineer, we use Chapter 9 as a bridge between the design issues of Chapter 4 and specific programming language constructs.

EXERCISES

The book contains many exercises of three types:

- short, paper exercises, aimed at extending the knowledge gained from the book or applying the knowledge more deeply; these exercises are interspersed throughout the chapters.
- longer paper exercises at the end of each chapter, requiring integration of the material in the chapter.
- term-projects requiring the development of some substantial software system by a small team.

Solutions to some of the exercises are provided at the end of each chapter. More exercise solutions are given in the Instructor's Manual.

CASE STUDIES

Several case studies are used in the text to demonstrate the integration of different concepts and to contrast different approaches in realistic situations. In addition, three case studies of real-life software engineering projects and their analyses are presented at the end of the book. These case studies may be read and studied at different times and for different purposes. From these case studies, the new student with little industrial experience can gain a quick view of the diversity of problems faced in industrial practice. The student with some experience perhaps will identify with certain aspects of these case studies and learn from others. The case studies may be read concurrently with the main text. Several exercises in the book refer to these case studies.

LABORATORY COURSE

Many software engineering courses combine lectures and a laboratory project. To do this in a single semester is rather difficult. The teacher will find himself discussing organizational issues while the students are concentrating on their daily forays into debugging. We believe that software engineering must be taught as all other engineering disciplines by first providing the student with a solid foundation in the "theory." Only after this has been achieved will laboratory experience enhance the student's knowledge. This implies that the student project must start closer to the middle of the semester rather than at the beginning. In our view, a better approach is to spend one semester on the theory and a second semester on the laboratory. The Instructor's Manual offers several ideas for organizing a laboratory course based on this text.

READING GRAPH

The book may be read in different sequences and at different levels. Each of Chapters 4 through 7 contains material that may be skipped on the first reading or for a less detailed study. Chapters 1 through 3 are required reading for the subsequent chapters. The following graph shows the dependencies among the chapters and the various paths through the book. The notation nP refers to a partial reading of Chapter n, skipping some sections; nC stands for a complete reading.

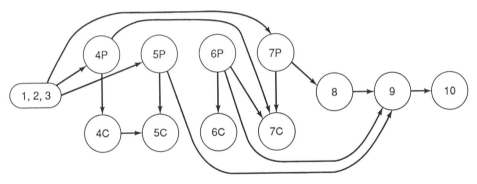

The Instructor's Manual discusses different course organizations based on the book. The conventional one-semester project software engineering course may follow the sequence: 1, 2, 3, 7P, 5P, 4P, 6P, 8, 9, 10. We ourselves prefer the sequence 1, 2, 3, 4P, 5P, 6P, 7P, 8, 9, 10. In either case, the students should start on the project after 5P.

ACKNOWLEDGEMENTS

We gratefully acknowledge reviews of earlier drafts provided by Reda A. Ammar of the University of Connecticut, Larry C. Christensen of Brigham Young University, William F. Decker of the University of Iowa, David A. Gustafson of Kansas State University, Richard A. Kemmerer of the University of California at Santa Barbara, John C. Knight of the University of Virginia, Seymour V. Pollack of Washington University, and K. C. Tai of North Carolina State University.

We would also like to thank the following people who have provided valuable feedback on various drafts of the manuscript: Vincenzo Ambriola, Paola Bertaina, David Jacobson, and Milon Mackey.

Hewlett-Packard Laboratories and Politecnico di Milano made it possible to conceive this book by supporting a course offered by Mehdi Jazayeri at the Politecnico di Milano during the spring of 1988. Alfredo Scarfone and HP Italiana provided us with support in Italy. We would like to acknowledge the support of management at Hewlett-Packard Laboratories, especially John Wilkes, Dick Lampman, Bob Ritchie, and Frank Carrubba in Palo Alto, and Peter Porzer in Pisa. We would like to thank Bart Sears for his help with various systems, and John Wilkes for the use of his data base for managing references. We have also received support from Consiglio Nazionale delle Ricerche.

Milano, Palo Alto, Pisa

Carlo Ghezzi
Mehdi Jazayeri
Dino Mandrioli

Chapter 1

Software Engineering: A Preview

Software engineering is the field of computer science that deals with the building of software systems which are so large or so complex that they are built by a team or teams of engineers. Usually, these software systems exist in multiple versions and are used for many years. During their lifetime, they undergo many changes–to fix defects, to enhance existing features, to add new features, to remove old features, or to be adapted to run in a new environment.

Parnas [1987] has defined software engineering as "multi-person construction of multi-version software." This definition captures the essence of software engineering and highlights the differences between programming and software engineering. A programmer writes a complete program, while a software engineer writes a software component that will be combined with components written by other software engineers to build a system. The component one writes may be modified by others; it may be used by others to build different versions of the system long after one has left the project. Programming is primarily a personal activity, while software engineering is essentially a team activity.

Indeed, the term "software engineering" was invented in the late 1960s after the realization that all the lessons learned about how to program well were not helping to build better software systems. While the field of programming had made tremendous progress–through the systematic study of algorithms and data structures and the invention of "structured programming"–there were still major difficulties in building large software systems. The techniques that were used by a physicist writing a program to calculate the solution to a differential equation for an experiment were not adequate for a programmer working on a team that was trying to build an operating system or even an inventory tracking system. What was needed in these complex cases was the classic engineering approach: define clearly the problem you are trying to solve, and develop standard tools and techniques for solving it.

To be sure, software engineering has made progress since the 1960s. There are standard techniques that are used in the field. But the field is still far from achieving the status of a classic engineering discipline. Many areas remain in the field that are still being taught and practiced on the basis of informal techniques. There are no generally accepted methods even for specifying what a software system should do. In designing an electrical engineering system, such as an amplifier, the system is specified precisely. All parameters and tolerance levels are stated clearly and are understood by the customer and the engineer. In software engineering, we are just beginning to define both what such parameters ought to be for a software system and–an apparently much harder task–how to specify them.

Furthermore, in classic engineering disciplines, the engineer is equipped with tools and the mathematical maturity to specify the properties of the product separately from those of the design. For example, an electrical engineer relies on mathematical equations to verify that a design will not violate power requirements. In software engineering, such mathematical tools are not well developed. The typical software engineer relies much more on experience and judgment rather than mathematical techniques. While experience and judgment are necessary, formal analysis tools are also essential in the practice of engineering.

In this book, we take the view that software engineering must be practiced as an engineering discipline. Our approach is to present certain principles that we believe are essential to the "multi-person construction of multi-version software." It is our view that such principles are much more important than any particular notation or methodology for building software. These principles will enable the software engineer to evaluate various methodologies and apply them when they are appropriate. Chapter 3 presents the principles; the rest of the book can be viewed as setting forth their application to the various problems in software engineering.

In this chapter, we review the evolution of software engineering and its relationship to other disciplines. The goal of the chapter is to place the field of software engineering in perspective.

1.1 THE ROLE OF SOFTWARE ENGINEERING IN SYSTEM DESIGN

A software system is often a component of a much larger system. The software engineering activity is therefore a part of a much larger system design activity in which the requirements of the software are balanced against the requirements of other parts of the system being designed. For example, a telephone switching system consists of computers, telephone lines and cables, telephones, perhaps other hardware such as satellites, and finally, software to control the various other components. It is the combination of all these components that is expected to meet the requirements of the whole system.

A requirement such as "the system must not be down for more than a second in 20 years" or "when a receiver is taken off the hook, a dial tone is played within half a second" can be satisfied with a combination of hardware, software, and special devices. The decision of how best to meet the requirement can only be made by considering many trade-offs. Power plant or traffic monitoring systems, banking systems, and hospital administration systems are other examples of systems that exhibit the need to view the software as a component of a larger system.

To do software engineering right, then, requires a broader look at the general problem of system engineering. It requires the software engineer to be involved when the requirements are being developed initially for the whole system. It requires that the software engineer attempt to understand the application area rather than just what abstract interfaces the software must meet. For example, if the system is aimed at users who are going to use primarily a menu system, it is not wise to develop a sophisticated word processor as a component of the system.

Above all, any engineering discipline requires the application of compromise. A classic compromise concerns the choice of what should be done in software and what should be done in hardware. Software implementation offers flexibility, while hardware implementation offers performance. For example, in Chapter 2, we will see an example of a coin-operated machine that could be built either with several coin slots, one for each type of coin, or a single slot, leaving it to software to recognize the different coins. An even more basic compromise involves the decision as to what should be automated and what should be done manually.

1.2 A HISTORY OF SOFTWARE ENGINEERING

The birth and evolution of software engineering as a discipline within computer science can be traced to the evolving and maturing view of the programming activity. In the early days of computing, the problem of programming was viewed essentially as how to place a sequence of instructions together to get the computer to do something useful. The problems being programmed were quite well understood–for example, how to solve a differential equation. The program was written by, say, a physicist to solve an equation of interest to him or her. The problem was just between the user and the computer–no other person was involved.

As computers became cheaper and more common, more and more people started using them. Higher level languages were invented in the late 1950s to make it easier to communicate with the machine. But still, the activity of getting the computer to do something useful was essentially done by one person who was writing a program for a well-defined task.

It was at this time that "programming" attained the status of a profession: you could ask a *programmer* to write a program for you instead of doing it yourself. This introduced a separation between the user and the computer. Now the user had to specify the task in a form other than the precise programming notation used before. The programmer then interpreted this specification and translated it into a precise set of machine instructions. This, of course, sometimes resulted in the programmer misinterpreting the user's intentions, even in these usually small tasks.

Very few large software projects were being done at this time–the early 1960s–and these were done by computer pioneers who were experts. For example, the CTSS operating system developed at MIT was indeed a large project, but it was done by highly knowledgeable and motivated individuals.

In the middle to late 1960s, truly large software systems were attempted commercially. The best documented of these projects was the OS 360 operating system for the IBM 360 computer family. The large projects were the source of the realization that building large software systems was materially different from building smaller systems. There were fundamental difficulties in scaling up the techniques of small program development to large software development. The term "software engineering" was invented around this time, and conferences were held to discuss the difficulties these projects were facing in delivering the promised products. Large software projects were universally over budget and behind schedule. Another term invented at this time was "software crisis."

It was discovered that the problems in building large software systems were not a matter of putting computer instructions together. Rather, the problems being solved were not well understood, at least not by everyone involved in the project or by any single individual. People on the project had to spend a lot of time communicating with each other rather than writing code. People sometimes even left the project, and this affected not only the work they had been doing but the work of the others who were depending on them. Replacing an individual required an extensive amount of training about the "folklore" of the project requirements and the system design. Any change in the original system requirements seemed to affect many parts of the project, further delaying system delivery. These kinds of problems just did not exist in the early "programming" days and seemed to call for a new approach.

Many solutions were proposed and tried. Some suggested that the solution lay in better management techniques. Others proposed different team organizations. Yet others argued for better languages and tools. Many called for organization-wide standards such as uniform coding conventions. There was no shortage of ideas. The final consensus was that the problem of building software should be approached in the same way that engineers had built other large complex systems such as bridges, refineries, factories, ships, and airplanes. The point was to view the final software system as a complex product and the building of it as an engineering job. The engineering approach required management, organization, tools, theories, methodologies, and techniques. And thus was software engineering born.

The above history emphasizes the growth of software engineering starting from programming. Other technological trends have also played significant roles in the evolution of the field. The most important influence has been that of the change in the balance of hardware and software costs. Whereas the cost of a computerized system used to be determined largely by hardware costs, and software was an insignificant factor, today the software component can account for far more than half of the system cost. The declining cost of hardware and the rising cost of software have tipped the balance further in the direction of software, setting in motion a new economical emphasis in the development of software engineering.

Another evolutionary trend has been internal to the field itself. There has been a growing emphasis on viewing software engineering as dealing with more than just "coding." Instead, the software is viewed as having an entire life cycle, starting from conception and continuing through design, development, deployment, and maintenance and evolution. The shift of emphasis away from coding has sparked the development of methodologies and sophisticated tools to support teams involved in the entire software life cycle.

We can expect the importance of software engineering to continue to grow for several reasons. First is economics: in 1985, around $140 billion were spent annually on software worldwide. It is anticipated that software costs will grow to more than $450 billion worldwide by 1995. This fact alone ensures that software engineering will grow as a discipline. Second, software is permeating our society. More and more, software is used to control critical functions of various machines such as aircrafts and medical devices. This fact ensures the growing interest of society in dependable software, to the extent of legislating specific standards, requirements, and certification procedures. No doubt, it will continue to be important to learn how to build better software better.

1.3 THE ROLE OF THE SOFTWARE ENGINEER

The evolution of the field has defined the role of the software engineer and the required experience and education. A software engineer must of course be a good programmer, be well-versed in data structures and algorithms, and be fluent in one or more programming languages. These are requirements for "programming-in-the-small," roughly defined as building programs that can be written in their entirety by a single individual. But a software engineer is also involved in "programming-in-the-large," which requires more.

The software engineer must be familiar with several design approaches, be able to translate vague requirements and desires into precise specifications, and be able to converse with the user of a system in terms of the application rather than in "computerese.' These in turn require the flexibility and openness to grasp, and become conversant with, the essentials of different application areas. The software engineer needs the ability to move among several levels of abstraction at different stages of the project, from specific application procedures and requirements, to abstractions for the software system, to a specific design for the system, and finally to the detailed coding level.

Modeling is another requirement. The software engineer must be able to build and use a model of the application to guide choices of the many trade-offs that he or she will face. The model is used to answer questions about both the behavior of the system and its performance. Preferably, the model can be used by the engineer as well as the user.

The software engineer is a member of a team and therefore needs communication skills and interpersonal skills. The software engineer also needs the ability to schedule work, both of his or her own and that of others.

As discussed above, a software engineer is responsible for many things. In practice, many organizations divide the responsibilities among several specialists with different titles. For example, an analyst is responsible for deriving the requirements, and a performance analyst is responsible for analyzing the performance, of a system. A rigid fragmentation of roles, however, is often counterproductive.

1.4 THE SOFTWARE LIFE CYCLE

From the inception of an idea for a software system, until it is implemented and delivered to a customer, and even after that, the system undergoes gradual development and evolution. The software is said to have a *life cycle* composed of several phases. Each of these phases results in the development of either a part of the system or something associated with the system, such as a test plan or a user manual. In the traditional life cycle model, called the "waterfall model," each phase has well-defined starting and ending points, with clearly identifiable deliverables to the next phase. In practice, it is rarely so simple.

A sample waterfall life cycle model comprises the following phases:

- **Requirements analysis and specification**. Requirements analysis is usually the first phase of a large-scale software development project. It is undertaken after a *feasibility study* has been performed to define the precise costs and benefits of a software system. The purpose of this phase is to identify and document the exact requirements for the system. Such study may be performed by the customer, the developer, a marketing organization, or any combination of the three. In cases where the requirements are not clear–e.g., for a system that has never been done before–much interaction is required between the user and the developer. The requirements at this stage are in end-user terms. Various software engineering methodologies advocate that this phase must also produce user manuals and system test plans.

- **Design and specification**. Once the requirements for a system have been documented, software engineers design a software system to meet them. This phase is sometimes split into two subphases: *architectural or high-level design* and *detailed design*. High-level design deals with the overall module structure and organization, rather than the details of the modules. The high-level design is refined by designing each module in detail (detailed design).

    Separating the requirements analysis phase from the design phase is an instance of a fundamental "what/how" dichotomy that we encounter quite often in computer science. The general principle involves making a clear distinction between *what* the problem is and *how* to solve the problem. In this case, the requirements phase attempts to specify *what* the problem is. There are usually many ways that the requirements may be met, including some solutions that do not involve the use of computers at all. The purpose of the design phase is to specify a particular software system that will meet the stated requirements. Again, there are usually many ways to build the specified system. In the coding phase, which follows the design phase, a particular system is coded to meet the design specification. We will see many other instances of the what/how dichotomy throughout the book.

- **Coding and module testing**. This is the phase that produces the actual code that will be delivered to the customer as the running system. The other phases of the life cycle may also develop code, such as prototypes, tests, and test drivers, but these are for use by the developer. Individual modules developed in this phase are also tested before being delivered to the next phase.
- **Integration and system testing**. All the modules that have been developed before and tested individually are put together–integrated–in this phase and tested as a whole system.
- **Delivery and maintenance**. Once the system passes all the tests, it is delivered to the customer and enters the maintenance phase. Any modifications made to the system after initial delivery are usually attributed to this phase.

Figure 1.1 gives a graphical view of the software development life cycle, that provides a visual explanation of the term "waterfall" used to denote it. Each phase yields results that "flow" into the next, and the process ideally proceeds in an orderly and linear fashion.

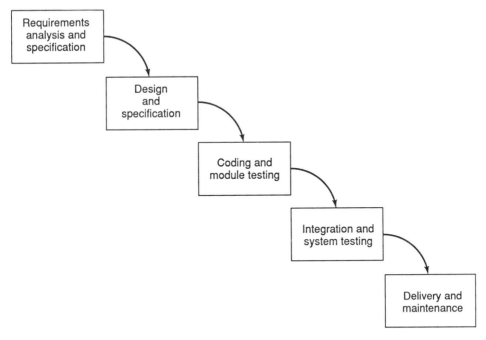

Figure 1.1   The waterfall model of the software life cycle.

A commonly used terminology distinguishes between *high phases* and *low phases* of the software life cycle: the feasibility study, requirements analysis, and high-level design contribute to the former, and implementation-oriented activities contribute to the latter.

As presented here, the phases give a partial, simplified view of the conventional waterfall software life cycle. The process may be decomposed into a different set of phases, with different names, different purposes, and different granularity. Entirely different life cycle schemes may even be proposed, not based on a strictly phased waterfall development. For example, it is clear that if any tests uncover defects in the system, we have to go back at least to the coding phase and perhaps to the design phase to correct some mistakes. In general, any phase may uncover problems in previous phases; this will necessitate going back to the previous phases and redoing some earlier work. For example, if the system design phase uncovers inconsistencies or ambiguities in the system requirements, the requirements analysis phase must be revisited to determine what requirements were really intended.

Another simplification in the above presentation is that it assumes that a phase is completed before the next one begins. In practice, it is often expedient to start a phase before a previous one is finished. This may happen, for example, if some data necessary for the completion of the requirements phase will not be available for some time. Or it might be necessary because the people ready to start the next phase are available and have nothing else to do. We will postpone these and other issues related to the software life cycle until Chapter 7.

Most books on software engineering are organized according to the traditional software life cycle model, each section or chapter being devoted to one phase. Instead, we have organized this book according to principles. Once mastered, these principles can be applied by the software engineer in all phases of software development, and also in life cycle models that are not based on phased development, as discussed above. Indeed, research and experience over the past decade have shown that there is a variety of life cycle models and that no single one is appropriate for all software systems. In Chapter 7, we will examine several different life cycle models.

1.5 THE RELATIONSHIP OF SOFTWARE ENGINEERING TO OTHER AREAS OF COMPUTER SCIENCE

Software engineering has emerged as an important field within computer science. Indeed, there is a synergistic relationship between it and many other areas in computer science: these areas both influence and are influenced by software engineering. In the following subsections, we explore the relationship between software engineering and some of the other important fields of computer science.

1.5.1 Programming Languages

The influence of software engineering on programming languages is rather evident. Programming languages are the central tools used in software development. As a result, they have a profound influence on how well we can achieve our software engineering goals. In turn, these goals influence the development of programming languages.

The most notable example of this influence in recent programming languages is the inclusion of modularity features, such as separate and independent compilation, and the separation of specification from implementation, in order to support team development of large software. The Ada programming language, for example, supports the development of "packages"–allowing the separation of the package interface from its implementation– and libraries of packages that can be used as components in the development of independent software systems. This is a step towards making it possible to build software by choosing from a catalog of available components and combining them, similarly to the way hardware is built.

In the opposite direction, programming languages have also influenced software engineering. One example is the idea that requirements and design should be described precisely, possibly using a language as rigorous and machine-processable as a programming language. As another example, consider the view that the input to a software system can be treated as a program coded in some "programming" language. The commands that a user can type into a system are not just a random collection of characters; rather, they form a language used to communicate with the system. Designing an appropriate input language is a part of designing the system interface.

Most traditional operating systems, such as OS 360, were developed before this view was recognized. As a result, the interface to them–the job control language (JCL)–is generally agreed to be extremely complicated to master. On the other hand, more recent operating systems, such as UNIX, really do provide the user with a programming language interface, thus making them easier to learn and use.

One result of viewing the software system interface as a programming language is that compiler development tools–which are quite well developed–can be used for general software development. For example, we can use grammars to specify the syntax of the interface and parser-generators to verify the consistency and unambiguity of the interface, and automatically generate the front end for the system.

User interfaces are an especially interesting case because we are now seeing an influence in the opposite direction. The software engineering issues revolving around the user interfaces made possible by the widespread use of graphical bit-mapped displays and mice have motivated programming language work in the area of "visual" or "pictorial" languages. These languages attempt to capture the semantics of the windowing and interaction paradigms offered by the new sophisticated graphical display devices.

Yet another influence of the programming language field on software engineering is through the implementation techniques that have been developed over the years for language processing. Perhaps the most important lesson learned has been that formalization leads to automation: stating a formal grammar for a language allows a parser to be produced automatically. This technique is exploited in many software engineering areas for formal specification and automatic software generation.

Another implementation influence is due to the two major approaches to language processing–compilation and interpretation–that have been studied extensively by compiler designers. In general, the interpretive approach offers more run-time flexibility and the compilation approach offers more run-time efficiency. Either is generally applicable to any software system and can therefore become another tool in the software engineer's toolbox. An example of their application outside the programming language area can be seen in the data-base field. The queries posed to a data base may be either compiled or interpreted. Common types of queries are compiled to ensure their fast execution: the exact search path used by the data-base system is determined before any queries are made to the system. On the other hand, since not all types of queries can be predicted by the data-base designer, so-called *ad hoc* queries are also supported, which require the data base to select a search path at run time. The *ad hoc* queries take longer to execute but give the user more flexibility.

1.5.2 Operating Systems

The influence of operating systems on software engineering is quite strong primarily because operating systems were the first really large software systems built, and therefore they were the first instances of software that needed to be engineered. Many of the first software design ideas originated from early attempts at building operating systems.

Virtual machines, levels of abstraction, and separation of policy from mechanism are all concepts developed in the operating system field with general applicability to any large software system. For example, the idea of separating a policy that an operating system wants to impose, such as assuring fairness among jobs, from the mechanism used to accomplish concurrency, such as time slicing, is an instance of separating the "what" from the "how"–or the specification from the implementation–and the changeable parts from what remains fixed in a design. The idea of levels of abstraction is just another approach to modularizing the design of a system.

In the opposite direction, the influence of software engineering on operating systems can be seen in both the way operating systems are structured and the goals they try to satisfy. For example, the UNIX operating system attempts to provide a productive environment for software development. A class of tools provided in this environment supports software configuration management–a way to maintain and control the relationships among the different components and versions of a software system.

Examples of the influence of software engineering techniques on the *structure* of operating systems can be seen in portable operating systems (again, see UNIX) and operating systems that are structured to contain a small "protected" kernel that provides a minimum of functionality for interfacing with the hardware and a "nonprotected" part that provides the majority of the functionality previously associated with operating systems. For example, the nonprotected part may allow the user to control the paging scheme, which has traditionally been viewed as an integral part of the operating system.

Similarly, in early operating systems, the command language interpreter was an integral part of the operating system. Today, it is viewed as just another utility program. This allows, for example, each user to have a personalized version of the interpreter. On many UNIX systems, there are at least three different such interpreters.

1.5.3 Data Bases

Data bases represent another class of large software systems whose development has influenced software engineering through the discovery of new design techniques. Perhaps the most important influence of the data-base field on software engineering is through the notion of "data independence," which is yet another instance of the separation of specification from implementation. The data base allows applications to be written that use data without worrying about the underlying representation of the data. This independence allows the data base to be changed in certain ways–for example, to increase the performance of the system–without any need to change the applications. This is a perfect example of the benefit of abstraction and separation of Separation of concernsconcerns, two key software engineering principles, as we will see in Chapter 3.

Another interesting impact of data-base technology on software engineering is that it allows data-base systems to be used as components of large software systems. Since data bases have solved the many problems associated with the management of concurrent access to large amounts of information by multiple users, there is no need to reinvent these solutions when we are building a software system–we can simply use an existing data-base system as a component.

One interesting influence of software engineering on data-base technology has its roots in early attempts to use data bases to support software development environments. This experience showed that traditional data-base technology was incapable of dealing with the problems posed by software engineering processes. For example, the following requirements are not handled well by traditional data bases: storing large structured objects such as source programs or user manuals; storing large unstructured objects such as object code and executable code; maintaining different versions of the same object; and storing objects, such as a product, with many large structured and unstructured fields, such as source code, object code, and a user manual.

Another difficulty dealt with the length of *transactions*. Traditional data bases support short transactions, such as a bank account deposit or withdrawal. Software engineers, on the other hand, need very long transactions: an engineer may require a long compilation to occur on a multimodule system or may check out a program and work on it for weeks before checking it back in. The problem posed for the data base is how to handle the locking of the code during these weeks. What if the engineer wants to work only on a small part of the program? Are all other access to the program forbidden?

There is presently considerable work going on in the data-base area to address such problems, ranging from introducing new models for data bases to adapting current data-base models.

1.5.4 Artificial Intelligence

Artificial intelligence is another field that has exerted influence on software engineering. The software systems built in the artificial intelligence research community have been among the most complex systems built. But they have been different from other software systems in significant ways. Typically, artificial intelligence systems are built with only a vague notion of how the system is going to work. The term "exploratory development" has been used for the process followed in building these systems.

This process is the opposite of traditional software engineering, in which we go through well-defined steps attempting to produce a complete design before proceeding to coding. These developments have given rise to new techniques in dealing with specifications, verification, and reasoning in the presence of uncertainty. Other techniques advanced by artificial intelligence include the use of logic in both software specifications and programming languages.

The logic orientation seems to be filling the gap between specification and implementation by raising the level of implementation languages higher than before. The logic approach to specification and programming is also called *declarative*. The idea is that we declare the specifications or requirements rather than specifying them procedurally; the declarative description is then executable. Logic programming languages such as PROLOG help us follow this methodology.

Software engineering techniques have been used in newer artificial intelligence systems–for example, in *expert systems*. These systems are modularized, with a clear separation between the facts "known" by the expert system and the rules used by the system for processing the facts–for example, a rule to decide on a course of action. This separation has enabled the building and commercial availability of "expert system shells" that include the rules only. A user can apply the shell to an application of interest by supplying application-specific facts. The idea is that the expertise about the application is provided by the user and the general principles of how to apply expertise to any problem are provided by the shell.

A different kind of symbiosis is currently taking place at the intersection of software engineering and artificial intelligence. Techniques of artificial intelligence are being applied to improve the software engineering tasks. For example, "programming assistants" are being developed to act as consultants to the programmer, watching for common programming idioms or the system requirements. Such "assistants" are also being developed to help in the testing activities of the software development, to debug the software.

The problem of providing interfaces for nonexpert users–for example, through the use of natural language–was first attacked by artificial intelligence. Cognitive models were also used to model the user. These works have influenced the very active area of user-interface design in software engineering.

1.5.5 Theoretical Models

Theoretical computer science has developed a number of models that have become useful tools in software engineering. For example, finite state machines have served both as the basis of techniques for software specifications and as models for software design and structure. Communication protocols and language analyzers are programs that have used finite state machines as their processing model.

Pushdown automata have also been used–for example, for operational specifications of systems and for building processors for such specifications. Interestingly, pushdown automata were themselves motivated by practical attempts to build parsers and compilers for programming languages.

Petri nets, of which we will have much more to say in Chapter 5, are yet another contribution of the theoretical computer science field to software engineering. While Petri nets were initially used to model hardware systems, in recent years they have been applied increasingly in the modeling of software. They are currently the subject of intensive study in many software engineering research organizations.

As another example, denotational semantics–a mathematical theory developed for describing programming language semantics–has been the source of recent developments in the area of specification languages.

Software engineering has also affected theoretical computer science. Algebraic specifications and abstract data type theory are motivated by the needs of software engineering. Also in the area of specifications, software engineering has focused more attention on non-first-order theories of logic, such as temporal logic. Theoreticians used to pay more attention to first-order theories than higher-order theories because the two are equivalent in power but first-order theories are more basic from a mathematical viewpoint. They are not as expressive as higher-order theories, however. A software engineer, unlike a theoretician, is interested both in the power and the expressiveness of a theory. For example, temporal logic provides a more compact and natural style for specifying the requirements of a concurrent system than do first-order theories. The needs of software engineering, therefore, have ignited new interest by theoreticians in such higher-order theories.

1.6 THE RELATIONSHIP OF SOFTWARE ENGINEERING TO OTHER DISCIPLINES

In the foregoing sections, we examined the relationship between software engineering and other fields of computer science. In this section, we explore how software engineering relates to other fields outside of computer science.

Software engineering need not be practiced in a vacuum. There are many problems that are not specific to software engineering and have been solved in other fields. Their solutions can be adapted to software engineering. Thus, there is no need to reinvent every solution. For example, the fields of psychology and industrial design can guide us in the development of better user interfaces.

1.6.1 Management Science

A large part of software engineering is involved with management issues. Such management has two aspects: technical management and personnel management. The generic issues in any kind of project management include project estimation, project scheduling, human resource planning, task decomposition and assignment, and project tracking. The personnel issues involve hiring personnel, motivating people, and assigning the right people to the right tasks.

Management science studies exactly these issues. Many models have been developed that can be applied in software engineering. By looking to management science, we can exploit the results of many decades of study.

In the opposite direction, software engineering has provided management science with a new domain in which to test management theories and models. The traditional management approaches to assembly-line production clearly do not apply to software engineering management, giving rise to a search for more applicable approaches.

1.6.2 Systems Engineering

Systems engineering is the field concerned with studying complex systems. The hypothesis is that certain laws govern the behavior of any complex system composed of many components with complex relationships. Systems engineering is useful when you are interested in concentrating on the system as opposed to the individual components. Systems engineering tries to discover common themes that apply to diverse systems–for example, chemical plants, buildings, and bridges.

Software is often a component of a much larger system. For example, the software in a factory monitoring system or the flight software on an airplane are just components of more complicated systems. Systems engineering techniques can be applied to the study of such systems. We can also consider a software system consisting of thousands of modules as a candidate complex system subject to systems engineering laws.

On the other hand, system engineering has been enriched by expanding its set of analysis models–which were traditionally based on classical mathematics–to include discrete models that have been in use in software engineering.

1.7 CONCLUDING REMARKS

Software engineering is an emerging *engineering* discipline. It is involved with building large software systems by teams of programmers. We have given a history of the evolution of the field, presented its relationship to other fields, and described the requirements of a software engineer. In this book, we will study the principles that are essential to the engineering activity of building software.

BIBLIOGRAPHIC NOTES

The definition of software engineering quoted at the beginning of the chapter is from Parnas [1987]. The distinction between programming in the small and programming in the large–and the recognition that software engineering deals with programming in the large–is due to DeRemer and Kron [1976].

The term "software engineering" was first used in a seminal NATO conference held in Garmisch, Germany, in 1968. A report on the conference appears in a book edited by Naur et al. [1976]. For standard terminology in the field, the reader may refer to the collection of standards published by IEEE [1989]. Boehm [1976] brought to the general attention the field of software engineering and its challenges.

The practical difficulties encountered in developing industrial software products are discussed in Brooks's classic book, on The Mythical Man-Month (Brooks [1975]). Boehm [1981] provides foundations for modeling and evaluating software costs.

The papers by Parnas [1985] and Brooks [1988] contain insightful discussions of the very nature of software and its inherent difficulties. A provocative view is contained in the debate reported in Denning [1989], which contains the text of an address by Dijkstra [1989] and rebuttals by many leading computer scientists.

For a discussion of the relationship between software engineering and programming languages, consult Ghezzi and Jazayeri [1987], which also provides a comprehensive view of programming languages, their concepts, and their evolution.

Much work in operating systems has influenced software design; in particular, we mention the early work of Dijkstra [1968a and b, and 1971]; Hoare [1972, 1974 and

1985]; and Brinch Hansen [1977]. The interaction between operating systems and software engineering is discussed by Browne [1980]. For a modern textbook on operating systems, consult Tanenbaum [1987]; Whiddett [1987] deals with concurrent programming for software engineers.

Data bases are studied by Ullman [1988]. The specific data-base requirements of software engineering are reviewed by Dittrich [1989].

The relationship between software engineering and artificial intelligence is analyzed in several papers and the views are often controversial. For example, Simon [1986] and Tichy [1987] argue that software engineering should inherit methods and tools from artificial intelligence, while Parnas [1988] argues the opposite and provides a critical view of artificial intelligence. Some approaches to knowledge-based software engineering are described by Kant and Barstow [1981], the special issue of *IEEE Transactions on Software Engineering* edited by Mostow (TSE [1985]), Goldberg [1986], and Rich and Waters [1988].

A discussion of the relationship between theoretical computer science models and software development can be found in Mandrioli and Ghezzi [1987].

Spector and Gifford [1986] discuss the relationship between software engineering and another engineering field, bridge design.

Neumann [1989] provides an alarmingly large list of documented risks to the public due to defective software, which raises the fundamental issue of the software engineer's social responsibility.

A thoughtful agenda for software engineering research is reported in the CSTB [1989] report issued by the Computer Science and Technology Board of the National Research Council (U.S.A.).

Other software engineering textbooks are by Conte et al. [1986], Fairley [1985], Lamb [1988], Pressman [1987 and 1988], and Sommerville [1989], where the reader may find complementary approaches and viewpoints to those presented in this book.

Chapter 2

Software: Its Nature And Qualities

The goal of any engineering activity is to build something–a product. The civil engineer builds a bridge, the aerospace engineer builds an airplane, and the electrical engineer builds a circuit. The product of software engineering is a "software system." It is not as tangible as the other products, but it is a product nonetheless. It serves a function.

In some ways software products are similar to other engineering products, and in some ways they are very different. The characteristic that perhaps sets software apart from other engineering products the most is that software is *malleable*. We can modify the product itself–as opposed to its design–rather easily. This makes software quite different from other products such as cars or ovens.

The malleability of software is often misused. While it is certainly possible to modify a bridge or an airplane to satisfy some new need–for example, to make the bridge support more traffic or the airplane carry more cargo–such a modification is not taken lightly and certainly is not attempted without first making a design change and verifying the impact of the change extensively. Software engineers, on the other hand, are often asked to perform such modifications on software. Because of its malleability, we seem to think that changing software is easy. In practice, it is not.

We may be able to change the code easily with a text editor, but meeting the need for which the change was intended is not necessarily done so easily. Indeed, we need to treat software like other engineering products in this regard: a change in software must be viewed as a change in the design rather than in the code, which is just an instance of the product. We can indeed exploit the malleability property, but we need to do it with discipline.

Another characteristic of software is that its creation is human intensive: it requires mostly engineering rather than manufacturing. In most other engineering disciplines, the manufacturing process is considered carefully because it determines the final cost of the product. Also, the process has to be managed closely to ensure that defects are not introduced. The same considerations apply to computer hardware products. For software, on the other hand, "manufacturing" is a trivial process of duplication. The software production process deals with design and implementation, rather than manufacturing. This process has to meet certain criteria to ensure the production of high-quality software.

Any product is expected to fulfill some need and meet some acceptance standards that set forth the qualities it must have. A bridge performs the function of making it easier to travel from one point to another; one of the qualities it is expected to have is that it will not collapse when the first strong wind blows or a convoy of trucks travels across it. In traditional engineering disciplines, the engineer has tools for describing the qualities of the product distinctly from the design of the product. In software engineering, the distinction is not yet so clear. The qualities of the software product are often intermixed in specifications with the qualities of the design.

In this chapter, we examine the qualities that are pertinent to software products and software production processes. These qualities will become our goals in the practice of software engineering. In the next chapter, we will present software engineering principles that can be applied to achieve these goals. The presence of any quality will also have to be verified and measured. We will introduce this topic in Section 2.4, and we will study it in Chapter 6.

2.1 CLASSIFICATION OF SOFTWARE QUALITIES

There are many desirable software qualities. Some of these apply both to the product and to the process used to produce the product. The user wants the software product to be reliable, efficient, and easy to use. The producer of the software wants it to be verifiable, maintainable, portable, and extensible. The manager of the software project wants the process of software development to be productive and easy to control.

In this section, we consider two different classifications of software-related qualities: internal versus external and product versus process.

2.1.1 External Versus Internal Qualities

We can divide software qualities into *external* and *internal* qualities. The external qualities are visible to the users of the system; the internal qualities are those that concern the developers of the system. In general, users of the software only care about the external qualities, but it is the internal qualities–which deal largely with the structure of the software–that help developers achieve the external qualities. For example, the internal quality of verifiability is necessary for achieving the external quality of reliability. In many cases, however, the qualities are related closely and the distinction between internal and external is not sharp.

2.1.2 Product And Process Qualities

We use a *process* to produce the software product. We can also attribute some qualities to the process, although process qualities often are closely related to product qualities. For example, if the process requires careful planning of system test data before any design and development of the system starts, product reliability will increase. Some qualities, such as efficiency, apply both to the product and to the process.

It is interesting to examine the word *product* here. It usually refers to what is delivered to the customer. Even though this is an acceptable definition from the customer's perspective, it is not adequate for the developer who requires a general definition of a software product that encompasses not only the object code and the user manual that are delivered to the customer, but also the requirements, design, source code, test data, etc. With such a definition, all of the artifacts that are produced during the process constitute parts of the product. In fact, it is possible to deliver different subsets of the same product to different customers.

For example, a computer manufacturer might sell to a process control company the object code to be installed in the specialized hardware for an embedded application. It might sell the object code and the user's manual to software dealers. It might even sell the design and the source code to software vendors who modify them to build other products. In this case, the developers of the original system see one product, the salespersons in the same company see a set of related products, and the end user and the software vendor see still other, different products.

Configuration management is the part of the software production process that is concerned with maintaining and controlling the relationship between all the related pieces of the various versions of a product. Configuration management tools allow the maintenance of families of products and their components. We will discuss configuration management in Chapter 7.

2.2 REPRESENTATIVE QUALITIES

In this section, we present the most important qualities of software products and processes. Where appropriate, we analyze a quality with respect to the classifications discussed above.

2.2.1 Correctness, Reliability, And Robustness

The terms "correctness," "reliability," and "robustness" are often used interchangeably to characterize a quality of software that implies that the application performs its functions as expected. At other times, the terms are used with different meanings by different people, but the terminology is not standardized. This is quite unfortunate, because these terms deal with important issues. We will try to clarify these issues below, not only because we need a uniform terminology to be used throughout the book, but also because we believe that a clarification of the terminology is needed to better understand and analyze the underlying issues.

2.2.1.1 Correctness

A program is *functionally correct* if it behaves according to the specification of the functions it should provide (called *functional requirements specifications*). It is common simply to use the term "correct" rather than "functionally correct"; similarly, in this context, the term "specifications" implies "functional requirements specifications." We will follow this convention when the context is clear.

The definition of correctness assumes that a specification of the system is available and that it is possible to determine unambiguously whether or not a program meets the specifications. With most current software systems, no such specification exists. If a specification does exist, it is usually written in an informal style using natural language. Such a specification is likely to contain many ambiguities. Regardless of these difficulties with current specifications, however, the definition of correctness is useful. Clearly, correctness is a desirable property for software systems.

Correctness is a mathematical property that establishes the equivalence between the software and its specification. Obviously, we can be more systematic and precise in assessing correctness depending on how rigorous we are in specifying functional requirements. As we will see in Chapter 6, correctness can be assessed through a variety of methods, some stressing an experimental approach (e.g., testing), others stressing an analytic approach (e.g., formal verification of correctness). Correctness can also be enhanced by using appropriate tools such as high-level languages, particularly those supporting extensive static analysis. Likewise, it can be improved by using standard algorithms or using libraries of standard modules, rather than inventing new ones.

2.2.1.2 Reliability

Informally, software is reliable if the user can depend on it.[1] The specialized literature on software reliability defines reliability in terms of statistical behavior–the probability that the software will operate as expected over a specified time interval; we will discuss this approach in Section 6.7.2. For the purpose of this chapter, however, the informal definition is sufficient.

Correctness is an absolute quality: any deviation from the requirements makes the system incorrect, regardless of how minor or serious is the consequence of the deviation. The notion of reliability is, on the other hand, relative: if the consequence of a software error is not serious, the incorrect software may still be reliable.

Engineering products are *expected* to be reliable. Unreliable products, in general, disappear quickly from the marketplace. Unfortunately, software products have not achieved this enviable status yet. Software products are commonly released along with a list of "Known Bugs." Users of software take it for granted that "Release 1" of a product is "buggy." This is one of the most striking symptoms of the immaturity of the software engineering field as an engineering discipline.[2]

In classic engineering disciplines, a product is not released if it has "bugs." You do not expect to take delivery of an automobile along with a list of shortcomings or a bridge

---

[1] "Dependable" is a term used as a synonym for "reliable."

[2] Dijkstra [1989] claims that even the sloppy term "bug," which is often used by software engineers, is a symptom of unprofessionalism.

with a warning not to use the railing. Design errors are extremely rare and worthy of news headlines. A bridge that collapses may even cause the designers to be prosecuted in court.

On the contrary, software design errors are generally treated as unavoidable. Far from being surprised with the occurrence of software errors, we *expect* them. Whereas with all other products the customer receives a guarantee of reliability, with software we get a disclaimer that the software manufacturer is not responsible for any damages due to product errors. Software engineering can truly be called an engineering discipline only when we can achieve software reliability comparable to the reliability of other products.

Figure 2.1 illustrates the relationship between reliability and correctness, under the assumption that the functional requirements specification indeed captures all the desirable properties of the application and that no undesirable properties are erroneously specified in it. The figure shows that the set of all reliable programs includes the set of correct programs, but not vice versa. Unfortunately, things are different in practice. In fact, the specification is a model of what the user wants, but the model may or may not be an accurate statement of the user's needs and actual requirements. All the software can do is meet the specified requirements of the model–it cannot assure the accuracy of the model.

Thus, Figure 2.1 represents an idealized situation where the requirements are themselves assumed to be correct, i.e., they are a faithful representation of what the implementation must ensure in order to satisfy the needs of the expected users. As we will discuss thoroughly in Chapter 7, there are often insurmountable obstacles to achieving this goal. The upshot is that we sometimes have correct applications that are designed for "incorrect" requirements, so that correctness of the software may not be sufficient to guarantee the user that the software behaves "as expected." This situations is discussed in the next subsection.

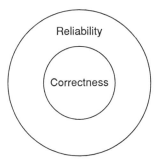

Figure 2.1   Relationship between correctness and reliability in the ideal case.

2.2.1.3 Robustness

A program is robust if it behaves "reasonably," even in circumstances that were not anticipated in the requirements specification–for example, when it encounters incorrect input data or some hardware malfunction (say, a disk crash). A program that assumes perfect input and generates an unrecoverable run-time error as soon as the user inadvertently types an incorrect command would not be robust. It might be correct, though, if the requirements specification does not state what the action should be upon entry of an incorrect command. Obviously, robustness is a difficult-to-define quality; after all, if we could state precisely what we should do to make an application robust, we would be able to specify its "reasonable" behavior completely. Thus, robustness would become equivalent to correctness (or reliability, in the sense of Figure 2.1).

Again, an analogy with bridges is instructive. Two bridges connecting two sides of the same river are both "correct" if they each satisfy the stated requirements. If, however, during an unexpected, unprecedented, torrential rain, one collapses and the other one does not, we can call the latter more robust than the former. Notice that the lesson learned from the collapse of the bridge will probably lead to more complete requirements for future bridges, establishing the resistance to torrential rains as a correctness requirement. In other words, as the phenomenon under study becomes more and more known, we will approach the ideal case shown in Figure 2.1, where specifications capture exactly the expected requirements.

The amount of code devoted to robustness depends on the application area. For example, a system written to be used by novice computer users must be more prepared to deal with ill-formatted input than an embedded system that receives its input from a sensor–although, if the embedded system is controlling the space shuttle or some life-critical devices, then extra robustness is advisable.

In conclusion, we can see that robustness and correctness are strongly related, without a sharp dividing line between them. If we put a requirement in the specification, its accomplishment becomes an issue of correctness; if we leave it out of the specification, it may become an issue of robustness. The border line between the two qualities is the specification of the system. Finally, reliability comes in because not all incorrect behaviors signify equally serious problems; some incorrect behaviors may actually be tolerated.

Correctness, robustness, and reliability also apply to the software production process. A process is robust, for example, if it can accommodate unanticipated changes in the environment, such as a new release of the operating system or the sudden transfer of half the employees to another location. A process is reliable if it consistently leads to the production of high-quality products. In many engineering disciplines, considerable research is devoted to the discovery of reliable processes.

2.2.2 Performance

Any engineering product is expected to meet a certain level of performance. Unlike other disciplines, in software engineering we often equate performance with efficiency. We will follow this practice here. A software system is efficient if it uses computing resources economically.

Performance is important because it affects the usability of the system. If a software system is too slow, it reduces the productivity of the users, possibly to the point of not meeting their needs. If a software system uses too much disk space, it may be too expensive to run. If a software system uses too much memory, it may affect the other applications that are run on the same system, or it may run slowly while the operating system tries to balance the memory usage of the different applications.

Underlying all of these statements–and also what makes the efficiency issue difficult–are the changing limits of efficiency as technology changes. Our view of what is "too expensive" is constantly changing as advances in technology extend the limits. The computers of today cost orders of magnitude less than computers of a few years ago, yet they provide orders of magnitude more power.

Performance is also important because it affects the scalability of a software system. An algorithm that is quadratic may work on small inputs but not work at all for larger inputs. For example, a compiler that uses a register allocation algorithm whose running time is the square of the number of program variables will run slower and slower as the length of the program being compiled increases.

There are several ways to evaluate the performance of a system. One method is to measure efficiency by analyzing the complexity of algorithms. An extensive theory exists for characterizing the average or worst case behavior of algorithms, in terms of significant resource requirements such as time and space, or–less traditionally–in terms of number of message exchanges (in the case of distributed systems).

Analysis of the complexity of algorithms provides only average or worst case information, rather than specific information, about a particular implementation. For more specific information, we can use techniques of performance evaluation. The three basic approaches to evaluating the performance of a system are *measurement*, *analysis*, and *simulation*. We can measure the actual performance of a system by means of monitors that collect data while the system is working and allow us to discover bottlenecks in the system. Or we can build a model of the product and analyze it. Or, finally, we can even build a model that simulates the product. Analytic models–often based on queuing theory–are usually easier to build but are less accurate while simulation models are more costly to build but are more accurate. We can combine the two techniques as follows: at the start of a large project, an analytic model can provide a general understanding of the performance-critical areas of the product, pointing out areas where more thorough study is required; then we can build simulation models of these particular areas.

In many software development projects, performance is addressed only after the initial version of the product is implemented. It is very difficult–sometimes even impossible–to achieve significant improvements in performance without redesigning the software. Even a simple model, however, is useful for predicting system performance and guiding design choices so as to minimize the need for redesign.

In some complex projects, where the feasibility of the performance requirements is not clear, much effort is devoted to building performance models. Such projects start with a performance model and use it initially to answer feasibility questions and later in making design decisions. These models can help resolve issues such as whether a function should be provided by software or a special-purpose hardware device.

The preceding remarks apply in the large, i.e., when the overall structure is conceived. They often do not apply in the small, where individual programs may first be designed with an eye toward ensuring correctness, and then be locally modified to improve efficiency. For example, inner loops are obvious candidates for efficiency-improving modifications.

The notion of performance also applies to a process, in which case we call it productivity. Productivity is important enough to be treated as an independent quality and is discussed as such in Section 2.2.10.

2.2.3 User Friendliness

A software system is user friendly if its human users find it easy to use. This definition reflects the subjective nature of user friendliness. An application that is used by novice programmers qualifies as user friendly by virtue of different properties than an application that is used by expert programmers. For example, a novice user may appreciate verbose messages, while an experienced user grows to detest and ignore them. Similarly, a nonprogrammer may appreciate the use of menus, while a programmer may be more comfortable with typing a command.

The user interface is an important component of user friendliness. A software system that presents the novice user with a window interface and a mouse is friendlier than one that requires the user to use a set of one-letter commands. On the other hand, an experienced user might prefer a set of commands that minimize the number of keystrokes rather than a fancy window interface through which he has to navigate to get to the command that he knew all along he wanted to execute. We will discuss user interface issues in Chapter 9.

There is more to user friendliness, however, than the user interface. For example, an embedded software system does not have a human user interface. Instead, it interacts with hardware and perhaps other software systems. In this case, the user friendliness is reflected in the ease with which the system can be configured and adapted to the hardware environment.

In general, the user friendliness of a system depends on the consistency of its user and operator interfaces. Clearly, however, the other qualities mentioned above–such as correctness and performance–also affect user friendliness. A software system that produces wrong answers is not friendly, regardless of how fancy its user interface is. Also, a software system that produces answers more slowly than the user requires is not friendly even if the answers are displayed in color.

User friendliness is also discussed under the subject "human factors." Human factors or human engineering plays a major role in many engineering disciplines. For example, automobile manufacturers devote significant effort to deciding the position of the various control knobs on the dashboard. Television manufacturers and microwave oven makers also try to make their products easy to use. User-interface decisions in these classical engineering fields are made, not randomly by engineers, but only after extensive study of user needs and attitudes by specialists in fields such as industrial design or psychology.

Interestingly, ease of use in many of these engineering disciplines is achieved through standardization of the human interface. Once a user knows how to use one television set, he or she can operate almost any other television set.[1] The significant

---

[1]Although the new remote control devices are quite complicated!

current research and development activity in the area of standard user interfaces for software systems will lead to more user-friendly systems in the future.

Exercise

2.1   Discuss the relationship between the human-interface aspects of software and reliability.

2.2.4 Verifiability

A software system is verifiable if its properties can be verified easily. For example, the correctness or the performance of a software system are properties we would be interested in verifying. As we will see in Chapter 6, verification can be performed either by formal analysis methods or through testing. A common technique for improving verifiability is the use of "software monitors," that is, code inserted in the software to monitor various qualities such as performance or correctness.

Modular design, disciplined coding practices, and the use of an appropriate programming language all contribute to verifiability.

Verifiability is usually an internal quality, although it sometimes becomes an external quality also. For example, in many security-critical applications, the customer requires the verifiability of certain properties. The highest level of the security standard for a "trusted computer system" requires the verifiability of the operating system kernel.

2.2.5 Maintainability

The term "software maintenance" is commonly used to refer to the modifications that are made to a software system after its initial release. Maintenance used to be viewed as merely "bug fixing," and it was distressing to discover that so much effort was being spent on fixing defects. Studies have shown, however, that the majority of time spent on maintenance is in fact spent on enhancing the product with features that were not in the original specifications or were stated incorrectly there.

"Maintenance" is indeed not the proper word to use with software. First, as it is used today, the term covers a wide range of activities, all having to do with modifying an existing piece of software in order to make an improvement. A term that perhaps captures the essence of this process better is "software evolution." Second, in other engineering products, such as computer hardware or automobiles or washing machines, "maintenance" refers to the upkeep of the product in response to the gradual deterioration of parts due to extended use of the product. For example, transmissions are oiled and air filters are dusted and periodically changed. To use the word "maintenance" with software gives the wrong connotation because software does not wear out. Unfortunately, however, the term is used so widely that we will continue using it.

There is evidence that maintenance costs exceed 60% of the total costs of software. To analyze the factors that affect such costs, it is customary to divide software maintenance into three categories: *corrective*, *adaptive*, and *perfective* maintenance.

Corrective maintenance has to do with the removal of residual errors present in the product when it is delivered as well as errors introduced into the software during its maintenance. Corrective maintenance accounts for about 20 percent of maintenance costs.

Adaptive and perfective maintenance are the real sources of change in software; they motivate the introduction of evolvability (defined below) as a fundamental software quality and anticipation of change (defined in Chapter 3) as a general principle that should guide the software engineer. Adaptive maintenance accounts for nearly another 20 percent of maintenance costs while over 50 percent is absorbed by perfective maintenance.

Adaptive maintenance involves adjusting the application to changes in the environment, e.g., a new release of the hardware or the operating system or a new data-base system. In other words, in adaptive maintenance the need for software changes cannot be attributed to a feature in the software itself, such as the presence of residual errors or the inability to provide some functionality required by the user. Rather, the software must change because the environment in which it is embedded changes.

Finally, perfective maintenance involves changing the software to improve some of its qualities. Here, changes are due to the need to modify the functions offered by the application, add new functions, improve the performance of the application, make it easier to use, etc. The requests to perform perfective maintenance may come directly from the software engineer, in order to improve the status of the product on the market, or they may come from the customer, to meet some new requirements.

We will view maintainability as two separate qualities: repairability and evolvability. Software is repairable if it allows the fixing of defects; it is evolvable if it allows changes that enable it to satisfy new requirements.

The distinction between repairability and evolvability is not always clear. For example, if the requirements specifications are vague, it may not be clear whether we are fixing a defect or satisfying a new requirement. We will discuss this point further in Chapter 7. In general, however, the distinction between the two qualities is useful.

2.2.5.1 Repairability

A software system is repairable if it allows the correction of its defects with a limited amount of work. In many engineering products, repairability is a major design goal. For example, automobile engines are built with the parts that are most likely to fail as the most accessible. In computer hardware engineering, there is a subspecialty called repairability, availability, and serviceability (RAS).

In other engineering fields, as the cost of a product decreases and the product assumes the status of a commodity, the need for repairability decreases: it is cheaper to replace the whole thing, or at least major parts of it, than to repair it. For example, in early television sets, you could replace a single vacuum tube. Today, a whole board has to be replaced.

In fact, a common technique for achieving repairability in such products is to use standard parts that can be replaced easily. But software parts do not deteriorate. Thus, while the use of standard parts can reduce the cost of software *production*, the concept of replaceable parts does not seem to apply to software repairability. Software is also different in this regard because the cost of software is determined, not by tangible parts, but by human design activity.

Repairability is also affected by the *number* of parts in a product. For example, it is harder to repair a defect in a monolithic automobile body than if the body were made of several regularly shaped parts. In the latter case, we could replace a single part more easily than the whole body. Of course, if the body consisted of too many parts, it would require too many connections among the parts, leading to the probability that the connections themselves might need repair.

An analogous situation applies to software: a software product that consists of well-designed modules is much easier to analyze and repair than a monolithic one. Merely increasing the number of modules, however, does not make a more repairable product. We have to choose the right module structure with the right module interfaces to reduce the need for module interconnections. The right modularization promotes repairability by allowing errors to be confined to few modules, making it easier to locate and remove them. In Chapter 4, we will examine several modularization techniques, including information hiding and abstract data types, in detail.

Repairability can be improved through the use of proper tools. For example, using a high-level language rather than an assembly language leads to better repairability. Also, tools such as debuggers can help in isolating and repairing errors.

A product's repairability affects its reliability. On the other hand, the need for repairability decreases as reliability increases.

2.2.5.2 Evolvability

Like other engineering products, software products are modified over time to provide new functions or to change existing functions. Indeed, the fact that software is so malleable makes modifications extremely easy to apply to an implementation. There is, however, a major difference between software modification and modification of other engineering products. In the case of other engineering products, modifications start at the design level and then proceed to the implementation of the product. For example, if one decides to add a second story to a house, first one must do a feasibility study to check whether this can be done safely. Then one is required to do a design, based on the original design of the house. Then the design must be approved, after assessing that it does not violate the existing regulations. And, finally, the construction of the new part may be commissioned.

In the case of software, unfortunately, people seldom proceed in such an organized fashion. Although the change might be a radical change in the application, too often the implementation is started without doing any feasibility study, let alone a change in the original design. Still worse, after the change is accomplished, the modification is not even documented *a posteriori*; i.e., the specifications are not updated to reflect the change. This makes future changes more and more difficult to apply.

On the other hand, successful software products are quite long lived. Their first release is the beginning of a long lifetime and each successive release is the next step in the evolution of the system. If the software is designed with care, and if each modification is thought out carefully, then it can evolve gracefully.

As the cost of software production and the complexity of applications grow, the evolvability of software assumes more and more importance. One reason for this is the need to leverage the investment made in the software as the hardware technology advances. Some of the earliest large systems developed in the 1960s are today taking advantage of new hardware, device, and network technologies. For example, the American Airlines SABRE reservation system, initially developed in the middle 1960s, is still evolving with new functionality. This is an amazing feat considering the increasing performance demands on the system.

Most software systems start out being evolvable, but after years of evolution they reach a state where any major modification runs the risk of "breaking" existing features. In fact, evolvability is achieved by modularization and successive changes tend to reduce the modularity of the original system. This is even worse if modifications are applied without careful study of the original design and without precise description of changes in both the design and the requirements specification.

Indeed, studies of large software systems show that evolvability decreases with each release of a software product. Each release complicates the structure of the software, so that future modifications become more difficult. To overcome this problem, the initial design of the product, as well as any succeeding changes, must be done with evolvability in mind. Evolvability is one of the most important software qualities, and the principles we present in the next chapter will help achieve it. In Chapter 4, we present special concepts, such as program families, which are intended exactly for the purpose of fostering evolvability.

Evolvability is both a product- and process-related quality. In terms of the latter, the process must be able to accommodate new management and organizational techniques, changes in engineering education, etc.

2.2.6 Reusability

Reusability is akin to evolvability. In product evolution, we modify a product to build a new version of that same product; in product reuse, we use it–perhaps with minor changes–to build another product. Reusability appears to be more applicable to software components than to whole products but it certainly seems possible to build products that are reusable.

A good example of a reusable product is the UNIX shell. The UNIX shell is a command language interpreter; that is, it accepts user commands and executes them. But it is designed to be used both interactively and in "batch." The ability to start a new shell with a file containing a list of shell commands allows us to write programs–scripts–in the shell command language. We can view the program as a new product that uses the shell as a component. By encouraging standard interfaces, the UNIX environment in fact supports the reuse of any of its commands, as well as the shell, in building powerful utilities.

Scientific libraries are the best known reusable components. Several large FORTRAN libraries have existed for many years. Users can buy these and use them to build their own products, without having to reinvent or recode well-known algorithms. Indeed, several companies are devoted to producing just such libraries.

Another successful example of reusable packages is the recent development of windowing systems such as X windows or Motif, for the development of user interfaces. We will discuss these in Chapter 9.

Unfortunately, while reusability is clearly an important tool for reducing software production costs, examples of software reuse in practice are rather rare.

Reusability is difficult to achieve *a posteriori*, therefore, one should strive for reusability when software components are developed. In the next two chapters, we will examine some principles and techniques for achieving reusability. One of the more promising techniques is the use of object-oriented design, which can unify the qualities of evolvability and reusability.

So far, we have discussed reusability in the framework of reusable components, but the concept has broader applicability: it may occur at different levels and may affect both product and process. A simple and widely practiced type of reusability consists of the reuse of people, i.e., reusing their specific knowledge of an application domain, of a development or target environment, and so on. This level of reuse is unsatisfactory, partially due to the turnover of software engineers: knowledge goes away with people and never becomes a permanent asset.

Another level of reuse may occur at the requirements level. When a new application is conceived, we may try to identify parts that are similar to parts used in a previous application. Thus, we may reuse parts of the previous requirements specification instead of developing an entirely new one.

As discussed above, further levels of reuse may occur when the application is designed, or even at the code level. In the latter case, we might be provided with software components that are reused from a previous application. Some software experts claim that in the future new applications will be produced by assembling together a set of ready-made, off-the-shelf components. Software companies will invest in the development of their own catalogues of reusable components so that the knowledge acquired in developing applications will not disappear as people leave, but will progressively accumulate in the catalogues. Other companies will invest their efforts in the production of generalized reusable components to be put on the marketplace for use by other software producers.

Reusability applies to the software process as well. Indeed, the various software methodologies can be viewed as attempts to reuse the same process for building different products. The various life cycle models are also attempts at reusing higher level processes. Another example of reusability in a process is the "replay" approach to software maintenance. In this approach, the entire process is repeated when making a modification. That is, first the requirements are modified, and then the subsequent steps are followed as in the initial product development. More details on this will be given in Chapter 7.

Reusability is a key factor that characterizes the maturity of an industrial field. We see high degrees of reusability in such mature areas as the automobile industry and consumer electronics. For example, in the automobile industry, the engine is often reused from model to model. Moreover, a car is constructed by assembling together many components that are highly standardized and used across many models produced by the same industry. Finally, the manufacturing process is often reused. The low degree of reusability in software is a clear indication that the field must evolve to achieve the status of a well-established engineering discipline.

Exercise

2.2   Discuss how reusability may affect the reliability of products.

2.2.7 Portability

Software is portable if it can run in different environments. The term "environment" can refer to a hardware platform or a software environment such as a particular operating system. With the proliferation of different processors and operating systems, portability has become an important issue for software engineers.

Even within one processor family, portability can be important because of the variations in memory capacity and additional instructions. One way to achieve portability within one machine architecture is to have the software system assume a minimum configuration as far as memory capacity is concerned and use a subset of the machine facilities that are guaranteed to be available on all models of the architecture (such as machine instructions and operating system facilities). But this penalizes the larger models because, presumably, the system can perform better on these models if it does not make such restrictive assumptions. Accordingly, we need to use techniques that allow the software to determine the capabilities of the hardware and to adapt to them. One good example of this approach is the way that UNIX allows programs to interact with many different terminals without explicit assumptions in the programs about the terminals they are using. The X Windows system extends this capability to allow applications to run on any bit-mapped display.

More generally, portability refers to the ability to run a system on different hardware platforms. As the ratio of money spent on software versus hardware increases, portability gains more importance.

Some software systems are inherently machine specific. For example, an operating system is written to control a specific computer, and a compiler produces code for a specific machine. Even in these cases, however, it is possible to achieve some level of portability. Again, UNIX is an example of an operating system that has been ported to many different hardware systems. Of course, the porting effort requires months of work. Still, we can call the software portable because writing the system from scratch for the new environment would require much more effort than porting it.

For many applications, it is important to be portable across operating systems. Or, looked at another way, the operating system provides portability across hardware platforms.

Exercise

2.3   Discuss portability as a special case of reusability.

2.2.8 Understandability

Some software systems are easier to understand than others. Of course, some tasks are inherently more complex than others. For example, a system that does weather forecasting, no matter how well it is written, will be harder to understand than one that prints a mailing list. Given tasks of inherently similar difficulty, we can follow certain guidelines to produce more understandable designs and to write more understandable programs.

Understandability is an internal product quality, and it helps in achieving many of the other qualities such as evolvability and verifiability. From an external point of view, the user considers the system understandable if it has predictable behavior. External understandability is a component of user friendliness.

2.2.9 Interoperability

Interoperability refers to the ability of a system to coexist and cooperate with other systems–for example, a word-processor's ability to incorporate a chart produced by a graphing package, or the graphics package's ability to graph the data produced by a spreadsheet, or the spreadsheet's ability to process an image scanned by a scanner.

While rare in software products, interoperability abounds in other engineering products. For example, stereo systems from various manufacturers work together and can be connected to television sets and recorders. In fact, stereo systems produced decades ago accommodate new technologies such as compact discs, while virtually every operating system has to be modified–sometimes significantly–before it can work with the new optical disks.

Once again, the UNIX environment, with its standard interfaces, offers a limited example of interoperability within a single environment: UNIX encourages applications to have a simple, standard interface, which allows the output of one application to be used as the input to another.

The UNIX example also illustrates the limitations of interoperability in current systems: the UNIX standard interface is a primitive, character-oriented one. It is not easy for one application to use structured data–say, a spreadsheet or an image–produced by another application. Also, the UNIX system itself cannot operate in conjunction with other operating systems.

Another example of the limitations of interoperability in current software is illustrated by most personal computer software.[1] Many vendors produce "integrated" products, meaning products that include several different functions. With better interoperability, the vendor could produce different products and allow the user to combine them if necessary. This would make it easier for the vendor to produce the products, and it would give the user more freedom in exactly what functions to pay for and to combine. In fact, in many instances, the vendor of the "integrated product" also has several independent products, each supporting a single function, but these products

---

[1]There are exceptions in the Macintosh environment, where applications are achieving increasingly higher levels of interoperability.

do not work together. Interoperability can be achieved through standardization of interfaces.

A concept related to interoperability is that of an *open system*. An open system is an extensible collection of independently-written applications that cooperate to function as an integrated system. An open system allows the addition of new functionality by independent organizations, after the system is delivered. This can be achieved, for example, by releasing the system together with a specification of its "open" interfaces. Any applications developer can then take advantage of these interfaces. Some of the interfaces may be used for communication between different applications or systems. Open systems allow different applications, written by different organizations, to interoperate.

An interesting requirement of open systems is that new functionality may be added without taking the system down. An open system is analogous to a growing organization that evolves over time, adapting to changes in the environment. The importance of interoperability has sparked a growing interest in open systems, producing some recent standardization efforts in this area.

Exercise

2.4   Discuss the relationship between evolvability and open systems.

2.2.10 Productivity

Productivity is a quality of the software production process; it measures the efficiency of the process and, as we said before, is the performance quality applied to the process. An efficient process results in faster delivery of the product.

Individual engineers produce software at a certain rate, although there are great variations among individuals of different ability. When individuals are part of a team, the productivity of the team is some function of the productivity of the individuals. Very often, the combined productivity is much less than the sum of the parts. Process organizations and techniques are attempts at capitalizing on the individual productivity of team members.

Productivity offers many trade-offs in the choice of a process. For example, a process that requires specialization of individual team members may lead to productivity in producing a certain product, but not in producing a variety of products. Software reuse is a technique that leads to the overall productivity of an organization that is involved in developing many products, but developing reusable modules is harder than developing modules for one's own use, thus reducing the productivity of the group that is developing reusable modules as part of their product development.

While software productivity is of great interest due to the increasing cost of software, it is difficult to measure. Clearly, we need a metric for measuring productivity–or any other quality–if we are to have any hope of comparing different processes in terms of productivity. Early metrics such as the number of lines of code produced have many shortcomings. In Chapter 8, we will discuss metrics for measuring productivity and team organizations for improving productivity. As in other engineering disciplines, we will see that efficiency of the process is affected strongly by automation. Modern software engineering tools and environments lead to increases in productivity. These tools will be discussed in Chapter 9.

Exercise

2.5   Critically evaluate number of lines of code as a productivity measure. (This issue will be analyzed in depth in Chapter 8.)

2.2.11 Timeliness

Timeliness is a process-related quality that refers to the ability to deliver a product on time. Historically, timeliness has been lacking in software production processes, leading to the "software crisis," which in turn led to the need for–and birth of–software engineering itself. Even now, many current processes fail to result in a timely product.

The following (real) example is typical of current (*circa* 1988) industry practice. The first release of an Ada compiler was promised by a computer manufacturer for a certain date. When the date arrived, the customers who had ordered the product received, instead of the product, a letter stating that since the product still contained many defects, the manufacturer had decided that it would be better to delay delivery rather than deliver a product containing defects. The product was promised for three months later.

In four months, the product arrived, along with a letter stating that many, but not all, of the defects had been corrected. But this time, the manufacturer had decided that it was better to let customers receive the Ada compiler, even though it contained several serious defects, so that the customers could start their own product development using Ada. The value of early delivery at this time had outweighed the cost of delivering a defective product, in the opinion of the manufacturer. So, in the end, what was delivered was late *and* defective.

Timeliness by itself is not a useful quality, although being late may sometimes preclude market opportunities. Delivering on time a product that is lacking in other qualities, such as reliability or performance, is pointless.

Timeliness requires careful scheduling, accurate work estimation, and clearly specified and verifiable milestones. All other engineering disciplines use standard project management techniques to achieve timeliness. There are even many computer-supported project management tools.

Standard project management techniques are difficult to apply in software engineering because of the difficulty in measuring the amount of work required for producing a given piece of software, the difficulty in measuring the productivity of engineers–or even having a dependable metric for productivity–and the use of imprecise and unverifiable milestones.

Another reason for the difficulty in achieving timeliness in the software process is continuously changing user requirements. Figure 2.2 plots user requirements against actual system capabilities and can show why most current software developments fail.

(The units of scale are not shown and can be assumed to be nonuniform.) At time t_0, the need for a software system is recognized and development starts with rather incomplete knowledge of the requirements. As a result, the initial product delivered at time t_1 does satisfies neither the initial requirements of time t_0, nor the user's requirements of time t_1. Between time t_1 and time t_3, the product is "maintained," in order to get closer to the user's needs. Eventually, it matches the original user's requirements at time t_2. For the reasons we have seen in Section 2.2.5.2, at time t_3 the cost of maintenance is so high that the software developer decides to do a major redesign. The new release becomes available at time t_4, but the gap with respect to the user's needs at that point is even greater than before.

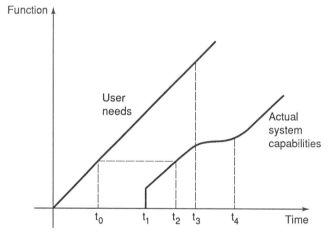

Figure 2.2   Software timeliness shortfall. (From Davis [1988], ©1988 IEEE, reprinted by permission of IEEE.)

One technique for achieving timeliness is through *incremental delivery* of the product. This technique is illustrated in the following–more successful–example of the delivery of an Ada compiler by a different (real) company from the one described before. This company delivered, very early on, a compiler that supported a very small subset of the Ada language–basically, a subset that was equivalent to Pascal with "packages." The compiler did not support any of the novel features of the language, such as tasking and exception handling. The result was the early delivery of a reliable product. As a consequence, the users started experimenting with the new language and the company took more time to understand the subtleties of the new features of Ada. Over several releases, which took a period of two years, a full Ada compiler was delivered.

Incremental delivery allows the product to become available earlier; and the use of the product helps in refining the requirements incrementally. Outside of software engineering, a classic example of the difficulty in dealing with the requirements of complex systems is offered by modern weapons systems. In several well-publicized cases, the weapons have been obsolete by the time they have been delivered, or they have not met the requirements, or, in many cases, both. But after ten years of development, it is difficult to decide what to do with a product that does not meet a requirement stated ten years ago. The problem is exacerbated by the fact that requirements cannot be formulated precisely in these cases because the need is for the most advanced system possible at the time of delivery, not at the time the requirements are defined.

Obviously, incremental delivery depends on the ability to break down the set of required system functions into subsets that can be delivered in increments. If such subsets cannot be defined, no process can make the product available incrementally. But a nonincremental process prevents the production of product subsets even if such subsets can be identified. Timeliness can be achieved by a product that can be broken down into subsets and an incremental process.

Incremental delivery of useless subsets, of course, is not of value. Timeliness must be combined with other software qualities. Chapter 4 will discuss many techniques for achieving product subsets, and Chapter 7 will discuss techniques for achieving incremental processes.

2.2.12 Visibility

A software development process is *visible* if all of its steps and its current status are documented clearly. The term that describes this quality best is the Russian word *glasnost*. Other terms are "transparency" or "openness." The idea is that the steps and the status of the project are available and easily accessible for external examination.

In many software projects, most engineers and even managers are unaware of the exact status of the project. Some may be designing, others coding, and still others testing, all at the same time. This, by itself, is not bad. Yet, if an engineer starts to redesign a major part of the code just before the software is supposed to be delivered for integration testing, the risk of serious problems and delays will be high.

Visibility allows engineers to weigh the impact of their actions and thus guides them in making decisions. It allows the members of the team to work in the same direction, rather than, as is often the case currently, in cross directions. The most common example of the latter situation is, as mentioned above, when the integration test group has been testing a version of the software assuming that the next version will involve fixing defects and will be only minimally different from the current version, while an engineer decides to do a major redesign to correct a minor defect. The tension between one group trying to stabilize the software while another person or group is destabilizing it– unintentionally, of course–is common. The process must encourage a consistent view of the status and current goals among all participants.

Visibility is not only an internal quality; it is also external. During the course of a long project, there are many requests about the status of the project. Sometimes these require formal presentations on the status, and at other times the requests are informal. Sometimes the requests come from the organization's management for future planning, and at other times they come from the outside, perhaps from the customer. If the software development process has low visibility, either these status reports will not be accurate, or they will require a lot of effort to prepare each time.

One of the difficulties of managing large projects is dealing with personnel turnover. In many software projects, critical information about the software requirements and design has the form of "folklore," known only to people who have been with the project either from the beginning or for a sufficiently long time. In such situations, recovering from the loss of a key engineer or adding new engineers to the project is very difficult. In fact, adding new engineers will often reduce the productivity of the whole project while the "folklore" is being transferred slowly from the existing crew of engineers to the new engineers.

The above points out that visibility of the process requires not only that all process steps be documented, but also that the current status of the intermediate products, such as requirements specifications and design specifications, be maintained accurately; that is, visibility of the product is required also. Intuitively, a product is visible if it is clearly structured as a collection of modules, with clearly understandable functions and easily accessible documentation.

2.3 QUALITY REQUIREMENTS IN DIFFERENT APPLICATION AREAS

The qualities we have described above are generic in the sense that they apply to any software system. But software systems are built to automate a particular application and therefore we can characterize a software system based on the requirements of the application area. In this section, we identify four major application areas of software systems and examine their additional requirements. We also show how they stress in different ways, some of the general qualities that we have discussed previously.

2.3.1 Information Systems

One of the largest and fastest growing application areas for computers is in the storage and retrieval of data. We call this class of systems "information-based systems" or simply "information systems" because the primary purpose of the system is managing information. Examples of information systems are banking systems, library-cataloguing systems, and personnel systems. At the heart of such systems is a *data base* against which we apply *transactions* to create, retrieve, update, or delete items.

Information systems have gained in importance because of the increasing value of information as a resource. The data that these systems manage is often the most valuable resource of an enterprise. Such data concern both the processes and the resources internal to the enterprise–plants, goods, people, etc.–and also information on external sources– competitors, suppliers, clients, etc. Increasingly, corporations are computerizing their manual procedures and trusting their data to computers. Their goal is to make their procedures more efficient and their data available on-line.

Information systems are data oriented and can be characterized on the basis of the way they treat data. Some of the qualities that characterize information systems are the following:

- **Data integrity.** Under what circumstances will the data be corrupted when the system malfunctions?
- **Security.** To what extent does the system protect the data from unauthorized access?

- **Data availability.** Under what conditions will the data become unavailable and for how long?
- **Transaction performance.** Because the goal of information systems is to support transactions against the information, the performance of such systems can be uniformly characterized in terms of the number of transactions carried out per unit time.

Another important characteristic of information systems is the need for providing interaction with end users who have little or no technical background, e.g., sales clerks, administrative staff, and managers. Thus, human-computer interaction requirements, such as user friendliness, are of prime relevance in this case. In particular, this requires that interaction with the application should take place via menus. Menus should be designed uniformly, and navigation among the different functions provided by the application should be easy. Users should never get the feeling of being lost; they should always be in control of the interaction with the application, and the application should guard against possible misuse by the users.

Modern information systems go further in this direction. Not only do they support easy access by the user, but also they encourage active user involvement in the creation of simple applications. Instead of relying on software specialists for providing *ad hoc* programs for, say, getting new kinds of reports from the data base, or querying the data base in an unforeseen manner, the end user may use facilities provided by the information system to solve such simple kinds of problems on his or her own. This feature is often called *end-user computing*.

2.3.2 Real-Time Systems

Quite apart from information systems is another large class of software systems called real-time systems. The primary characteristic of these systems is that they must respond to events within a predefined and strict time period. For example, in a factory-monitoring system, the software needs to respond to a sudden increase in temperature by immediately setting certain switches or sounding an alarm. Or a missile guidance system constantly needs to monitor the environmental conditions and current position of the missile and correct the trajectory accordingly.

While the real-time classification is usually used to refer to factory automation, surveillance systems, etc., real-time requirements can be found in many more traditional settings. An unusual but interesting example is the mouse-handling software in a computer system that needs to respond to mouse click interrupts within a certain time period. For example, in some systems, a single mouse click is a command to select an object while a double-click, if the two clicks are sufficiently close in time, is a (different) command to "open" the object. This kind of interface establishes a real-time requirement on the software because the software must process the first click quickly enough so that it can accept the second interrupt and determine whether the user initiated a double-click or two successive single-clicks.

There is a common misconception regarding real-time systems that says that a real-time system is one that requires "fast response times." This is neither true nor sufficiently precise. "Fast" is a qualitative property of an application; what is required for a real-time system is a quantitatively specifiable and verifiable notion of response time. Also, in some real-time systems, a response that comes too early may be as incorrect as a response that comes too late. In the previous mouse-click example, if the first click is processed "too fast," the double-click may not be detected correctly.

Real-time systems have been studied extensively in their own right. We can call information systems data oriented, and real-time systems control oriented. At the heart of real-time systems is a "scheduler" that orders or "schedules" the actions of the system. There are two basic types of scheduling algorithms used: deadline and priority. In priority scheduling, each action has an associated priority. The action with the highest priority is the one executed next. In deadline scheduling, each action has a specified time by which it must be started or completed. It is the responsibility of the scheduler to ensure that actions are scheduled in such a way as to satisfy the scheduling requirements.

In addition to the generic software qualities, real-time systems are characterized by how well they satisfy the response time requirements. Whereas in other systems response time is a matter of performance, in real-time systems response time is one of the correctness criteria. Furthermore, real-time systems are usually used for critical operations (such as patient monitoring, defense systems, and process control) and have very strict reliability requirements.[1]

In the case of highly critical systems, the term *safety* is often used to denote the absence of undesirable behaviors that can cause system hazards. Safety deals with requirements other than the primary mission of a system and requires that the system execute without causing unacceptable risk. Unlike functional requirements, which describe the intended correct behavior in terms of input-output relationships, safety requirements describe what should never happen while the system is executing. In some sense, they are negative requirements: they specify the states the system must never enter.

Finally, other software qualities may be important in the case of real-time systems also. We have shown that human-computer aspects are relevant in the case of information systems. They may be most relevant for real-time systems also. For example, the external interface with a control system monitoring a critical industrial plant must be designed in such a way that the operator perfectly understands the state of the system under control, so that he or she can always operate the plant safely.

2.3.3 Distributed Systems

Advances in processor and network technology have made it possible to build so-called distributed systems, which consist of independent or semi-independent computers connected by a communication network. The high-bandwidth, low-error-rate network makes it possible to write distributed software systems, that is, systems with components that run on different computers.

While the generic software qualities apply to distributed software, there are also some new requirements. For example, the software development environment must support the development of software on multiple computers, where users are compiling and perhaps linking on different computers.

---

[1]The term "mission critical" is used to characterize such systems.

Among the characteristics of distributed systems are (1) the amount of distribution supported–for example, is the data distributed, or the processing, or both? (2) whether the system can tolerate the partitioning of the network–for example, when the network link makes it impossible for two subsets of the computers to communicate; and (3) whether the system tolerates the failure of individual computers.

One interesting aspect of distributed systems is that they offer new opportunities for achieving some of the qualities discussed. For example, by replicating the same data on more than one computer, we can increase system reliability. Or by distributing the data on more than one computer, we can increase the performance and the reliability of the system. Of course, replicating or distributing data is not so simple and requires significant design work. There are many established techniques for dealing with these issues. We will see some of these in Chapter 4.

2.3.4 Embedded Systems

Embedded systems are systems in which the software is one of many components and often has no interface to the end user; rather, the software has interfaces with the other system components and probably controls them. Embedded software is now used in airplanes, robots, microwave ovens, dishwashers, refrigerators, automobiles, and other appliances.

What distinguishes embedded software from other kinds of software is that the interface of embedded software is with other devices rather than humans; for example, the software sends speed control data to the motors of a robot instead of displaying such data as a curve on the screen. This removes some requirements from the interface design and allows trade-offs to be made in deciding what the system interface will be like. For example, it is often possible to modify the software interface–thereby complicating the software–in order to simplify the design of a hardware device.

Consider a coin-operated vending machine which accepts different-sized coins. We can either build a hardware device to determine the monetary value of each inserted coin–perhaps even having a different slot for each acceptable kind of coin–or let the hardware decide the weight and dimension of the coin and report them to the software, which will then make the decision about the value of each coin and whether enough money has been inserted. Putting the decision-making capability in software allows a more flexible system because changing the machine to accept newly released coins or to raise the price of dispensed items or to work in a different country will not require the design of a new hardware device, but perhaps will require just the resetting of some internal switches, if the software is designed right.

Although we have discussed the four preceding application areas as distinct, in practice many systems exhibit characteristics that are common to several of these areas. For example, it is easy to imagine an information system that may also have some real-time requirements. Such a system may, of course, be distributed. Furthermore, the system may be embedded in a larger monitoring system. As another example, embedded systems are often real time in nature.

A hospital patient-monitoring system is a good example. It must maintain a data base of patient histories. It can be distributed to allow entry and retrieval of data from nurses' stations or various laboratories. It may have some real-time characteristics–for example, for the monitoring of devices in the emergency room. And finally, it may have some requirements of embedded systems because it may interact with laboratory devices in order to update patient records automatically on the basis of test results.

2.4 MEASUREMENT OF QUALITY

Once we have decided on the qualities that are the goals of software engineering, we need principles and techniques to help us achieve them. We also need to be able to *measure* a given quality.

If we identify a quality as important, it is incumbent upon us to measure it to determine how well we are achieving it. This, in turn, requires that we define each quality precisely so that it is clear what we should be measuring. Without measurements, any claims of improvement are without basis. But without defining a quality precisely, there is no hope that we can measure it precisely–let alone quantitatively.

The established engineering disciplines have standard techniques for measuring quality. For example, the reliability of an amplifier can be measured by determining the range within which it operates. The reliability of a bridge can be measured by the amount of pressure it can withstand. Indeed, these tolerance levels are released with the product as part of the product specification.

Although some software qualities, such as performance, are measured relatively easily, for most qualities, there are unfortunately no universally accepted metrics. For example, whether a given system will evolve more easily than another is usually determined subjectively. Notwithstanding, metrics are needed, and indeed much research work is currently under way for defining objective metrics. In Chapter 6, we will examine this issue in depth.

2.5 CONCLUDING REMARKS

Software engineering is concerned with applying engineering principles to the building of software products. To arrive at a set of engineering principles that apply uniformly to widely differing software products, the first step is to devise a set of qualities that characterize the products. That is what we have done in this chapter. We have presented a set of qualities that determine the merit of any software product. Our next task is to learn what principles to apply so that we can build software products that achieve these qualities. That is the topic of the next chapter.

FURTHER EXERCISES

2.6   In this chapter, we have discussed the software qualities that we consider to be the most important. Some other qualities are testability, integrity, ease of use, ease of operation, and learnability. Define each of these–and possibly other–qualities, giving examples, and relate them to the qualities we have discussed in the chapter.

2.7 Classify each of the qualities discussed in this chapter as internal, external, product or process, giving examples. The classes are not mutually exclusive.

2.8 Show graphically the interdependence of the qualities discused in this chapter: draw a graph where each node represents a software quality and an arrow from node A to node B indicates that quality A contributes toward achieving quality B. What does the graph show you about the relative importance of the software qualities? Are there any cycles in the graph? What does a cycle imply?

2.9 Sometimes, new managers use many of the techniques they used on their most recent project. Using this as an example, discuss the concept of reusability applied to the software process.

2.10 If you are familiar with the ARPA protocols for ftp and telnet, discuss their role in interoperability.

2.11 We have discussed interoperability as a product-related quality. We can also talk about the interoperability of processes. For example, the process followed by a quality assurance organization must be compatible with that followed by the development organization. Another example is offered by a company that contracts with an independent organization to produce the documentation for a product. Use these examples and others of your own to analyze interoperability as applied to a process.

HINTS AND SKETCHY SOLUTIONS

2.1 In some cases, human-interface decisions may affect the reliability of a system. For example, one should ensure that two switches which issue two commands with entirely opposite effects are not placed close to each other, in order to prevent the inadvertent choice of one switch instead of the other.

2.2 As components are more and more reused, they are likely to become more and more reliable, since residual errors are progressively eliminated.

BIBLIOGRAPHIC NOTES

For a discussion of software, its nature, and its characteristics, refer to Boehm [1976], Wegner [1984], Parnas [1985], Freeman [1987a], Brooks [1988]. Weinberg [1971], and Weinberg and Schulman [1974] deal with human aspects of software development.

Different views of the software production process are provided by Boehm [1981], Agresti [1986], Curtis et al. [1988], and Humphrey [1989].

A classification of software qualities is presented by Boehm [1976] and discussed in detail by Boehm et al. [1978]. For each quality, in turn, there is a specialized bibliography. The International Conference on Reliable Software by ACM [1975] had an important role in stimulating research in the area.

Musa et al. [1987] gives an in-depth view of software reliability following a statistical approach. Program correctness is studied by Manna [1980] and Mandrioli and

Ghezzi [1987]. We will return to these issues in Chapter 6. The concept of software safety has been investigated by Leveson [1986]. The concept of security has been formalized by McLean [1990]. The concept of trusted computer systems is illustrated by Ames et al. [1983].

General texts on performance are Ferrari [1978] and Smith [1989]; the classic on computational complexity is Aho et al. [1974]. Practical approaches to writing efficient programs are illustrated by Bentley [1986 and 1988].

For user friendliness and the issue of human-computer interaction, refer to Rubinstein and Hersch [1984], Schneiderman [1987], and the special issue of *IEEE Software* [1989a].

Maintenance and software evolution are extensively studied by Lientz and Swanson [1980], Belady and Lehman [1979], and Lehman and Belady [1985]. The distinction between corrective, adaptive, and perfective maintenance is due to Lientz and Swanson, who also report the figures we gave in this chapter.

Reusability is discussed by Freeman [1987b] and Biggerstaff and Perlis [1989].

Kernighan and Pike [1979] illustrate how the UNIX environment influences interoperability.

Productivity is discussed at length by Boehm [1981] and Capers Jones [1986].

A characterization of real-time systems is given by Wirth [1977] and Stankovic [1988].

The state of the art in software quality metrics is illustrated by Basili [1980] and Conte et al. [1986]; recent advances are illustrated in the special issue of *IEEE Software* [1990b].

Chapter 3

Software Engineering Principles

In this chapter, we discuss some important and general principles that are central to successful software development. These principles deal with both the *process* of software engineering and the final *product*. The right process will help produce the right product, but the desired product will also affect the choice of which process to use. A traditional problem in software engineering has been the emphasis on either the process or the product to the exclusion of the other. Both are important.

The principles we develop are general enough to be applicable throughout the process of software construction and management. Principles, however, are not sufficient to drive software development. In fact, they are general and abstract statements describing desirable properties of software processes and products. But, to apply principles, the software engineer should be equipped with appropriate *methods* and specific *techniques* that help incorporate the desired properties into processes and products.

In principle, we should distinguish between methods and techniques. Methods are general guidelines that govern the execution of some activity; they are rigorous, systematic, and disciplined approaches. Techniques are more technical and mechanical than methods; often, they also have more restricted applicability. In general, however, the difference between the two is not sharp. We will therefore use the two terms interchangeably.

Sometimes, methods and techniques are packaged together to form a *methodology*. The purpose of a methodology is to promote a certain approach to solving a problem by preselecting the methods and techniques to be used. *Tools*, in turn, are developed to support the application of techniques, methods, and methodologies.

Figure 3.1 shows the relationship between principles, methods, methodologies, and tools. Each layer in the figure is based on the layer(s) below it and is more susceptible to change, due to passage of time. This figure shows clearly that principles are the basis of all methods, techniques, methodologies, and tools. The figure can also be used to explain the structure of this book. In this chapter, we present essential software engineering principles. In Chapters 4, 5, and 6, we present methods and techniques based on the principles of this chapter. Chapter 7 presents some methodologies, and Chapter 9 discusses tools and environments.

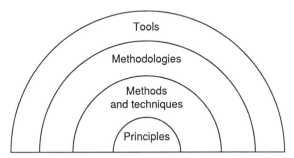

Figure 3.1   Relationship between principles, techniques, methodologies, and tools.

In our discussion of principles, we try to be general enough to cover every type of application. The same applies to the specific methods and techniques we develop in the chapters that follow. The emphasis we place on some principles and the particular methods and techniques we have selected, however, are deliberate choices. Among the qualities that were discussed in the previous chapter, we stress reliability and evolvability; and this choice, in turn, affects the emphasis on principles, methods, and techniques.

As mentioned in Chapter 1, we consider the case where the software to be developed is not just an experiment to be run a few times, maybe only by its own developer. Most likely, its expected users will have little or even no knowledge of computers and software. Or it might be required to support a critical application, where the effects of errors are serious, perhaps even disastrous. For these and other reasons, the application must be reliable.

Also, we assume that the application is sufficiently large and complex that special effort is required to decompose it into manageable parts. This is especially true in the likely case where the project is done by a team. But it is also true in the case of a single software engineer doing the job. In both cases, there is a need for an approach to software development that helps to overcome its complexity.

In all the above circumstances, which represent typical situations in software development, reliability and evolvability play a special role. Clearly, if the software does not have reliability and evolvability requirements, the need for software engineering principles and techniques diminishes greatly. In general, the choice of principles and techniques is determined by the software quality goals.

In this chapter, we discuss seven general and important principles that apply throughout the software development process: rigor and formality, separation of concerns, modularity, abstraction, anticipation of change, generality, and incrementality. The list, by its very nature, cannot be exhaustive, but it does cover the important areas of software engineering. Although often the principles appear to be strongly related, we prefer to describe each of them separately below in quite general terms. They will be taken up in more concrete, detailed, and specific terms in the chapters that follow. In particular, the principle of modularity will be presented in Chapter 4 as the cornerstone of software design.

3.1 RIGOR AND FORMALITY

Software development is a creative activity. There is an inherent tendency in any creative process to be neither precise nor accurate, but rather to follow the inspiration of the moment in an unstructured manner. *Rigor*, on the other hand, is a necessary complement to creativity in every engineering activity: it is only through a rigorous approach that we can produce more reliable products, control their costs, and increase our confidence in their reliability. Rigor does not need to constrain creativity. Rather, it enhances creativity by improving the engineer's confidence in creative results, once they are critically analyzed in the light of a rigorous assessment.

Paradoxically, rigor is an intuitive quality that cannot be defined in a rigorous way. Also, various degrees of rigor can be achieved. The highest degree is what we call *formality*. Thus, formality is a stronger requirement than rigor: it requires the software process to be driven and evaluated by mathematical laws. Of course, formality implies rigor, but the converse is not true: one can be rigorous even in an informal setting.

In every engineering field, the design process proceeds as a sequence of well-defined, precisely stated, and supposedly sound steps. In each step, the engineer follows some method or applies some technique. The methods and techniques applied may be based on some combination of theoretical results derived by some formal modeling of reality, empirical adjustments that take care of phenomena not dealt with by the model, and rules of thumb that depend on past experience. The blend of these factors results in a rigorous and systematic approach–the methodology–that can be easily explained and applied time and again.

There is no need to be always formal during design, but the engineer must know how and when to be formal, should the need arise. For example, the engineer can rely on past experience and rules of thumb to design a short bridge, to be used temporarily to connect the two sides of a creek. She would instead use a mathematical model to verify whether the design is safe if the bridge were a long one that is supposed to stand permanently. She would use a more sophisticated mathematical model if the bridge were exceptionally long, or if it were built in a seismic area. In this case, the mathematical model would consider factors that could be ignored in the previous case.

Another–perhaps striking–example of the interplay between rigor and formality may be observed in mathematics. For example, textbooks on the calculus of functions are rigorous, but seldom formal: proofs of theorems are done in a very careful way, as sequences of intermediate deductions that lead to the final statement, where each deductive step relies on an intuitive justification that should convince the reader of its validity. Almost never, however, is the derivation of a proof stated in a formal way, in terms of mathematical logic. This means that very often the mathematician is satisfied with a rigorous description of the derivation of a proof, without formalizing it completely. In critical cases, however, where the validity of some intermediate deduction is unclear, the mathematician may try to formalize the informal reasoning to assess its validity or falsity.

These examples show that the engineer (and the mathematician) must be able to understand the level of rigor and formality that should be achieved, depending on the conceptual difficulty of the task and its criticality. The level may even vary for different parts of the same system. For example, critical parts may deserve a formal description of their intended functions and a formal approach to their assessment. Well-understood and standard parts would require simpler approaches.

The same happens in the case of software engineering. Chapter 5 will go deeply into this issue in the context of software specifications. We will show that the description of what a program does may be given in a rigorous way by using natural language; it can also be given formally by providing a formal description in a language of logical statements. The advantage of formality over rigor is that formality may be the basis of mechanization of the process. For example, one may hope to use the formal description of the program to create the program (if the program does not yet exist) or to show that the program corresponds to the formal description (if the program and its formal specification exist).

Traditionally, there is only one phase of software development where a formal approach is used: programming. In fact, programs are formal objects: they are written in a language whose syntax and semantics are fully defined. Programs are formal descriptions that may be automatically manipulated by compilers: they are checked for formal correctness, transformed into an equivalent form in another language (assembly or machine language), "pretty-printed" so as to improve their appearance, etc. These mechanical operations, which are made possible by the use of formality in programming, can effectively improve the reliability and verifiability of software products.

Rigor and formality are not restricted to programming: they should be applied throughout the software process. Chapter 4 shows these concepts in action in the case of software design. Chapter 5 describes rigorous and formal approaches to software specification. Chapter 6 does the same for software verification.

So far, our discussion has emphasized the influence of rigor and formality on the reliability and verifiability of software products. Rigor and formality also have beneficial effects on maintainability, reusability, portability, understandability, and interoperability. For example, a rigorous, or even formal, software documentation can improve all of these qualities over informal documentation, which is often ambiguous, inconsistent, and incomplete.

Rigor and formality also apply to software processes. Rigorous documentation of a software process helps in reusing the process in other similar projects. Based on this documentation, managers may foresee the steps through which the new project will evolve, assign appropriate resources as needed, etc. Similarly, rigorous documentation of the software process may help maintain an existing product. If the various steps through which the project evolved are documented, one can modify an existing product starting from the appropriate intermediate level of its derivation, not the final code. More will be said on this crucial point in the following chapters. Finally, if the software process is specified rigorously, managers may monitor it accurately, in order to assess its timeliness and improve productivity.

3.2 SEPARATION OF CONCERNS

Separation of concerns allows us to deal with different individual aspects of a problem, so that we can concentrate on each separately. Separation of concerns is a commonsense practice that we try to follow in our everyday life to master the difficulties we encounter. The principle should be applied also in the case of software development, to master its inherent complexity.

More specifically, there are many decisions that must be made in the development of a software product. Some of them concern features of the product as such: functions to offer, expected reliability, space and time efficiency, relationship with the environment (special hardware or software resources required), user interfaces, etc. Others concern the development process: development environment, team organization and structure, scheduling, control procedures, design strategies, error recovery mechanisms, etc. Still others concern economic and financial matters. These different decisions may be unrelated to one another. In such a case, it is obvious that they should be treated separately.

Very often, however, many decisions are strongly related and interdependent. For instance, a design decision (e.g., swapping some data from main memory to disk) may depend on the size of the memory of the selected target machine (and hence, the cost of the machine), and this, in turn, may affect the policy for error recovery. When different design decisions are strongly interconnected, it is practically impossible to take all the issues into account at the same time or by the same people.

The only way to master the complexity of the project is to separate the different concerns. First of all, one should try to isolate issues that are less intimately related to the others. Also, when issues are taken into account separately, related issues should not be considered in all details, but only insofar as they have an impact on the main issue under consideration.

There are various ways in which concerns may be separated. First of all, one can separate them in *time*. As an everyday life example, consider the case of a university professor who decides to deal with teaching activities by concentrating classes, seminars, office hours, and department meetings from 9 a.m. to 2 p.m. Monday through Thursday and leaving the rest of the time to research, except for Friday, which is devoted to consulting. Such temporal separation of concerns allows for precise planning of activities and eliminates overhead that would arise through switching from one activity to another in an unconstrained way. As we saw in Chapter 1 and will see in more detail in Chapter 7, separation of concerns in terms of time is the underlying motivation of the software life cycle, a rational model of the sequence of activities that should be followed in software production.

Another type of separation of concerns is in terms of *qualities* that should be treated separately. For example, in the case of software, we might wish to deal separately with the efficiency and the correctness of a given program. One might decide first to design software in such a careful and structured way that its correctness is expected to be guaranteed *a priori* and then to restructure the program partially to improve its efficiency. Similarly, in the verification phase, one might first check the functional correctness of the program and then its performance. Both activities can be done rigorously, applying some systematic procedures, or even formally, i.e., using formal correctness proofs and complexity analysis. Verification of program qualities is the subject of Chapter 6.

Another important type of separation of concerns allows different *views* of the software to be analyzed separately. For example, when we analyze the requirements of an application, it may be helpful to concentrate separately on the data that flow from one activity to another in the system and the flow of control that governs the way different activities are synchronized. Both views help us understand the system we are working on better, although neither one gives a complete view of it.

Still another type of separation of concerns allows us to deal with *parts* of the same system separately; here separation is in terms of size. This is a fundamental concept that we need to master to dominate the complexity of software production. It is so important that we prefer to detail it below as a separate point under modularity.

One may suspect that there is an inherent disadvantage in separation of concerns: by separating two or more issues, we might miss some global optimization that would be possible by tackling them together. Often, however, this objection overemphasizes our ability to make "optimized" decisions. By combining concerns, we are likely to make wrong decisions because we are unable to overcome complexity. Instead, the complexity of the global problem can be overcome much better by concentrating on different aspects separately, even at the expense of missing some potential optimizations.

Note that if two issues of one problem are intrinsically intertwined (i.e., the problem is not immediately decomposable into separate issues), it is often possible to make some overall design decisions first and then effectively separate the concern on the different issues. For example, consider a system where on-line transactions access a data base concurrently. In a first implementation of the system, each transaction is supported by the underlying machine by locking the entire data base at the start of the transaction and unlocking it at the end. Suppose now that a preliminary performance analysis shows that some transaction, say t_i (which might print some complex report extracting many data from the data base), takes longer than we can afford to have data base unavailable to other transactions. Thus, the problem is to revise the implementation in order to improve its performance yet maintain the overall correctness of the system. Clearly, the two issues–functional correctness and performance–are strongly related. Thus, a first design decision must concern both of them: t_i is no longer implemented as an atomic transaction, but is split into several subtransactions $t_{i1}, t_{i2}, \ldots, t_{in}$, each being atomic. The new implementation may affect the correctness of the system, because of the interleaving that may occur between execution of any two subtransactions. Now, however, the two concerns of checking the functional correctness and analyzing performance have been separated, and two independent analyses can be made, maybe even by two different designers with different expertise.

As a final remark, notice that separation of concerns may result in separation of responsibilities in dealing with separate issues. Thus, the principle is the basis for dividing the work on a complex problem into specific work assignments, possibly for different people with different skills. For example, by separating managerial and technical issues in the software process, we allow two types of people to cooperate in a software project. As another example, having separated requirements analysis and specification from other activities in a software life cycle, we may hire specialized analysts with expertise in the application domain, instead of relying on internal resources. The analyst, in turn, may concentrate separately on functional and nonfunctional system requirements.

Exercise

3.1   Write a simple program in which you show that you can deal separately with correctness and efficiency.

3.3 MODULARITY

A complex system may be divided into simpler pieces called *modules*. A system that is composed of modules is called *modular*. The main benefit of modularity is that it allows the principle of separation of concerns to be applied in two phases: when dealing with the details of each module in isolation (and ignoring details of other modules) and when dealing with the overall characteristics of all modules and their relationships in order to integrate them into a coherent system. If the two phases are temporally executed in the order mentioned, then we say that the system is designed *bottom up*; the converse denotes *top-down* design.

Modularity is an important property of most engineering processes and products. For example, in the automobile industry, the construction of cars proceeds by assembling building blocks that are designed and built separately. Furthermore, parts are often reused from model to model, perhaps after minor changes. Most industrial processes are essentially modular, made out of work packages that are combined in simple ways (sequentially or overlapping) to achieve the desired result.

Exercise

3.2   Describe the work packages involved in building a house, and show how they are organized sequentially and in parallel.

We will emphasize modularity in the context of software design in the next chapter. Modularity, however, not only is a desirable design principle, but permeates the whole of software production. In particular, there are three goals that modularity tries to achieve in practice: capability of decomposing a complex system, of composing it from existing modules, and of understanding the system in pieces.

The *decomposability* of a system is based on dividing the original problem top down into subproblems and then applying the decomposition to each subproblem recursively. This procedure reflects the well-known Latin motto *divide et impera* (divide and conquer), which describes the philosophy followed by the ancient Romans to dominate other nations: divide and isolate them first and conquer them individually.

The *composability* of a system is based on starting bottom up from elementary components and proceeding to the finished system. As an example, a system for office automation may be designed by assembling together existing hardware components such as personal workstations, a network, and peripherals; systems software such as the operating system; and productivity tools such as document processors, data bases, and spreadsheets. A car is another obvious example of a system that is built by assembling components. Consider first the main subsystems into which a car may be decomposed: the body, the electrical system, the power system, the transmission system, etc. Each of them, in turn, is made out of standard parts; for example, the battery, fuses, cables, etc., form the electrical system. When something goes wrong, defective components may be replaced by new ones.

Ideally, in software production we would like to be able to assemble new applications by taking modules from a library and combining them to form the required product. Such modules should be designed with the express goal of being reusable. By using reusable components, we may speed up both the initial system construction and its fine-tuning. For example, it would be possible to replace a component by another that performs the same function but differs in computational resource requirements.

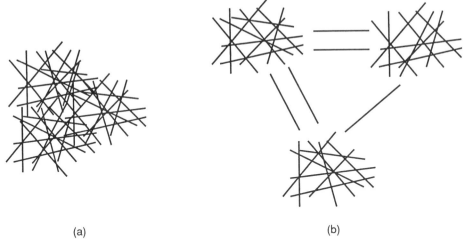

(a)   (b)

Figure 3.2   Graphical description of cohesion and coupling (**a**) A highly coupled structure. (**b**) A structure with high cohesion and low coupling.

The *capability of understanding* each part of a system separately aids in modifying a system. The evolutionary nature of software is such that the software engineer is often required to go back to previous work to modify it. If the entire system can be understood only in its entirety, modifications are likely to be difficult to apply, and the result unreliable. When the need for repair arises, proper modularity helps confine the search for the source of malfunction to single components.

To achieve modular composability, decomposability, and understanding, modules must have *high cohesion* and *low coupling*.

A module has high cohesion if all of its elements are related strongly. Elements of a module (e.g., statements, procedures, and declarations) are grouped together in the same module for a logical reason, not just by chance; they cooperate to achieve a common goal, which is the function of the module.

Whereas cohesion is an internal property of a module, coupling characterizes a module's relationship to other modules. Coupling measures the interdependence of two modules (e.g., module A calls a routine provided by module B or accesses a variable declared by module B). If two modules depend on each other heavily, they have high coupling. Ideally, we would like modules in a system to exhibit low coupling, because if two modules are highly coupled, it will be difficult to analyze, understand, modify, test, or reuse them separately. Figure 3.2 provides a graphical view of cohesion and coupling.

A good example of a system that has high cohesion and low coupling is the electric subsystem of a house. Because it is made out of a set of appliances with clearly definable functions and interconnected by simple wires, the system has low coupling. Because each appliance's internal components are there exactly to provide the service the appliance is supposed to provide, the system has high cohesion.

Modular structures with high cohesion and low coupling allow us to see modules as black boxes when the overall structure of a system is described and then deal with each module separately when the module's functionality is described or analyzed. This is just another example of the principle of separation of concerns.

Exercises

3.3   Suppose you decide to modularize the description of a car by splitting it into small cubes 15 inches on a side. Discuss this modularization in terms of cohesion and coupling. Propose a better way of modularizing the description, if any. Draw general conclusions about how one should modularize a complex system.

3.4   Explain some of the causes of and remedies for low cohesion in a software module.

3.5   Explain some of the causes of and remedies for high coupling between two software modules.

3.4 ABSTRACTION

Abstraction is a process whereby we identify the important aspects of a phenomenon and ignore its details. Thus, abstraction is a special case of separation of concerns wherein we separate the concern of the important aspects from the concern of the unimportant details.

What we abstract away and consider as a detail that may be ignored depends on the purpose of the abstraction. For example, consider a quartz watch. A useful abstraction for the owner is a description of the effects of pushing its various buttons, which allow the watch to enter various functioning modes and react differently to sequences of commands. A useful abstraction for the person in charge of maintaining the watch is a box that can be opened in order to replace the battery. Still other abstractions of the device are useful for understanding the quartz watch and mastering the activities that are needed to repair it (let alone design it). Thus, there may be many different abstractions of the same reality, each providing a *view* of the reality and serving some specific purpose.

Exercise

3.6   Different people interacting with a software application may require different abstractions. Comment briefly on what types of abstractions are useful for the end user, the designer, and the maintainer.

Abstraction is a powerful technique practiced by engineers of all fields for mastering complexity. For example, the representation of an electrical circuit in terms of resistors, capacitors, etc., each characterized by some model in terms of equations, is an idealized abstraction of a device. On the one hand, the equations are a simplified model that approximates the behavior of the real components; on the other, the model we build often ignores details such as the fact that there are no "pure" connectors between components and that these connectors should also be modeled in terms of resistors, capacitors, etc. Both facts can be ignored by the designer because the effects they describe are negligible in terms of the results that we wish to observe.

This example illustrates an important general idea: the models we build of phenomena–such as the equations for describing devices–are an abstraction from reality, ignoring certain facts and concentrating on others that are deemed relevant. The same holds for the models built and analyzed by software engineers. For example, when the requirements for a new application are analyzed and specified, software engineers build a model of the proposed application. As we will see in Chapter 5, this model may be expressed in various forms, depending on the required degree of rigor and formality. No matter what language we use for expressing requirements–be it natural language or the formal language of mathematical formulas–what we provide is a model that abstracts away from a number of details that we decide can be ignored safely.

Abstraction permeates the whole of programming. The programming languages that we use are abstractions built on top of the hardware: they provide us with useful and powerful constructs so that we can write (most) programs ignoring such details as the number of bits that are used to represent numbers or the addressing mechanism. This helps us concentrate on the problem to solve rather than the way to instruct the machine on how to solve it. The programs we write are themselves abstractions. For example, a computerized payroll procedure is an abstraction over the manual procedure it replaces: it provides the essence of the manual procedure, not its exact details.

Abstraction is an important principle that applies to both software products and processes. For example, the comments that appear in the header of a procedure are an abstraction that describes the effect of the procedure. When the documentation of the program is analyzed, such comments are supposed to provide all the information that is needed to understand the other parts of the program that use the procedure.

As an example of the use of abstraction in software processes, consider the case of cost estimation for a new application. One possible way of doing cost estimation consists of identifying some key factors of the new system and extrapolating from the cost profiles of previous similar systems. The key factors used to perform the analysis are abstractions of the system.

Exercises

3.7   Variables appearing in a programming language may be viewed as abstractions of memory locations. What details are abstracted away by programming language variables? What are the advantages of using the abstraction? What are the disadvantages?

3.8   A software life cycle model, such as the waterfall model outlined in Chapter 1, is an abstraction of a software process. Why?

3.5 ANTICIPATION OF CHANGE

Software undergoes changes constantly. As we saw in Chapter 2, changes are due both to the need for repairing the software–eliminating errors that were not detected before releasing the application–and to the need for supporting evolution of the application as new requirements arise or old requirements change. This is why we identified maintainability as a major software quality.

The ability of software to evolve does not come for free–it requires special effort to anticipate how and where the changes are likely to occur. When likely changes are identified, special care must be taken to proceed in a way that will make future changes easy to apply. We will see this important point in action in Chapter 4 in the case of design. We will show how software can be designed such that likely changes that we anticipate in the requirements, or modifications that are planned as part of the design strategy, may be incorporated in the application smoothly and safely. Basically, likely changes should be isolated in specific portions of the software in such a way that changes will be restricted to such small portions.

Anticipation of change is perhaps the one principle that distinguishes software the most from other types of industrial productions. In many cases, a software application is developed while its requirements are not entirely understood. Then, after being released, based on feedback from the user, the application must evolve as new requirements are discovered or old requirements are updated. In addition, applications are often embedded in an environment, such as an organizational structure. The environment is affected by the introduction of the application, and this generates new requirements that were not present initially. Thus, anticipation of changes is a principle that we can use to achieve evolvability.

Reusability is another software quality that is strongly affected by anticipation of change. As we saw, a component is reusable if it is directly usable to produce a new product. More realistically, it might undergo slight changes before it can be reused. As such, reusability may be viewed as low-grain evolvability, i.e., evolvability at the component level. If we can anticipate the changes of context in which a software component might be embedded, we may then design the component in a way that such changes may be accommodated easily.

Anticipation of change requires that appropriate tools be available to manage the various versions and revisions of the software in a controlled manner. It must be possible to store and retrieve documentation, source modules, object modules, etc., from a data base that acts as the central repository of reusable components. Access to the data base must be controlled. A software system must be kept consistent, even when changes are applied to some of its components. As we mentioned in Section 2.1.2–and as we will see again in Chapters 7 and 8–the discipline that studies this class of problems is called *configuration management*.

In our discussion of anticipation of change, we focused attention more on software products than on software processes. Anticipation of change, however, also affects the management of the software process. For example, managers should anticipate the effects of personnel turnover. Also, when the life cycle of an application is designed, it is important to take maintenance into account. Depending on the anticipated changes, managers must estimate costs and design the organizational structure that will support the evolution of the software. Also, managers should decide whether it is worthwhile investing time and effort in the production of reusable components, either as a by-product of a given software development project, or as a parallel development effort.

Exercise

3.9   Take a sorting program from any textbook. Discuss the program from the standpoint of reusability. Would you be able to reuse it if the type of the components changes? What if the sequence of values to sort is so long that it should be stored on secondary storage? How would you modify the program to improve its reusability under these circumstances? Based on this experience, produce a list of general suggestions that would favor anticipation of change in a program.

3.6 GENERALITY

The principle of generality may be stated as follows:

> Every time you are asked to solve a problem, try to focus on the discovery of a more general problem that may be hidden behind the problem at hand. It may happen that the generalized problem is not more complex–it may even be simpler–than the original problem. Being more general, it is likely that the solution to the generalized problem has more potential for being reused. It may even happen that the solution is already provided by some off-the-shelf package. Also, it may happen that by generalizing a problem you end up designing a module that is invoked at more than one point of the application, rather than having several specialized solutions.

On the other hand, a generalized solution may be more costly, in terms of speed of execution, memory requirements, or development time, than the specialized solution that is tailored to the original problem. Thus, it is necessary to evaluate the trade-offs of generality with respect to cost and efficiency, in order to decide whether it is worthwhile to solve the generalized problem instead of the original problem.

For example, suppose you are asked to merge two sorted sequential files into a sorted sequential file. Based on the requirements, you know that the two source files do not contain any records with identical key values. Clearly, if you generalize your solution to accept source files that may contain different elements with the same key value, you provide a program that has higher potential for reusability. Also, you may be able to use a merge program that is available in your system library.

As another example, suppose you are asked to design an application to handle a small library of recipes. Suppose the recipes have a header–containing information such as a name, a list of ingredients, and cooking information–and a textual part describing how to apply the recipes. Apart from storing recipes in the library, it must be possible to do a sophisticated search for recipes based on available ingredients, maximum calories, etc. Rather than designing a new set of facilities, these searches can be viewed as a special case of a more general set of text-processing facilities, such as those provided by the AWK language under UNIX. Before starting with the design of the specialized set of routines, the designer should consider whether the adoption of a generalized text processing tool would be more useful. The generalized tool is undoubtedly more reliable than the specialized program to be designed, and it would probably accommodate changes in the requirements or even new requirements. On the negative side, however, there may be a cost of acquisition, and possibly overhead, in the use of the generalized tool.

Generality is a fundamental principle if our goal as software engineers is to develop general tools or packages for the market. The success of such tools as spreadsheets, data bases, and word processors is that they are general enough to cover the practical needs of most people when they wish to handle their personal business with a computer. Instead of customizing specific solutions for each personal business, it is more economical to choose among the products already available on the market.

Such general-purpose, off-the-shelf products represent a rather general trend in software. For every specific application area, general packages that provide standard solutions to common problems are increasingly available. If the problem at hand may be restated as an instance of a problem solved by a general package, it may be convenient to adopt the package instead of implementing a specialized solution.

This general trend is identical to what happens in other branches of industry. For example, in the early days of automobile technology, it was possible to customize cars according to the specific requirements of the customer. As the field became more industrialized, customers could only choose from a catalogue of models–which correspond to pre-packaged solutions–provided by each manufacturer. Nowadays, it is not possible to ask for a personal car design, unless one is ready to pay an enormous amount of money.

3.7 INCREMENTALITY

Incrementality characterizes a process that proceeds in a stepwise fashion, in increments. The desired goal is reached by successively closer approximations to it. Each approximation is reached by an increment of the previous one.

Incrementality applies to many engineering activities. When applied to software, it means that the desired application is produced as an outcome of an evolutionary process.

One way of applying the incrementality principle consists of identifying useful *early subsets* of an application that may be developed and delivered to customers, in order to get *early feedback*. This allows the application to evolve in a controlled manner in cases where the initial requirements are not stable or fully understood. The motivation for incrementality is that in most practical cases there is no way of getting all the requirements right before an application is developed. Rather, requirements emerge as the application–or parts of it–is available for practical experimentation. Consequently, the sooner we can receive feedback from the customer concerning the usefulness of the application, the easier it is to incorporate the required changes into the product. Thus, incrementality is intertwined with anticipation of change and is one of the cornerstones upon which evolvability may be based.

Incrementality applies to many of the software qualities discussed in Chapter 2. We may progressively add functions to the application being developed, starting from a kernel of functions that would still make the system useful, although incomplete. For example, in some business automation systems, some functions would still be done manually, while others would be done automatically by the application.

We can also add performance in an incremental fashion. That is, the initial version of the application might emphasize user interfaces and reliability more than performance, and successive releases would then improve space and time efficiency.

When an application is developed incrementally, intermediate stages may constitute *prototypes* of the end product; that is, they are just an approximation of it. The idea of rapid prototyping is often advocated as a way of progressively developing an application hand in hand with the understanding of its requirements. Obviously, a software life cycle based on prototyping is rather different from the typical waterfall model described earlier, where we first do a complete requirements analysis and specification and then start developing the application. It is based on a more flexible and iterative development model. This difference will of course have an effect not only on the technical aspects of the projects, but also on organizational and managerial issues. More on this point will be said in Chapter 7.

As we mentioned in connection with anticipation of change, evolutionary software development requires special care in the management of documents, programs, test data, etc., developed for the various versions of software. Each meaningful incremental step must be recorded, documentation must be easily retrieved, changes must be applied in a controlled way, and so on. If this is not done carefully, an intended evolutionary development may quickly turn into undisciplined software development, and all the potential advantages of evolvability would be lost.

Exercise

3.10 Discuss the concept of software prototype illustrated here as opposed to the concept of prototype used by engineers in other industrial branches (e.g., the prototype of a bridge or a car).

3.8 CONCLUDING REMARKS

In this chapter, we have discussed seven important software engineering principles. These principles apply throughout the software development process and during software evolution. Because of their general applicability, we have presented them separately, as the cornerstones of software engineering, rather than in the context of any specific phase of the software life cycle. Another reason for presenting them separately is that the terminology used in software is not standardized, and often the same term is used by different people with a different meaning. Understanding software principles early will allow us to use the relevant terms unambiguously in the rest of the book.

Software engineering principles, as stated here, might seem too abstract. We will make them concrete with more details in the rest of this book in the context of software design, specification, verification, and management. This will be done partly explicitly, by pointing out the relevant principles (where appropriate), and partly implicitly, leaving their recognition to the reader.

We emphasized the role of general principles before presenting specific methods, techniques, and tools. The reason is that software engineering–as any other branch of engineering–must be based on a sound set of principles. Principles, in turn, are the basis for the set of methods used in the discipline and the specific techniques and tools used in everyday life.

As technology evolves, software engineering tools will evolve. Methods and techniques will evolve, too–although less rapidly than tools–as our knowledge of software increases. In this picture, principles will remain more stable; they constitute the foundation upon which all the rest may be built. Also, they are the key that must be used by the reader to interpret the concepts discussed in the rest of this book.

FURTHER EXERCISES

3.11 Suppose you are writing a program that manipulates files. Among the facilities you offer is a command to sort a file in both ascending and descending order. Among the files you manipulate, some are kept automatically sorted by the system. Thus, you might take advantage of that fact: if the file is already sorted, you do not do any action; or you apply a reverse function if the file is sorted in the opposite order. Discuss the pros and cons of using specialized solutions instead of simply calling the sort routine every time the sort command is issued.

3.12 Discuss briefly the relationships between generality and anticipation of change.

3.13 Discuss briefly the relationships between generality and abstraction.

3.14 Discuss the relation between incrementality and timeliness.

3.15 Discuss the principles that may be useful in software development, and show how they relate to the principles discussed here.

HINTS AND SKETCHY SOLUTIONS

3.4 Dividing a long program into contiguous pieces does not necessarily generate a good structure with high cohesion. Grouping together statements that realize some conceptual function gives higher cohesion. (This corresponds to the conventional decomposition of programs into subroutines.) It is even better if we can group together the data and the routines that access the data, because this enhances readability and modifiability.

3.5 Modules that do not interact with each other have minimum coupling, but this also means that they do not "cooperate" in any sense. If one module can access the local variables of another–i.e. if it can directly modify the state of the other module–the coupling is higher than if a module calls a procedure defined in another module.

3.6 The end user is interested only in an abstract description of how to operate the application; all details concerning how the application has been designed and implemented may be (and should be) abstracted away. The designer should know what the requirements are and, when designing a part, should have an abstract view of the rest of the system that allows him or her to have a clear picture of how that part interacts with the rest, but ignoring the details of the rest. When maintaining a system, one should also have an abstract view of the rationale of the design (why certain design decisions were made and why others were discarded). This would allow a system to be modified in a reliable way and without deteriorating its structure.

3.8 We will see in Chapter 7 that the waterfall life cycle is an idealized view of software development. For example, the model of Figure 1.1 ignores the fact that some steps must be repeated as one phase reveals inconsistencies or mistakes in the previous phase.

3.10 This is evolutionary prototyping, whereas in other fields we see more of throwaway prototypes. These terms will be discussed in Chapter 7.

3.14 By delivering an application incrementally, we might deliver a useful subset of the application earlier. That is, we can be early on the market with a product, although it is incomplete.

BIBLIOGRAPHIC NOTES

Several textbooks emphasize formal approaches to programming; among these we mention Alagic and Arbib [1978], Gries [1981], and Mills et al. [1987a]. Landmark contributions to the field are given by Wirth [1971], Dahl et al. [1972], and Dijkstra [1976]. Liskov and Guttag [1986] provide rigorous foundations for programming in the large; the approach they propose is deeply rooted in the concept of data abstraction.

Parnas's work on design methods and specification is the major source of insight into the concepts of separation of concerns, modularity, abstraction, and anticipation of change. All of Parnas's papers referenced in the bibliography help enlighten these fundamental issues. In particular, Parnas [1978] illustrates important software engineering principles.

The concepts of cohesion and coupling are discussed by Yourdon and Constantine [1979] and Myers [1978], which attempts to provide objective measures for the "goodness" of a design.

Anticipation of change, generality, and incrementality are justified by the work of Belady and Lehman [1979], Lehman and Belady [1985], and Lientz and Swanson [1980] on software evolution.

Configuration management is discussed by Babich [1986], Tichy [1989], and later in Chapters 7 and 9. The language AWK is presented by Aho et al. [1988].

Rapid prototyping is discussed by Boehm et al. [1984]; the special issue of *IEEE Computer* edited by Tanik and Yeh (Computer [1989]) contains several papers on the subject.

Chapter 4

Software Design

Once we have determined the need for a software system and we have decided on its desirable qualities, we must proceed to design that system. This chapter starts by discussing the design activity and its fundamental goals. It shows how we can achieve the desired qualities illustrated in Chapter 2; in particular, it emphasizes the need for designing systems that are reliable and evolvable.

The principle of rigor and formality will inspire us to adopt appropriate notations for describing the resulting designs. Separation of concerns, modularity, and abstraction will be applied to tame the complexity of the design activity and produce designs that are characterized by high understandability, to enhance our confidence in the correctness of our solutions. Finally, anticipation of change and incrementality will allow us to design systems that can evolve easily as requirements change, or systems that can be enriched progressively in their functions, starting from a small initial version with only limited functionality. *Design for change* is the motto we adopt from Parnas to stress the principles of anticipation of change and incrementality in the context of design.

We also tackle the problem of designing families of applications. Very often the applications we design are not just individual products, but a family of products that may differ in the functions they offer, the hardware configuration on which they run, the set of services they provide, etc. Despite their differences, there is much in common that can be analyzed and designed once for the whole family. The principles of generality and anticipation of change support the design of program families. In fact, various members of the family may be designed as the results of changes applied to an existing member– that is, by evolving that member.

To achieve high quality of design, two crucial and strictly related issues must be addressed by the software engineer. First, a careful definition of the modular structure of the system must be provided–what the modules are and what are their relationships. These concepts are discussed in Section 4.2.1. Second, appropriate criteria must be chosen for decomposing a system into modules.

The main criterion we introduce in Section 4.2.2 and discuss throughout the book is *information hiding*: a module is characterized by the information it hides from other modules, which are called its clients. The hidden information remains a secret to client modules. Information hiding is further analyzed and specialized to deal with the changeable nature of data, leading to the concept of abstract data types, presented in Section 4.2.4. Further techniques supporting design for change are discussed in Section 4.2.5.

Section 4.2.6 introduces a popular design technique: stepwise refinement. Stepwise refinement produces software designs in a top-down manner, whereas information hiding proceeds mainly bottom up. Design strategies (top down vs. bottom up) are contrasted in Section 4.2.7 from several viewpoints. In discussing all of these design issues, we use a notation to describe designs, introduced in Section 4.2.3. This notation, necessary for stating concepts rigorously, is based on a highly simplified subset of the Ada programming language. Semantic aspects of designs will be described in this chapter by means of informal comments; formal specification of module semantics will be discussed in Chapter 5.

A particular design technique, called object-oriented design, is presented in Section 4.3. Object-oriented design is a technique that pushes the application of the concepts of information hiding and abstract data types to their extreme consequences. Furthermore, object-oriented design organizes software into modular structures that are more elaborate than those provided by more conventional modular structures. These structures are defined with the goal of supporting the production of highly reusable software.

To achieve the goal of reliability, we deal with the problem of designing software that can respond to adverse events and behave in an acceptable manner even when it enters anomalous processing states. A careful design activity must address this robustness requirement, which is extremely important in critical applications. These issues are treated in Section 4.4.

In Section 4.6, we discuss is how concurrency, distribution, and real-time issues affect the design. We do not go very deeply into this subject here for several reasons. First, a discussion of how concurrent components may interact and be synchronized is a specialized topic that deserves a separate treatment. Traditionally, this is studied in the context of courses and textbooks on operating systems, distributed systems, real-time software, etc. Second, the issue is highly related to the specific constructs available in the operating system or the programming language used to implement concurrency. Thus, going deeply into details would require dealing with several different notations. Accordingly, we stick to general concepts and refer to selected concurrency schemes in our discussion, without aiming for completeness. We will address concurrency and real-time issues by extending the concepts and the notations we develop to deal with traditional sequential software.

The principles of good design cannot be taught as a fixed set of rules that can be applied according to a rigid recipe. If they are formulated in abstract terms, they do not provide designers with deep insights and convincing suggestions. Their effectiveness is best communicated through examples. Unfortunately, for reasons of space, it is impossible to illustrate the complete designs of real applications in a textbook. Thus, we illustrate the various design concepts through small practical examples. We do, however, provide a more comprehensive design case study in Section 4.5.

Designs are ultimately mapped onto programs, i.e., the structures and components we identify during the design activity will be represented in terms of constructs of the programming language that we use to implement our software. This mapping of designs onto programs can be done more easily for some languages than for others; in particular, there are languages for which the design techniques we present can lead to programs almost directly. For example, information hiding and the design structures illustrated in this chapter may be easily mapped onto the Ada programming language. As another example, object-oriented languages would be the natural candidates for implementing object-oriented designs. The problem of mapping designs onto programming languages will be delayed to Chapter 9, which deals with tools and environments.

Design is a difficult and critical activity; it is also highly creative. This chapter is about the methods we can use to tame these difficulties, and to guide and discipline creativity. Systems, however, may be complex, requirements may be conflicting, and the general methods to apply are far from precise prescriptions. Unfortunately (or fortunately?), in software design there are no general and easy-to-use recipes that can be adopted once and for all and followed faithfully in all circumstances. Specific prescriptions are applicable only in restricted domains. The designer must be equipped with general principles and methods whose practical application will then depend on the application area and other constraints such as the qualities desired of the product, composition of the development team, and schedules. It is important for the designer to practice applying the principles and methods we present here so that they become second nature to him or her just like the laws of mathematics.

In order to ease the application of good principles and methods, some have been prepackaged into standardized methodologies. There is high demand for such methodologies from industry because they tend to standardize software development by making the application of methods more uniform within an organization. Standardization, in turn, makes it easier to cope with turnover in software development groups. Some of these methodologies are widely adopted in practical software development, although quite often they are just based on common sense and lack truly convincing, general, and rigorous foundations. We briefly account for some of the important methodologies in Chapter 7, which deals with the organization of the software life cycle. In this chapter, we concentrate on general, application-independent design principles that can be used to meet the software quality goals stated in Chapter 2.

4.1 SOFTWARE DESIGN ACTIVITY
AND ITS OBJECTIVES

The design activity is a fundamental phase in the process that progressively transforms the system requirements through a number of intermediate stages into a final product. Its output is a *software design*.[1] We define a software design as a *system decomposition into modules*– description of what each module is intended to do and of the relationship among the modules. Such a description is often called *the software architecture*, or the *software structure*. Thus, the goal of the design activity is the definition of the software architecture.

We can view design as a process in which the architecture is described through steps of increasing detail. Each new step implements the requirements identified in the previous one, the final step being the implementation, which completes the transformation of the software architecture into programs.

The modularity principle is of paramount importance in the design of software; this is why the components of a system identified during the design activity are called, simply, modules. If we look carefully at the literature, however, the concept of module is rather elusive. Sometimes it is used to name a boxlike iconic symbol in a blueprint that is intended to represent a design. In other cases, it is used to denote a well-identified piece of a program, such as a collection of routines. In still other cases, it is used to denote individual work assignments within a complex system. We will clarify our idea of a module in the following sections; for now, we will rely upon an intuitive notion that may encompass all of the foregoing possibilities.

The decomposition of a system into modules can be accomplished in several ways and in several steps. For example, one might first do a decomposition in which the system is decomposed into higher level modules called subsystems. Relations among the subsystems are then defined, and the intended behavior of each subsystem is agreed upon by the designers. Next, each subsystem is analyzed separately, and the procedure is iterated until we reach the point where the complexity of each component is sufficiently small that it can be implemented readily by a single person.

When a module M is decomposed into other modules, we say that these are used to *implement* M. Thus, in this approach, implementation is performed by recursive (sub)module decomposition into modules, until we reach the point where implementation can be done in terms of a programming language in a straightforward way.

The reader will recognize here several of the principles and concepts that were presented in Chapter 3, in addition to modularity. Rigor and formality are useful in the description of the software architecture. The more precise the description, the easier it is to divide software development into separate tasks that can proceed in parallel, with little risk of inconsistencies. Also, precision makes it easier to understand the system, should the need arise to modify it. Finally, the effectiveness of the aforementioned design process depends on how well the selected techniques for modularization allow us to deal with each module separately, according to the principle of separation of concerns. Using two concepts already introduced in Chapter 3, modules should have high cohesion and low coupling.

According to the definition we gave in Chapter 3, the process of module decomposition just described can be called *top down*. It is also possible to proceed in a *bottom-up* manner. For example, a module may be designed to provide an easy, abstract

---

[1] Note that often the term "design" is used to denote both the activity and its result. When an ambiguity may arise, we try to be consistent and explicitly call the former "design activity" and the latter "software design" or "architecture."

way of accessing a peripheral device, masking the low-level hardware-oriented primitives provided by the device. The module acts like a layer that applies cosmetics (i.e., abstraction) to the device and lets it appear with a better and easier-to-deal-with look. Here, the process is intrinsically bottom up: we start from an existing, but intricate, object, and we build an abstraction around it.

According to a bottom-up strategy, the design process consists of defining modules that can be iteratively combined together to form subsystems. This is typical in the case where we are reusing modules from a library to build a new system, instead of building such a system from scratch. The entire system is constructed by assembling lower level components in an iterative fashion.

This discussion of bottom-up versus top-down design will be taken up later in Section 4.2.7. We will see that it is possible–and often convenient–to combine the two, for different parts of the system or at different points in the design activity.

Before discussing the criteria that may be followed to modularize a system, we examine two important goals for a software architecture: *design for change*, in Section 4.1.1, and *program families*, in Section 4.1.2. Design for change is a way to do a software design that can be reused easily as requirements change. Similarly, the concept of a program family allows us to view several end products as one single application that is reused–specialized and modified in varying degrees–in different contexts, giving rise to different versions. Thus, both of the concepts of design for change and program families fall within the general framework of software reusability and support software evolvability.

4.1.1 Design for Change

In Chapter 3, we presented anticipation of change as a general software principle to cope with the evolutionary nature of software. To apply this principle in the context of software design means that during the design activity we anticipate the changes that the software may undergo during its lifetime and, as a result of this anticipation, produce a software design that will accommodate the changes easily. Following Parnas, we refer to the techniques used to accomplish this goal as *design for change*.

Design for change promotes a design that is flexible enough to accommodate changes easily. This, however, cannot be achieved in general, for *every* type of change. Special care in the initial phase is necessary to anticipate likely changes when the requirements for software are stated. At this initial stage, one should not concentrate exclusively on what is *presently* needed in terms of functions to offer or, more generally, qualities to achieve. One should also concentrate on the expected or possible evolution of the system. In fact, very often, the application we are designing is a first step of a known, preplanned sequence of steps that will lead to the final automated system. In such cases, we must make sure that the initial design will easily accommodate the anticipated evolution.

Still more often, however, required changes are not precisely known *a priori*, although they will almost inevitably arise afterwards. Here, the previous experience of the software engineer and the deep understanding of the problem domain by the end user may play a major role in identifying potential areas of change and the future evolution of the system. After the requirements for changes are identified, the design should try to make those changes easily applicable.

Software engineers must realize the importance of design for change. A common mistake is to design a system for today's requirements, paying little or no attention to likely changes. The consequence of this approach is that even a marvelous design may turn out to be extremely difficult and costly to adapt to requests for changes, and it will have to be redone almost completely in order to incorporate even seemingly "minor" changes. Another unfortunate consequence is that in the process of trying to accommodate changes, the designer may have to clutter the initial elegant structure, resulting in an application that is more and more difficult to maintain and that inspires little confidence in its reliability.

4.1.1.1 What changes? The nature of evolvability

What are the types of changes that a design should try to anticipate? To understand this issue, we must go back to the problems we discussed in Chapter 2 under maintainability and, in particular, to the notion of evolvability (Section 2.2.5.2). As we saw, it has been reported in the literature that maintenance usually accounts for more than 60 percent of software costs. One reason these costs are so high is that software engineers tend to overlook the issue of maintainability during software development. They do not anticipate it at all.

Recall from Chapter 2 that maintenance may be classified into three categories: perfective, adaptive, and corrective maintenance. Adaptive and perfective maintenance are the real sources of change in software; they motivated the introduction of evolvability as a fundamental software quality and anticipation of change as a general principle that should guide the software engineer.

The following changes may fall under perfective and adaptive maintenance. They are not exhaustive of all such changes, but they are a sample of common ones.

Change of algorithms. This change is probably the best understood type of change that we can apply to software–to improve the efficiency of some part, deal with a more general case, etc.

Consider the well-known case of sorting algorithms. In order to choose among the many existing algorithms, we should know the size of the list to be sorted, the probable distribution of the data in the list, etc. Consequently, the choice of the most suitable algorithm to be used in the application may depend on experimental data acquired after the system is operational. We might start with a simple and straightforward algorithm as our initial choice and then replace it with a better solution as more experimental data are acquired. If the algorithm is confined to a well-identified module (a routine of the programming language), the change will be easy to apply because the portion of the program that requires changing is easily identified, being bound by its unique entry and exit points.

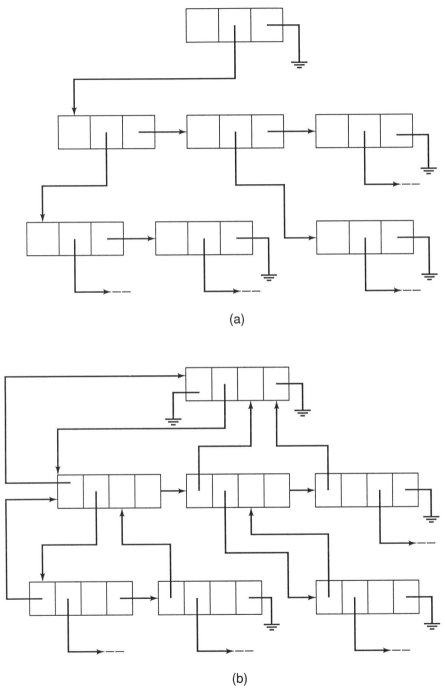

Figure 4.1   Two sample data structures representing a tree.

Exercise

4.1   Give an example of two sorting algorithms whose execution profiles change considerably depending on the distribution of data in the array to be sorted. Discuss how data distribution affects the execution profiles.

Change of data representation. The efficiency of a program can change dramatically by changing the structure used to represent some relevant data. As an example, changing the structure used to represent a table from a sequential array to a linked list or to a hash table can change the efficiency of the operations accessing the table. Typically, inserting an element into an array is costly if array entries are to be kept sorted according to, say, increasing index values. In fact, inserting an element at position i must be preceded by an operation that shifts all the elements at positions i through n, n being the number of stored entries, in order to provide room for the entry to be stored at position i. This shift operation, whose average cost in terms of processing time is proportional to n, is not needed if we choose a linked list implementation of the table.

Another example is the case of a tree data structure, implemented via pointers. Each node of the tree has two pointer fields, one pointing to its right sibling if any, the other pointing to its first direct descendant if any (see Figure 4.1(a)). Suppose we wish to add one more pointer, in order to make it easy (more efficient) to move along the data structure from the leaves towards the root of the tree. The pointer we add connects any node to its parent node, if there is any (see Figure 4.1(b)).

As another example of change of data representation, not dictated by efficiency issues, one might wish to add fields to (or delete fields from) records as more (or less) information is needed to be saved in a file. One instance of this is when a new field is added to records representing students enrolled in a class in order to store the data on the other courses the student is currently taking.

It has been reported that changes in data structures have a profound influence on the costs of maintenance (about 17 percent of total maintenance costs!).[1]

Although we have discussed change of algorithms and change of data structures separately, they are often related. For example, we may apply a change in a data structure in order to provide a better algorithm. Or, vice versa, a change in algorithms may require changes in data structure.

Exercise

4.2   Discuss some possible motivations for changing the tree data structure presented in Figure 4.1. Discuss whether (and why) the change of data structure requires a change of algorithms.

Change of underlying abstract machine. The programs we write are run by some abstract (or virtual) machine. The machine coincides with the hardware in the (happily

---

[1]See Lientz and Swanson [1980].

unlikely) case where no higher level languages are available for programming. More frequently, the abstract machine we use corresponds to the high-level language in which we write programs, the operating system to which we issue system calls, possibly the data-base management system we use to store and retrieve long-lived data, etc. The abstract machine, by itself, hides details of the underlying physical machine.

Very often, however, we need to modify applications in order to be able to run them under a new release of the operating system, taking full advantage of the new facilities offered by it. Similarly, there may be new releases available of the compiler we use, and the new version might perform additional optimizations in order to generate faster and smaller object code. Or there might be a new version of the DBMS that saves disk space and offers improved functions in terms of protection from undesired access and recovery from failures. This means that the underlying abstract machine changes, and the changes may affect our application. Sadly, the benefits do not come for free. For example, if the new DBMS is able to store our data in half the original space, we have to reformat our existing data bases. We may also have to change our data access programs to take advantage of the saving in space. Even if the functions offered by our software remain totally unchanged, the change in the underlying abstract machine affects the software.

Exercise

4.3   Do you have any personal experience with software changes in the underlying abstract machine? Briefly present your experience and discuss what made your software difficult to change.

Change of peripheral devices. A change of peripheral devices is strongly related to a change of the underlying abstract machine. We can view it as a specialization of that type of change in such cases as embedded computer applications, avionic systems, and process control systems, where control software needs to interact with many different and special-purpose peripheral devices. Such devices may be subject to change; in particular, they are progressively becoming "more intelligent," i.e., data-processing functions are being progressively decentralized to be performed locally, without disturbing the main application running on the main machine. Ideally, we would like to be able to accommodate such changes without affecting, or redesigning the entire application.

Change of social environment. A change of social environment is similar to the previous two types of change. It is, however, not motivated by the need for modification arising in the software itself. Rather, the social environment in which the application is embedded requires our software to change.

For example, in a tax application, suppose that a change in legislation requires the rules for deductions to change slightly. Then the concept of a deductible item remains, but the list of deductible items changes. Software must change accordingly, in order to make the application valid for the new tax rules.

As another example, there is a never-ending discussion within the Italian government as to whether to introduce a new Lira, called a "heavy Lira", worth 1,000 Lire. The reason is that the current Lira is worth about 0.0007 U.S. dollars, and thus prices are given with many digits! This change in the Italian legislation will affect existing software. Think of banking applications or any type of financial system that must deal with the new heavy Lira instead of (or in addition to) the old one.

Exercise

4.4   For some existing or hypothetical application, give an example of a software change that might be due to a change in the social environment.

Following the motivation we discussed in Chapter 3, software is often developed incrementally. Incrementality is another source of change that requires special care. For example, we may try to isolate useful portions of the application and release them so that the customer can start using the system and give us feedback based on experience. Later, when new parts are added to the system, it is important that we concentrate on the new developments and leave the early subsets unchanged. To make the approach feasible, the new and old parts must fit together cleanly, so that no need for complex software changes arises as the new parts are released and integrated with the previously running, but incomplete, application.

4.1.2 Program Families

In many practical situations, changes consist of building new versions of the same software; every version constitutes an individual product, but the set of versions constitutes a *family*. Often, a new version is supposed to supersede the previous one; say, it eliminates some known errors or adds improved features to the product. In other cases, a new version is simply another product that coexists with the previous one; maybe it works on a different hardware, or it has special requirements in terms of memory available, or it provides different functions for some parts of the system. The reason we regard the different versions of a software product as a family, rather than a set of different products, is that all members in the family have much in common and are only partially different. By designing *all* members of the family jointly, rather than doing separate designs for each member in the family, we avoid the cost of designing the common parts separately.

A simple example is given by an application that is required to be used by inexperienced users who need to interact with the system in their native language. The application intrinsically has to exist in multiple versions, each version being specialized to a different language in which messages, screens, menus, and commands must be provided. Another example is a data-base management system that is required to run on different machines, possibly on different operating systems, and for various configurations.

It is quite intuitive that the differences among the various versions are greater in the latter case than in the former. In both cases, however, we should identify commonalities among the different versions of the software and delay the point where any two versions start being different. The more we stress commonality, the less work is done for each new version. This reduces the chance of inconsistencies and reduces the combined maintenance effort expended on all the products.

Very often we do not pay special care to designing program families as a whole, but rather we proceed from version to version in a sequential manner. A common mistake is illustrated by the trees shown in Figure 4.2. Starting from the requirements, version 1 of the application (corresponding to node 3 in Figure 4.2(a)) is developed through a sequence of design steps (represented in the figure by directed edges). Nodes represented by circles stand for intermediate design descriptions; nodes represented by squares represent a complete, executable version. Thus Figure 4.2(a) illustrates that the requirements are first transformed into the intermediate design stage 1, then 2, and finally into version 1 of the program.

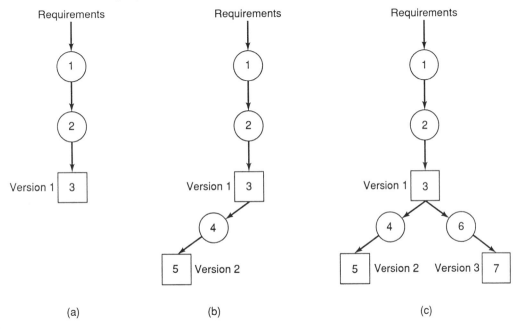

(a)   (b)   (c)

Figure 4.2   Sequential design of a program family.

At this point, if the need for a new version–version 2–arises, we start modifying version 1. Initially, the application is put in the intermediate design stage represented by node 4 (Figure 4.2(b)), by deleting parts of the code of version 1; then it is transformed into a fully operational version, represented by node 5. Node 5 may be the starting point of the derivation of further versions, not illustrated in the figure. Also, a branch representing a different version may start from node 3, as illustrated in Figure 4.2(c).

This type of approach for deriving the members of a program family is not satisfactory. In fact, the family illustrated in Figure 4.2 is biased by the design decisions made while version 1 was initially developed, since versions 2 and 3 are derived as modifications of version 1. No effort was made to isolate what is common to all versions and, iteratively, what is common to smaller and smaller subsets of the family. Thus, the derivation of a new member of the family becomes particularly difficult if the new member differs substantially from the previous member.

New versions of software are derived by modifying the code of the previous version because often intermediate design steps (represented in the figure by circles) are not documented. Programs are the only available trustable descriptions that can be used as a starting point for modifications. But programs (even well-written and well-documented programs) may be difficult to understand in sufficiently precise terms to allow modifications to be applied reliably. We can never be sure whether a modification done to a part of the system will adversely affect other parts. Also, we may inadvertently make design decisions that were discarded before, but never documented.

A systematic approach to the design of program families that solves these problems will be presented in Section 4.2. This approach is based on the general principle of design for change, where changes are restricted to capturing the differences among the various members of the family.

4.2 MODULARIZATION TECHNIQUES

In this section, we discuss techniques that can be used during design to achieve the objectives stated in Section 4.1. In particular, we distinguish between two complementary aspects of design; one (Section 4.2.1) that addresses the problem of defining the overall structure of the architecture in terms of relationships among modules and the other (Section 4.2.2) that deals with the design of each module, to which we apply the principle of information hiding.

As stated in Chapter 1, these two aspects are often called *architectural* (or *high-level*) *design* and *detailed design*. Even though several design methodologies suggest that the two be performed as two consecutive steps, we do not see them as separate steps, where the second necessarily follows the first. Rather, we view design as a continuum in which the interplay between these two activities takes place in a flexible way.

In order to document and analyze our designs, we will need a *design notation*. While several such notations are in use today, there is no standard one and each has its shortcomings. Rather than use one of the existing notations, which would distract us with the details of its syntax and other idiosyncrasies, we introduce a simple design notation in Section 4.2.3. The purpose of this notation, which comes in both a textual and a graphical form, is to serve our pedagogical needs in this book. It is not intended that the notation be used in industrial software development. The notation is analogous to "Pidgin Algol."[1]

After introducing information hiding as a general method, we illustrate a particular instance of it that leads to the important concepts of abstract objects and abstract data types, defined and illustrated in Section 4.2.4. Then we analyze design strategies and distinguish between top-down and bottom-up design. The two approaches are compared critically in Sections 4.2.6 and 4.2.7. We then specialize our design concepts to the case of object-oriented design. Finally, two more aspects are discussed, the first having to do

---

[1]Pidgin Algol is used by Aho et al. [1974] for describing and analyzing algorithms.

with the design of responses to undesirable events–a fundamental issue in systems that demand high reliability–and the second having to do with concurrency.

4.2.1 The Module Structure And Its Representation

A module is a well-defined component of a software system. It is quite common to equate modules and routines, but this view of a module is too narrow. A module is a software fragment that corresponds to more than just a routine. It may be a collection of routines, a collection of data, a collection of type definitions, or a mixture of all of these. In general, we may view a module as a *provider of computational resources or services*.

When we decompose a system into modules, we must be able to describe the overall modular structure precisely and state the relationships among the individual modules.

We can define many relationships among modules. For example, we may define a relation that states that one module must be implemented before another, or that it is more important than another. The first relation may be used by a manager to monitor the development of the system; the second may be used as a guideline for assigning work to programmers, according to their skills and experience.

What we are interested in here, however, are the kinds of relations on modules that define the software architecture and that help us understand and control it; for example, whether a module uses the facilities provided by another module or is a part of the other module. As we will see soon, these are two useful relationships among modules that may be used to define our system architecture.

In what follows we address the following issues: What is the structure of software in terms of its constituent modules? How can we define that structure precisely? And what are the desirable properties of such a structure?

First, from an abstract viewpoint, the modular structure of a system can be described in terms of various types of mathematical relations. Let S be a software system, composed of modules $M_1, M_2,..., M_n$, that is,

$$S = \{M_1, M_2, \ldots, M_n\}$$

A *relation* r on S is a subset of $S \times S$. If two modules M_i and M_j are in S, we represent the fact that the pair $<M_i, M_j>$ is in r by using the infix notation $M_i\ r\ M_j$. Since we are interested in describing the mutual relationships among different modules, we will always implicitly assume the relations of interest in this text to be *irreflexive*. This means that $M_i\ r\ M_i$ cannot hold for any module M_i in S.

The *transitive closure* of a relation r on S is again a relation on S, written r^+. Let M_i and M_j be any two elements of S. Then r^+ can be defined recursively as follows: $M_i\ r^+\ M_j$ if and only if $M_i\ r\ M_j$ or there is an element M_k in S such that $M_i\ r\ M_k$ and $M_k\ r^+\ M_j$. A relation is a *hierarchy* if and only if there are no two elements M_i, M_j such that $M_i\ r^+\ M_j$ and $M_j\ r^+\ M_i$.

The transitive closure of a relation captures the intuitive notion of *direct* and *indirect* relationships. For example, for two modules A and B, A CALLS$^+$ B implies that either A CALLS B directly or indirectly through a chain of CALLS.

Mathematical concepts can usually be grasped more effectively and intuitively if we can give them a graphical representation. Relations are a good example of this general

principle. A relation can be represented in graphical form as a directed graph whose
nodes are labelled by elements in S, and a directed arc exists from the node labelled M_i to
the node labelled M_j if and only if M_i r M_j.

A relation is a hierarchy if and only if there are no cycles in the graph of the
relation; this type of graph is called a DAG (directed acyclic graph). Figure 4.3(a)
illustrates a generic graph, and Figure 4.3(b) represents a hierarchy (a DAG).

The following two sections discuss two types of relations among modules that are
very useful for structuring software designs: USES and IS_COMPONENT_OF. One
more type of relation, INHERITS_FROM, will be described in Section 4.3 in the specific
context of object-oriented design.

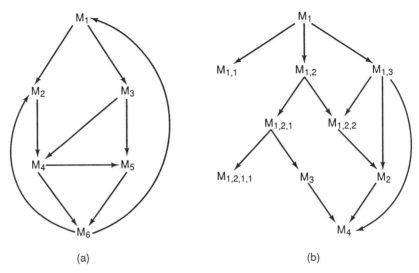

(a)   (b)

Figure 4.3   Graph representation of a relation among modules. **(a)** General graph.
(b) Directed acyclic graph (DAG).

4.2.1.1 The USES relation

A useful relation for describing the modular structure of a software system is the so-
called USES relation. For any two distinct modules M_i and M_j, we say that M_i USES M_j if
and only if correct execution of M_j is necessary for M_i to complete the task described in
its specification. If M_i USES M_j, we also say that M_i is a *client* of M_j, since M_i requires the
services that M_j provides.

An obvious instance of a USES relation is when module M_i contains a call to a
procedure contained in module M_j. In fact, a procedure call often corresponds to the
USES relation. (This will be the case in most of the examples we will discuss in this
book.) USES, however, is not equivalent to "contains a call to a procedure of." There are
examples of calls that do not imply USES, as well as USES that do not correspond to
calls. As an example of the first case, consider a module M_i that is requested to report
some anomaly discovered at run time by calling a procedure H contained in some other
module M_j. Issuing the call is all that is requested from M_i, and M_i is correct no matter

what the module M_j actually does after being called. An example of the other case is the situation of two modules M_i and M_j executing concurrently and asynchronously, where M_i requests a service from M_j by sending it a message through a mailbox and then suspends itself waiting for a response to be received through another mailbox. Yet another example is given next.

Example 4.1

Suppose we are designing a C program in which a global data structure is stored in the static area that is accessible to several subprograms. Each subprogram is viewed as a module and represents an operation on the shared data structure. You may imagine the data structure to represent a table (say, a phone directory) and each subprogram to provide a service to access the table for inserting, deleting, and retrieving information. For simplicity, suppose that the table is represented as an array and that a shared variable TOT contains the number of entries stored in the table.

In this case, the various modules that access the shared data structure use one another, even though they do not call each other. In fact, if the specification of, say, the retrieval subprogram says that it should be able to retrieve the value of all inserted entries that have not been deleted so far, then the retrieval program USES the insertion program even though it does not call it. For example, suppose that the subprogram performing insertion of a new entry in the table (incorrectly) does not update the value of TOT. The insertion program would prevent the correct functioning of the retrieval program because one of the entries inserted and not deleted from the table would not be retrievable. Thus, the module performing retrieval would not complete its task as prescribed in its specification. The point is that the operation implemented by a module–insert, in this case–must put the globally visible data structure in a correct state so that other modules may perform their tasks as specified.   ∎

A good restriction to impose on the USES relation is that it should be a hierarchy. Hierarchical systems are easier to understand than nonhierarchical ones: once the abstractions provided by used components are understood, client components may be understood without looking at the internals of the used modules. In other words, separation of concerns can be applied by traversing the USES structure, starting with the nodes of the DAG that do not use any other nodes up to the nodes that are not used by any other node. When we encounter a node, the corresponding module may be understood by referring to the abstractions provided by used modules (if any) that have been previously encountered and understood.

As a consequence of the hierarchical USES structure, we obtain another beneficial practical effect: quoting Parnas, if the structure is not hierarchical, "we may end up with a system in which nothing works until everything works." [1] In fact, the presence of a cycle in the USES relation implies a strong coupling between all the modules in the cycle, meaning that no subsets of the modules in the cycle may be used or tested in isolation.

The restriction to a hierarchy has a methodological implication, too: the resulting structure defines a system through *levels of abstraction*. This often-used (and misused)

---

[1] Parnas [1979].

term can be illustrated by reference to Figure 4.3(b). At the most abstract level, the entire system can be viewed as providing the services defined by module M_1. To implement such services, module M_1 uses modules $M_{1,1}$, $M_{1,2}$, and $M_{1,3}$. In turn, the abstract services offered by, say, $M_{1,2}$ are implemented by using the lower level modules $M_{1,2,1}$ and $M_{1,2,2}$.

We define the *level* of a module as follows: the level of a module that is not used by any other module is 0, and the level of any other module M is i, where i is the length of the longest path in the DAG that connects a level-0 module to the node M. A system described by a hierarchical USES relation may be understood in terms of successive levels of abstraction: a level i module USES only modules at any level j where i < j. For example, in Figure 4.3(b), the levels of $M_{1,3}$, M_2, and M_4 are 1, 3, and 4, respectively; $M_{1,3}$ USES M_2 and $M_{1,3}$ USES M_4.

Given any two modules M_i and M_j whose levels are i and j, respectively, we say that M_i is a *higher level* module than M_j if and only if i < j.

Another common term used in connection with a hierarchical USES relation, especially in the case of the structure of operating systems, is *abstract (virtual) machine*. We already introduced this term in Section 4.1.1.1. Its meaning is that the modules at a certain level–say i–provide a set of services that correspond to an abstract (or virtual) machine. Such services are used by higher level modules to implement the services they are expected to provide. In the implementation of such services, the services provided by modules at level i are used as if they were provided by some virtual machine. Virtual machines are progressively detailed by using others, until no further levels are given.

As an example, consider the case of a module M_R that provides input-output of record values. Let M_R use another module M_B that provides input-output of a single byte at a time. When used to output record values, M_R's job consists of transforming the record into a sequence of bytes and isolating a single byte at a time to be output by means of the output operation provided by M_B. As viewed from its clients, module M_R is a virtual machine that implements input and output operations for record values. But in order to perform its services, M_R uses a lower level module M_B that corresponds to a simpler virtual machine.

The USES relation among modules is defined statically; that is, the identification of all pairs $<M_i, M_j>$ belonging to USES is independent of the execution of the software. In fact, it is exactly the purpose of design to define the relation once and for all. To clarify this issue, consider a module M that uses modules M_1 and M_2 by calling one of their procedures. If the client module M contains the code structure:

if cond **then** proc1 **else** proc2

where proc1 is a procedure of module M_1 and proc2 is a procedure of module M_2, then M USES M_1 and M USES M_2, although during any particular execution it may well happen that either M_1 or M_2 is invoked, but not both.

As another example, consider the case of dynamic reconfiguration of a distributed system: at run time, module M_i may use module M_j up to the point where dynamic reconfiguration causes M_i to use module M_k. M_j and M_k provide exactly the same functionality, but reside on different nodes of the distributed system. Upon failure of the node where M_j resides, any request for the services that were provided by M_j is redirected to M_k. Thus, in terms of the USES relation, we have both M_i USES M_j and M_i USES M_k, although only M_j is actually used in the normal case.

The graphical view of the relation USES provides an intuitive, although partial, description of the coupling among modules. If each node of the graph is connected to every other node of the graph (i.e., the graph is complete: there is a pair $<M_i, M_j>$ in USES for each M_i, M_j in S), then the modular structure is very intricate, and does not provide a manageable partitioning of the entire system into parts.

Actually, these comments also hold for most other relations among modules. If the graph of a relation r is complete, then every module is related to every other module, and no part is independent of the whole. In such a case, the cardinality of r is n^2, where n is the cardinality of S. On the opposite side, if r is empty, then the relation describes a modular structure in which no two modules are related. Thus, the system is split into parts that can be designed and understood in complete isolation. While an empty r is unrealistic in practice, this situation shows that we should try to achieve modular structures in which the cardinality of r is much smaller than n^2.

The USES relation provides a way to reason about coupling in a precise manner. With reference to the USES graph, we can distinguish between the number of outgoing edges of a module (called the module's *fan-out*) and the number of incoming edges (called *fan-in*). A good design structure should keep the fan-out low and the fan-in high. A high fan-in is an indication of good design because a module with high fan-in represents a meaningful–i.e., general–abstraction that is used heavily by other modules.

In order to evaluate the quality of a design, however, merely evaluating the structure of the USES relation is not sufficient. Also important is the nature of the interaction among modules. Here are examples of how modules may actually use one another:

1. An unstructured type of use occurs when a module modifies local data–or even instructions–of another module. This may happen in the case of assembly language programs.

2. A module may use another module by communicating with it through a common data area, like a C static variable or a FORTRAN COMMON block.

3. The data exchanged between two modules may be "pure" data, or they can be control information, such as flags. Exchanging control information often results in a tricky kind of interaction that impairs the readability of programs.

4. In a concurrent environment, a used module may communicate with a client module via messages. In a similar fashion, in the Ada programming language, a module M enclosing task T_M may use a module M' enclosing task $T_{M'}$ by having, in T_M, a call to an entry of task $T_{M'}$. This is a disciplined way of letting two concurrent modules communicate.

5. Finally, a used module may communicate with its client through subprogram parameters. This is a disciplined and traditional way of letting two sequential modules interact.

Exercises

4.5   Provide a mathematical formula that formally defines the concept of the level of a module.

4.6   Consider procedure calls that may be considered instances of the USES relation. Mutually recursive modules do not form a hierarchy. Direct recursion within a module, however, is allowed in a hierarchy. Are these statements correct? If so, what is the justification?

4.7   Can you define the concept of level for a general graph rather than for a DAG? Why? Why not? What does this imply about a USES relation that is not a hierarchy?

4.8   Suppose that procedure calls correspond to USES, and consider the case of procedure parameters. For example, module M_i may call a procedure P of module M_j, passing to it as a parameter procedure Q of module M_k. Define the USES relation for M_j, considering the modules it uses through calls to its formal procedure parameter.

4.2.1.2 The IS_COMPONENT_OF relation

Two other relations among modules that are useful for describing designs are IS_COMPONENT_OF and COMPRISES. These relations allow designers to describe an architecture in terms of a module that is composed of other modules that may themselves be composed of other modules, and so on.

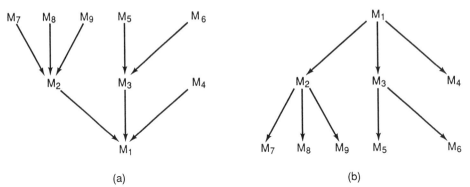

Figure 4.4   (a) An example of the IS_COMPONENT_OF relation. (b) The COMPRISES relation corresponding to (a).

Let S be a set of modules. For any M_i and M_j in S, M_i IS_COMPONENT_OF M_j means that M_j is realized by aggregating several modules, one of them being M_i. COMPRISES is defined as the inverse relation of IS_COMPONENT_OF, i.e., for any two elements M_i and M_j in S, we say that M_i COMPRISES M_j if and only if M_j IS_COMPONENT_OF M_i. Let $M_{S,i}$ be a subset of S defined as follows:

$$M_{S,i} = \{ M_k \mid M_k \text{ is in S and } M_k \text{ IS\_COMPONENT\_OF } M_i \}$$

Then we can say that M_i IS_COMPOSED_OF $M_{S,i}$ and, conversely, $M_{S,i}$ IMPLEMENTS M_i.

If a module M_i is composed of a set of other modules $M_{S,i}$ then the modules of set $M_{S,i}$ actually provide all of the services that M_i should provide: they are the result of M_i's decomposition into components, and therefore, they implement M_i.

In design, once M_i is decomposed into the set $M_{S,i}$ of its constituents, it is replaced by them, that is, M_i is an abstraction that is implemented in terms of simpler abstractions. The only reason to keep M_i in the modular description of a system is to be able to refer to it, thus making the design structure more clear and understandable. At the end of the decomposition process, however, only the modules that are not composed of any other modules can be viewed as composing the software system. The others are kept just for descriptive purposes.

The relation IS_COMPONENT_OF can also be described by a directed graph, as shown in Figure 4.4(a). It is irreflexive and is also a hierarchy. In it, we can thus define one module as being at a higher level than another module, as we did in the case of the USES relation. In practice, it is more useful to introduce the concept of level with reference to the relation COMPRISES. Figure 4.4(b) describes the system of Figure 4.4(a) in terms of this relation.

The concept of level defined by COMPRISES is such that if M_i IS_COMPOSED_OF $\{M_{i,1}, M_{i,2}, \ldots, M_{i,n}\}$, then M_i is higher level than $M_{i,1}, M_{i,2}, \ldots, M_{i,n}$. Note that the concept of a level of abstraction used in design descriptions is ambiguous, unless we explicitly specify whether it is intended as the level with respect to the USES relation, or the COMPRISES relation, or any other relation on modules (such as IS_COMPONENT_OF). In the case of USES, all modules $M_{i,1}, M_{i,2}, \ldots, M_{i,n}$ used by a given module M_i are lower level than M_i; M_i provides the services it exports to its clients by using the services provided by the lower level modules $M_{i,1}, M_{i,2}, \ldots, M_{i,n}$. In the case of COMPRISES, all modules implementing a given module M_i are lower level than M_i: they actually stand for M_i–i.e., M_i is refined by substituting $M_{i,1}, M_{i,2}, \ldots, M_{i,n}$ for it.

The graphical representation of IS_COMPONENT_OF also describes IS_COMPOSED_OF, IMPLEMENTS, and COMPRISES. For example, in Figure 4.4, M_2, M_3, and M_4 are components of M_1; M_1 IS_COMPOSED_OF $\{M_2, M_3, M_4\}$; $\{M_2, M_3, M_4\}$ IMPLEMENTS M_1; and M_1 COMPRISES M_i, for $2 \leq i \leq 4$. The entire software system is composed of modules M_4, M_5, M_6, M_7, M_8, M_9. The other modules that appear in the graph do not have a physical existence; their only purpose is to help describe the modular structure in a hierarchical way.

For example, suppose that Figure 4.4 describes the modular structure of an application in which M_2 is the module providing input facilities, M_3 is the heart of the system, providing all the processing, and M_4 provides output facilities. In turn, module M_2 is composed of various modules (M_7, M_8, M_9), each providing certain input services, such as input through digitalization of input forms, input through I/O terminals, etc. Module M_3 is decomposed into M_5 and M_6. The final system contains only physical modules that correspond to the elements of the IS_COMPOSED_OF relation that are not further decomposed into other modules–in the example, M_4, M_5, M_6, M_7, M_8, and M_9.

So far, in our discussion of IS_COMPONENT_OF, we have assumed that a module is a component of at most one module. Although this represents the typical case, we do not impose such a restriction in the definition of the IS_COMPOSED_OF relation. Therefore, it is possible to complete the graph of Figure 4.4 with a directed arc from node

M_6 to, say, node M_4, to indicate that M_6 is a component of both M_3 and M_4. When a module M_i is a component of both modules M_j and M_k, one can give an obvious alternative description where M_i is a component of just M_j and use a copy $M_{i'}$ of M_i as a component of M_k. Another solution adopted by some languages (e.g., Ada) consists of defining a so-called *generic* module and then generating instances to be used in the different contexts in which they become actual components. We will elaborate on this later.

The two relations USES and IS_COMPONENT_OF can be, and usually are, used together. For example, we may start a higher level description of a system's architecture by saying that SYSTEM is composed of modules M_1, M_2, and M_3, where M_1 uses both M_2 and M_3. Later, we specify M_1 as composed of M_4 and M_5, and so on.

Exercises

4.9   Are IS_COMPOSED_OF and IMPLEMENTS relations on S?

4.10 Suppose you decide to adopt the following policy: a module M_1 may be implemented before a module M_2 if M_1 has no components and it does not use M_2 or any module composing M_2. Formally describe this as a relation between modules.

4.2.1.3 Program families revisited

We can use the relations USES and IS_COMPONENT_OF to restate some points concerning program families.

Suppose you are designing a system S that you decompose into the set of modules M_1, M_2,..., M_i, with some USES relation on it. Then, suppose you turn to the design of any of such modules, say M_k, $1 \leq k \leq i$. At this point, you may realize that any design decision you take will separate one subset of family members from others; for example, M_k is an output module, and its design may need to discriminate between textual output and graphical output, to be dealt with by two different family members. Suppose you make the decision to follow one of the design options (in the example, the graphical output), which leads you to decompose M_k into $M_{k,1}$, $M_{k,2}$,..., $M_{k,ik}$, with some USES relation defined on this set.

You should record these design decisions carefully, so that future changes will be made reliably. Suppose that at some later point a different member of the family needs to be designed (for example, the system that provides support for textual output). You should never allow yourself to modify the final implementation by changing the code in order to meet the new requirements. Rather, the recorded documentation of the structure of the modules should force you to resume the design from the decomposition of module M_k, so that you may provide a different implementation in terms of lower-level components. Note, however, that the rest of the system will remain untouched, i.e., modules M_1,..., M_{k-1} and M_{k+1},..., M_i will not be affected by the design of the new family member.

4.2.2 Interface, Implementation, And Information Hiding

The relations USES and IS_COMPONENT_OF provide only a rough description of the software architecture. For example, more remains to be said regarding the exact nature of the interaction between two modules participating in the USES relation and about the details of IS_COMPONENT_OF. That is, when a module M_i that uses module M_j is refined into its components $M_{i,1}, M_{i,2}, ..., M_{i,n}$, it is necessary to state exactly what the USES relation between the modules in the set $\{M_{i,1}, M_{i,2}, ..., M_{i,n}\}$ and M_j means.

Intuitively, we would like to divide the software into components such that each component can be designed independently of the other components. If each component becomes a work assignment to a different programmer on a team, then each programmer should be able to work on a component with as little knowledge as possible about how other members of the team are building their components. Once again, this is the essence of separation of concerns and modularity, as discussed in general terms in Chapter 3.

To be more precise, we must define how the interaction among modules actually takes place–that is, the exact nature of the USES relation between any two modules. The set of services that each module provides to its clients (i.e., the purpose of the module as it relates to other modules) is called its *interface*. The corresponding services are said to be *exported* by the module and *imported* by the clients. The way these services are accomplished by the module is called the module's *implementation*. A clear distinction between the interface of a module and its implementation is a key aspect of good design, because it supports the separation of concerns.

The interface of a module M describes exactly what the client modules need to know in order to avail themselves of the services provided by M. The interface is an abstraction of the module as viewed by its clients. The designer who is in charge of M, while working on the design, only needs to know the interfaces of the other modules used by M and may ignore their implementation. M's interface is viewed by the designer as his or her task description: the goal is to provide exactly these services through a suitable implementation. By an implementation of a module is meant the decomposition of the module in terms of components–described by the relation IS_COMPONENT_OF–or, if the module is sufficiently simple, its representation in terms of code in some programming language, wherein it possibly uses the services provided by other low-level modules.

The interface of a module M may be viewed as a *contract* between M and its clients; i.e., the interface records all and only the facilities the designer in charge of M agrees to provide to other designers. Clients may depend only on what is listed in the interface. Thus, as long as the interface remains the same, M may change without affecting its clients.

In most practical cases, interfaces describe computational resources, such as variables that are shared among modules in order to provide a form of interaction, or procedures (functions) that must be called to have some operation performed. The examples we give here also make this assumption. Interfaces, however, are not limited to these types of resources. For example, information concerning the response time of an exported routine may be part of the interface description in the case of a real-time application. It is a kind of information that clients should know in order to decide whether to use the module.

We can go deeper into the distinction between an interface and an implementation by introducing the concept of *information hiding*. The clients of a module know about its services only through its interface; the implementation is hidden from them. This means that the implementation may change without affecting the module's clients, provided that the interface remains unchanged. Thus, a crucial aspect of design consists of defining precisely what goes into a module's interface–and therefore is visible to its potential clients–and what remains hidden in the implementation and can be changed at any time without affecting the clients.

The following section illustrates these concepts in more depth and discusses how to design module interfaces.

Exercise

4.11   (For the Ada programmer.) Consider the specification part of Ada packages as a module interface description. What is the difference between exporting a type and exporting a private type? Describe this difference in terms of the exported functionality.

4.2.2.1 How to design module interfaces

A commonly used analogy to describe the concepts of an interface, an implementation, and information hiding is illustrated in Figure 4.5: a module is like an iceberg, the interface–the visible part–is like its tip, and the implementation is what is hidden by the surface of the sea. The tip is just a small part of the whole.

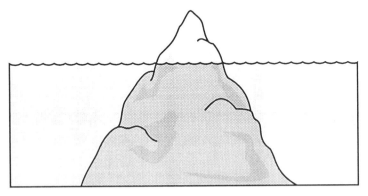

Figure 4.5   The interface as the tip of the iceberg.

If we scratch the surface of this analogy, however, we observe that it is far from satisfactory: the tip does not provide a very satisfactory abstraction of the iceberg as viewed, for example, by a ship. Relying upon the shape of the tip does not prevent the ship from crashing into the iceberg! As opposed to the tip of the iceberg, the interface describes all that must be known to operate the module correctly.

The iceberg analogy throws light on a very important point. What should go in the description of the interface and what should remain hidden in the implementation? Clearly, the interface of a module should reveal as little information as possible, but sufficient information for other modules to use the services provided by the module. Revealing unnecessary information makes the interface unnecessarily complex and reduces the understandability of the design of the system. Also, by revealing knowledge of internal details that are not necessary, it is more likely that a change to a module will affect not only its implementation, but also its interface. Even worse, other modules might take advantage of the information we make public by operating on it in an undesirable manner. On the other hand, not exporting services that need to be imported by clients would make the module useless.

Exercise

4.12   Discuss a TV remote controller as an interface for the user who wants to watch TV. Is the interface adequate if the user wants to connect the appliance to other devices (e.g., a stereo system, VCR, or video camera) through its input and output channels?

Exercise 4.12 illustrates an important concept. The interface we design depends on what services we wish to offer to clients and, conversely, on what we decide to hide within the module. We can hide certain things if we expect that the clients will not use them, but we cannot hide them if the clients are expected to use them. The art of designing module interfaces consists of balancing carefully what we want to hide and what we need to provide. If everything is hidden, then modules neither communicate nor cooperate with one another; they are autonomous subsystems. If everything is visible, then the module structure is intricate and characterized by too high a coupling.

Example 4.2

Suppose we are designing an interpreter for a very simple programming language MINI, operating on integers and integer arrays. We provide a symbol-table module that is used to store information about the variables of a program; in particular, the value of a variable may be retrieved by calling a procedure GET of the symbol-table module, passing it the symbolic name of the variable whose value is needed and, possibly, the value of the index (in the case of an array). Similarly, a procedure PUT must be called to store a new value for a given variable. When a new variable declaration is encountered, a new entry is created in the symbol table by calling a procedure NOTIFY, passing it the name of the variable and its size (the number of integer entries it represents).

The purpose of the interface we are designing is to hide the physical structure of the table from the clients of the symbol-table module. In order to warn clients when they try to read or write the value of a variable that does not exist, or access an array with an illegal index value, the procedures GET and PUT return an additional parameter POS. If the value returned for POS is less than or equal to zero, it means that no such variable is stored in the table. Otherwise, the value represents the starting address of the contiguous block of cells where the variable is stored.

This design can be criticized because of the redundancy of the interface. If our purpose is just to provide operations to store and retrieve data (and signal the case where access to the data is incorrect), then we are providing additional information (i.e., the position in the table where the data are stored). Such redundancy has negative side effects on ease of change, as we will show shortly. It also provides a loophole into information hiding.   ∎

How should we proceed in the design of modules through information hiding in order to improve cohesion and reduce coupling–in terms of both the number of interconnections in the graph of the USES relation and the type and amount of information exported through interfaces?

To answer this question, we should first define what the overall primary goal of our design actually is. As before, we assume here that changeability is a primary goal: we want our design to be able to evolve easily and reliably according to some anticipated changes and possibly others. The next section gives some guidelines on how to design modules that can accommodate future changes.

Exercise

4.13   Consider changing the interface of the module of Example 4.2 to have a separate call for asking whether the previous call was successful. Discuss this change in terms of the quality of the modular structure, the efficiency of the system, etc.

4.2.2.2 Module secrets and design for change

To maximize evolvability, the interface of a module should export the minimum possible amount of detail. Another goal is to hide low-level details and provide an abstract interface in order to make the design more understandable–as a consequence of the principles of abstraction and separation of concerns. Once the changes we wish to facilitate are identified, we can structure the system in such a way that changeable decisions are hidden in the implementation part of some modules, whereas module interfaces represent stable information, i.e., information that is not affected by the changes.

We say that the changeable, hidden information becomes the *secret* of the module; also, according to a widely used jargon, we say that such information is *encapsulated* within the module implementation.

Example 4.3

The secret of the symbol-table module of Example 4.2 is the data structure chosen for internal representation. We may choose to use a linear array, a hash table, a linked list, a binary tree, or even other more sophisticated data structures. The important goal we wish to reach is the ability to change the data structure without affecting client modules. The reason is that we want to design and implement the system quickly, by first concentrating on the module structure, without spending too much time designing and tuning the data structures in each module. We want to postpone the decision about the nature of the internals of each module, such as the "best" type of data structure, to a later point, after we have completed the entire design of the interpreter and, maybe, collected some execution profiles.

If we examine the interface closely enough, however, we see that it reveals too much; in particular, it reveals part of its (supposed) secret. By knowing the address of the storage area for a variable (revealed by both GET and PUT), we are allowed to access it directly, without being obliged to go through the interface procedures. Thus, for example, if a portion of code repeatedly accesses the same simple variable–say, X–it would be possible to obtain the value of POS (for example, by calling PUT with a fictitious initial value) and then use it directly for all accesses that refer to variable X. Of course, this method would work correctly only if the position at which the value is stored did not change. This would be the case in a simple implementation of the symbol-table module in which new declarations encountered were simply appended at the end of a sequential data structure.

Even if the software would work in this case, which may correspond to the initial release of the system, it would become incorrect as soon as we decided to change the implementation to one in which, say, a sequential data structure was kept sorted as new entries were added to it. In fact, as new declarations were encountered, they would have to be recorded in the appropriate position in the data structure, and this might imply shifting some existing entries, invalidating the values previously returned by POS. ▌

As we anticipated in Section 4.1.1.1, details of an interface to the abstract machine underlying the software are examples of information that should be hidden. This includes details of some operating system calls or intricacies of the interaction with some special peripheral devices. The main reason for hiding these details is to protect the application against changes in the underlying abstract machine. Such changes may result from anticipated hardware evolution or to achieve application portability. Another strong reason for encapsulating abstract-machine dependent aspects in *ad hoc* modules is separation of concerns: mixing low-level machine-dependent details with higher level application-dependent features would hamper understandability.

For example, instead of using the low-level primitives offered by the file system for data storage and retrieval, we might define a module that provides more abstract ways for doing that, hiding the data structure, the algorithms, and the policies used for implementing the services. This would make the client modules more understandable and would also protect them from possible changes in the file system and in the implementation of the abstract services.

Example 4.4

Suppose that a computer is used to control a remote plant, such as a flexible manufacturing system. The computer must provide input acquisition to get measures from some physical devices located at different points in the plant. For example, it would receive the value of the temperature at points P_1, P_2, and P_5, the value of the pressure at points P_1, P_3, and P_4, etc. As a function of input data, control signals must be sent back to the controlled plant and a history log must be kept in a file to facilitate maintenance of the plant. Input data are presently received as sequences of bytes that must be decoded by the control application being designed. It is anticipated, however, that the system will evolve to a new distributed configuration, where physical inputs will be processed remotely by special devices and sent to the controlling computer as record-like structured information.

An appropriate design here would define an input acquisition module whose secret would be the physical way input data are acquired. Such a module would provide client modules with a query operation to be invoked when one wanted to know what the next input datum is (what kind of measure it was, where it was measured, etc.) and the value of the measure (an integer or real value, depending on the type of measure).   ∎

In conclusion, the purpose of information hiding is to design modules that protect some changeable design decision by making it a secret and to provide a meaningful abstraction through stable module interfaces. The identification of likely changes is crucial to this approach. A tentative set of likely changes should be found in the requirements document that sets the goals for the application. As already mentioned, when the requirements of a new system are being determined, special attention should be paid to define not only what is needed now, but also what is likely to be needed in the future. Example 4.4 illustrates this point. Other points are illustrated by the following example.

Example 4.5

Suppose that the requirements for the control application of Example 4.4 contain a description of how historical data must be processed. Suppose they also describe a predefined set of fixed-format queries that can be used to extract information in the maintenance phase. Future enhancements of the system are anticipated that will allow natural language-like queries.

A good modularization in this case will encapsulate in one module the physical structure of the files used to store the historical data; that is, the module will provide procedures to access the various items stored in the data structure. Another module will provide abstract queries; that is, it will encapsulate the way queries are actually provided by the user–in natural language or in fixed format–and how they must be analyzed in order to extract the exact meaning of the user's request.   ∎

As we saw in Chapter 3, an important class of likely changes has to do with the strategy followed to produce the application. The strategy of incremental development tries to identify useful subsets of the application that might be developed and delivered earlier than others. Although some parts of the system are not dealt with at some point and are delayed to a later effort, special care is needed in the design stage to define exactly the interfaces with respect to the parts that are left for later development. This will allow later additions to be done without disturbing the previously delivered functions. In other cases, in the initial stage, some parts of the system are deliberately implemented in a highly simplified manner. They are then redesigned and reimplemented at a later stage. The symbol table of Example 4.2 is one such example. Another example is illustrated next.

Example 4.6

Suppose we are developing a completely new type of data-base management system that–we hope–will become a revolutionary item in the marketplace. The great new features of the system are in the language used for queries, which permits sophisticated use of both natural language and pictorial interaction.

Before starting development of this new system, we would like to be able to assess the validity of the approach with respect to its innovative human-computer interaction aspects. Thus, we decide to implement the user interface, but delay the implementation of the "real" data-base management system (i.e., the definition of the physical file structures, the various algorithms for storage and retrieval, recovery procedures, etc.).

What we will implement is a *prototype* of the application that can only deal with a limited amount of information, because all data will be kept in main memory using arrays. Potential users will be asked to play with the system and give feedback to the designers regarding its usability. They will be warned that the performance of the prototype has nothing to do with the expected performance of the future system: they should only pay attention to the way queries may be submitted with a mixture of natural language and pictures.

If the interface between the module providing human-computer interaction and the module providing data-base access has been designed carefully, then the two modules may evolve independently. For example, we may concentrate first on implementing a robust version of the human-computer interaction module and later turn the prototype implementation of the data-base module into a realistic version without affecting the rest of the system. In other words, if we design stable interfaces among the various modules, then modules may evolve independently from the prototype implementation to their final version.   ∎

4.2.2.3 More on likely changes

The examples we gave in the previous sections are just a small sample of requests for software changes that may be encountered in practice, but we can divide all possible changes that we might anticipate into a few classes. Information hiding modules should then be designed to accommodate these classes of changes reliably and efficiently. In Section 4.1.1, we discussed a list of likely changes: in algorithm, in data representation, in the underlying abstract machine, and in the social environment. Encapsulation via information hiding modules supports such changes. For example, if we use a procedure to encapsulate an algorithm, changing the algorithm requires changing the procedure body, and this can be done without affecting the procedure's clients. Similarly, by hiding a data structure and providing abstract interface operations to access and modify it, we can protect the users of the data structure from changes in the representation of data.

Policies are another kind of design decision that should be encapsulated within information hiding modules. Such a policy might involve the order in which certain operations are performed. For example, suppose we are designing a module to provide clients with a sorted list of items. Suppose it must be possible to INSERT an item in the list, DELETE it from the list, and PRINT the list of item names in alphabetical order. Then INSERT, DELETE, and PRINT constitute the module's interface.

This module can hide various kinds of policies–for example, the list is kept sorted as each item is inserted or deleted; or it is sorted just prior to printing it; or it is never kept sorted, but the PRINT operation simply prints the items in the right order. We may view these three policies as covering a spectrum from an eager to a lazy policy. Note, however, that a change in the policy would leave the clients unaffected, as the policy is a secret of the module. The policy, however, would affect the execution time for each operation. That is, an eager policy makes it possible to support a fast PRINT at the expense of a slow INSERT and DELETE, since these must keep the list sorted.

As another example of this issue, consider the case of concurrent applications, where it is vital to distinguish between *mechanisms* and *policies*. In this type of application, we need mechanisms to suspend processes if they need to access some shared resource (e.g., a printer or a buffer). The underlying *scheduler* should then use some policy to resume suspended processes; for example, it might resume processes based on a purely first-in–first-out basis, or it might use more complicated policies based on, say, priorities or execution times. Either of these policies can be implemented by providing a module that exports the mechanisms to suspend and resume processes:

- suspend (P) would be invoked to suspend process P;
- resume (P) would be invoked to resume the next process; it also provides the identifier of the resumed process in the output parameter.

The module would hide the policy used to select the next process to be resumed. Future changes in the policies will then integrate smoothly with the rest of the system: only performance will be affected, not correctness.

What can be hidden depends also on the type of application. For example, in many real-time applications, scheduling policies cannot be hidden from client modules. They are thus made part of the interface. They are not hidden in the implementation since they cannot be changed irrespective of the clients' wishes. Rather, the fact that, say, certain events are handled according to one policy or another (e.g., FIFO versus LIFO) may affect the ability of a module to react to some incoming stimuli within specified time constraints. And a failure in this regard may cause serious, dangerous, or even catastrophic effects in the real-time system.[1]

Exercise

4.14   Discuss the previous example of the sorted list of items in the case of real-time applications. Can a change of policy affect the clients? Why? Why not?

---

[1] Actually, note that often it is not necessary–or useful–to make the policy manifest in the interface. For example, one can provide a more abstract view of it by stating constraints on response times of certain operations.

4.2.2.4 Summing up

No matter what method we follow to modularize an application, module interfaces should represent all and only the information that client modules need to know in order to avail themselves of the module's services. By examining just the interface, the designers of other modules must be able to decide whether they may benefit from using the module. This obviously requires a way to describe module interfaces precisely, so that no ambiguities arise in the interpretation of the exported services. This issue is studied in the next section (and partly in Chapter 5). Before tackling this problem, however, two summary comments are in order here.

First, a clear distinction between the interface and the implementation and a precise definition of the interface are necessary for module (re)usability. A module may be (re)used in any context, provided that the services listed in its interface match the clients' expectations, no matter what the implementation is.

Second, the interface must contain all the information that is needed to characterize the module's behavior as viewed by the clients. As we pointed out, in most cases interfaces provide descriptions of routines to be invoked by client modules. They can also provide a description of shared data. Furthermore, in real-time applications, the response time of an exported operation is part of the interface.

4.2.3 Design Notations

We have so far discussed software design issues informally: architectures have been described in a colloquial style, using English prose. But English prose, or any other form of natural language description, is not an adequate medium for describing artifacts like software designs. More precision, rigor, and even formality are required for an unambiguous description. Thus, software engineers need special notations to specify their designs.

Actually, this is true for every field of engineering. For example, electrical engineers produce blueprints in which complex appliances are described in terms of interconnected iconic symbols representing elementary devices, such as resistors, capacitors, and transistors. These elementary devices may be viewed as standard components that may be assembled to produce a new system. Suitable annotations describe the types of elementary devices to be assembled–for example, the voltage to be supplied between two given points or the value, in ohms, of resistors. The layout of such blueprints is standardized, and no ambiguities arise when such descriptions are interpreted in the construction phase, to build the circuit. Actually, before implementation, the blueprint may be analyzed to uncover inconsistencies or errors. Similar considerations apply to the case of civil or mechanical engineering. In all such cases, designs are expressed in a standardized, graphical notation.

No standardized notation for expressing software designs has emerged yet, although there are several proposals and some have been adopted in practice. In the next two subsections, we illustrate two notations, one based on a programming language-like syntax (called TDN) and the other based on a graphical interface (called GDN). These notations have many similarities to the notations used in practice. The reason we chose our own notation is twofold: first, we did not want to be distracted by details of syntax that do not add much to the expressiveness of the notation; second, so far, no notation has emerged as a standard to which we should adhere.

The notations we introduce here describe the software architecture by specifying modules and their relationships. Each notation is formal as far as the *syntax* of interfaces is concerned. For example, it says how to formulate a request for a service exported by a module in a syntactically correct form. But it does not formally specify the *semantics* of the exported services, i.e., what a service actually accomplishes for the clients, along with possible constraints or properties that clients need to know. Semantics is only described informally, by means of comments. The issue of formally specifying module semantics will be studied in Chapter 5.

4.2.3.1 TDN: A textual design notation

TDN, the textual design notation we illustrate here, is based loosely on the syntax of the Ada programming language, although some features are added and a large number of details of the language are deliberately ignored in order to provide a design notation that does not depend heavily on any particular language and is sufficiently simple and abstract. Also, some aspects of the language are deliberately left informal and can be filled in by the designer, depending on his or her taste, the type of application being designed, the programming language that will be ultimately used for implementation, etc. Above all, assuming that the reader knows a programming language such as Pascal, Modula-2, C, or Ada, the notation should be self-explanatory.

We assume that a module may export any programming language type of resource: a variable, a type, a procedure, a function, or any other entity defined by the language. As we mentioned, comments are used to provide semantic information about the exported services. In particular, comments are used to specify the *protocol* to be followed by the clients so that exported services are correctly provided. For example, the protocol might require the clients of a table handling module not to insert items into the table if the table is full. Or, in the case of a module that exports a square-root routine, the protocol might require clients not to pass negative arguments.

In general, if a module requires a special protocol to be followed in order to request one of its exported services, then this requirement should be stated as a comment associated with the syntactic description of the exported service in the module interface. Although written informally, the protocol is an essential part of the contract between the module's clients and the module's implementer, and it should be agreed upon by the designers and users of all such modules.

Comments are also used to describe the exact nature of the exported resource, once the required protocol is satisfied by the clients. Finally, comments are used to specify aspects of the interface that do not correspond to computational resources, such as routines or variables, but that deal with response times or other aspects. Time bounds and any other kind of additional constraints or properties of the exported entities may be stated as comments written in natural language when appropriate.

The parts of the module's description discussed so far define the interface, i.e., what is visible to client modules. TDN, however, supports the description of other aspects of the architecture that may be necessary for its proper documentation. In particular, a **uses** part specifies the names of used modules (if any) and an **implementation** part gives a high-level description of the implementation, which may be useful for understanding the module's rationale. Typically, the **implementation** part gives the list of internal components, according to IS_COMPOSED_OF. Using informal comments, we may also describe which secrets are encapsulated within the module and why.

Figure 4.6 provides a sample TDN module description, and the reader is invited to read it carefully before proceeding. Note that the TDN description does not specify a module by itself, but rather a module that is part of an architecture.

> **module** X
> **uses** Y, Z
> **exports var** A : integer;
>   **type** B : **array** (1. .10) **of** real;
>   **procedure** C (D: **in out** B; E:**in** integer; F: **in** real);
>   *Here is an optional natural language description of what*
>   *A, B, and C actually are, along with possible constraints*
>   *or properties that clients need to know; for example we*
>   *might specify that objects of type B sent to procedure C*
>   *should be initialized by the client, and should never*
>   *contain all zeroes.*
> **implementation**
>   *If needed, here are general comments about the rationale*
>   *of the modularization, hints on the implementation, etc.*
>   **is composed of** R, T
> **end** X

Figure 4.6   A sample module description.

What characterizes a module from its client's viewpoint, i.e. its interface, is exactly what appears in the **exports** section. The rest of the description does not deal with the interface, but serves to document the architecture in a precise manner. Thus, a change in the **exports** clause will affect the functional correctness of the clients, whereas changes to other sections do not.

The benefit of using a design notation like TDN instead of an unstructured and colloquial description lies not only in its rigor and precision, but also in the fact that the design description can be checked for consistency and completeness. The check can be done manually, by carefully examining the textual description, or mechanically, if we provide a specific tool to perform it.

In the example of Figure 4.6, eventually modules R and T must be defined; if they aren't, we have a manifest case of incompleteness. Since R and T actually replace X, one or both must use one of Y or Z, or both. (Otherwise the **uses** clause of X would be wrong.) In addition to importing from Y and Z, R and T may import from one another. Also, what X exports should be a subset of the union of the sets of resources exported by R and T.[1] All of these constraints should be checked to assess the consistency and completeness of the description. One correct description of modules R and T is given in Figure 4.7.

---

[1] For simplicity, we assume that the sets exported by R and T are disjoint.

```
module  R
uses  Y
exports  var  K : record  . . .end;
          type  B : array  (1. .10) of real;
          procedure   C (D: in out  B; E: in integer; F: in real);
implementation
          .
          .
end  R
```

```
module  T
uses  Y, Z, R
exports  var  A : integer;
implementation
          .
          .
end  T
```

Figure 4.7   Sample components of module X in Figure 4.6.

The **uses** clause in a module specification describes exactly the USES relation introduced in Section 4.2.1.1. As such, it simply states that a module may access any resource exported by another module. It may be useful to refine the **uses** clause by stating exactly which resources are imported by the module. Should this be required, we will use the notation

　　　　uses <module_name> **imports** (<resource_name_list>);

If no **imports** clause is provided, all exported resources may be imported by the module. An example of a module W using modules X and XX is shown in Figure 4.8. The example shows that W imports selectively from X, whereas it imports all of the resources exported by XX.

```
module  W
uses  X imports  (B, C),
          XX
exports  . . .
implementation
          .
          .
end  W
```

Figure 4.8   An example of a module with selective import.

When we refer to an entity E exported by a module M, we can use the dot notation M.E or, if no ambiguity arises, simply E. We might keep on adding new features to TDN and defining all the syntactic and semantic details. For example, if a module uses several modules and imports resources from them that have the same name in the exporting modules, the language might provide a way to resolve naming conflicts by renaming imported resources. We will not follow this path, however, in order to keep TDN as concise and general as possible. By adding features to TDN, we would make it closer to some programming language, and this would reduce its generality. We leave it up to the designer to add new features to the language if doing so turns out to be useful.

If TDN is to be used only with a specific programming language, it is possible to extend it with some language-specific features. But this must be done carefully, since a useful design notation should stay away from the low-level details of a programming language.

Example 4.7

Examples 4.2 and 4.3 introduced the problem of writing an interpreter for the MINI programming language. Here we address the problem of defining a compiler for MINI. One possible architecture is the following:

```
module COMPILER
exports procedure MINI (PROG: in file of char;
                        CODE: out file of char);
        MINI is called to compile the program stored in PROG and
        produce the object code in file CODE
implementation
        A conventional compiler implementation. ANALYZER performs
        both lexical and syntactic analysis and produces an abstract
        tree as well as entries in the symbol table;
        CODE_GENERATOR generates code starting from the abstract
        tree and information stored in the symbol table. Module MAIN
        acts as a job coordinator.
is composed of ANALYZER, SYMBOL_TABLE,
        ABSTRACT_TREE_HANDLER,
        CODE_GENERATOR, MAIN
end COMPILER
```

Modules MAIN, ANALYZER, and CODE_GENERATOR are specified as follows:

```
module MAIN
uses ANALYZER, CODE_GENERATOR
exports procedure MINI (PROG: in file of char;
                        CODE: out file of char);
        .
        .
        .
end MAIN

module ANALYZER
uses SYMBOL_TABLE, ABSTRACT_TREE_HANDLER
exports procedure ANALYZE (SOURCE: in file of char);
```

SOURCE is analyzed; an abstract tree is produced by using the services provided by the handler, and recognized entities, with their attributes, are stored in the symbol table.

end ANALYZER

module CODE_GENERATOR
uses SYMBOL_TABLE, ABSTRACT_TREE_HANDLER
exports procedure CODE (OBJECT: **out file of** char);

The abstract tree is traversed using the operations exported by the ABSTRACT_TREE_HANDLER and accessing the information stored in the symbol table in order to generate code in the output file.

end CODE_GENERATOR

The reader is invited to complete the description of the remaining modules as an exercise. In particular, for the symbol-table module, we suggest going back to Examples 4.2 and 4.3.   ∎

Exercise

4.15   Does the module structure described in Figure 4.6 represent a hierarchy? If not, how could you turn it into a hierarchy? If so, how could you turn it into a non-hierarchical structure?

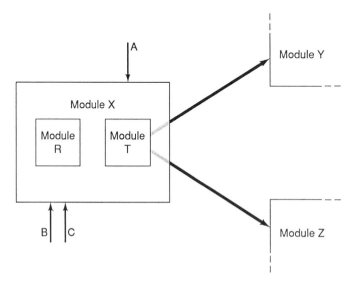

Figure 4.9   Graphical description of module X of Figure 4.6.

4.2.3.2 GDN: A graphical design notation

The reason engineers customarily adopt pictorial notations for their blueprints is that graphical descriptions can be more intuitive and easier to grasp than textual descriptions. (A picture is worth a thousand words, according to folk wisdom.) In this section, we provide a graphical design notation (GDN) that reflects the textual description we defined in Section 4.2.3.1 and that is based on the graphical descriptions referred to earlier to describe module relations.

A module is represented by a box whose incoming arrows represent its interface, i.e., the exported resources. The reason exported resources are represented by incoming arrows is motivated by the fact that exported resources are accessible from the outside, i.e., they represent an access path *into* the module.

Figure 4.9 gives a graphical description of the module X described textually in Figure 4.6. The fact that X uses modules Y and Z is shown by bold directed edges connecting X to Y and Z. Details of the exported resources–such as the number of procedure parameters, their type, and the type of variables–are omitted for simplicity, but may be added as annotations on the incoming arrows.

A box is empty if the module is elementary, i.e., if it is not composed of any subcomponents. This is not the case with module X, which is composed of R and T. Since modules R and T are components of X, we can expand their definition, according to Figure 4.7, inside X; the resulting description is shown in Figure 4.10.

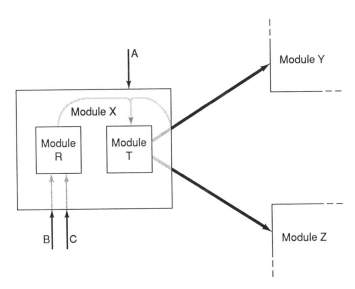

Figure 4.10   Module X is composed of modules R and T.

Figure 4.10 shows explicitly which inner modules actually originate the resources exported by module X: B and C are provided by R, and A is provided by T. Graphically, this is shown by using shadow lines to connect export arrows of module X with the corresponding export arrows of modules R and T. Similarly, shadow bold lines are used to specify which of R and T actually use the modules used by X. Figure 4.10 actually says something more than the corresponding textual notation: it shows selective import of resource K from module R to module T, whereas the textual description of Figure 4.7 simply states that T uses R.

If a module M is a component of both modules L and N, we draw a box labeled M in both L and N. Should M be composed of other modules, the IS_COMPONENT_OF structure for M is described separately. This is sketched in Figure 4.11 in the case where M exports A and B and is composed of G and H.

Exercises

4.16   Give a TDN description of module T of Figure 4.10.

4.17   Describe the module structure of Example 4.7 using GDN.

4.18   Describe the architecture of Figure 4.11 using TDN.

4.2.4 Categories of Modules

Although the designer can design a module that exports any combination of resources (variables, types, procedures and functions, labels, etc.), most modules can be classified into standard categories. Such a categorization is useful because it provides a uniform classification scheme for documentation and, possibly, for retrieval from a component library. Also, using a limited set of module categories makes a design more uniform and standard. As we discussed in Chapter 2, standard parts are the sign of the maturity of an engineering discipline. Categorization of modules is a step towards the development of standard software engineering components.

In this section, we illustrate three standard categories: procedural abstractions, libraries, and common pools of data. Two more general and abstract categories–abstract objects and abstract data types–are illustrated in the sections that follow.

A useful–and commonly well-known–type of module provides just a procedure or a function, corresponding to some abstract operation. Such modules implement a *procedural abstraction* and are used to encapsulate an algorithm. Typical examples are sorting modules, fast Fourier transform modules, and modules performing translation from one language into another. The usefulness of procedural abstractions has been recognized since the early times of computing, and programming languages provided special support for them via subprograms.

A module may also contain a *group* of related procedural abstractions. A typical and very successful case is represented by libraries of mathematical routines. Such libraries provide solutions to the most commonly used problems of calculus, e.g., computation of limits, derivatives, and integrals. Another example is a library of routines that provide algebraic operations on matrices. Still another is a library of graphical routines–for example, to direct a plotter. Modules of this type are used to package together a related set of routines. We use the term *library* to denote this class of modules.

Another common type of module provides a *common pool of data*. Once the need for sharing data among several modules is recognized, we can group such data together in a common pool that is imported by all client modules. All client modules are then allowed to manipulate the data directly, according to the structure used to represent the data, which is visible to them.

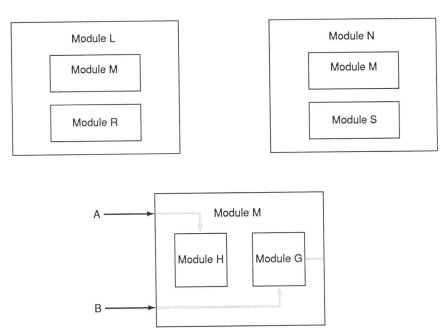

Figure 4.11   Module M is a member of both L and N.

An interesting use of a common data pool module is one that groups system configuration constants. For example, suppose that the supervisor of a control system is parameterized with respect to the number of input lines and the length of buffers in which inputs are temporarily stored. Each installation of the control system requires constant values to be assigned to these parameters, which are accessed by the modules that comprise the supervisor. A typical solution consists of grouping all configuration constants in a common pool of data that may be easily accessed for configuration purposes.

In general, however, a common pool of data is a rather low-level type of module. Such a module does not provide any form of abstraction: all details of the data are visible and manipulable by all clients. The ability to group shared data in a common block only provides limited help in terms of readability and modifiability.

Establishing common pools of data is easily implementable in conventional programming languages. For example, it can be done in FORTRAN by means of the COMMON construct, or in C using static variables.

Most of the examples we gave in Sections 4.2.2 and 4.2.3, however, demand more abstract modules that can *hide* particular data structures as secrets of the module. For example, the symbol-table module used in the interpreter (Examples 4.2 and 4.3) and in the compiler (Example 4.7) of language MINI hides the specific data structure used to represent the table and exports the operations used to access it. This module is an example of the important class of modules that package together both data and routines; they will be discussed in the next subsection.

4.2.4.1 Abstract objects

We have already mentioned that nearly 17 percent of the costs involved in software maintenance are due to changes in the representation of data. Thus, a very important type of encapsulation is one that hides the details of data representations and shields clients from changes in them.

A symbol-table module illustrates a typical module that hides a data structure as a secret and exports routines that may be used to access the hidden data structure. Should the data structure change, all we need to change are the algorithms that implement the access routines, but client modules continue to use the same calls to perform the required accesses and thus do not need to change, as long as the interfaces to the access routines remain the same.

From their interface, these types of modules look like libraries. But they have a special property that, for example, mathematical libraries do not exhibit: they have a permanent, hidden, encapsulated data structure in their implementation part that is visible to routines that are internal to the module, but is hidden from client modules. In the symbol table example, the data structure is used to store the entries as they are inserted into the table.

The hidden data structure provides these modules with a *state*. In fact, as a consequence of calls to the routines exported by the module, the values stored in the data structure may change from call to call; therefore, the results provided by two calls with exactly the same parameters may be different from time to time. This behavior is different from the case of a pool of procedures or functions that constitute a library, because the library does not have a state: two successive calls with the same parameters always provide the same result.

The difference between a module with a state and library modules does not show through the syntax of the interface. In both cases, the module exports just a set of routines. We, however, distinguish between these two types of modules in our classification scheme. Modules that exhibit a state will be called *abstract objects*. We use a comment to indicate that a module is an abstract object.

Example 4.8

Arithmetic expressions may be written in parenthesis-free form using so-called Polish postfix notation, where operators follow their operands. An example of an expression written in Polish postfix form is

    a b c + *

which corresponds to the infix expression

a * (b + c)

We restrict our attention to arithmetic expressions with only binary operators and integer operands. Also, we assume here that the input string is a correct postfix expression.

A way to evaluate arithmetic postfix expressions is to use a last-in–first-out data structure–a stack. The expression is scanned from left to right and operands are pushed onto the stack as they are encountered. When an operator is encountered, the two topmost operands are taken off the stack, the operator is applied to the two operands, and the result is pushed on top of the stack. As an example, the reader is invited to simulate by hand the evaluation of the expression a b c + * when a = 2, b = 3, and c = 5.

Stacks can be implemented in several different ways, as any textbook on data structures illustrates. If their size is bounded, we may use an array; otherwise, we may use a linked list.

If we wish to encapsulate the stack in a module, we may define the following interface:

exports
        procedure PUSH (VAL: **in** integer);
        procedure POP_2 (VAL1, VAL2: **out** integer);

Procedure PUSH is used to insert a new operand on top of the stack; procedure POP_2 is used to extract the pair of topmost operands in the stack.

The hidden part of the module may then choose any data structure to represent the stack; the data structure is a secret of the module.   ∎

The design of the abstract object described in Example 4.8 may be criticized with respect to its reusability. First, it provides a specialized primitive to pop two elements at a time. This is useful when we have only binary operators; it fails when we extend the expression evaluator to a more general case where we can also have unary operators. In order to accommodate both binary and unary operators, one could provide a pop operation that pops one element at a time and let client modules call the operation twice when needed. Second, the design has been based on the assumption that the expression to be evaluated is correct. If this is not the case, a run-time error would occur when we try to, say, pop an element from the stack when it is empty.

A more reliable design would define another interface routine, called EMPTY, that would deliver a Boolean result depending on whether the stack is empty. Of course, this design does not prevent the run-time error, but it provides a way for the client to avoid it. Notice that this revised solution requires more from the client, but it is the price we pay to make our design more reusable and reliable.

Exercises

4.19   Redesign the interface of the stack module according to the previous comments. Also, discuss the use of a fixed-size data structure to implement the stack. Under what assumption is the interface correct? Is the module easily reusable? If not, how can you improve its reusability?

4.20   An output module is used to print single characters. As viewed by client modules, output is performed one character at a time. The output module, however, hides the exact way output is performed. This allows a family of programs to be designed, where the different members differ in the type of devices to which the output is directed. Some devices output data on a character-by-character basis, while others group characters in longer sequences and add special control (e.g., parity) characters.

Would you classify this output module as a procedural abstraction or as an abstract object? Sketch the TDN and GDN descriptions of the output module in the case where physical output is performed by a (hardware) module that buffers up to 16 characters. Give an example of a module that should not use this module because it needs to know the module's secret.

4.2.4.2 Abstract data types

In this section, we introduce *abstract data types* as another category of modules that help in structuring our designs in a uniform and standard manner. We use Example 4.8 to motivate the introduction of this new category. The example used a stack abstract object. What if an application requires more than one stack? We need the ability to define a type and then generate instances of that type. We also need a way to (a) associate a set of procedures with the type in order to manipulate instances of that type, and (b) encapsulate the details of the type in the module, in order to hide the type and make its changes possible without affecting the interface. Figure 4.12 illustrates this kind of module using our textual design notation.

```
module  STACK_HANDLER
exports
        type  STACK = ?;
        This is an abstract data type module; the data structure
        is a secret hidden in the implementation part.
        procedure   PUSH (S: in out  STACK ; VAL: in integer);
        procedure   POP (S: in out  STACK ; VAL: out integer);
        function  EMPTY (S: in STACK) : BOOLEAN;
            :
            :
end STACK_HANDLER
```

Figure 4.12   An abstract data type module in TDN.

A new notational device is introduced in the figure: the "?" symbol. It is used to export a type definition, leaving the details of the corresponding data structure hidden in the implementation part of the module. The fact that a type is exported allows client modules to declare variables of that type; the fact that the type definition is hidden, however, implies that variables of that type can only be manipulated by procedures or functions exported by the module, since they are the only ones that "know" about the secret. Client modules must pass the variables of the type in question as parameters to the exported routines for proper manipulation.

An *abstract data type* is a module that exports a type, along with the operations that must be invoked to access and manipulate objects of that type; it hides the representation of the type and the algorithms used in the operations. Such a module can be implemented directly in Ada by exporting a (limited) private type, or in Modula-2 by exporting an opaque type.

Instances of an abstract data type are abstract objects that behave exactly like those discussed before. In particular, they can only be manipulated by the routines implemented and exported by the abstract data type module.[1] Such routines may include those needed to assign an abstract object to a variable and those needed to compare two abstract objects for equality. To simplify the notation, instead of listing these operators among exported routines, we use the conventional operators ":=" and "=" for them, and list these operators after the "?" symbol in the type clause. Thus, writing:

type A_TYPE: ? (:=, =);

in a module interface means that clients can assign an object of type A_TYPE to a variable of the same type and can compare two objects of type A_TYPE for equality. Should ":=" or "=" be missing from the type declaration, the corresponding operations would not be available to clients.

Example 4.9

Suppose we are designing a simulation system for a gasoline station, the purpose of which is to find the optimal size (in terms of number of service lines, length of lines, etc.) of the station, given the expected arrival rates of cars together with their requests for service. Each request for a service is characterized by a certain duration.

We represent each service line (gasoline, car wash, etc.) by an abstract object that represents the cars waiting for their turn to be served. There will be an operation to place a car in a service line, another to extract a car from the line, another to check whether the line is empty, and another to merge two lines associated with the same kind of resource, should the resource provided by one of them be exhausted. The policy is strictly first in–first out for all services.

We introduce an abstract data type module FIFO_CARS that describes FIFO queues of cars. We also assume that cars are described by another abstract data type module CARS, used by FIFO_CARS to perform operations on the cars extracted from the queues. The following is a sketch of module FIFO_CARS:

> **module** FIFO_CARS
> **uses** CARS
> **exports**
> > **type** QUEUE : ?;
> > **procedure** ENQUEUE (Q: **in out** QUEUE ; C: **in** CARS);
> > **procedure** DEQUEUE (Q: **in out** QUEUE ; C: **out** CARS);
> > **function** IS_EMPTY (Q: **in** QUEUE) : BOOLEAN;
> > **procedure** MERGE (Q1, Q2 : **in** QUEUE ; Q : **out** QUEUE);

---

[1] The only syntactic difference in the case of an abstract data type instance is that the object to which an operation must be applied is a parameter of the operation.

> *This is an abstract data type module representing queues of*
> *cars, handled in a strict FIFO way; queues are not assignable or*
> *checkable for equality, since ":=" and "=" are not exported*

end FIFO_CARS

This module allows other modules to declare instances of type QUEUE, such as

        gasoline_1, gasoline_2, gasoline_3: QUEUE;
        car_wash: QUEUE;

and operate on them using the exported operations. For example, we might write

        ENQUEUE (car_wash, that_car);
        MERGE (gasoline_1, gasoline_2, gasoline_3);   ∎

There is an important reason for distinguishing between abstract objects and abstract data types, even though an abstract object can certainly be obtained by generating an instance of the abstract data type.[1] The reason is that there is a difference, at least in the way these concepts may be implemented, in some programming languages (e.g., Ada). Intrinsically, an abstract data type can generate any number of instances, but we know *a priori* that abstract objects exist in only a single instance. Also, an abstract object module has a state, and an abstract data type module does not.

Exercise

4.21   A key-manager module provides a different key every time a key is requested by a client. A client can assign keys, compare them for equality, and determine which of two keys is smaller. Design the key manager module and describe the design using TDN.

4.2.4.3 Generic modules

In this section, we present an extension of TDN that provides a powerful tool for writing reusable components. This extension, called *generic modules*, can be motivated by going back to the abstract objects of Exercise 4.20. In that exercise, the physical way of performing integer I/O was hidden from clients through an interface that listed–among other things–the appropriate operation to be invoked for character output. Should we need to output values of any other type, we must provide new, specialized modules.

Suppose that the types we want to deal with are physically represented as blocks of contiguous locations, and suppose that the implementation language we use provides a

---

[1] In rigorous terms, we should say "generating an instance of the hidden type exported by the abstract data-type module." However, if no ambiguity arises, for simplicity we call *abstract data type* both the module and the type defined by that module. Also, we call *abstract object* both the instance of an abstract data-type module and a module of the kind illustrated in the previous section.

facility to scan objects byte by byte. All of the specialized modules we are going to design for the various types differ in their interface because of the type of the parameters used for the exported routines. (For example, imagine a routine to output an integer, and one to output an array of 100 integers.) All of the specialized modules, however, are very similar: they are based on exactly the same scheme and differ only in a few places. For example, all of them perform the output by unpacking the object into bytes and then packing bytes as requested by the protocol imposed by the physical output device.

It would be useful to be able to provide a single (abstract) description for all such I/O modules, by factoring all the variations into a single module, instead of duplicating a number of almost identical modules. By providing just one description for all modules, we eliminate the chance (and danger) of having inconsistencies among different modules; moreover, we localize the effect of possible modifications to exactly one unit. What we obtain is a single, highly reusable component.

A solution to this problem is given by enriching TDN to support generic modules. A generic module is a module that is parameterized with respect to a type. In our case, we would write

generic module GENERIC_I/O (T)
       T is required to be either a scalar, a record, or an array
uses . . .
exports procedure WRITE (ITEM : **in** T);
      .
      .
      .
end GENERIC_I/O

Here, module GENERIC_I/O is generic with respect to type T and procedure WRITE uses this type for its input parameter. A generic module is not directly usable by clients. In fact, rather than being a module, it is a *module template*. In order to be used, it must first be instantiated by providing actual parameters. For example, in order to instantiate an output module for integers, we should write

module INTEGER_I/O **is** GENERIC_I/O (INTEGER)

If there are constraints on the possible types to be sent as parameters at instantiation time, these constraints should be specified via comments in the interface of the generic module. In our example, we assumed that the generic I/O module works correctly only with scalars, arrays, and records; it is not guaranteed to work correctly for, say, linked lists and other kinds of dynamic data structures.

If the generic module requires its parameter type to support a particular operation, this must be specified in the module header. For example,

generic module M (T) **with** OP(T)
uses ...
      .
      .
      .
end M

indicates that the operation OP must be supported by any type that is provided to module M when it is instantiated. At instantiation time, an actual procedure must be passed as a parameter along with the type, as in the declaration:

module M_A_TYPE **is** M(A_TYPE) PROC (M_A_TYPE)

As the previous examples have shown, generic modules allow software designers to factor several algorithms into a single, abstract, generic representation that is instantiated before being used. Another typical example would be a generic sorting module, which is left parametric with respect to the type of the elements to be sorted. Thus, intrinsically, a generic module is a reusable component, because it factors several modules into a unique abstraction that is easily reused in different contexts by simple instantiation.

Similar situations arise in the case of abstract data types that can often be written as generic modules and then instantiated in various specialized module instances. For instance, in Example 4.9, we introduced a module to represent FIFO queues of cars. Suppose now that we wish to model the tellers in a bank, where bank customers queue up waiting to be served. In both cases we must describe what a queue is, the only difference being in the types of items we end up queueing in our abstract objects. Thus, again, we might solve the problem by defining a generic abstract data-type module (call it GENERIC_FIFO_QUEUE) and then generating as many module instances as are necessary.

The use of generic modules can be viewed as an application of the principle of generality: instead of solving a specific problem for, say, integers, we solve a more general problem for a class of types. Special-case solutions can then be derived from the general solution. Viewed in this way, generic modules can be useful for developing families of programs.

Exercises

4.22   Define precisely module GENERIC_FIFO_QUEUE, and instantiate a module that represents the abstract data type "queue of integer values." Show how you can then generate an abstract object instance.

4.23   We have described a generic module as parameterized by types. Propose other possibilities for parameterizing modules.

4.24   Give an example of a module that provides the possibility of sorting an array of elements of any type. The constraint is that it must be possible to compare elements of such a type to see which is bigger.

4.2.5 More Techniques for Design for Change

So far in this chapter, we have presented a body of general methods that may be used for designing well-structured software–software that can be easily understood and, most important, easily modified. These methods are valuable also for achieving the important goals of producing families of programs and generating reusable components.

Modularization via information hiding may be used to encapsulate the differences between family members, so that such differences cannot be visible outside. Similarly, the definition of simple, non-redundant, and clear interfaces can favor module reuse: in order to understand whether a component is reusable, one should conform to its interface. As we mentioned, reusability is further enhanced by genericity.

As a complement to the general principle of information hiding and the methods we have been discussing so far, the following sections illustrate some specific techniques for implementing modules that accommodate change easily.

4.2.5.1 Configuration constants

One difficulty with software modifications is that the specific information that is going to change may be wired into and spread throughout the program. As a simple example, consider the size of an integer table that is initially set to 10, but is required to become 50. The initial system might contain declarations like

> a: **array** (1. .10) **of** integer;

if we want a to store a local copy of the table. If we want to check whether an integer k used as an index in the table does not exceed its bounds, the program might contain a statement like

> **if** k ≥1 **and** k ≤ 10 **then**
> > *perform indexing;*
> **else**
> > *do other actions;*
> **end if**;

Clearly, changing the array upper bound to 50 requires changing both declarations and statements like the previous ones. In cases like this, however, where the required changes in software can be factored out into a set of constants (called *configuration constants*), the problem may be solved by changing the value of such constants and then recompiling the program.

Languages like C, Pascal, Modula-2, and Ada provide symbolic constants as a simple solution to the problem of making programs easily adaptable to a change of configuration constants. Being constants, configuration data may not be changed inadvertently by the program; being symbolic, they may be given names that suggest their meaning, in order to improve readability and modifiability.

As we mentioned before, configuration constants may be grouped together in a module that provides a common pool of data. This module would then be used by all clients that need to access the configuration data.

Another example of the use of symbolic configuration constants is the case of a device handler in which the length of buffers may vary from configuration to configuration. Each configuration may be viewed as a different member of the same family, and different family members may be generated by recompiling the application with different values of configuration constants.

Exercise

4.25 Changing the value of a configuration constant requires recompilation. Is it always necessary to perform a *complete* recompilation (i.e., a compilation of all the modules)? Discuss the issue by giving examples in C, Pascal, Modula-2, or Ada.

4.2.5.2 Conditional compilation

Configuration constants support only simple ways of representing multiple-version software. More flexible and general schemes may be provided by means of conditional compilation.

With this approach, all versions of a family are represented by one single source copy, and the differences between various versions are taken into account by conditional compilation. Source code that is relevant to only some versions is bracketed by macro commands that are recognized by the compiler. When the compiler is invoked, some parameters must be specified that describe which version of object code is to be produced; the compiler automatically ignores source statements that are not part of the proper version.

Example 4.10

Suppose we are requested to write a program in which some parts (e.g., device drivers) must be tailored to a specific hardware configuration. During design, we try to factor out all parts that do not depend on the specific hardware. If the final program is to be written in the C programming language, we may use the C preprocessor to specify what parts are to be tailored to the chosen hardware architecture. This is a sketchy example of what the C program would look like:

```
          ...source fragment common to all versions...
# ifdef hardware-1
          ...source fragment for hardware 1 ...
# endif
#ifdef hardware-2
          ...source fragment for hardware 2 ...
# endif
 .
 .
 .
```

If, at compilation time, we specify the switch D = hardware-1, only the code associated with hardware-1 will be compiled.   ∎

Exercises

4.26 Discuss the effectiveness of conditional compilation as the differences between the various versions become complex.

4.27   How can you use the generic facility in Ada to achieve the same task as in Example 4.10, without resorting to conditional compilation?

4.2.5.3 Software generation

Symbolic constants and conditional compilation achieve evolvability by allowing programs to be sufficiently general to cover some anticipated changes and to be able to be specialized at compilation time. Another appealing strategy is to generate automatically a new solution for each requested change.

Generators have been used successfully in restricted application domains. A typical example is a compiler generator, such as yacc in the UNIX environment, which can generate (part of) a compiler, given the formal definition of the language to be translated. If we decide to change the source language for which we have developed a compiler, we do not need to modify the compiler directly; rather, we rerun yacc on the newly defined language. This approach is particularly useful when the source language is not frozen yet and is subject to modifications.

Another example is a system for generating user interfaces that can be found in most data-base management systems on personal computers. In such systems, the layout of the panels used for human-machine interaction is directly "painted" on the computer screen. This declarative description is then automatically transformed into run-time actions that support the interaction of the user with the application. Changing the layout of the screen according to the user's taste can be accomplished quite easily and does not require any coding, just re-generation.

Other examples of software generators will be given in Chapter 5, where we show that certain specification languages may be executable. In some cases, execution is achieved by translating a specification into an implementation, i.e., by generating the application directly from some abstract description. Although this approach is not in common practice today, it is used in restricted domains in many software production environments. We discuss this point further in Chapter 9.

4.2.6 Stepwise Refinement

Modern introductory programming courses focus the attention of students on systematic approaches to program design and validation. The most popular approach followed is called *design by stepwise refinement*. Such design strategy is easy to describe and understand.

As its name states clearly, stepwise refinement is an iterative process. At each step, the problem to be solved is decomposed into subproblems that are solved separately. The subsolutions that comprise the solution of the original problem are then linked together by means of simple control structures. They may be executed in a sequence, or they may be selected alternatively, or they may be iterated in a loop. Thus, if P is the statement of the original problem, P_1, P_2,..., P_n are the statements of the subproblems, and C is a Boolean expression that represents a condition, P may be decomposed and solved according to one of the following patterns:

(1) $P_1; P_2; ... ; P_n$

(2)   **if** C **then**
                    $P_1;$
         else
                    P2;
         end if;

(3)   **while** C **loop**
                    $P_1;$
         end loop;

Often we need to express multiple branch selection. Thus, instead of using deeply nested **if** statements, which may adversely affect program readability, we may use a generalized **case** statement:

(2')   **case**
                    C1: P_1;
                    C2 : P_2;
                    . . . ;
                    Cn : P_n;
                    otherwise P_0;
         end case;

Each C_i represents a Boolean expression, and all C_i's are required to be mutually disjoint.

Problem statements at each step of decomposition are usually given as natural language-like descriptions. Each refinement step is represented by rewriting the natural language description in terms of subproblem statements glued together by means of the control structures represented by the above patterns. Subproblem statements, in turn, are made more detailed at the next refinement step.

Thus, the design process starts with an overall description of the problem to be solved (the "top" function), recursively applies functional decomposition, and terminates as we reach the point where each subproblem is easy to express in terms of a few lines of code in the chosen programming language. (In turn, one may view programming language statements as formal statements of very simple subproblems whose solution is directly provided by the underlying abstract machine.)

Example 4.11

The following is a description of the derivation of the sort-by-straight-selection algorithm by stepwise refinement.

Step 1
         let n be the length of the array a to be sorted;
         i := 1 ;
         while i < n **loop**
                    interchange the smallest of a_i .. .a_n and the element at position i;

```
                i := i + 1;
        end loop;
```

Step 2

```
        let n be the length of the array a to be sorted;
        i := 1 ;
        while i < n loop
                j := n;
                while j > i loop
                        if a(i) > a(j) then
                                interchange the elements at positions j and i ;
                        end if;
                        j := j - 1;
                end loop;
                i := i + 1;
        end loop;
```

Step 3

```
        let n be the length of the array a to be sorted;
        i := 1 ;
        while i < n loop
                j := n;
                while j > i loop
                        if a(i) > a(j) then
                                x := a(i); a(i) := a(j); a(j) := x;
                        end if;
                        j := j - 1;
                end loop;
                i := i + 1;
        end loop;                                                                ∎
```

Design by stepwise refinement can be represented graphically by means of a *decomposition tree* (DT). A DT is a tree in which the root is labelled by the name of the "top" problem, every other node is labelled by the name of a subproblem, and the child nodes of any given node are labelled by the names of the subproblems that detail it in a refinement. The left-to-right order of child nodes of a given node represents the order in which subproblems are to be solved during program execution. Nodes representing alternative subproblems are identified by a dotted line that groups the arcs that connect the nodes to their parent node; arcs are also labelled by the condition under which the connected subproblems must be chosen. Iteration is represented by a solid line, to which the condition governing the **while** structure is added as a label.

For example, Figure 4.13 represents the DT corresponding to the following stepwise refinement:

Step 1

```
        P;                              P is the problem to solve.
```

Step 2

P$_1$; P$_2$; P$_3$;   *P is decomposed into the*
                                       sequence of P$_1$, P$_2$, and P$_3$.

Step 3

P$_1$;
while C **loop**
                P$_{2,1}$;   *P$_2$ is decomposed into*
end loop;   *an iteration.*
P$_3$;

Step 4

P$_1$;
while C **loop**
                if C$_1$ **then**   *P$_{2,1}$ is decomposed into*
                        P$_{2,1,1}$;   *a selection.*
                else
                        P$_{2,1,2}$;
                end if;
end loop;
P$_3$;

One might wonder about the relationships between a DT and the graph of the IS_COMPOSED_OF relation or, equivalently, between top-down design obtained through iterative decomposition of a module in terms of its components and stepwise refinement. Indeed, they are similar concepts; but there are differences, too.

For example, suppose you wish to describe the stepwise refinement illustrated in Figure 4.13 in terms of the IS_COMPONENT_OF relation, representing problems and subproblems in the figure in terms of modules. Then the IS_COMPONENT_OF description of the stepwise refinement would introduce modules M for P, M$_1$ for P$_1$, M$_2$ for P$_2$, and M$_3$ for P$_3$. We cannot, however, simply state the relation

M IS_COMPOSED_OF {M$_1$,M$_2$,M$_3$}

because there would be no agent in the system responsible for arranging for the sequential execution of M$_1$,M$_2$, and M$_3$, which is implicit in the figure. Thus, we need to introduce an additional module M$_4$ to impose the sequential control flow from M$_1$ to M$_2$ to M$_3$. This would allow us to state the following relation:

M IS_COMPOSED_OF {M$_1$,M$_2$,M$_3$,M$_4$}

In turn, M$_2$ would be decomposed in terms of M$_{2,1}$ (associated with P$_{2,1}$) and M$_{2,2}$, which acts as a control module used to impose iterative use of M$_{2,1}$:

M$_2$ IS_COMPOSED_OF {M$_{2,1}$, M$_{2,2}$}

Finally, $M_{2,1}$ would be decomposed into $M_{2,1,1}$, $M_{2,1,2}$ (associated with $P_{2,1,1}$ and $P_{2,1,2}$, respectively), and $M_{2,1,3}$, which acts as a control module performing selection between $M_{2,1,1}$ and $M_{2,1,2}$ according to the value of C_1:

$$M_{2,1} \text{ IS\_COMPOSED\_OF } \{M_{2,1,1}, M_{2,1,2}, M_{2,1,3}\}$$

This example shows that a design produced by stepwise refinement may also be described top down in terms of the IS_COMPOSED_OF relation. In fact, the method we used may be applied in general to transform one description into the other. The resulting description in terms of IS_COMPONENT_OF, however, does not correspond to a meaningful modularization. Actually, stepwise refinement should be considered more a method for describing the logical structure of a given algorithm, implemented by a single module, rather than a method for describing the decomposition of a system into modules. The description of the sorting program we gave above is an illustration of the virtue of the method when it is applied in the small. A complex and large system cannot be designed and described via stepwise refinement; rather, its design requires decomposition into modules, separate development of each module, and consistent application of information hiding.

Exercises

4.28 Describe the USES relation among the modules we introduced to represent the stepwise refinement illustrated in Figure 4.13 and show the module structure using GDN.

4.29 Describe the stepwise refinement of the sort-by-straight-selection example discussed above in terms of the corresponding decomposition tree.

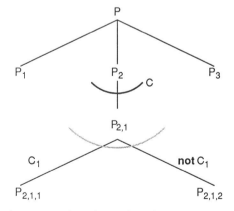

Figure 4.13   Graphical representation of stepwise refinement.

4.2.6.1 An assessment of stepwise refinement

A common misconception about stepwise refinement is that it can provide a strategy for finding a solution, by suggesting a smooth and almost mechanical way of recursively decomposing a problem into simpler subproblems. This misconception derives from illustrative examples of derivations found in some introductory textbooks, where the program seems to come out naturally by stepwise refinement. Contrary to appearances, however, the process of deriving a program may be highly creative and may require exploration of various alternatives before the appropriate solution is found. Take a well-known problem like sorting; it is certainly not by following stepwise refinement carefully that we can invent a good solution like, say, quicksort as opposed to, say, bubblesort or sort by straight selection!

What is certainly true is that stepwise refinement is an effective way of describing a solution after it has been invented. It is a way of describing–*a posteriori*–the rationale behind an algorithm by positing an ideal and rational derivation process. As such, it can be a good program documentation technique. Furthermore, if code is written by following stepwise refinement systematically, the resulting program is easy to understand.

Stepwise refinement is an effective technique for describing small-sized programs. It fails, however, to scale up to systems of even moderate complexity. It is a method that works in the small, but fails in the large. In particular, it does not match the goals that information hiding tries to solve, and more specifically, it does not help designers reuse components from previous applications or design reusable components when applied to larger programs. Here are a few reasons that explain these shortcomings:

Subproblems tend to be analyzed in isolation. No emphasis is put by stepwise refinement on trying to generalize subproblems in a way that would make them reusable at different points within the derivation of the system, let alone across different designs.

When a problem is to be made more detailed, it is studied in the context of the decomposition subtree in which it appears. On the other hand, when a problem is being decomposed into subproblems, it may be useful to see whether a suitable generalization of the problem would make it similar to another problem being solved elsewhere, so that we can unify the two problems and design a single module for them.

No attention is paid to information hiding. Stepwise refinement does not draw the designer's attention to the need for encapsulating changeable information within modules. In fact, the modules we derive when we apply stepwise refinement are pure procedural abstractions. A problem represented by some abstract function is recursively decomposed into subproblems, all of which are represented by abstract functions.

In stepwise refinement, the strategy never emphasizes the need for grouping together functions to define an abstract object or data type, nor is there a way to derive modules that provide selective export of a collection of resources. The only principle that guides functional decomposition by stepwise refinement is the striving for readability of the resulting solution.

No attention is paid to data. This is a corollary of the previous point. Stepwise refinement does not stress the use of information-hiding modules. For example, the method does not stress the derivation of modules that hide a data structure and export abstract operations to access it.

The top function may not exist. The method starts by stating the top problem, which is recursively detailed in terms of subproblems. A minor, but annoying, issue is that the top problem may be unnatural to state. Remember that the top problem should describe the problem as a very high-level function that transforms the input data into the expected results. Such a function, however, does not always exist.

For example, what is the function performed by a word processor? A word processor is a system that reacts to input commands that create a text, append or insert new characters into an existing file, and can do complex text manipulation in response to commands supplied by the user. Of course, one can always write the top function as "respond to all user commands." but this is of very little help in the future decomposition.

There is a premature commitment to the control structures that govern the flow of control among modules. The case study of translating the stepwise refinement of Figure 4.12 into a hierarchy of IS_COMPOSED_OF illustrates this point clearly. When P_2 is decomposed into the iteration of $P_{2,1}$, two modules are introduced conceptually: $M_{2,1}$ and $M_{2,2}$. $M_{2,1}$ corresponds to $P_{2,1}$; $M_{2,2}$ is just a control module that simply contains the statement

> **while** C **loop** $P_{2,1}$ **end loop**;

to force repeated execution of $M_{2,1}$. A similar situation then arises in the decomposition of $M_{2,1}$. This concept is further emphasized by the following example.

Example 4.12

Suppose we are designing a program to check the syntactic correctness of programs written in a given programming language. Following stepwise refinement, we may write:

Step 1

> Recognize a program stored in a given file f;

Step 2

> correct := true;
> analyze f according to the language definition;
> **if** correct **then**
> > *print message* "program correct";
> **else**
> > *print message* "program incorrect";
> **end if**;

Step 3

> correct := true;
> perform lexical analysis:
> > *store the program as a sequence of tokens in file f_t and the*
> > *symbol table in file f_s, and set the Boolean variable*
> > *error_in_lexical_phase according to the result of lexical analysis;*

if error_in_lexical_phase **then**
        correct := false;
else
        perform syntax analysis on file f_t and set the
        Boolean variable error_in_syntactic_phase according to the
        result of syntax analysis;
        if **error_in_syntactic_phase** then
            correct := false;
        end if;
end if;
if correct **then**
        print message "program correct";
else
        print message "program incorrect";
end if;

Without proceeding any further with the example, we can see that we have made strong commitments about the flow of control from the early stages of our development. For example, we decided that lexical analysis should come first, that it should operate on the entire input program, and that it should produce the corresponding sequence of tokens in an intermediate file, to be used by the subsequent phase of syntax analysis.

Suppose now that we decide to change strategy–for example, we decide that we do not want to perform recognition in two passes, but we wish to let the syntactic analyzer, drive the process. In this case, the syntactic analyzer repeatedly activates the lexical analyzer asking for the next token. This change has a profound impact on the structure of the program as described by stepwise refinement: everything must be redone starting from step 3.

The impact of this change would not be so dramatic, however, if we followed an approach based on information hiding–for example, by defining the following sample modules:

- CHAR_HOLDER: hides the physical representation of the input file and exports an operation for accessing the source file on a character-by-character basis;
- SCANNER: hides the details of the lexical structure of the language from the rest of the system and exports an operation for providing the next token in the sequence;
- PARSER: hides the data structure used to perform syntax analysis (the parse tree), which might be encapsulated in an internal abstract-object module (PARSER).   ∎

Exercise

4.30 Complete the design of the language recognizer. Use both TDN and GDN to describe your design. Describe what changes are needed to transform a two-pass solution into a one-pass solution.

4.2.7 Top-Down Versus Bottom-Up Design

What strategy should we follow when we design a system? Should we proceed top down, by recursively applying decomposition through IS_COMPOSED_OF, until we break down the system into manageable components? Or, starting from what we wish to encapsulate within a module, should we proceed bottom up, recursively defining an abstract interface and then grouping together several modules to form a new higher level module that comprises them?

Stepwise refinement is an intrinsically top-down method. Some of the criticisms we raised about the method must be attributed to its peculiarities. In particular, the premature commitment to control structures and the orientation to design in the small are due to the programming language-based style used to describe the refinements. Other major criticisms, however, apply to the top-down strategy in general. Among these are the facts that subproblems tend to be analyzed in isolation, that no emphasis is placed on the identification of commonalities or on reusability of components, and that little attention is paid to data and, more generally, to information hiding.

Information hiding proceeds mainly bottom up. It suggests that we should first recognize what we wish to encapsulate within a module and then provide an abstract interface to define the module's boundaries as seen from the clients. Note, however, that the decision of what to hide inside a module (such as the decision to hide certain policies) may depend on the result of some top-down design activity. Since information hiding has proven to be highly effective in supporting design for change, program families, and reusable components, its bottom-up philosophy should be followed in a consistent way.

Design, however, is a highly critical and creative human activity. Good designers do not proceed in a strictly top-down or strictly bottom-up fashion. For example, should they decide to proceed top down, they also tend to pay attention to identifying commonalities and possible reusable components, i.e., they combine a predominantly top-down strategy with a bottom-up attitude.

A typical design strategy may proceed partly top down and partly bottom up, depending on the phase of design or the nature of the application being designed, in a way that might be called *yo-yo design*. As an example, we might start decomposing a system top down in terms of subsystems and, at some later point, synthesize subsystems in terms of a hierarchy of information-hiding modules.

The top-down approach, however, is often useful as a way to document a design. Despite our claim that the design activity should not be constrained to proceed according to a fixed, rigid pattern, but should be a blend of top-down and bottom-up steps, we also recommend that the *description* of the resulting design be given in a top-down fashion. Even if a system has not been designed top down, we should describe it as if it were designed top down, because this makes the system easier to understand.

4.3 OBJECT-ORIENTED DESIGN

Object-oriented design is a technique that pushes to the extreme a design approach based on abstract data types. It has become popular in the past few years due to the appearance of new programming languages (and the rediscovery of older ones) that enforce the technique by supporting an adequate notation and, in particular, due to the expectations raised by the technique for producing reusable software components.

Unfortunately, the terminology of object-oriented methods is not well standardized, and there is not even agreement as to what object-oriented design really is. The same holds in the programming language area, where there is no general consensus on what characterizes an object-oriented programming language.

In this section, we will address object-oriented design in rather general terms that will encompass several of the forms in which the concept has been described in the literature. Unlike most object-oriented languages, however, we continue using well-understood terms like "procedure" (or "routine") and "procedure call" instead of the terms *method* and *message* that are used in some object-oriented jargon.

> **module** EMPLOYEE
> **uses** SITE, MONEY, UNIQUE_NUMBER
> > *Modules SITE , MONEY, and UNIQUE_IDENTIFIER are abstract data type modules that are not presented here; e.g. instances of type SITE are objects representing the various locations of the company.*
> **exports**
> > **function** FIRST_NAME: string_of_char;
> > **function** LAST_NAME: string_of_char;
> > **function** AGE: positive_integer;
> > **function** WHERE: SITE;
> > **procedure** HIRE (LAST_N: **in** string_of_char;
> > > FIRST_N: **in** string_of_char;
> > > INIT_SALARY: **in** MONEY;
> > > ID: **out** UNIQUE_IDENTIFIER);
> > *This operation hires an employee with the given first and last names, and assigns an initial salary. Also, it assigns a unique identifier by calling the appropriate module.*
> > **procedure** FIRE;
> > **procedure** ASSIGN (S: **in out** SITE);
> > *It is not possible to assign an employee to a site if it is already assigned to it (i.e., WHERE must be different from S). The client must ensure that this incorrect behavior does not arise. The effect of the operation is to add the employee to those in S and delete the employee from those in WHERE; in addition, WHERE is set to S.*
> > **function** SALARY: MONEY;
> > :
> > :
> **end** EMPLOYEE

(a) continued on next page

Figure 4.14   An example of inheritance. (**a**) Textual design description.
(**b**) Graphical design description.

module ADMINISTRATIVE_STAFF **inherits** EMPLOYEE
uses FOLDER
> *One must list specific modules used in this module; in this case we list FOLDER, an abstract data type module whose instances represent folders containing work to be done by the administrative employee*

exports
> *Here we list the additional resources that the module exports, apart from those it inherits from its parent*
> **procedure** DO_THIS (F: **in** FOLDER);
> *The current employee receives a folder f containing the work to do*
> .
> .
> .

end ADMINISTRATIVE_STAFF

module TECHNICAL_STAFF **inherits** EMPLOYEE;
uses PROJECT
> *Module PROJECT is an abstract data type whose instances are projects on which technicians are working*

exports
> **procedure** ASSIGN (P: **in out** PROJECT);
> *Assigns the current object (a technician) to a project*
> .
> .
> .

end TECHNICAL_STAFF

(a) continued from previous page

Figure 4.14   An example of inheritance. (a) Textual design description.
(b) Graphical design description.

In object-oriented design, there is one single kind of module: the abstract data-type module. Thus, we modify TDN to express the fact that all modules implicitly implement just abstract data types. Instead of using the notation "**type** XX = ?" in the interface of some module X to introduce the type's name, we let client modules use the module's name directly. Hence, instead of declaring, say, an object of the abstract data type XX defined by module X as "a: XX", we would write "a: X".

Another substantial change occurs in the operations that are invoked on instance objects. In the case of the abstract data type module X exporting XX, in order to manipulate object a, operation op is invoked by X's client modules as

>   op (a, other_parameters)

In the case of object-oriented design, we would write

>   a.op (other_parameters)

indicating invocation of precisely operation op provided by instance a of module (i.e., abstract data type) X. Thus, all operations exported by an object-oriented module implicitly operate on a *current instance object*, which is not named as a parameter.

Besides the USES and the IS_COMPONENT_OF relations, one more relation is provided by object-oriented design: INHERITS_FROM. As we will see shortly, through inheritance one may design one component as a (constrained) modification of another. Thus, in most object-oriented notations–and in the extended TDN notation we illustrate here–if M_1 INHERITS_FROM M_2, then M_1 has visibility into the internal structure (the secrets) of M_2. This is a radical departure from the behavior of the USES relation, where the internals of a module are hidden.

The relation INHERITS_FROM defines a hierarchy on modules. If M_2 INHERITS_FROM M_1, we say that M_1 is the *parent module* and M_2 is the *heir module*.

One way of looking at inheritance is as a *classification scheme* for abstract data types. For example, in a business application we may classify employees of a given company as technical staff and administrative staff. To do so, we define a module EMPLOYEE and two heir modules TECHNICAL_STAFF and ADMINISTRATIVE_STAFF (see Figure 4.14).

All employees–i.e., instances of EMPLOYEE–are characterized by certain operations that are provided by the module for manipulation. For example, they may be hired, by which they receive a unique identifier and an initial salary; they may be fired, by which the unique identifier is released; they may be promoted; they may be assigned

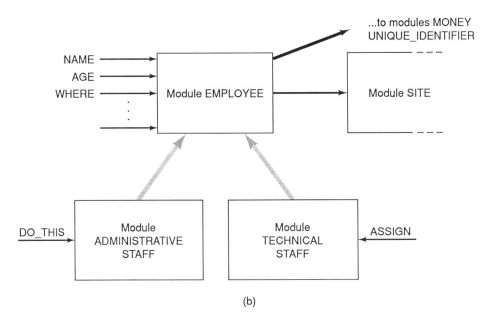

(b)

Figure 4.14   An example of inheritance. (a) Textual design description.
(b) Graphical design description.

to a work site of the company; and they may be asked for their name, age, salary, etc. Some employees are members of the technical staff, others are members of the administrative staff, and still others are neither technical nor administrative.

A member of the administrative staff enjoys all properties of employees. From an abstract data-type viewpoint, this means that it may be manipulated by all operations defined by the parent module, plus others that characterize the heir module itself. In object-oriented terminology, we say that all such operations are automatically inherited by the heir from the parent. For example, members of the administrative staff may be hired, fired, etc., and they may be assigned some work to do by passing them a folder. The latter operation is specific to the heir module: it is not inherited from its parent module. Similarly, members of the technical staff, apart from the operations inherited from their parent module, may be manipulated by an operation that assigns them to some project. Finally, there are also individuals that are neither members of the technical staff nor members of the administrative staff. According to the hierarchy of Figure 4.14, they are just members of module EMPLOYEE, without belonging to any particular heir module.

Figure 4.14 describes the modules using an extended version of TDN (part (a)) and GDN (part (b)).

The EMPLOYEE example shows a particular way of looking at inheritance as a *classification scheme for abstract data type*s. According to this view, an heir module is more *specialized* than its parent module. This view is useful when the system is initially designed. It helps the designer concentrate first on what is common among all abstract objects of a given set and then on the differences among subsets. Commonalities are factored out in a parent module, while differences are singled out in the heirs.

This procedure is a step in the direction of improving reusability. In fact, we may try to factor out in a module all features that are likely to be sufficiently general to be easily reused. The additional features needed in specific applications may be added afterwards by means of heir modules.

We can also look at inheritance as a *way of building software incrementally*. Thus, inheritance facilitates system evolution as new requirements arise. More generally, it can make maintenance easier to perform. The idea is that whenever the need arises to modify an existing module M_1 in order to obtain a new behavior as described in a module M_2, instead of modifying M_1, we inherit from M_1 and apply the changes that would transform M_1 into M_2. The type of changes we have examined so far consists exclusively of adding new operations to the abstract data types, but this restriction will be relaxed below.

In essence, we used incrementality to define the two heirs of EMPLOYEE. The two heir modules were defined by just listing the differences with respect to the parent module. To be more precise, the heir module is obtained from its parent module as a copy of its implementation with some new resources added to it.

As the example of Figure 4.14 shows, we took advantage of the fact that, through inheritance, we may access the internal details of the parent module. This is necessary because in order to *modify* a module, one must have access to its details. In fact, the internal data structure used to implement the abstract data type must be known in order to provide the heir with the ability to define additional operations. This is different from the case of USES, where the client only needs to know the interface of the used module, not its internal secrets. This view of inheritance, however, has been criticized in the literature since a change in the internal part of the parent module has an impact on the correctness of the heirs, which must change accordingly. This raises the question as to whether the useful effects of inheritance–classification (or specialization) and incremental modification–may be obtained without violating the principle of information hiding.

Example 4.13

Let us modify the simulation of a gasoline station outlined in Example 4.9. Suppose that the gas station has several service lines for gas and that two queues may be merged if a gas dispenser becomes empty. Suppose also that there is one queue for car repair and that the car repair service is available only when the mechanic is on duty.

One approach consists of designing a NEW_FIFO_CARS module–possibly an instance of the GENERIC_FIFO_QUEUE module defined in Exercise 4.22–and two heir modules–one for gas lines and one for repair–that add specialized operations. The first heir module, called GAS_QUEUE, allows two queues to be merged into one queue. The second, called REPAIR_QUEUE, provides an operation for the mechanic to signal that he or she is on duty, and an operation for car drivers to check whether the service is currently available. The following fragment shows such a solution:

```
module NEW_FIFO_CARS is GENERIC_FIFO_QUEUE (CAR)
        Module FIFO_QUEUE has been provided by Exercise 4.22; you
        can easily rephrase it here in OO notation. It provides facilities
        to place items in and take items out of the queue.
module GAS_QUEUE inherits NEW_FIFO_CARS


exports
        procedure MERGE (Q: GAS_QUEUE);
        Q is merged into the current queue.


end GAS_QUEUE

module REPAIR_QUEUE inherits NEW_FIFO_CARS


exports
        procedure SET_AVAILABLE;
        procedure SET_UNAVAILABLE;
        These procedures are called by an abstract object representing
        the mechanic, to signal that the service is or is not available.
        procedure IS_AVAILABLE;
        This procedure is called to see whether the mechanic is
        available.


end REPAIR_QUEUE                                                  ∎
```

In order to provide additional support for incrementality and changeability, other types of incremental modifications are usually permitted through inheritance, besides simply adding operations by the heir modules. Unfortunately, however, these types of inheritance are not provided by all languages that claim to support object-oriented design. Also, some of the issues they raise are highly controversial and not fully understood yet. As a consequence, we state the problems in rather general terms, without providing any notational details, and ignore the underlying subtleties.

A rather simple extension of the previously introduced inheritance mechanism is when an heir provides a different implementation for one of the parent's resources. An example is when the parent exports a routine (say, a sort routine) and the heir provides a different implementation for it, with no change in the routine's interface, just in the algorithm. What happens here is a *redefinition*–not an addition–of an operation of the abstract data type in the heir module, so that objects of the heir module will be manipulated by the redefined operation, not by the operation with the same name that is inherited from the parent module.

More subtle cases, however, arise if we allow redefinition of (parts of) the data structure hidden in the parent module. Still more critical problems arise if we wish to use inheritance more liberally, as some object-oriented languages would actually permit, supporting unconstrained redefinition of both the data and the routines of the parent module. Finally, there are cases where the heir may change the definition of what is exported and what is hidden among the whole set of resources defined by its parent module.

Another important and controversial issue is whether the design notation should provide ways to describe *multiple inheritance*. In fact, not everything may be organized in a tree-like fashion (as we have done so far), with each heir having only one parent. Often, one would like to define a new module by combining the features provided by two or more parent modules. For example, we might want to define an object FIFO_EMPLOYEE_QUEUE that inherits from both FIFO_QUEUE and EMPLOYEE. Multiple inheritance, however, is not provided by all object-oriented notations and is even less understood. Thus, we do not exploit it here.

All the ways we have discussed of viewing inheritance make it clear that the concept has enormous potential from a software engineering viewpoint. It can help support design for change, incremental development, design of program families, and reusable components. Through inheritance, one may progressively add new features to a module, according to an incremental design philosophy. The various members of a program family may be designed as heirs of a parent module that contains features that are common to all family members. Reusable components may be customized by providing heir modules that only describe the differences with respect to the original component.

More generally, we can recognize the potential advantages of the inheritance mechanism by examining it in the light of the general principles set forth in Chapter 3. Inheritance supports the application of all of the following:

- *separation of concerns*, by allowing us to concentrate on the common properties of a set of objects and the special properties of the particular objects at different times;
- *modularity*, by encouraging a particular kind of modularity in terms of classification of objects;
- *abstraction*, by allowing us to separate the common properties of a set of objects from the details of the individual objects;

- *anticipation of change*, by supporting the derivation of new modules through systematic modification of existing modules;
- *generality*, by allowing us to design general modules that can be specialized in different ways;
- *incrementality*, by supporting the extension of existing modules to build new ones that offer more performance, more functionality, etc.

The difficult and controversial points we have raised above, however, show that the field is still open to research contributions and subject to rapid evolution. More important, there are deep conceptual differences among the object-oriented languages available today. In particular, if we wish to make heavy use of inheritance–one of the features that gives to object-oriented design its special flavor and provides its power and flexibility–we should take into account the specific features offered by the programming language we intend to use for implementation. In other words, if you are going to use an object-oriented programming language that provides inheritance, then we recommend making use of inheritance as the language allows. Instead, if you are using a language that does not provide inheritance, then mapping the inheritance hierarchy onto the implementation may lead to programs that are difficult to design and understand. In such a case, we suggest relying on the general design concepts we have illustrated so far, without using inheritance at all, or use a very simple type of inheritance so that the mapping of the design onto the chosen programming language will be smooth.

4.4 HANDLING ANOMALIES

A systematic design approach followed by a rigorous and disciplined implementation is the best way of dominating the complexity of software and building reliability into the products. Unfortunately, software products can be very complex, rendering software production subject to human fallibility. No matter how careful we are during development, we should never trust our software unconditionally. This can be frustrating to the conscientious programmer, after much care, effort, and money has been spent to build a truly reliable product. The only solution to this problem is humility. The software engineer must be aware of the criticality of many applications; as mentioned, software errors may cause great financial losses or endanger human lives. We must do all that we can to minimize the risks of such disasters.

The designer must employ *defensive design*. By this, we mean that the designer not only should strive for maximum reliability in developing a system, but also should try to shield the application from errors that–unfortunately–may creep in during development or may arise due to adverse circumstances during program execution. That is, we must build *robust* systems: our programs should continue to behave reasonably even in the case of unexpected and unforeseen circumstances.

We define a module to be *anomalous* if it fails to provide a service as expected and specified in its interface. So far, our design descriptions–whether textual or graphical–are mainly syntactic in nature and do not support a formal description of the semantics of the services exported by a module. A semantic enrichment of the notation may be given according to the concepts we will discuss in Chapter 5. For simplicity, here we assume that semantics is specified by means of comments appearing in the interface, as explained in Section 4.2.3. We do, however, extend our design notations to associate a set of exceptions (defined below) with each service exported by a module. The *exceptions* associated with a service denote the anomalies that may occur while that service is being performed. For simplicity again, we assume that the services exported by a module correspond to routines; what we say here, however, may be restated for other types of services.

Either a module executes correctly, in which case it performs the requested service and returns to the client in a normal way, or it enters an anomalous state. Defensive design requires that in the latter case the module should signal the anomaly by *raising an exception* to the client. In other words, we distinguish between the correct behavior of the module and the anomalous behavior. If something goes wrong and the module cannot complete the requested service correctly, the module should return an exception.

In order to state clearly that an anomalous state was entered, the module should not return normally, as if nothing had happened. Rather, it should return abnormally, by raising an exception. An exception may be viewed as an event that is signalled to the client. The module executing the service requested terminates execution, and the client, notified of the occurrence of the exception, responds by suitably handling the exception.

Why should a module M fail to provide its service as specified? Following what we said in Section 4.2.2, this may happen because M's client does not satisfy the required protocol for invoking one of M's services. It may also happen if M does not satisfy the required protocol when trying to use a service exported by another module–say, N. In the latter case, N's failure is signalled back to M and M's *exception handler* is activated accordingly. The handler may try to recover from the anomaly, or it may simply do some cleanup of the module's state and–in turn–let the routine fail, in its turn signalling an exception to its caller.

If the recovery is successful, M would not fail; otherwise, cleanup may be necessary to ensure that subsequent uses of M by other clients do not find the module in an inconsistent state. Note, however, that exception handlers are hidden in the module body; i.e., the exact way an exception is handled by a module is part of the module's secret. Therefore, we do not go deeply into the issue here. We do not examine how signalled exceptions are bound to handlers, or what happens if a client module does not possess a handler for the signalled exception. These issues are very much dependent on the programming language we choose for the implementation and will be taken up in Chapter 9, which deals with implementation issues.

Apart from the previously discussed types of failures, a module may fail to provide its service because of an unforeseen condition, such as an overflow or an array index out of bounds, occurring during execution of the module. In the latter case, we assume that the underlying abstract machine is able to trap the abnormal condition and pass it on to the software for appropriate handling. If the underlying implementation language supports this feature, the failure may also arise if some logical assertion on correctness is violated during execution. Once such failures are passed to the software, they are treated as were the previous types of exceptions.

Hereafter, we extend TDN interface descriptions so that a list of exception names may be associated with exported services. These are the names of exceptions that may be raised by the service to signal its anomalous completion. The policies adopted by the module to handle anomalies that are signalled to it may be specified in comments, if necessary, to document the design.

Let us give some examples. Suppose that when interfaces are defined, designers agree on certain restrictions that apply to parameters of a procedure P enclosed in some module M. For example, they might agree that P should receive a nonnegative value for parameter X. This decision is recorded in M's interface as a comment (see Figure 4.15). Of course, in a perfect world, there is no reason to suspect that client modules do not satisfy this requirement. Defensive design, however, requires that we not trust clients to behave properly and protect M by sending back an exception if P is called with a negative value for X.

> **module** M
> **exports** . . .
>   **procedure** P (X: INTEGER; . . .)
>   **raises** X_NON_NEGATIVE_EXPECTED,
>   INTEGER_OVERFLOW;
>   *X is to be positive; if not, exception*
>   *X_NON_NEGATIVE_EXPECTED is raised;*
>   *INTEGER_OVERFLOW is raised if internal*
>   *computation of P generates an overflow*
>   :
> **end** M

Figure 4.15   A design fragment describing exceptions.

> **module** L
> **uses** M **imports** P (X: INTEGER; . . .)
> **exports** . . .;
>   **procedure** R (. . .)
>   **raises** INTEGER_OVERFLOW;
>   :
> **implementation**
>   *If INTEGER_OVERFLOW is raised when P is invoked, the*
>   *exception is propagated*
>   :
> **end** L

Figure 4.16   A design fragment of a propagated exception.

As another example, consider Figure 4.16 in which module L uses module M of Figure 4.15. Should the exception INTEGER_OVERFLOW occur when procedure P is called by procedure R of L, we might decide that R's handler do some cleanup and bookkeeping and then raise an appropriate exception (perhaps INTEGER_OVERFLOW again) to be handled by R's client. The same policy might then be followed by the client, and so on. Indeed, this can be a way of performing an organized shutdown of the system as a consequence of an unrecoverable error.

From the fragment of Figure 4.16, we observe that L does not raise an exception corresponding to the condition X_NON_NEGATIVE_EXPECTED, which may be raised by P. This means that either L guarantees that the exception never arises, or L will recover from it.

Exercise

4.31   Suppose we are asked to build a cross-reference table for the variables appearing in a program. A cross-reference program is an aid to reconstruct documentation from existing programs that are, by assumption, correct. Thus, according to the specification, it should never happen that a variable is used without or before being declared. For simplicity, we assume that the language does not provide scoping rules: all variable names are global.

We design a cross-reference table module CRT–an abstract object–that exports two operations: (1) Procedure NOTIFY is called to insert a variable's name in the table, along with the number of the line where the declaration of the variable occurred. (2) Procedure OCCUR is called to record the occurrence of a variable in a statement, by specifying a variable's name and an occurrence line.

As part of the contract with client modules, we specify in the interface that NOTIFY cannot be called if a variable with the same name is already in the cross-reference table. Also, OCCUR can be called only if the variable we are transmitting as a parameter has already been declared (again, it was in the cross-reference table). These protocols are consistent with the assumption that the source program is correct.

Design a robust CRT module and provide its TDN description. Implement your design in a programming language of your choice, assuming that suitable other modules drive CRT. Discuss the pros and cons of the language as far as exception handling is concerned.

4.5 A CASE STUDY IN DESIGN

In this section, we illustrate the concepts presented in the previous sections in the context of a case study in design. Our goal is not to provide a general recipe of "what makes a good design." Design is a creative activity that cannot be done mechanically; it requires human insight. Accordingly, we examine here a hypothetical design process in action, showing some of the problems that may arise in practice and discussing examples of what makes a good module.

Let us consider a small group of software engineers designing the compiler of yet another programming language–MIDI. MIDI is considerably more complex than the MINI language of Examples 4.2. and 4.7. In particular, it is an ALGOL-like, block-structured programming language. The overall design of Example 4.7 is supposed to be valid here, too, and is not discussed any more. In what follows, we concentrate our attention on the design of the module SYMBOL_TABLE. The designers are told that the programs to be compiled are created by means of a special-purpose syntax-directed editor that enforces the syntactic correctness of programs. Blocks are correctly bracketed by **begin**, **end** pairs, and–for reasons of style–the editor does not permit the creation of programs with more than seven levels of block nesting.

SYMBOL_TABLE is an abstract object that hides the physical data structure used to represent the table it creates. Its interface is tentatively represented by the TDN fragment in Figure 4.17. According to the figure, client modules may insert an identifier, along with its attributes into the table via procedure INSERT. Clients are also allowed to retrieve the attributes of previously recorded identifiers via procedure RETRIEVE. Attributes are supposed to be stored in a descriptor. Operations are available to signal when a new lexical scope is entered (procedure ENTER_SCOPE) and when a scope is exited (procedure EXIT_SCOPE). Finally, an operation (LEVEL) should be available to compute the lexical nesting level of an identifier. The level is zero if the identifier is declared locally, i.e., in the most recently entered, and not yet exited, scope; the level is one if the identifier is nonlocal and declared in the previously entered scope; and so on.

> **module** SYMBOL_TABLE
> > *Supports up to 7 nesting levels (enter, exit); pairs of calls*
> > *must be properly nested; each exit call must match a*
> > *unique previous enter call* ;
> **uses** ... **imports** (IDENTIFIER, DESCRIPTOR)
> **exports procedure**   INSERT (ID: **in** IDENTIFIER;
> > > > DESCR: **in** DESCRIPTOR);
> > **procedure**   RETRIEVE (ID:**in** IDENTIFIER;
> > > > DESCR: **out** DESCRIPTOR);
> > **procedure**   LEVEL (ID: **in** IDENTIFIER; L:**out** INTEGER);
> > **procedure**   ENTER_SCOPE;
> > **procedure**   EXIT_SCOPE;
> **end** SYMBOL_TABLE

Figure 4.17   TDN fragment representing the initial version of the symbol table interface.

The designers of the MIDI compiler soon realize that the current version of the SYMBOL_TABLE interface has the following shortcomings:

1. Operation INSERT should return a parameter if insertion cannot be accomplished because an identifier with the same name was already declared in the current scope.

2. Operations RETRIEVE and LEVEL should return a parameter if an identifier with the specified name is not currently visible.

3. Operations ENTER_SCOPE and EXIT_SCOPE are guaranteed to be correctly invoked by the assumption that programs are created by the syntax-directed editor. For the sake of robustness, however, they should raise an exception if invoked abnormally. This would allow the system to work robustly even if an error is present in the syntax-directed editor, or if the source program is not created by the special editor but, say, is obtained from an independent supplier.

Based on these three points, the designers produce a revised version of the SYMBOL_TABLE interface, shown by the fragment in Figure 4.18.

> **module** SYMBOL_TABLE
> **uses** ... **imports** (IDENTIFIER, DESCRIPTOR)
> **exports**
> > *Supports up to 7 nesting levels; (**enter** , **exit**) pairs of calls must be properly nested; each **exit** call must match a unique previous **enter** call;*
> > **procedure** INSERT (ID: **in** IDENTIFIER;
> > > DESCR: **in** DESCRIPTOR;
> > > RESULT: **out** boolean);
> > > *RESULT will be false if ID is multiply defined*
> > **procedure** RETRIEVE (ID: **in** IDENTIFIER;
> > > DESCR: **out** DESCRIPTOR;
> > > RESULT: **out** boolean);
> > > *RESULT will be false if ID is not visible in the current scope*
> > **procedure** LEVEL (ID: **in** IDENTIFIER;
> > > L: **in** INTEGER;
> > > RESULT: **out** boolean);
> > > *RESULT will be false if ID is not visible in the current scope*
> > **procedure** ENTER_SCOPE **raises** EXTRA_LEVELS;
> > > *EXTRA_LEVELS is raised in the abnormal case where the number of nesting levels > 7*
> > **procedure** EXIT_SCOPE **raises** EXTRA_END;
> > > *EXTRA_END is raised in the abnormal case where there is no matching **enter** for an **exit***
> **end** SYMBOL_TABLE

Figure 4.18   TDN fragment representing a revised version of the symbol table interface.

Let us now follow the job of the designer of SYMBOL_TABLE. The program's block structure requires that information concerning the various scopes be allocated and deallocated according to a LIFO policy. When a new scope is entered, a new block of descriptors is allocated. The block is deallocated upon scope exit. We can, therefore, use a stack for storing descriptors. Thanks to the information on the maximum nesting level, the designer decides to use an array of lists, each list representing the declarations occurring in a block in terms of <identifier, descriptor> pairs.

Defining a list is not a new problem for our designer. She has faced the same problem over and over–redefining a new list from scratch every time it is needed–and this is quite frustrating! Thus, the designer decides to define a rather general list-handling module that will be reusable in future designs.

LIST is designed as a generic abstract data type. Being generic, it can be instantiated to a module that handles a list of elements of any specific type. Being an abstract data type, it allows several list objects to be instantiated. A tentative version of the module's interface is shown by the TDN fragment of Figure 4.19.

```
generic module   LIST(T) with MATCH (EL_1,EL_2: in T)
exports
          type LINKED_LIST:?;
          procedure  IS_EMPTY (L: in LINKED_LIST): BOOLEAN;
          Tells whether the list is empty.
          procedure  SET_EMPTY (L: in out  LINKED_LIST);
          Sets a list to empty.
          procedure  INSERT (L: in out  LINKED_LIST; EL: in T);
          Inserts the element into the list
          procedure  SEARCH (L: in LINKED_LIST; EL_1: in T;
                             EL_2: out T; FOUND: out boolean);
                     Searches L to find an element EL_2 that
                     matches EL_1 and returns the result in FOUND.
     end LIST(T)
```

Figure 4.19   TDN fragment representing the initial version of the interface for a list handling module.

LIST exports a SEARCH procedure that searches the list to find an element that "matches" a given parameter. In the SYMBOL_TABLE example, since T is an <identifier, descriptor> pair, two elements of type T match if their identifiers are the same. In general, what "match" means should be specified by a procedure associated with the formal parameter T and sent as actual parameter when the module is instantiated. Also, the module provides a procedure INSERT to store an element of type T. Where the element is actually stored is not specified in the interface: it may be at the beginning of the list, at the end, or at any intermediate point (e.g., in order to keep the list sorted). The choice is thus left to the implementation.

In many practical cases of list handling, the clients must know whether the item is stored at the beginning, at the end, or at a specific intermediate point. In such cases, we should extend the given module LIST, in order to provide various specialized kinds of INSERT. If we adopt an object-oriented design method, we may design such redefinitions or extension in terms of inheritance. The same considerations hold in the case where we wish to add new operations to LIST that make it a truly general-purpose module.

At this point, we leave it to the reader to develop the example in all its details, using both TDN and GDN. Some of the details that we have omitted to mention here will show up, and this will help the reader to understand the design more deeply.

4.6 CONCURRENT SOFTWARE

So far, we have assumed that the application we are designing has a single stream of execution (often called "thread of control"), i.e., that it is a purely sequential system.

Unfortunately, many applications do not fall into this class, and the consequence is additional complexity of both design and analysis. Such classes of applications are so important that they deserve special treatment. Usually they are studied as a separate topic in the courses and textbooks on operating systems or real-time systems. Here, we put these applications in relation to other types of software, by showing how the previously examined design techniques are affected by concurrency.

One of the key problems in designing concurrent software is to ensure the consistency of data that are shared among concurrently executing modules. We will discuss this problem and solutions to it in Section 4.6.1. We will then consider two particular classes of concurrent software, real-time software in Section 4.6.2 and distributed software in Section 4.6.3.

4.6.1 Shared Data

Let us generalize the concepts of modularity we have studied to the case where we have an abstract object that is accessed by more than one sequential activity (or *process*) at a time. For example, suppose we have the abstract object BUFFER of type QUEUE of characters. This object might be an instance of a type obtained by first instantiating the generic type of Exercise 4.22, i.e.,

module QUEUE_OF_CHAR **is** GENERIC_FIFO_QUEUE (CHAR)

and then instantiating a variable

BUFFER : QUEUE_OF_CHAR.QUEUE;

assuming that QUEUE is the name of the type exported by GENERIC_QUEUE and using dot notation to specify selection of a resource exported by a specific instance.

We assume here that the following operations are available on objects of type QUEUE of characters:

- PUT: inserts a character in a QUEUE;
- GET: extracts a character from a QUEUE;
- NOT_FULL: returns **true** if its QUEUE parameter is not full;
- NOT_EMPTY: returns **true** if its QUEUE parameter is not empty.

Object BUFFER is accessed concurrently by client processes that produce characters (say, PRODUCER_1, PRODUCER_2, etc.) and call operation PUT to insert a new character in the buffer. It is also accessed concurrently by client processes that remove characters (say, CONSUMER_1, CONSUMER_2, etc.), and call procedure GET to extract one character from the buffer. Assume that operation PUT may be called only if the buffer is not full and that operation GET may be called only if the buffer is not empty.

To use the module BUFFER correctly, we might try to embed calls to GET and PUT issued from the clients into the following structures:

(i)   **if** QUEUE_OF_CHAR.NOT_FULL (BUFFER) **then**
                    QUEUE_OF_CHAR.PUT (X);
           end if;

(ii)   **if** QUEUE_OF_CHAR.NOT_EMPTY (BUFFER) **then**
                    QUEUE_OF_CHAR.GET(X);
           end if;

Unfortunately, this does not suffice to access the buffer correctly. For it may happen that CONSUMER_1 checks the buffer and does not find it empty. Thus, it chooses to enter the **then** branch and gets ready to GET. Before it actually executes GET, however, CONSUMER_2 also checks the buffer and finds it nonempty; it, too, enters the **then** branch and gets ready to GET. If BUFFER initially contained only one character, we reach an illegal state where two authorizations to GET a character have been issued. This will certainly lead to an error during execution.

Exercise

4.32   Suppose that the code implementing operation PUT contains the statement TOT := TOT + 1, TOT being the total number of buffered characters, while operation GET contains the statement TOT := TOT - 1. Also, suppose that PRODUCER_1 and CONSUMER_2 are concurrently performing PUT and GET on the buffer. Show that the system may enter an illegal state.

The BUFFER example illustrates the need for *synchronization* of concurrent activities. Two concurrent activities proceed in parallel as long as their actions do not interfere with one another. But if they need to cooperate or compete for access to a shared resource, such as BUFFER in the example, then they cannot simply proceed independently and must synchronize their actions.

There are several ways to effect synchronization of processes. One is to ensure that any shared resource the processes access is used in *mutual exclusion*. When a process is executing a PUT (or a GET), no other process should be allowed to access BUFFER; otherwise an error, as in Exercise 4.32, might arise. Also, (i) and (ii) above show that when a consumer executes operation (ii), it should access the object in mutual exclusion, i.e., no other process should be allowed to execute any other operation on the shared buffer. The same holds if a producer executes operation (i).

More generally, operations that affect the internal state of a shared object should always be executed in mutual exclusion, so that they leave the object in a consistent state. The same holds for sequences of operations that test the value of an object and possibly modify the value depending on the result of the test.

The problem of accessing shared data in a concurrent environment is actually a generalization of the problem in the sequential environment. Variables that are shared among modules in a sequential environment also require special care, because two successive calls to a module M may observe different values of a variable due to an intervening call to M issued by some other module. This arrangement may be intentional (in the case of an abstract object), or it may be an error. In the sequential environment, such interactions of modules are explicit in the design of the application.

In a concurrent environment, however, the interactions are dependent not only on the design of the application, but also on the particular implementation of concurrency on the execution system. The added difficulty is due to the fact that the order of execution of operations (e.g., accesses to the shared data), in general cannot be determined by the program as it is written, but depends on the speed of execution of the various tasks.

The trouble spots we observed in the case of producers and consumers concurrently accessing the buffer are due to the unfortunate occurrences of particular sequences of actions. It may happen that the system works correctly in the majority of executions, but when the actions occur in some particular sequence, the system fails. Different sequences of actions in the access to the buffer may correspond to different speeds of execution of processes. Indeed, when several processes are executing concurrently, their speed of execution depends on the processor(s) on which they execute.

There are several ways of influencing the speed of execution of processes. First, processes may share the same processor, and the scheduler may assign them a fixed quantum of processing time periodically. Or, alternatively, some processes may have a higher priority than others. Or each process may run on a separate, dedicated physical processor. In these three cases, the speed of execution of these processes is subject to great variation.

We would like to be able to design our software in a way that its correct behavior is ensured, independently of the speed of execution of processes. The system should have the same correct behavior no matter whether it is executed on a uniprocessor or a multiprocessor, whether the time-shared uniprocessor uses fixed time slices or priorities, and so on. This would make our solution more general, allowing it to work for a family of implementations of the underlying abstract machines. Thus, changing the underlying abstract machine would affect only the performance of the software, not its correctness. Also, reasoning about the correctness of the design would be facilitated, since the design could be assessed without taking execution speeds of processes into consideration.

To do this, we extend the concepts and the notation of abstract objects and abstract data types to the case of concurrent software. In particular, we follow two common paradigms of concurrent software design. These paradigms, in turn, are reflected in the constructs provided by some existing concurrent programming languages.

The first approach–inspired by the Concurrent Pascal programming language–leads to the notions of *monitors* and *monitor types*, which represent concurrently accessed objects as protected passive entities. This approach will be called *monitor based*. The second approach–inspired by the Ada programming language–leads to the concept of a *resource guardian*, which is used to represent a concurrent active object. The mechanism used for synchronization is called rendezvous, and thus we call this approach *rendezvous based*.

Although the approach chosen for describing a software design is independent of the implementation language, the mapping of a design onto a program is more direct if the two are based on the same philosophy. The issue of mapping designs onto existing programming languages is taken up in Chapter 9. It should be clear, however, that certain design structures (e.g., a rendezvous-based design) are easier to map onto a certain language (e.g., Ada). Also, considerably more effort goes into the implementation if the language we use is sequential, and concurrency must then be achieved via calls to the underlying operating system.

4.6.1.1 Monitors and monitor types

A *monitor* is an abstract object accessed in a concurrent environment. As viewed by clients, the operations exported by a monitor through its interface are assumed to be executed in mutual exclusion. Suppose that a process P requires execution of an operation while some other process is already executing an operation of the same monitor M. Then P gets suspended until the thread of control of no other process is internal to M, so that P may gain legal access to M.

From the clients' viewpoint, mutual exclusion is guaranteed by the monitor through its interface; the way it is actually provided by the monitor depends on the monitor's implementation. If we implement our system in a language like Concurrent Pascal, mutual exclusion is guaranteed directly by the language. If the language does not provide any automatic way of enforcing mutual exclusion, then we must guarantee it in implementing our application.

Of course, mutual exclusion in the execution of individual operations is not sufficient to guarantee correctness in the access to shared objects. As we saw above, two consumers may invoke operation NOT_EMPTY to check whether the buffer is not empty, and both may be authorized to perform the removal of a character, but if the buffer originally contained a single character, the second attempt to remove a character would generate an erroneous state.

> **concurrent module**   CHAR_BUFFER
> > *This is a monitor, i.e. an abstract object module in a concurrent environment*
>
> **uses** . . .
> **exports**
> > **procedure** PUT (C : **in** CHAR) **requires** NOT_FULL;
> > **procedure** GET (C: **out** CHAR) **requires** NOT_EMPTY;
> > *NOT_EMPTY and NOT_FULL are hidden Boolean functions yielding TRUE if the buffer is not empty and not full, respectively. They are not exported as operations, because their purpose is only to delay the calls to PUT and GET if they are issued when the buffer is in a state where it cannot accept them*
> > :
> > :
> **end** CHAR_BUFFER

Figure 4.20   A monitor example.

To solve problems of this kind, we extend our textual design notation by permitting exported operations to be coupled with an optional **requires** clause. As viewed by clients, this clause is automatically checked when the operation is called. If its result is **true**, then the operation is executed normally, but in mutual exclusion. If the result is

false, the process issuing the call is suspended and waits for the condition to become **true**. Suspension releases the mutual exclusion that was previously acquired, so that other processes may be allowed to enter the monitor. At some point, a process executing some monitor operation might cause the condition on which other processes were suspended to become **true**. Such processes would then become eligible for resumption; when resumed, a process executes the operation in mutual exclusion, as if it had requested the operation just then. In this way, testing the **requires** clause and executing the associated operation result in an atomic action.

All the suspensions and resumptions needed to handle the **requires** clause properly are not visible to the clients, but are automatically provided by the monitor implementation. If we choose Concurrent Pascal as a programming language, the **requires** clause is automatically handled by the language implementation. If we use a sequential programming language, mutual exclusion and the **requires** clause may be implemented by appropriate calls to the operating system.

Figure 4.20 gives the example of a monitor representing a buffer of characters. We simply add the keyword **concurrent** to specify the monitor's semantics for the module.

Monitor types can be defined accordingly and can be generic. An example of a generic monitor type representing FIFO queues of any component type is illustrated in Figure 4.21.

> **generic concurrent module**   GENERIC_FIFO_QUEUE (EL)
>   *This is a generic monitor type, i.e. an abstract data type*
>   *accessed in a concurrent environment*
> **uses** . . .
> **exports**
>   **type** QUEUE: ?;
>   **procedure** PUT (Q1:**in out** QUEUE; E1: **in** EL)
>   **requires** NOT_FULL (Q1: QUEUE);
>   **procedure** GET (Q2:**in out** QUEUE; E2: **out** EL)
>   **requires** NOT_EMPTY(Q2: QUEUE);
>
>   .
>   .
> **end** GENERIC_FIFO_QUEUE (EL)

Figure 4.21   A monitor type example.

Operations exported by a monitor may raise exceptions, and the syntax for specifying the exception associated with an operation is the same as before. For example, in the case of the CHAR_BUFFER monitor, suppose that the interface specifies that the character sent to PUT should satisfy some constraint. The specification of PUT would then be modified to read

> **procedure** PUT (C : **in** CHAR) **requires** NOT_FULL
>   **raises** PAR_ERROR;

where PAR_ERROR is the exception raised by PUT if the parameter does not satisfy the constraints specified in the interface.

We conclude our brief discussion of monitors and monitor types at this point, without trying to add details to our design notation. Going further into details would raise several critical issues that would make our notation more intricate and more programming-language oriented.

Exercise

4.33   Extend GDN by providing a graphical notation for monitors and monitor types.

4.6.1.2 Guardians and the rendezvous

The approach we have followed so far views a software system as composed of two kinds of entities: active entities, i.e., processes, which have independent threads of control, and passive objects. Passive objects may be either instances of an abstract type or single-instance abstract objects. Passive objects may be shared among processes or may be used as private resources by a process. A shared object must be either a monitor or an instance of a monitor type; otherwise, there would be no guarantee that access to the object would preserve a consistent state.

As we anticipated, there are other paradigms on which we can base the design of a concurrent system. One such paradigm is exemplified by the approach taken by the Ada programming language, among others. In this approach, private objects are the only passive entities of a system. Active objects come in two "flavors": processes, as before (called tasks in Ada), and *guardians* of shared resources.

Guardians are themselves tasks whose sole purpose is to guarantee orderly access to a hidden secret representing an encapsulated resource, possibly a data structure. Guardians are never-ending tasks that await requests to perform some operation. Requests may be accepted or not, depending on some condition based on the internal state of the resource controlled by the guardian. Requests are accepted by the guardian one at a time.

A task issuing a request to a guardian becomes suspended until the guardian accepts the request and completes execution of the corresponding action. Following Ada terminology, this form of interaction between a task and a guardian is called a *rendezvous*.

The same syntactic notation we gave before in the case of the monitor-like approach may be used to describe a design based on the rendezvous-like approach. What changes, of course, is the semantics. As an example, take the concurrent module CHAR_BUFFER of Figure 4.20. If we interpret the design notation in the context of the rendezvous-based approach, CHAR_BUFFER is a task that accepts requests to operate on its guarded state by performing either GET or PUT. A GET request is accepted only if the buffer is not empty; a PUT request is accepted only if the BUFFER is not full. A task issuing one of these requests (via a suitable call) is suspended until the request is fulfilled by the guardian, i.e., until the guardian finds the **requires** clause true, decides to respond to the request, and executes the body of the request. The guardian repeatedly accepts valid requests in a never-ending loop.

In order to clarify these issues, one may consider that, in a rendezvous-based language, the internals of module CHAR_BUFFER might look like the sketchy program of Figure 4.22. The program describes the structure of a guardian implementing the CHAR_BUFFER concurrent module of Figure 4.20. It is written in a self-explaining Ada-like style. A more detailed description of Ada tasking is given in Chapter 9, when we discuss programming languages. Our purpose here is simply to clarify the issues involved in the rendezvous-based approach.

```
loop
        select
                when NOT_FULL
                        accept  PUT (C: in CHAR);
                        This is the body of PUT; the client  calls it as if it
                        were a normal procedure
                        end ;
                or
                when NOT_EMPTY
                        accept  GET (C:out CHAR);
                        This is the body of GET; the client  calls it as if it
                        were a normal procedure
                end ;
        end select  ;
        end loop  ;
```

Figure 4.22   Typical internal structure of a guardian task.

Both the monitor-based approach and the rendezvous-based approach provide *nondeterministic* solutions to concurrency problems. The CHAR_BUFFER guardian is specified as a server accepting requests to access the buffer, either to add new characters or to remove characters. Requests to add new characters are accepted if the buffer is not full; similarly, requests to extract symbols from the buffer are honored if the buffer is not empty. From the client's viewpoint, when the buffer is neither full nor empty, pending requests (if any) are handled nondeterministically, as is suggested by the **select ... or ... end select** construct of Figure 4.22. Note that we do not specify what happens when several requests of the same kind (e.g., GET) are issued to the same guardian. Here, too, we may assume that the choice of which request to fulfill is made nondeterministically.[1] Similarly, in the monitor-based approach, several processes may be waiting for the mutual exclusion condition to be released. Which of them is actually resumed when the monitor is freed? Finally, if some processes are suspended on a **requires** clause and the condition becomes true, which of them is chosen?

In all these cases, the module's behavior, as viewed by its clients, is nondeterministic. That is, the interface does not reveal how the module actually makes its choices. Nondeterminism is an important property at the specification level, because it allows us not to overspecify the behavior of the system being designed. Thus, our design

---

[1] Actually, Ada says that these requests must be handled in a first-in-first-out fashion.

is not sensitive to the ways the nondeterminism is resolved later. The programming language we use to implement the system may make specific choices where we have left things nondeterministic; and other choices may be made by the abstract machine that supports the execution of the programming language. Whatever choices will be made, the system will be correct, and only performance will be affected.

Exercise

4.34   Consider a programming environment composed of a sequential programming language (e.g., C) and an operating system (e.g., UNIX). Provide implementation guidelines for both monitor-based and rendezvous-based designs.

4.6.2 Real-Time Software

In the previous section, we solved the problem of concurrent access to shared data by assuming that we can resolve contention by suspending the execution of competing processes for a period of time. For example, in the case of the monitor-based design, producers could be suspended if the buffer they were accessing was full.

Unfortunately, suspension of processes is not always feasible. For example, an operation invoked on the abstract object may belong to the thread of control of a process that cannot be suspended, perhaps because the process is a physical activity existing in the environment whose temporal evolution is not under the control of the computer system. Continuing with the previous example, suppose that one producer is a physical line that carries sampled data acquired from a controlled chemical plant sent to the controller (a computer). In this case, there is no way to, say, slow down or suspend the plant! If a datum sent by the plant is not accepted in time by the controller, it will simply be lost. It is the controller's job to comply with the speed requirements of the plant in such a way that the data sent on the line are accepted, with no data losses. Problems of this kind characterize real-time systems.

Real-time systems may be defined as systems for which reasoning about correct behavior requires dealing with the speed of execution of the processes that comprise the system. When we design such systems, we must comply with requirements that specify time limits within which certain operations must be executed. If some operations are not executed within the limit–i.e., if they occur either too early or too late–the system is incorrect.

This time constraint shows the fundamental difference between a pure concurrent system and a real-time concurrent system. A concurrent system is designed by ignoring the speed of processes. By applying suitable design principles, we may ensure correctness of the system independently of the speeds of processes that comprise the system. Processes may be explicitly suspended (i.e., they may be slowed down as much as we wish) in order to ensure the validity of certain logical properties. For example, in the case of the monitor-based solutions discussed in the previous section, we are able to say, "at the future point where the producer will be allowed to perform a PUT operation, the buffer will have some free space to store the value delivered by the client." This was

concurrent module   REACTIVE_CHAR_BUFFER
This is a monitor-like object working in a real-time environment.
uses ...
exports
        reactive procedure   PUT (C: **in** CHAR);
        PUT is used by external processes, and two consecutive
        PUT requests must arrive more than 5 msec. apart;
        otherwise, some characters may be lost
        procedure   GET (C: **out** CHAR);
         :
         :
end REACTIVE_CHAR_BUFFER

(a)

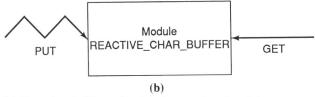

(b)

Figure 4.23   (a) Textual and (b) graphical design notation describing events.

stated by means of the **requires** clause. Statements like this do not make any sense in the case of a real-time system. If incoming signals arrive at a time frequency of, say, one every 5 milliseconds and no incoming signal must be lost for security reasons, knowing that "eventually the incoming signal will be buffered" does not solve our problems: the signal *must* be buffered within 5 milliseconds, i.e., before the next signal arrives; otherwise the signal is lost.

To deal with real-time issues in our design notations, we do not propose any specialized constructs, but rather suggest using comments to attach the needed requirements. For example, a comment may be used to say that the execution time of a certain exported routine is bounded by given lower and upper bounds.

Real-time systems often interact with an external environment that produces stimuli autonomously, at unpredictable times. Therefore, such systems may be viewed as reactive systems that respond to incoming stimuli provided by the external world.[1] It is thus useful to have a way to specify that a given routine represents the response to an unpredictable request coming from the external environment. In TDN, we specify that by using the keyword **reactive**. Similarly, in GDN we indicate it by means of a zigzag arrow (see Figure 4.23).

If an operation is classified as **reactive**, it means that its execution cannot be delayed–for example, by suspending the caller and resuming it at a later convenient time.

---

[1] The fact that the environment activates some operation at unforeseen time instants is typical of, though not exclusive to, real-time systems.

In practice, reactive operations are specified by stating constraints on their execution times; e.g. "the operation can occur every x milliseconds, with $5 \leq x \leq 15$." Thus, it is the designer's responsibility to make sure that when an incoming request for such an operation arrives, no other operation of the module is being executed. Otherwise, the result would be unpredictable.

Practical experience has shown that timing issues are extremely critical, and this is what makes real-time systems difficult to design and verify. The complexity of design and verification scales up as we move from purely sequential systems to concurrent systems and from purely concurrent systems to real-time systems, and what makes the difference is time. In the case of sequential systems, time only has to do with the performance of a program. In the case of a concurrent system, we can suitably organize the system so that proper synchronization ensures correctness in a time-independent manner. Thus, again, time only affects the performance of the resulting program. In the case of real-time systems, however, time affects correctness. Thus, it introduces one more dimension that must be taken into account when we design, implement, and verify our systems.

Besides being intrinsically complex, real-time systems often provide critical functions, so that the effect of errors may be disastrous, possibly causing heavy financial losses or even loss of human lives. Unfortunately, the present body of knowledge about real-time systems is not entirely adequate. By contrast, in the case of sequential systems, the state of the art is much more advanced. There, we find good design and verification methods and we can use several tools, such as good programming languages, to assist us in software development. To a lesser degree, the same applies to concurrent systems, but it does not apply at all to real-time systems. For all these reasons, real-time systems are still the subject of much research, from their design to their verification.

4.6.3 Distributed Software

One important class of concurrent software consists of concurrent activities that run on different computers that are connected by a communication network. For example, it is now commonplace to find an organization's computers connected by a local area network. Such a network allows the users of the different computers to communicate (e.g., via electronic mail), share resources (e.g., printers and files), and otherwise cooperate. It is important to be able to design software that can take advantage of these kinds of environments.

In this chapter, we have structured a software design based on modules and several relationships among them. Distribution imposes additional requirements. The resource guardian modules, as developed in Section 4.6.1, are directly applicable in a distributed application and can serve as a unit of distribution. We must, however, impose certain restrictions on the USES relation between two modules that reside on different machines. In particular, because the modules on different machines have independent address spaces, we cannot allow one module directly to access variables defined in other modules. We will allow, however, indirect access of such variables through access procedures exported by the module, described in Section 4.6.3.3.

With distributed software, these are the main new issues that we must consider in design:

- **Module-machine binding.** Sometimes a module is required to run on a particular machine. For example, if the module's purpose is to provide a printing service, the module may have to run on a computer that is attached to a printer. Other times, the module may be able to run on any number of a class of machines–for example, those that have a gateway connection to enable them to reach networks outside the organization.

- **Intermodule communication.** If two modules reside on different machines, how should they communicate? We have seen that modules that reside on the same machine can communicate by using a shared global area: one module records some information in the global area and the other reads the information. This approach–which works for both sequential programs and concurrent programs–does not extend directly to the distributed environment because the two modules are on different machines. Another approach to intermodule communication in the sequential environment is through parameter passing at procedure call and return times. The procedure call mechanism has been extended to a *remote procedure call* in which the caller and the callee are not required to be on the same machine. A final approach to intermodule communication in a distributed environment is by sending *messages*.

- **Efficient access to abstract objects.** We have identified abstract objects as important types of modules that are derived naturally during the design of a system. In a sequential system, we do not incur a large cost by encapsulating a piece of data needed by module M_1 as part of an abstract object M_2. In a distributed system, however, if the two modules are located on different machines, M_1 pays a vary high cost in terms of time for accessing data in M_2 rather than local data in M_1–such access may take as much as ten times longer than in the local case. Two approaches to making abstract objects more efficient in a distributed environment are *replication* and *distribution*.

We examine the above issues more closely in Sections 4.6.3.2 through 4.6.3.4. But first, in Section 4.6.3.1, we discuss briefly a particular model for structuring a distributed system–the *client-server* model.

4.6.3.1 The client-server model

We have said that the role of modules is to provide services to other modules that are called client modules. This model is directly applicable to distributed architectures. The most popular architecture for a distributed application is in terms of clients and servers residing on different machines. For example, consider a printing service facility on a network of computers. In this network, some computers have printers attached to them and others do not. We can design the printing service to consist of client and server modules. The server receives a file and prints it on a printer. The client accepts a file name and sends the contents of the file to a server module, along with information about the user who requested the print operation.

Some of the modules that we have encountered already can be viewed naturally as server modules in a client-server architecture. For example, a module similar to the BUFFER example of Section 4.6.1 can be used by client modules of the printing service application to deposit the files to be printed. The server module is then the consumer of the application. More generally, the resource guardian modules of Section 4.6.1.2 can model servers in a distributed application.

Exercise

4.35   The same module may be a client in one context and a server in another. For example, consider a printing service facility that consists of a number of client modules running on machines without printers, a number of BUFFER modules running on any machine, and a number of server modules running on machines that have printers. Discuss whether the BUFFER is a client or a server.

4.6.3.2 Binding a module to a machine

As we said before, an issue that we face in a distributed software architecture is that of binding modules to machines. Sometimes, as in the print server example, the binding is imposed by necessity. Other times, there is a choice, and this choice may be guided by several considerations. For example, in order to reduce the cost of communication, we may want to place server modules on machines that are close to their clients, perhaps even on the same machine, if possible.

Another issue is whether the binding is static or dynamic. A static binding is simpler, but the ability to choose the location of execution of a module dynamically allows us, for example, to choose a lightly loaded system in order to improve the application's performance. This ability is also essential for supporting highly reliable systems because the failure of one machine can be tolerated by moving the modules that were running on it to another machine. This dynamic movement of processes is called *migration*. We will not deal with the many details of this problem which may be found in the specialized literature.

A special issue regarding static or dynamic binding of modules to machines is whether a module can be instantiated (i.e., created) dynamically in the first place. Some systems support the creation of processes at run time, and others do not. If processes may be created dynamically, then the application can determine at run time how many instances of the process it needs to run. The ability to create a process on a specific machine is an additional feature. In designing our software, we must keep the capabilities of the underlying machine in mind because of the great variation of different languages and operating systems.

TDN and GDN can be further extended to cope with the design of distributed software. In GDN, in order to define the binding of a module to a machine, we represent machines as circles and we draw the box representing a module within the circle representing the machine where the module is allocated. If the module is bound statically to a machine, we use a double-headed double arrow to connect the module box to the machine circle. The absence of such an arrow means that the module may migrate dynamically. In some cases, however, we wish to state that a module may migrate only to a restricted set of machines; this is indicated by inserting dotted replicated boxes representing a module in the machines where migration is permitted.

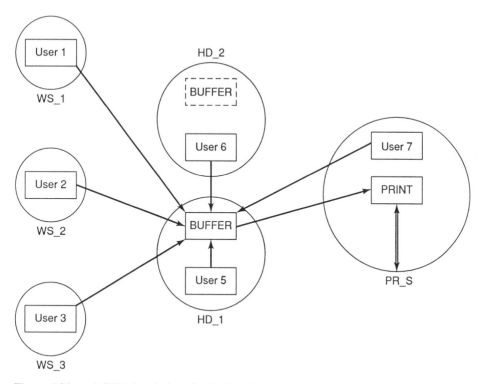

Figure 4.24   A GDN description of a distributed system.

Figure 4.24 is the GDN description of a system containing a print server (PR_S), two machines provided with a hard disk (HD_1 and HD_2), and several diskless workstations (WS_1, WS_2,...). Several USER modules residing on different machines may send print requests to a BUFFER module, which prepares output files to be sent to the PRINT module in a special format. The BUFFER module is initially allocated to HD_1; should the need for reconfiguration arise, it may only migrate to HD_2, because it needs to use the hard disk.

Exercises

4.36 Extend TDN to deal with the problem of binding a module to a machine. Then use it to specify a printing service that is composed of three modules: a client module that accepts user requests for printing a file, a BUFFER module that stores the print requests, and a service module that picks up requests from BUFFER and performs the requests. Which modules have to be concurrent? Does the client module have to be concurrently accessible?

4.37 Explain why in real-time systems dynamic creation of processes may not be desirable.

4.38 Consider an application that is required to be accessible from any machine on a particular network. There are thousands of machines on the network, but we expect that the application will not be run by more than ten users at any one time. Design a solution to this problem. Is dynamic binding of modules to machines useful in this example? How can you use process migration in this application? What would your solution be if you are required to have a static binding of modules to machines?

4.6.3.3 Intermodule communication

Two models of communication are used in distributed applications: remote procedure call and message passing.

The remote procedure call mechanism is an extension of the traditional procedure call that allows the calling and the called modules to reside on different machines. Commercial packages are available that support this type of interaction under different operating systems. Because of its similarity to traditional procedure calls, using this model of inter-module interaction allows us to design our application as before, without making any distinction between service requests for local and remote modules: any module interface that is written in terms of procedure calls can be supported in a distributed application. In practice, however, there are many details that hamper this approach.

As an example, even if the ideas of a procedure call and a return are implemented rather naturally, not all forms of parameter passing can be supported so easily. For example, since the calling and called modules reside in two different address spaces, the two modules cannot communicate in terms of pointers. This means that parameter passing by reference, or passing linked data structures, is problematical, if possible at all. The commercial remote procedure call systems adopt appropriate restrictions on the kinds of parameters that can be passed.

Another example of the difference between remote and local procedure calls is in exception handling. In practice, there does not seem to be a good way for a remotely called procedure to signal an exception to its caller. The details of these problems may be found in the specialized literature.

The message-passing paradigm for intermodule interaction is based on the idea of a mailbox. Each module may be considered to have a mailbox in which it can receive messages from other modules. Client modules can send requests to the mailbox of a server module. A server picks up a request from its mailbox, acts upon it, and, if necessary, sends a reply to the mailbox of the appropriate client. The chief consideration in the use of message passing involves the size of mailboxes (how many message can be buffered) and whether a module can choose a target mailbox dynamically or the choice is static.

Although the two paradigms of remote procedure call and message passing are equal in power, in that each can be simulated with the other, they are appropriate for different software architectures. The most significant difference between the two is that remote procedure call is inherently a synchronous form of interaction and message passing is asynchronous, that is, a module making a procedure call must wait until the callee returns, but a client sending a message may continue with its thread of control. This difference engenders different software designs.

Exercises

4.39   Examine the Ada tasking facilities. Are they based on remote procedure call or message passing?

4.40   Consider an application in which a sensor module reads a series of values on an incoming line and sends these values to a recorder module for further processing. If these two modules are distributed on two different machines, which form of inter-module communication would you choose to use? Why?

4.41   For the previous exercise, sketch each module in a suitable extension of TDN once using remote procedure call and once using message passing.

4.6.3.4 Replication and distribution

The final consideration in software design for a distributed environment is to make access to data efficient. In particular, we have emphasized that one useful type of module is an abstract object, which provides client modules with access to an encapsulated data structure. This means that the client module makes a request–usually through a procedure call–for any data that it wants to access. The cost of accessing a piece of data through a procedure call rather than through memory directly–which is done for local data–is considered excessive even in some sequential applications. Many compilers support in-line procedure call expansions to speed up this kind of access. The cost is considerably higher if the abstract object is on a remote machine. The cost of a remote access on the fastest networks is around four times the cost of a local access and can be as much as an order of magnitude higher. We therefore need a way to make access to abstract objects efficient if we are going to use them in a distributed application. Two general methods exist for doing this.

The first approach is to replicate the distributed object on several machines–on every machine in the extreme case. In the latter case, each client has access to the abstract object locally. The problem now is that the copies of the object must be kept consistent so that the different clients continue to observe the same abstract object rather than many different objects. Many techniques have been developed, both in the operating system and data-base areas, for solving this problem.

Another solution is to distribute the abstract object on different machines. That is, even though logically the object is a single object, we can partition it physically and store the partitions on different machines, with each partition close to the clients that are likely to access it.

For each particular abstract object, we must consider whether it makes sense to replicate it, partition it, do both, or do neither. But replication and partitioning give us a systematic method for distributing a software architecture that we have derived according to the principles in this chapter.

Exercises

4.42 Extend both TDN and GDN to cope with the problems of dynamic allocation, intermodule communication, replication, and distribution.

4.43 Consider a printing service application. A BUFFER module stores the job requests. Should we partition or replicate BUFFER? Why or why not?

4.44 Consider an application for managing bank accounts in a bank. There is an abstract object that represents all the customer accounts in the bank. The bank has many branches all over the country. Each branch has a computer that is used to access the customer-account object. Would you replicate or partition the object? Why or why not?

4.45 Sketch the design of a conference room reservation application. Hundreds of rooms may be reserved for any particular time. The application may be accessed from thousands of machines on the network.

4.46 Consider an application that is expected to receive stock market data that arrives on an incoming wire service and make it available to all the computers on the network for different types of queries. We decide to use an abstract object to represent the stock market data. Would you partition or replicate the data? Why or why not?

4.7 CONCLUDING REMARKS

In this chapter, we have examined the various facets of software design. Most of the general software principles we presented in Chapter 3 have been examined in more depth here, in the context of software design. In particular, we emphasized modularity, which is the very essence and the common theme underlying the whole chapter. Separation of concerns, abstraction, generality, and incrementality have also been discussed extensively. In particular, they have been viewed as derived qualities that should follow from appropriate modularization techniques. Finally, rigor and formality have been shown to be essential qualities of the documentation of our designs. They inspired the definition of a design notation that was presented in two forms, one textual (TDN) and one graphical (GDN). Such notations provide a clear way of documenting a software design, to facilitate communication among software designers and future maintainers of the system.

As we already mentioned, design is a critical and creative activity. It can be inspired by general principles and guidelines, but it cannot be mechanized by fixed absolute rules or theorems. We have shown that design consists of defining an architecture in terms of a set of–preferably hierarchical–relations on modules and defining module interfaces. These activities may be driven by the general principles that the architecture should have low coupling and high cohesion, and that interfaces should enforce information hiding. Putting these principles into practice, however, requires insight, design maturity, and experience. The principles are not recipes.

Information hiding was assumed as a cornerstone upon which a solid design is based. Thus, we paid much attention to the question of how to design interfaces through information hiding. In particular, we identified several categories of modules that may be used as guidelines during design. Most notable among these were abstract objects and abstract data types.

Abstract objects and abstract data types led to the concept of object-oriented design, a promising approach to software design that is now becoming a reality because of the existence of new programming languages that support the approach by providing linguistic features that are missing in traditional languages.

Object-oriented design, with its related languages, takes the idea of information hiding to its logical consequences, with the aim of helping software designers get closer to such goals as design for change, design of program families, incremental development, the production of reusable components, and ease of maintenance. Even though this is a promising viewpoint, there is open debate on deep underlying semantic issues, which presently results in a variety of notations. The field is still an active research area and will become more practical and settled in the future. In this chapter, we have stressed the general principles of design without relying on any specific object-oriented design notation.

Among the qualities of software design, we stressed design for change and reliability. Design for change is achieved by the above principles. Reliability is also a by-product of a disciplined approach to design. Good methods help overcome the complexity of design and hence promote the likelihood that flaws are absent from a particular design. But we also addressed the issue of defensive design, by showing that possible anomalies should be considered during the design phase and described in the documentation.

Finally, we addressed the issue of design for concurrent, real-time, and distributed systems, by extending the design principles and the proposed design notation to these cases. Our goal here was to show that the principles and the approaches that we presented for designing sequential software may be extended to deal with concurrency, real-time, and distribution.

FURTHER EXERCISES

4.47 Define some useful relations among modules other than the relations discussed in this chapter.

4.48 Classify the changes discussed in Section 4.1.1.1 as either perfective, adaptive, or corrective maintenance.

4.49 Consider a program you have written in the past in a programming language like Ada, Modula-2, C, or Pascal (Here we consider Ada, but the exercise can be adapted quite easily to any of these languages.) Consider Ada library units as corresponding to the concept of a module that we are using in this chapter. Also, define a relation CALLS between any two modules such that M_i CALLS M_j if and only if a call to a procedure or function in M_j is issued within M_i.

    a. Unlike the assumption we made in Section 4.2.1, would it make any sense to define CALLS as a reflexive relation?

    b. What follows from requiring CALLS to be a hierarchy?

    c. Draw the CALLS graph for your sample program and check whether it is a DAG or not.

4.50 Prove that the inverse of a hierarchy is also a hierarchy.

4.51 With reference to Figure 4.4, we may say that

$\{M_1\}$ ENCAPSULATES $\{M_4, M_5, M_6, M_7, M_8, M_9\}$
$\{M_2\}$ ENCAPSULATES $\{M_7, M_8, M_9\}$
$\{M_3\}$ ENCAPSULATES $\{M_5, M_6\}$

Thus, the relation ENCAPSULATES relates each module with the set of elementary modules that comprise it. Define ENCAPSULATES formally.

4.52 Discuss the coupling of the modules described in Example 4.1. Is this a good design?

4.53 Study the COMMON construct of FORTRAN, and discuss the difference between labelled and unlabelled COMMON, as well as their possible use. Also, discuss the mechanisms provided by FORTRAN to initialize COMMON areas.

4.54 Describe how to use C to define a common area for storing data. Do the same for Pascal.

4.55 We have criticized the POP_2 interface to the stack of Example 4.8 on the grounds of being too *specialized*. We said that if we *generalize* the interface to POP, clients have more flexibility in its use. Specialization, however, is sometimes necessary for efficiency reasons. For example, consider a stack that is implemented on one node of a distributed system. Compare POP and POP_2 in terms of efficiency of the interface for clients.

4.56 According to the definition of the Ada programming language, what is the difference between **private** and **limited private** types exported by a package, as far as client modules are concerned?

4.57 Example 4.9 used objects of type FIFO_CARS to represent any queue at the gas station. We would like, however, to treat a queue of cars waiting for gas differently from a queue of cars waiting for, say, a tune-up. In particular, if there is no gas left, we do not want to merge the two queues. In Example 4.9, the proper handling of queues was left to the client modules. Clients would choose appropriate names for objects (such as gasoline_1 or car_wash) in order to avoid merging inhomogeneous queues inadvertently. Suggest a better solution using generic modules.

4.58 In Section 4.2.4.3, we have described generic modules parameterized by types. Study the Ada manual and describe other possibilities for parameterizing modules.

4.59 We did not provide an enrichment of GDN to describe exceptions and exception handling. Propose a notation to describe the fact that an exception may be raised by a module when a request for a service is being served. Your notation should also provide a way to show that an exception is propagated after being signalled to a client.

4.60 Suppose you wish to model the elevator system of a multifloor building. The system is composed of m floors and n elevators. Each elevator has a set of buttons, one for each floor. These light up when pressed and cause the elevator to visit the corresponding floor. The light goes out upon the elevator's reaching the floor. Each floor (except for the ground and top floors) has two buttons, one to request an up elevator and one to request a down elevator. The illumination goes out when the elevator visits the floor and is either moving in the desired direction or has no outstanding requests. Each elevator has an emergency button which, when pressed, causes a warning signal to be sent to the site manager. The elevator is then deemed "out of service." Each elevator has a mechanism to cancel its out-of-service status.

    a. Model this system in an object-oriented style.

    b. Suppose that the elevators are divided into two sets, the first comprising the elevators that serve floors zero through m_1, the second serving floors m_1 through m. What would change in your design to accommodate this feature?

4.61 After the first step of design described at the beginning of Section 4.5, the designer of the SYMBOL_TABLE module anticipates that he will store the information of the various blocks in contiguous locations. Therefore, the algorithms for RETRIEVE and LEVEL will be almost identical: to search for the value of a variable, first the most recently entered block is searched, and then, if the variable is not found, the previously entered block is searched, and so on. The designer proposes to his colleagues to take advantage of this near-identity of algorithms and change the interface. Instead of having procedures RETRIEVE and LEVEL, he will provide a procedure (RETRIEVE_LEVEL) that merges the two. Its proposed interface is as follows:

      procedure RETRIEVE_LEVEL (ID: **in** IDENTIFIER;
                             DESCR: **out** DESCRIPTOR; L: **out** integer);

After some discussion, the designer's colleagues convince him that merging the two operations into one is not a good idea. Do you agree with this decision? Why? Why not?

4.62 Referring to the module QUEUE_OF_CHAR discussed in Section 4.6, do you expect two concurrent executions of NOT_EMPTY and NOT_FULL to require execution in mutual exclusion? Why? Why not? How about concurrent execution of NON_EMPTY and GET?

4.63 Is it completely correct to say that the **requires** clause defined in Section 4.6.1.1 is part of the interface of a concurrent module? Why? Why not?

4.64 Do the operations NOT_FULL and NOT_EMPTY exported by the module in Figure 4.20 provide any useful abstraction when called by the module's clients? Why? Why not?

4.65 What difficulties may be encountered if a monitor operation is allowed to use another monitor operation (perhaps even exported by the same monitor)?

4.66 Study concurrency features in Ada, and provide a detailed description of the case where any number of consumers (defined by a task type) and one producer may access a given buffer to append and remove characters.

4.67 "A real-time system is such that a function that produces the correct result would be incorrect if the result is produced too early or too late." Give examples of systems that illustrate this definition.

4.68 Examine case study A at the back of the book. Show how the company would have been able to deal with the different needs of different customers by exploiting some of the techniques illustrated in this chapter.

HINTS AND SKETCHY SOLUTIONS

4.9 IS_COMPOSED_OF and IMPLEMENTS cannot be defined as mathematical relations on S because they relate an element of S with a subset of elements of S.

4.32 Observe that the two statements are actually performed as a sequence of more elementary actions. It may happen, then, that both processes read TOT, then PRODUCER_1 increases the read value and stores it back into TOT, and finally CONSUMER_2 decreases the read value and stores it back into TOT!

4.47 A semantic equivalence relation between modules is useful for deciding whether one module can replace another one during software evolution. As far as compilation is concerned, there can be order relations between modules, of the type "M_1 must be compiled before M_2". In distributed systems, there could be a relation stating that two modules must be allocated to the same machine. See also Exercise 4.51.

4.61 A different implementation might cache the descriptors of all visible identifiers at block entry, without caching the level. This would invalidate the proposed interface.

4.63 Strictly speaking, a concurrent module can be used properly even without knowing the **requires** clause. The clause, however, provides useful information for a better understanding of the effect of the associated operations. It also has an impact on performance analysis, since it helps find possible delays due to the mutual exclusion it enforces.

4.64 Clients cannot rely on the result they get back, because other processes may change them in the meantime.

4.65 Such a feature may increase the risk of deadlock.

4.68 By using, say, object-oriented design, the company could first have factored out in a few modules all information and operations that are needed by all legal offices. Later, legal offices could have been specialized by applying inheritance to cope with different classes of needs. This approach would also have supported an incremental construction and delivery of the system.

Also, by following the approach suggested by Example 4.6, the company could have concentrated both design and promotion efforts on the innovative features of the system.

BIBLIOGRAPHIC NOTES

The work of D.L. Parnas is the major source of inspiration of the view of design presented in this book.

Dijkstra ([1968a, 1968b, and 1971]) was the first to teach how to use the powerful principles of separation of concerns and levels of abstraction to deal with complexity of design.

Parnas pioneered all subsequent work on software design: Parnas [1972b] introduced the concept of information hiding–the cornerstone of good software design structures–while Parnas [1972a] introduced the notion of module specification, which we address in the next chapter. Subsequent work gave additional insights into the issues of program families (Parnas [1976]) and program modification for extension and contraction (Parnas [1979]). Parnas [1974] discusses the need for precision when we talk about hierarchical systems. Britton et al. [1981] discuss abstract interfaces for device interface modules. Hester et al. [1981] illustrates the use of good design documentation.

The textbook by Lamb [1988] is permeated by Parnas's design approach. Hoffman [1989] discusses the issue of interface design and specification in a practical–yet rigorous–fashion. Hoffman [1990] discusses criteria for designing good module interfaces.

Work on module interconnection languages addresses the issue of providing linguistic mechanisms to describe the interconnection of software modules; examples are surveyed by Prieto-Diaz [1986].

The notion of an abstract data type is rooted in the work of Dahl et al. [1972] and Liskov [1974]. Liskov and Guttag [1986] illustrate a methodical approach to software construction based on the recognition of abstractions.

Lientz and Swanson [1980] discuss the causes of change in software and report figures showing the influence of various factors (such as change in the data).

The TDN notation we used to illustrate designs is based on the programming languages Ada (see AJPO [1983]) and Modula-2 (see Wirth [1983]). The graphical representation we use resembles the HOOD notation, defined by the European Space Agency (see HOOD [1989]). Wasserman et al [1990] describe another proposal; Buhr [1984] provides a graphical notation to describe Ada designs.

The issue of application generators is discussed in Software [1990c]. For conditional compilation, see Babich [1986], which places it in the context of configuration management.

Object-oriented design is illustrated by Booch [1986, 1987a, and 1987b] in the context of the Ada programming language. It is illustrated by Meyer [1988] in the context of the Eiffel programming language. We have adopted Meyer's view of what "object oriented" means and his approach to exception handling. Our discussion of top-down versus bottom-up design was also inspired by Meyer. Snyder [1986] criticizes the fact that heir modules may access the secrets of their parent modules, in conflict with the information-hiding principle. Wegner [1987] presents a clear explanation and classification of the issues surrounding object-oriented language designs.

Concurrent software design was addressed by Brinch Hansen [1977], who defined the programming language Concurrent Pascal. Rendezvous-based mechanisms were inspired by CSP–Communicating Sequential Processes–defined by Hoare [1985] and found their systematic application in the Ada programming language. Weihl [1989] discusses abstract data types in a concurrent environment.

Systematic development of concurrent software is described by Bustard et al. [1988]. Mani and Chandy [1988] present a foundation for parallel program design, including a promising theory illustrated with numerous examples.

The issues of real-time systems are described by Wirth [1977] and Stankovic [1988]. Design of distributed systems is discussed by Shatz and Wang [1989]. The guardian concept in the context of distributed systems is due to Liskov and is the basis of the design of the ARGUS system (Liskov [1988]).

A design issue not specifically addressed in this book concerns user interfaces. The interested reader may refer to Schneiderman [1987], Coutaz [1985], and the special issue of *IEEE Software* [1989a].

For a view of programming languages and their support of software design, refer to Ghezzi and Jazayeri [1987].

Other approaches to design are described in various books on "structured design," such as Yourdon and Constantine [1979] and Myers [1978]. These approaches are based on a system decomposition into functional modules. The methods are part of a larger methodology, called Structured Analysis/Structured Design (SA/SD); we will address this methodology in Chapter 7. For a detailed discussion of the concepts of cohesion and coupling, refer to Yourdon and Constantine [1979] and Myers [1978].

Surveys of software design techniques are presented by Bergland [1981] and Yau and Tsai [1986].

Chapter 5

Software Specification

Every nontrivial engineering system must be *specified*. For instance, one can state that a bridge must support at least 1,000 tons, must be 30 meters wide, etc. In this sense, the specification is a precise statement of the requirements that the system–in this case, the bridge–must satisfy. Of course, we may specify not only the final system, but also the subsystems and components that will be used to make up the system. So the bridge designer will also specify the requirements for the columns, the cables, the bolts, etc.

In traditional engineering disciplines, the word *specification* has a precise meaning. In software engineering, however, the term is used in several contexts with slightly different meanings. We have even used it informally several times in the previous chapters.

In general, we can view a specification as the statement of an agreement between a producer of a service and a consumer of the service, or an implementer and a user. Depending on the context, the implementer and the user are different, and the nature of the specification is different. A *requirements specification* is an agreement between the end user and the system developer. A *design specification*–for example in terms of the USES hierarchy–is an agreement between the system architect (or designer) and the implementers. A *module specification* is an agreement between the programmers using the module and the programmer implementing the module. For example, the **exports** clause of the modules in a TDN description can be viewed as a (syntactic) specification of those modules.

As these examples show, the term "specification" is used at different stages of system development. Furthermore, a *specification* at some level states the requirements for the *implementation* at a lower level. Since the specification is an agreement between the user and the implementer, we can view it as a *definition* of what the implementation must provide.

This relationship between the specification and the implementation is often explained in terms of the *what versus how* dichotomy described in Chapter 1. The specification states *what* a system should do; the implementer decides *how* to do it. In practice, however, the distinction between the two is not often so sharp. For instance, in some cases, the decision as to whether to distribute a banking system throughout the bank's branches or to keep it centralized in the main branch and use remote terminals at the other branches can be considered a design matter, i.e., a *how* matter. So one can claim that physical distribution of the system is not a requirement, but an implementation issue. In other cases, the user can explicitly require a distributed architecture, which then automatically becomes part of the system specification. So an implementation that realizes all required functions but uses a single mainframe would be rejected as incorrect.

Furthermore, sometimes a simple way to describe *what* one wants is just to give an example of *how* it can be done. This implies not that it must be done in exactly that way, but that it must behave *as if* it were done that way. For instance, one can state that the execution of several concurrent transactions in an information system must be performed as if each transaction were executed in a noninterruptible way. This does not necessarily require the implementer to let each transaction run to completion before starting another one–which would be highly inefficient in the case of long transactions. Rather, the implementer is free to interleave the execution of different transactions, as long as each is perceived by the user to have run without interruption.

The specification activity is a critical part of the whole design process. Specifications themselves are the result of a complex and creative design activity; they are subject to errors just as are the products of other activities, such as coding. As a consequence, all the design principles discussed in Chapter 3 should be applied as well to the specification process.

In this chapter, we will first analyze the *uses* of specifications. Next, we will point out the main specification *qualities* that should be kept in mind when writing specifications. Then we will analyze some of the most relevant techniques of writing specifications, by classifying them according to different *specification styles*. We will also discuss the *applicability* of each class to various application areas. Finally, we will discuss the problems in, and techniques for, *managing* the specifications of real systems, which inevitably tend to be complex and tedious.

5.1 THE USES OF SPECIFICATIONS

Software specifications can be used for different purposes. Here are their major uses.

Statement of user needs. A main purpose of a product's specification is to define the needs of the product's users. Sometimes, the specification may be part of a contract signed between the producer and the user. It could also form part of the user manuals.

A user's needs are sometimes not clearly understood by the developer. If this is the case, a careful analysis–involving much interaction with the user–should be devoted to reaching a clear statement of requirements, in order to avoid possible misunderstandings.

Sometimes, at the beginning of a project, even the user has no clear idea of what exactly the desired product is. Think, for instance, of user interfaces. A user with no previous experience with computer products may not appreciate the difference between, say, menu-driven interaction and a command line interface. Even an exact formulation of system functions and performance may be missing in an initial description produced by an inexperienced user.

Other times, however, the requirements and the specifications can be very clear. In traditional engineering, in fact, standard specifications exist for such things as nails, screws, and tiles. Such standards enable different producers to produce the "same" product. In software engineering, a programming language (and a target architecture) can be viewed as a standard specification for a compiler. This also enables different producers to build a product based on the same specification.

Many times, major failures occur because of misunderstandings between the producer and the user. Such misunderstandings are more likely to occur when the culture and the "language" of the two are widely different–for instance, when the user is a lawyer or in the humanities. Case study A at the back of the book is an example of this problem.

When these problems occur, unfortunately, going back to the specifications usually reveals an ambiguity that supports both the user's and the producer's interpretation. This situation shows a need for the ability to *verify* the specifications, e.g., to check whether they adequately define what the product has to be, before implementing the product. For instance, submitting a specification document to the end user may help uncover previous misunderstandings of actual user needs. This way, improper definitions may be avoided by discovering them early. We will analyze in more depth the issue of specification verification in Section 5.4. The issue of involving the user in specification verification will be discussed in Section 5.7.3. More will be said about the specification of user needs in Chapters 6 and 7.

A statement of the requirements for the implementation. Specifications are also used as a reference point during product implementation. In fact, the ultimate goal of the implementation is to build a product that meets the specifications. Thus, specifications are used by the implementer during design to make design decisions and during the verification activity to check that the implementation complies with the specifications.

We have already remarked that the whole design process is a chain of definition-implementation-verification steps. Thus, it is likely that several different specification documents will exist. As already mentioned, a specification that defines the external behavior of the system is called a *requirement specification*, and a specification of the software architecture, possibly at several levels of abstraction, is called a *design specification*.

In general, different uses of the specifications stress the required qualities in different–perhaps even contrasting–ways. For instance, if specifications must be used as part of a contract, they must be understandable by all parties to the contract. This may restrict the *language* used for writing them, since technical terminology and notation may not be acceptable to many users. On the other hand, the specification of, say, a module interface, is more useful for driving its implementation if it is written in a formal notation of the type introduced in Chapter 4.

A reference point during product maintenance. In Chapters 2 and 4 we have seen that several kinds of maintenance may occur during a product's life cycle. All of them involve specifications.

In the case of corrective maintenance, usually only the implementation is changed. Thus, specifications are needed to check whether the new implementation corrects the errors contained in the previous version of the product. An exception could be when the error is in the specification, but is not discovered until the product is used. In this case, one must first correct the specification and then modify the implementation accordingly.

Adaptive maintenance occurs because of a change in the requirements. Among such changes are modifications of the functionality of the product–say, coping with a new tax law in a payroll system–and modifications in the operating environment–say, a change in the automatic teller mechanisms in a banking system. In such cases, the original specifications must be adapted to the new requirements. Then the new implementation must be checked against them again for correctness. Experience has shown unequivocally that attempts to reduce development time by changing the implementation only is counterproductive, producing inconsistencies between specification and implementation. One of the worst examples of this approach is when "patches" are applied to the object code, as in Case Study A. Such patches produce inconsistencies even between the source and the object code.

In perfective maintenance, sometimes the requirements do not change. For example, one may wish to restructure the design in an attempt to gain an improvement in performance. In other cases, such as the inclusion of new functions or the modification of an existing function, the requirements also change. Again, what is important is the use of specifications to understand the impact of the change clearly and to accomplish the change reliably.

5.2 SPECIFICATION QUALITIES

Of course, one can write good specifications or bad ones. Most of the qualities listed in Chapter 2 as general software qualities contribute to the production of good specifications. For instance, user friendliness is a relevant feature for specifications as well as for the whole software product. As with software, user friendliness implies different requirements, depending on who the user of the specification actually is–e.g., the end user or the implementer. Maintainability is also desirable for specifications. As we saw in the previous section, specifications are likely to change during a product's life as the product itself changes.

In this section, we will discuss three qualities that are especially relevant for specifications. The first quality required of specifications is that they should be *clear, unambiguous*, and *understandable*. This claim sounds obvious, but it cannot be overemphasized. In particular, informal specifications, written in a natural language, are likely to hide subtle ambiguities.

Consider a common example of a word processor providing a **select** command, specified in the following way:[1]

---

[1]From the Manual of *Microsoft Word 4.0*.

> Selecting is the process for designating areas of your document that you want to work on. Most editing and formatting actions require two steps: first you select what you want to work on, such as text or graphics; then you initiate the appropriate action.

Such a definition does not specify exactly what the term "area" means. It turns out that in most products this is intended as a "*contiguous* sequence of characters." This can sometimes be inferred by carefully reading the manuals or, more likely, by direct experimentation. One might however interpret the term "area" as the union of *scattered* sequences of characters, so that one could go through a text, selecting different–not necessarily contiguous–words, and then, say, italicizing all of them by a single command. This is not possible in standard word processors. The main point, however, is that the original specification does not make clear whether it is possible or not.

Another example is the following fragment of a specification taken from the documentation of a real project for a mission-critical system:

> The message must be triplicated. The three copies must be forwarded through three different physical channels. The receiver accepts the message on the basis of a two-out-of-three voting policy.

Intuitively, this specification states that, for reasons of reliability, messages are triplicated. Upon receiving them, the receiver determines the content of the transmitted message by comparing the copies: if two of them match, their content is assumed correct.

It is not clear, however, whether the message should be considered received *as soon as* two identical copies have been received, without waiting for the third one, or whether the receiver should wait for all three copies before comparing their contents. Since we are talking about a real-time system, this point can make a significant difference in acting on the message.[1]

The application of rigor and formality can help significantly in achieving these and many other qualities of specifications. For instance, the ambiguity in the voting policy just mentioned was discovered because it was decided to formalize the informal specification. Later in this chapter, we will see how to formalize the voting policy to remove all ambiguities.

The second major quality requirement for specifications is *consistency*. For instance, in a word processor one could state that:

- The whole text should be kept in lines of equal length, with the length specified by the user.
- Unless the user gives an explicit hyphenation command, a carriage return should occur only at the end of a word.

---

[1]By looking at the design documentation, we found that, actually, neither of the two suggested interpretations was chosen by the implementer. In fact, the receiver polled the three channels periodically, so that an implicit time-out was defined: if the three copies were received within a given time, all of them were compared; if, however, after a given period of time only two of them were available, and they matched, then the message was accepted without waiting for the third transmission.

This definition, however, does not cover the case where a particular word is longer than the length specified for lines. In such a case, the specification is self-contradictory, or *inconsistent*. Therefore no implementation can satisfy it. The probability of inadvertently including some inconsistency in a specification increases as the specification documents become longer and more complex, which is often the case in real-life projects.

The third prime quality requirement for specifications is that they should be *complete*. There are two aspects of completeness. First, the specification must be internally complete. This means that the specification must define any new concept or terminology that it uses. A glossary is often helpful for this purpose. For example, if the specification of an elevator system states that "in the absence of any outstanding requests, the elevator enters a *wait-for-request* state," the specification must also define the meaning of *wait-for-request* state.

The second aspect of completeness refers to completeness with respect to requirements: the specification must document all the needed requirements. In the elevator example, if it is required that an elevator that has no outstanding requests must go to the first floor and open its doors, this must be stated explicitly and not left to the designer's discretion.

Often, response-time performance is not specified for most non-real-time systems– e.g., word processors. Upon using the product, however, the customer may complain that the system is too slow. Exceptional cases are also rarely specified, yet they are quite relevant; for instance, one would not be very happy if a power failure caused all open files to be lost.

In any case, it is often unrealistic to ask for complete specifications in a strict sense. This is because many requirements can be identified clearly only after some experience with the system. Moreover, too many details would need to be specified. More realistically, some requirements are considered to be common to every system. This assumption, in turn, may lead us to accept some amount of imprecision. For instance, one will often be satisfied with sentences of the type "response times should be about two seconds" or "the system should be robust with respect to power failures." The aim, however, is to keep such imprecision within limits that avoid the risk of dangerous ambiguities of the type mentioned earlier. It is the responsibility of both the user and the producer to decide when some imprecisions can be accepted on a commonsense basis and when they must be avoided as dangerous.

Because of the difficulties in achieving complete specifications, the use of the *incrementality* principle is especially important in deriving specifications. That is, one may start off with a fairly incomplete specification document and expand it through several steps, maybe after some experience with early prototypes. We will see examples of this point later in the chapter.

Exercises

5.1   Go through all the software qualities listed in Chapter 2, and state clearly which are relevant for specifications and which are not.

5.2   Give a specification for the *justify* function in a word processor.

5.3 CLASSIFICATION OF SPECIFICATION STYLES

We may classify the many different styles of specifications according to two different, orthogonal criteria.

Specifications can be stated *formally* or *informally*. Informal specifications are written in a natural language; they can, however, also make use of figures, tables, and other notations to help understanding. They can also be structured in a standardized way. When the notation gets a fully precise syntax and meaning, it becomes a *formalism*. In such a case, we talk of *formal specifications*. It is also useful to talk of *semiformal* specifications, since, in practice, we sometime use a notation without insisting on a completely precise semantics. The TDN and GDN notations introduced in Section 4.2.3.1 are an example of semiformal notations, since they put together a formal syntactic description of module interfaces and an informal statement of their meaning. We will see later how the informal comments in our TDN module specifications can be made precise by formalization.

The second major distinction between different specification styles is between operational and descriptive specifications. *Operational specifications* describe the intended system by describing the *desired behavior*, usually by providing a model of the system, i.e., an abstract device that in some way can simulate its behavior. By contrast, *descriptive specifications* try to state the *desired properties* of the system in a purely declarative fashion.

For example, suppose you give the following specification of a geometric figure E:

E is the path of the point that moves so that the sum of its distances from two fixed points P_1 and P_2 is constant.

What we have given is an operational definition of the curve known in geometry as an ellipse whose foci are P_1 and P_2. An alternative definition of the same curve would be given by providing its equation, $ax^2 + by^2 + c = 0$.

The example shows that an operational definition easily allows us to check whether the specification describes the kind of curve that we had in mind when we gave the specification. It is in fact easy to draw a curve with paper and pencil following the specification and then examine whether the curve satisfies, say, the aesthetic requirements we had in mind (see Figure 5.1). Of course, the implementation of the curve might turn out to be entirely different from what is given in the specification; for example, it might be a curve to be displayed on a graphical terminal. Nevertheless, experimentation helps us understand whether the specification we gave is correct. On the other hand, if we want to check whether, say, a given point P lies on the curve, we can do it more easily by referring to the equation. The equation might also help in assessing the adequacy of the requirements: the curve might be the trajectory of a robot, point P might represent the site where a human should work, and safety reasons might require that the robot never reach point P.

For a software example, consider the following informal operational specification of the sorting of an array:

Let a be an array of n elements. The result of sorting a is an array b of n elements such that the first element of b is the minimum of a (if several elements of a have the same value, any one of them is acceptable), the second element of b is the minimum of the array of n - 1 elements obtained from a by removing its minimum element; and so on until all n elements of a have been removed.

This specification suggests a natural and simple (although not very efficient) way of implementing the sorting of an array. The suggestion, however, does not imply that a sorting algorithm *must* sort a in that way: it must only produce the same result. Thus, quicksort is a perfectly adequate implementation of the specification. The problem with this kind of specification, however, is that it is difficult for the reader to determine what is important about the specification and must be implemented and what is not important and may be ignored.

A descriptive specification of the sorting of a is the following:

The result of sorting a is an array b which is a permutation of a and is sorted.

If the concepts of *permutation* and of being *sorted* are not considered clear enough, they can be further defined in a natural (and descriptive) way.

There are several trade-offs between descriptive and operational specification styles. It is sometimes claimed that descriptive specifications are *more abstract* than operational specifications because they do not bias the reader towards any particular implementation. In essence, they help focus on essential properties of the system without modeling the behavior of any implementation. Although this is basically true, we must recognize that some hidden implementation schema is present in *any* specification. For instance, the above descriptive specification of sorting an array suggests the following trivial implementation: "Enumerate all permutations of the original array. The first permutation that is sorted is an acceptable output for a sorting algorithm." Thus, both specifications of sorting suggest a particular implementation schema. Neither one appears to be the best

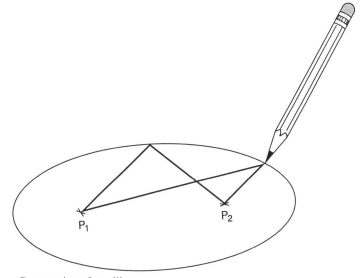

Figure 5.1   Construction of an ellipse.

implementation; the second is just far less efficient than the first.

One could also write specifications that are in some sense halfway between operational and descriptive. For instance, one could define a new operation to be applied to an array a in the following way:

- First, a must be sorted; where the definition of "sorted" is given in the previous descriptive way;
- Then any duplicate elements of the sorted array must be deleted from the array.

This specification is operational in the sense that it specifies a sequence of two operations to be performed to obtain the desired result. But part of it–the meaning of the term "sorted"–is given in a descriptive way.

In summary, the distinction between operational and descriptive specifications is not always sharp and is sometimes subjective. It is, however, an adequate distinction for categorizing different specification styles.

In Sections 5.5 and 5.6, we develop a deeper understanding of specification styles, techniques, and goals by describing and critically evaluating some sample specification techniques. While we have selected these techniques because they are important representatives of specification styles, it is not the particular choices that are our main subject. Since there is no style that is right for all circumstances, our purpose is to help the reader develop the ability to analyze a specification technique or style critically and select or reject it depending on the situation. The appropriate style or notation can help a designer express a design or problem clearly. An inappropriate notation makes it difficult to do so.

On the other hand, no style or notation–formal or informal–can guarantee that the designer will come up with a good design or an insightful formulation of a problem. Good design requires experience and creativity. Since so much in the design activity depends on subjective criteria, it is important to develop a critical intuition that enables one to adapt the right specification style, technique, and notation to the problem at hand.

Exercise

5.3   Give a completely descriptive specification of the previous example that used a mix of descriptive and operational styles to describe an array operation.

5.4 VERIFICATION OF SPECIFICATIONS

We have stated that one important use of specifications is to serve as a reference against which we can verify the implementation. But we also observed that the specification itself must be verified.

In Chapter 2, we saw that the correctness of an application does not automatically imply that the functions performed by the application are exactly the ones that were meant by the user. The same observation holds for all software qualities. Even if the implementation eventually satisfies the specification, we may still end up with a product that does not match the user's expectations. It is thus important that specifications be verified prior to starting an implementation, in order to assess their correctness.

There are two general ways of verifying a specification. One consists of observing the dynamic behavior of the specified system in order to check whether it conforms to the intuitive understanding we had of the behavior of the ideal system. The other consists of analyzing the properties of the specified system that can be deduced from the specification. The properties that are deduced are then checked against the expected properties of the system.

The effectiveness of both techniques increases depending on the degree of formality of the specification. In fact, in a completely formal setting, a way of observing the dynamic behavior of the specified system may consist of providing an interpreter of the formal language in which the specifications are written and then executing formal specifications on sample input data. Similarly, deducing new properties from the ones stated as part of the (descriptive) specification can be made mechanical in some formal logic setting, as we will see.

In the ellipse example shown in Figure 5.1, the observation of the dynamic system behavior can also be called *simulation*. Simulation is obtained by executing the formal specification, and this, following the concepts we introduced in Chapter 2, yields a *prototype* of the specified system, before any implementation has been started. In a less formal setting, execution may be simulated in the human mind, rather than mechanically, and this more easily accommodates informality. Similarly, *property analysis* can be done by human inspection, especially if the specifications are not fully formal.

It is perhaps useful to compare software engineering with more traditional engineering fields. There, descriptive specifications are often given in terms of (or on the basis of) mathematical equations that model the system. Think of a bridge of a given shape connecting two banks of a river: the mathematical model provided by the engineer supports a property analysis, in terms of whether or not the bridge can sustain a given distribution of static or dynamic forces. An operational model of the system is often built as a mock-up (a prototype, in our terminology), which is usually viewed not as a specification, but rather as an aid in verifying the specifications.

So far, we have only discussed the verification of functional specifications. It is also important to verify the completeness and consistency of specifications. Again, with formal specifications, some of this verification may be done mechanically (e.g., verifying that all terms used in the specification document are defined); some verification, on the other hand, may require the use of more sophisticated proofs. Informal specifications are harder to verify automatically, but even for them some mechanical checks are possible and should be used.

The issues of requirements verification will be taken up later in this chapter and also in Chapters 6, 7, and 9.

5.5 OPERATIONAL SPECIFICATIONS

In this section, we describe a few widely known and widely applied notations for giving specifications in an operational style. We start from a semiformal notation that is adopted mainly for the description of information systems. Then we illustrate a formal model that is suitable for describing control aspects in system modeling.

5.5.1 Data Flow Diagrams: Specifying Functions of Information Systems

Data flow diagrams (DFDs) are a well-known and widely used notation for specifying the functions of an information system. They describe systems as *collections of data* that are manipulated by *functions*. Data can be organized in several ways: they can be stored in *data repositories*, they can flow in *data flows*, and they can be transferred to or from the external environment.

One of the reasons for the success of DFDs is that they can be expressed by means of an attractive graphical notation that makes them easy to use.

The basic elements of a DFD are:[1]

- *Bubbles*, used to represent functions.
- *Arrows*, used to represent data flows. Arrows going to bubbles represent input values that belong to the domain of the function represented by the bubble. Outgoing arrows represent the results of the function, i.e., values that belong to the range of the function.
- *Open boxes*, used to represent data stores. Arrows entering (exiting) open boxes represent data that are inserted in (extracted from) the data store.
- *I/O boxes*, used to represent data acquisition and production during human-computer interaction.

Figure 5.2 gives examples of the above graphical symbols. Figure 5.3 shows how the symbols can be composed to form a DFD. The DFD describes the arithmetic expression

$$(a + b) * (c + a * d)$$

assuming that the data a, b, c, and d are read from a terminal and the result is printed. The figure shows that arrows can be "forked" to represent the fact that the same datum is used in different places.

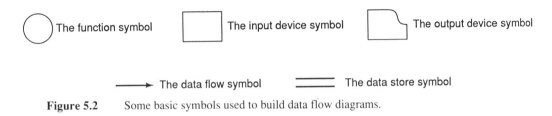

Figure 5.2   Some basic symbols used to build data flow diagrams.

---

[1]The DFD notation is not standardized. The literature contains several slightly different definitions.

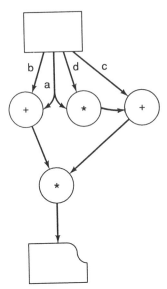

Figure 5.3   A data flow diagram for specifying the arithmetic expression
(a + b) * (c + a * d).

Example 5.1

Figure 5.4 describes a simplified information system for a public library. The data and
functions shown are not necessarily computer data and computer functions. The DFD
describes physical objects, such as books and shelves, together with data stores that are
likely to be, but are not necessarily, realized as computer files. Getting a book from the
shelf can be done either automatically–by a robot–or manually. In both cases, the action
of getting a book is represented by a function depicted by a bubble. The figure could
even represent the organization of a library with no computerized procedures.

The figure also describes the fact that, in order to obtain a book, the following are
necessary: an explicit user request consisting of the title and the name of the author of the
book and the user's name; access to the shelves that contain the books; a list of authors;
and a list of titles. These provide the information necessary to find the book.

The way the book is actually obtained, however, is not at all mentioned in the figure.
If we did not use our previous experience about the way one borrows a book from a
library, there would be no way to deduce this information from the figure. Thus, we
should consider this DFD as a *first approximation* of the description of a library
information system.   ∎

A finer description of how a book can be selected from the library shelves is given
in Figure 5.5, which can be seen as a *refinement* of (a part of) Figure 5.4. Figure 5.5 is
still somewhat imprecise, in that it does not specify whether both the title and the name
of the author are necessary to identify a book, or whether only one of them is enough. We

do know that, in general, one is sufficient, but occasionally, both are necessary. This distinction, however, is not explained by the figure. More generally, Figures 5.4 and 5.5– and DFDs in general–lack a precise meaning, chiefly for the following reasons:

1. The *semantics* of the symbols used is specified only by the identifiers chosen by the user. Sometimes this is sufficiently precise: e.g., the symbol '+' clearly denotes the function "add," and no further explanation is needed. Other times, however, more explanation is necessary. For instance, the function "Find book position" of Figure 5.5 has some intuitive meaning, but does not fully specify what happens if some information is missing. A realistic definition could be as follows:

    If the user supplies both author name(s) and book title **then**
          determine book position (if the book exists;
          otherwise give an appropriate message)
    elsif only the author is given **then**
          supply a list of all existing books by that
          author and ask the user for a selection;
    elsif only the title is given ...
        .
        .
        .
    end if

2. *Control* aspects are not defined by the model. For example, Figure 5.6 shows a simple DFD where the outputs of three bubbles, A, B, and C, are input to D and D's two outputs are inputs to the bubbles E and F. By itself, this diagram does not specify clearly the way in which inputs are used and outputs are produced by the function D. In particular, there are many different, equally possible alternatives, for both input and output. For the inputs:

    • D may need all of A, B, and C–not being able to execute unless they are all present together.
    • D may need only one of A, B, and C to execute; that is, the associated data transformation could take place when only one of the three is present.

    For the outputs:

    • D may output a result just to one of the two output bubbles E and F, again in a nondeterministic but exclusive way.
    • D may output the same data to both E and F.
    • D may output distinct data to both E and F.

    Other interpretations of D's inputs and outputs are also compatible with Figure 5.6.

    Another case where DFDs leave synchronization between components of a system completely unspecified is shown in Figure 5.7, where two bubbles A and B are connected by a single data flow, with A's output being B's input. There are at least two possible interpretations of this DFD:

- A produces a datum and then waits until B has consumed it. (This is often the case when A and B denote arithmetic operations on simple data.)
- A and B are autonomous activities that have different speeds, but there is a buffering mechanism between them (some sort of bounded queue or unbounded pipe) that ensures that no data are lost or duplicated (for instance, if A denotes computing the time spent by employees in their work and B denotes computing a payroll).

In sum, DFDs are an attractive graphical notation suitable for capturing, in a fairly immediate and intuitive way, the flow of data and the operations involved in an information system. However, they, lack a precise semantics.

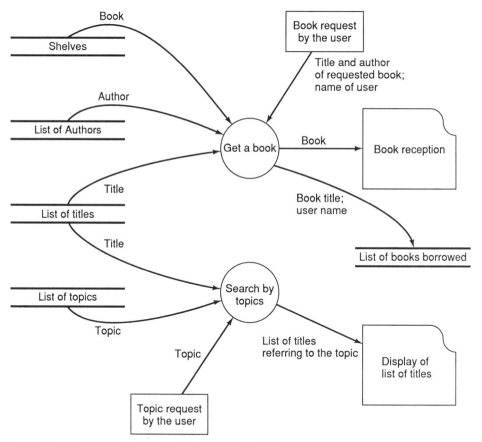

Figure 5.4   A DFD describing a simplified library information system.

This drawback has some negative consequences. First, if a rough description of the system modeled is not sufficient, and we need a precise and detailed definition, DFDs simply cannot do the job. Second, imagine you want to build a machine to simulate the system modeled, in order to test whether the specifications reflect the user's expectations.

Such a machine cannot be derived *directly* from the DFD, because no machine execution is possible without a precise semantics for the notation. A human reader is able to fill the semantic gap thanks to the intuitive meaning of the identifiers. But the machine, lacking intuition, will not be able to interpret a notation of the type given in Figure 5.7.

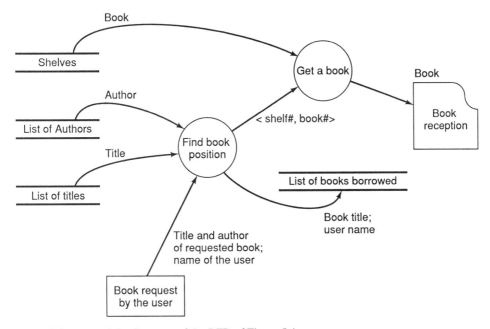

Figure 5.5   Partial refinement of the DFD of Figure 5.4.

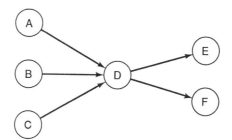

Figure 5.6   A DFD that is ambiguous in its use of inputs and outputs.

Figure 5.7   A DFD that does not specify synchronization between modules.

For these reasons, we say that traditional DFDs are a *semiformal notation*. Their syntax–i.e., the way of composing bubbles, arrows, and boxes–is sometimes defined precisely, but their semantics is not.

Several ways have been tried to overcome these difficulties in the use of DFDs. Essentially, they can be classified as follows:

- *Using a complementary notation to describe those aspects of the system that are not captured adequately by DFDs.* Thus, the complete system specification will consist of the integration of different descriptions provided in different notations. Some hints on the application of this technique will be given in Section 5.7.1.

- *Augmenting the DFD model in order to cope with aspects that are not captured by its traditional version.* For instance, we can handle control aspects by introducing *control flow arrows*. A control flow arrow going to a bubble means that the computation of the function associated with the bubble may occur only when a signal is present in the arrow. Figure 5.8 shows the notation and an example of the use of control flow arrows.

- *Revising the traditional definition of a DFD, to make it fully formal.* For example, one could define a formal DFD model that would make it possible to express all desirable interpretations of original DFDs in an unambiguous fashion. Thus, one might use different notations to distinguish the case where the arrow between two bubbles specifies the flow of a single datum from that where the arrows represents a pipe. Or, one could annotate the diagram to specify whether all input data flows are needed or whether only one is required to compute the function performed by a given bubble. Finally, one could provide a notation that would formally specify the function performed by a bubble.

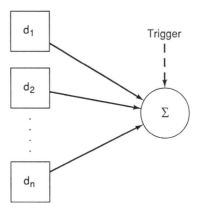

Figure 5.8   A partial DFD augmented with control flow arrows. The trigger is a control flow arrow. It is dashed rather than continuous. The function "sum" associated with the bubble is applied to all data existing in the boxes as soon as a trigger occurs.

In the sections that follow, we will present other system specification notations that are defined in a completely formal way.

Exercises

5.4   Give a more complete description of a library information system, including several other operations such as returning or reserving a book or doing a bibliographic search. Then, refine them up to a level where all of them are explained in sufficient detail.

5.5   Give a completely detailed specification of a reasonably powerful and realistic function, "finding book position." You are invited to reflect on how many details are involved in the full specification of such a small and seemingly simple part of a seemingly simple information system.

5.6   List some ambiguities in the use of the DFD notation other than those that have been pointed out in this section.

5.5.2 Finite State Machines: Describing Control Flow

In the description of information systems, the emphasis is on the organization of data and related operations. We saw, however, that to make specifications more precise, some attention must be paid to *control* aspects as well. For instance, sooner or later, one must specify in a DFD whether the execution of a function must wait for all inputs or whether it can start as soon as some of them are available. In a similar way, programming languages have constructs both to describe data organization and to describe the flow of control.

In the specification of different systems, the balance between data and control flow may be different. For instance, in a communication system one might first like to state requirements such as

- One must not write into a full buffer or read from an empty one;
- One should not access a buffer while another process is writing into it;
- Reading from a buffer must have a higher priority than writing into it;
- Every message must be forwarded through some channel within 2 milliseconds.

Then, one could also attend to functional aspects such as the following:

- For each message received, the parity must be checked;
- For every 10 messages received, a new message is synthesized that is the concatenation of the 10 messages preceded by a header that specifies the address of the receiving station.

Thus, both information systems and control systems–and, indeed, all other kinds of systems–have functional and data aspects as well as control aspects. The models used, however, could put different emphases on the two according to the nature of the systems.

Finite state machines (FSMs) are a simple, widely known, and important model for describing control aspects. An FSM consists of

1.   a finite set of states, Q;
2.   a finite set of inputs, I;
3.   a transition function $\delta : Q \times I \rightarrow Q$. δ can be a partial function, i.e., it can be undefined for some values of its domain.

Graphically, an FSM is shown by a graph whose nodes represent states; an arc labeled i goes from q_1 to q_2 if and only if $\delta(q_1, i) = q_2$. Figure 5.9 shows a simple FSM.

As the term itself suggests, FSMs are suitable for describing systems that can be in a finite set of states and that can go from one state into another as a consequence of some event, modeled by an input symbol. For instance, a lamp can be either on or off and can go from on to off as the consequence of an external action consisting of pushing the switch button. Pushing the button again causes the opposite transition. This simple system is described by the FSM of Figure 5.10. Another simple example of the use of FSMs is given next.

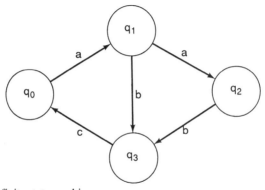

Figure 5.9   A finite state machine.

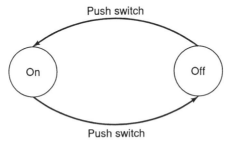

Figure 5.10   A finite state machine description of a lamp switch.

Example 5.2

Consider the control of a (small part of a) chemical plant. Temperature and pressure levels must be monitored for safety reasons. Sensors are installed to generate appropriate signals when either of these levels exceeds some predefined values. A trivial policy for managing the plant is the following: when either one of the signals is raised by the corresponding sensor, the control system shuts the plant off and raises an alarm signal; the system is restarted manually when the cause of the failure has been rectified. All this is described by the FSM of Figure 5.11.

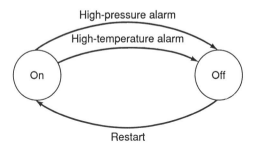

Figure 5.11   An FSM describing the control of a chemical plant.

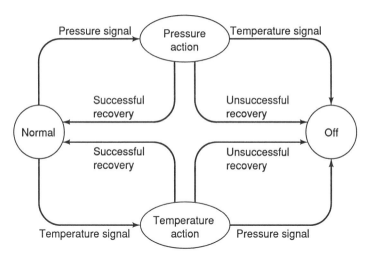

Figure 5.12   A refined policy for the control of a chemical plant described by an FSM.

This simple policy is obviously inadequate. A better way of managing the plant is as follows. When one of the two signals is raised, a recovery action is automatically invoked (there is a "temperature action" and a "pressure action"). If, after a while, the recovery action succeeds, the system is automatically reset to the "normal" state, and a message "everything OK" is issued to the external environment. Otherwise, the alarm signal must be raised and the plant must be shut off. The system must also be switched off if it is trying to recover from one kind of anomaly–temperature or pressure–and the other signal is raised. It is assumed that the two signals cannot occur simultaneously. This new policy is described by the FSM of Figure 5.12.   ∎

FSMs are often used to specify sets of acceptable strings (i.e., formal languages). In such a case, they are augmented by defining an *initial state* $q_0 \in Q$ and a subset F of Q, called the set of *final* or *accepting* states, graphically denoted by doubly circled nodes. The set I is the set of characters used to form the input strings.

An input string is *accepted* by the FSM if and only if there is a path in its graphical representation leading from q_0 to any final state such that the catenation of the labels of the edges of the path is the input string. For instance, the machine of Figure 5.13 accepts the words **begin** and **end**. The machine of Figure 5.14 accepts any legal identifier of the Ada programming language.

Sometimes, FSMs are augmented with the possibility of producing *output signals*. In this case, the transition function δ is augmented as

$$\delta: Q \times I \rightarrow Q \times O$$

where O is the finite set of output symbols. Graphically, the label <i/o> labels an arc going from q_1 to q_2 if and only if $\delta(q_1, i) = <q_2, o>$.

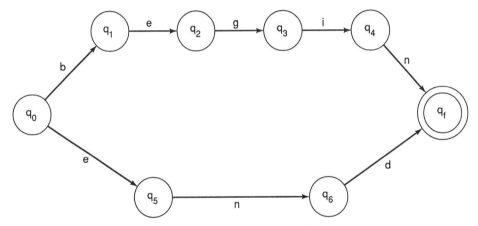

Figure 5.13   An FSM accepting the keywords **begin** and **end**.

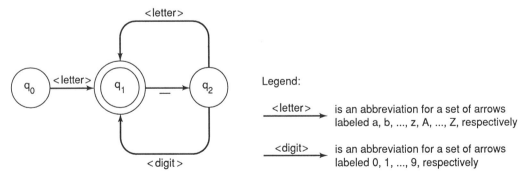

Figure 5.14   An FSM accepting Ada identifiers.

FSMs are a simple and widely used model. Their applications range from the specification of control systems to compilation, pattern matching, hardware design, and even applications outside of computer science. The simplicity of the model, however, may become a weakness in some more intricate cases. We will discuss the most relevant ones from the point of view of system specification, with primary reference to the specification of control systems, which is one of their major fields of application.

First, FSMs are a finite memory device, as their name suggests. This implies that in many cases their "computational power" is limited. For instance, in Example 5.2, suppose that the response to abnormal temperature is

> attempt a cooling effort that is
> 2 * (present_temperature - standard_value)

The cooling effort in this case cannot be modeled by a finite state device because its possible values are infinite.

Even when the range of possible values is finite–which is the case for many physical quantities of practical interest–the description of the responses may become extremely cumbersome. The quoted sentence is a much better specification than an FSM that uses a different arc for each different integer temperature value within, say, a 50-degree range. Similarly, even though the physical memory of any computer is always finite, it consists of an unmanageably large number of states: describing an eight-bit register by means of an FSM requires 2^8 different states!

When such situations occur, we can cope with them in different ways:

- We may give up on describing all details of the system and be satisfied with an approximation that ignores requirements of the type above. After all, Figure 5.11 provides some meaningful information, even without specifying the "amount of cooling effort."
- We may change models. Actually, a large variety of other models have been proposed to overcome this and other problems. Some appear as modifications of the original FSM; others are totally different models.
- We may *enrich* the model by adding new features to the description to cope with the new requirement.

For instance, in the system of Example 5.2, we can state, whether formally or informally, that the transition from the "normal" state to the "temperature-recovering" state must be accompanied by an action described as

> cooling-effort := 2 * (present_temperature - standard_value)

Also, one could add more complex *predicates* for effecting state transitions, as in the following description:

> **if** temp ≤ very_dangerous_value **then**
> > apply transition to Temperature_action
> **else**
> > apply transition to Off
> **end if**;

Actually, if we carry such a way of enriching the original model to its logical extreme, we end up with a full definition of a new FSM-like model. We will see that this has been done several times, both for FSMs and for many other models, in order to provide new *ad hoc* formal specification languages.

FSMs have another drawback that is somewhat typical of control system descriptions. This shortcoming is illustrated by the following example.

Example 5.3

A producer process produces messages and puts them into a two-slot buffer. A consumer process reads the messages and removes them from the same buffer. If the buffer is full, the producer must wait until the consumer process has emptied a slot. Similarly, if the buffer is empty, the consumer process must wait until a message has been inserted by the producer. The two processes and the buffer may be described separately by the FSMs of Figure 5.15.

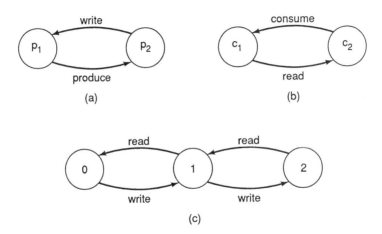

Figure 5.15   Three separate FSMs describing a producer-consumer system.
(**a**) Producer. (**b**) Consumer. (**c**) Buffer.

Although it can be useful to examine the three components separately, it is clear that the two processes, together with the buffer, are a single, synchronized system that must also be described as a whole.

A natural way of attacking this problem is to compose the different FSMs to obtain a new FSM that describes the whole system. Intuitively, the resulting state set should be the Cartesian product of the component state sets; furthermore, arcs denoting the same action in different components should become single arcs in the resulting graph. Applying this composition to Figure 5.15, we would obtain the result shown in Figure 5.16. In this FSM, a state such as $<0, p_2, c_2>$ corresponds to the buffer's being empty, the producer's being in state p_2, and the consumer's being in state c_2.

The approach is not without drawbacks. First, we see that, even in the fairly simple case under consideration, the cardinality of the state space grows dramatically: if we compose n subsystems, each one with k_i states, the resulting system has a cardinality of $k_1 \cdot k_2 \cdot \ldots k_n$.

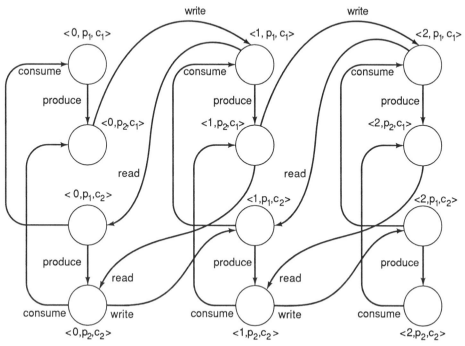

Figure 5.16   An integrated FSM description of a producer-consumer system.

This objection, however, is mitigated somewhat by the consideration that we need is actually a complete description of the system, not a complete FSM describing the system. Thus, we can argue that full information about the system is given by the three components of Figure 5.15, augmented with precise–even algorithmic–rules for composing FSM "modules" into "full FSMs," with no need for the explicit description of Figure 5.16. In some sense, we have built a modular specification of the system, leaving its integration to a straightforward "FSM linker." We will see a more explicit example of this technique in Section 5.7.2.2.

There is, however, a more serious objection to the use of FSMs for the description of systems that consist of several concurrent units. If we look at Figure 5.16, we realize that it is an adequate description of the system under certain somewhat restrictive assumptions. Basically, the system described is always in a unique state and performs exactly one action at any instant of time. There is, however, no reason to impose a serialization between production by the producer and consumption by the consumer, two actions that are absolutely independent.

A possible rebuttal to this objection is that Figure 5.16 is still an adequate specification of the concurrent system because the effect of two concurrent–and compatible–actions, say a write and a consume, is the same as the effect of *any serialization* of the two actions, either write followed by consume or consume followed by write. This answer is partially true. It works fairly well if we can assume that the time for any transition is short enough that we can say at any instant t, "the present state of the system is, say, <1, p_1, c_2>." In such a case, we could even define new transitions that are the "parallel execution" of elementary transitions in order to cope with truly simultaneous events.

Instead, suppose that the various operations take fairly different execution times; e.g., consuming is longer than producing, which in turn is far longer than reading from and writing into the buffer. In this case, it may happen that the producer and consumer start together (producing and consuming, respectively). After a while, the producer is finished with producing and may start writing. This, again, may be finished before the consumer is finished with its original operation, and a new instance of production may start. Thus, we see that the transitions of the various components occur in an *asynchronous way* that is no longer described well by the FSM of Figure 5.16.   ∎

Example 5.3 shows that FSMs are essentially a *synchronous model*. (At any time, a global state of the system must be defined and a single transition must occur.) Other models are more appropriate for describing systems consisting of concurrent and asynchronous components, more so if timing aspects–i.e., stating time constraints for the completion of several transitions–are important. In the next section, we present and evaluate an operational model that is explicitly aimed at the description of concurrent systems.

Exercises

5.7 Using FSMs, describe a lighting system consisting of one lamp and two buttons. If the lamp is off, pushing either button causes the lamp to switch on, and conversely.

5.8 Describe a system with two lamps and one button. When the light is off, pushing the button causes the first lamp to go on. Pushing the button again causes the second lamp to go on and the first to go off. Pushing the button yet again causes both lamps to go on, and pushing it once more switches both lamps off.

5.9 Modify the specification given by the FSM of Figure 5.12 in order to cope also with simultaneous signals.

5.10 Modify the specification given by the FSM of Figure 5.12 by considering the case where temperature and pressure each have two different associated signals, one indicating a slight deviation from the acceptable value and the other a dangerous deviation from the acceptable value. In the latter case, the system must be shut off immediately.

5.5.3 Petri Nets: Specifying Asynchronous Systems

Petri nets are a graphical formalism for systems specification. They are formed from:

1. a finite set of *places*;
2. a finite set of *transitions*; and

3.   a finite set of *arrows* connecting either places to transitions or transitions to places.[1]

Graphically, places are represented by circles and transitions by bars. Whenever useful, a double-headed arrow connecting a place P and a transition t will be considered as an abbreviation for a pair of arrows, one going from P to t, the other going from t to P. Figure 5.17 shows a sample Petri net.

A Petri net (PN) is given a *state* by marking its places. A *marking* of a PN consists of assigning a nonnegative integer to each place. This is represented graphically by inserting a number of *tokens* in every place of the net. Figure 5.18(a) shows one marking of the PN of Figure 5.17. The evolution of a PN, i.e., its progression through state changes, is regulated by the rules explained below.

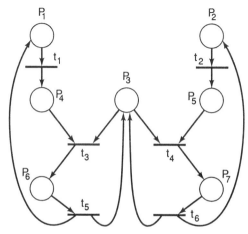

Figure 5.17   A Petri net.

A transition may have one or more input and output places. If an arrow goes from a place to a transition, the place is said to be one of the transition's *input places*; if an arrow goes from a transition to a place, the place is said to be one of the transition's *output places*. A transition is said to be *enabled* if there is at least one token in each of its input places.

An enabled transition may *fire*. This means that one token is removed from each input place and one token is inserted in each output place of the transition. In Figure 5.18(a), both t_1 and t_2 are enabled; no other transition is enabled. In such a case, the marking of the net may evolve in two different ways, either by firing t_1 or by firing t_2. Thus, the model is *nondeterministic*, in the sense that given an initial marking, different evolutions of the PN are possible. In the case of Figure 5.18(a), the firing of t_1 produces the marking of Figure 5.18(b), whereas the firing of t_2 produces the marking of Figure 5.18(c). Notice that, after t_1 fires, t_2 is still enabled and could fire. Correspondingly, t_1

---

[1]We usually consider only the case where at most one arrow connects the same pair <place, transition> and <transition, place>. The few exceptions should not cause any problem.

would still be enabled if t_2 fires first. In either case, one would reach the marking of Figure 5.18(d). At this point, t_3 and t_4 are both enabled, and either can fire in a nondeterministic way. This time, however, the firing of one prevents the other from firing. For example, if t_3 fires, t_4 will no longer be enabled.

A *firing sequence* of a given PN with a given initial marking is a sequence of transition firings, denoted as a string of transition labels $<t_1, t_2,..., t_n>$, such that t_1 is enabled in the initial marking, t_2 is enabled in the marking obtained by firing t_1, and so on.

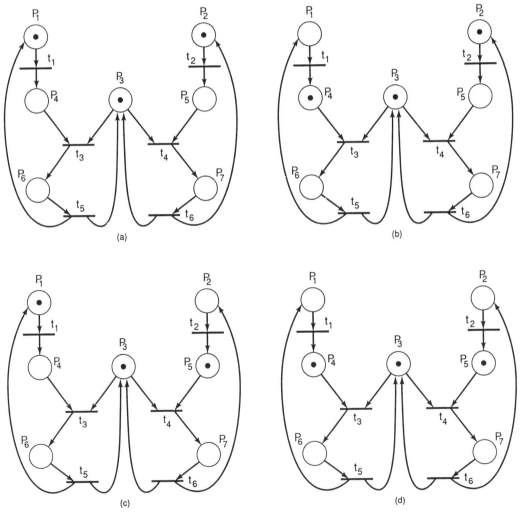

Figure 5.18   Evolution of a Petri net.
(a) Initial marking. (b) t_1 fires from initial marking.
(c) t_2 fires from initial marking. (d) t_1 and t_2 fire from initial marking.

Before going further into the analysis of the behavior of PNs, let us interpret them as a model for the description of concurrent systems. In a PN, a transition usually models an event or an action, and its firing represents the occurrence of the event or execution of the action. Thus, a transition is enabled if the *conditions* are satisfied that allow the occurrence of the modeled event or action. The presence of a token in a place denotes the existence of some condition. For instance, a place may model a resource, and the existence of one or more tokens in that place means the availability of one or more instances of that resource.

Let us look at the net of Figure 5.18(a). We can interpret its two parts, consisting of transitions t_1, t_3, t_5, and t_2, t_4, t_6, respectively, as two independent activities flowing through the events modeled by the transitions. The two activities share a common resource, modeled by place P_3. They could be two different programs using the same CPU, or two students sharing a book, etc.

Initially, the two activities can proceed in an independent and asynchronous way. In fact, t_1 and t_2 are both enabled, and the firing of one does not prevent the other from firing. In such a case, we say that the two transitions are *concurrent*. This arrangement could model, say, the independent editing of two programs at different terminals, or the reading of personal lecture notes by two students. After both transitions have fired,[1] however, both activities are again enabled to proceed, but in mutual exclusion. This is shown in Figure 5.18(d). The resource modeled by P_3 is actually available, but only for one of the two activities, the choice being nondeterministic. In this case, we say that the two transitions are in *conflict*.

Suppose that the resource is given to the activity on the left-hand side of the figure. Then the net can proceed through t_3 and t_5, leaving the other activity temporarily blocked. The firing of t_5 frees the resource that now is again available for further use. At this point, t_4 could fire. But it is also possible that, on the contrary, t_1 fires again, and then, the choice between t_3 and t_4 is resolved once more in favor of t_3. This can be repeated forever.

The model does not impose any policy to resolve conflict situations. In the concurrent system terminology, a process that never receives access to a needed resource, is said to suffer *starvation*. Thus, a firing sequence where only transitions t_1, t_3, t_5 occur lead to starvation of the activity on the righthand side of the figure.

Now, assume that the initial marking of the PN has two tokens in P_3 instead of one. This means that two indistinguishable resources are available. As a consequence, t_3 and t_4 are no longer in conflict, but are concurrent. If the two activities represent computer processes and two CPUs are available for them in a multiprocessor machine, the two processes may be executed in parallel.

Figure 5.19 is a modification of Figure 5.18(a). It models the case where the two activities need two identical copies of a resource to proceed. These copies are modeled by two tokens in place R. After an activity starts–say the leftmost–by firing t_1, it may obtain any one of the available resources (firing t_3') Then, it attempts to obtain also the other resource (firing t_3''). Once the activity has obtained both resources, execution can proceed, eventually releasing both (firing t_5).

---

[1]Notice that this does not necessarily happen. For example, after t_1 has fired, t_3 could fire. This would disable t_2 until t_5 fires.

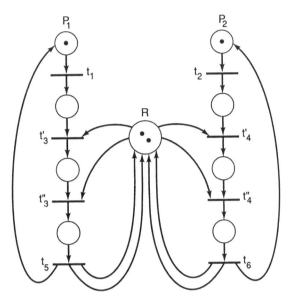

Figure 5.19   A Petri net that can enter a deadlock state.

Consider, however, the firing sequence $<t_1, t'_3, t_2, t'_4>$, which leads to a marking where no transition is enabled. Thus, the net is prevented from any further progress. Each of the activities has obtained one of the two resources and needs the other one to go further. But this cannot happen because the needed resource is owned by the other activity, which is also waiting for one more resource.

This is a typical *deadlock* situation, which is modeled quite well by a PN. Formally, a PN with a given marking is said to be in deadlock if and only if no transition is enabled in that marking. A PN where no deadlock can ever occur starting from a given marking is said to be *live*.

It is interesting to observe that we were able to derive the deadlock property of a system by doing manual analysis of the PN that models the system.

Exercises

5.11 Show that the modification of the PN of Figure 5.19 given in Figure 5.20 is live. How do you interpret the modification introduced?

5.12 Consider the PN of Figure 5.21. It is clear that it is live. The activity modeled by transitions t_2 and t_4, however, can go into starvation. In fact, a marking can be reached from which the two transitions can never be enabled. Comment briefly on the difference between this type of starvation and the one illustrated before.

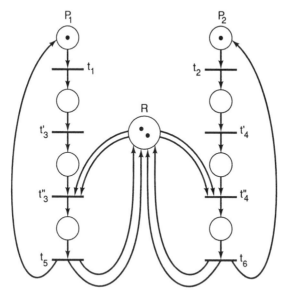

Figure 5.20   A modification of the Petri net of Figure 5.19 that is live.

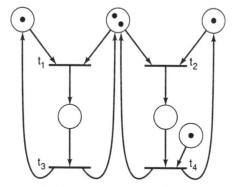

Figure 5.21   A Petri net, a part of which can go into starvation.

Example 5.4

Let us go back to the producer-consumer system modeled as an FSM in Example 5.3. The three separate components of the system can be described by the PNs of Figure 5.22.

Graphically, the composition of the three subsystems into a PN is shown in Figure 5.23. The figure shows that the major drawbacks of the corresponding FSM representation (given in Figure 5.16) are now resolved satisfactorily. First, the graphical complexity of the figure does not multiply the state space of the components, but is only additive. In fact, in Figure 5.16 the number of nodes coincided with the number of states.

In Figure 5.23, the number of states is given by the number of possible markings. The reader is invited to compare a PN describing a system of two producers and three consumers using a four-position buffer with the corresponding FSM representation.

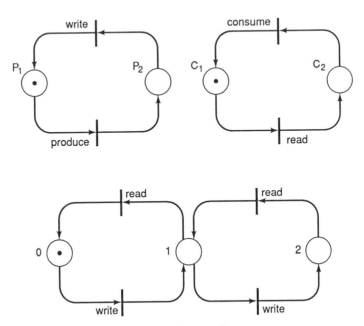

Figure 5.22   Three separate Petri nets describing a producer-consumer system.

Second–and more important–in Figure 5.23, the concurrency of independent activities is described properly. In fact, if the system is in the state $<1, p_1, c_2>$, i.e., a token is in each one of those places, both of the transitions produce and consume are enabled. That is, the two transitions are concurrent. (They can be executed in parallel without preventing each other from firing). Also, looking at the firing sequence

<produce, write, produce, read, consume, write, read, consume>

shows immediately which actions could happen concurrently and which ones have to be serialized because the termination of one is necessary for the start of the other.   ∎

Exercises

5.13   Give examples of firing sequences for the net of Figure 5.18(a).

5.14   Describe some of the systems previously described by FSMs by means of PNs, and compare the different specifications.

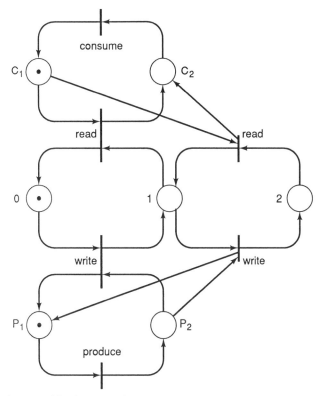

Figure 5.23   An integrated Petri net describing a producer-consumer system.

5.5.3.1 Limitations and extensions of Petri nets

Even though PNs model certain aspects of systems quite well, their use in applications has revealed some weaknesses also. First, they are–like FSMs–a control-oriented model. Tokens typically represent the flow of control in the execution of several actions. The tokens, however, are *anonymous*. For example, the presence of a token in some place may denote only the presence of a message in a buffer, not what the message says.

This simplicity may be useful. Often–for example, when we are interested in analyzing the flow of messages within a communication network–the important issue is whether or not a message that has been produced somewhere will be delivered somewhere else. In such cases, the actual content of the message may be an irrelevant detail.

But this is not always the case. For example, suppose you wish to specify a system in which a message is to be forwarded through one of two different channels: $channel_1$ is selected if the message is well formed; $channel_2$–the "error" channel–is selected if the message is incorrect. The message is well-formed if it contains an even number of 1's (i.e., if it has correct parity).

Figure 5.24 shows a tentative PN specification of such a system. This net, however, suggests that the choice between the two channels is nondeterministic when a message is ready to be forwarded (represented by a token in place P). It is not an adequate description of the system we have described with words, since the choice between the channels is dictated by the contents of the message.

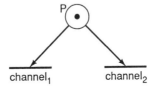

Figure 5.24   A portion of a Petri net describing the forwarding of messages through different channels.

In our example, the firing of a transition *should* depend on what the message says, which is represented by the token. But this is clearly impossible, since the token says nothing at all; a token merely denotes the presence of a message. Besides being able to associate what messages say (their *values*) with tokens, it would also be useful to be able to *compute* the value of the tokens. Then, on receipt of a message, a station could modify the message before forwarding it, e.g., by adding an additional address field. These problems are common to all control-oriented models.

Another drawback of PNs is the fact that, in the general case, it is not possible to specify a *selection policy* between different transitions that are enabled. For instance, going back to the net of Figure 5.18(a), we already noticed the possibility of the firing sequence $<t_1, t_3, t_5>$ repeating indefinitely, starving the activity consisting of $<t_2, t_4, t_6>$. To avoid starvation in this case, we could enforce an alternation policy by modifying the net slightly as shown in Figure 5.25. This modified net prevents t_3 from firing a second time before t_4 has fired once.

It can be mathematically proved, however, that, in the general case, PNs do not have the ability to describe a selection policy such as

> **if** transition t is enabled **then**
>   fire t;
> **else**
>   fire the first enabled transition
>   according to some ordering criterion
> **end if**;

Timing issues are another critical aspect of some systems. As we have seen in Chapters 2 and 4, in some real-time systems, failure to compute an answer within a given time has the same severe effect as not computing it at all or computing it incorrectly. Also, the result of a computation may depend on the speed of execution of some actions.

For instance, suppose that an external line sends messages to a computer at some given speed. Every message that is received is put into a buffer and then processed. If a message is not taken from the buffer before the next message arrives, it is overwritten. Thus, the results of the processing may vary depending on the arrival times of the messages.[1]

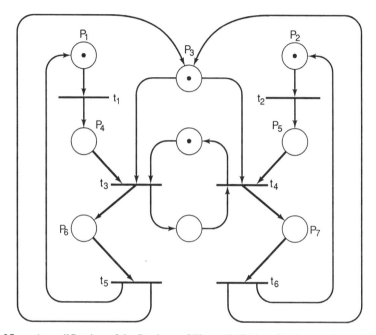

Figure 5.25   A modification of the Petri net of Figure 5.18(a), enforcing an alternation policy.

Unfortunately, most models of computer systems, including PNs, do not take time into account explicitly. The consequence is a lack of depth in modeling and analysis. For instance, consider again the PN of Figure 5.18(a). If t_1, t_3, and t_5 take 1 second each to be completed, and t_2 takes 5 seconds, it is clear that the firing sequence $<t_1, t_2, t_3, t_5, t_4>$ is not feasible, contrary to what is suggested by the net. In fact, suppose that at time 0 both t_1 and t_2 start. At time 1, t_3 can start but t_2 is not completed. Thus, if the firing of a transition models the complete execution of the corresponding activity, the firing of t_2 cannot occur before the firing of t_3.

Luckily, the flexibility of the model has allowed it to be extended in several directions while maintaining its original "philosophy." Let us review some fairly standard modifications of PNs that have proved useful in several circumstances.

Assigning values to tokens. Tokens can be modified to carry a value of an appropriate type: an integer, an array of bytes, or even a full *environment* consisting of several variables and associated values. Accordingly, *predicates* and *functions* are associated with transitions with the following meaning: a transition with k input places and h output

---

[1]This is the classical problem of missing interrupts.

places is enabled if there exists a k-tuple of tokens–one for each input place–such that the predicate associated with the transition is satisfied by the values of the tokens of the tuple. These tokens are together called a *ready* tuple.

Notice that the predicate is evaluated on exactly one token for each input place. Thus, there could be more than one ready tuple for some transition; that is, the same token could belong to different ready tuples. When an enabled transition fires, this implies all of the following:

- the cancellation of all tokens that belong to a ready tuple from the input places (if there is more than one ready tuple, its choice is nondeterministic);
- the evaluation of h new token values on the basis of the values of the ready tuple by applying the function associated with the transition (thus, such a function has a domain of k-tuples and a range of h-tuples);
- the production of one token for each output place, the value of which is computed by the function associated with the transition.

For instance, consider the PN of Figure 5.26, where tokens are assumed to carry integer values. The notation is self-explanatory: the name of a place in a predicate or function stands for a token in that place. Both transitions t_1 and t_2 are enabled. Transition t_1 has two ready tuples, namely <3, 7> and <3, 4>, since both tuples satisfy the predicate $P_2 > P_1$. Transition t_2 has one ready tuple, namely <4, 4>, which satisfies the predicate $P_3 = P_2$. The token valued 1 in P_2 does not belong to any ready tuple. Thus, the firing of t_1 by using the tuple <3, 4> would produce a token with value 7 in P_4 and would therefore disable t_2, since the tokens 3 and 4 would disappear respectively from P_1 and P_2. Instead, the firing of t_1 by using <3,7> would produce the value 10 in P_4. After that, t_2 could still fire, producing the value 0 in P_4 and 8 in P_5.

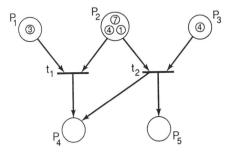

Figure 5.26   A Petri net whose tokens carry values. The predicate $P_2 > P_1$ and the function $P_4 := P_2 + P_1$ are associated with t_1; the predicate $P_3 > P_2$ and the functions $P_4 := P_3 + P_2$ and $P_5 := P_2 + P_3$ are associated with t_2.

This first enrichment to the PN model allows a natural and simple solution to the problem of Figure 5.24. In fact, it is sufficient to consider tokens as carrying a value of the type of messages, say, sequences of bits. The predicate "P has an even number of 1's" can then be attached to transition $channel_1$ and similarly for transition $channel_2$. Also, if the forwarding of the messages through the channels implies some modification of the message, this can be done in a natural way by adding appropriate functions to the transitions.

Exercise

5.15 Use the above PN extension to describe a message dispatcher that works along the following lines. The dispatcher receives messages from two different channels. It checks the parity of each message. If the parity is wrong, it sends a "nack" through a reply channel (there is one such channel for each input channel); if the parity is right, it places the received message into a buffer. The buffer may store ten messages. When the buffer is full, the dispatcher sends the whole contents of the buffer to a processing unit through another channel. No message can be placed into a full buffer.

Specifying scheduling policies. When the pure nondeterminism of the Petri net model is not adequate, we face the problem of specifying a policy for selecting a transition to fire among all the enabled transitions. A fairly simple way of doing this is to attach priorities to transitions. Then we modify the firing rule in the following way: if, in some state, several transitions are enabled, only the ones with maximum priority are actually allowed to fire.

Priorities are usually defined statically. If tokens carry a value, however, we can define dynamic priorities whose values depend on the values of the tokens of the input places of the transitions.

Exercise

5.16 Add suitable priorities to the PN you have built to solve Exercise 5.15. If the dispatcher is in a condition where it can either receive a message from an input channel, or send a "nack" reply, or forward the buffer contents to the processor, then it must order its priorities as follows: first get the message, then send the "nack," then forward the buffer contents.

Timed Petri nets. Subtle theoretical problems arise when one wants to introduce time within formal computation models. This, however, is not the place to go deeply into such theoretical issues. We just mention that the notion of time has been added to Petri nets in several ways. Here we describe one of the most simple and natural ways of introducing time into PNs by scratching only the surface of this hard problem.

Timed PNs are PNs in which a pair $<t_{min}, t_{max}>$ is associated with each transition. Again, such values could be constant or computed as functions of the values of tokens at the input places. The idea is that once a transition is enabled, it must wait for at least t_{min} time to elapse before it can fire. Also, if enabled, it *must* fire before t_{max} time has elapsed, unless it is disabled by the firing of another transition before t_{max}. A timed PN is equivalent to an original PN if, for every transition, $t_{min} = 0$ and $t_{max} = \infty$.

Temporal and other modifications can obviously be combined. So if we attach both times and priorities to transitions, care is needed in determining which transition can or must fire at which time. A natural rule is that if several transitions can fire (this does not mean only that they are enabled, but also that each is enabled during its $[t_{min}, t_{max}]$ interval), then only transitions with maximum priorities can actually fire, within a time that is less than or equal to their own t_{max}.

For instance, consider the net of Figure 5.27. Suppose that at time $t = 0$ the marking is modified by the arrival of a token in P_2, so that both t_1 and t_2 are enabled at the same time. In such a case, it may happen that t_1 fires within a time less than 2. If it does not fire within that time, however, then it cannot fire any more, because at time $t = 2$ t_2 can fire too, and it has a higher priority than t_1. Now, if at time $t = 1$ a token is produced into P_4, then during the interval $1 \le t < 2$, both t_3 and t_1 can fire, but t_1 cannot fire before t_3, because it has lower priority.

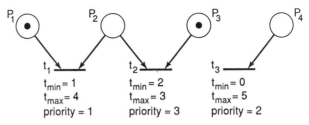

Figure 5.27   A timed Petri net.

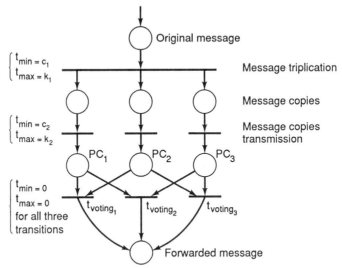

Figure 5.28   A possible formalization of message replication and selection through augmented Petri nets. The predicate $PC_1 = PC_2$ is associated with $t_{voting1}$. The predicate $PC_1 = PC_3$ is associated with $t_{voting2}$. The predicate $PC_2 = PC_3$ is associated with $t_{voting3}$. The predicate true is associated with all other transitions. The identity function is associated with all transitions. c_1 and k_1 (c_2 and k_2) are the lower (upper) bounds of the duration of operation Message triplication (Message copies transmission).

Now, let us go back to the problem of giving a precise meaning to the informal specification

> The message must be triplicated. The three copies must be forwarded through three different physical channels. The receiver accepts the message on the basis of a two-out-of-three voting policy.

which was discussed in Section 5.2. Timed PNs, augmented with tokens carrying values, can easily provide a precise description of the possible interpretations of this informal specification.

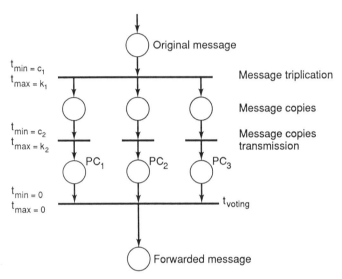

Figure 5.29   An alternative formalization of message replication and selection. The predicate $PC_1 = PC_2$ **or** $PC_2 = PC_3$ **or** $PC_1 = PC_3$ is associated with t_{voting}. The function "**if** $PC_1 = PC_2$ **then** PC_1 **elsif** $PC_2 + PC_3$ **then** PC_2 **elsif** $PC_1 = PC_3$ **then** PC_1 **else** "ERROR" **end if**" is associated with t_{voting}. The predicate **true** is associated with all other transitions. The identity function is associated with all other transitions.

The first interpretation suggested in Section 5.2 was that the message should be considered received as soon as two identical copies have been received. This interpretation is formalized by the PN of Figure 5.28. With this formulation, as soon as two tokens with the same value are present in P_1, P_2, or P_3, the corresponding transition fires.

A different interpretation of the informal requirements, based on the decision to wait for receipt of all three copies before performing the comparison, is formalized by the net of Figure 5.29.

This example of the triplicate messages shows that the use of a formal model allows us to attach a precise meaning to a system specification. Furthermore, the formal model may be the basis of a rigorous *analysis*. For example, if we are interested in determining the maximum time that may be spent to deliver an incoming message, we can easily see that it is $k_1 + k_2$ in both cases. If, however, we assume that transmission of the copies through the three channels takes a time that is randomly distributed within c_2 and k_2, we find that the probability of receiving the message in place Forwarded Message within time t is higher in the case of Figure 5.28 than in the case of Figure 5.29.

Now, assume that each channel has some probability of failure during transmission. (This could be modeled by adding more transitions, connected to the "message copies" places, that simply destroy the tokens that represent the messages.) Then the model of Figure 5.28 would have a lower probability of global failure–i.e., not forwarding the message to place Forwarded Message–than the model of Figure 5.29. Since message triplication is apparently done just to enhance performance and/or fault tolerance, it is clear that such a difference between the two interpretations of the informal specification is quite useful.

The above analysis could have been made even more precise by further enriching the PN model with stochastic features, such as probabilistic distributions of firing times and probabilistic distributions of the firing of enabled transitions. The interested reader can find models of this type in the literature suggested in the bibliographic notes.

Exercises

5.17   Give a formalization, in terms of augmented PNs, of the third interpretation mentioned in Section 5.2, in which the receiver polls the three channels periodically. If three copies are received within a given time, all of them are compared. If only two are received within the given time, and they coincide, however, then the message is accepted.

5.18   The formalization of Figure 5.28 has a minor flaw that may become relevant if the PN is part of a cyclic system. Find and fix the error, i.e., modify the PN in such a way that it behaves properly even if repeated cyclically.

5.5.3.2 A case study using Petri nets

Let us now apply the Petri net model–and some of its variations–to describe a more complex and realistic system, namely, an elevator system. Consider the following informal specification, which has been proposed and used in the literature as a benchmark for evaluating the applicability of specification techniques and tools to real life problems. It is quoted directly:

An n elevator system is to be installed in a building with m floors. The elevators and the control mechanisms are supplied by the manufacturer. The internal mechanisms of these are assumed (given). The problem concerns the logic to move elevators between floors according to the following constraints:

1. Each elevator has a set of buttons, one for each floor. These illuminate when pressed and cause the elevator to visit the corresponding floor. The illumination is canceled when the corresponding floor is visited by the elevator.

2. Each floor has two buttons (except the ground and the top floors), one to request an up-elevator and one to request a down-elevator. These buttons illuminate

when pressed. The illumination is cancelled when the elevator visits the floor and is either moving in the desired direction, or has no outstanding requests. In the latter case, if both floor request buttons are pressed, only one should be cancelled. The algorithm to decide which to service first should minimize the waiting time for both requests.

3. When an elevator has no requests to service, it should remain at its final destination with its doors closed and await further requests (*or model a "holding" floor*).

4. All requests for elevators from floors must be serviced eventually, with all floors given equal priority (*can this be proved or demonstrated?*).

5. All requests for floors within elevators must be serviced eventually, with floors being serviced sequentially in the direction of travel (*can this be proved or demonstrated?*).

6. Each elevator has an emergency button which, when pressed causes a warning signal to be sent to the site manager. The elevator is then deemed "out of service". Each elevator has a mechanism to cancel its "out of service" status.

Before going into the exercise of translating the above statements into a formal model, let us substantiate the value of doing so. Although people are generally familiar with this type of system, the specifications should be examined with some attention. It would be interesting for the reader to postpone reading the following comments and first try to analyze and perhaps formalize the specifications by him- or herself.

Let us focus our attention on point 2. First, we read that every floor, except the first and the last, has two buttons. Note that there is no implication here–or elsewhere in the specifications–that rules out as incorrect a system implementation where the first floor has 9 buttons and the last one 4. This remark, however, could appear to be overly critical: there is an "obviously correct" interpretation, i.e., that the first floor has only the button to go up and the last floor has only the button to go down. We make this interpretation because it is part of our ordinary knowledge about elevators and we can easily integrate this knowledge with explicitly stated requirements. This remark could even be used as an argument in favor of informality in specifications: a formal definition would have compelled us to specify in full detail even things that are perfectly understood, resulting in wasted effort.

In general, formality is a tool for achieving precision *whenever needed*. Full precision may be useless and even boring, if the intended reader of the specifications is a human being. Thus, it is the responsibility of the specifier to choose an appropriate *level of formality*. Sometimes, the simplicity, immediateness, and generality of natural language may be preferable to the semantic rigor of mathematical formalisms. Other times, a–perhaps graphical–semiformal notation can give a quick and sufficiently clear idea of the desired system. In still other cases, especially if the system is complex or critical, the effort of going through full formalization may be worthwhile. In general, formality is required when we cannot afford the risk of being misinterpreted.

Now, let us go further into the analysis of point 2. The rule states:

> The illumination is cancelled when the elevator visits the floor and is either moving in the desired direction, or ...

This sentence can be interpreted in at least two different ways. Consider an elevator going up. (The case when the elevator is going down is symmetric.) Then the rule could mean either of the following:

- Switch off the up button as soon as the elevator reaches the floor coming from below. (This interpretation has an exception if the floor is the first or the last one).
- Switch off the up button after an elevator reaches the floor and starts moving in the up direction.

By examining different elevators, we can see that both interpretations have been used in practice. It has been observed empirically that, in general, one does not realize the ambiguity in a sentence like the one above until one builds a formal model of it.

Finally, notice the imprecision in the requirement

> The algorithm to decide which to service first should minimize the waiting time for both requests.

What does it mean to "minimize the waiting time for both requests"? Here are two possible interpretations:

- In no other way should it be possible to serve either request in a shorter time. This interpretation could be infeasible: minimizing the waiting time of one request could require a longer waiting time for the other request;
- The sum of the two waiting times should be minimized. But why just the sum?

Even worse, the waiting time that is forecast at the moment of making the decision could be changed by the coming of other requests during the service. For imagine that, at floor 2, we decide to go up with an elevator to serve a request issued at floor 60, but. when going up, the elevator stops for a new call issued at floor 40. This new call was not anticipated when it was decided to choose the elevator that was chosen to serve the original request.

Exercise

5.19 Continue with the analysis of the above specifications, trying to discover ambiguous or questionable points.

Let us try to specify the elevator system by means of a Petri net. A very sketchy view of the system is provided by the net of Figure 5.30. This description has some intuitive attraction: it gives a pictorial display of the elevators' position and of the events that determine their movement. It stresses the fact that in order to move from one floor to an adjacent floor, some button must be illuminated, and that the movement, in turn, is the result of pressing it.

The description in Figure 5.30, however, is far from satisfactory. Here are a few of its shortcomings:

1. The description is terribly incomplete: many other facts must be taken into account. There are not only internal, but also external, buttons. The movement of the elevator can be caused by any of the buttons: even an elevator at floor 1 can move up as a consequence of pushing the down button of floor 40. The net does not explain how a button is reset. What about the case of an elevator that is going from, say, floor 4 to floor 27 and the external up button of floor 20 is pressed just when it is crossing that floor? What is the latest acceptable calling time in such a case?

2. The description shows immediately that the full formalization of the system is likely to be enormous and totally unmanageable. Think of a system with 100 floors and 7 elevators!

3. The description is clearly wrong in many details. For instance, Figure 5.30 suggests that a button is illuminated when it is pushed; this is modeled by the presence of a token in place "button illumination." If the button is pressed twice before it is reset, however, we have two tokens in that place, so that when the request is eventually serviced and one token is consumed, the other token remains, thus describing incorrectly that the button is still illuminated.

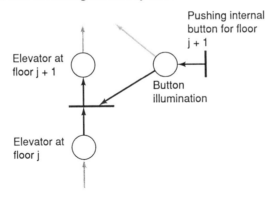

Figure 5.30   A first formalization of button switching through a Petri net.

Exercise

5.20 Find other inadequacies and trouble spots in the above initial formalization.

Despite the above shortcomings, Figure 5.30 can be taken as a starting point to obtain a correct and full specification of the system by means of Petri nets.

First, let us face the problem of managing the complexity of the system. Here, we must recall that specification is a *design* activity and that a complete specification document is in general the result of many trials and corrections. It is not a document that is to be built from scratch and never modified. Thus, we must apply all of the design principles that have been illustrated in Chapters 3 and 4 to the design of the specifications as well.

In particular, it is quite useful in this case to define suitable specification *modules*, intended as portions of a final PN. Each module describes a component of the system. A complete description is the result of integrating all the modules together. In this case, it seems natural to use different portions of the net to represent the elevators' positions, and the setting and resetting of internal and external buttons.

Also, it is clear that, with the exception of the first and last floors, the description of what happens at floor j will be identical to what happens at floor k. And since the same will hold for elevators and buttons, this suggest a *parameterized* specification that refers to generic floor j, elevator m, button of floor h, etc., as it was to some extent already suggested in the shape of Figure 5.30. Thus, we obtain the following natural structure for the specification.

System description. The overall specification is decomposed into modules. There are n specification modules of type ELEVATOR and m specification modules of type FLOOR. Each module is described by a suitably extended PN, with suitable module interconnections.

Each module of type ELEVATOR is decomposed into two submodules, one of type ELEVATOR_POSITION, which represents the position of each elevator, the other of type ELEVATOR_BUTTONS, which represents the state of buttons internal to the elevator. More precisely, the latter can be decomposed into m modules of type BUTTON, each of which represents one of the m buttons internal to each elevator.

Each module of type FLOOR, in turn, is decomposed into two modules of type BUTTON, which represent the calls to elevators to go up or down. The modules representing the first and last floor are an exception, since they are described by only one module of type BUTTON, representing calls to go up and down, respectively.

Now let us face individual problems of description, going problem by problem. We start with the rules for button illumination, which seem fairly simple, but contain an apparent mistake in the first attempt. We will make use of timed PNs with priorities.

Button description. Modules of type BUTTON may be described as in Figure 5.31. Pushing a button is represented by the firing of transition Push. If the button is off (a token is in Off) and Push fires, then Set immediately fires (thus, $t_{min}(Set) = t_{max}(set) = 0$) and sets the button to on (a token is in On). To prevent meaningless accumulation of tokens in P, one can set $t_{min}(Push) = 0.1$ and $t_{min}(C) = t_{max}(C) = 0.005$ (transition C acts as a token consumer).[1] In such a way, an on button can be pushed many times (with a minimum idle time of 0.1) without any undesirable consequences.

The firing of transition Reset represents the resetting of the button. The way other modules can reset a module of type BUTTON will be described later. This means that other arrows not shown here will be connected to Reset.

---

[1]By default, time is given in seconds.

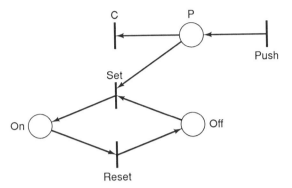

Figure 5.31   Switching the buttons on.

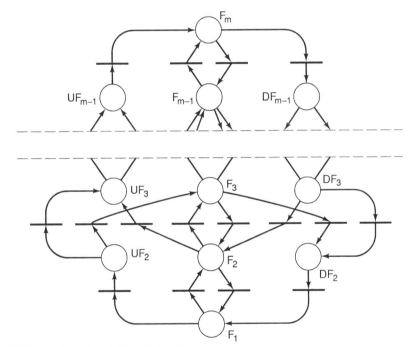

Figure 5.32   A first description of elevator movement.

Exercise

5.21   Give an alternative specification of button illumination by using PNs augmented with priorities instead of timed PNs. Discuss the differences between the two representations.

Description of elevator position and movement. As a first rough approximation, each module of type ELEVATOR_POSITION can be represented as in Figure 5.32. Intuitively, the figure describes how an elevator can move from one floor to the next in each direction. A token in place F_i, $1 \leq i \leq m$, represents an elevator *standing* at floor i. A token in place DF_i (UF_i), $2 \leq i \leq m - 1$, represents an elevator *passing* through floor i moving downwards (upwards). Appropriate times should be associated with the transitions, in order to account for the elevator's speed.

We insist on the importance of describing complex facts in an incremental way. Thus, Figure 5.32 gives first an idea of elevator movement, by distinguishing between the case of standing and moving elevators. In a more detailed view, the conditions that cause an elevator to move upwards are expressed by the net fragment of Figure 5.33, with reference to an elevator initially standing at floor F_j. (The conditions that cause the elevator to move downwards can be modeled in much the same way.)

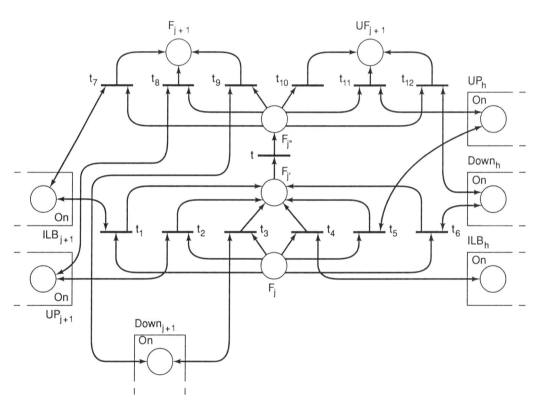

Figure 5.33   A more precise description of elevator movement.

Let h be any integer greater than j + 1 and less than or equal to m. An elevator standing at floor j can move up if there is either an internal request to stop at floor j + 1 or at some floor h; or an external request at floor j + 1 or any floor h. Such requests are modeled by the presence of a token in the place On of the nets of type BUTTON that represent internal and external buttons. In Figure 5.33, ILB_{j+1} and ILB_h are nets of type BUTTON that represent the internal buttons for stops at floors j + 1 and h, respectively.

Similarly, UP_{j+1}, $DOWN_{j+1}$, UP_h, and $DOWN_h$ represent the buttons for external calls from floors j + 1 and h, to go up or down, respectively.[1]

The specification of Figure 5.33 uses two intermediate places F_j' and F_j'' between F_j and both F_{j+1} and UF_{j+1}. The firing of transitions t_1 through t_6 represent the response of the elevator to a request to move up; as a consequence, a token enters place F_j'. The firing of transition t between F_j' and F_j'' represents the time needed to move from floor j to floor j + 1; in fact, we define $t_{min}(t) = t_{max}(t) = \Delta t$, Δt being the time needed to move from one floor to an adjacent floor. (For simplicity, we ignore that such time is not constant, because it may include a noninfinite acceleration.) For every other transition of Figure 5.33, we set $t_{min} = t_{max} = 0$. (This, again, corresponds to the assumption that times taken to make a decision whether or not to stop at some floor can be ignored. This assumption is an abstraction of the supposed real situation, where the mechanism that governs the system, e.g., a microprocessor, has negligible reaction times compared to the times that are required by the mechanical system.)

Transitions t_7 through t_{12} represent the (nondeterministic) choice among requests for service. In this way, we model the fact that the elevator may service also incoming requests concerning floor j + 1, provided that they occur during the transfer time from floor j to floor j + 1.

The description of an elevator in transit through floor j + 1 (represented by a token in place UF_{j+1}) can be given similarly (but not identically) to that just given Note that a token appears in place UF_{j+1} only if there are pending (internal or external) requests for service to some higher floor h.

In our description, so far we have not made any assumptions about a decision policy for selecting a request to be served if there is more than one request pending. Thus, at the stage we are now, the model is still highly nondeterministic. For example, the model does not require the elevator to stop at floor j + 1 if an internal request to stop there is issued before passing floor j + 1 in the upward direction. Our choice is to concentrate all policy decisions within a SCHEDULER module, which is discussed below.

Let us now browse through the specification of the remaining aspects of the elevator system.

Switching the buttons off. Figure 5.34 models how an internal button ILB_j is switched off when the elevator reaches floor j. (We have drawn a box around the components of ILB_j.) Transition Reset has $t_{min} = t_{max} = 0$ and the highest priority, so that we are guaranteed that the light is switched off as soon as the elevator reaches the corresponding floor. Again, notice how the specification is built up in parts, i.e., in a modular way. In this figure, we are referring to place F_j without repeating all the previous connections to it.

Figure 5.35 sketches how floor buttons UP_j ($1 \le j \le m - 1$) are switched off. Transition t_i' is the duplication of any transition t_i ($1 \le i \le 6$) of Figure 5.33. (They are all treated identically.) Transitions t_i' also have $t_{min} = t_{max} = 0$, but have higher priority than transitions t_i; in this way, a transition t_i' is chosen to fire instead of the corresponding t_i if the floor button is to be switched off. Transition Reset fires to reset the button when

---

[1]Floors 1 and m are an exception, because they only have buttons UP_1 and $DOWN_m$

there are no pending requests. We define t_{min} (Reset) = t_{max} (Reset) = dp, where dp is the delay time needed to model a person entering the elevator and pushing a button. Floor buttons $DOWN_i$ ($2 \leq i \leq m$) are modeled in the same way. As a consequence, both floor buttons are switched off if no internal service request occurs in due time. (Note that here we are changing the informal requirements slightly.) Notice that the formalization of Figure 5.35 disambiguates the informal statement about switching the button off by choosing the second of the two interpretations we suggested in analyzing the deficiencies of the informal requirements.

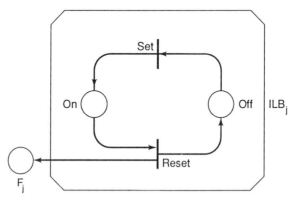

Figure 5.34   Switching the internal buttons off. The box only shows the grouping of the places and transitions related to the elevator button; it has no semantic significance.

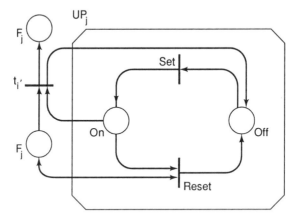

Figure 5.35   Switching the floor buttons off.

Exercises

5.22 Formalize the first of the two interpretations of the rule on switching the button off that were discussed in our assessment of the informal specification.

5.23 Formalize the original rule of the informal specifications, i.e., "in the latter case, if both floor request buttons are pressed, only one should be cancelled," instead of the present choice that switches both buttons off.

Decision policies. The model described so far is highly nondeterministic. The reason is that we decided to encapsulate all decision policies in a module called SCHEDULER. This is a sample application of information hiding to specifications: encapsulation will allow us to change policies without affecting the mechanisms described by the rest of the net; for example, we will be able to fine tune the system's performance at the requirements specification level by simulating different policies in the model.

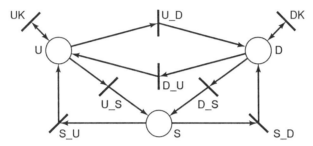

Figure 5.36   A simple scheduling policy.

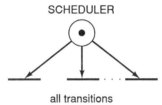

all transitions

Figure 5.37   A more general way of representing scheduling policies. Each transition has a predicate of the type OK(Scheduler) (in conjunction with other possible conditions). The token in SCHEDULER stores all information about the system state that is useful for the selection of which transition to fire. The token is "permanent," since it is always reproduced after the firing of any transition and after possibly being updated.

Here, we simply sketch a simplest instance of SCHEDULER. The chosen policy differs from the fuzzy requirement of the informal specifications: it guarantees the *fairness* among the service requests–i.e., it guarantees that every request will be served eventually (but does not try to "minimize waiting times," whatever that means). Thus, no request will ever suffer starvation.

We assign each elevator a "direction state," which is either U (up), D (down), or S (standby)–see Figure 5.36. A token in U (D) means that the elevator direction is up (down). A token can be in S only if the elevator is at some floor and there are no calls. Our policy consists of keeping the direction state unchanged as long as there are calls that would force the elevator to go in that direction. Otherwise, transitions U_D, D_U, U_S, and D_S fire when the direction of movement changes from up to down, down to up, up to standby, or down to standby, respectively. U_K denotes any transition of the overall net (e.g., $t_1,..., t_{12}$) representing an upwards movement; D_K denotes any transition of the overall net representing a downwards movement. Transitions U_K and D_K have higher priority than U_D and D_U, which, in turn, must have higher priority than U_S and D_S. All transitions of Figure 5.36 have $t_{min} = t_{max} = 0$. Furthermore, in the portion of the net of Figure 5.33, and in similar ones, we give higher priority to transitions t_7, t_8, and t_9 than to transitions t_{10}, t_{11}, and t_{12}. This way, an elevator is forced to stop at any floor if there are internal or external requests to serve that floor.

Other policies could be defined in several ways. If, however, one wants to describe scheduling policies in a fairly general way–such as taking into account service times and minimizing them according to some reasonable definition–a different approach may be more useful. In the general case, one could define a place, SCHEDULER, whose token is not anonymous, but carries information about the overall state of the system. Suitable predicates are associated with transitions in such a way that the enabled transitions are exactly those that are allowed to fire according to the scheduling policy. This is sketched in Figure 5.37.

Once we have completed the formalization of the elevator system in terms of PNs, we can analyze it to verify whether it defines the intended behavior properly. As we anticipated in Section 5.4, the simplest way to verify the adequacy of a specification is by *simulating* it. In our case, simulation through PNs is quite natural: we just need to apply the firing rules to the model, starting with an initial state.

For instance, we could consider an initial marking where an elevator is at floor 1– i.e., a token is in place F_1–and all of the internal and external buttons are off. Now assume that somebody enters the elevator and pushes the internal button 2. This corresponds to the firing of transition Push in the portion of the net describing the button (see Figure 5.31). Set fires immediately, which corresponds to switching the button on. Thus, transition t_4 in the net of the type of Figure 5.33 is enabled and fires immediately. After a time Δt, a token will be in F_2'', enabling transition t_7. This transition will fire immediately. Just after this, transition Reset for the internal button of the elevator corresponding to floor 2 fires (see Figure 5.34).

This simulation allows us to conclude that, if an elevator is at floor 1, and no button is On when its internal button 2 is pushed, then after Δt seconds the elevator will reach floor 2 and the button will be reset. Notice that we could not have deduced this statement if we assumed that other buttons were On at the initial time or were pushed within Δt seconds after the pushing of button 2. This is due to the nondeterministic definition of the system and should be verified by the reader as an exercise.

Similarly, one could simulate external calls by using the rules formalized in Figures 5.31 and 5.35. This would make apparent the chosen interpretation for the informal requirement

> The illumination is cancelled when the elevator visits the floor and is either moving
> in the desired direction, or...

If it turns out that this is not the interpretation meant by the customer, the specification must be modified accordingly (see Exercise 5.22).

We have seen a strong reason in favor of using a formal model for giving specifications: specifications can be simulated automatically with the help of an interpreter for the model. The benefits of this should be quite obvious. The usefulness of simulation, however, depends on the model. Interpreting an FSM–even a fairly complex one–is easy and efficient. Interpreting a PN is conceptually simple, but its efficiency is affected by the nondeterminism of the model, which may require the use of time-consuming backtracking techniques. In fact, suppose you are executing a PN to state whether, from a given marking m, a different marking m' can be reached. During the interpretation, nondeterministic choices are taken whenever several transitions are enabled. If it turns out that these choices do not produce the marking m', we must undo some of them to try different ones. We will comment further on the use of models to verify specifications in Sections 5.6.2.4 and 5.7.3.

Exercise

5.24   Give reasonable interpretations of the phrase "minimize the waiting times" in the informally stated requirements of the elevator system. Formalize the chosen interpretations as selection functions to be attached to a PN schema of the type of Figure 5.37. Check whether your policy still guarantees that all requests will eventually be served.

5.6 DESCRIPTIVE SPECIFICATIONS

As we stated in Section 5.3, descriptive specifications try to describe the desired properties of a system rather than its desired behavior. In this section, we start a short review of descriptive specification notations with a semiformal and widely used model. Then we move to completely formal notations.

A natural way of specifying system properties precisely is through the use of *mathematical formulas*. Unlike natural language, mathematical formulas have a precise syntax and semantics. Furthermore, they can be managed by automatic devices as well as formal operational models.

Many mathematical formalisms have been proposed for the description of system properties. In this section, we will review two major approaches: one based on the use of mathematical logic–in the style of the so-called Floyd-Hoare specifications–and one based on the use of algebra.

5.6.1 Entity-Relationship Diagrams

We have seen that DFDs are a useful notation to describe the operations used to access and manipulate the data of a system–typically, of an information system. However, this is often not enough to specify all the interesting features of the system. A conceptual description of the structure of data and of their relations is also necessary.

Actually, it is unclear which of the two descriptions (operations and data structures) should come first. Understanding the operations to be provided by the system helps in

understanding the logical structure of the data. On the other hand, the logical structure
holds irrespective of the operations performed on the data. One may even argue that it
represents our knowledge of the application area, which is more stable than the
operations provided by the application.

The two views are clearly complementary, and both are useful for understanding and
specifying an application. Therefore, we start our review of descriptive specifications
with the *entity-relationship* model, a widely known and adopted notation for describing
the relations among the data of an information system.

The entity-relationship model (*ER model*) was motivated by the need for a
conceptual model of data suitable for specifying user views and logical requirements in
information systems and, more generally, in applications that are centered around large
collections of interrelated data. The model is based on three primitive concepts: *entities*,
relations, and *attributes*. The model has an associated graphical language, which is
particularly easy to understand; the descriptions given in the graphical language are
called *ER diagrams*.

Figure 5.38 shows a simple example of an ER diagram that describes the entities
STUDENT and CLASS with the relationship ENROLLED_IN that may hold between a
STUDENT and a CLASS. An entity–represented by a box–stands for a collection of items
that share common properties; the concept is thus similar to that of a type in
programming languages. The properties of an entity are its attributes and the relations in
which it participates. Attributes are listed next to the entity, and relations are represented
as diamond-shaped boxes. In our example, STUDENT is a collection of individuals;
NAME, AGE, and SEX are attributes of STUDENT; and every student is characterized by
a triple of values–representing the student's name, age, and sex. A relation on two
entities–such as STUDENT and CLASS–is a set of pairs <a, b>, where a is an element of
STUDENT and b is an element of CLASS. The relation shown in Figure 5.38 could
represent the fact that student a is enrolled in class b.

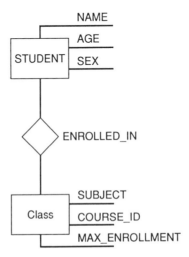

Figure 5.38   An ER diagram describing a relationship between students and classes.

Unfortunately, ER diagrams have not been standardized. This means that there is no official, universally recognized version of the notation, but many variations exist in practice. Some ER languages allow relations to be n-ary, i.e., they may relate any number of entities; others support binary relations only. Also, some permit relations to have attributes while others do not. If attributes of relations were permitted, we could define the attribute PROFICIENCY to be associated with ENROLLED_IN. Then the attribute associated with any given pair <a, b> in ENROLLED_IN would represent the proficiency of student a in class b. Finally, some ER languages support a kind of inheritance among entities, often called the IS_A relation in ER jargon. For example, one could define UNDERGRADUATE and GRADUATE as two subentities of STUDENT, inheriting the properties of STUDENT and adding new ones in terms of attributes and participation in relations (UNDERGRADUATE IS_A STUDENT).

Most ER languages allow relations to be partial; i.e., not every element in the related entities has to participate in the relation. In addition, they often allow the relation to be annotated as one to one, one to many, many to one, or many to many. If a relation R between A and B is one to one, then for any <a, b> in R, there exists no a' in A such that <a', b> is in R and a'≠ a; and, conversely, there exists no b' in B such that <a, b'> is in R and b'≠ b. If R is many to one, it is only required that for any <a, b> in R, there exists no b' in B such that <a, b'> is also in R and b'≠ b, etc. Graphically, this is represented as in Figure 5.39. We can see from Figure 5.38 that the relation ENROLLED_IN is many to many.

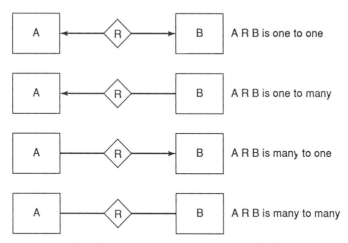

Figure 5.39   Annotations describing constraints on the relationship R.

The annotations in Figure 5.39 describe simple constraints on the relationship. In practice, however, when we specify requirements, we would like to be able to state more general and complex kinds of *constraints* on our data that might characterize some important properties of the world we are modeling. Unfortunately, the power of the ER language is rather limited, and more complex concepts must be expressed separately by using a different notation. For example, there is no way to specify graphically that a class can exist only if the number of enrolled students is greater than five, and that the number cannot exceed the value MAX_ENROLLMENT that is an attribute of each class. If we want, this can be stated as a comment in natural language, associated with the diagram as further documentation.

According to the classification discussed in Section 5.2, ER diagrams are a semiformal notation because their syntax and semantics are not stated precisely and because their lack of expressive power forces us to add properties as informal comments. Also, they are a descriptive notation, because they state what the entities and their properties are in terms of attributes and participation in relations. In Section 5.6.2, we will comment on the relation between ER diagrams and the formal descriptive notation provided by logic.

ER diagrams are widely used in practice. Since they are graphical, they are highly expressive and easy to understand by nonspecialists. It is also claimed that they are effective for the assessment of requirements, since even end users may be trained to understand them and thus may verify whether the description provided by the software engineer captures the requirements adequately. Another important point is that ER notations are now supported by many existing tools (see Chapter 9).

Exercises

5.25 Suppose that your ER language does not support attributes associated with relations, but does support n-ary relations. Following the discussion in Section 5.6.1, how would you represent the students' proficiency levels in a given class?

5.26 Augment the ER diagram of Figure 5.38 by introducing the entity PROFESSOR and suitable relations TEACHES (with entity CLASS) and SUPERVISES (with entity STUDENT). How can you specify a (funny) constraint like "a student cannot take a class that is taught by his or her supervisor"?

5.6.2 Logic Specifications

A formula of a *first-order theory* (FOT) is an expression involving variables, numeric constants, functions, predicates, and parentheses, as in traditional arithmetic. The usual logical connectives–**and, or, not, implies**, and ≡ (which denotes logical equivalence)– are also used. In fact, the type of the result of a first-order theory formula must be Boolean. As opposed to the Boolean-valued formulas of many programming languages, however, FOT formulas may also use *quantifiers*–i.e., the symbols **exists** and **for all** that can be applied to variables.

Following are a few examples of FOT formulas:

1. $x > y$ **and** $y > z$ **implies** $x > z$;
2. $x = y \equiv y = x$;
3.   **for all** x, y, z ($x > y$ **and** $y > z$ **implies** $x > z$);
4. $x + 1 < x - 1$;
5.   **for all** x (**exists** y ($y = x + z$));
6. $x > 3$ **or** $x < -6$.

The semantics of such formulas should be sufficiently clear from the intuitive meanings of the symbols used.

Notice that some of the above formulas are true, others are false, and still others are true or false depending on the values of the unquantified variables. So formulas 1 and 2 are true regardless of the values of x, y, and z, formula 4 is false regardless of the value of x, and formula 6 is true for some values of x, and false for others.

A variable that occurs in a formula is said to be *free* in that formula if it is not quantified; a variable that is not free is said to be *bound*. So x is free in formula 1 and is bound in formula 3. If all variables in a formula are quantified, the formula is said to be *closed*. Thus, formula 3 is closed. A closed formula is always either true or false. The *closure* of a formula is obtained by quantifying all of its free variables with the **for all** quantifier. So the closure of formula 4 is **for all** x (x + 1 < x - 1). If a formula is true for all values of its free variables, its closure is also true. Thus, the closure of formula 1 is true, but the closure of formula 4 is false.

In some cases, the truth of a formula depends on the domain chosen for its variables. For instance, the formula

7.   for all x (x ≥ 1) **or** (x ≤ -1) **or** (x = 0)

is true if x is an integer; it is false if x is a real number. Here, however, we will deal with variables whose domains should be understood without ambiguity. In particular, numeric variables will be assumed to be integers, unless stated otherwise.

Earlier, we observed that ER diagrams can be classified as a semiformal descriptive notation. We can illustrate these property by showing that ER diagrams may be easily restated in terms of logic; moreover, logic provides a formal notation to express the constraints that are not expressible in terms of ER diagrams. For example, in the discussion relating to Figure 5.38, the constraint that "a class can exist only if the number of enrolled students is greater than five, and the number cannot exceed the value MAX_ENROLLMENT" can be stated as

> **for all** a **in** CLASS
>   5 ≤ **cardinality** {b | <a, b> **in** ENROLLED_IN} ≤
>   a.MAX_ENROLLMENT

where we use the dot notation to denote the value of an entity's attribute. Also, the function **cardinality** has been introduced to indicate the number of elements in a set.

Next, we will demonstrate the use of logical formulas in program specification in two stages. First, we will show how complete programs can be specified by stating logical formulas that relate the program's input and output. These are called *input-output assertions*. Next, we will show the use of *intermediate assertions*. These are logical formulas that are used to specify program fragments by making statements about the state of the program execution at particular points of the program. Finally, we will use both types of specification to present the case study of the elevator system in terms of logical specifications.

Exercises

5.27   Build the closures of formulas 1 through 7 above.

5.28   Is the closure of formula 6 true?

5.6.2.1 Specifying complete programs: input-output assertions

We start with the simplest use of mathematical formulas to express software properties. Let P be a sequential program. Let $<i_1, i_2,..., i_n>$ denote the sequence of P's input values and $<o_1, o_2,...., o_m>$ the sequence of P's output values. More precisely, assume that P reads all input values from and writes all output values into sequential files; $<i_1, i_2,..., i_n>$ is the sequence of values stored in the input file in the order in which P reads them, and $<o_1, o_2,..., o_m>$ is the sequence in which P writes its output.

A *property*, or *requirement*, for P is expressed as a formula of the type

$$\{\text{Pre } (i_1, i_2,..., i_n) \}$$
$$\text{P}$$
$$\{\text{Post } (o_1, o_2,..., o_m, i_1, i_2,..., i_n)\}$$

where $\text{Pre } (i_1, i_2,..., i_n)$ denotes a FOT formula having $i_1, i_2,..., i_n$ as free variables and $\text{Post } (o_1, o_2,..., o_m, i_1, i_2,..., i_n)$ denotes a FOT formula having $o_1, o_2,..., o_m$ and, possibly, $i_1, i_2,..., i_n$, as free variables. Pre is called the *precondition* of P, and Post is the *postcondition* of P. The meaning of the above formula is that if Pre holds for the given input values before P's execution, then, after P's execution, Post must hold for the output and input values.

Let us give some simple examples of program specifications in terms of pre and postconditions.

1. $\{\textbf{exists } z \ (i_1 = z * i_2)\}$
            P
            $\{o_1 = i_1 / i_2\}$

This states that, if the input value i_1 is a multiple of the input value i_2, then the output must be the result of the division i_1/i_2. A stronger requirement for a division program is the following:

2. $\{ i_1 > i_2 \}$
            P
            $\{i_1 = i_2 * o_1 + o_2 \textbf{ and } o_2 \geq 0 \textbf{ and } o_2 < i_2\}$

This requirement is stronger in the sense that it imposes fewer constraints on the input values and more constraints on the output values. A precondition of {true} does not place any constraint on input values; it always holds, regardless of the input values, implying that the program will achieve its result for all input values. The specification

3.   {true}
        P
        $\{(o = i_1 \textbf{ or } o = i_2) \textbf{ and } o \geq i_1 \textbf{ and } o \geq i_2\}$

requires that P produce the greater of i_1 and i_2. The specification

4. $\{i_1 > 0 \textbf{ and } i_2 > 0\}$
        P
        $\{(\textbf{exists } z_1, z_2 \ (i_1 = o * z_1 \textbf{ and } i_2 = o * z_2)$
        and not
        $(\textbf{exists } h \ (\textbf{exists } z_1, z_2 \ (i_1 = h * z_1 \textbf{ and } i_2 = h * z_2) \textbf{ and } h > o))\}$

requires that P compute the greatest common divisor of i_1 and i_2.

Assuming that n is a positive value denoting the length of the input sequence, the specification

5. $\{n > 0\}$
        P
        $\{o = \sum_{k=1}^{n} i_k\}$

requires that P compute the sum of the sequence. Finally, the specification

6. $\{n > 0\}$
        P
        $\{\textbf{for all } i \ (1 \leq i \leq n) \textbf{ implies } (o_i = i_{n-i+1})\}$

requires that P produce the reverse of its input sequence, assuming that the input sequence is not empty.

Exercises

5.29 Give a logic specification for a program that reads a sequence of n + 1 values and checks whether the first value also appears in the next n input values.

5.30 Give a logic specification for a program that first reads two words, i.e., two sequences of alphabetic characters, separated by a blank and terminated by the special character '#'. The second word may be null; the first may not. Then, the program reads a sequence of other words, separated by blanks and terminated by '#', and rewrites the sequence, substituting all occurrences of the first word by the second.

You should just sketch the solution without going into all the details. Then, you should go back to the exercise after reading the rest of this section.

The previous examples and exercises have shown that the formulas needed to specify even simple problems may require many details and may be hard to understand. We have already faced this inconvenience in our previous examples of operational specifications. We will consider the problem of managing complex specifications in full generality in Section 5.7. We anticipate, however, some suggestions for improving the readability of logic specifications, just as we did when building nontrivial specifications with PNs and FSMs.

Consider, for instance, the problem given in Exercise 5.30. The major source of trouble is that even simple and intuitive concepts, such as "word," have no predefined meaning in the FOT syntax. Thus, if we want to formalize a sentence such as "two words are equal" or "one word is substituted by another one," we have to go through many details. This, however, can be done once and for all by the use of suitable *definitions*.

We could introduce the predicate input_word (m, n) to state that the sequence of characters in the input stream, from the mth through the nth positions, is a word. This is formalized by the formula

$$\text{input\_word } (m, n) \equiv (\textbf{for all } i \ (m \le i \le n) \ \textbf{implies} \ \text{alphabetic } (c_i))$$

where, in turn, alphabetic (c) means that c is an alphabetic character. (The formalization of this predicate is a trivial exercise.)

Now we can use the predicate input_word as a compact and understandable *abbreviation* whenever needed. In particular, we can define the predicate input_text (m, n) to state that the sequence of elements of the input file from the mth through the nth positions is a piece of text, that is, a sequence of words separated by a blank (' ') and bracketed by a pair of symbols, '#'. Precisely;

$$\begin{aligned}
&\text{input\_text}(m,n) \equiv \\
&\quad (i_m = \text{'\#' } \textbf{and } i_n = \text{'\#' } \textbf{and} \\
&\quad\quad (\textbf{exists } k \ (\textbf{for all } j \ (1 \le j \le k) \ \textbf{implies} \\
&\quad\quad\quad (\textbf{exists } h_j, m_j \ (\text{input\_word}(m_j, m_j + h_j) \ \textbf{and} \\
&\quad\quad\quad\quad m_1 = m + 1 \ \textbf{and } m_k + h_k + 1 = n \ \textbf{and} \\
&\quad\quad\quad\quad (1 \le j < k) \ \textbf{implies } (m_{j+1} = m_j + h_j + 2 \ \textbf{and} \\
&\quad\quad\quad\quad i_{mj + hj + 1} = \text{' '})))))))
\end{aligned}$$

Once this is stated, one can go on to define suitable predicates for the output file and, eventually, an overall relation between input and output files based on the previous definitions. This is left to the reader.

Exercise

5.31   Find some detail of the informal specification of Exercise 5.30 that was not defined precisely, and check it against the formal definition.

5.6.2.2 Specifying program fragments: intermediate assertions

We have, so far, used pre- and postconditions on I/O values to specify *complete programs*. Often, however, it is useful to specify portions of programs. For instance, if we are building a library of general-purpose modules, we do not even know the context in which some procedures will be executed.

Such a generalization is quite straightforward. All we need do is allow expressions in pre- and postconditions to refer to program variables as well as to I/O values. For instance, suppose you want to specify a procedure search with input parameters element, table (an array of integers), and n, the number of elements stored in table. The procedure is to check whether element exists in table. This can be done as follows:[1]

7.   {n > 0} -- n is a constant value
      procedure search (table: **in** integer_array; n: **in** integer;
                                    element: **in** integer; found: **out** Boolean);
      {found ≡ (**exists** i (1 ≤ i ≤ n **and** table (i) = element))}

Similarly, one could write the following specification for a subprogram that reverses the contents of an array of integers:

8.   {n > 0 }
      procedure reverse (a: **in out** integer_array; n: **in** integer);
      {**for all** i (1≤ i ≤ n) **implies** (a (i) = old_a (n - i +1))}

In this specification, we needed to state a relation between the values of the program variables before and after the execution of the procedure. Thus, we used the auxiliary variable old_a to denote a's value prior to execution of the procedure.

The following is a specification for a sort procedure:

9.   {n > 0}
      procedure sort (a: **in out** integer_array; n: **in** integer);
      {sorted (a,n)},

As we did before, we define the new predicate

      sorted (a,n) ≡ (**for all** i (1 ≤ i < n) **implies** a (i) ≤ a (i + 1))

Exercise

5.32   Is the specification 9 above an appropriate specification for a sorting procedure? Why? If not, give an appropriate specification for a sorting procedure.

Specifying properties of the state of program execution, rather than just I/O relations, becomes even more important when we deal with nonterminating programs, such as operating systems, and even more so, when we need to specify systems that

---

[1]We implicitly assume here that the lower bound of arrays is 1.

include non-software components, such as the elevator system of Section 5.5.3.2. Consider, for example, the classical producer-consumer system. Informally, a major requirement for such a system is that the sequence of items produced matches the sequence of items consumed. If the two processes are in **repeat-forever** loops, however, the two sequences are not even defined (a sequence has to be finite). Actually, what we are interested in is that, at any given *critical point*, the two sequences coincide. This property must hold infinitely many times, independently of how many items are produced and consumed. Thus, we say that it must be *invariant* during system execution.

In general, an *invariant property* is a predicate on a system state that must hold repeatedly anytime the system reaches some predefined points.

Let us examine a producer-consumer system in more detail.

Example 5.5

Consider the producer-consumer system of Section 4.6.1.1. To specify the desired system behavior, we need to state a predicate based on the sequences of characters that are read and written. These are neither I/O nor program variables in the strict sense. (There is neither a declaration nor any use of such variables.) We may refer to them, however, as if they were program variables in the same way as we did when referring to the value of the same variable at different points in the execution of a sequential program.

Thus, we define the variables INPUT_SEQUENCE and OUTPUT_SEQUENCE, and we assume that each PUT operation of a producer (into CHAR_BUFFER) appends the written character at the end of INPUT_SEQUENCE and that each GET operation of a consumer appends the character read at the end of OUTPUT_SEQUENCE.

Now, we realize that it is not exactly true that we want the two sequences to be always the same. In fact, they may differ up to the present contents of the buffer. Thus, the invariant property that can be assumed as a specification is

input_sequence = append (output_sequence,
                                           contents(CHAR_BUFFER))

where the meanings of the APPEND and CONTENTS operations should be obvious.

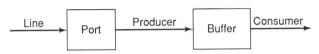

Figure 5.40   A simple producer-consumer system.

Analyzing this property more deeply, however, we realize that even its new formulation cannot be claimed to be an invariant property in a strict sense. In fact, when, say, the consumer is executing the monitor procedure GET, the buffer contents and OUTPUT_SEQUENCE are not even well defined. We do not, however, need such a strong requirement on the invariance of the desired property. For our purposes, it is perfectly satisfactory that the invariant property hold whenever the system is not executing a monitor procedure.

Thus, the *critical execution points* at which we need to guarantee that the invariant property holds are at the entry and the exit of monitor procedures. (In fact, the variables of interest are affected only by monitor procedures.)   ▌

More examples of specifications of execution state properties will be given in Chapter 6.

Exercises

5.33 Specify a procedure that is intended to merge two sorted arrays into a single one. You should distinguish two different cases:

    a. Duplicate elements in input arrays should appear as duplicates in the output array;
    b. Input and output arrays should contain no duplicate elements.

5.34 Consider the system outlined in Figure 5.40. It consists of three processes: Line, Producer, and Consumer. Line represents the external environment of the system. It writes single characters into Port, from which Producer gets them. The two are synchronized through a monitor. Producer puts the character into Buffer through another monitor, from which Consumer gets packets of $n \leq$ size(Buffer) characters. The consumer does not have to wait until the buffer is full. Formalize a correct behavior of this system by means of an appropriate invariant assertion.

5.6.2.3 A case study using logic specifications

To tackle a larger problem, let us now apply logical formalism to the elevator case study analyzed in Section 5.5.3.2. This will allow us to compare and contrast it with the PN analysis used there. The first step of our specification effort is to define a set of elementary predicates that describe relevant properties about the system state or the system operation. For instance, at (E, F, T) could be used to state that elevator E is at floor F at time T. Similarly, start (E, F, T, up) could state that elevator E left floor F at time T in the up direction; and so on.

Then, one could write a set of formulas that describe the behavioral rules of the system. For instance;

$$\text{(at } (E, F, T) \text{ \textbf{and} on } (EB, F_1, T) \text{ \textbf{and} } F_1 > F) \text{ \textbf{implies} start } (E, F, T, up)$$

specifies that, if at time T elevator E is at floor F, and its internal button referring to floor F_1, with $F_1 > F$, is on, then, at the same time, the elevator starts moving in the up direction.

Notice that here we are predicating properties of system objects such as elevators, floors, etc., in the same way that in previous examples we stated properties of program variables. We introduce new predicates (e.g., at, and on) and specify their semantics through FOT formulas in the same way that we could state the property

$$x > y \text{ \textbf{and} } y > z \text{ \textbf{implies} } x > z$$

for the predicate '>' in arithmetic.

This is a good example of the different uses of specifications. If we specify properties of system objects such as elevators and buttons, we are specifying *system requirements*; if we specify properties of program variables, we are specifying program *design* and *implementation*.

For syntactic convenience, we denote variable identifiers by strings beginning with uppercase letters and predicates by strings beginning with lowercase letters.[1] Notice also that time is explicitly taken into account as a system variable. This will allow us to state time constraints between the occurrence of different events; e.g., the request for an elevator and its arrival at the floor.

To continue formalizing the elevator system further requires a systematic approach, such as the one we adopted in Section 5.5.3.2 based on PNs. First, we partition the set of elementary predicates that are intended to describe the system's evolution into *elementary states* and *events*.

States describe a condition of the system that has a nonnull duration. The global notion of a system state at a given time is the conjunction of all elementary states that hold during that time. For the sake of brevity, in the following we will call *elementary states* just *states*. The term *global state* will identify the state of the whole system.

Events describe conditions that can hold only at a particular instant of time. For example, the event

arrived (E, F, T)

means that elevator E arrived at floor F at time T, while the state

standing (E, F, T_1, T_2)

means that elevator E has been parked at floor F from time T_1 to time T_2.

In this description, then, time is represented explicitly–by a single time value for events, which are by definition instantaneous, and a pair of time values for states, where the pair denotes the time interval during which the state holds.

The behavior of the system is described by implicative formulas, or *rules*, i.e., by a set of premises followed by the keyword **implies** followed by the consequence of the premises. The rules allow one to deduce the occurrence of an event or the change of a state at a particular moment, as the consequence of a set of events or states holding at that moment or before, possibly under certain conditions. Since a state changes with the occurrence of an event, another group of rules extends the period of time during which a state exists, until a modifying event occurs.

For the sake of simplicity, a few assumptions are made. First, we assume *zero decision times,* as we also assumed in Section 5.5.3.2. Furthermore, we exclude *simultaneous events*. This does not affect our specification substantially, but allows a simplification of certain rules. If they turn out to be unrealistic, these assumptions may be removed easily–at the price of a slight increase in the number of formulas used.

---

[1]This convention is borrowed from PROLOG, a programming language based on first-order logic.

Next, we give a sample of events, states, and rules that constitute the system specification. Exercises will then lead the reader through a completion of the specification and some variations. Remember that there are m floors and n elevators. The system is turned on at t_0.

Events

- arrival (E, F, T)   E in [1..n], F in [1..m], T $\geq$ t_0 (t_0 is the initial time)

represents the arrival of elevator E at floor F at time T. This event does not say whether the elevator, once it has arrived, would stop at that floor or leave immediately for another floor; nor does it say anything about the direction of motion of the elevator or about the floor the elevator is coming from.

- departure(E, F, D, T)   E in [1..n], F in [1..m], D in {up, down}, T $\geq$ t_0

describes the departure of elevator E from floor F in direction D at time T. We will see in the rules that this event puts elevator E in the state of motion from floor F in direction D.

- stop (E, F, T)   E in [1..n], F in [1..m], T $\geq$ t_0

represents the arrival and stopping of elevator E at floor F at time T. The stop is for servicing an internal or external request. We will see in the rules that this event puts elevator E in the state of standing at floor F.

- new_list (E, L, T)   E in [1..n], L in [1..m]*, T $\geq$ t_0

At every instant T, each elevator has an associated list L of integers[1] between 1 and m. The list represents the set of floors at which the elevator will eventually stop, according to the scheduling decisions performed, up to that time, by the control component of the system. A list is associated with each elevator because this way the scheduling strategy for internal and external requests can be easily and naturally expressed by rules–to be given later–managing the lists of the different elevators. At any instant, each elevator "decides" what to do according to the contents of its list. new_list (E, L, T) means that the list associated with elevator E becomes L at time T; thus, this predicate represents the event that transforms the control state of elevator E by setting its reservation list to L.

- call (F, D, T)
- request (E, F, T)   E in [1..n], F in [1..m], D in {up, down}, T $\geq$ t_0

These two predicates denote events generated from outside the system: external calls from floor F in direction D at time T and the reservation of floor F from inside elevator E

---

[1]The * indicates the transitive closure operation; a* stands for a sequence of zero or more a's.

at time T, respectively. These events are associated with the pushing of the corresponding buttons by someone who wants to make a reservation. If $F = 1$ or $F = m$, there is a further condition on the parameter values: D must be equal to up and down, respectively.

States

Since states are properties of objects that have a duration, all predicates that refer to states have two time parameters that represent the boundaries of the time interval during which the property holds. We use the convention that time intervals associated with state predicates are closed at the left and open at the right; that is, the lower extreme of the time interval is included in the interval and the upper extreme is excluded from the interval. (The notation adopted to indicate such time intervals is $[T_1, T_2[$.) This choice is motivated by the fact that any effects of events are assumed to be instantaneous, so that a new state holds from the time instant (included) when the event that generates it occurs up to the time instant (excluded) when the event that determines the next, instantaneous, state change occurs.

From the definition of a state, it is clear that if a property that characterizes a state holds during a given time interval, it will hold during any time interval contained in the given interval. Also, given a time interval during which a state holds, the state may also hold during a larger time interval. For example, if we state that

$$\text{moving } (E, F, D, T_1, T_2)$$

i. e., the state of movement of elevator E from floor F in direction D holds in the time interval $[T_1, T_2[$, it must be possible to deduce

$$\textbf{for all } T_3, T_4 \ (T_1 \leq T_3 < T_4 \leq T_2) \text{ moving } (E, F, D, T_3, T_4)$$

Nothing, however, prevents

$$\text{moving } (E, F, D, T_3, T_4)$$

with $T_3 < T_1 < T_2 < T_4$ from holding as well. We will later give appropriate rules to enforce these assumptions about the semantics of states.

Next, we provide a list of elevator states:

*   standing (E, F, T_1, T_2) E in $[1..n]$, F in $[1..m]$, $t_0 \leq T_1 < T_2$

states that in the time interval $[T_1, T_2[$, elevator E is standing at floor F. As just pointed out, this does not imply that elevator E arrived at floor F at time T_1 or that it will leave at time T_2.

*   moving (E, F, D, T_1, T_2) E in $[1..n]$, F in $[1..m]$, $t_0 \leq T_1 < T_2$

specifies that in the time interval $[T_1, T_2[$, elevator E is moving in direction D, and the last floor traversed was F.

- list (E, L, T_1, T_2) E in $[1..n]$, L in $[1..m]^*$, $t_0 \leq T_1 < T_2$

specifies that in the time interval $[T_1, T_2[$, the list associated with elevator E is L. Unlike the predicates standing and moving, which denote a physical property of the elevators, the predicate list denotes a control property.

We now illustrate the rules that describe the behavior of the system. We will give the rules that describe the movement of elevators, followed by those that express the control strategies. In each group, the rules will be partitioned into those leading to the deduction of events and those leading to the deduction of states.

Elevator rules that relate events and states

The rules that govern the relationships between states and events in the system are first given in English and then stated as a formal expression of logic.

R_1. Elevator E, upon arrival at floor F, leaves immediately if that floor does not require service and the list is not empty. If the next floor to be serviced is higher than the one being passed, the departure is in the upward direction; otherwise, it is in the downward direction. We adopt the convention that the floor to be serviced is the one in the first position in the list. (This is denoted by the function first applied to the variable L.)

> arrival (E, F, T_a) **and**
> list (E, L, T, T_a) **and**
> first $(L) > F$
> **implies**
> > departure (E, F, up, T_a).

There is a similar rule in the case of departure in the opposite direction.

R_2. Elevator E, upon arrival at floor F, stops there if that floor must be serviced, that is, if the floor number appears as the first element of the list associated with the elevator.

> arrival (E, F, T_a) **and**
> list (E, L, T, T_a) **and**
> first $(L) = F$
> **implies**
> > stop (E, F, T_a).

R_3. If elevator E arrives at a floor F with an empty list, it will stop there. Assuming that all elevators are moving to service the floors that appear in their list, they should leave from, and arrive at, floors with nonempty lists. This rule then becomes significant if the scheduling policy allows for *cancelling* elements from the list of a moving elevator (see control rules below).

> arrival (E, F, T_a) **and**
> list $(E, empty, T, T_a)$ **and**
> **implies**
> > stop (E, F, T_a).

R_4. We assume that elevators have a fixed and known service stop time Δt_s. If the elevator list is not empty at the end of such a time interval, the elevator leaves the floor immediately.

> stop (E, F, T_a) **and**
> list (E, L, T, $T_a + \Delta t_s$) **and**
> first (L) > F,
> **implies**
>   departure (E, F, up, $T_a + \Delta t_s$).

There is a similar rule for departures in the opposite direction.

R_5. At the end of the period of service, if there are no floors to be serviced–i.e., if the elevator list is empty–the elevator will leave only when the list becomes nonempty.

> stop (E, F, T_a) **and**
> list (E, L, T_p, T) **and**
> $T_p > T_a + \Delta t_s$ **and**
> list (E, empty, $T_a + \Delta t_s$, T_p) **and**
> first (L) > F
> **implies**
>   departure (E, F, up, T_p).

As usual, a similar rule describes the departure in the opposite direction.

R_6. As we did with PNs, we assume that the time Δt taken by an elevator to move from one floor to the next, in either direction, is known and fixed. The arrival at a floor then takes place at a time Δt after the departure time from the previous floor.

> departure (E, F, up, T)
> **implies**
>   arrival (E, F + 1, T + Δt).

There is a similar rule for departure in the opposite direction.

R_7. The event of stopping at floor F at time T initiates a state of standing at the floor that lasts at least for the time interval [T, T + Δt_s[.

> stop (E, F, T)
> **implies**
>   standing (E, F, T, T + Δt_s).

R_8. At the end of a service stop of length Δt_s, if there are no floors to be serviced, the elevator will remain standing at the floor as long as the list remains empty.

> stop (E, F, T_s) **and**
> list (E, empty, $T_s + \Delta t_s$, T)

implies
        standing (E, F, T_s, T).

R_9. The event of the departure of elevator E from floor F in direction D at time T initiates a state of movement that lasts for the time interval [T, T + Δt[.

        departure (E, F, D, T)
implies
        moving (E, F, D, T, T + Δt).

R_{10}. If a state is proven to hold for the time interval [T_1,T_2[, then it is possible to infer that it also holds for all time intervals [T_3, T_4[that are included in [T_1, T_2[.

        standing (E, F, T_1, T_2) **and**
        $T_1 <= T_3$ **and** $T_3 < T_4$ **and** $T_4 < T_2$
implies
        standing (E, F, T_3, T_4).

There are similar rules for all other states.

Control Rules

Control rules are rules that allow one to deduce events of the type new_list and states of the type list; in other words, they express the scheduling strategy. As an example, we give the rules that express the simple strategy according to which requests that come from inside elevators are immediately inserted in the elevator's list in such a way that the list is sorted either in the order from the current floor to the top if the elevator is moving up, or in the reverse order if the elevator is moving down. The elements in each list are canceled as soon as the elevator stops at the corresponding floor. External calls can be managed similarly, e.g., by inserting the requested floor in the list of the closest elevator that is moving in the right direction or in elevator that is standing.

R_{11}. The event of reserving a floor F from inside an elevator E that is not standing at that floor causes an instantaneous update to the list L associated with E, according to the above policy.

        request (E, F, T_R) **and**
        not (standing (E, F, T_a, T_R)) **and**
        list (E, L, T_a, T_R) **and**
        LF = insert_in_order(L, F, E)
implies
        new_list (E, LF, T_R).

The relation insert_in_order is a function that produces the new list by inserting F based on the position and direction of elevator E, according to the above policy. Its detailed formalization is left to the reader as an exercise. We hide the service policy in one function so that a change of policy would require only the replacement of the insert_in_order function. This is an example of the principle of design for change, applied to writing specifications.

R_{12}. The effect of the arrival at floor F of an elevator E that stops there is to remove the first element F from the list.

> arrival (E, F, T_a) **and**
> list (E, L, T, T_a) **and**
> F = first (L) **and**
> L_t = tail (L)
> **implies**
> > new_list (E, L_t, T_a).

The predicate tail (L) means the remaining part of L, after having deleted its first element.

R_{13}. The control state of an elevator E is represented by the list that specifies all reservations scheduled for E; it remains unchanged as long as no modifications occur to its list.

> new_list (E, L, T_1) **and**
> **not** (new_list (E, L, T_2) **and** $T_1 < T_2 < T_3$)
> **implies**
> > list (E, L, T_1, T_3).

Exercises

5.35 Complete the above set of events, states, and rules. In particular, describe the events that switch internal and external buttons on and off. Define the policy for canceling external reservations in both interpretations described in Section 5.5.3.2.

Warning: You should pay attention to the consistency between the contents of lists and button illumination. That is, if an internal button is illuminated, the corresponding floor must appear in the elevator's list. Also, some inconsistency could arise between the rule R_{12} and the policy of switching external buttons off only when the elevator leaves the floor in the desired direction. Why? How can you avoid the risk of inconsistency?

5.36 Is the policy described here to serve internal and external requests the same as that in Section 5.5.3.2?

5.37 Define and formalize other service policies.

5.6.2.4 Verifying specifications: a comparison of descriptive and operational style

In the previous section, we used logic to specify an elevator system. We gave rules that describe system behavior in the sense of defining how the system reacts to some stimuli when it is in a certain state. Now let us analyze the elevator's specification as we did in the case of Petri nets. We can "simulate" the system by assuming a given system state at a given time and checking the effect of the occurrence of some events. This is formalized by formulas that are assumed to be true *a priori* (and therefore that denote *facts*). Then, the above rules can be used to *deduce* the consequences of these facts.

For instance, we can define the elevator state

standing (2, 3, 5, 7);

i.e., that elevator 2 has been at floor 3 at least from time 5 to time 7. Also, we can state

list(2, empty, 5, 7);
request(2, 8, 7);

Then, by applying the rules of the specification, we can deduce the fact

new_list(2, {8}, 7),

and, if we exclude the occurrence of other events,

departure (2, up, 7 + Δt_s);
arrival (2, 8, 7 + Δt_s + $\Delta t_a \cdot (8 - 3)$)

by means of a few simple logical deductions.

Thus, the logical formalism describes the system's operation by means of *deductions*. Now, the set of formulas is a specification of the system in the sense that every implementation must guarantee that all of the given rules are true. But if this is so, then all of the consequences of the rules will be guaranteed.

Logical deduction can be applied not only to simulate system behavior, but also to *analyze* system properties. In fact, in a descriptive specification such as the above logical description of the elevator system, a system property is just another formula on system variables. For instance, the property that all requests will eventually be served can be formalized as

new_list (E, L, T) **and** F $\in$ L **implies**
    new_list (E, L$_1$, T$_1$) **and** F $\notin$ L$_1$ **and** T$_1$ > T$_2$.

If we succeed in deducing this formula from the previous system specification, we will be able to rely on its truth in any valid implementation of the system. Thus, proving properties of a logic specification is just the same logical deduction activity as deducing system dynamics.

Here we see a major difference between operational and descriptive specification styles. In operational specifications, the description of the *state* of the system is quite different from the description of the *properties* of the system. This fact has a major impact on the way we can use a–possibly automatic–specification interpreter to verify specifications. For instance, we could use a PN interpreter to verify that, after initializing an elevator system with 30 floors, 4 elevators, a given speed, and a given sequence of calls, all requests will be serviced with a maximum delay of 30 seconds. The interpreter, however, cannot provide a *proof* that for any system with n floors, m elevators, and speed z, for any sequence of no more than y calls per minute, the maximum delay between a call and its service is **w**, **w** being a suitable function of n, m, z, and y. In other words, a PN interpreter could be used to simulate specifications, but not to prove their properties–at least directly.

These remarks apply in general to all operational and descriptive styles and to all properties. For instance, consider FSMs. If we want to know what the state of the system will be when starting from a given state and applying a given sequence of transitions, we just have to "execute the automaton." If, instead, we want to know whether the system can behave periodically, we must check the graph that represents the FSM for the presence of cyclic paths.

As a further example, consider the property of a system's being deadlock free. PNs are provided with a clear formal definition of this property, as we saw in Section 5.5.3. A PN interpreter, however, cannot be used to *decide* whether a given net is deadlock free; we can, at most, *test* the model in several different cases to check whether in those cases a deadlock occurs. Thus, if we want to decide whether a system modeled by a PN has the risk of running into a deadlock, we must analyze the model in some different way than executing it.[1]

Instead, suppose you have given a formal definition of the same system using FOT formulas. Then the desired property is, again, an FOT formula, such as

for all s_1, s_2 ((state (s_1) **and** state (s_2) **and** reachable (s_2, s_1)) **implies**
exists s_3 (state (s_3) **and** $s_3 \neq s_2$ **and** reachable (s_3, s_2))

i.e., for any state s_1, and for any state s_2 that is reachable from s_1, the system can evolve into a new state s_3, that is reachable from s_2. As a consequence, we can use the same interpreter of FOT formulas to simulate a system or to decide system properties. Of course, an undecidable property will not become decidable just because we used a descriptive style to express it: we only have a homogeneous language to describe both the system and its properties.

On the other hand, executing logical specifications–i.e., building interpreters for them–may not be as simple as it is for operational specifications. For instance, "interpreting" a set of FOT formulas requires applying rules of deduction, that, in general, involve much nondeterminism: often, from a set of premises, several partial conclusions may be derived, and many of them do not necessarily lead to the desired final conclusion.

It is worth recalling that the problem of *proving theorems*, within FOTs, is undecidable; in other words, we cannot automatically decide whether a given property (an FOT formula) is implied by a given specification (another FOT formula). Executable logic languages such as PROLOG, however, succeed fairly well in *approximating* the deductive power of FOTs through effective interpretation techniques. For this reason, they can be used as *prototyping languages*. We refer the interested reader to the more specialized literature for deeper explanations of this issue.

---

[1] It turns out that deadlock freedom is decidable for "pure PNs," i.e., PNs given according to the original definition, but that the problem is of intractable complexity to apply decision algorithms in practice.

In conclusion, operational formalisms seem more naturally oriented towards simulation of systems, whereas descriptive formalisms are more naturally applied to analysis of properties.

Exercise

5.38 Define (not prove!) a property of the elevator system stating that the waiting time for each request is bounded. Formalize this property as a FOT formula.

5.6.3 Algebraic Specifications

Another popular descriptive specification style is based on the use of *algebra* rather than logic as the underlying mathematical formalism. Essentially, algebraic specifications define a system as a *heterogeneous algebra*, i.e., a collection of different sets on which several operations are defined.

Traditional algebras are *homogeneous*. A homogeneous algebra consists of a single set and several operations. For instance, the integers, together with the addition, subtraction, multiplication, and division operations, are a homogeneous algebra. By contrast, alphabetic strings (i.e., sequences of characters), together with the operations of concatenation and length, are not a homogeneous algebra, since the range of the length operation is the set of integers, not the set of strings. Thus, strictly speaking, we say that this algebra consists of two sets—strings and integers—on which the two above operations are defined.

It turns out that many software systems can be naturally defined as heterogeneous algebras; after all, the definition "collection of sets together with operations" is quite close to the notion of an abstract data type introduced in Section 4.2.4.2. We will state some important connections between heterogeneous algebras and abstract data types in Section 5.7.2.1.

Let us explore the essential features of algebraic specifications through a few examples. As a starting point, consider the simple case of strings.

Example 5.6

Imagine that we want to specify a system to manage strings. The first relevant facts that one should record are the operations needed and the sets involved in such operations. In this case, assume we want to manage strings by

- creating new, empty strings (operation new);
- concatenating strings (operation append);
- adding a new character at the end of a string (operation add);
- checking the length of a given string (operation length);
- checking whether a string is empty (operation isEmpty);
- checking whether two strings are equal (operation equal).

A short inspection of the above list shows that the sets involved, besides the set of strings itself, here called String, are

- Char: the set of alphabetic characters;
- Nat: the set of natural numbers;
- Bool: the set of logical values, {true, false}.

The collection of sets that form the heterogeneous algebra is called its *signature*. Each set, in turn, is called a *sort* of the algebra. Thus, to define a heterogeneous algebra, we first need to specify its signature, the involved operations, and their domains and ranges. This definition is called the algebra's *syntax* and can be expressed in any of several notations. We are going to adopt here a notation based on the Larch specification language. The notation is quite intuitive and is fairly close to that of other algebraic languages. Here is the syntax of the algebra for strings in a "Larch-like" notation:

> **algebra** StringSpec;
> **introduces**
> > **sorts** String, Char, Nat, Bool;
> > **operations**
> > > new: () → String;
> > > append: String, String → String;
> > > add: String, Char → String;
> > > length: String → Nat;
> > > isEmpty: String → Bool;
> > > equal: String, String → Bool.

Sort String is just one of the sets involved. The fact that we are actually interested in its definition, and that natural numbers and Booleans are in some sense "auxiliary sorts," has only intuitive relevance and is noted by the name given to the algebra in the first line. Also, notice that the new operation has no arguments, i.e., no domain. This is a conventional way to denote constant values. In fact, a function with no argument may have just one value. In this case, this is the "empty string."

The meaning intended for the above operations, in this instance, is quite clear. Nevertheless, such a meaning must be defined precisely. This is done in the algebra's *semantics*, using *equations* that are intended to define essential *properties* that must always be true when the operations are applied. For this reason, such equations are also called the *axioms* of the algebra.

Some obvious properties of the String algebra operations are that the string created by the new operation is the empty string (this is actually more a definition than a property); that by concatenating the empty string to any other string, we obtain that same string (i.e., the empty string is a *unit* with respect to concatenation); and that no string obtained by adding a character to any other string can be empty.

The formalization of these and other properties in our Larch-like notation yields the following construct:

> **constrains** new, append, add, length, isEmpty, equal **so that**
> **for all** [s, s_1, s_2: String; c: Char]
>   isEmpty (new ()) = true;
>   isEmpty (add (s,c)) = false;
>   length (new ()) = 0;
>   length (add (s,c)) = length (s) + 1;
>   append (s, new ()) = s;
>   append (s_1, add (s_2,c)) = add (append (s_1,s_2),c);
>   equal (new (),new ()) = true;
>   equal (new (), add (s,c)) = false;
>   equal (add (s,c), new ()) = false;
>   equal (add (s_1, c), add (s_2, c) = equal (s_1,s_2);
> **end** StringSpec.

Let us examine the above equations. To start with, observe that we used five undeclared and undefined symbols, namely 0, 1, +, true, and false. The other symbols, including parentheses and '=' (not to be confused with the operation "equal"), are either symbols of the notation or have been declared in the syntax. If we wanted to be absolutely rigorous, we should have declared '+' as an operation of the Nat algebra and 0, 1, true, and false as constants (i.e., functions with zero arguments) of their respective sorts. Furthermore, we should have given axioms to specify properties of those algebras; in particular, according to Peano's classical axiomatization of arithmetic, we should have stated that actually '1' is the result of applying the elementary operation "successor" to the constant '0'. To avoid an excessive number of fairly obvious equations, however, we left them as implicit–and as an exercise for the reader.

Next, let us proceed to analyze of the above specification. There is no doubt that the equations of this specification describe "truths" about strings. What we are interested in, however, is the ability to derive other properties from them, as we did with logic specifications: it is for this reason that the equations are called *axioms*.

For instance, consider the property

$$\text{append (new (), add (new (), c)) = add (new (), c)}$$

that should clearly hold for every character c. It can be derived from the above axioms in the following way. If we let s_1, s_2 = new () in the axiom

$$\text{append } (s_1, \text{add}(s_2,c)) = \text{add (append}(s_1,s_2),c)$$

we obtain

$$\text{append (new (), add (new (),c)) = add (append (new (), new ()), c)} \qquad \textbf{(i)}$$

Then, by substituting s = new () in the axiom append (s, new ()) = s, we obtain append (new (), new ()) = new (). Using this for substitution in (i), we obtain the desired property.

Similarly, let $<c_1,..., c_n>$ be an abbreviation for

add (add...(add (new (), c_1),...), c_n).

Then it is an easy exercise to prove that

append ($<c_1,c_2>$, $<c_3, c_4>$) = $<c_1,c_2,c_3,c_4>$

for every c_1,c_2,c_3,c_4.

Now, consider properties such as

append(new(), s) = s   **(ii)**

and

append (s_1, append (s_2,s_3))= append (append (s_1,s_2),s_3)   **(iii)**

These two properties can be proved by induction. We do so for (ii). Now, (ii) holds for s = new () by applying the axiom append (s, new ()) = s with s = new (). Assume that (ii) holds for a given string s_1, and let s be add (s_1,c). Then append (new (), s) = append (new (), add (s_1,c)) = add (append (new (),s_1),c) = add (s_1,c) = s. Thus, (ii) holds for s, too.

The above intuitive reasoning, however, assumes that every string s, other than new (), is of the type add (s_1, c), for some s_1, c. The operations new and add are thus called the *generators* of the algebra StringSpec. Although this sounds obvious intuitively, it is not explicitly stated in the formalization of StringSpec. To specify this fact, we modify the header of the earlier semantic definition as follows:

> **constrains** new, append, add, length, isEmpty, equal **so that**
>   StringSpec **generated by** [new, add]
>   **for all** [s, s_1, s_2: String; c: Char]

This constrcuts states explicitly that all elements of sort String can be obtained as a suitable combination of the operations new and add. Similarly, all natural numbers can be generated by the constant '0' and the "successor" operation.

Now, let us assume that the previous algebra has been enriched by introducing constant characters, such as 'a', 'b',.... (The constants are enclosed within quotes.) Formally, these constants are introduced by defining them as functions with no arguments, as we did for the new operation; e.g., a: () $\rightarrow$ Char. 'a' will be used as an abbreviation for a(). Then, consider the property

equal (add (s, 'a'), add (s, 'b')) = false

Intuitively, this certainly appears to be true. There is, however, no way to prove that it is true[1] within the framework of the system.

---

[1]The reader should pay some attention to the intricacies of mathematical formulas.   Here, we want to prove, i.e., to state the truth of, a formula that states the falsity of another formula. We should keep in mind that, in general, the fact that there is no proof of a formula does not mean

This shows that the previous axioms are *incomplete*, i.e., they do not allow us to deduce all the desired "truths" of our algebra. Happily, in this case, the specifications formalized by previous equations can easily be *completed* (it is not, however, always so simple to achieve completeness!) by

- adding the new operation equalC, defining *equality between characters*. This operation should be *constrained* by equations of the type

  equalC ('a', 'a') = true;
  equalC ('a', 'b') = false;
  .
  .
  .

- replacing the last equation of the previous semantics by

$$\text{equal (add } (s_1, c_1), \text{ add } (s_2, c_2)) = \text{equal } (s_1, s_2) \text{ and equalC } (c_1, c_2) \qquad \textbf{(j)}$$

Clearly, in writing algebraic specifications, as with other styles styles of specifications, incompleteness is not the only risk. We could *overspecify*–i.e., unduly constrain–a system, as would happen, for instance, if we wrote the axiom

$$\text{equal (add } (s_1, c_1), \text{ add } (s_2, c_2)) = \text{equal } (s_1, s_2) \text{ and} \qquad \textbf{(jj)}$$
$$\text{equalC } (c_1, c_2) \text{ and not equalC } (c_1, \text{'a'})$$

instead of the previous (j). In fact, (jj) improperly states that two strings can be equal only if they do not contain the character 'a'!

We could also write contradictory or inconsistent specifications, as would happen if we added

  equal (add (s,c), s) = true

to the axioms. In general, a set of algebraic equations is *contradictory*, or *inconsistent*, if it allows us to prove true = false.

We could write *redundant* specifications if we added, say,

  append (new (), s) = s

to the set of axioms, since it can already be proved as a consequence of the other axioms. In practice, redundancy in algebraic specifications is a much smaller problem than inconsistency and incompleteness and can usually be ignored.

---

that the formula is false. There is no proof of equal (add (s, 'a'), add (s, 'b')) = true. There is also no proof that equal(add(s, 'a'), add(s, 'b')) = false, but we "feel" that this formula should be true and we would like to be able to prove it. Again, our exposition of these theoretical issues relies much on the reader's intuition and leaves a deep mathematical treatment of the topic to the appropriate literature.

In conclusion, an algebraic specification defines a system as the collection of all sets and related operations stated in the signature of the specification, whose elements satisfy all equations of the semantic part of the specification and, therefore, even all equations derivable from them.   ∎

We now gain better insight into algebraic specifications through a larger example.

Example 5.7

Suppose you want to specify a text editor. The specification must indicate the data types on which the editor must operate–i.e., the sorts, the available operations, and their meaning. Initially, let us consider an oversimplified text editor, suitable for handling simple text files, with the following set of operations:

- newF: creates a new, empty file (the suffix F is used to indicate that the operation is related to files; in fact, in some cases, there are similar operations for different sets);
- isEmptyF: states whether a file is empty;
- addF: adds a string of characters at the end of a file;
- insertF: inserts a string at a given position of a file. The rest of the file will be rewritten just after the inserted string (word);
- appendF: concatenates two files;
- other operations that will be discussed later or can be imagined by the reader as an exercise.

Thanks to the similarity with the previous example, the following algebraic specification for the text editor should be sufficiently clear:

> **algebra** TextEditor;
> **introduces**
> > **sorts** Text, String, Char, Bool, Nat;
> > **operations**
> > > newF: () → Text;
> > > isEmptyF: Text → Bool;
> > > addF: Text, String → Text;
> > > insertF: Text, Nat, String →Text;
> > > appendF: Text, Text → Text;
> > > deleteF: Text →Text;
> > > lengthF : Text → Nat;
> > > equalF : Text, Text → Bool;
> > > addFC: Text, Char → Text;
> > > > {This is an auxiliary operation that will be needed to define addF and other operations on files. Also, we assume that all operations previously introduced in StringSpec are still available. To make clear the distinction between the two kinds of operations, the

latter are suffixed by 'S'. We assume that the syntax
and the semantics of these belong to TextEditor also,
without explicitly copying them}

constrains newF, isEmptyF, addF, appendF, insertF, deleteF **so that**
TextEditor **generated by** [newF, addFC]
for all [f, f_1,f_2: Text; s: String; c: Char; cursor: Nat]

    isEmptyF (newF ()) = true;
    isEmptyF (addFC (f, c)) = false;
    addF (f, newS ()) = f;
    addF (f, addS (s, c)) = addFC (addF (f, s), c);
    lengthF (newF ()) = 0;
    lengthF (addFC (f, c)) = lengthF (f) + 1;
    appendF (f, newF ()) = f;
    appendF (f1, addFC (f_2, c)) = addFC (appendF (f_1, f_2), c);
    equalF (newF (),newF ()) = true;
    equalF (newF (), addFC (f, c)) = false;
    equalF (addFC (f, c), new ()) = false;
    equalF (addFC (f_1, c_1), addFC (f_2, c_2) =
                          equalF (f_1, f_2) **and** equalC (c_1, c_2);
    insertF (f, cursor, newS ()) = f;
    (((equalF (f, appendF (f_1, f_2)) **and** (lengthF (f_1) = cursor - 1))
    implies
        equalF (insertF (f, cursor, s), appendF (addF (f_1, s), f_2))) = true;
  end TextEditor.

The last equation looks rather complicated. To make such equations more understandable, we may write them as

  if ((equalF (f, appendF (f_1, f_2)) **and** (lengthF (f_1) = cursor - 1)) **then**
        (insertF (f, cursor, s) = appendF (addF (f_1, s), f_2))

These kinds of equations are called *conditional equations*.

Let us examine the real meaning of the operations defined by the above equations. Algebraic equations state relations among the elements of the sets involved, not relations on *variables that store values*. Thus, it would be plausible, but not necessary, to deduce from the previous equations that the result of applying insertF (f, cursor, s) is the *modification of the state of file* f consisting of inserting the string s between portions f_1 and f_2 on the file. This formula just states a property of the value of type file that is the result of the operation. In order to stress the difference with the concepts of conventional programming languages, our syntax for algebraic specifications uses the keyword **operations** rather than the traditional keywords **procedure** and **function**.

Thus, both of the following two *implementations* of the insert operation would be adequate with respect to the above specification:

• Implementation 1: The operation modifies f in the specified way;

- Implementation 2: The operation creates a new file whose value is computed in the specified way.

In general, of course, direct-access file systems tend to work according to implementation 1 (if no explicit command states the opposite), whereas sequential, batch processing file systems necessarily work according to implementation 2.

Even though the above specification contains a considerable number of equations (the reader should not forget that some of them have been left implicit), it is still far from specifying a realistic text editor. The way to achieve such a goal, however, should now be clear. ∎

Algebraic specifications are a useful notation for specifying the semantics of modules such as abstract data types. They do not deal with time-dependent behavior, however. In the past few years, researchers have been trying to add the notion of time to algebraic specifications, although without much success. Currently, algebraic specifications do not seem appropriate for describing such systems as our earlier elevator system.

Exercises

5.39 Prove that the following properties hold for the StringSpec algebra introduced in this section:

equal (<'a','c', 'a', 'd'>, <'a','c', 'a', 'd'>) = true
equal (<'a','c', 'a', 'd'>, <'a','c', 'd', 'a'>) = false

5.40 If we imagine that the operations of Example 5.7 are interactive user commands to manipulate text files, these are definitely too limited. The main shortcoming is the fact that the user has no way to *name* files. It is possible only to build new files and then operate on them. Augment the previous specification to include a naming facility. The user must be able to give identifiers to files when creating them and use an identifier to specify the file to which an operation must be applied.

You may consider the name, or identifier, of a file as different from the previous variables f, f_1, and f_2 of sort Text. In other words, the name should be an attribute of a file, uniquely identifying it.

5.41 Augment the specification given in Example 5.7 with operations such as the following:

- change (f, s_1, s_2): substitutes all occurrences of s_1 in f with s_2;
- find(f, s): returns a Boolean value that states whether s is in f, and, if it is, returns the position of the first character of s in f. (There are a couple of trouble spots in this informal definition; can you spot them?)

5.7 BUILDING AND USING SPECIFICATIONS IN PRACTICE

In the previous section, we have seen a sample of models and notations that can be used for giving specifications of different systems. Although most of the examples we used were inspired by real software problems, the systems involved were very simple. In this section, we look at the problem of applying specification techniques to real-life systems. After examining what more is needed for writing and using specifications in practice, we look at a few ways that help tackle the practical problems of dealing with large and complex systems.

5.7.1 Requirements for Specification Notations

Let us examine critically the benefits obtained and the problems raised by the use of the formalisms introduced in Sections 5.5 and 5.6. Certainly, by exploiting the principles of rigor and formality, we were able to make clear and precise many specifications that otherwise might have been left vague or ambiguous until later design or implementation phases.

It turned out, however, that even for specifying relatively simple systems, many details had to be taken into consideration. For instance, a full description of a skyscraper elevator system in terms of PNs would be a huge, unmanageable, unintelligible network; and the algebraic specification of a even a toy text editor would require many equations, both explicit and implicit.

Thus, building requirements specifications for real-life systems is likely to be as complex an activity as designing the implementation of these systems: the resulting specification document–whether we use a formal notation or English–would be as complex as the design documentation and code itself. Consequently, all principles stated in Chapter 3 should be applied to the construction of complex specifications.[1] Even many "design techniques" examined in Chapter 4 are highly useful for managing the "design" of complex specifications.

Having emphasized the importance of rigor and formality in previous sections, let us briefly examine a few other principles separately. All "specification languages" we have presented so far–finite state machines, DFDs, PNs, logic, and algebraic equations–are related to real specification languages in the same way that so-called toy programming languages, such as those of the "MiniPascal style" used in many introductory computer science courses, are related to real programming languages. They grasp the essentials of the real languages, but they are suitable only for expressing simple systems, such as how to code sorting algorithms and trigonometric functions, and not, say, real-life payroll systems or compilers. What they lack most with respect to (good) real programming languages are abstraction and modularization mechanisms. The next section shows that specification formalisms may be provided with such mechanisms, in much the same way as in the case of programming languages.

The principle of *separation of concerns* also has some natural implications for specifications. For instance, whenever possible, *functional specifications*, i.e., the definition of what the system should do as a consequence of the given input, should be kept separate from *performance specifications*, i.e., the definition of efficiency requirements, from *user interface specifications*, and so on.

---

[1]In fact, our presentation of the derivation of the elevator system specification was carried in a *modular* way, even if we did not give a formal definition of "PN module" or "FOT module."

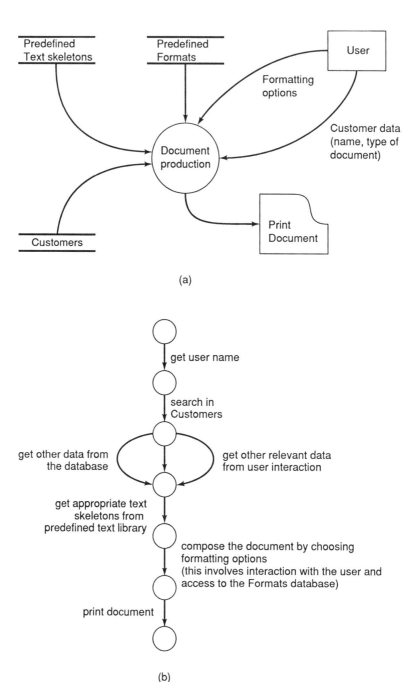

(a)

(b)

Figure 5.41   Two views of document production.
(a) Data view through a DFD. (b) Control view through an FSM.

Sometimes, separation of concerns may even result in using different notations for specifying different aspects of a system. For instance, imagine that you wanted to describe the production of a document in an office automation system. The DFD of Figure 5.41(a) describes which sources of information and what kind of data are necessary to produce the document: a library of predefined Text_skeletons (say, contracts of several types in which specific data such as names, dates, and amounts, are missing); a data base of Customers that already have been in touch with the office; the customers themselves; and a predefined set of Formats to be selected to print the document.

The figure, however, does not specify the order of execution for the actions that lead to the composition and printing of the document. This is specified by the FSM of Figure 5.41(b), which shows that, after having gotten the customers name, we may get further data–the customer's address, date of birth, etc.–either from the Customer data base or through more interaction with the customer. There is intuitive evidence that if the customer's record is already in the data base, then the edge "get other data from the data base" is followed. The alternative edge is followed if the customer's record is not in the data base. This, however, is not stated explicitly in the figure. If we wanted to be more precise, we could augment the model by adding suitable labels to the edge to specify the conditions under which it could be followed.

Similarly, we already noticed in Section 5.6.1 that DFDs and ER diagrams can complement each other by supplying different "views" of system descriptions, the former being oriented to the specification of system functions, the latter to the description of the relations among data.

Incrementality is perhaps even more important for specifications than for implementation. It is seldom the case that all requirements are well understood at the very beginning of a software project. More often, their final formulation is the result of a long process involving much trial and error. Furthermore, it is in any case wise initially to focus attention on the most relevant and critical requirements of a system. Later on, even minor requirements must be taken into consideration and stated clearly in the appropriate documents.

Incrementality should be applied in the construction of specifications even to the level of rigor and formality, in the sense that initially things can hardly be formulated in an absolutely precise way. (In general, things are not very precise even in the mind of the person stating the requirements.) Thus, initial formulations are likely to be informal and rather fuzzy notes, whether written in a natural language or sketched in some graphical notation. Then, if an effort is made to state them more precisely, it is likely that they are going to change and that even the "language" in which they are expressed will move from informal to semiformal or formal.

Several examples of specifications given in Sections 5.5 and 5.6 have been derived in an incremental way, both by moving from an informal statement to a formal one (recall the elevator system, particularly with reference to switching the button lights on and off) and by modifying earlier formulations given in the same formalism (again, the case of switching the button lights of the elevator system on and off is illustrative).

In writing specifications, a full and complete formalization of the document is not usually necessary. We already remarked in Chapter 3 that even mathematicians, when formulating and proving theorems, proceed by incrementally adding details and formality in the critical steps of definitions and proofs. In the same way, a specification document could be a mixture of informal natural language sentences, semiformal figures, and fully formalized models, when needed, under the complete responsibility of the designer.

Another reason to adopt combinations of "languages" for specifications is that specifications are often used by different people with different purposes, as we pointed out in Section 5.1. For example, it is quite unlikely that a contract for a software product will be signed on the basis of a document written in mathematical logic. Thus, further requirements may be imposed on specification documents if they must be managed by the end users. We will briefly examine a few techniques for tackling this problem in Section 5.7.3.

In summary, talking about *specification languages* is at least as difficult as talking about programming languages. A specification document is not likely to be just a huge, yet well-structured and well-modularized PN. Nor is it likely to be a single FOT formula. In many cases, a specification document could even use different formalisms to achieve different purposes. Thus, the specifier may naturally wish to integrate several formal, informal, and/or semiformal specifications, into a unique document whose major goals are clarity, precision, and immediate understandability. Quite often, a full description in a single formal language looks more like implementation code than like system definition. Therefore, the "ideal specification language" is even less realistic than the "ideal programming language." This, however, is certainly not a good reason for using no specification language at all!

Finally, the process of writing, analyzing, modifying, and using specifications to check an implementation can benefit highly from the use of appropriate tools. In the most trivial case, one can use just a word processor to edit and modify documents written in a natural language. It is clear, however, that much more is desirable, much more is already available, and still much more is likely to be offered in the future to help the whole process. For instance, graphical editors to help writing, say, DFDs or PNs are already widely available. Some remarks on the main features of tools for specification analysis have already been given, and the issue will be considered further in Chapter 9.

Exercises

5.42 Can performance specifications be separated from functional specifications in real-time systems? Justify your answer.

5.43 Give a PN control view of the production of a document.

5.44 Discuss the application of the principles of generality and anticipation of change to the construction of specifications.

5.7.2 Building Modular Specifications

This section is devoted mainly to showing how appropriate constructs, suitably embedded in the specification language, can help in applying the principles of modularity, abstraction, and incrementality to specifications. First, we will present a language based on algebraic equations. Then we will show how appropriate constructs can be added, in principle, to any language, to make it more suitable for writing specifications in practice.

5.7.2.1 A sample algebraic specification language

Let us go back to the TextEditor algebra of Example 5.7. We have already noticed that many equations are missing: equations to define strings, equations to define natural numbers, those to define characters, and those to define Booleans. In some sense, writing in full detail all of the equations to specify a text editor would entail as much effort as implementing the system in Pascal by using only the Boolean data type and the array constructor.

Whether we use Naturals, Booleans, etc., as algebras or as Pascal data types, they always denote sets and operations that are widely known and widely used, so that one should not need to redefine them every time they are needed. In Pascal and other programming languages they are built in, i.e., they are defined and implemented once and are accessible to all users. Also, *libraries* of other widely useful data types and operations are often provided by language implementers or system administrators. So we have trigonometric routines, I/O packages, and even packages to handle tables and the like. Furthermore, and most important, we have mechanisms to build our own abstractions and modules and to build complex systems by integrating them.[1]

This kind of support is provided by several specification languages also. Let us briefly see how this happens by taking inspiration from Larch. As we said in Section 5.6.3, Larch is a well-developed specification language based on the algebraic style. Basically, Larch's modules are algebras. In Larch, one can define *hierarchies* of algebras by means of suitable relations that are based on the same principles described in Chapter 4. Let us start illustrating them with a simple example.

We saw that the StringSpec algebra used some elementary sets and operations, such as Nat, Bool, Char, and '+'. Assume that these have been previously defined as independent algebras as follows:

> **algebra** BoolAlg;
> **introduces**
> > **sorts** Bool;
> > **operations**
> > > true () → Bool;
> > > false () → Bool;
> > > **not** : Bool → Bool;
> > > **and**: Bool, Bool → Bool;
> > > **or**: Bool, Bool→ Bool;
> > > **implies**: Bool, Bool→ Bool;
> > > ≡: Bool, Bool→ Bool;
> > **constrains** true, false, **not**, **and**, **or**, **implies**, ≡ **so that**
> > Bool **generated by** [true, false]

----

[1]This is especially true in the case of object-oriented programming languages.

for all [a, b: Bool]
   not (true) = false;
   not (false) = true;
   a **and** b = **not** (**not** (a) **or not** (b));
   a **implies** b = **not** (a) **or** b;
   .
   .
   .

end BoolAlg.

algebra NatNumb;
introduces
   sorts Nat, Bool;
   operations
     0: () $\rightarrow$ Nat;
     Succ[1]: Nat $\rightarrow$ Nat;
     + : Nat, Nat $\rightarrow$ Nat;
     - : Nat, Nat $\rightarrow$ Nat;
     = : Nat, Nat $\rightarrow$ Bool;[2]
   .
   .
   .

constrains 0, Succ, +, -, =,..., **so that**
NatNumb **generated by** [0, Succ]
   .
   .
   .

end NatNumb.

algebra CharAlg;
introduces
   sorts Char, Bool;
   operations
     'a': () $\rightarrow$ Char;
     'b' : () $\rightarrow$ Char;
     .
     .
     .

end CharAlg.

StringSpec may now be defined completely by *using* these specifications. This is done in Larch through the **imports** clause, which simply states that the imported algebra is enclosed in the new one, in the sense that all its sorts and operations may be used, with their given meanings, in the new algebra. The clause specifies, additionally, that their semantics *cannot be modified* by additional constraints in the new theory; it can only be

---

[1]This is the "successor" operator, which increments a natural number by one unit.

[2]Strictly speaking, we should use a different operation symbol, such as "equalN", to denote equality between naturals, since '=' is a reserved symbol of the algebra's syntax. However, to avoid the heavy notation equalN (5,5), we have decided to overload the two operation symbols.

used. In other words, we should not expect that the properties of, say, '+' are further specified in StringSpec. In our case, we just need the following declaration:

> **algebra** StringSpec;
> **imports** BoolAlg, NatNumb, CharAlg;
> **introduces**
> > **sorts** String, Char, Nat, Bool;
> > **operations**
> > > new: () $\rightarrow$ String;
> > > .
> > > .
> > > .
>
> **end** StringSpec.

After that, everything may proceed as before.

Notice that **imports** defines a relation between algebras. Semantically, it implies the USES relation between modules, but it says something more than this. In fact, the USES relation simply states that if M_1 USES M_2, then M_1's correctness depends on M_2's correctness. The **imports** clause states also that M_1 can use M_2, through its operations. The **imports** clause is required to be a hierarchy, whereas USES is not, although we saw in Chapter 4 that hierarchical relations are desirable. Also, in both cases, the semantics of operations exported by M_2 cannot be affected by M_1.

Exercise

5.45   Build the TextEditor algebra of Example 5.7 by importing suitable other algebras. In so doing, you should notice that a problem of identifying the scope of identifiers arises in the same way as in programming languages. For instance, different "new" operations are needed for different sorts. The problem is not taken into consideration here, since it can be handled by applying traditional techniques–hiding rules, overloading, etc. You are invited, however, to define your own scope rules for the Larch-like language that is going to be defined.

Example 5.8

We often deal with several types of data structures: stacks, queues, sets, etc. These different data structures have some properties in common and others that distinguish them from each other. These properties, however, are rarely stated precisely, and, in general, we find different definitions for them. Here, we seek to find out common and different aspects of many classical (dynamic) data structures and arrange them in a well-structured algebraic hierarchy that resembles the inheritance hierarchy of object-oriented design.

First, observe that any data structure is a place for storing data, i.e., it is a *data container.* Thus, assuming that all items to be stored are of sort, say, DataType, we start by defining a Container algebra, with the idea that all other data structures should be seen as particular cases of this structure. (Thus, we see an application of the principle of generality.) Elements of type Container can be created via the usual new operation, items may be stored in them through an insert operation, they may be either empty or nonempty, and they have a specific size. Since all possible configurations of any data structure may be reached by appropriately inserting some elements into the data structure, new and insert are generators of the Container algebra, just as new and add are generators for the StringSpec algebra. Thus, we have the following simple algebra:

```
algebra Container;
imports DataType, BoolAlg, NatNumb;
introduces
        sorts Cont;
        operations
                new: () → Cont;
                insert: Cont, Data → Cont;
                    {Data is the sort of algebra DataType, to which
                    elements to be stored in Cont belong}
                isEmpty: Cont → Bool;
                size: Cont → Nat;
constrains new, insert, isEmpty, size so that
Cont generated by [new, insert]
for all [d: Data; c: Cont]
        isEmpty (new ()) = true;
        isEmpty (insert (c, d)) = false;
        size (new ()) = 0;
end Container.
```

Our next step is to define a TableAlg algebra as a specialization of Container. That is, we consider a table as a particular case of a data container with more operations, and maybe with slightly different meanings. Here, we assume that a table insert is done in an ordered way, by inserting the new item as the *last* element of the table. Thus, last and rest are two other simple operations belonging to the algebra. Furthermore, we want to check tables for equality, and we want to delete elements from a table. (Since the same element could be inserted several times into the table, we want to delete all of its occurrences, if any.) The following new definition makes use of the new relation **assumes** between algebras:

```
algebra TableAlg;
assumes Container;
introduces
        sorts Table;
        operations
                last: Table → Data;
                rest: Table → Table;
                equalT : Table, Table → Bool;
                delete: Table, Data → Table;
constrains last, rest, equalT, delete, isEmpty, new, insert so that
for all [d, d₁, d₂: Data; t, t₁, t₂: Table]
```

last (insert (t, d)) = d;
rest (new ()) = new ();
rest (insert (t, d)) = t;
equalT (new (), new ()) = true;
equalT (insert (t, d), new ()) = false;
equalT (new (), insert (t,d)) = false;
equalT (t_1,t_2) = equalD^1(last (t_1), last (t_2)) **and**
                                    equalT (rest (t_1),rest (t_2));
delete (new (), d) = new ();
delete (insert (t,d),d) = delete (t, d);
if not equalD(d_1, d_2) **then**
                delete (insert (t, d_1), d_2) = insert (delete (t, d_2), d_1);
    end TableAlg.

As with **imports**, the **assumes** clause gives access from the "assuming algebra" to the signature and semantics of the "assumed" one. Also, both **imports** and **assumes** are transitive in the sense that they allow access to operations of other algebras further imported or assumed by the assumed–or imported–algebra. Again, we do not deal here with any newly generated problems of scope; we simply add appropriate suffixes to common operations, such as new, and equal.[2]

The difference between **import** and **assumes** is that **assumes** allows modification of the semantics of the assumed operations, whereas imports does not. In our example, TableAlg equations impose new constraints on the new and insert operations. This is not the same as, say, using the '+' operation anywhere, without altering its meaning. Thus, the **assumes** clause states a typical *inheritance* relation between algebras, in the same sense that this relation has in the object-oriented terminology.

Another type of data container is a *FIFO queue*. FIFO queues have operations last and equal, as do tables. Their delete operation, however, is both syntactically and semantically different from the table delete. Furthermore, they have a first operation, which returns the first element that has been inserted into the queue and has not yet been removed. Next, we provide the definition of QueueAlg; Figure 5.42.a summarizes the algebras defined so far and the relations among them.

algebra QueueAlg;
assumes Container;
introduces

---

[1]We assume that algebra DataType is provided with an equality operation.

[2]Another important issue we do not deal with here is that of *error conditions*. For instance, suppose that the delete operation is applicable only if the element to be deleted exists in the table. Then we must specify that delete (t,d) results in an error in such a case. Also, last (new ()) should result in an error. The reader is invited to augment these and other sets of equations with appropriate error conditions, by introducing the keyword **error**.

    sort Queue;
    operations
        last: Queue $\rightarrow$ Data;
        first: Queue $\rightarrow$ Data;
        equalQ : Queue , Queue $\rightarrow$ Bool;
        delete:Queue $\rightarrow$ Queue;
constrains last, first, equalQ, delete, isEmpty, new, insert **so that**
for all [d: Data; q, q_1, q_2: Queue]
        last (insert (q, d)) = d;
        first (insert (new(), d) = d
        first (insert (q, d)) = **if not** isEmpty (q) **then** first (q);
        equalQ (new (), new ()) = true;
        equalQ (insert (q, d), new ()) = false;
        equalQ (new (), insert (q, d)) = false;
        equalQ (insert (q_1, d_1), insert (q_2, d_2)) = equalD (d_1, d_2) **and**
                                                    equalQ (q_1,q_2);

        delete (new ()) = new ();
        delete (insert (new (), d)) = new ();
        if not equalQ (q, new ()) **then**
            delete (insert (q,d)) = insert (delete (q), d);
    end QueueAlg.   ∎

Exercise

5.46   Build the algebras shown in Figure 5.42(b), which completes Figure 5.42(a). Notice that equality has different meanings in different algebras. For instance, multisets are sets with possible repetitions of elements, but in which the order is not relevant. Thus, {a, b, a, c} = {b, a, c, a} ≠ {a, b, b, c}. Sets are considered a specialization of multisets, since they can be obtained by adding more equations to the equations for equality between multisets.

    The mechanisms introduced to build hierarchies of algebras exploit the principle of incrementality since they allow the construction of complex new algebras as modifications of existing ones. Incrementality is favored by algebraic specification languages in other ways also: in general, it might be difficult to obtain a complete and consistent set of equations stating the properties of an algebra at the first writing, even applying suitable modularization mechanisms; such a set of equations, however, can be obtained incrementally, allowing early versions of specifications to be partially incomplete.

    For instance, consider the queue equality operation of Example 5.8. One could first write the equation

$$\text{equalQ (insert } (q_1, d_1), \text{ insert } (q_2, d_2)) = \text{equalD } (d_1, d_2) \textbf{ and}$$
$$\text{equalQ } (q_1,q_2)$$

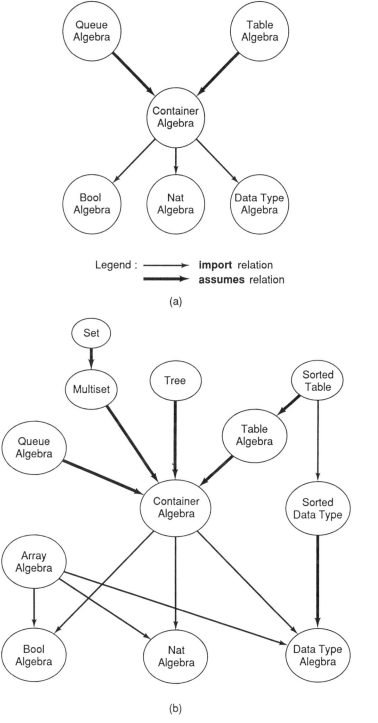

Figure 5.42   Hierarchies of algebras. **(a)** A simple hierarchy. **(b)** A richer hierarchy: SortedDataType assumes DataType and adds a total ordering to it (operation '<'). SortedTable contains sorted tables, with no duplicate elements.

which seems to contain the essential aspects of the desired operation. Then, further equations may be added to cope with "extreme conditions." It is also possible to do the opposite: first clarify special cases, and then cope with the general one. In both ways, the set of equations is built incrementally, focusing attention on different aspects at different moments.

In some sense, we could call the above two ways of exploiting incrementality, *incrementality in the large* and *incrementality in the small*. The former deals with the construction of families of algebras, the latter with the construction of a single algebra.

Exercises

5.47 Why did we not add the equation size (insert (c, d)) = size(c) + 1 in the specification of the Container algebra?

5.48 Discuss technical differences between **assumes** and the object oriented INHERITS_FROM, in one or more of its forms discussed in Chapter 4.

5.49 QueueAlg and TableAlg given in Example 5.8 actually have more in common than just Container. Define an "intermediate algebra" that contains all that is common to the two.

Going from specification to implementation

The whole design process can be seen as a chain of definition-implementation steps, often resulting in a hierarchy of modules. The IS_COMPOSED_OF relation is an example of such a hierarchy. During the process of design, several "languages" can be used, according to different needs. For instance, one could write initial specifications in an algebraic language, then design a software architecture using the notation introduced in Section 4.2.3.1, and finally code the system in Ada.

The transition between different levels of the definition-implementation hierarchy may proceed more or less naturally, depending also on the languages used. For instance implementing the hierarchy of modules of Figure 5.42(b) in terms of the notation of Section 4.2.3.2 is a smooth transition.

In the case of Larch, several *interface languages* have been defined, with the purpose of helping to effect a natural transition from specifications written in the basic language outlined above (called the Larch *shared language*, since it is common to any design, independently of the programming language used) to the implementation, which may be coded in different languages. Thus, there is a Larch/CLU language and a Larch/Pascal language, and others can be defined.

Let us briefly examine the essential features of the Larch/Pascal language. As a first step, it is quite natural to see an algebra as an abstract data type. The most obvious way of implementing an abstract data type in Pascal is to see it as type declarations coupled with function and/or procedure declarations.

Here, we must take into account the most relevant difference between shared Larch and Pascal. The former is *purely functional*–that is, its operations do not modify any execution state; the latter is operational–that is, procedures, and even functions, can have side effects. Thus, translating a specification written in shared Larch into a Pascal-like notation essentially consists of defining which operations become functions, which operations become procedures, and which variables the procedures can modify. This is easily explained through an example.

Consider the StringSpec algebra described in Example 5.6. Its signature is transformed, in Larch/Pascal, into the following declaration:

> **type** String **exports** isEmpty, add, append,...
> > {Notice that new has been dropped; in fact, we could either use the Pascal **new** statement, which would force us to implement strings through pointers, or accept the limitation of not being able to create string variables at run time}
>
> **based on** Boolean, integer, character
> > **function** isEmpty (s: String) : Boolean
> > > **modifies at most** [ ] {i.e., it has no side effects};
> >
> > **procedure** add (**var** s : String; c : char)
> > > **modifies at most** [s]
> > > {it has no effects on execution state other than modifying the string parameter s};
> >
> > **function** length (s: String) : integer
> > > **modifies at most** [ ] ;
> >
> > **procedure** append (**var** s_1, s_2, s_3: string)
> > **modifies at most** [s_3]
> > {although we decided, for convenience in the implementation, that all procedure parameters are passed by reference, actually only s_3, which is meant as the result of the operation, is modified};
> > .
> > .
> > .
>
> **end** StringSpec.

This translation from Larch signature into a notation closer to Pascal can be obtained, in principle, as the result of an interactive, syntax-directed translation. A translator could, in fact, automatically generate portions of the code, interacting with the designer, who decides whether an operation is to be implemented as a procedure or as a function and which elements–not necessarily parameters–can be modified.

The Larch/Pascal interface language is an example of a transition technique that helps along the complex process leading from specifications to implementation. In principle, it can also be applied to other specification and implementation languages.

5.7.2.2 Modularizing other specification formalisms

In this section, we show that appropriate modularization mechanisms can be designed for any formalism. Since the basic aspects of modularization should now be well understood, we will sketch the main ideas and leave the details to exercises.

Let us consider FSMs first. We already noticed in Section 5.5.2 that "exploding" Figure 5.15 into a complete FSM that describes the producer-buffer-consumer system would result in a fairly complex automaton even for such a simple case. We do not, however, need to go into a figure such as Figure 5.16 to understand the behavior of the system. We just need a structure whose semantics is the same as that of Figure 5.16, but that is more understandable.

For instance, consider Figure 5.43, which introduces a notation inspired by Statemate, one of the existing specification languages based on the FSM formalism. The figure describes the collection of the three components of the system as an AND chart, defining the state space of the whole system as the Cartesian product of the states of its components, but without displaying the state space explicitly. To make things clearer, we added two states with respect to the original description of Figure 5.14, namely, an initialization state and a concluding state. The arrows going from init to p_1, 0, and c_1 mean that, when the system is started (transition start occurs), it is positioned in the state that corresponds to the triple $<p_1,0,c_1>$. Similarly, the arrows connecting p_1, 0, and c_1 to end indicate that system operation can terminate when the three components are in those respective states.

Several other modularization mechanisms can be designed for structuring FSMs. One of these is suggested in the following exercise.

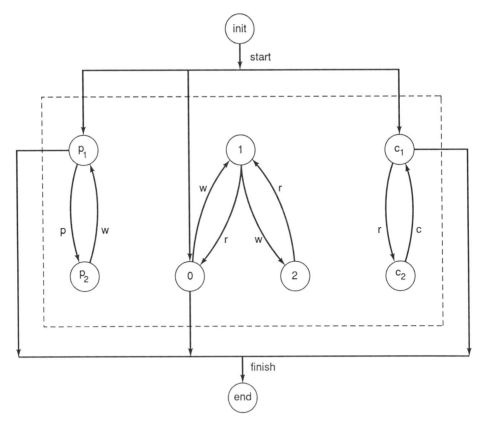

Figure 5.43   Modular description of a producer-buffer-consumer system in terms of "structured finite state machines".

Exercise

5.50 Consider an OR chart for structuring FSMs as illustrated in Figure 5.44. The *compound state* $\bar{q}$ in part (b) of the figure denotes a high-level view of the system in which it is irrelevant to distinguish between q_1 and q_2. The arrow labeled d going from $\bar{q}$ to q_0 represents a pair of arrows going from q_1 and q_2 to q_0. The arrow labeled b that goes from q_0 to $\bar{q}$ only states, at a high level, that $\bar{q}$ is reached. The "default" arrow into q_1 from no other state, however, denotes that if $\bar{q}$ is entered, its "substate" q_1 has to be selected for a more precise assignment. It is also possible that an arrow directly accesses a substate of a compound state (e.g., the arrow labeled a going from q_3 to q_2). Thus, OR charts are a way of describing FSMs in a compact way whenever a subsystem is reachable by many external states and–at least at some initial stage–one may ignore which individual states of the subsystem are actually connected to external states.

Give examples of systems that can be usefully described by OR charts.

5.7.3 Specifications for the End User

Specifications can be used as a common reference for the producer and the user of an application. When used this way, it is unlikely that the user would understand a document written in mathematical formalism. The only common language between producer and user is the natural language.

The last statement should not be considered an argument against the use of formal models. Rather, formal system description could be used to help the producer-user interaction in two different ways. First, once one has used formal models to spot and disambiguate informal and imprecise specifications, it is easy to "retranslate" the formalization into a prose description. The advantage of this approach is that the description obtained in this way does not suffer from the problems of ambiguity or incompleteness.

For instance, we realized in Section 5.5.3.2 that the informal specifications of the elevator system did not state in a clear way when buttons had to be switched off. Once a precise definition has been achieved through formalization, however, it is not difficult to reformulate it as an English sentence that states precisely what we want from the system.

Second, one may even go further and build a prototype of the system by providing an interpreter of the specification language. This could be supplied to the user in order to check whether requirements have been properly understood by the producer. Clearly, there are some cases when the prototype can be operated directly by the user and others when it cannot. An appropriate *user interface*, however, can make the prototype always manageable directly by the end user.

Another conclusion that may be drawn from the elevator example is that the PN specification cannot be understood by the end user. We could, however, use the PN description as an *internal form* and provide the user with an abstract view in terms of intuitive iconic symbols. The end user would see an elevator icon moving up and down the screen. (This is the result of translating a token flow in terms of icon movement.) The user could also see some buttons to click with the mouse; this would correspond to the pushing of a button in the real system, etc. Such an activity is usually called *system animation*. Obtained here as a result of using formal, executable models, animation is an active area of research today.

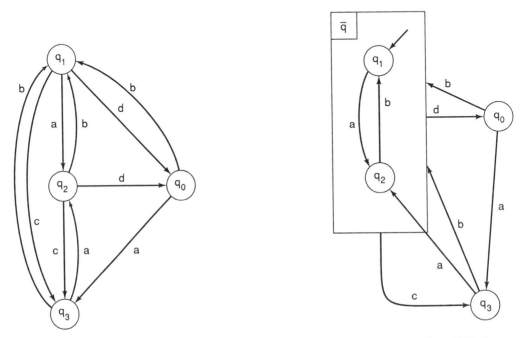

Figure 5.44   OR chart for structuring FSMs. **(a)** An FSM. **(b)** Transformation of the FSM of (a) into a structured OR chart.

5.8 CONCLUDING REMARKS

This chapter has been devoted to the subject of software specification. A specification is a precise statement. Specifications can help document many things in a software engineering project such as the following:

- what the users need from a system (requirements specification);
- the design of a software system (design specification);
- the features offered by a system (functional specification);
- the performance characteristics of a system (performance specification);
- the external behavior of a module (module interface specification);
- the internal structure of a module (internal structural specification).

Depending on its nature, the specification is intended for a particular user: the system designer, the system implementer, the end user, the system manager, etc. Similar principles can be used to develop good specifications for these different users.

After having discussed the major desirable qualities for specifications, we classified specification techniques as formal or informal, and operational or descriptive. We presented major representative techniques from each of the last two classes: data flow diagrams, finite state machines, and Petri nets (operational techniques), and entity-relationship diagrams, logic, and algebraic specifications (descriptive techniques). Data flow and entity relationship diagrams are examples of the semiformal approach; logic specifications are an example of the formal approach. We contrasted the operational and descriptive approaches by using an elevator system as a case study.

Like software systems, specifications can be large, complex objects that undergo many changes during their lifetime. We therefore need appropriate principles and techniques for managing the development of specifications. Accordingly, we showed that the principles of Chapters 3 and 4 apply as well to building and managing specifications as to software. We developed the requirements for managing the writing of complex specifications and examined the impact of these requirements on the different styles of specifications. We argued that modularity is the key to managing complex specifications and showed how the different specification styles may be used to develop modular specifications.

We have stressed that there is no ideal specification style or language. Considering the variety of details that need to be specified for a complex system, it is likely that the best approach is to use several styles and languages, either for the different parts of the same system, or for different views, or even for different users of the specifications. Such an eclectic approach can encompass a mixture of formal and informal specifications, as well as descriptive and operational ones.

We also discussed the use of specifications in enhancing the interaction between the end user and the developer, with an eye toward producing more accurate specifications. In particular, we discussed system animation and rapid prototyping. The software specification literature contains a dichotomy between specifying and prototyping. The idea is that you either go from (nonexecutable) specifications to code, or you build a prototype that is a first version of the system and develop it into the final system. We saw, however, that there is no contradiction between the two approaches: we can start with a–possibly executable–specification that is our first prototype. The organizational issues related to this topic will be discussed in Chapter 7. In the next chapter, we will examine one of the most important uses of specifications–that of software verification.

FURTHER EXERCISES

5.51   Consider the following specification of a change command for a word processor:

change (p,q) **is defined by**:
for any sequence of characters s in the text
        if p = s **then**
            replace p by q;

          end if;
      end change;

Is this specification formal or informal? Is it operational or descriptive? Is it ambiguous or not?

5.52   Build an FSM that accepts the set of strings that contain an even number of 0's and an odd number of 1's, and that begin with 1 and end with 0.

5.53   Give an FSM description of a system consisting of several independent programs that share the same CPU, the same memory device, and the same I/O devices in such manner that access to them occurs in mutual exclusion.

5.54   Modify the preceding exercise by considering a system with different instances of physical resources (CPUs, disks, etc.), but in which programs may share some files. Is the model used in the previous case still adequate? Why?

5.55   Show that any FSM can be "translated" into an equivalent PN–i.e., a PN whose set of acceptable firing sequences is the same as the transition sequences of the FSM. Also, show that the converse operation is not always possible.

How can you analyze the deadlock-freedom property by means of FSMs?

5.56   The processing time of some data often depends on some property of the data. For example, sorting a sequence of items depends on the size of the sequence. Imagine that some transition of a PN models a process of this type. Provide a modification of the timed PN model presented here that is able to cope with this case.

5.57   Consider the portion of a PN given in Figure 5.45. Suppose you want to model a requirement of the type "Once a token is produced in place P_3, it can be consumed, either through transition t_1 or through transition t_2, within a time t_{max}. If neither of these alternatives happens, the token cannot be consumed any more." Show that timed PNs as defined in this chapter cannot describe such a requirement. Outline an alternative way of defining timed PNs that could cope with this problem.

5.58   Complete the specification of the elevator system given in Section 5.5.3.2 with a description of the emergency button and its effects.

5.59   Complete the specification of the elevator system given in Section 5.5.3.2 by describing the opening and closing of the doors.

5.60   Modify the specification of the elevator system given in Section 5.5.3.2 by taking into account the fact that Δt–the transfer time between two adjacent floors–depends on whether an elevator does or does not stop at a floor. Consider also the case in which the elevator moves from a floor where it is standing.

5.61   Sketch how the elevator system described in Section 5.5.3.2 could be specified in terms of FSMs. You don't need to go into all the details. Rather, you should point out what FSMs are able to describe and where they fail to capture the desired requirements.

5.62   Use PNs to model office organization and automation. You should describe all relevant activities that occur in the office (producing documents, computing invoices and salaries, etc.), the data they involve and the way they operate on them, and the precedence relations between different activities (e.g., one cannot mail a letter if it has not been written). You do not need to produce a long list of activities and data stores. Rather, you should focus attention on *a few* of them and analyze them in some depth. You may refer to Section 5.7.1 for hints on this project.

5.63   Augment the ER diagram of Figure 5.38 so that you can specify the prerequisites for each class (i.e., which classes must be taken before taking the given class).

5.64 Give an ER diagram complementing the DFD of Figure 5.5, in order to describe the entities involved in the application and their relationships.

5.65 Give a logic specification for a program that computes the integer square root of nonnegative integers.

5.66 Augment the specification of Exercise 5.65 by imposing the requirement that, if the input value is negative, an appropriate error message is printed.

5.67 Go back to the specification of the search procedure (number 7) given in Section 5.6.2.2. Would it still be adequate if the variable table were a global variable instead of an input parameter?

5.68 Modify the logic specification of the elevator system by taking elevator acceleration into consideration.

5.69 Go back to the PN of Figure 5.30. Is it incomplete? Is it inconsistent? Why?

5.70 Describe, in both an operational style and a descriptive style, the following *problem* (not its solution!):

A farmer has to carry a goat, a cabbage, and a wolf from one side of a river to the other side. She has a boat to do so, but the boat cannot carry more than three items, whether farmer, goat, cabbage, or wolf. If she leaves both the goat and the cabbage on the same side of the river or in the boat, without being present, the goat will eat the cabbage. Similarly, the wolf will eat the goat if left unattended.

Compare the two specifications from several points of view.

5.71 Describe, in both an operational style and a descriptive style, the fact that a fixed number of processes can access any of a fixed number of common resources in mutual exclusion. Compare the two specifications.

5.72 Write a paper comparing the specification of Section 5.5.3.2 with the specification of Section 5.6.2.3 from several points of view.

5.73 Here is an example of a real-time specification that does not involve mission-critical systems (it has been mentioned in Section 2.3.2). In the Macintosh personal computer, the user may use the mouse by clicking or *double-clicking* it. If two clicks occur within a given time Δt, their meaning is different from the case in which they are separated by a longer time interval. Describe the Macintosh click and double-click semantics both in an operational–e.g., by means of timed PNs–and in a logic style. Compare the two specifications.

5.74 Build a PN interpreter that will work both interactively and in batch. In the former case, the nondeterminism of the model can be resolved by the user through a dialog. In the latter case, nondeterministic choices should be taken randomly, but the user should be able to give appropriate scheduling options before execution, possibly on the basis of previous experiences. For instance, one could ask for "complete execution." In this case, the interpreter should provide all firing sequences, up to a predefined point. Alternatively, one could start from an existing firing sequence and ask for a change in some firing choices to obtain a new firing sequence as a modification of the previous one.

5.75 How could you analyze the property of equivalence between two different systems described in terms of FSMs? Could you make use of an FSM interpreter?

5.76 Give a complete description of the library system described in Figures 5.4 and 5.5, possibly integrating the use of DFDs with other notations.

5.77 Give an algebraic specification of the module FIFO_CARS introduced in Example 4.9.

5.78 Discuss an enrichment of the Larch specification language described in Section 5.7.2.1 by allowing genericity.

5.79 The signatures of algebraic specifications are often given in graphical notation wherein sorts are represented by nodes and operations are represented by multisource arrows going from the domain to the range. Figure 5.46 describes the signature of the StringSpec algebra.

Define a new version of the Larch shared language that is based on the graphical representation of the signature. (The semantic equations may still be defined textually.) Then, define translation mechanisms into the Larch/Pascal interface language that is still textual.

5.80 Define a specification-design language for algebraic equations based on Larch and on the design notation of Section 4.2.3.1. Give examples of the use of this language, and sketch its translation into a programming language. The main idea is to move from the definition of an algebra to the definition of an abstract data type by specifying which operations become procedures and which become functions.

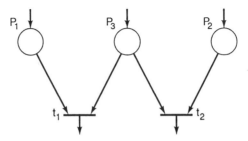

Figure 5.45   A portion of a Petri net.

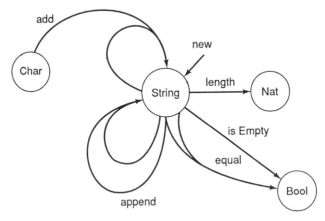

Figure 5.46   Graphical representation of the signature of StringAlg. (Multiple arrows do not define the *order* of the operands. If this is relevant, a suitable graphical convention must be given.)

5.81 Give *examples* of translations from DFD descriptions into skeletons of code in some programming language, e.g., the declarative part of an Ada package. You do *not* need to define *algorithms* for the translation.

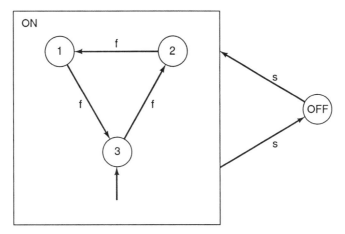

Figure 5.47   An OR chart describing a room-lighting system.

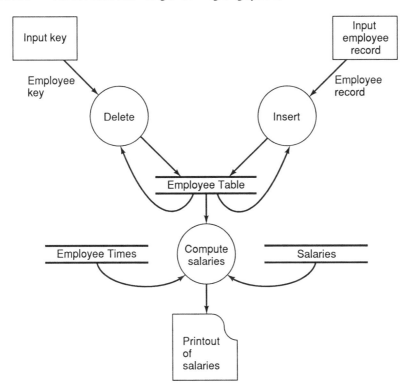

Figure 5.48   A DFD describing part the computation of employees' salaries.

5.82   Give constructs to build modular logic specifications. You may borrow ideas from Larch or from programming languages.

5.83 Discuss how to build modular PNs.

5.84 Give rules to build complex DFDs by stepwise refinement of higher level ones.

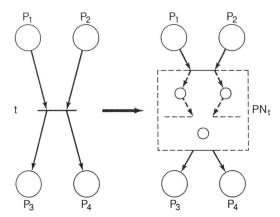

Figure 5.49   Refinement of a Petri net transition.

HINTS AND SKETCHY SOLUTIONS

5.19 **a.** In point 4, what does "with all floors given equal priority"mean ?

- That all floors must be served in a nondeterministic way, provided that eventually they will be served?
- That all floors must be served in a FIFO way?
- Consider the case in which there are two elevators at floor 2, with one request for floor 60 and one request for floor 3. Then both elevators go to floor 60 first, and then both go to floor 3. Is this case compatible with the specification?

b. Why do points 4 and 5 state different requirements for external and internal requests? (Point 5 is more precise than point 4.)

c. From the point of view of the *organization* of the specifications, it should be noticed that there is a mixture of specifications defining the behavior of the system (e.g., switching buttons), specifications stating requirements on system properties (e.g., "all requests must be serviced"), and specifications on scheduling decisions ("the algorithm...should minimize...").

5.24 In the general case, the token in place SCHEDULER should contain information about the whole state of the system, i.e., elevator positions and button illuminations, because the waiting times depend on these. Once this information is stored in SCHEDULER, a *decision* function could be attached to a transition connected only to SCHEDULER. Such a function embeds the algorithm chosen to minimize waiting times and must be computed in a time that is negligible with respect to the dynamics of the system. In other words, the maximum time associated with the transition must be very small compared with the time Δt that is required for an elevator's moving from one floor to an adjacent one.

5.25 Introduce a third entity, PROFICIENCY, and define a ternary relation.

5.31 The informal specification did not state how many blanks could exist between two consecutive words. Also, it was not stated whether the terminator '#' should immediately follow the last character of the last word or whether a blank was needed before it. The formal specification makes this clear. It is quite easy to change options if desired.

5.32 No. The procedure

```
procedure sort (a: in out integer_array) is
begin
        for i in a'first. . a'last loop
            a (i) := i;
        end loop;
end
```

would satisfy the given requirement.

An appropriate specification for a sorting procedure is

```
{n > 0}
P
{perm(a,old_a) and sorted (a,n)}
```

where perm (x, y) states that x is a *permutation* of y. (However, when giving a full definition of perm, you should pay attention to the case in which some element occurs more than once in the array.)

5.40 The new operation name : Text $\rightarrow$ Identifier is defined; the other operations are modified accordingly–for instance,

newF: Identifier $\rightarrow$ Text.

A sample of semantics modification is the following.

```
name (newF (id)) = id;
if name (f1) = name (f2) then f1 = f2;
if (equalF(f, appendF (f1, f2)) and (length F (f1) = cursor) and name (f) = id) then
(insertF (id, cursor, s) = appendF (addF (f1,s), f2) and name (insertF (id, cursor, s) = id)
```

5.41 (Second part)

First, the range of the operation is the Cartesian product Bool $\times$ Nat, with obvious restrictions.

Second, if s is the empty string, it always occurs in f in any position.

Third, what if s occurs several times in f? What if some occurrences are intersecting? Some of these remarks apply even to the change command.

5.48 We saw in Chapter 4 that the INHERITS_FROM relation is still quite controversial and different definitions are given for it in different languages. Whenever unconstrained redefinition of inherited operations is allowed, it makes inheritance different from **assumes**, since **assumes** can only add new properties to the inherited operations, without canceling previous equations. There are Object-Oriented languages, however, that at least aim at a semantics of the inheritance relation that coincides with **assumes**.

5.50 An example of systems that can be usefully described through OR charts is the following:

A room-lighting system consists of three lamps. The system is operated by two different buttons. One switches the system from off to on and conversely. The other flips illumination among the three lamps in a circular way. Figure 5.47 gives an OR chart for the system.

5.55 PNs can have an infinite number of states because in some cases the marking of places can grow unboundedly.

5.57 A simple solution consists of attaching pairs $\langle t_{min}, t_{max} \rangle$ to places, instead of transitions. Thus, if a token is produced into a place P, it cannot be consumed before t_{min} has elapsed. Furthermore, if at time t_{max} an output transition of P is enabled, it must fire at t_{max}; if several are enabled, the choice is, as usual, nondeterministic. If t_{max} elapses and the token has not been consumed, it can never be consumed by any transition, i.e., it is "lost."

A more general solution that could handle many different timing situations is outlined as follows.

Each token carries a *time stamp*, which is a value representing the time when it has been produced. Predicates associated with transitions are defined on the time stamps of the tokens in the input places. A definition of the semantics of these nets is given by Ghezzi et al. [1989].

5.67 No, because the procedure could modify table during execution. In this case, the output assertion would require the variable found to be true if and only if the value element exists in table after execution, not before. Thus, the postcondition should be changed by using *old_*table instead of table.

5.72 Simulating PNs is simpler and more natural than simulating logical specifications by deductions, whether this is done by hand or automatically. By contrast, analyzing properties is perhaps easier in logic.

Dealing with–and changing–implementation policies is easier in a logic style. In fact, for PNs, we could need strong changes in the model.

"Putting together" several components of the specifications is perhaps more complex with PNs. In fact, the graphical representation becomes unmanageable. The difficulty is in checking possible inconsistencies among several components. In a set of logical rules, we have the same problem, but following the flow of logical deductions to check possible inconsistencies is perhaps more systematic.

5.78 Apply the same examples and techniques used in Chapter 4.

5.81 The DFD of Figure 5.48 can be translated into the Ada package interface outlined as follows.

```
package Employees is
        Empl_Table:...
        Empl_Record:... --contains an Empl_Key declaration--
        Empl_Time:...
        Salaries:...
        procedure Insert (Empl_Record: in...; Empl_Table: in out...);
        procedure Delete (Empl_Key: in...; Empl_Table: in out...);
        procedure Comp_Sal (Empl_Times: in...;
                                    Empl_Table: in...; Salaries: out...);
    end Employees;
```

5.83 PNs can be described in several structured ways. In particular, one could see a transition as describing a fairly complex activity that could be further detailed by suitable subnets. Figure 5.49 gives a hint on how to produce this kind of *refinement*. Alternatively, one could define several components of a PN as independent subnets. That are to be aggregated by following suitable *composition rules*. Figures 5.22 and 5.23 can be used as a source of inspiration for defining such rules.

5.84   Apply *functional decomposition* to operations denoted by bubbles. For instance, a "compute salary" function may be decomposed into "compute number of hours at work," "compute gross salary," "compute taxes," and "compute net salary."

BIBLIOGRAPHIC NOTES

Cohen et al. [1986] and Gehani and McGettrick [1986] are two monographs on software specification. Davis [1988] compares different specification techniques, expanded to book form in Davis [1990]. For the basic terminology on specification refer, to the IEEE Standards [1989].

Boehm [1984b] distinguishes between verification (compliance with the specified requirements) and validation (the system serves its intended purpose). Parnas [1972a] is a seminal paper advocating a clear distinction between specification and implementation. Parnas [1977] provides a lucid introduction to, and requirements for, specifications. Heninger [1980] is an example of rigorously structured specifications based on natural language.

Data flow diagrams are one of the most popular notations for software specification. They are presented, in many slightly different versions, in many papers and books such as DeMarco [1978]. Ward and Mellor [1985] have extended DFDs with control flow arrows and other features in order to make them suitable for real-time systems analysis and specification. Real-time specifications are also described by Hatley and Pirbhai [1987].

FSMs are probably the most widely known, most simple, and most used model in computer science. They are described in much detail in many different textbooks, such as Mandrioli and Ghezzi [1987].

Petri nets are due to Petri [1972], who defined them originally to describe interacting finite state machines. They are described by Peterson [1981] and Reisig [1985]. Among the many variations and extensions that have been proposed for the basic model, we mention predicate-transition networks by Genrich [1987], in which tokens are allowed to carry values and the firing of transitions may depend on those values through predicates that are associated with transitions. Time has been added to Petri nets in several ways; the one presented here is due to Merlin and Farber [1975]. Ghezzi et al. [1989a] present a general way to introduce time into Petri nets. AjmoneMarsan et al. [1984] propose a stochastic extension, by making the firing of transitions probabilistic.

The case study on the elevator system has been used extensively in the literature as a benchmark for specification methods and languages. The informal definition presented here is taken from the call for papers of the 4th IEEE International Workshop on Software Specification and Design [1987], where it was explicitly proposed as a challenging exercise. Its formalization in terms of Petri nets is from Ghezzi and Mandrioli [1987].

The entity-relationship model was introduced by Chen [1976].

The application of mathematical logic to computer science was pioneered by McCarthy [1963], Floyd [1967], and Hoare [1969]. The text by Manna and Waldinger

[1985] is an excellent introduction to mathematical logic, with particular emphasis on computer science applications. A shorter introduction is also provided in the theoretical computer science text by Mandrioli and Ghezzi [1987]. The application of logic to the specification of concurrent and real-time systems has been undertaken on the basis of the initial work of Hoare [1972].

Much interest is presently devoted to the use of temporal logic. A good tutorial on this extension to classical logic and its applications to computer science is provided by Kroeger [1987]. Ostroff [1989] discusses the application of temporal logic to real-time systems. The elevator formalization in terms of logic is taken from Garzotto et al. [1987].

The use of algebraic formalisms for software specification has been advocated by several researchers. Initial efforts were due to Guttag [1977] and Goguen et al. [1975]. The language Larch discussed in this chapter is due to Guttag and Horning [1983, 1986a and 1986b] and Guttag et al. [1985a and 1985b]. Jalote [1989] discusses how to test the completeness of specifications given in an algebraic style.

A similar approach is taken by specifications based on assertions about *traces*. These assertions state desired properties of sequences of calls to the functions provided by a given module. They have been introduced by Bartussek and Parnas [1978] and formalized by McLean [1984].

CCS (calculus of communicating systems), due to Milner [1980], is a well-known and extensively studied algebraic approach to the specification of concurrent systems.

Two other important examples of specification languages that have found industrial application are VDM (Vienna definition method), presented by Bjorner [1982], Bjorner and Prehn [1983], and Jones [1986a and b]; and Z, presented by Spivey [1989]. Both languages are based mainly on the so-called *denotational approach* to formal semantics. This is a descriptive method that consists of defining the meaning of a notation as the solution (minimal fixed point) of a suitable set of equations in suitable domains.

Many specification languages have been developed on the basis of the models presented in this chapter. Some of them have been associated with appropriate tools to support their use. A partial list of these languages is the following:

- RSL (Requirement Statement Language) is based on the so called R-Nets–a semiformal extension of FSMs. It is part of the Software Requirements Engineering Methodology (SREM) developed by TRW for the U.S. Strategic Defense Command. RSL is presented by Alford [1977].
- PSL (Problem Statement Language) is an operational language developed by Teichrow and Hershey [1977]. It is a computer-aided technique for structured documentation and analysis of information processing systems.
- SADT has been developed by Ross [1977] as part of a complete methodology.
- PAISLey (Process-oriented, Applicative and Interpretable Specification Language) has been described by Zave [1982 and 1984]. Zave and Schell [1986] present the support environment for PAISLey.
- Statecharts is a specification language for reactive, real-time systems. It is based on an extension of FSMs–as mentioned in Section 5.7.2.2. Statecharts are described by Harel et al. [1990].

- Prot-Nets are an extension of Petri nets in which tokens have values and firing times are attached to transitions. They have been developed by Bruno and Marchetto [1986].
- Ina-Jo is a specification language developed by System Development Corporation. The language is based on first-order predicate calculus. It is discussed by Berry [1987] and Wing and Nixon [1989].
- ASLAN, developed by Auernheimer and Kemmerer [1985], is also based on first-order predicate calculus. It has been extended to deal with real-time systems by Auernheimer and Kemmerer [1986].
- AFFIRM is a specification language based on algebraic techniques and presented by Musser [1980]. Sunshine et al. [1982] discuss its application to the specification and verification of communication protocols.,
- OBJ2 is a specification language that derives from Goguen's early work on algebraic specifications. The language is described by Futatsugi et al. [1985]; Nakagawa et al [1988] describe a practical application of the language.
- PLUSS is another algebraic specification language (Bidoit et al. [1985]).
- LOTOS is a specification language for communications applications, based on Milner's CCS. It is described by Bolognesi and Brinksma [1987].
- RT-Lucid, described by Skillicorn and Glasgow [1989], is a data flow-based language extended to cope with timing aspects.

Other specification languages and techniques are reviewed and compared by Davis [1988 and 1990] and by Yadav et al. [1988].

Writing specifications is difficult and error prone. This is why we need to verify (validate) them, according to Boehm [1984]. The issue of executing specifications has been advocated by Kemmerer [1985]. Prototyping is discussed by Luqi and Ketabchi [1988], Luqi et al. [1988]. The special issue of *IEEE Computer* edited by Tanik and Yeh (Computer [1989a]) may be consulted for a sample of rapid prototyping techniques and applications. Boehm et al. [1984] compare software design based on specification with an approach based on prototyping.

Moriconi and Hare [1986] and Harel [1988] advocate the use of *visual languages* to make specifications more understandable. Roman and Cox [1989] illustrate the use of animation for visualizing concurrent computations. An interesting special case of animation applied to scientific computing is reported in the special issue of *IEEE Computer* edited by Nielson (Computer [1989]).

An eclectic approach to writing specifications has been advocated by Ghezzi and Mandrioli [1987] and Sanden [1989b].

Chapter 6

Verification

In Chapters 3, 4, and 5, we have seen how to develop software methodically so that the product meets its intended uses. In a perfect world, we could stop here.

Human beings, however, are fallible, and they make mistakes: even if they adopt the most sophisticated and thoughtful design techniques, erroneous results can never be avoided *a priori*. Consequently, the product of any engineering activity–a bridge, an automobile, a television set, or a word processor–must be *verified* against its requirements throughout its development.

During the design and construction of, say, a bridge, one must repeatedly verify the product in all its intermediate development stages. For instance, the first blueprints of the bridge are verified by using suitable equations to forecast whether the bridge will sustain the required loading. Possibly, a physical model is also built to further enhance the reliability of the forecast. Finally, in some cases, the real bridge is checked by loading it with a number of trucks of a given weight before opening it to the public.

Not only the *products* of bridge design and construction are verified, but even the *process* must be checked. For instance, before starting the actual construction of the bridge, one should verify that the building site has been prepared appropriately–maybe including schools for the children of the workers if the bridge has to be built in an undeveloped area. There are even government agencies that must approve the design before any work can begin. The site, likewise, must be prepared by the contractor and approved by an appropriate agency.

Software, of course, must be verified in much the same spirit. In the present chapter, however, we will learn that verifying software is perhaps more difficult than verifying other engineering products. We will try to clarify why this is so.

This chapter is devoted to software verification and is organized as follows. First, the goals and requirements of the verification activity are discussed. Then, major verification techniques are presented, compared, and evaluated.

Before we proceed with the technical details, however, we should discuss some issues regarding terminology. The field of software verification is progressing rapidly, and there is no consistent terminology. The terms *verification* and *validation*, in particular, are used with many, often inconsistent, meanings. We will avoid the term *validation* and only use *verification* in this chapter. By verification, we mean all activities that are undertaken to ascertain that the software meets its objectives. As we will see, these efforts encompass a wide spectrum, including testing and mathematical proofs as well as informal reasoning.

At the beginning of the chapter, we will use the terms error and defect interchangeably in place of the more common and affectionate (but sloppy) term, "bug." We will define these and other terms more precisely later in the chapter.

6.1 GOALS AND REQUIREMENTS OF VERIFICATION

Just as in the bridge verification example and any other engineering work, both the process of software development and all of its products must be verified. With small programs, with programs we write for our own use, and with programs that do not have critical requirements to meet, program verification often consists of trying a few sample cases to see whether the results of running the code match our expectations. Although this practice is unprofessional and cannot be approved even for such simple programs, the consequence of errors in these cases can usually be tolerated. Unfortunately, people are often tempted to carry over this same approach to the verification of software *products*.

Trying a few sample cases, however, is too limited to provide us with any confidence in the software. In fact, even if after such testing one could be confident that the product computed the desired function–although we will see that this will never be obtained in an absolute way–we would still be quite far from software that we can trust: the software might perform poorly, or its documentation might be inadequate, preventing its effective use or its evolution. Furthermore, performing verification only after the running code is available would make it very difficult to repair any defects that were detected. Experimental data from practical projects have shown that the cost of removing an error after the software has been completely developed is much higher than if errors are eliminated earlier.

In sum, the verification activity–just like other software design activities–must follow rigorous principles and suitable techniques; it cannot be left exclusively to human insight, experience, or luck.

Let us now go through the requirements for verification in a more systematic way.

6.1.1 Everything Must Be Verified

In principle, all design processes and all of the products os these processes must be verified. We already have discussed the issue of verifying specifications in Chapter 5, and we showed that simulation and property analysis are two means for achieving it.

In some sense, even *verification must be verified*. In fact, once we have tested a system for proper behavior, we should check whether our experiments were made properly themselves. Verifying the validity of experiments is standard practice in established scientific disciplines. Going back to the bridge example, after having tested the strength of the bridge in several cases, we should check whether all the experiments have been carried out in the right way and whether more experiments are needed. Similarly, if we have been able to prove some desirable property of our system, we must critically analyze whether the proof we made is "correct." Of course, such a "recursive" application of the verification activity must eventually stop.

Also, *every software quality must be verified*. Not only must we check, through verification of correctness, whether the implemented software behaves according to the specification document(s), but also, we must certify the software's portability, performance, modifiability, etc.

The above remarks suggest that verification may be performed at different points of time by different people with different goals and by applying different techniques. For instance, in some cases it may be useful for a product to be verified by a person other than its implementer; in other cases, verification could be performed by applying precise algorithms, etc. These organizational issues will be treated in part in Chapters 7 and 9. Here, we are concerned mainly with principles and related techniques to be applied during the verification activity.

6.1.2 The Results of Verification May Not Be Binary

We tend to think of verification as a "yes or no" activity: after having performed as many tests as needed and as much analysis as required, eventually the result of the verification is either acceptance or rejection of the final product. Even though it is true that, ultimately, the producer either decides to deliver the product or not and the user decides to accept it or not, there are many verification activities whose results cannot be reduced to a binary answer.

As we observed in Chapter 2, even correctness itself, i.e., compliance with functional specifications, is a matter of degree. In other words, it cannot be stated that a piece of software is absolutely error free, but an approximation of ideal correctness is often considered satisfactory and may in some way be certified. It is common to hear or read sentences such as "The new release of this product corrects several errors," i.e., it is more correct than the previous release. This implies that:

- The presence of defects in large and complex software cannot be avoided completely in practice.

- Sometimes, some defects can be tolerated. (Recall from Chapter 2 that correctness is related to, but is not the same as, reliability or robustness.)

- In practice, correctness is relative. But, unfortunately, this does not imply that it is easy to measure.

Efficiency is a typical example of a software quality that can be exhibited at different levels. Efficiency is often explicitly mentioned in requirements documents and can be measured in several ways: for instance, it could be expressed as a complexity formula of the type "The time required to perform computations is given by the function $f(n)$ of the length n of the input stream"; or, one could experimentally build tables that state the number and kind of resources needed to run a system in several representative cases.

Furthermore, we will see at the end of this chapter that one can apply statistical criteria to define, measure, and thus verify reliability.

6.1.3 Verification May Be Objective Or Subjective

Some instances of verification may be the result of an objective activity, such as performing a test by supplying some input data to the system and checking the output, or measuring the response time of an interactive system to given stimuli.

Not all qualities, however, can be quantified in such an objective way. For instance, portability and maintainability can be made precise only by specifying an environment–porting a software system from a given architecture to another specific one, or modifying existing software in order to meet a precisely stated new requirement. In many cases, one would like to state a generic level of portability even though one is unable to specify exactly the technical features of possible new architectures. Similarly, one would like to estimate reusability even when one cannot specify exactly in which new context the software will have to be reused.

In such cases, objective measures must be replaced by or integrated with subjective estimates. For instance, we stated in Chapter 4 that the use of object-oriented techniques may be expected to enhance reusability. We substantiated this claim by providing examples showing that "essential parts" of existing code could be naturally adapted to operating conditions different from their original ones. Such a claim, however, could not be related to any objective measure of the reuse of code, say the number of lines of unaffected code. Even this rough quantification of reusability could be misleading: it would imply that complexity of software reuse is measured by the number of lines of code–an often assumed, but questionable, hypothesis.

Thus, one needs to estimate a level of modifiability even in the absence of an objective criterion to measure it.

Example 6.1

Consider the following real case showing how, in practice, reusability may be empirically evaluated. Manufacturer A wants to buy a screen-oriented editor to market with their new line of computers. Software vendor B claims to have developed an editor that could easily be adapted to various environments. The editor already runs on the processors that the manufacturer is using. What manufacturer A is really interested in is whether the editor may be adapted to support different kinds of terminals. B claims that this can be done easily and that the editor already supports many different types of terminals. In the absence of any objective measure for evolvability of the code, A and B agree on an experiment: A will try to add the support for a new terminal. If this can be done in less than a week, then A will buy the software. While the goal of "modifiability" was a subjective one for B during the development of the editor, it became the deciding factor for making the sale, based on a precise, although subjective, experiment.   ▮

Other aspects of software products are even more intrinsically subjective–after all, bridges and other artifacts may also be more or less beautiful. Certainly, understandability and user friendliness are by definition subject to human judgment, and such judgments may vary from person to person.

All this suggests that subjective evaluation must be a part of the whole verification process, even if the results of subjective evaluations are generally less dependable. In much the same way, despite its greater fallibility, subjective evaluation is not avoided in other engineering fields. Instead, precautions are taken to reduce the associated risks. For instance, committees–and supercommittees–are set up to contrast several opinions against each other.

6.1.4 Even Implicit Qualities Must Be Verified

The desired software qualities should be stated explicitly in the requirements specification document. Some requirements, however, may have been left out, either because they are implicit, or because they were forgotten. In Chapter 2 we used the term *robust* to characterize a software whose functional behavior remains acceptable, even in unspecified circumstances.

Let us consider the case of implicit requirements. For example, requirements for conventional EDP systems often state only functional requirements, and even those are often incomplete. This does not mean that such systems have no performance requirements. They are omitted because they are not considered to be critical, and they can be left to professional judgment and common sense. For instance, everybody should understand that a transaction at an automatic teller *normally* should not exceed one minute; and furthermore, the term "normally" should be quantified as–say–about 95% of the time.

Maintainability is a typical example of a software quality that is seldom explicitly asked for, yet is often highly desirable. We also saw that it is hardly quantifiable. This notwithstanding, a good software engineer should strive not only to design maintainable software, but also to verify the maintainability of the product during each step of the design process. For instance, once the requirements for a user interface are specified, one should ask how, when, and why they are likely to change. Similarly, suppose you have decided to buy some piece of software to be integrated into a system you are building. If you are not completely sure that such a piece of software will meet all your present and future needs, you should analyze the implications of changing your decision in the future, maybe by redeveloping the same piece of software. Example 6.1 illustrates this point: the software of company B was adequate for the needs of company A, but company A needed to perform an experiment to ensure that the decision to buy from company B would not preclude them from supporting different terminals later.

Exercise

6.1   Go back to the software qualities discussed in Chapter 2. Classify all of them with respect to the following verifiability issues:

    a.   Are they objective or subjective?

    b.   Are they binary or not?

    c.   Are they more or less relevant in different applications and environments?(Variability of relevance.)

6.2 APPROACHES TO VERIFICATION

There are two fundamental approaches to verification. The first consists of *experimenting with the behavior* of a product to see whether the product performs as expected (i.e., *testing* the product.) The other consists of *analyzing* the product–or any design documentation related to it–to deduce its correct operation as a logical consequence of the design decisions. The two categories of verification techniques are also classified as *dynamic* or *static,* since the former requires–by definition–executing the system to be verified, while the latter does not. Not surprisingly, the two techniques turn out to be nicely complementary.

We already saw an instance of the difference between dynamic and static verification in Chapter 5, when we discussed the issue of the verification of specifications. There, we distinguished between simulating the specifications and analyzing the properties that can be deduced from the specifications. In this chapter, we will focus our attention mainly on the verification of software correctness. As suggested in the previous section, however, much of the proposed techniques can and should be applied also to the verification of other qualities. We will provide some hints on this topic later in the chapter. In particular, we will discuss the problem of assessing the more subjective qualities, such as understandability and modifiability, and we will present some techniques for doing so, along with their difficulties and trouble spots.

The rest of this chapter is organized as follows. Section 6.3 addresses testing, and Section 6.4 deals with analysis. Section 6.5 introduces symbolic execution, a less standard, but promising technique that can be seen as a middle way between analysis and testing. Section 6.6 examines the role of debugging in software verification. Verification of other software qualities is discussed in Section 6.7.

6.3 TESTING

The most natural, and customary, way of verifying any piece of work is just to operate it in some representative situations and verify whether its behavior is as expected. In general, it is impossible to test it under all possible operating conditions. Thus, it is necessary to find suitable *test cases* that provide enough evidence that the desired behavior will be exhibited in all remaining cases. This is often a difficult, and sometimes even impossible, job. Furthermore, in the case of software testing, the usual analogies between traditional engineering fields and software engineering fail to provide useful suggestions.

Consider our familiar example of bridge construction, and assume you wish to test the bridge's ability to sustain weight. If you have verified that the bridge can sustain 1,000 tons, then it will sustain any weight less than or equal to 1,000 tons, under the same circumstances.

The same criterion cannot be applied to software, as shown by the following example.

Example 6.2

Consider the following binary search procedure:

```
procedure binary-search (key: in element; table: in elementTable;
        found: out Boolean) is
begin
        bottom := table'first; top := table'last;
        while bottom < top loop
            if (bottom + top) rem 2 ≠ 0 then
                middle := (bottom + top - 1) / 2;
            else
                middle := (bottom + top) / 2;
            end if;
            if key ≤ table (middle) then
                top := middle;
            else
                bottom := middle + 1;
            end if;
        end loop;
        found := key = table (middle);
end binary-search;
```

What happens if we leave out the **else** clause of the first **if** statement? The procedure will still work properly for all tables whose size is such that the **if** condition will always be true (i.e., the size is a power of 2), but this does not guarantee that it works properly for all tables of smaller size.   ∎

The difference between the software and the bridge stems from the fact that the features of most engineering constructions have a *continuity* property, so that we can rely on the fact that small differences in operating conditions–for example, between test operation and normal operation–will not result in dramatically different behaviors. Such a continuity property is totally lacking in software, as the above example emphasizes.

Testing is a critical activity in software engineering and should be performed as systematically as possible by stating clearly what result one expects from it and how one expects to obtain that result. On the contrary, often in practice, testing is performed in an unstructured way without applying any criterion. In the following sections, we first state testing goals and then give some precise terminology and explicitly point out the theoretical limitations of the testing activity. Finally, we explain testing strategies and how testing can be organized.

Exercise

6.2   Show that the procedure of Example 6.2 contains a subtle error: it does not work for tables of a certain size. Which size is that?

6.3.1 Goals for Testing

Program testing can be used to show the *presence* of bugs, but never to show their absence.

This famous statement by Dijkstra (in Dahl et al. [1972]) is a perfect synthesis of the goals of testing: if the results delivered by the system are different from the expected ones in just one case, this unequivocally shows that the system is incorrect; by contrast, a correct behavior of the system on a finite number of cases does not guarantee correctness in the general case. For instance, we could have built a program that behaves properly for even integer numbers but not odd numbers. Clearly, any number of tests with even input values will fail to show the error.

This, of course, does not imply that testing is useless in verifying software. We should simply keep in mind that no absolute certainty can be gained from a pure testing activity. On the other hand, absolute certainty can hardly be obtained on the basis of any human activity. Even mathematical proofs, which are a more reliable means of guaranteeing any property than informal reasoning, are error prone; many of them have even been found to contain errors after years of usage. Thus, testing should be considered only one of the means to analyze the behavior of a system and should be integrated with other verification techniques in order to enhance our confidence in system qualities as much as possible.

Testing should be based on sound and systematic techniques so that, after testing, we may have a better understanding of the product's reliability. For instance, a natural approach such as using randomly generated test cases turns out to be inappropriate in many situations. In fact, consider the following program fragment:

```
read (x); read (y);
if x = y then
        z := 2;
else
        z := 0;
end if;
```

```
      write (z);
```

Suppose that the programmer incorrectly wrote z := 2 instead of z := 22. The error is immediately discovered by supplying the program equal values for the variables x and y. If x and y are–say–integers, however, and we use a random number generator for supplying their values to the program, it is very unlikely that the condition x = y will be tested.

Testing should help *locate* errors, not just detect their presence. The result of testing should not be viewed as simply providing a Boolean answer to the question of whether the software works properly or not. Tests should be organized in a way that helps isolate errors. This information can then be used in *debugging*.

Testing should be *repeatable*, i.e., tests should be arranged in such a way that repeating the same experiment–supplying the same input data to the same piece of code– produces the same results. This remark sounds fairly obvious–even more so if we compare it with some classical experimental laws such as "At sea level, pure water will boil at 100 degrees centigrade–212 degrees Fahrenheit." Hard-to-repeat experiments, however, are not infrequent, and they are responsible for the major difficulties surrounding the debugging activity.

A major source of lack of repeatability in software testing is the influence of the execution environment on the semantics of erroneous programs. A typical example is the case of uninitialized variables. For instance, suppose that a piece of program contains the statement

```
      if x = 0 then
            write ("abnormal");
      else
            write ("normal") ;
      end if;
```

and that variable x is not initialized before this statement in the program code. Then if the language implementation does not provide any check against this type of error–which is often the case for reasons efficiency of execution–the statement will be executed by reading the contents of the physical memory cell corresponding to x. This will probably have an unpredictable value. Thus, in many executions of the program, we will read the output normal, but, in an absolutely unforeseeable way, some execution of the same program, with the same input data, will provide the opposite result. The issue of repeatability becomes even more critical with concurrent software.as we will see in Section 6.3.7.

Finally, testing should be *accurate*. This will increase the reliability of testing. Here, we should observe that the *accuracy* of the testing activity depends on the level of precision–and maybe even formality–of the software specifications. For instance, suppose that in a real-time system specification it has been stated that, as a consequence of input stimulus x, the system should produce output y within Δt milliseconds. This suggests using input x as a test to check whether the appropriate output y is produced within Δt milliseconds. But if the requirement reads "As a consequence of input stimulus x, the system should produce output y within Δt milliseconds, no matter which other events happen in the system during this time," a careful designer would probably test the system by supplying x in several different contexts, in order to check whether the response time is still acceptable in a busy system.

Furthermore, if a formula expresses a property of software outputs in a mathematical way, it will be easier to check, possibly automatically, whether the output produced exhibits that property. For instance, consider the formula

$$\{ \textbf{ for all } i \, (1 \leq i < n) \textbf{ implies } (a(i) \leq a(i+1)) \}$$

which specifies that the variable array a is sorted. By checking whether a satisfies this formula after program execution, we obtain an effective way to verify whether the program has produced a valid a.

Since it may be unclear whether the result of an execution is indeed correct, verifying it against a formal specification can enhance the reliability of the testing activity.

6.3.2 Theoretical Foundations of Testing

In this section, we introduce the testing terminology in a precise manner and show the limitations of testing from a mathematical point of view. The terminology, however, is not standardized, so that the same terms may be used somewhere else with a different meaning.

Let P be a program, and let D and R denote its input domain and its range, respectively; that is, D is the set of all data that can correctly be supplied to P, and the results of P's executions, if any, are elements of R. Obviously, both D and R may contain (possibly unbounded) sequences of data if P contains several I/O statements, perhaps embedded within loops.

For simplicity, we will assume that P behaves as a *function*–possibly partial[1]–with domain D and range R. This is quite often the case, at least for sequential programs. It is not difficult, however, to extend the basic definitions and properties to the more general case where P determines a *relation*[2] between D and R. Thus, we will denote the result of executing P on input datum d as P(d).

Let OR denote the requirement on output values of P as stated in P's specification– whether in a formal notation or not. Then, for a given d ∈ D, P is said to be *correct for* d if P(d) satisfies OR. Thus, P is correct if and only if it is correct for every d in D.

The presence of an *error* or *defect* is demonstrated by showing that P(d) is incorrect for some d–that is, that it does not satisfy the output requirements. We call such a situation a *failure*. A failure is a manifest symptom of the presence of an error. We know well, however, that the presence of an error does not necessarily cause a failure. Thus, testing tries to increase the likelihood that program errors cause program failures, by selecting appropriate test cases.

---

[1]The function may be partial since, for some input data, the result is undefined; i.e., a run-time error occurs.

[2]This may happen when P is coded in a language that deals with concurrency and/or nondeterminism.

A *fault* is an incorrect intermediate state that may be entered during program execution–say, a variable being assigned a value that is different from what it should be. Obviously, a failure occurs only if a fault happens during execution, and a fault occurs only if an error exists in the program, but the two converse statements do not hold, in general.

A *test case* is an element d of D. A *test set* T is a finite set of test cases, that is, a finite subset of D. P is correct for T if it is correct for all elements in T. In such a case, we also say that T is *successful*[1] for P.

A test set T is said to be *ideal* if, whenever P is incorrect, there exists a d ∈ T such that P is incorrect for d. In other words, an ideal test set always shows the existence of an error in a program, if an error exists. Obviously, for a correct program, any test set is ideal. Also, if T is an ideal test set and T is successful for P, then P is correct.

A *test selection criterion* C is a subset of 2_F^D, where 2_F^D denotes the set of all finite subsets of D. In other words, C specifies a condition that must be satisfied by a test set. For instance, for a program whose domain D is the set of integers, C could require that test sets contain at least three elements, one of them being negative, one positive, and one zero. A test set T *satisfies* C if it belongs to C. In general, C may be described by a suitable formula that must be satisfied by all elements of any of the subsets of D that belong to C. For example, the aforementioned requirement of C is described by the formula

$$C = \{<x_1, x_2, ..., x_n> \mid n \geq 3 \text{ and exists } i, j, k \, (x_i < 0, x_j = 0, x_k > 0)\}$$

A selection criterion C is *consistent* if, for any pair of test sets T_1 and T_2, both satisfying C, T_1 is successful if and only if T_2 is. Thus, if one is provided with a consistent criterion, there is no theoretical reason to make a specific choice of a test set among those satisfying C. We will later see, though, that there are practical reasons for preferring one test set over another.

A criterion C is *complete* if, whenever P is incorrect, there is an unsuccessful test set that satisfies C. Thus, were we provided with a consistent and complete criterion C, any test set T satisfying C could be used to decide P's correctness.

For instance, suppose that P is a program to sort sequences of integers and that P works properly only if the length of the sequence to be sorted is a power of two. Then a complete and consistent criterion for P is to request that any test contain at least one sequence whose length is not a power of two. By contrast, a criterion that requires that either all sequences in T have length that is a power of two, or none of them have this property, is complete but not consistent.

Finally, we say that a *testing criterion* C_1 is *finer* than C_2 if, for any program P, for every test set T_1 satisfying C_1, there exists a subset of T_1, say T_2, that satisfies C_2.

Unfortunately, none of the above definitions is *effective*: we cannot derive an algorithm that states whether an object–a program, a test set, or a criterion–has the desired property.

---

[1]Some authors define a test case's being successful in exactly the opposite way: a test succeeds if it causes the program to fail. See the bibliographic notes for more explanation on this definition.

First, consider the correctness of a program P. Suppose you may formally specify the functional requirements as a first-order formula FR (d, u), having d and u as free variables, and let P (d) be the function associated with the program. Then the correctness of P may be formally stated as

for all d **in** D, u **in** R (u = P(d) **implies** FR (d, u))

This statement, however, cannot be decided, since doing so would mean we would have to decide the truth of any first-order formula–an undecidable problem. Second, in some cases, it could even be impossible to decide whether a value d is in a test set T or not, depending on how T is defined–another well-known undecidable problem. Thus, it is impossible to decide whether a test is ideal, whether a criterion is consistent and/or complete, etc. These are in the long list of major program properties–such as correctness, termination, and equivalence–that are undecidable.

Furthermore, we will next see that many criteria used in practice are themselves undecidable, i.e., it is not decidable whether a given test set satisfies them or not, and whether there exists a test set that satisfies them. As always with undecidable problems, this means that full mechanization is not possible, and our approach to verification must be based on common sense and ingenuity. In practice, mechanical support tools can provide clerical help, but they require human interaction at some critical points.

The next section proposes and evaluates some possible criteria for the selection of test sets.

Exercise

6.3 We say that C_1 is *more reliable* than C_2 if, whenever a program P is incorrect, it cannot happen that a test set T_2 satisfying C_2 causes P's failure whereas T_1 satisfying C_1 does not. Show that C_1 *finer* than C_2 does not necessarily imply C_1 *more reliable* than C_2. Give a condition that guarantees such an implication.

6.3.3 Empirical Testing Principles

We observed that, in general, the only testing of any system that can provide absolute certainty about the correctness of system behavior is *exhaustive testing*, i.e., testing the system under all possible circumstances. Unfortunately, such testing can never be performed in practice. Thus, we need testing *strategies*, i.e., some criterion for selecting significant test cases. The notion of the *significance* of a test set, however, cannot be formalized, but it is an important intuitive notion, being an empirical approximation of the concept of an ideal test set.

A significant test case is a test case that has a high potential to uncover the presence of an error. Thus, the successful execution of a significant test case increases our confidence in the correctness of a program. Intuitively, rather than running a large number of test cases, our goal in testing should be to run a sufficient number of significant test cases. If a significant test set T_1 is a superset of another significant test set

T_2, we can certainly rely more on T_1 than on T_2. On the other hand, since testing is costly, we must limit the number of possible experiments.

Example 6.3

This simple example shows that the number of test cases in a test set does not necessarily contribute to the significance of the test set. Suppose you have written the following wrong program fragment to compute the maximum of two numbers:

```
if x > y then
        max := x;
else
        max := x;
end if;
```

In this case, the test set {x = 3, y = 2; x = 2, y = 3} is able to detect the error, whereas { x = 3, y = 2; x = 4, y = 3; x = 5, y = 1} is not, although it contains more test cases.   ∎

In spite of the theoretical limitations emphasized in the previous section, testing criteria are needed in practice to define significant test sets. A testing criterion attempts to group elements of the input domain into classes such that the elements of a given class are expected to behave in exactly the same way. This way, we can choose a single test case as representative of each class. If the classes D_i are such that $\cup D_i$ = D, we say that the testing criterion satisfies the *complete coverage principle*. We will see that many well-known practical testing criteria satisfy this principle.

Example 6.4

Suppose you have to build a program to compute the factorial of any number. The specification of the program reads as follows:

> If the input value n is < 0, then an appropriate error message must be printed. If $0 \leq n < 20$, then the exact value of n! must be printed. If $20 \leq n \leq 200$, then an approximate value of n! must be printed in floating point format, e.g., using some approximate method of numerical calculus. The admissible error is 0.1% of the exact value. Finally, if n > 200, the input *can* be rejected by printing an appropriate error message.

In this case, it is quite natural to divide the input domain into the classes {n < 0 }, {0 $\leq$ n < 20}, {20 $\leq$ n $\leq$ 200}, and {n > 200} and to use test sets containing one element from each class. Suppose that the results are correct for the data belonging to one test set, e.g., {-10,5,175}. Then the assertion that the program will behave correctly for any other value is just a reasonable expectation, not the truth!   ∎

If we divide the input domain into disjoint classes D_i such that $D_i \cap D_j$ = Ø for i ≠ j, i.e., if the classes constitute a *partition* of D, then there is no particular reason to choose one element over another as a class representative. The classes of Example 6.4 are an example of a partition. If the classes are not disjoint, however, we have the possibility of choosing representatives to minimize the number of test cases. For example, if $D_i \cap D_j \neq \varnothing$, a test case in $D_i \cap D_j$ exercises both D_i and D_j.

For instance, consider the following testing criterion: the program must be tested with classes D_1, D_2, and D_3 of values for x, where

$$D_1 = \{d_i|\ d_i \bmod 2 = 0\}$$
$$D_2 = \{d_i|\ d_i < 0\}$$
$$D_3 = \{d_i|\ d_i \bmod 2 \neq 0\}$$

Here, since $D_1 \cap D_2 \neq \varnothing$ and $D_2 \cap D_3 \neq \varnothing$, we can choose just two test cases to exercise the program and still satisfy the complete coverage principle. For instance, the test set {x = 48; x = - 37} would be acceptable.

The complete coverage principle is subject to many interpretations, including several trivial ones. At one extreme, we could insist that each class consist of a single element; this would lead to exhaustive testing, which has already been ruled out as infeasible. At the other extreme, we could group all input data into just one class, which would lead to trying the system in just one case. Thus, we may evaluate how good a testing criterion is based on how significant the representatives of the classes obtained by its decomposition are. The application of the principle to produce significant tests is quite a challenging task.

Ideally, the complete coverage principle should help approximate consistent and complete criteria in the following way. If the input domain D is decomposed into several subsets D_i, then a test set may be chosen such that it contains at least one representative from each D_i, with the goal that if a test set T_1 differs from T_2 only with respect to which representative is chosen from each set D_i, then the results of test sets T_1 and T_2 coincide (in terms of failure or success). In such a case, the partition would provide a consistent criterion. On the other hand, completeness would be achieved if, in case the program contains an error, there is at least one D_i such that any representative of D_i exposes the error. Although we know from the previous section that, in general, it is impossible to find such a decomposition in an automatic way, common sense and insight can help in finding subsets that exhibit some degree of consistency and completeness.

In Example 6.3, any test set that causes the execution of both branches of the **if-then-else** statement would most likely show the error in the program fragment, no matter which data are selected from the classes {x > y} and {x ≤ y}. As an exercise, the reader is invited to find the exceptions.

Thus, a careful selection of test cases, with the goal of satisfying the complete coverage principle, can in some sense approximate consistent and complete criteria. We can increase the reliability of such criteria by choosing more than one element from each class. For example, if we feel that a particular partition is "rather" consistent and complete, but that there could be some exceptions, we could improve the method by generating several cases–maybe randomly–from the same class.

It turns out that this general principle can be applied in many different–and sometimes complementary–ways. Next, we review how the testing activity can be organized in practice and how we can describe various empirical approaches to the determination of significant test sets in light of the complete coverage principle. We will do so by first distinguishing between *testing in the small* and *testing in the large*. Testing in the small addresses the issue of testing individual software components. Testing in the large, instead, addresses the issue of decomposing and organizing the testing activity according to the modular structure of complex programs. We discuss testing in the small in Section 6.3.4 and testing in the large in Section 6.3.5.

6.3.4 Testing in the Small

Testing in the small addresses the testing of individual modules. There are two main approaches: *white-box testing* and *black-box testing*. Testing a piece of software as a black box means operating the software without relying on any knowledge of the way it has been designed and coded. Test sets are developed, and their results evaluated, solely on the basis of the specification. By contrast, testing software as a white box means using information about the internal structure of the software and maybe even ignoring its specification. The choice of partitioning possible test cases for the program of Example 6.3 into the classes { x > y} and {x ≤ y} is an example of white-box testing, and Example 6.4 is an instance of black-box testing.

Intuitively, both strategies are useful and somewhat complementary. White-box testing tests what the program *does*, while black-box testing tests what it is *supposed to do*. Thus, they can both increase the level of confidence in the reliability of the component. The following two sections describe the two approaches in some detail.

6.3.4.1 White-box testing

White-box testing is also called *structural testing* because it uses the internal structure of the program to derive the test data. The following example illustrates the concept.

Example 6.5

Consider the following well-known algorithm of Euclid:

```
begin
        read (x); read (y);
        while x ≠ y loop
            if x > y then
                x := x - y;
            else
                y := y - x;
            end if;
        end loop;
        gcd : = x;
end;
```

Observe that the **while** condition suggests two possible cases to be exercised by tests: x = y and x ≠ y. In fact, in the former case, the program computes its output without executing the **while** loop at all. In the latter case, the loop is executed at least once. Thus, by supplying as input data x = 3, y = 3, and x = 4, y = 5, we obtain a first kind of "completeness" with respect to exercising the main loop.

Continuing with this strategy, we could refine the condition $x \neq y$ by exercising both the cases $x > y$ and $x < y$. Notice that by choosing, say, the test set $\{<x = 3, y = 3>, <x = 4, y = 3>, <x = 3, y = 4>\}$, we exercise the program in such a way that all of its statements are executed at least once. This is called the *statement coverage criterion* and is discussed next.   ∎

Statement coverage criterion. Intuitively, the statement coverage criterion is based on the observation that an error cannot be discovered if the parts of the program containing the error and generating the failure are not executed; thus, we should strive for complete coverage of statements. The criterion, however, has some obvious weaknesses.

First, it is clear that executing some statement once and observing that it behaves properly is no guarantee that it is correct. But this is a quite general remark that depends on the very nature of software.

Second, in block-structured languages, where statements may be part of more complex statements, it is not even clear what we mean by a *statement*. A natural assumption is to stick to the traditional BNF syntactic definition of programming languages and to assume as an *elementary statement* any statement that is derived from the <statement> nonterminal without producing any recursive occurrence of the same nonterminal. Thus, in a simple, conventional block-structured language, elementary statements are assignment statements, I/O statements, and procedure calls. With this assumption, the criterion can be stated as follows.

> **STATEMENT COVERAGE CRITERION.** Select a test set T such that, by executing P for each d in T, each elementary statement of P is executed at least once.

In general, the same input datum causes the execution of many statements. Thus, we are left with the problem of trying to minimize the number of test cases and still ensure the execution of all statements.

For instance, consider the following program fragment:

```
read (x); read (y);
if x > 0 then
        write ("1");
else
        write ("2");
end if;
if y > 0 then
        write ("3");
else
        write ("4");
end if;
```

Let us denote by I_1, I_2, W_1, W_2, W_3, and W_4 the first and second **if** statements and the write ("1"), write ("2"), write ("3"), and write ("4"), statements, respectively. Also, let D_i

denote the class of input values that cause execution of Wi, for i = 1,..., 4. Clearly, D_1 = {x > 0}, D2 = {x ≤ 0}, D3 = {y > 0}, and D4 = {y ≤ 0}. Thus, if a representative is chosen from each of the classes, we are guaranteed that all of W_1, W_2, W_3, and W_4 are executed at least once.

Therefore, we might choose the following test set:

$$\{<x = 2, y = 3>, <x = -13, y = 51>, <x = 97, y = 17>, <x = -1, y = -1>\}$$

This test set, however, is not minimal with respect to the criterion, since every input datum belongs to two classes. Thus, we may reduce the number of test cases to two, for example, by selecting the following representatives:

$$\{<x = -13, y = 51>, <x = 2, y = -3>\}$$

A weakness of the statement coverage criterion is illustrated by the following fragment:

```
if x < 0 then
          x := -x;
end if;
z := x;
```

Choosing a test set such that, at the beginning of execution of the fragment, x is negative, would result in the execution of all statements of the fragment. Not exercising the case x ≥ 0, however, is in some sense a lack of completeness. In fact, we could see the fragment as a short notation for

```
if x < 0 then
          x := -x;
else
          null;
end if;
z := x;
```

In this formulation, the statement coverage criterion would require executing even the **null** statement, and this experiment could show an error. Thus, different syntactic conventions could lead to different instantiations of the same criterion. We will deal with this problem later.

Edge coverage criterion

The complete coverage principle may also be applied to criteria on the basis of the program structure, described by a graphical representation of the program control flow. Assume again the case of a simple block-structured language.

For any program fragment P its *control flow graph* G_P is built inductively in the following way:

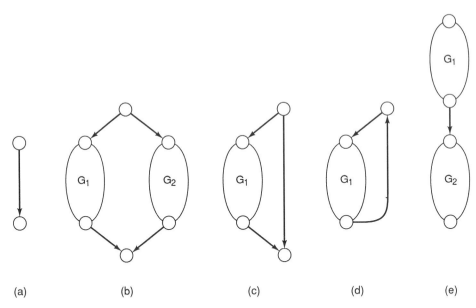

Figure 6.1   Construction of the control-flow graph of a program.
(**a**) Graph of an I/O, assignment, or procedure call statement.
(**b**) Graph of **if-then-else** statement. (**c**) Graph of **if-then** statement.
(**d**) Graph of **while** loop. (**e**) Graph of two sequential statements.

1.   For each I/O, assignment, or procedure call statement, a graph of the type of
     Figure 6.1(a) is built. The graph has an edge, representing the statement.[1] The
     edge connects two nodes that represent entry into, and exit from, the statement.

     If needed, a unique label, labeling both the statement and the edge of the graph,
     may be used to make the correspondence between edges and statements
     explicit.

2.   Let S_1 and S_2 denote two statements, and G_1 and G_2, denote their
     corresponding graphs. Then

     • The graph of Figure 6.1(b) is associated with the statement

> **if** cond **then**
> S_1;
> **else**
> S_2;
> **end if**;

     • The graph of Figure 6.1(c) is associated with the statement

---

[1]More often, the control flow graph is defined in the literature by representing statements
with nodes.

if cond **then**
    S_1;
end if;

• The graph of Figure 6.1(d) is associated with the statement

while cond **loop**
    S_1;
end loop;

• The graph of Figure 6.1(e) is associated with the statement

S_1;
S_2;

Since we are interested in the flow of control in a program, we may consider a sequence of edges of the type of Figure 6.2, with no other edges leading to any node $n_2,\ldots, n_{k-1}$, or leaving any of them, as equivalent to a single edge going from n_1 to n_k. This construction may thus be used to simplify a control flow graph.

Figure 6.3 shows the control flow graph of Euclid's algorithm given in Example 6.5.

Once we have associated a control flow graph with a program fragment, we can state the following criterion:

EDGE COVERAGE CRITERION. Select a test set T such that, by executing P for each d in T, each edge of P's control flow graph is traversed at least once.

We can see that the test sets derived by the edge coverage criterion exercise all conditions that govern the control flow of the program, in the sense that the criterion requires test cases that make each condition generate both true and false values (at different times).The reader might prove that, in general, the edge coverage criterion produces different results from, and is finer than, the statement coverage criterion. As an exercise, the reader should also verify that the test we derived for Euclid's algorithm in Example 6.5 actually provides edge covering.

Condition coverage criterion

The edge coverage criterion can be further strengthened, to make it more likely to expose errors. Consider the following fragment, which searches for an element within a table (implemented as an array of items):

```
found := false;
if number_of_items ≠ 0 then counter := 1;
    while (not found) and counter < number_of_items loop
        if table (counter) = desired_element then
            found := true;
        end if;
        counter := counter + 1;
    end loop;
end if;
if found then write ("the desired element exists in the table");
else write ("the desired element does not exist in the table");
end if;
```

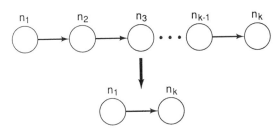

Figure 6.2   Equivalent portions of control flow graphs.

This code contains a trivial and common error: "<" appears instead of "≤" in the loop condition. Let us choose the following test sets:

1.   A table with no items, i.e., number_of_items = 0; this causes execution of the fragment without any iteration of the loop body.

2.   A table with three items, the second being the desired one; this causes execution of the loop body twice, the first time without executing the **then** branch, the second time executing it. Notice that both branches of the final **if-then-else** statement are executed, so that the edge coverage criterion is fulfilled.

The error is not discovered by the test set. Closer inspection of the program shows that the loop condition has two parts: "**not** found" and "counter < number_of_items". The two test cases we provided exercised the two possible values of the first part (one for each iteration), but only one of the possible outcomes of the second. A stricter criterion, requiring that both possible values of the second constituent of the condition are exercised, would have revealed the error.

In general, a compound Boolean expression may be true or false depending on the values of its constituent expressions. For example, if C is a compound Boolean expression written as the conjunction or disjunction of several elementary clauses (i.e., C is of the type c_1 **and** c_2 **or** c_3..., with c_i being either an atomic formula[1] or its negation,) then these atomic formulas are called constituents, and their values affect the value of C. Often, as in the example, the different values taken by each individual constituent expression characterize significant test cases.

We can thus derive a new testing criterion that is finer than the edge coverage criterion:

CONDITION COVERAGE CRITERION. Select a test set T such that, by executing P for each element in T, each edge of P's control flow graph is traversed, and all possible values of the constituents of compound conditions are exercised at least once.

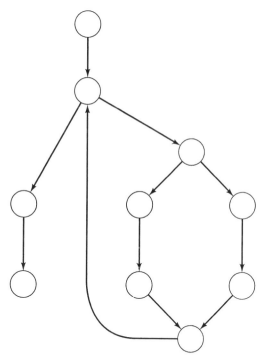

Figure 6.3   Control flow graph of Euclid's algorithm coded in Example 6.5.

Another way of looking at this situation is to observe that a statement like

if c_1 **and** c_2 **then**
        s_t;
    else

---

[1]An atomic formula consists of a relational expression (i.e., a relational operator such as =, $\neq$, or $\leq$, applied to arithmetic expressions) or a Boolean variable.

$$s_f;$$
end if;

is equivalent to

if c_1 **then**
   if c_2 **then**
     $s_t;$
   else
     $s_f;$
   end if;
  else
    $s_f;$
  end if;

If one applies the edge coverage criterion to the second form, one actually generates test sets that exercise all edges of the control flow graph and all possible values of atomic conditions. Thus, the condition coverage criterion enhances the edge coverage criterion by making explicit the edges that might be "hidden" in the control flow graph of the program.

The idea of exercising the various values of the constituents of the conditions has given rise to other criteria; the reader can find some interesting ones in Exercises 6.6 and 6.7.

Path coverage criterion

The following example, shows that the edge coverage criterion may fail to identify significant test cases.

Example 6.6

In the program fragment

if $x \neq 0$ **then**
  $y := 5;$
else
  $z := z - x;$
end if;
if $z > 1$ **then**
  $z := z / x;$
else
  $z := 0;$
end if;

the test set $\{<x = 0, z = 1>, <x = 1, z = 3>\}$ causes the execution of all edges but fails to show the risk of a division by zero. Such a risk would become evident by the test set $\{<x = 0, z = 3>, <x = 1, z = 1>\}$, which would exercise other possible flows of control through the fragment. ∎

Example 6.6 suggests that traversing single edges may not be enough to ensure the traversal of all important flows of execution. A natural extension would therefore lead to the following new testing criterion:

PATH COVERAGE CRITERION. Select a test set T such that, by executing P for each d in T, all paths leading from the initial to the final node of P's control flow graph are traversed.

Clearly, this new criterion is finer than the edge coverage criterion. In the above example, the path consisting of the **else-then** branches of the two **if** statements would have shown the error. Unfortunately, however, in the general case, the number of possible execution paths, even in simple programs, is very large–too large, in practice, if not infinite. Traversing all control paths is almost as infeasible as exercising all possible input data. Thus, the path coverage criterion turns out to be impractical in almost all cases.

The criterion, however, can be kept as a "reference guide" in order to determine a few critical paths, among the many possible ones, to be exercised. For instance, going back to the previous program fragment that searches for an element within a table, there is some intuitive evidence that an important sample of execution paths could be the following:

- Skipping the loop (the table is empty);
- Executing the loop once or twice and then finding the desired element;
- Searching the entire table without finding the desired element.

More generally, we could suggest the following empirical guideline for testing loops: Look for conditions that execute loops

1. zero times (or a minimum number of times in special cases such as repeat-until loops);
2. a maximum number of times;
3. an average number of times (according to some statistical criterion).

Furthermore, when dealing with complex combinations of alternatives (several **if** or **case** statements), one should try to combine paths as much as possible. The major source of complexity is nested loops.

Before closing this section, we wish to discuss an important point. After we have chosen a coverage criterion (say, statement coverage or edge coverage), we get to the point of determining actual input values that would guarantee fulfillment of the criterion. For instance, consider the following fragment, and suppose we are trying to follow the statement coverage criterion:[1]

---

[1]A similar reasoning applies to any other criterion.

```
read (x);
z := 2 * x;
if z = 4 then
        statement ...
```

Here, it is obvious that, if we want to execute the *statement*, we need to supply the value 2 to the read statement. In the following fragment, however, there is no input value that will cause the execution of *statement*.

```
if x > 0 then
        if x < 0 then
                statement ...
```

This example shows that coverage of *all* statements in a program may be impossible if the program contains unreachable statements. Of course, one may still reformulate the criterion by requiring that *all reachable statements* be covered at least once by test data. In the general case, however, it is not decidable whether suitable input data exist that guarantee the execution of some given statement in a given program–i.e., whether some given statement is reachable. Consequently, the criterion is not effective.

As a consequence, if we try to enforce the testing policy that "100% of statement coverage must be achieved," not only may the goal be unachievable, but also, we cannot decide algorithmically whether the 100% coverage was not reached because we were unable (or too lazy) to find test cases, or because of the presence of unreachable statements.

This is yet another case where the theory of testing unveils unsolvable problems: whatever coverage criterion we try to fulfill, we face problems that cannot be solved in a purely mechanical fashion, but require human intervention at some point. More will be said on this topic in Section 6.4.3. and in Chapter 9.

Finally, we anticipate that in Chapter 9 we will discuss tools that help evaluate the thoroughness of testing by computing the percentage of coverage reached, based on some coverage criterion. Such percentages can be used to "verify" the testing activity.

Exercises

6.4   Consider the following two program fragments:

a.

```
found := false; counter := 1;
while (not found) and counter < number_of_items loop
        if table (counter) = desired_element then
                found := true;
        end if;
        counter := counter + 1;
end loop;
if found then
```

```
                write ("the desired element exists in the table");
        else
                write ("the desired element does not exist in the table");
        end if;
```

b.

```
        found := false; counter := 1;
        while (not found) and counter < number_of_items loop
                found := table (counter) = desired_element;
                counter := counter + 1;
        end loop;
        if found then
                write ("the desired element exists in the table");
        else
                write ("the desired element does not exist in the table");
        end if;
```

State whether the edge coverage criterion may lead to different test sets in the two cases.

6.5   Let $\{C_i\}$ denote the set of all Boolean conditions used in a program P to govern the flow of execution. (For simplicity, we assume that control is driven only by Boolean conditions; for instance, **case** statements of Pascal are ruled out.) The edge coverage criterion requires that a test set $\{d_j\}$ must be such that each c_i is made true and false by some d_j at least once.

For each C_i, let D_i and $\overline{D}_i$ denote, respectively, the sets of input data that cause C_i to be true and false during P's execution. Then the edge coverage criterion is satisfied by test sets T that must contain at least one element of D_i and one element of $\overline{D}_i$ for each C_i. This does not define a partitioning of D, however. Why?

As a consequence, there may be different test sets, with different cardinality, satisfying the edge coverage criterion. Thus, the problem arises of finding minimal test sets that satisfy the criterion. For the following fragments, find minimal test sets compatible with the edge coverage criterion:

a.		b.		c.	
if x > z **then**		**if** x > z **then**		**if** x > z **then**	
	y := 3;		y := 3;		y := 3;
else		**else**		**else**	
	y := 2;		y := 2;		x := z + 2;
end if;		**end if**;		**end if**;	
if x > z + 1 **then**		**if** a > b **then**		**if** x > z + 1 **then**	
	w := 3;		w := 3;		w := 3;
else		**else**		**else**	
	w := 2;		w := 2;		w := 2;
end if;		**end if**;		**end if**;	

6.6   Let $\{C_i\}$ be defined as in Exercise 6.5. Consider the *truth assignment criterion* defined as follows:

Let $\langle tr_1,..., tr_n \rangle$ denote any truth assignment to conditions $\{C_i\}$, i.e., $\langle tr_1,..., tr_n \rangle$ is an n-tuple of Boolean values to be assigned to each condition of P. For any such assignment, let

D_r denote the set of values of D that make all C_i's true or false according to the assignment.

Show that $\{D_r\}$ is a partitioning of D. Show that the truth assignment criterion is finer than the edge coverage criterion.

6.7   Let $\{C_i\}$ be defined as in Exercise 6.5. The *multiple condition coverage criterion* can be defined as follows: each test set must make all conditions C_i true and false in all possible ways, based on the values of their constituents. For instance, if C_i is c_{i1} **and** c_{i2}, then we must generate four cases that would make c_{i1} true and c_{i2} true, c_{i1} false and c_{i2} true, etc.

Give (possibly minimal) test sets satisfying the multiple condition coverage criterion for the following program fragment.

```
if x > z and x > 3 then
        a := 1;
else
        a := 2;
end if;
if a > b or z < x then
        w := 1;
else
        z := x;
end if;
```

Clearly, the multiple condition coverage criterion is finer than the edge coverage criterion. Which is finer, the multiple condition coverage criterion or the truth assignment criterion? Which is finer, the multiple condition coverage criterion or the condition coverage criterion?

6.8   Would the truth assignment criterion guarantee the discovery of the error in the fragment of Example 6.6?

6.9   Compute the maximum number of possible execution paths for the two programs of Exercise 6.4 as a function of table size.

6.3.4.2 Black-box testing

Black-box testing, also called *functional testing*, is based on the definition of what a (piece of) program is intended to do, i.e., on the program's specification, rather than on its structure. We can apply the complete coverage principle to black-box testing. Suppose that the specification of a program reads:

> The program receives as input a record describing an invoice. (A detailed description of the format of the record is given.) The invoice must be inserted into a file of invoices that is sorted by date. The invoice must be inserted in the appropriate position: if other invoices exist in the file with the same date, then it should be inserted after the last one. Also, some consistency checks must be performed: the program should verify whether the customer is already in a corresponding file of customers, whether the customer's data in the two files match or not,... .

An intuitive way to test this program could be as follows:

1. Provide an invoice whose date is the current date.

2. Provide an invoice whose date is before the current date (in some systems this operation could be forbidden by law, depending on the country where the system is operated). This case, in turn, can be split into the two following subcases:

    2.1. Provide an invoice whose date is the same as that of some existing invoice.

    2.2. Provide an invoice whose date does not exist in any previously recorded invoice.

3. Provide several incorrect invoices, checking different types of inconsistencies.

This informal procedure is the result of decomposing the specifications into a set of relevant classes and analyzing the behavior of the program in at least one case for each class.

Here, again, we see a major motivation for being rigorous, and possibly even formal, in writing specifications: the more precisely the operating conditions of the system and the expected results are defined, the more precisely can one categorize input data and compare the observed results against the expected ones. Furthermore, when specifications are given in a formal notation, test sets could even be derived (semi)automatically by tools that apply the very same philosophy and technique as in the case of white-box testing.

Next, we present three approaches to white-box testing: *syntax-driven testing*, which is applicable to programs whose input is formally described by a grammar; *decision table-based testing*, which is applicable whenever a specification is described by a decision table; and the *cause-effect graphs* technique.

Syntax-driven testing

A classical example of the application of formal specifications to drive testing can be seen in compiler verification. In this case, we have a complete formal specification of the syntax of the language, namely its BNF or some equivalent definition. The specification can be used to generate test sets–i.e., sample programs to be compiled–in several ways. For instance, a simple criterion is to supply to the compiler a set of test programs such that each syntactic production of the BNF is applied at least once in some program. This criterion is called *syntax-driven testing*.

Example 6.7

Suppose your program is an interpreter of simple arithmetic expressions, defined by the following BNF grammar:

> <expression> ::= <expression> + <term>|<expression> - <term> | <term>
> <term> ::= <term> * <factor> | <term> / <factor> | <factor>
> <factor> ::= ident | (<expression>)

A way to do syntax-driven testing is to take any rule of the grammar (say, <term> ::= <term> * <factor>) and then generate a string, starting from the grammar's axiom

<expression> so that the rule is applied. This means that the complete coverage principle is applied here in such a way that all grammar rules are covered by at least one test case. For example, we might choose the following derivation:

<expression> ⇒ <expression> + <term> ⇒ <expression> + <term> * <factor>

We may then complete the generation in any way, e.g., by generating the shortest possible derivation:

<expression> + <term> * <factor> ⇒ <term> + <term> * <factor> ⇒
<factor> + <factor> * <factor> ⇒ ident + ident * ident

This procedure generates a test case for each rule of the grammar. Some rules, however, are exercised as a consequence of trying to exercise some other rule. For example, in the previous derivation, we exercised the following rules:

<expression> ::= <expression> + <term>
<term> ::= <factor>
<factor> ::= ident

We can therefore reduce the number of test cases by keeping track of the rules that have already been exercised by previous test cases.   ∎

The previous example shows that there are many ways of generating tests based on a grammar. For example, we chose to generate the shortest possible derivation that exercises each rule, but other strategies are also possible. In general, the syntax of most classical ALGOL-like languages is such that we can even generate a single program that would exercise all statements of the language. That is, the whole test set could consist of one rather long single test case.

Thus, the question arises as to what criteria should be followed to generate the test set. The notion of a *minimal test set* should be considered with some care in the case of syntax-driven testing. In fact, we usually refer to it by comparing the cardinality of two test sets T_1 and T_2. But should we consider a test set T_1 consisting of one program of 1,000 characters as preferable to a test set T_2 consisting of two programs of 100 characters each? Perhaps the sum of the lengths of the programs contained in the test set would be a better measure.

Exercises

6.10   Define a simple Pascal-like language by means of a BNF. Then find one or more test sets that satisfy the syntax-driven testing criterion. Is it possible to have a test set consisting of just one program?

6.11   Explain how syntax-directed techniques can be applied to programs that are not language processors.

Decision table-based testing

Decision tables are a simple formalism to describe how different combinations of inputs may generate different outputs. They are in practical use, especially in data processing applications. Their tabular form makes them easy to understand and supports a systematic derivation of tests. In what follows, we introduce them through an example.

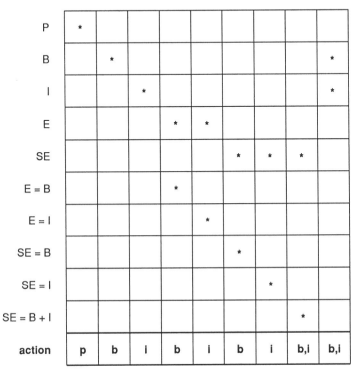

Table 6.1   Decision table specifying the word processor of Example 6.8.

Example 6.8

Consider the following informal specification for a word processor:

> The word processor may present portions of text in three different formats: plain text (p), boldface (b), and italics (i). The following commands may be applied to each portion of text: make text plain (P), make boldface (B), make italics (I), emphasize (E), superemphasize (SE). Commands are available to dynamically set E to mean either B or I. (We denote such commands as E = B and E = I, respectively.) Similarly, SE can be dynamically set to mean either B (command SE = B), or I (command SE = I), or B and I (command SE = B+I).

The decision table corresponding to the specification is given in Table 6.1. The table describes the conditions on the rows (here, the commands given to the word processor);

columns represent rules, i.e., the actions that are the result of the exercising conditions. As an example, the rule represented by the leftmost column of the table shows that condition P generates output p. (To avoid cluttering the table with too many entries, we show only true conditions, marked with an asterisk, "*".)

One can generate test cases naturally on the basis of the decision table, trying to apply the complete coverage criterion so that each column of the table is exercised by at least one test. This "blind" application of the principle, however, may be too expensive in terms of the number of experiments to be carried out, due to the exponential growth of the number of test classes with respect to the number of conditions. In fact, in general, the number of columns can go up to 2^n, where n is the number of conditions. Thus, we may need some technique to select a *significant subset* of all possible input classes. A way to tackle this problem is discussed in the next section. ∎

The cause-effect graph technique

The cause-effect graph technique is based on a formal way of structuring complex input-output specifications called *cause-effect graphing*. In order to apply cause-effect graphing, one must first transform the specification of inputs and outputs into Boolean values and the transformation performed by the program into a Boolean function. We describe the technique in the following example.

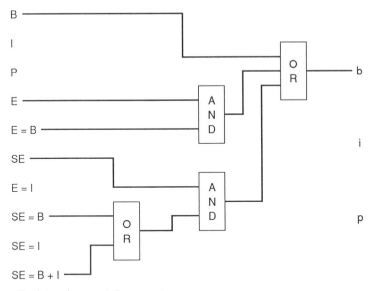

Figure 6.4   Partial and-or graph for a word processor.

Example 6.9

Consider the informal specification for a word processor given in Example 6.8. An input command in {B, I, P, E, SE, E = B, E = I, SE = B, SE = I, SE = B+I} can be represented by a 10-tuple of Booleans (called *causes*). Thus, for example, <true, false, false, false, false, false, false, false, false, false> represents command B, and <false, false, false, true,

false, true, false, false, false, false> represents E = B and E. The same technique obviously applies to outputs, called *effects*. In our example, an output is an element in {b, i, p}; for instance, <false, false, true> denotes a plain text output.

Once both the input and the output domains are restated in terms of Booleans representing causes and effects, the function is also restated as a Boolean function. In particular, it is synthesized as a combination of the logical operators **not, and,** and **or** and is graphically represented by using any one of the well-known techniques. Figure 6.4 gives a pictorial representation of how a boldface output may be obtained; the reader should complete the graph as an exercise.

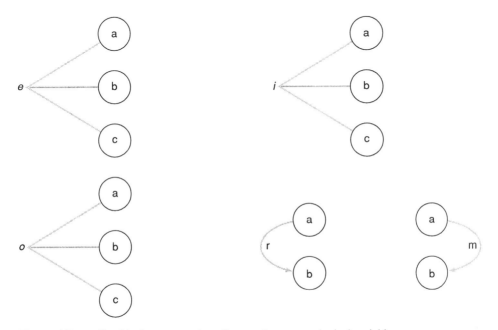

Figure 6.5   Graphical representation of constraints among logical variables.

Suppose now that the informal requirements also specify the following constraints:

Both B and I exclude P (e. g., one cannot ask for both plain text and italics for the same portion of text). E and SE are mutually exclusive.

In our example, since B and P are mutually exclusive, the tuple <true,false,true,...> would not describe legal input commands, because it would mean a request for both bold and plain text. The following notation may be used to specify *constraints*:

- A dotted connection labeled *e* of the type of Figure 6.5 joining the logical variables a, b, and c states that *at most one* among a, b, and c may be true.
- A dotted connection labeled *i* states that at least one of the arguments a, b, and c must be true.

•   A dotted connection labeled *o* states that one and only one of a, b, and c must be true.

•   A dotted directed connection from a to b labeled r states that a *requires* b, that is, a **implies** b.

•   A dotted directed connection from a to b labeled *m* states that a *masks* b, that is, a **implies not** b.

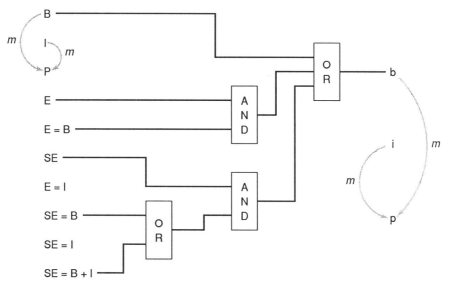

Figure 6.6   The fragment of Figure 6.4 augmented with diagram showing constraints among the variables.

Similar constraints can be imposed on output variables as well. When such constraints are specified on both inputs and outputs, their *compatibility* must be verified. Figure 6.6 is an enrichment of Figure 6.4 that displays all constraints on input and output variables.   ∎

The graph that is obtained by following the procedure set out in Example 6.9 is called the *cause-effect graph* of a program specification. The cause-effect graph can be used to drive program verification by applying the complete coverage principle in a fairly obvious way, i.e., by generating all possible combinations of inputs and checking whether the outputs correspond to the specification. Actually, it can also be used to assess the specification itself. In fact, it can show a possible inconsistency, if, say, the output corresponding to an admissible input violates the graph's compatibility constraints. Also, it can show possible incompleteness, if, say, no input value is found that supplies an admissible output.

If the size of the test set is considered excessive, the following procedure can be applied to reduce the size: for each admissible combination of output values, find *some* combinations of input values that cause that combination of output values by tracing back through the graph.[1] The combinations of input values are selected among all possible ones by means of the following heuristic rules:[2]

1. In tracing back through an **or** node whose output is true, we use only input combinations that have only one true value. This way, each cause is tried independently, based on the assumption that combining two causes does not alter the effect of each cause. For instance, if the output of an **or** node must be true, and l_1, l_2 are the inputs, we consider only $\{<l_1 = true, l_2 = false>, <l_1 = false, l_2 = true>\}$.

2. Similarly, in tracing back through an **and** node whose output is false, we use only input combinations that have only one false value.

Exercises

6.12   Consider a cause-effect graph in which you also represent constraints (e.g, take the graph shown in Figure 6.6). How can you represent constraints by means of a decision table?

6.13   Give a mathematical definition of how the input-output specification of a program may be transformed into a Boolean function, as required by the cause-effect graph technique. State when this approach is ineffective and when it is not applicable at all.

6.3.4.3 Testing boundary conditions

We have based our testing criteria–both white box and black box–mostly on partitioning the input domain of the program into suitable *classes*, on the assumption that the behavior of the program is "similar" for all elements of each class. Some typical programming errors, however, just happen to be at the boundary between different classes.

For instance, quite often programmers use '<' instead of '≤', or conversely. This error is unlikely to be detected by applying any of the previous techniques. It is also one of the main reasons why pure random testing works poorly.

More precisely, suppose that a program fragment is of the type

```
if x > y then
        S₁;
else
        S₂;
end if
```

Many of the white-box testing criteria would lead to selecting at least one pair of values for x and y such that x > y and at least one such that x ≤ y. This by no means implies that

---

[1]For simplicity, let us ignore any actions to be performed if some inconsistency or incompleteness is discovered during this procedure.

[2] These rules are a simplified version of those given by Myers [1979].

one has to select one pair with x = y, which would be the most natural way to detect the error of writing '>' instead of '≥'.

This remark leads to a natural suggestion: after having partitioned the input domain D into several classes, test the program using input values not only "inside" the classes, but even at their boundaries. Notice that the suggestion applies to white-box techniques as well as to black-box techniques. This natural way of complementing many of the previous testing criteria is usually called *testing boundary conditions*.

In practice, the different testing criteria should always be applied in combination, because none is completely effective by itself. We will ask you to ponder this point in Exercise 6.57.

6.3.5 Testing in the Large

So far, we have been concerned with testing single pieces of software, i.e., individual modules that will be combined with other modules to form a complete system. Actually, they could also be complete programs considered as a whole, i.e., programs whose testing was considered with respect to an overall definition of their expected behavior.

The combinatorial explosion of many of the techniques we illustrated in the previous sections might make them applicable only to small programs. Of course, when we are dealing with complex systems, we need techniques to master the complexity of their verification–and of their testing in particular–just as for their design and specification. The present section deals with this problem.

6.3.5.1 Testing and modularity

The organization of the testing activity should in some way reflect the organization of the design activity. This implies that the modular architecture of the system is a natural candidate to drive the verification of the system. Just as we build a complex system by first designing it as a collection of well-connected modules, we should be able to test modules separately, one by one, and eventually test the whole system. There are several obvious benefits in testing a system modularly: it is easier to localize errors; it is easier to discover them at early stages of development, and it is easier to classify errors according to their scope, i.e., whether they are design errors or coding errors, etc.

Thus, good design techniques result in better software, not only in the sense that the software is likely to contain less errors, but also in the sense that it is easier to catch and fix the errors that do occur. In other words, good design techniques enhance verifiability also.

We will discuss module testing, integration testing, and system testing. *Module testing* is intended to verify whether a given module has been implemented correctly with respect to its expected external behavior: no matter which modules are interacting with it, provided that these modules are using its interfaces correctly. *System testing* is intended to check whether a whole collection of modules behaves properly–possibly on the basis of the assumption that all of its constituent modules behave properly by themselves.

Systems are often integrated gradually: collections of modules are put together to form a subsystem, and this may be progressively integrated with other modules and/or subsystems. Partial systems may thus be created and tested. We call the testing that is performed while a system is being integrated *integration testing*. At the very final stage of integration that begets the whole system, integration testing coincides with system testing. In general, however, system testing is executed in the actual delivery environment (or as close as possible to it), as opposed to the development environment, in which module testing and integration testing take place. Depending on the application also, some levels of integration and system testing are not pure software testing–e.g, testing an embedded application consisting of the hardware and the software running on it.

6.3.5.2 Module testing in context

A single module should be tested on the basis of the techniques described as testing in the small. A module, however, often cannot be executed by itself. Using the terminology of Chapter 4, if M_i USES M_h and M_i USES M_k, then correct execution of M_i requires a correct version of M_h and M_k to be available. If we wish to execute M_i in isolation, e.g., since M_h and M_k are not yet available, then we need to provide a temporary *context* for M_i's execution that simulates the real context that will be provided by M_h and M_k.

Modules are ultimately mapped into different programming constructs–say, a procedure, a package, a task, or even a full program that cooperates in a system of programs interacting through an operating system to provide a complete application. In order to support the testing of a single module, we need a complete environment that provides all that is necessary for the execution of the module and is not included within the module itself. In particular, it may happen that

- the module uses an operation–say, it calls a procedure–that does not belong to it;
- it accesses nonlocal data structures; or
- it is itself used (called) by another module.

All these situations must be simulated in order to make the testing of the module possible.

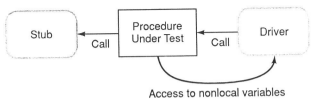

Figure 6.7   A procedure under test, with a stub providing a functional abstraction and a driver.

Consider the case of an external procedure call occurring during module execution. If the procedure that is called is not yet available(because it is still being developed), the simplest way to manage the call is to build a *stub*, i.e., a procedure that has the same I/O parameters as the missing procedure, but a highly simplified behavior. For example, it might produce its expected results by reading them from a file or asking them from a human tester interactively, or it might even do nothing and simply print some diagnostic message, should this be acceptable by the caller. The stub will then be linked with the module just as if it were the real procedure.

The following example shows the development of a stub to replace a sorting procedure. The procedure is intended to sort sequences of n integers according to the following declaration:

```
type sequence (max_size: NATURAL) is
        record
                size : INTEGER range 0. . max_size:= 0;
                contents = array (1..max_size) of INTEGER;
        end record;
```

The stub looks like this:

```
procedure sort (seq : in out sequence) is
begin
        write ("the sequence to be sorted is the following:");
        for i in 1 .. seq.size loop
            write (seq.contents (i));
        end loop;
        write ("enter the result of sorting the sequence");
        for i in 1 .. seq.size loop
            read (seq.contents (i));
        end loop;
        --- a safer version of the stub could verify the consistency of
        --- the user-supplied data with respect to procedure specification
    end sort;
```

In much the same way, one can build *drivers*, i.e., pieces of code that simulate the use of the module being tested by other modules of the system, and set the shared data as they would be set in the real application by other modules that are yet to be designed. Figure 6.7 gives an intuitive picture of a module being tested. The module consists of a procedure, together with a stub and a driver.

As an example of a driver, suppose that you have built a procedure (called insert_table) that inserts an item (of type element_type) in a table in the appropriate order. Suppose that procedures to initialize (init_table) and print (print_table) a table are already available; a procedure (input) is also available to read values of type element_type via suitable interaction with the user. Then a driver to help test procedure insert_table could be built along the following lines (the details are left to the reader as an exercise):

```
init_table;
input (el1);
insert_table (el1);
--check whether insertion was done properly
```

```
print_table;
input (el2);
insert_table (el2);
--check whether insertion was done properly
print _table;
        .
        .
        .
```

All the support software developed for module and integration testing, including the stubs, is sometimes called test *harness* or *scaffolding*. The term "scaffolding" is used in analogy to the scaffolding that is used to hold buildings up during their construction: they are not part of the final building, but they certainly are necessary.

Here we see another case where we can envisage the future use of formal, executable specifications when the appropriate technology is available. In fact, suppose that a module M has been formally specified by means of, say, a logic language that is executable. Then its formal specification can be easily turned into a stub that is more reliable and effective than, say, a stub that is completely simulated by user interaction.

Example 6.10

Imagine a module compute_monthly_incomes. To do its job, this module accesses a data base that stores all invoices issued by the company. Access to the data base is performed through appropriate procedures, which belong to a module DBM encapsulating all of the "secrets" of the data base. These procedures include a **select** operation that, given a predicate, returns an array of invoices that satisfy the predicate.

The DBM module is not available yet, so that compute_monthly_incomes requires a stub to be executed. The **select** operation allows queries to specify sophisticated and complex logical selection policies that cannot be handled by a conventional data-base system. So we cannot resort to conventional data bases as temporary stubs.

A possible solution to the problem of implementing compute_monthly_incomes without the DBM module, with present-day technology, might be to use the logical power of a language like PROLOG, provided that a suitable run-time connection is established between PROLOG and our programming language. In such a case, PROLOG may be viewed as an approximation to an executable specification language.   ∎

Exercises

6.14 Sometimes, your stub can use some existing facilities, provided, for example, by the operating system. Explain how to use the sort package provided on most systems in the above stub. If you can use the sort package in your stub, why not use it in the final product?

6.15 Suppose you have built a module that implements a complete abstract data type fifo_queue, provided with operations is_empty, enqueue, dequeue, etc., with their natural meaning. Build a facility to drive the execution of such a module, consisting of a small program that allows the user to test the module.

6.3.5.3 Bottom-up and top-down integration

integration testing can be performed by following different strategies. At one extreme, one could first test all of a system's modules separately and then the whole system at once. This is called *big-bang testing*. With big-bang testing, integration testing disappears, and we proceed abruptly from module testing to system testing. The problem with big-bang testing is that all intermodule dependencies are tested during the system test phase. If the system consists of many modules, there are many interactions being tested at once. A more disciplined approach is needed in order to test the intermodule dependencies incrementally.

An alternative to big-bang testing is *incremental testing*. There are several reasons to apply the incrementality principle to integration testing. First, since modules are developed one at a time, there is no reason to delay integration testing until all the modules os a system have been implemented; rather, we can start integration testing as soon as a reasonable subset of the modules has been developed.

Second, it is easier to localize errors incrementally. For instance, if a subset of n modules has been successfully and carefully tested, and a fault occurs when adding a new module, that has itself been successfully tested, it is likely that the error is in the interface between the new module and the previous ones. If, by contrast, we integrate a whole set of modules at once, localization of errors is more difficult.

Third, partial aggregations of modules often constitute important subsystems that can have some autonomy. For instance, a complex office information system can integrate modules that perform financial computations, processing of documents, etc. Each of these modules, in turn, may consist of several modules, such as invoiceDB, lettersDB, and personnelFiles. Clearly, it is worthwhile to test the integration of all the modules related to document processing independently of those having to do with financial processing, and conversely. This kind of testing will also help focus attention on critical relationships between the modules when moving to higher level integration. Furthermore, if the subset provides a meaningful subsystem, it may be delivered to the users according to an incremental delivery strategy.

Fourth, incremental testing can reduce or obviate the need for stubs or drivers. For instance, suppose you have a module file_manager that exports a set of traditional operations on files. After having tested this module separately, you may turn to testing a module table_manager that manages several kinds of tables, whether stored in memory or in secondary storage. Thus, it uses the file_manager module. You could decide to link table_manager to file_manager immediately and test the two of them together. This will allow you to avoid the construction of stubs that simulate the operations of file_manager, and you will be able to test table_manager independently, maintaining a good chance to localize possible errors.

Once the incrementality principle is accepted, the question arises, In which order should modules be aggregated. Two natural approaches to answering this question are *bottom-up* and *top-down* aggregation. The former means starting aggregation and testing from the leaves of the USES hierarchy. It requires the implementation of drivers to substitute for higher level modules. The latter means starting from top-level modules and using stubs to simulate lower level ones. The complementary benefits of the two approaches should be fairly obvious and are left to the reader as an exercise. Also, mixed solutions could easily be designed to cope with peculiar cases.

The top-down and bottom-up approaches may be used–and combined–in several ways by following a software architecture that is described in terms of both the USES and the IS_COMPOSED_OF relations. For example, consider the GDN structure of Figure 6.8. We may test M_1 by providing a stub for M_2 and a driver for M_1. Later, we can provide an implementation for $M_{2,1}$ and a stub for $M_{2,2}$. Alternatively, one can first implement $M_{2,2}$ and test it using a driver. Then one can design $M_{2,1}$ and test the combination of $M_{2,1}$ and $M_{2,2}$–which constitutes M_2–using a driver. Finally, one can implement M_1 and test it along with M_2 using a driver for M_1.

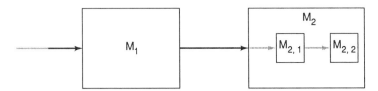

Figure 6.8   A GDN structure showing that M_1 USES M_2 and M_2 IS_COMPOSED_OF $\{M_{2,1}, M_{2,2}\}$.

Exercises

6.16   Design an incremental testing strategy for the software architecture given in Example 4.7.

6.17   Discuss the advantages and disadvantages of top-down integration with respect to bottom-up integration.

6.3.6 Separate Concerns in the Testing Activity

Testing a whole system is a complex activity that involves, in general, several phases, with different goals, performed by different people. For instance, some testing could be done by the developers of the software themselves, some testing could be done by other people belonging to the same company that produces the system, some testing could be done by the customer. Also, some tests could be done to ensure functional correctness, others to ensure robustness, etc. Applying the principle of separation of concerns is a key to a successful testing strategy.

Let us recall from Section 6.1.1 that all software qualities should be verified and, therefore, possibly tested. This suggests that testing should address not only compliance with precisely stated functional requirements, but also performance, robustness, user friendliness, and all other requested qualities. We can use the principle of separation of concerns to design test cases for different qualities: one test set is designed to check functional behavior, another is designed to check performance, and so on.

One should not, however, forget that even qualities that are not explicitly specified in the requirements document are worth verifying. As we saw in Chapter 2, in practice it is often impossible to point out exhaustively and exactly all the requirements of a system; it is therefore wise to test more than what is asked for officially.

In the following, we give a sampling of the different concerns that we can address with specific kinds of tests.

Overload testing. Suppose that a transaction system is required to execute at least 20 transactions per second with an average response time not to exceed 30 seconds. It would be prudent to test how the system behaves during peak conditions, when, say, 30 transactions are requested in a second. Such testing is called *overload testing*. It is likely that many ideas and suggestions for overload testing arise after system implementation, rather than during system specification. Of course, many of the results derived during such overload testing will be a source of inspiration for future enhancements of the system and also for future development of similar systems.

Testing for robustness. For much the same reason as in overload testing, it is advisable to test the system under unexpected conditions, such as erroneous user commands and power failures. Strictly speaking, it could seem a waste of time to schedule the testing of the system under unexpected conditions; instead, why not specify the expected response explicitly in the requirements document? The relevance of many unexpected conditions, however, may become clear only after some experience with early versions of the system.

Regression testing. Another concern that should be kept in mind during testing is that software is going to be modified during its lifetime, as we already have emphasized several times. For instance, suppose you are going to add new functionality to your software, or you are going to modify a module to improve its response time. The changes, of course, may introduce errors into software that was previously correct. For example, suppose the program fragment

```
x := c +1;
proc (z);
c := x + 2;
x := 3;
```

works properly. Now suppose that in a subsequent redesign it is transformed into

```
proc(z);
c := c + 3;
x := 3;
```

in an attempt at program optimization. This may result in an error if procedure proc accesses variable x.

Thus, we need to organize testing also with the purpose of verifying possible *regressions* of software during its life, i.e., degradations of correctness or other qualities due to later modifications. Properly designing and documenting test cases with the purpose of making tests repeatable, and using test generators, will help regression testing. Conversely, the use of interactive human input reduces repeatability and thus hampers regression testing.

Finally, we must treat test cases in much the same way as software. It is clear that such factors as evolvability, reusability, and verifiability are just as important in test cases as they are in software. We must apply formality and rigor and all of our other principles in the development and management of test cases. We will examine some organizational issues related to software evolution and testing in Chapter 7.

6.3.7 Testing Concurrent And Real-Time Systems

We have seen in Chapters 4 and 5 that concurrent systems are, in general, more difficult to design and specify than sequential systems. Not surprisingly, they are also more difficult to verify. In this section, we will discuss the additional problems that may arise in testing concurrent programs.

In principle, all of the testing techniques we have discussed so far should be applicable to sequential as well concurrent programs. Making tests repeatable, however, becomes a critical issue in concurrent programming. In fact, in traditional programming languages such as Pascal, COBOL, FORTRAN, etc., the semantics of a program is a function from the set of possible input data to the set of output data. This means that, if we provide the same input to a program twice, the program must produce the same results both times. This property does not hold in the case of concurrent and real-time systems, as we discussed in Chapter 4. The issue is taken up here in the context of the Ada programming language.

Example 6.11

Consider the following fragment of an Ada program that is a slight modification of the guardian task given in Figure 4.21:

```
task Char_Buffer_Handler is
        .
        .
        .
loop
            .
            .
            .
        select
                when NOT_full accept PUT
                    --code of PUT
            .
            .
            .
        or
                when NOT_empty accept GET
                    --code of GET
            .
            .
        end select;
        .
        .
        .
end loop;
        .
        .
        .
end Char_Buffer_Handler;
```

As we discussed in Section 4.6, this code defines a task whose job is to manage the use of a buffer of characters by other tasks–producers, who may write (PUT) characters into the buffer, and consumers, who may read (GET) characters from it.

The critical issue here is the *nondeterminism* of the behavior of the task. The task Char_Buffer_Handler can serve requests for writing or reading, provided that their respective conditions hold. If are requests of both types pending, however, and the buffer is neither full nor empty, both requests can be accepted: the task may choose which request to serve in a way that is not specified by the programmer.

Let us examine the impact of nondeterminism on guaranteeing the repeatability of testing. If we apply the complete coverage principle to a system composed of the Char_Buffer_Handler task and a set of producers and consumers, it sounds natural to test the system in such a way that the above loop is entered at least once with a full buffer, at least once with an empty buffer, and maybe once with a buffer that is neither full nor empty.

Now, imagine the programming error of leaving out the **when** NOT–Full clause. Intuitively, in testing the system with the buffer full, a failure should occur, in much the same way as if we had forgotten an **if** x ≠ 0 clause before executing a division by x. When we are testing the effect of a PUT operation on a full buffer, however, a GET request may be issued by some consumer. Since we have neither control over nor knowledge of the policy used by the Char_Buffer_Handler to serve pending requests, it may happen that the GET request is served first. After that, at the next loop iteration, the PUT operation will be performed without any trouble.

This experiment, however, does not guarantee at all that by running the same system of tasks with the same input data on a different machine, the program will behave correctly. In fact, a different implementation could select, under the same condition as above, the option to serve the PUT request, thus generating a fault. Even running the same system on the same machine with the same input data could provide different results if, for example, the operating system worked under a time-sharing policy that sometimes led to slowing down the consumer tasks and other times to slowing down the producer tasks.   ∎

The difficulties of testing concurrent systems become even more apparent when we move from testing in the small to testing in the large. In fact, it is intuitively clear that testing repeatability is much more difficult when we operate different modules running concurrently than when they run sequentially. The above producer-consumer program is an example of this.

Real-time systems are even more difficult to verify, for similar reasons. In fact, their correctness, by definition, depends on execution speeds. Clearly, verifying such systems requires taking into consideration many more details than in traditional systems; typically, many aspects that are "implementation details" that can be abstracted away in traditional systems–such as scheduling policies, machine architecture, and speed–must be taken into account here.

In conclusion, the general testing principles we have discussed so far are certainly applicable to concurrent and real-time systems. Much more care and technical details, however, must be taken into consideration, and, in general, many more test cases need to be considered. In fact, the number of possible execution paths is further increased by the possible execution interleavings of several concurrent units, and in the case of real-time systems, completeness should be pursued even from the point of view of relative processing speeds. For example, with a producer-consumer system, one should test the case when production is fast relative to consumption, and conversely.

The topic of testing concurrent and real-time systems is an active research area. Thus, we do not go further into the topic here, but instead refer the interested reader to the appropriate literature in the bibliographic notes.testing

Exercises

6.18   Consider a system of three tasks: a producer, a consumer, and a Char_Buffer_Handler, of the type outlined in Example 6.11. Consider also a fixed sequence of external stimuli and a fixed size of the buffer. (Say, the buffer has length 3, and the producer gets four items from the external environment to be put into the buffer.)

Assume that concurrency is simulated on a uniprocessor with the following different scheduling policies:

- Policy 1: every task runs until it is blocked by asking for an unavailable resource.
- Policy 2: every task runs until it reaches a synchronization point. At that point, the producer has higher priority than the consumer. (The Char_Buffer_Handler has the lowest priority, since it depends on the task it has to serve.)
- Policy 3: every task runs until it reaches a synchronization point. At that point the producer has lower priority than the consumer.

Discuss execution flows and the possibility of detection of failure with respect to the error discussed in Example 6.11.

6.19   Consider the following real-time version of the previous producer-consumer system. The Char_Buffer_Handler has no guard to block writing operations. Furthermore, when both PUT and GET requests are pending, the policy used to manage the **select** statement gives precedence to the PUT request. On the other hand, producers may be suspended only for a limited time on the PUT request, after which they skip the statement. Try to design a significant test set for such a system, by taking into account possible (minimum and maximum) process execution speeds, the specified scheduling policy, etc.

6.4 ANALYSIS

In Section 6.3, we discussed verification by experimentation, that is, testing. In this section, we will discuss verification by means of analysis. Analyzing any piece of work means inspecting it to understand its properties and capabilities. We observed that in the case of engineering products, analysis complements and integrates with experimental verification. For instance, one can check the minimum distance necessary to stop a car at a given speed by driving it at that speed and braking, perhaps repeating the experiment several times. Or, alternatively, one can try to derive the braking distance by applying appropriate mathematical formulas that take into account such properties of the car as its speed, weight, and center of gravity, and the friction between the wheels and the road.

Cast in terms of software, testing characterizes a *single* execution, whereas analysis characterizes a *class* of executions. While this observation seems to show the advantage of analysis over testing, both approaches have advantages and disadvantages that somewhat complement each other. Analysis is subject to the fallibility of our reasoning. Also, it is generally based on a *model* of the product rather than on the product itself. Thus, it abstracts away from elements that could be crucial. Experiments, on the other hand, are bound to the context in which they are performed, and their generality is not always clear. For instance, what about the braking distance of a car on a wet road, after an experiment on a dry road?

In the case of software, we have already noticed that testing is better suited to show the existence of errors rather than their absence. Is analysis, however, able to *prove* freedom from error?

Verification of a piece of software in order to check a desired property is similar to the activity of a mathematician in proving–or disproving–a theorem. Initially, a statement is formulated that is supposed to be true. At this point, it is a conjecture. Then, we start the process of trying to prove the truth of the conjecture, i.e., to show that it is a theorem. Probably, some intuitive reasoning that supports the conjecture will be available, but more evidence, i.e., a more convincing proof, is needed. If the initial attempt to build a proof fails, we might start to doubt the truth of the statement. We can try to show its falsehood unequivocally by a counterexample, the search for which might be driven by the failure of our previous attempt at proof. Conversely, verifying that the conjecture is actually true in some critical case may provide useful suggestions to derive a full proof. Eventually, the mathematician may come to either a proof of the theorem or a counterexample of the conjecture. It could also happen that neither a proof nor a counterexample can be found. In fact, the truth of a statement in a nontrivial theory–as well as the correctness of a program–is undecidable.

Unfortunately, when decisions or proofs cannot be performed mechanically, we are subject to human fallibility, and, in general, there is no guarantee that the right decision will be taken. Even in pure mathematics, erroneous theorems and proofs are sometimes accepted as valid, although this happens less frequently than the acceptance of software as error free when it is not. Once more, formality, when applicable, can help reduce–but not avoid–the risks of fallibility.

Software design analysis can apply many different techniques with different purposes. It can address the verification of highly different qualities (correctness, performance, etc.). It can be done by humans, whether the authors of the design or colleagues or customers, or with the aid of machine instruments. It can apply formal techniques or be based on intuition and experience. It can be applied to any step of the development process and to the related products, etc.

For instance, in the case of high-level language code, much analysis is performed automatically by the compiler during program translation. Thanks to such analyses, we are helped in fixing many trivial errors, such as violating the type constraints of a variable. Unfortunately, less trivial errors are less easy to detect and require a deeper analysis. Here, we are concerned with this type of analysis.

6.4.1 Informal Analysis Techniques

The most natural and simple analysis technique consists of just looking at the software–the requirements or design specification, or the code–and trying to imagine its behavior by manual simulation, maybe with some help from pencil and paper to focus attention on the most relevant facts.

In this case, the cooperation of people other than the designers is helpful. In fact, in examining one's own work, it is easy to be biased by the same reasoning that was used in the design and thus fail to spot errors. Another person, with no previous misconceptions, is more likely to detect the errors.

The success of informal reasoning in software verification has led to attempts to organize this activity. Two particularly successful organized approaches are *code walk-throughs,* presented in Section 6.4.1.1, and *code inspections*, discussed in Section 6.4.1.2.

It is possible, however, to apply informal analysis techniques to something other than code. Consider, for example, the case of specifications. Completeness and consistency can be checked manually, even for informal specifications. One should check that every concept used is uniquely defined and that no undefined concepts are left in the specification document. If cross-references, glossaries, or decision tables are available, they can be helpful in this phase. If they are not available, or if they are incomplete, they can be created.

6.4.1.1 Code walk-throughs

A code walk-through is an informal analysis of code as a cooperative, organized activity by several participants. The analysis is based mainly on the game of "playing the computer." That is, participants select some test cases (the selection could have been done previously by a single participant) and simulate execution of the code by hand. This is the reason for the name *walk-through*: participants "walk through the code" or through any design notation. States of execution may be recorded either on private storage (a piece of paper) or on shared memory (a blackboard).

Several guidelines have been developed over the years for organizing this naive but useful verification technique to make it more systematic and reliable. Of course, these guidelines are based on personal experience, common sense, and many subjective factors. Thus, they should be considered more as examples than as rules to be applied dogmatically.

In general, the following prescriptions are recommended:

- The number of people involved in the review should be small (three to five).
- The partecipants should receive written documentation from the designer a few days before the meeting.
- The meeting should last a predefined amount of time (a few hours).
- Discussion should be focused on the *discovery* of errors, not on fixing them, nor on proposing alternative design decisions.
- Key people in the meeting should be the designer, who presents and explains the rationale of the work,[1] a moderator for the discussion, and a secretary, who

---

[1]Experience shows that most errors are discovered by the designer during the presentation, while trying to explain the design to other people.

is responsible for writing a report to be given to the designer at the end of the meeting.

- In order to foster cooperation and avoid the feeling that the designers are being evaluated, managers should not participate in the meeting.

The success of code walk-throughs hinges on running them in a cooperative manner as a team effort: they must avoid making the designer feel threatened.

6.4.1.2 Code inspections

Another organized activity devoted to analyzing code is called *code inspection*. The organizational aspects of code inspection are similar to those of code walk-throughs (i.e., the number of participants, duration of the meeting, psychological attitudes of the partecipants, etc., should be about the same), but there is a difference in goals.

In code inspection, the analysis is aimed explicitly at the discovery of commonly made errors. In other words, the code–or, in general, the design–is examined by checking it for the presence of errors, rather than by simulating its execution. In such a case, it is useful to state *beforehand* the type of error for which we are searching. For instance, consider the classical error of writing a procedure that modifies a formal parameter and calling the procedure with a constant value as the actual parameter.[1] It is more likely that such an error will be discovered by looking for it in the code, than by simply hand-simulating execution of the procedure.

Since many errors in programs can be classified according to well-known categories, we can hope to discover most of them just by looking for them. The following is a list of some classical programming errors:

- use of uninitialized variables;
- jumps into loops;
- incompatible assignments;[2]
- nonterminating loops;
- array indexes out of bounds;
- improper storage allocation-deallocation;
- actual-formal parameter mismatches in procedure calls;
- comparisons of equality for floating point values.

Many of the above errors–as well as others not listed here–have different symptoms and impacts depending on the programming language. For instance, improper storage

---

[1]In some cases, the compiler provides automatic protection against this type of error.

[2]Even though most modern programming languages have a strong typing system–i.e., they allow all type checks to be done at compile time–some incompatibilities in assignments will necessarily be detectable only at run time. For instance, suppose you have a type week_day that includes the seven days of the week as possible values and a *subtype* work_day that is restricted to values from Monday to Friday. Then, if x and y are two variables declared of the two types, respectively, most compilers will–reasonably–accept the assignment y := x. But this may result in a run-time error if x's value is Sunday at execution time.

allocation-deallocation is not even possible for static languages such as FORTRAN. Or, in Pascal, many mismatches between actual and formal parameters can be caught at compile time, but there might be an exception for procedure parameters, etc. We might also use a language-specific list based on the error-prone features of the language.

Furthermore, we will see in Chapter 9 that, despite the undecidability of most of the errors listed above, many analytical tools exist to help in detecting such errors. In general, the human inspectors should concentrate on what cannot be inspected automatically. The reviewers should receive the reports produced by the analysis tools.

Exercises

6.20   Discuss the above list of errors from the point of view of the programming language being used.

6.21   Complete the above list of errors by including a discussion of their impact, depending on the programming language adopted.

6.4.2 Correctness Proofs

Informal analysis techniques are useful, but more rigorous and even formal approaches are needed to make verification more reliable. The following example illustrates how informal reasoning can fail to detect an erroneous fragment in a program.

Example 6.12

The following incorrect program fragment is intended to merge two sorted arrays of n elements each:

```
i := 1; j := 1; k := 1;
while k ≤ 2 * n loop
        if a(i) < b(j) then
                c(k) := a(i);
                i := i + 1;
        else
                c(k) := b(j) ;
                j := j + 1;
        end if;
        k := k + 1;
end loop;
```

An informal analysis of this code may read as follows:

> Three counters are defined: i for a, j for b, and k for c. They are all initialized to 1. At each step, the ith element of a and the jth element of b are compared. The smaller one is stored into c as the kth element. Then k and the counter of the array containing the selected element are incremented. The step is repeated until c is all built.

Superficially, this reasoning seems to confirm the correctness of the program, but actually it hides the subtle error that when the end of, say, a is reached (i.e., i = n), the loop may be executed again, and if a(n) < b(j), i becomes n + 1, which is an error. Even testing may fail to show the error, since the program could access some physical location that does not correspond to any program variable, perhaps producing an appropriate result to the test a(i) < b(j).   ∎

Formal program analysis is a verification aid that may enhance program reliability. Indeed, a program is a formal object, since the syntax and the semantics of programming languages can be defined formally. Once the program's specification has been given in a formal way, proving program correctness amounts to the–nontrivial–task of building a mathematical proof of the equivalence between the program and its specification. Such a proof, of course, would enhance our confidence in the program, as is the case whenever we apply mathematical reasoning in an analysis.

In this section, we briefly describe the fundamentals of correctness proofs, trying to avoid excessive mathematical detail, but also trying not to hide their intricacies. This will enable us to assess the practical application of the approach. We organize our presentation in the following way: Section 6.4.2.1 introduces the basic notions of program correctness: Section 6.4.2.2 extends the concepts to a richer set of statements, including the ability to deal with arrays: finally, Section 6.4.2.3 addresses the issue of how to deal with formal verification in practice.

6.4.2.1 Basic concepts of correctness proofs

To introduce the basic concepts of correctness proofs, consider the following simple example, which consists of a program and its specification. The specification uses the Hoare-like notation introduced in Section 5.6.2.1.

```
{true}
begin
        read (a); read (b);
        x := a + b;
        write (x);
end
{output = input₁ + input₂}
```

Due to the semantics of the write statement, the postcondition output = $input_1$ + $input_2$ holds after its execution if and only if, just before its execution, the predicate {x = $input_1$ + $input_2$} holds. Since the assignment statement stores the value of a + b into x, the previous predicate is guaranteed to hold after execution of x := a + b if and only if the predicate {a + b = $input_1$ + $input_2$} holds just before its execution. Finally, since read (a) and read (b) will give a and b, respectively–the values of the first two input values $input_1$–and $input_2$, we realize that {a + b = $input_1$ + $input_2$} will certainly hold before execution of "x := a + b". As a consequence, we can conclude that the whole program guarantees the truth of {output = $input_1$ + $input_2$} at the end of its execution; that is, the program is correct.

The above reasoning is a formal derivation of the correctness of a program with respect to a specification given in Hoare's notation. Essentially, it is based on the fact that for any postcondition Post on program variables, and for any assignment statement x := exp, where exp is an expression containing program variables, a necessary and sufficient condition for Post to hold *after* statement execution is that Post itself holds *before* its execution with exp substituted for any occurrence of x. Such substitution[1] is called *backward substitution,* and the resulting predicate is called a *precondition.*

The reader can reinforce his or her understanding of backward substitution by considering the following tautologies (i.e., statements that are always true):

$$\{x = 5\} \ x := x + 1 \ \{x = 6\}$$
$$\{z - 43 > y + 7\} \ x := z - 43 \ \{x > y + 7\}$$

Input and output statements can be treated as if they were assignment statements from the input file and to the output file, respectively. In the previous example, since we knew that the input file contained two values (to be read into a and b), we could treat the two read statements as if they were written as

$$a := input_1; \ b := input_2;$$

Similarly, we could treat the only output statement as if it were

$$output := x$$

The general way to deal with input and output, though, is more complicated, and will be discussed in Section 6.4.2.2.

Backward substitution can be applied easily to *sequences* of assignment statements. In fact, if $\{z - 43 > y + 7\}$ is a necessary and sufficient condition for $\{x > y + 7\}$ to hold after x := z - 43–that is, if

$$\{z - 43 > y + 7\}$$
$$x := z - 43$$
$$\{x > y + 7\}$$

and if $\{a + b - 43 > y + 7\}$ is a necessary and sufficient condition for $\{z - 43 > y + 7\}$ to hold after z := a + b–that is, if

$$\{a + b - 43 > y + 7\}$$
$$z := a + b$$
$$\{z - 43 > y + 7\}$$

---

[1]For simplicity, we assume here that the evaluation of the expression on the right-hand side does not generate any side effects, which could happen if it involved a function call. As an exercise, the reader may verify why this hypothesis is needed and should modify the backward substitution rule to cope with side effects.

then $\{a + b - 43 > y + 7\}$ is a necessary and sufficient condition for $\{x > y + 7\}$ to hold after $z := a + b$; $x := z - 43$–that is,

$$\{a + b - 43 > y + 7\}$$
$$z := a + b; x := z - 43$$
$$\{z - 43 > y + 7\}$$

More generally, suppose that, for any two statements S_1 and S_2, you have separately proved that

$$\{F_1\} \, S_1 \, \{F_2\},$$

and

$$\{F_2\} \, S_2 \, \{F_3\}$$

i.e., that the truth of F_1 guarantees that F_2 holds after execution of statement S_1 and the truth of F_2 guarantees that F_3 holds after execution of statement S_3. Then, you can deduce

$$\{F_1\} \, S_1; S_2 \, \{F_3\}$$

i.e., that if F_1 holds, then F_3 will hold after the execution of S_1 followed by S_2.

We can state this reasoning in the form of a *proof rule* for sequencing statements, as expressed in *Hoare's notation*:

$$\frac{\{F_1\}S_1\{F_2\}, \ \{F_2\}S_2\{F_3\}}{\{F_1\}S_1;S_2\{F_3\}}$$

This notation is used in the following way: If Claim_1 and Claim_2 have been proved, one can deduce Claim_3 from the rule

$$\frac{\text{Claim}_1, \ \text{Claim}_2}{\text{Claim}_3}$$

The proof rule for sequencing statements can even be stated more strongly. Suppose that F_0 implies F_1, F_2 implies F_2' and F_3 implies F_4. Then, from $\{F_1\} \, S_1 \, \{F_2\}$ and $\{F_2'\} \, S_2 \, \{F_3\}$, you can deduce $\{F_0\} \, S_1; S_2 \, \{F_4\}$. That is,

$$\frac{F_0 \text{ implies } F_1, \ F_2 \text{ implies } F_2', \ F_3 \text{ implies } F_4, \ \{F_1\} \, S_1 \, \{F_2\}, \ \{F_2'\} \, S_2 \, \{F_3\}}{\{F_0\} \, S_1; S_2 \, \{F_4\}}$$

All this should sound quite natural, and the reader is invited to check his or her understanding through the following exercise.

Exercise

6.22 Prove the following two properties:

1. $\{x > 0 \text{ and } y > 0\}$ **2.** $\{x > 0\}$

    z := x * y   y := x ** 2;

    $\{z > - 1\}$;   z := sqrt (y);

                                   $\{z > 0\}$

Of course, programs do not consist exclusively of sequences of assignment and I/O statements. Thus, we need *proof rules* for all the different constructs of a given programming language in order to prove correctness with respect to a particular set of specifications. In what follows, we summarize the essential proof rules for a restricted set of ALGOL-like language constructs; for simplicity, we will restrict ourselves to programs that manipulate integers. The reader is referred to the more specialized literature for a more complete treatment of the topic.

First, let us examine conditional statements. As an introductory example, consider the following formula:

```
{true}
if x ≥ y then
        max := x;
else
        max := y;
end if
{(max = x or max = y) and (max ≥ x and max ≥ y)}
```

This formula states that, whatever the values of x and y are before execution of the code, the value of variable max must equal the maximum of the two after execution of the code.

Now, assume that $x \geq y$ at the beginning. Then the **then** branch of the statement is executed. Backward substitution of the desired postcondition yields $\{(x = x \text{ or } x = y) \text{ and } (x \geq x \text{ and } x \geq y)\}$, and the predicate is implied by the condition $x \geq y$, which guarantees execution of this branch. The same happens if $x < y$. Thus, we may deduce that *in all cases*–this is the *meaning* of the true precondition–the desired postcondition will hold after execution of the conditional statement.

More generally, let

        if cond **then** S_1; **else** S_2; **end if**;

be any conditional statement, where S_1 and S_2 are any two statements. Then we can state the following proof rule for conditional statements:

$$\frac{\{\text{Pre and cond}\}\ S_1\ \{\text{Post}\},\{\text{Pre and not cond}\}\ S_2\ \{\text{Post}\}}{\{\text{Pre}\}\ \textbf{if}\ \text{cond}\ \textbf{then}\ S_1;\ \textbf{else}\ S_2;\ \textbf{end if};\ \{\text{Post}\}}$$

The proof rules that we are building for ALGOL-like constructs can be arbitrarily composed and nested. For example, **if-then-else** statements may contain other **if-then-else** statements in their **then** or **else** branches (see Exercise 6.23 at the end of this section).

Let us now consider while loops; other kinds of iterative statements may be modeled in a similar way. Let I be any assertion. The proof rule for **while** loops is

$$\frac{\{\text{I and cond}\}\ S\ \{\text{I}\}}{\{\text{I}\}\ \textbf{while}\ \text{cond}\ \textbf{loop}\ S;\ \textbf{end loop};\ \{\text{I and not cond}\}}$$

Intuitively the meaning of this rule is the following. Suppose we have been able to prove that, if assertion I holds, then executing the loop body S under condition cond preserves I's truth. Then I is a *loop invariant*, i.e., it is a predicate that holds at loop entry and exit no matter how many times we execute the loop. As a consequence, we may infer that, whenever I holds at loop entry, I will still be true at loop exit, along with **not** cond.

A trivial application of the above rule is the following:

```
{x ≥ 0}
while x > 0 loop
        x := x - 1;
end loop;
{x = 0}
```

The formula $\{x \geq 0\}$ is a loop invariant for the loop. This is can be seen in the fact that backward substitution through x := x - 1 yields $\{x - 1 \geq 0\}$, which is implied by $\{x \geq 0$ **and** $x > 0\}$ since x is an integer. Thus, application of the rule gives the postcondition $\{x \geq 0$ **and not** $(x > 0)\}$, that is, $\{x = 0\}$.

We emphasize that this proof rule allows the derivation of a postcondition of a **while** loop that is guaranteed to hold at loop exit, *if the loop is ever exited*. In other words, having proved the invariance of a loop assertion does not prove that the loop will eventually terminate, as is shown by the predicate

```
{x > y}
while x ≠ 0 loop
        x := x - 2;
        y := y -2;
end loop;
{x > y and x = 0}
```

which can easily be proved to hold on the basis of the loop proof rule. The loop, however, will never terminate if x is odd upon entry to the loop.

As a consequence, the proofs that we will be able to provide with this technique are called *partial correctness proofs*; i.e., the validity of a formula

> {Pre} Program {Post}

only guarantees that if the precondition Pre holds before the execution of Program, and *if the program ever terminates*, then the postcondition Post will be achieved.

A *total correctness proof*, on the other hand, is a mathematical proof that Pre guarantees Program's termination *and* the truth of Post. Total correctness proofs require a *termination proof* in addition to a partial correctness proof. For termination proofs, we refer the reader to the more specialized literature in the bibliographic notes. In what follows, we will focus on partial correctness proofs, assuming that termination is verified separately.

We are now able to build correctness proofs of complete programs by applying the foregoing proof rules. Let us start with the following, simplest, case.

Example 6.13

Consider the following program and its assertions:

```
{input₁ > 0 and input₂ > 0}
begin
        read (x); read (y);
        div := 0;
        while x ≥ y loop
            div := div + 1;
            x := x - y;
        end loop;
        write (div); write (x);
end;
{input₁ = output₁ * input₂ + output₂ and 0 ≤ output₂ < input₂}
```

The predicates of this program provide a specification of an integer division algorithm. Our goal is to prove that the implementation is correct with respect to the given specification.

Backward substitutions through the output statements leave us with the job of proving

```
{input₁ > 0 and input₂ > 0}
begin
        read (x); read (y);
        div := 0;
        while x ≥ y loop
            div := div + 1;
            x := x - y;
        end loop;
{input₁ = div * input₂ + x and 0 ≤ x < input₂}
```

At this point, we need to be able to invent a suitable loop invariant. Actually, many assertions are invariant–in a more or less trivial way–for the above loop. For instance, $z + w = 2$, $div \geq 0$, and $div > 10,000$, are all invariant for the loop. (Prove the invariance of these assertions as an exercise.) These invariants, however, are useless for us: we need an invariant that, conjoined with the negation of the loop condition, implies the truth of the assertion

$$\{input_1 = div * input_2 + x \text{ and } x < input_2\}$$

The choice of a loop invariant is a key point in the correctness proof. Its discovery, in general, requires insight into the algorithm of the program. In this example, the job of the loop is to increment div by one unit at every iteration and to decrement x by the value of y. This can be formalized as the following candidate invariant: I_1: $input_1 = div * y + x$.

Backward substitution through the loop body immediately shows that this formula actually is an invariant. It is not sufficiently strong, however, to prove that the required postcondition holds at exit; i.e., we cannot prove that I_1 **and** $x < y$ **implies** $\{input_1 = div * input_2 + x$ **and** $x < input_2\}$. To prove this we need to strengthen I_1 so that $y = input_2$ **and** $x \geq 0$ also hold. Since these additional conditions are also invariant, we deduce the following stronger loop invariant:

$$I_2\colon input_1 = div * y + x \text{ and } x \geq 0 \text{ and } y = input_2$$

It is easy to verify that the conjunction of this invariant with $x < y$ (the negation of the loop condition) implies the desired postcondition. Finally, we easily verify the fragment

```
{input₁ > 0 and input₂ > 0}
begin
        read (x); read (y); div := 0;
{I₂: input₁ = div * y + x and x ≥ 0 and y = input₂}
```

and this completes the proof.   ∎

Proof rules allow us to derive formulas that are assertions about properties that hold at intermediate points in the program. We saw in Section 5.6.2.2 that these assertions are called *intermediate assertions*. An intermediate assertion is associated with a particular point in the program and states a property that must hold at that point–in any execution of the program. Loop invariants are a kind of intermediate assertion that characterize the semantics of a loop. The assertion $\{input_1 = div * input_2 + x$ **and** $0 \leq x < input_2\}$ holding before the output statements of the program discussed in Example 6.13 is another example of an intermediate assertion. We will see in Section 6.6 that intermediate assertions may be useful in the error removal phase of software development.

Exercises

6.23 Prove formally that the following program fragments each store the maximum among x, y, z, and w into variable max:

a. if $x \geq y$ and $x \geq z$ and $x \geq w$ then
        max := x;
  elsif $y \geq x$ and $y \geq z$ and $y \geq w$ then
        max := y;
  elsif $z \geq x$ and $z \geq y$ and $z \geq w$ then
        max := z;
  else
        max := w;
  end if;

c. if $x \geq y$ and $x \geq z$ and $x \geq w$ then
        max := x;
  end if;
  if $y \geq x$ and $y \geq z$ and $y \geq w$ then
        max := y;
  end if;
  if $z \geq x$ and $z \geq y$ and $z \geq w$ then
        max := z;
  end if;
  if $w \geq x$ and $w \geq y$ and $w \geq z$ then
        max := w;
  end if;

b. if $x \geq y$ and $z \geq w$ then
    if $x \geq z$ then
        max := x;
    else
        max := z;
    end if;
  elsif $x \geq y$ then
    if $x \geq w$ then
        max := x;
    else
        max := w;
    end if;
  elsif $z \geq w$ then
    if $z \geq y$ then
        max := z ;
    else
        max := y;
    end if;
  else
    if $w \geq y$ then
        max := w;
    else
        max := y;
    end if;
  end if;

6.24 Does the proof of Example 6.13 hold also with the weaker precondition $input_1 \geq 0$ **and** $input_2 \geq 0$? Can the assumed precondition be weakened? How?

6.25 Build correctness proofs for the following fragments:

a. $\{input_1 > 0$ **and** $input_2 > 0\}$
  read (z); read (y);
  x := 1;
  j := 1;
  while $y \geq j$ **loop**
    j := j + 1;
    x := x * z;
  end loop;
  write (x);
  $\{output = input_1{}^{input_2}\}$

b. $\{input_1 > 0$ **and** $input_2 > 0\}$
  read (x) ; read (y) ;
  while $x \neq y$ **loop**
  if $x > y$ **then**
    x := x - y;
  else
    y := y - x;
  end if;
  end loop;
  write (x);
  $\{GCD (input_1, input_2, output)\}$

In the second fragment, the predicate GCD (x, y, w)–read "w is the greatest common divisor of x and y"–stands for:

exists z_1, z_2 $(x = w^*z_1$ **and** $y = w^*z_2)$

and not exists h (**exists** z_1, z_2 $(x = h^*z_1$ **and** $y = h^*z_2)$ **and** $h > w$

6.4.2.2 Programs with arrays

The proof rules used so far help in proving the correctness of very simple programs. But real programming languages involve a richer set of statements for which adequate proof rules must be given. We do not try to cover a detailed treatment of all programming language constructs here. These may be found in the specialized literature. There is, however, one major issue of conceptual relevance that we must address.

Consider the following assignment statement involving the use of an indexed variable

a(i) := 4;

If we apply the previous proof rule for assignment statements, we would obtain an assertion of the type

{a(3) = 2}
a(i) := 4;
{a(3) = 2 **and** a(i) = 4}

which is false if i = 3 when the statement is executed. Clearly, the problem arises because the effect of the statement depends on the value of the index variable. In order to cope with this problem, when the left-hand side of an assignment statement is an indexed variable, the backward substitution rule must be generalized. We show how to effect such a generalization next.

For any assertion Post, and for any statement of the type a(i) := expression, let Pre denote the assertion obtained from Post by substituting every occurrence of an indexed variable a(j) by the term

if j = i **then** expression **else** a(j);

Then we can use the rule

{Pre} a(i) := expression; {Post}

for our correctness analysis.[1]

Applying the new rule to the previous example, we obtain

{ (**if** 3 = i **then** 4 **else** a(3)) = 2 **and** (**if** i = i **then** 4 **else** a(i)) = 4}
a(i) := 4;
{a(3) = 2 **and** a(i) = 4}

which is simplified to

---

[1]A few mathematical intricacies have been omitted to simplify the notation. However, the simplified rule can be used safely in most practical situations.

$\{i \ne 3$ **and** $a(3) = 2\}$
$a(i) := 4;$
$\{a(3) = 2$ **and** $a(i) = 4\}$

As a first application of the new rule, consider the following program fragment that is intended to insert an integer x into a table of n elements. The table is implemented as an array with nmax elements of type integer. If, before execution of the code, n is less than nmax, then the program must guarantee that x will be inserted into the table. A formal proof of this requirement calls for the verification of the following formula:

```
{n < nmax}
if n < nmax then
        n := n + 1;
        table (n) := x;
end if;
{n ≤ nmax and (exists i (1 ≤ i ≤ n and table (i) = x))}
```

By applying the augmented backward substitution rule we obtain the following predicate:

```
{n + 1 ≤ nmax and
    (exists i (1 ≤ i ≤ n + 1 and
                (if i = n + 1 then x else table (i)) = x))
    )
}
```

Now, n < nmax implies n + 1 ≤ nmax. On the other hand,

(exists i (1 ≤ i ≤ n + 1 **and (if** i = n + 1 **then** x **else** table (i)) = x))

is obviously satisfied by i = n + 1. Thus, the stated precondition guarantees the desired postcondition.

As another example, let us prove the following formula:

```
{n ≥ 1}
i := 1; j := 1;
found := false;
while i ≤ n loop
        if table (i) = x then
                found := true;
                i := i + 1
        else
                table (j) := table (i);
                i := i + 1; j := j + 1;
        end if;
end loop;
n := j - 1;
```

{**not exists** m (1 ≤ m ≤ n **and** table (m) = x) **and**
found ≡ **exists** m (1 ≤ m ≤ *old*_n **and** *old*_table (m) = x)}

In this formula *old*_table and *old*_n are constants that denote the values of table and of n, respectively, before execution of the program fragment. (Recall from Section 5.6.2 that, sometimes, in formal specifications, we need to refer to values held by variables at previous points of the execution flow.)

Intuitively, the above specification states that the program should delete from the table all occurrences of the value x, if any, and should store in the variable found a Boolean value indicating whether or not x occurred in table before execution. It is not explicitly requested, however, that all other elements of table should be preserved.

Let us prove the correctness of the foregoing program fragment by means of the following loop invariant:

I: {(j ≤ i) **and** (i ≤ *old*_n + 1)
            and (**not exists** m (1 ≤ m < j **and** table (m) = x))
            and (n = *old*_n)
            and found ≡ **exists** m (1 ≤ m < i **and** *old*_table (m) = x)}

First, it is easy to prove that I **and** i > n implies the result of backward substitution of the postcondition through n : = j - 1.

Second, let us prove I's invariance through the loop. Backward substitution through the **then** branch yields

{(j ≤ i + 1) **and** (i + 1 ≤ *old*_n + 1)
            and (**not exists** m (1 ≤ m < j **and** table (m) = x))
            and (n = *old*_n) **and exists** m (1 ≤ m < i + 1
            and *old*_table (m) = x)}

which is implied by I **and** i ≤ n **and** table(i) = x.

The **else** branch produces

{(j + 1 ≤ i + 1) **and** (i + 1 ≤ *old*_n + 1)
            and (**not exists** m (1 ≤ m < j + 1
            and (**if** m = j **then** table (i) **else** table (m)) = x))
            and (n = *old*_n)
            and found ≡ **exists** m (1 ≤ m < i + 1 **and** *old*_table (m) = x)}

The fact that I **and** i ≤ n **and** table(i) ≠ x imply the first two clauses is obvious. Let us show that they also imply

(**not exists** m (1 ≤ m < j + 1 **and** (**if** m = j **then** table (i) **else** table (m)) = x))

To see that they do, note that, for all m, with $1 \leq m < j$, the statement is implied by the invariant; when m = j, it is implied by the condition of the **if** statement. In quite the same way, we may also prove

$$found \equiv \mathbf{exists}\ m\ (1 \leq m < i + 1\ \mathbf{and}\ old\_table\ (m) = x)$$

Finally, it is plain that the precondition $n \geq 1$ implies the result of backward substituting I through i := 1; j := 1; found := false. This completes the correctness proof.

The technique we have presented here to deal with arrays also allows us to deal with input-output statements in a formal way. In fact, we can view the files input and output as unbounded arrays having associated indexes c_i and c_o, respectively, that are initialized to 1 and automatically incremented after any input-output operation. Specifically, statement read (x) may be viewed as an abbreviation of

$$x := input\ (c_i);$$
$$c_i := c_i + 1;$$

Similarly, write (x) may be considered an abbreviation of

$$output\ (c_o) := x;$$
$$c_o := c_o + 1;$$

Exercise

6.26 Augment the above specification of the delete operation by requiring that no elements of *old*_table other than x be deleted and no other elements be added. Also, specify that the number of elements should never exceed nmax. Prove the correctness of the program with respect to the new assertions.

6.4.2.3 Using correctness proofs in practice

The examples and the exercises in the previous section demonstrate that formal correctness proofs are intricate even for fairly simple programs. Thus, the question naturally arises, "What about proving the correctness of a software system that is 10,000 lines or more?" In other words, we must assess the applicability of the proof technique to practical situations. In fact, formal verification techniques were proposed by theoreticians over 20 years ago, but their application in practical projects is still an exception, and much debate goes on about their practical usefulness.

Some of the major objections raised against the use of formal verification techniques are the following:

1. Formal proofs are often even longer and more complex than the programs they are intended to prove. Thus, they are at least as error prone as those programs.

Hence, a correctness proof does not increase our confidence in the program's correctness.

2. Formal proofs require too much mathematical background to be used by the average software designer.

3. Formal proofs overwhelm designers with details that could easily be dispensed with using an informal analysis.

4. Even if we can achieve mathematical certainty of the correctness of a program, we cannot rely on it in an absolute way because there could be a failure in the implementation of the language (the compiler) or even in the hardware.

5. Formal proofs do not deal with the physical limitations of the computing device. For instance, a limited number of bits is used to approximate real numbers. Thus, assertions that are true in the idealized mathematical world may turn out to be false when actual computations are performed.

Some of these objections are serious. In evaluating the applicability of formal verification techniques, however, we must also consider counterobjections. Let us start by refuting the last two claims above.

Of course, even when we have proven the formal correctness of a program for, say, air traffic control, we cannot rely 100 percent on the air traffic control *system*. An earthquake could destroy the hardware on which the program is running, or the hardware itself could have a failure, or an error could be present in the compiler that translated the application program.

But this is not a new situation. Even if the design of a car is perfect, there could be an error in the assembly procedure or a defect in the material used to build the brakes, and the resulting product would not be reliable any more. Still, we feel safer if the design has been in some manner certified. In a complex system, all components must be verified, and the application program is just a component of the whole system. Also, mathematical properties can be proven on mathematical models that are an abstraction of the real world. Thus, having verified that a mathematical model of a bridge tolerates certain circumstances does not guarantee that the real bridge will not collapse under those same circumstances. However, we justifiably accept conclusions drawn on the basis of the analysis of the model, as long as we keep in mind that some risks are not considered by the model.

On the other hand, the literature on formal correctness analysis does not deal, in general, with the problem of approximating infinite sets by the finite memory of the computer. This problem, however, is well understood, and powerful solutions are available in the literature on numerical calculus.

Let us now focus attention on the remaining objections. It is true that a formal analysis takes longer and is more difficult and even more tedious than an informal analysis. And errors do exist in formal reasonings. Formal reasoning is nonetheless considered universally to be a fundamental tool for deriving reliable conclusions. In the history of science, the introduction of formal objects has always been motivated by failures of previous, less rigorous, attempts. And pure mathematics, as we have observed, has used much informal reasoning to build sound and important theorems. The discovery of trouble spots such as paradoxes has even led to more formal approaches to, say, set theory and mathematical logic. In general, when we have good reasons not to rely too much on informal reasoning, that try to gain more confidence by using formulas, and this attempt often leads to the discovery of subtle errors.

To be useful in practice, formal verification techniques should be applied in conjunction with the modularity and incrementality principles, just as they are applied together in the design and specification activities. The following examples illustrate this point.

Suppose we have defined and implemented an abstract data type TABLE along the following lines:

> **module** TABLE;
> **exports**
> > **type** Table_Type (max_size: NATURAL): ?;
> > *no more than max_size entries may be stored in a table*
> > *user modules must guarantee this*
> > **procedure** Insert (Table: **in out** TableType ; ELEMENT: **in** ElementType);
> > **procedure** Delete (Table: **in out** TableType; ELEMENT: **in** ElementType);
> > **function** Size (Table: in Table_Type) **return** NATURAL;
> > *provides the current size of a table*
> > .
> > .
> > .
> **end** TABLE

Each abstract operation can be specified formally by means of suitable pre- and postconditions, as exemplified in the following

> {true}
> Delete (Table, Element);
> {Element ∉ Table};
>
> {Size (Table) < max_size}
> Insert (Table, Element)
> {Element ∈ Table};

At this point, we can easily–and formally–prove properties about the abstract data type TABLE by using its abstract specification. For instance, we could prove that applying a Delete operation after an Insert operation guarantees that the deleted element is not present in the table if the Insert operation is applied when the table is not full. In fact, this follows easily from the above two formulas about Insert and Delete.

To prove the correctness of module TABLE's implementation, we must know what data structure is used to represent tables. Suppose that type TableType is implemented as

```
type TableType (max_size: NATURAL) is
        record
                size : INTEGER range 0. . max_size:= 0;
                contents = array (1.. max_size) of INTEGER;
        end record;
```

Then it is explicitly stated that predicate Element ∈ Table is true if and only if there exists a value i such that $1 \leq i \leq size \leq max\_size$ **and** Table.contents(i) = Element, it is a simple exercise to prove the correctness of the procedures that implement the operations on Table.

The previous specifications, however, are too weak to prove a natural and desirable property such as

```
{Table.size < max_size}
Insert (Table, Element);
Delete (Table, Element);
{Table = Old_Table - {Element}}[1]
```

which states that after the above two operations, the table is the same as it was except that Element is missing (see Exercises 6.27 and 6.28 below).

This example has shown once more that modularization must be exploited not only in the construction of software, but throughout its specification, design, and verification, including any possible formal analysis. In particular, the idea may be pushed even further in the verification of a modular system, where we can profitably integrate testing and analysis. A critical module should be specified formally and its implementation checked carefully against the formal specification, perhaps by applying formal proof techniques, whereas other components of the system could be left to a more informal verification.

For example, a good candidate for formal specification and analysis is a library package that is used by many users or that is used in critical applications. Certainly, the reusability of a component can be enhanced if its potential users understand its functionality fully and can rely on its correctness.

As an example of how formal program proofs can be reserved for critical portions of a program, let us go back to the merge program of Example 6.12, which is repeated as follows for convenience:

```
i := 1; j := 1; k := 1;
while k ≤ 2 * n loop
        if a(i) < b(j) then
                c(k) := a(i);
                i := i + 1;
        else
                c(k) := b(j) ;
                j := j + 1;
        end if;
        k := k + 1;
end loop;
```

---

[1]The symbol '-' denotes set difference here.

Initially, a simple informal analysis could raise the question of whether the indexes i, j, and k are guaranteed to remain within the ranges 1..n, 1..n, and 1..2 * n, respectively. The question may be easily rephrased as whether the assertion

I: {1 ≤ i ≤ n **and** 1 ≤ j ≤ n **and** 1 ≤ k ≤ 2 * n}

is a loop invariant.

An attempt to prove this assertion invariant–with the aid of the further relation k = i + j -1–would fail much more clearly in a formal than in an informal analysis. In fact,

I **and** k = i + j– 1

does not imply

{1 ≤ i + 1 ≤ n **and** 1 ≤ j + 1 ≤ n **and** 1 ≤ k + 1 ≤ 2 * n}

i.e., the result of the latter's backward substitution through the loop body.

Actually, as we know, the program fragment is incorrect; after correcting it, we would be able to prove the assertion. The assertion, however, is not a complete specification of the fragment, but only contains facts that we consider critical. In reality, going through a complete specification and its related correctness proof would be quite complicated (see Exercise 6.67). But the example shows that we do not need to go through a complete specification and its correctness proof to assess the program. If there are critical facts that we want to verify (in the example, indexing in the arrays), then we may still specify and prove them in a formal way. This is an instance of the principles of separation of concerns and abstraction, namely, deal with the critical issues only, and is particularly valuable when the program is large and complex.

We should also emphasize that program assertions–pre- and postconditions and intermediate assertions–can be used as a formal way of expressing program comments. As such, they can be used both to drive correctness proofs and to debug programs. In other words, the activity of formally specifying properties of the execution states at some critical points can be used both to help localize and repair errors (debugging) and to prove their absence (proving correctness). We will return to the topic of debugging, using assertions, in Section 6.6.

The usefulness of formal analysis techniques can be enhanced further by the use of (semi)automatic tools. In fact, in a formal correctness proof, there are a few critical points where ingenuity must be applied (typically, the invention of loop invariants and the proof of logical implications), and there are many "clerical" steps that can easily be automated (typically, backward substitutions and some algebraic simplifications). It is natural to leave the carrying out of the latter to the computer and allow the user to concentrate on the critical aspects. Some remarks on tools that aid in formal analysis will be given in Chapter 9; here, however, we observe that the existence of such tools for proving program correctness may foster the practicality of the technique and counter the previous objections 1 and 3.

We believe that a good knowledge of formal analysis techniques will eventually enhance the reliability of even informal analysis. In fact, rigor and formality always enhance the reliability of even informal, everyday types of reasoning.

Exercises

6.27 Is the following provable with respect to the specification given for module TABLE in this section? Why? Why not?

{max_size > 1}
Delete (Table, Element);
Insert (Table, Element);
{Element ∈ Table}

6.28 Modify the specifications given in Section 6.4.2.3 for operations Insert and Delete in such a way that both

{Size (Table) < max_size}
Insert (Table, Element);
Delete (Table, Element);
{Table = *Old*_Table - Element}

and

{Size (Table)> 1}
Delete (Table, Element);
Insert (Table, Element);
{Element ∈ Table}

become provable. Then give an implementation, and either prove it correct with respect to the augmented specifications, or, if it is not correct, modify the implementation accordingly.

6.5 SYMBOLIC EXECUTION

Symbolic execution is a verification technique that can be classified as somewhere in between testing and correctness analysis: it is a synthesis of experimental and analytical approaches to software verification.

Consider the following simple program:

```
read (a); read (b);
x := a + b;
write (x);
```

A computer needs to read some specific input values in order to perform its computation and to produce the appropriate output. By contrast, a human analysis (for instance, during a walk-through) can go along the following lines:

Let A and B be the first two values of the input file. They are assigned to variables a and b, respectively. Thus, the result of assignment x := a + b is that x gets the value A + B. Finally, A + B is printed as the result.

The advantage of this kind of reasoning over actual numerical computation is more generality: A and B represent *any actual values* for the input variables. Thus, they allow us to conclude that the program's output is their sum, no matter what their actual values are. By contrast, if we just test the program by supplying, say, 3 and 4 as input values, the fact that the output is the value 7 provides little evidence that the program's function was just a sum.

The main difference between computer execution and hand simulation of the previous program is that in computer execution variables receive actual numeric[1] values, whereas in hand simulation we give them *symbolic values*. Thus, we said that a's value was A and that, after execution, x got the value A + B.

Without going into a formal theory of symbolic execution, for which we refer the reader to the specialized literature referenced in the bibliographic notes, we can say that the technique is based on the fact that the domain of possible values for program variables is the set of expressions made up of symbolic values and operation symbols. We do not need many mathematical definitions to convince the reader that the results of symbolically evaluating the following programs are the expressions within square brackets:

```
read (a); read (b);
x := a + 1; y := x *  b;
write (y);
[(A + 1) * B]

read (a); read (b);
x := a + 1; x := x + b + 2;
write (x);
[A + B + 3]
```

We see from the second example that some simplification of formulas can be applied naturally to the symbolic results.

Symbolic evaluation is a candidate technique for general and reliable program analysis. For instance, consider the following asserted program fragment:

```
{true}
read (a);
x := a * a;
x := x + 1;
write (x);
{output > 0}
```

Symbolic evaluation of this fragment easily produces the result output = A^2 + 1. Thus, a simple arithmetic deduction allows us to conclude that the specification is met. The method we follow is similar to what we did in correctness proofs. Also, much of the

---

[1] In this section, we talk about *numeric computation* and *numeric values* as opposed to symbolic computation and symbolic values, respectively. Thus, the attribute "numeric" applies not only to genuine numeric values, but also to values that, strictly speaking, are of nonnumeric type, such as characters and Booleans.

symbolic transformation involved in such an analysis can be performed automatically, just as backward substitution is done in correctness proofs.

The situation, however, becomes more intricate as soon as we deal with nontrivial programs. For instance, in the program fragment

```
read (a);
if a > 0 then
        DO_CASE_1;
else
        DO_CASE_2;
end if;
```

symbolic execution cannot proceed when it reaches the conditional, because a's symbolic value does not carry enough information to support the choice of either DO_CASE_1 or DO_CASE_2. To deal with such branches, a basic approach is to select a particular branch and continue along it.

We will describe how this kind of problem can be treated in Section 6.5.1, which provides the basic concepts behind symbolic execution of a simple ALGOL-like language. The more intricate details that are needed to symbolically execute programs with arrays are discussed in Section 6.5.2. Section 6.5.3 discusses the use of symbolic execution in testing. Finally, Section 6.5.4 suggests how the theory of symbolic execution may be extended to deal with concurrent programs.

6.5.1 Basic Concepts of Symbolic Execution

Consider the following program fragment, and assume that at the beginning of its execution the symbolic values of the variables are $x = X$, $a = A$, and $y = Y$:

```
x := y + 2;
if x > a then
        a := a + 2;
else
        y := x + 3;
end if;
x := x + a + y;
```

After execution of the first statement, we have $x = Y + 2$, with all other variables remaining unchanged. At the branching point, since the comparison $Y + 2 > A$ may yield either true or false, we make an arbitrary choice, say the **else** branch. This leads to the final state $\{a = A, y = Y + 5, x = 2 * Y + A + 7\}$. We must, however, record the fact that such a result is obtained by selecting the **else** branch of the **if** statement. This can be done by keeping track of the path executed, say, by referring to the control flow graph of the program, and by recording the condition the symbolic values must satisfy in order to guarantee the traversal of the selected path. In this case, the condition is $Y + 2 \leq A$. As a result, we may claim that the symbolic execution we have described produces the triple

$$<\{a = A, y = Y + 5, x = 2 * Y + A + 7\}, <1, 3, 4>, Y + 2 \le A>$$

where <1, 3, 4> denotes the execution path with reference to the control flow graph shown in Figure 6.9.

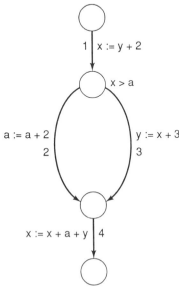

Figure 6.9   An annotated control flow graph. The branching node is marked
by the corresponding condition in the program fragment, and
edges are marked by the corresponding statements.

The condition that guarantees the execution of a given path is called the *path condition*. Once a path condition is given, the corresponding execution path can be derived immediately from the program, and conversely. Thus, only one of the two is necessary to fully describe the symbolic execution. For the moment, however, we will keep both. Indeed, we will see later that the execution path is actually needed for concurrent programs.

In general, let P denote a program fragment, and let G_P denote P's control flow graph. Then the result of symbolically evaluating P on a path of G_P is the *symbolic state* of P, defined as the triple <symbolic_variable_values, execution_path, path_condition>. The set symbolic_variable_values describes the bindings of variables with their symbolic values by equations of the type

variable_identifier = symbolic_expression

where symbolic_expression is composed in the usual way from identifiers that denote symbolic variable values. (For simplicity, we use lowercase letters for variable identifiers and uppercase letters for symbolic values.) The execution path is a sequence of contiguous edges in G_P. The path condition is a logical expression involving symbolic values and denotes the condition that the symbolic values must meet to guarantee traversal of the execution path.

Before starting symbolic execution, the symbolic state of the interpreter is initialized to show the symbolic values of variables as undefined, the execution path as null, and the condition path as true. As new statements are encountered, the symbolic interpreter updates the symbolic state in the following way:

1. The execution of an input statement read (x) causes the binding x = X to be added to the state, where X is a *newly introduced* symbolic value that does not occur in any previous state, and causes any previous binding for x to be deleted.

2. The execution of an assignment statement x := expression causes the construction of the symbolic value of the expression, SV, from the symbolic values of the variables involved in the expression. (The details of such construction should be obvious from the previous examples.) Subsequently, the binding x = SV is stored into the state, replacing the previous binding for x, if any.

3. The execution of an output statement write(expression) causes the symbolic evaluation of the expression as before and the binding output(n) = computed_symbolic_value, where n denotes a counter associated with the output file. The counter n is initialized to one and is automatically incremented after each output statement.

4. After execution of the last statement of a sequence that corresponds to an edge of G_P, the edge is appended to the execution path.

5. The execution of a conditional statement of the type **if** cond **then** S_1; **else** S_2; **end if**, or of a **while** cond **loop**...**end loop** statement causes the following sequence of steps to be executed:

   a. The condition is evaluated by substituting in it the current symbolic values for variables. Let eval (cond) denote the symbolic result.

   b. If it can be deduced that eval (cond) is true or false, independently of the values of the symbolic identifiers,[1] then execution proceeds by following the appropriate branch. Otherwise:

   c. A nondeterministic choice of true or false is made for the condition. In the former case, eval (cond) is conjoined to the current path condition. In the latter case, **not** (eval (cond)) is conjoined to the path condition. Then, execution proceeds along the corresponding edge of G_P.

By applying the above symbolic execution procedure to the previous fragment, we obtain two different triples as results. Besides the one already mentioned, we also have the following triple that is obtained by selecting the **then** branch of the conditional statement.

---

[1]Remember that evaluating logical implications of symbolic expressions is, in general, undecidable. Thus, it cannot be done completely mechanically and may require human interaction.

$$<\{a = A + 2, y = Y, x = 2 * Y + A + 4\}, <1, 2, 4>, Y + 2 > A >$$

Clearly, in many cases, the set of possible triples that are the result of symbolically executing a program fragment may be infinite, as may be the number of paths in the control flow graph.

Symbolic execution of traditional programming constructs such as **if-then-else** and **while** loops establishes a one-to-one correspondence between the execution path and the path condition; that is, a given path condition unequivocally determines an execution path, and conversely. This is due to the deterministic nature of these constructs–i.e., for any actual execution state, when variables have numeric values, the next statement to be executed is determined uniquely. In such a case, we can drop the execution path component from the symbolic state; this would not be possible, however, if the language provides nondeterministic control structures or, as we will see in Section 6.5.4, in the case of concurrent programs.

Exercises

6.29 Give symbolic evaluation rules for classical programming constructs such as **case**, **repeat-until**, and other constructs.

6.30 Compute some symbolic evaluation triples by increasing the length of the execution paths for the programs of Exercise 6.25.

6.5.2 Programs with Arrays

Symbolic execution becomes more intricate when dealing with arrays for much the same reasons as in proving correctness. We will briefly sketch two possible ways of tackling the problem.

In the first approach, any access to a given array whose index value is not numerically known is considered as if it were a branch, with an edge for each possible index value. In other words, let a be an array with 10 elements. Then, the statement a(i) := exp is considered a shorthand notation for

```
case i of
      when 1 => a(1) := exp;
      when 2 => a(2) := exp;
         ⋮
```

This approach is simple, but produces a proliferation of execution paths. It could be used in practice only in interactive execution or with small-sized arrays.

A more general approach is to let any assignment to an array value produce a new symbolic value for the whole array and to record suitable relationships between the old value and the new value. For instance, let A_1 be the symbolic value of array a at a given point where statement a(i)= exp is executed. Then, after execution, a receives the new symbolic value A_2, which we will denote as $A_2 = A_1<i, exp>$, which is a shorthand notation for

for all k **if** $k = i$ **then** $A_2(k) = exp$ **else** $A_2(k) = A_1(k)$

We can see a similarity between this formula and the backward substitution rule given for correctness proofs.

We explain the second method with the help of the following example.

Example 6.14

Consider the following program fragment, where x denotes an integer array variable of length 5:

```
1.      read (i);
2.      y := x(i);
3.      x(3) := 9;
4.      read (i);
5.      x(i) := 3 + y;
6.      y := x(2);
7.      read (i);
8.      x(i) := x(i) - 1;
9.      y := y + x(i);
```

Let execution start in an initial state in which the symbolic value X_1 is bound to x. Then, executing statements 1 through 9 produces the following bindings:

1.	read (i);	$i = I_1$
2.	y := x(i);	$y = X_1(I_1)$
3.	x(3) := 9;	$x = X_2$ **where** $X_2 = X_1 < 3, 9 >$
4.	read (i);	$i = I_2$
5.	x(i) := 3 + y;	$x = X_3$ **where** $X_3 = X_2 < I_2, 3 + X_1(I_1) >$
		that is, $X_3(I_2) = 3 + X_1(I_1)$[1]
6.	y := x(2);	$y = X_3 (2)$
7.	read (i);	$i = I_3$
8.	x(i) := x(i) - 1;	$x = X_4$ **where** $X_4 = X_3 < I_3, X_3(I_3) -1 >$
9.	y := y + x(i);	$y = X_3(2) + X_4(I_3)$

Notice that the symbolic state can be expressed as a function of the symbolic values read and x's initial value X_1, using substitutions that "unfold" the additional relations stored into the state. By performing such operations, we obtain, at the end of the execution of the fragment,

---

[1]Here, some optimization could be performed. In fact, since x has not been referenced since its last assignment, we could simply update its current value by means of the modification $x = X_2$ **where** $X_2 = X_1 < 3, 9 >< I_2, 3 + X_1(I_1)>$.

$$y = X_1 < 3,\ 9 > < l_2,\ 3 + X_1(l_1) > (2) +$$
$$X_1 < 3,\ 9 > < l_2,\ 3 + X_1(l_1) > < l_3,\ X_1 < 3,\ 9 > < l_2,\ 3 + X_1(l_1) > (l_3) - 1 > (l_3) \quad \blacksquare$$

Exercise

6.31 Compute several execution paths for the program of Example 6.12. (Try the case where you execute the loop just once, and observe how the treatment of arrays becomes simpler in the particular case where indexes have a numeric value even during symbolic evaluation.)

6.5.3 The Use of Symbolic Execution in Testing

Symbolic execution is a powerful tool that can be seen as an interesting middle ground between the generality and rigor–but also tedium and complexity–of correctness proofs and the simplicity–but also unreliability–of testing. In fact, the results of symbolic execution are *formulas* that in one way or another help in deducing program properties. The technique, however, is still evolving, and its practical applicability is questionable in the case of large and complex programs.

Symbolic execution, however, can be used indirectly as a testing aid. More precisely, it can help in the selection of test data for a particular execution path. In fact, once a given path in the control flow graph of a program has been selected (for example, to reach a statement in the case of the statement coverage criterion), a suitable path condition that guarantees its traversal can be built algorithmically. Thus, the problem of guaranteeing path traversal is reduced to proving the satisfiability of a mathematical formula.

For instance, consider the following program fragment (which was discussed in Section 6.3.4.1), whose control flow graph is given in Figure 6.10:

```
found := false; counter := 1;
while (not found) and counter < number_of_items loop
        if table (counter) = desired_element then
                found := true;
        end if;
        counter := counter + 1;
end loop;
if found then
        write ("the desired element exists in the table");
else
        write ("the desired element does not exist in the table");
end if;
```

If we symbolically execute the path <1,2,3,5,6,7,9>, we obtain the path condition

```
table(1) = desired_element
```

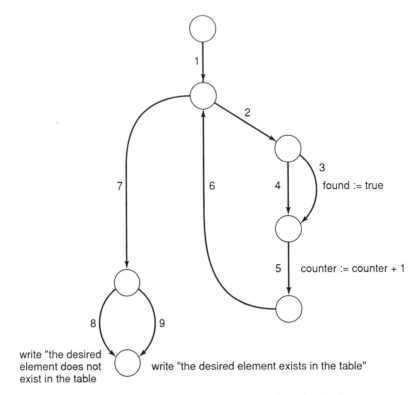

Figure 6.10   Control flow graph of the program fragment of Section 6.5.3.
Edges are labeled by the relevant assignment statements.

On the other hand, if we try to execute the path <1,2,3,5,6,2,3,5,6,...>, we obtain, as a
partial path condition,

        1 < number_of_items
        and table(1) = desired_element
        and not (true)
        and 2 < number_of_items

which clearly is a contradiction, showing that the path in question is infeasible. In fact,
the loop can be executed only once if the **then** branch of its inner **if** statement is
executed.

       Of course, in general, deciding the satisfiability of path conditions is still an
undecidable problem. But finding values that make a formula true is often easier than
directly looking for values that guarantee path traversal. In other words, symbolic
execution can help make test data selection more systematic. Indeed, for special cases,
such as linear path conditions, the process can be made algorithmic.

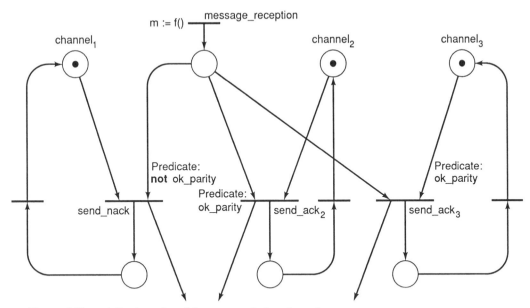

Figure 6.11   A Petri net describing a transmission channel.

6.5.4 Symbolic Execution of Concurrent Programs

In this section, we examine the use of symbolic execution in the analysis of concurrent software. Specifically, we base our analysis on Petri nets; the remarks we give, however, are general and do not depend on the particular formalism we use for describing a concurrent system.

Let us consider augmented Petri nets in which tokens have values and each transition has an associated action and a predicate that determines whether the transition can fire based on the values of incoming tokens. Symbolic execution allows us to use symbolic values for tokens and evaluate the transition predicates symbolically.

In a sequential and deterministic program, at any given point, the state of the symbolic interpreter is given by a triple <symbolic_variable_values, execution_path, path_condition>, where path_condition fully determines the execution path. In a concurrent system, the execution path is a sequence of atomic execution steps. In the particular case of a Petri net, an atomic step is modeled by the firing of a transition, which consumes a tuple of tokens from its input places. If we make the simplifying assumption that no more than one token will ever be present in each place, a sequence of atomic steps can be modeled by a firing sequence, which resolves the nondeterminism that is due to several transitions being enabled. Thus, the triple <symbolic_variable_values, execution_path, path_condition> can be used to model the symbolic state of the interpreter provided that we interpret execution_path as the firing sequence.

Consider the specification of a concurrent system given in Figure 6.11. The Petri net represents messages that may be received and dispatched on one of three channels. The action that generates a message in the mailbox is modeled by the statement m := f(). Function f with no argument states that messages are sent to the system by the external environment, without any relationship to the internal state of the system. Thus, f is actually used as a random number generator.

When we execute a Petri net symbolically, we start with an initial value of true for the path condition. A transition can fire only if its associated predicate is implied by the path condition. If we decide to fire it, then the execution path (i.e., the firing sequence) is updated. A transition can also fire if the path condition implies neither the truth nor the falsity of its associated predicate. If we decide to fire it, then not only is the execution path updated as before, but the path condition is also updated by the conjunction of the evaluated predicate.

Now consider the path condition

$$M_1.ok\_parity \text{ and not } M_2.ok\_parity \text{ and } M_3.ok\_parity$$

where M_1, M_2, and M_3 are the symbolic values of messages received (i.e., the tokens generated by the transition message_reception) and $M_i.ok\_parity$ (i = 1,2,3) indicates whether or not the parity bit of M_i is correct. We can see that the path condition makes the following firing sequence possible:

<message_reception, send_ack$_2$, message_reception, send_nack, message_reception, send_ack$_3$>

In this example, when the path condition contains $M_i.ok\_parity$, two transitions may fire, because the associated predicate is true. The firing sequence resolves the choice between the two.

Thus, both the path condition and the firing sequence are needed to characterize an execution path uniquely. We can then use the pair <firing sequence, path condition> to drive the testing activity. For example, if the net of Figure 6.11 is the specification of a communication system, we could use the path condition to derive constraints on the input messages submitted to the system when it is being tested and then check whether the system executes its actions in the same sequence as specified in the pair. Unfortunately, because of the presence of nondeterminism, other sequences of actions would also be considered valid, and we should check whether the observed sequence is actually valid according to the net description in the figure.

On the other hand, if we want to reproduce exactly the same sequence of actions as specified in the pair, we may get into problems, because we must be able to resolve nondeterminism exactly as it is stated in the firing sequence member of the pair. This may be difficult to achieve if some actions are performed by the external environment in an unpredictable manner, as may be the case here for messages received in the mailbox. On this very specific topic, we refer the interested reader to the specialized literature mentioned in the bibliographic notes.

6.6 DEBUGGING

In our discussion of testing, we have said several times that the goal of testing is the discovery of errors ("bugs") in programs. According to the terminology introduced in Section 6.3.2, we can say that a program's failure is a clear symptom of the presence of an error, but the presence of an error does not necessarily cause a failure. The goal of testing is to discover program executions in which errors lead to failures. As we said before, however, the choice of an appropriate testing criterion enables us to view successful testing as more than an uninteresting experiment: it should, indeed, increase our confidence in the correctness of the program.

Debugging is the activity of locating and correcting errors. It can start once a failure has been detected. Unfortunately, going from the detection of a failure to correcting the error that is responsible is far from trivial. Although debugging is not a verification activity and thus–strictly speaking–should not be treated in this chapter, it is so intimately related to verification that we have decided to discuss it here briefly.

Debugging is one of the least understood activities in software development and is practiced with the least amount of discipline. It is often approached with much hope and little planning. While there is still much to be learned about debugging and, in particular, about what leads to successful debugging, our previous discussion of the testing and analysis of programs enables us to analyze debugging carefully, leading to a disciplined approach.

First, a failure is actually a behavior that does not match the program specifications. Thus, one should first consult the specifications themselves, to determine whether they are clear enough and to consider the possibility that the error is in the specifications, rather than in the implementation. Second, the location of the error, assuming that the error is in the implementation, is not always apparent. The failure could even be caused by a combination of several errors.

Thus, rigor and care must be used in locating errors during debugging. Certainly, a clear separation between testing in the small and testing in the large, i.e., modularizing the testing activity, helps in debugging. For instance, if two modules behave properly when operated separately, and a failure occurs when they are integrated, their interface should be checked for consistency.

Even when an error has been clearly localized to a given module, however, the module could still be too large and complex to enable the immediate detection of the error. Thus, in some sense, we need to practice some "testing in the smaller" *a posteriori*, e.g., by breaking the module into small fragments whose intended behavior we understand clearly.

A simple and powerful principle to aid in localizing errors is *closing up the gap between faults and failures*. To understand this notion, recall from our terminology from Section 6.3 that we consider as fault an incorrect state during program execution, say a variable value that is not correct. The problem is that faults do not always lead to failures and therefore may go undetected.

We can, however, expose faults by means of suitable techniques. For instance, consider the old-fashioned technique of producing a *memory dump*: printing out the

contents of memory at some given point of program execution. In principle, this
technique tries to make any fault result in a failure. By dumping the memory, we are
making the state of the program–i.e. the contents of the memory–an output of the
program so that any discrepancy in any part of the memory shows up as a failure in the
output produced by the program. Of course, this requires that we state precise
requirements for the results of memory dumps just as for other program outputs. If we are
able to do this–and to check such requirements–then we have turned a fault into a failure
at the point of the dump, and we have closed the gap between the two.

The obvious drawback of this approach is that too many details are needed, in
general, to analyze the result of a dump (even if it is represented symbolically). That is,
the specification of the whole memory state is too complex to define and to check. But
the principle of pushing faults closer to failures by adding the specification of the
program state can be applied in other, more flexible, ways.

A natural middle ground between examining dumps and examining only the
program's output is to restrict our attention to some particular variables at some particular
execution points. This can be done by using software monitors. A monitor used to inspect
the value of a variable is called a *watch point* (or a *spy point*).

We can implement a watch point by inserting an output statement in the appropriate
place in the program. We will see in Chapter 9 that debuggers make it possible to insert
watch points in a program without modifying the program manually. This eliminates
many practical problems involved with adding ad hoc debugging statements to the
program manually. For example, in the manual modes, we have to be sure that after
finding and fixing the error, we remove any debugging statements we have inserted.

In this section, however, we are interested only in the concept of a watch point, and
we will use output statements. So if, for instance, we wish to check the value of array
index variable i at a given point where the array is accessed, we just modify the code, say,

```
a: array (1..10) of INTEGER;
        .
        .
        .
a(i) := ...
```

to

```
a: array (1..10) of INTEGER;
        .
        .
        .
write (i);
a(i) := ...
```

Suppose, however, that we are really interested not in the particular value of the
variable, but rather in the fact that it satisfies a particular condition. For example, suppose
the watch point on variable i is intended to check whether the array index is in the first
half of the array–i.e., we are interested in the truth or falsity of the assertion $\{1 \leq i \leq 5\}$ at
the point where we have inserted write (i).

In Section 6.4.2, we saw the use of intermediate assertions for exactly this purpose.
There, we tried to produce a proof that the assertion holds in any execution of the
program when execution reaches the point at which the assertion occurs. In debugging,

we attempt to verify that the assertion holds for a particular execution. In program debugging, whether we realize it or not, whether we do it formally or informally, we are testing the validity of assertions. These assertions may have been embedded by the programmer in the program or may have been manufactured by the person doing the debugging as hypotheses about the location and nature of the error.

An effective way to add executable debugging assertions to a program is to use a procedure called assert that accepts a Boolean input. This procedure will evaluate its input and will do nothing if its input is true; it will produce a message or terminate the program if its input is false. Using the assert procedure in the above example instead of write(i), we could use assert (i > 0 and i < 6). One advantage of this approach is that calls to assert can be removed from the program relatively easily after debugging is completed (through conditional compilation, the use of comments, etc.).

Example 6.15

Consider the following procedure, intended to merge two sorted sequences with no duplicate elements into a single sorted sequence with no duplicate elements. The procedure is given together with appropriate type declarations and a formal specification written as a pair of logical formulas (pre- and postconditions):

```
type sequence (max_size: NATURAL) is
        record
                size : INTEGER range 0. . max_size:= 0;
                contents = array (1.. max_size) of INTEGER
        end record;

{(1 ≤ l < m ≤ a.size) implies a.contents (l) < a.contents (m)) and
(1 ≤ l < m ≤ b.size) implies b.contents (l) < b.contents (m))}

procedure strict_merge (a, b : in sequence; c : out sequence) is
        i, j, k : integer;
begin i := 1; j := 1; k := 1;
while i ≤ a.size and j ≤ b.size loop
        if a.contents (i) < b.contents (j) then
                c.contents (k) := a.contents (i);
                i := i + 1;
        else
                c.contents (k) := b.contents (j) ;
                j := j + 1;
        end if;
        k := k + 1;
end loop;
while i ≤ a.size loop
        c.contents (k) := a.contents (i);
        i := i + 1; k := k + 1;
end loop;
```

```
while j ≤ b.size loop
        c.contents (k) := b.contents (j);
        j := j + 1; k := k + 1;
end loop;
c.size := k - 1;
end;
```

{(1 ≤ l < m ≤ c.size} **implies** c.contents (l) < c.contents (m)) **and**
(**for all** x
            ((**exists** l (x = a.contents (l)) **or exists** m (x = b.contents (m)))
            implies exists p (x = c.contents (p))) **and**
            (**exists** p (x = c.contents (p)) **implies**
            (**exists** l (x = a.contents (l)) **or exists** m (x = b.contents (m))
            ))
}

Executing the procedure with input data

$$a = \{1,3,5,7\} , b = \{2, 3, 8\}$$

produces the erroneous result c = {1,2,3,3,5,7,8}, which violates the output requirement

{(1 ≤ l < m ≤ c.size) **implies** c.contents (l) < c.contents (m))}

We can help localize the error by noting that, at each iteration of the first loop (as well as at each iteration of other loops), c should exhibit the property stated in the assertion up to the portion so far constructed. This can be formalized by the loop invariant

{(1 ≤ l < m < k} **implies** c.contents (l) < c.contents (m))}

Now, if we test the validity of the loop invariant during program execution by inserting the statement

if k > 2 **and then** c.contents (k - 2) ≥ c.contents (k - 1) **then**
        write ("iteration #:"); write (k - 1); write ("monotonicity error in c");
end if

as the last statement of the first loop, the fault will occur at the fourth loop iteration, and pinpointing this fact helps identify its source.   ∎

In Section 6.4.2, we saw the central role of intermediate assertions, such as loop invariants, in program correctness proofs; here we have seen their application in the very practical debugging activity.

As another example, consider the following fragment of code appearing in a client of the table manipulation module sketched in Section 6.4.2.3.

```
read (Element);
Insert (Table, Element);
        .
        .
Delete (Table, Element);
write (element);
```

In order to check whether the table is used correctly, we could insert the following intermediate assertions within the code:

```
read (Element);
{Size (Table) < max_size}
Insert (Table, Element);
{Element ∈ Table};
        .
        .
{Size (Table) > 0}
Delete (Table, Element);
{Element ∉ Table};
write (Element);
```

These assertions may be checked at run time in order to help detect and localize errors.

In conclusion, inserting and checking intermediate assertions within the code can be seen as a "specification *a posteriori*" of small program fragments. (In fact, we have used the same notation as for logic specification of whole programs.) In other words, the program is overspecified by adding details about its states of execution. The result is that whenever such more detailed specifications are violated, a program failure will occur—that is, more failures are generated from program faults. Insertion of intermediate assertions can also be viewed as an attempt during debugging to check a proof of correctness for a particular execution of the program.

Yet another function of intermediate assertions is as formal comments used for program documentation. The benefit of formality is that debugging can be performed systematically by checking the truth of such assertions.

We will see in Chapter 9 that appropriate tools can support the use of assertions in design and coding, as well as debugging.

Exercise

6.32 Modify the procedure of Example 6.15 by eliminating the second loop. Describe how you can use intermediate assertions to detect the errors in the program.

6.7 VERIFYING OTHER SOFTWARE PROPERTIES

At the beginning of this chapter, we stated that all software qualities should be verified, although we deliberately restricted our attention to the verification of functional correctness. In this section, we briefly address the topic of verification of other relevant qualities. As usual, we do not try to be exhaustive. Rather, we want to help develop the reader's intuition in the complex verification process. First, we address the issue of a classical "objective" quality, namely, performance. Then, we go into the more elusive topic of measuring qualities such as reliability, understandability, and modifiability.

6.7.1 Verifying Performance

Performance has always been a major concern in software systems, whether one is dealing with strictly real-time systems, with more traditional electronic data-processing systems, or with end-user productivity tools. Since performance is a measurable software property, several methods have been developed to verify it.

Performance evaluation is a subject in its own right. It is treated in specialized books and courses outside of software engineering. Rather than summarizing these texts here, we wish to provide just a framework to put the different specialized techniques for evaluating software performance in a unified perspective.

Performance can be verified from several standpoints and with several techniques. In general, these all complement each other. One can be interested in *worst case analysis*, where the focus is on proving that the system response time is bounded by some function of the external requests to the system, say, the number of incoming interrupts per second and the size of a file to be processed. In other cases, we might be interested in the *average behavior* of the system, wanting to know the average response time rather than its maximum value.

Another relevant factor in performance is the standard deviation. Clearly, both worst case and statistical factors are pertinent here. Sometimes, though, these may be in conflict. For instance, one of the best sorting algorithms, Quicksort, has a worst case performance that is $O(n^2)$, n being the number of elements to be sorted, whereas other algorithms that are worse on the average have worst case performance that is $O(n * \log n)$.

Both worst case analysis and statistical analysis are supported by established models, techniques, and tools. In the former, computational complexity theory, and in the latter, statistics, probability and queueing theory, provide many analytical models.[1]

As with functional correctness, performance can be verified either by *analyzing* suitable models of the software or by *experimenting* directly with the system behavior. Also, we can talk about static versus dynamic verification techniques, each with advantages and disadvantages. An important technique is that of *simulation*, which derives knowledge about system performance by running a mathematical model of the system. It is therefore considered a dynamic verification technique, even though it does not require running the real system. In general, simulation applies statistical models of the system. We can view simulation as a rapid prototyping technique devoted to the

---

[1]In some specialized literature, the term *performance evaluation* is reserved only for statistical analysis.

analysis of performance. It is fairly surprising that it was used for a long time before analogous techniques were applied to the verification of functional specifications and before the term became commonplace.

6.7.2 Verifying Reliability

Statistical and probabilistic methods work quite well for measuring those of a system's properties which we cannot measure with absolute certainty. In the case of software, we saw in the previous section that performance may naturally be modelled and evaluated in a statistical way. In general, many properties of engineering artifacts, such as *reliability*, are measured and verified in this way. For instance, the reliability of an electrical appliance may be measured in terms of its probability of failure within a given time. This measure is helpful whenever we cannot guarantee absence of failures absolutely.

In the case of software, we have already seen in Chapter 2 that reliability is used intuitively to denote a broader and often more useful property than correctness. In fact, we saw that in many cases one may even accept an incorrect system, assuming that its defects are not serious and/or that failures do not occur too frequently. For instance, a word processor whose spell-checker sometimes fails to catch some unusual misspelling may still be considered reliable if this error occurs not too frequently and other functions, such as saving files are guaranteed to work.

Thus, it sounds rather natural to try to measure the reliability of software on a probabilistic basis, as has been done in other engineering fields. Unfortunately, however, there are some difficulties with this approach. First, as we remarked at the beginning of this chapter, the notion of continuity is generally lacking in software. This prevents us from quantifying in a rigorous and measurable way concepts such as "small defect" and "acceptable failure". Furthermore, traditional probabilistic models are based on hypotheses that do not hold in the case of software.

For instance, we can assume that, *normally*, the separate events of two different customers entering a bank to ask for some service are *independent* in the same way that the results of flipping the same coin two times are independent. This independence allows us to estimate quantities such as the mean service time spent with some teller and the average length of the waiting queues. Similarly, the events of two different chip failures in the same processor can generally be considered independent. This allows us to state the probability of system failure both in the case where the whole system depends on both chips and in the case where the functioning of one chip is enough to guarantee system operation.

This is not so, however, in the case of software: independence of *failures* can hardly be assumed. For instance, consider the following fragment:

```
if x > 0 then
        write (y);
else
        write (z);
        write (x);
end if;
```

Suppose that two independent errors have been made by the programmer. One generates the fault of making x's value incorrect, and the other makes z's value incorrect. But if the value of x is 6 instead of 7, evaluation of the above condition still produces a correct result, and thus, neither error will cause a failure during execution. By contrast, if x is 0 instead of 1, both failures will occur; and if x is 2 instead of 0, we can infer the error in x (because y is printed instead of z and x), but not the error in z.

Nevertheless, measuring statistical reliability properties, such as the mean time between two software failures, is an attractive goal and has been pursued by researchers.

First of all, let us point out that reliability is concerned with measuring the *probability of the occurrence of failure*, that is, the probability of the observable effects of errors. Second, several quantities are taken into consideration as meaningful parameters for estimating software reliability including, typically, the following:

- The *average total number of failures*, AF(t), observed at a given time. The average is obtained with respect to different observations on different installations of the same system. Ideally, experiments should be performed in such manner that n identical instantiations of the same system are initialized identically. Then, these n instantiations start operating independently (say, with different, unrelated, users). For each of them, the total number of failures at time t is next computed. Finally, the average of such numbers with respect to the n instantiations is AF(t).

- The *failure intensity*, FI(t), i.e., the number of failures per time unit. FI(t) is the derivative of AF(t) with respect to time t, using the terminology of continuous mathematics.

- The *average time interval between two failures*, also called the *mean time to failure* (MTTF). Clearly, MTTF(t) = 1/ FI(t).

In the above quantities, the time variable may be intended in different ways. It may denote either the actual *execution time* of the software under consideration, or the *calendar time*, which includes also the time when the system is off, or even the machine *clock time*, that is, all the time that the hardware is running–including time spent on other programs. Clearly, these three times are related: in a system that is in a state of equilibrium, the ratio of any one to any of the other two can be thought of as constant. In more dynamic cases (e.g., when the number of applications running on the same processor varies over time), more complex and deeper analysis is needed. We will talk here about execution time only, without going into the subtleties of the differences among such measures.

Thus, it is assumed that the occurrence of software failures follows some law of randomness. Here, we could discuss philosophical issues on determinism, nondeterminism, and randomness. In fact, some claim that even the result of throwing a coin is regulated by deterministic laws, so that, by knowing the strength applied when flipping the coin, the density of air, the weight and the shape of the coin, etc., one could, in principle, forecast the result of a coin toss. However, since all of these elements are combined in a far too complex way for us to know what they are, a random model is much more practical for analyzing such a phenomenon. Of course, we will not be able to forecast the exact result of a single coin toss, but we can state that, for a large enough number of tosses, about 50% will be heads and 50% will be tails.

Similarly, it is claimed that software construction is often so complex that human

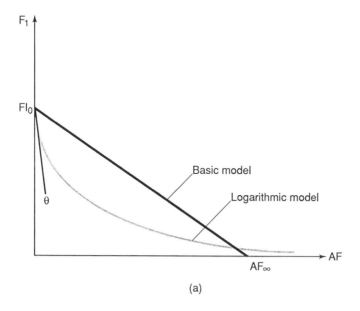

(a)

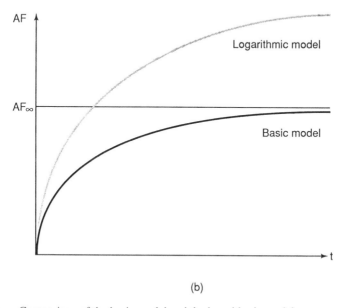

(b)

Figure 6.12   Comparison of the basic model and the logarithmic model.
(a) Failure intensity as a function of average number of total failures observed.
(b) Average number of total failures observed as a function of time.

programming errors that cause failures are distributed randomly,[1] and their effects occur randomly. In other words, failures, as well as the environment (external stimuli, input values, etc.) within which software must operate, are arranged randomly. Therefore, several classical models of random processes have been used to describe the variables involved. Two major models are discussed next.

The *basic model* assumes that the decrement per failure experienced–i.e., the derivative with respect to the number of detected failures–of the failure intensity function is constant. In other words, the FI variable is a function of AF according to the law

$$FI(AF) = FI_0 (1 - AF/AF_\infty)$$

where, FI_0 is the initial failure intensity and AF_∞ is the total number of failures.

Obviously, this law is based on the assumption that a decrease in failures is due to the fixing of the errors that were the sources of the failures. We know that detecting a failure is one thing, and finding its cause and removing it is quite another, even without considering the risk of introducing a new error. The basic model is based on the optimistic hypothesis that the total number of failures is finite. Also optimistic is the hope that the ability to remove errors does not vary in time. In practice, however, the errors detected first are usually easier to remove than subtle errors that occur in very intricate situations.

By contrast, the *logarithmic model* assumes, more conservatively, that the decrement per failure of FI decreases exponentially, i.e.,

$$FI(AF) = FI_0 \exp (- \theta \cdot AF)$$

where θ is called the *failure intensity decay* parameter. A comparison of the two models is given in Figure 6.12.

If failures actually occur according to either of these models, that model can be used to predict system reliability. In fact, it is sufficient to measure FI_0 and other constant parameters in the above formulas by performing a sufficient amount of testing so that average values are reasonably stable. Then, the application of the chosen formula allows the estimation of, say, the expected MTTF after 100 hours of execution time.

We must evaluate a given model on the basis of how it matches the actual failure phenomenon. Unfortunately, it is not clear whether and which statistical hypotheses can be assumed in regard to error and failure distribution. For instance, the basic model assumes that the total number of failures is finite, and the logarithmic model assumes the opposite. In other cases, we see claims of the type "After a reasonable amount of system experimentation, the number of remaining errors is likely to be proportional to the number detected so far," which clearly contradicts both models' assumptions.

Experimental evidence has been used to show that any of these models–basic, logarithmic, and others–does indeed work well for some class of applications. The fact that there exist arguments in favor of different models, however, shows at least that the applicability of these models must be restricted to carefully selected fields. For instance, the claim about the proportional relationship of detected to undetected errors is based on

---

[1]Randomly does not mean *uniformly*.

the observation of an old and very complex system–the OS 360 operating system–that was not built with a rigorous approach. The main reason for this pessimistic assumption was the observation that trying to fix a detected error caused the introduction of new errors as a side effect.

We do not go deeper into the subject here, since it would require developing much ad hoc theory. The topic is much debated in the scientific community, and its industrial application is only beginning. We will refer the reader to the relevant literature in the bibliographic notes. Here, we simply stress the point that by building a suitable formal model of the phenomenon at hand–in this instance, reliability–we can use the results of mathematics to gain some control over the phenomenon, such as the ability to predict. The critical issue, however, is whether and how well the formal models of reliability capture the peculiarities of software.

Exercise

6.33   Consider an application that contains errors causing an improper alarm. The consequence of these failures is that the operator must restart the system. An independent error, however, is also present in the initialization routines executed by the operator. This error does not cause a fault every time that the system is restarted. Rather, the fault, and the failure, too, occur depending on some external parameters set by the operator during the restart procedure. Discuss the correlation between the two types of failures.

6.7.3 Source-Code Metrics

We often assess software qualities such as understandability, modifiability, and portability. on the basis of common sense and experience. For instance, in Chapter 4, we insisted that good modularization is important to achieve many of the desired qualities. But we did not give any objective measure to determine whether one program is modularized "better" than another. There have been attempts, however, to make this measurement more precise. In some books and manuals, for example, one can even read suggestions of the type "a module length should not exceed 50 lines of code, or one page." Such recommendations, however, are too simplistic. They measure the size of a module independently of the module's logical organization. What if we are not able to build a procedure or an abstract data type in fewer than 51 lines? Should we split it anyway just to satisfy the above requirement? Even the notion of a *line of code* is rather elusive: does a module become more acceptable (shorter) just because we write several statements on the same line?

Another common and well-known claim–based on a famous remark by Dijkstra–is that a program containing GOTO statements may easily become unreadable. Should we therefore reject a program based on a count of its GOTO statements? Or should we consider one program better than another just because it contains fewer GOTO statements? But we know that one can build well-structured programs with GOTO statements and obscure ones without using GOTOs.

In short, no doubt, we need to be able to evaluate software qualities in more systematic ways in order to increase the objectivity of our assessments. But unfortunately, the easy attempts to translate our common sense into mathematical formulas intended to measure software qualities may often be readily criticized by finding obvious counter-examples. Using the number of lines as a metric to evaluate a module is a good example of a simplistic attempt. Even the more elaborate models proposed so far have proven to be controversial.

To conclude the chapter, we give a brief account of two of the best known models for measuring program complexity.[1] Since the metrics of these models are based on quantities that are measured from the source program, they are called *source-code metrics*.

6.7.3.1 Halstead's theory

Software science is an approach–due to Halstead–to measuring software qualities on the basis of objective code measures. It is based on information theory, which in turn is based on the following measurable quantities, defined for a given program coded in any programming language:

- η_1, the number of unique, distinct operators appearing in the program;
- η_2, the number of unique, distinct operands appearing in the program;
- N_1, the total number of occurrences of operators in the program;
- N_2, the total number of occurrences of operands in the program.

Although the terms "operator" and "operand" have an intuitive meaning, a precise definition of them is needed to avoid ambiguities that may arise between different programming languages. For instance, a pair of parentheses, as well as a **begin**-**end** pair, is considered a single operator. A label is considered an operator if it is used as the target of a GOTO statement, since its purpose is to effect control; otherwise, it is considered a comment. A GOTO statement applied to a label is considered an operator. An **if-then-else-end if** 4-tuple is considered a single operator. A ';' is considered a single operator. And other conventions hold as well. The following exercises are intended to convince the reader that much care is needed to define terms precisely. (In some cases, several answers are possible.)

Exercises

6.34 How should a reference to an array element of the type a (i, 4) be considered? Should it be viewed as a single operand? As an operator a applied to the operands i and 4 ? What about the comma?

6.35 How should a procedure identifier be considered, both when declared and when called? What about the identifier of a procedure that is passed as a parameter to another procedure?

---

[1]Do not confuse this with computational complexity!

Once we have defined η_1 and η_2 precisely, we can define the program vocabulary η and the program length N as

$$\eta = \eta_1 + \eta_2$$

and

$$N = N_1 + N_2$$

At this point, we can already consider some relations between the above quantities. A first obvious relation is

$$\eta \le N$$

Also, we can derive an upper limit on N as a function of η, based on the observation that it is quite unlikely that a program has several identical parts–in formal language terminology, substrings–of length greater than η. In fact, once a piece of code occurs identically in several places, it is usually made into a procedure, or a function, or a common subexpression to be stored in a temporary variable. Since repeated pieces of code are quite unlikely to contain all of a program's operands and operators, we can safely assume that any program of length N consists of N/η substrings of length η such that none of them occurs more than once in the program. Now, for any given alphabet of size k, there are exactly k^r different strings of length r. Thus, $N / \eta \le \eta^{\eta}$, and $N \le \eta^{\eta + 1}$. Also, since operands and operators in a program tend to alternate, we can further refine the upper bound into $N \le \eta \cdot \eta_1^{\eta_1} \cdot \eta_2^{\eta_2}$.(see Exercise 6.72).

Now, let us quote Halstead [1977], who derives an estimate $\hat{N}$ for the length of a program with η_1 operators and η_2 operands in the following way:

Now the upper limit $N \le \eta \cdot \eta_1^{\eta_1} \cdot \eta_2^{\eta_2}$ must include not only the single ordered set of N elements that is the program we seek, but it must also contain all possible subsets of that ordered set. Fortunately, the family of all possible subsets of a set of N elements is so well known that it has a name, "the Power Set", and this family itself has 2^N elements. Consequently we may equate the number of possible combinations of operators and operands with the number of elements in the power set, and solve for the length of an implementation of an algorithm in terms of its vocabulary. From

$$2^N = \eta \cdot \eta_1^{\eta_1} \cdot \eta_2^{\eta_2}$$

we have

$$N = \log_2 (\eta_1^{\eta_1} \cdot \eta_2^{\eta_2}) \text{ or } N = \log_2 \eta_1^{\eta_1} + \log_2 \eta_1^{\eta_2}$$

yielding the equation

$$\hat{N} = \eta_1 \log_2 \eta_1 + \eta_1 \log_2 \eta_2$$

where the "hat" has been placed on N to distinguish the quantity obtained, the calculated length, with this equation from the value of the length N obtained by direct observation.

We decided to quote Halstead's reasoning directly since, in spite of its intuitive attractiveness, it suffers from flaws that make it questionable. The major flaw is that a program is not a "single ordered set of N [distinct!] elements", but a string, with possible repetitions. Consider, for instance, the string aba, for which the set of all possible strings obtained by "picking up" any subset of its elements, in any order, is

$$\{\varepsilon \text{ (the empty string), a, b, ab, aa, ba, aba, baa, aab}\}$$

which contains more than 2^3 elements. (It could contain even less. When?)

Disregarding the questionable reasoning that leads to its formulation, $\hat{N}$ is an *estimate* of possible program length, not its measured value. Thus, it is interesting and necessary to compare $\hat{N}$ and N on some relevant samples. Some statistics performed on published algorithms seem to indicate an average value of the relative error $(N - \hat{N}) / N$ to be less than 10%.

As defined by Halstead, program length is a reasonable formalization of conceptual length, but does not coincide with more traditional notions of the term (the number of characters in the source code, the number of lines of code, the number of statements, etc.). Clearly, the physical length of the program (here, we assume the physical length to be the number of characters in the code) depends on factors such as the choice of identifiers for operators and operands. To avoid this type of dependency, which would produce highly different measures for "essentially the same program," the notion of program volume is introduced; i.e.,

$$V = N \log_2 \eta$$

Intuitively, the program volume V is the minimum number of bits needed to code the program. In fact, in order to represent η different identifiers, we need at least $\log_2 \eta$ bits.

Then, the notion of potential volume V^* is defined as the volume of the most succinct program in which an algorithm can be coded. Reasonably enough, it is claimed that such a form is given by assuming that the available programming language has just a single operator to perform the computation of the given algorithm, say op. Thus, if the algorithm operates on input and output data $d_1, d_2,..., d_n$, the most succinct program is

$$op (d_1, d_2,..., d_n)$$

which implies $\eta_1 = 2$ (commas are not considered operators here!), $\eta_2 = n$, and, therefore, $V^* = (2 + \eta_2) \cdot \log_2 (2 + \eta_2)$.

The notion of potential volume is then used to introduce the concept of program level, viz.,

$$L = V^* / V$$

L is an attempt to measure the *level of abstraction* of the formulation of an algorithm, assuming that the most abstract possible formulation is that having volume V^*. Again, there is some intuitive evidence in favor of such a definition, although it can be criticized more or less in the same way as have been the previous definitions.

Another important quantity introduced by Halstead's theory is the *effort* E, defined as V/L. Halstead argues that E may be interpreted as the number of mental discriminations required to implement a program (the implementation effort) and also as the effort required to read and understand the program. Experience has shown that, for small programs, E is well correlated with the effort needed for maintenance.

Halstead's software science goes further, giving formal definitions to such concepts as language level, intelligence contents, program purity, and so on. As a result, the theory defines a set of parameters that may be measured in programs (or estimated before development). Such parameters may be used for the quantitative assessment of properties in order to evaluate whether one program is better than another–for example, which of two programs solving the same problem has a higher complexity and hence requires more maintenance, or which has a higher abstraction level.

In conclusion, Halstead's theory tries to provide a formal definition for such qualitative, empirical, and subjective software qualities as program complexity, ease of understanding, and level of abstraction, based on the count of some low-level quantities, such as the number of operators and operands appearing in a program. The goal is to be able to predict the level of these qualities a program will have before the start of a project and then measure the level mechanically to assess the quality of the resulting product. In the next section, we review another theory that has the same goals as Halstead's software science, but is based on other quantities that can be measured in the source code.

Exercise

6.36 It is interesting to examine how the ratio $(N - \hat{N} / N$ varies when a program is divided into parts. (Actually, some experiments show that the partitioning of vocabularies due to program modularization maintains the stability of the ratio $(N - \hat{N}) / N$.) Two extreme situations may occur:

a. η_1 and η_2 are the same for all parts;

b. η_1 and η_2 are partitioned into disjoint subsets by modularization.

Compute the variations of $\hat{N}$ for a program with $N = \hat{N} = 72$, $\eta_1 = 4$, and $\eta_2 = 16$ when the program is divided into two parts, under the two extreme assumptions.

Warning: It may be difficult to "divide" a program in such a way as to satisfy the latter assumption. (At least one procedure definition and call must share an identifier.) For large values of the quantities involved, however, we can assume that, at least, η_1 and η_2 have small intersections with respect to their size.

6.7.3.2 McCabe's theory

Another source-code metric has been developed by McCabe, who observed that the quality of a program depends on the complexity of its control flow, rather than on operators and operands, as in Halstead's theory. McCabe's complexity metric C is based on the control flow graph, and is defined as

$$C = e - n + 2p$$

where e is the number of edges, n is the number of nodes, and p is the number of connected components of the graph (usually, 1).

In graph-theoretic terms, C is called the cyclomatic number of the graph, and thus McCabe's metric is called *cyclomatic complexity*. C defines the number of linearly independent paths in a program. It is possible to prove that, for structured programs with single-entry, single-exit constructs (i.e., with no GOTO statements), the cyclomatic number is equal to the number of conditions plus one. Also, for planar graphs, it is equal to the number of regions into which the graph divides the plane. For example, in the case of Euclid's algorithm, whose control flow graph is shown in Figure 6.3, the cyclomatic complexity is 5.

According to McCabe, the number of conditions that govern the control flow is an indication of how difficult the component is to understand, test, and maintain. McCabe also contends that well-structured modules have a cyclomatic complexity in the range 3-7, and C = 10 is a reasonable upper limit for the complexity of a single module, confirmed by empirical evidence.

Much research and experimental activity has been reported on validating Halstead's and McCabe's theories. Some experiments seem to support them, while others are inconclusive. Some researchers have tried to combine Halstead's, McCabe's, and even other metrics. We give an account of the field in the bibliographic notes.

Exercise

6.37   Evaluate McCabe's cyclomatic number for the merge program of Example 6.15.

6.8 CONCLUDING REMARKS

This chapter has been devoted to the verification of software qualities, primarily correctness. After reviewing the goals and requirements of verification, we examined major verification techniques. We provided a classification of these techniques based on analysis versus experimentation, or, alternatively, as static versus dynamic. Program testing is experimental. Code inspections, walk-throughs, and correctness proofs are analytic. Symbolic interpretation is a mixture of the two.

This classification may be criticized because it does not always characterize the different techniques clearly, e.g. a walk-through involves manual execution and symbolic execution is hard to classify. Because in practice many verification methods are combinations of static and dynamic techniques, other classifications have been proposed in the literature, with the aim of characterizing such hybrid methods better.

We have covered testing in depth. Starting from the basic terminology and some important theoretical results, we examined several classifications of testing techniques, such as testing in the small versus testing in the large and white-box testing versus black-box testing. We suggested that many different testing criteria can be understood in the light of the general *complete coverage principle* . We examined several such criteria and testing techniques in detail. In general, the different testing techniques have been shown to have complementary features, leading to many hybrid techniques being proposed in the literature.

Many experimental studies have tried to assess the success of various testing techniques. Their results, however, should be examined very carefully, because they depend on so many factors that are hard to control. For example, the order of application affects the results: usually one applies a simple technique to detect many simple errors, and then more sophisticated techniques to detect (fewer) more subtle errors. Also, we should not consider one technique to be more powerful than another just because it seems to detect more errors. We should also take the "difficulty" of the errors into account.

We then reviewed analysis techniques, informal as well as formal. To date, the practical use of formal analysis techniques has been limited but significant; e.g., in protocol verification, compiler verification, and operating system security. There is still much debate about the practical importance of these techniques but it should be clear from this chapter that their judicious use can enhance the practice of software engineering.

We discussed debugging as a natural complement to testing and examined its relationship to formal analysis.

Next, we considered the problem of assessing software qualities other than functional correctness. For some qualities, such as performance, well-established models exist. For others, such as reliability, stochastic models that work well in other engineering disciplines are more controversial as far as applicability to software goes. These models are the subject of much active research.

Finally, we gave a brief account of source-code metrics, which try to provide quantitative models of such subjective qualities as complexity of understanding and maintaining a program, ease of testing, and abstraction level. The approaches discussed are controversial, and much research is still necessary in the field.

FURTHER EXERCISES

6.38   Consider the following program fragment:

```
read (x); read (y);
if x > 0 or y ≤ 0 then
        write ("1");
else
        write ("2");
end if;
if y > 0 then
        write ("3");
else
        write ("4");
end if;
```

Discuss how to generate test cases using the statement coverage criterion.

6.39 Define how to construct control flow graphs for programs containing other structured statements such as **repeat-until**, **case**, and **if-then-elsif-else-end if**.

6.40 Give rules to build control flow graphs associated with program fragments containing GOTO statements in addition to structured statements. Also, give rules to transform a classical flowchart into a control flow graph.

6.41 Build the control flow graph of the binary search procedure of Example 6.2.

6.42 Prove that the edge coverage criterion produces different results from, and is finer than, the statement coverage criterion.

6.43 Suppose you reformulate the condition coverage criterion so that you require, not that all edges, but just that the constituents of compound conditions, of the control flow graph be exercised. Prove why this criterion would not be finer than the edge coverage criterion.

6.44 Compute the maximum number of possible execution paths for Euclid's algorithm given in Example 6.5 as a function of the maximum number of input values.

6.45 Consider the following sorting program fragment:

```
for i in 2 .. n loop
        x := a(i);
        a(0) := x;
        j := i - 1;
        while x < a(j) loop
                a(j + 1) := a(j);
                j := j - 1;
        end loop;
        a(j + 1) := x;
end loop;
```

Select a number of "significant" execution paths and find values of array a that cause their traversal.

6.46 In addition to the usual logical operators for composing Boolean expressions, Ada allows operators **or-else** and **and-then**. Give rules for building control flow graphs for statements that use these operators.

6.47 Consider the system described in Figure 6.13. In this system, two modules, M_1 and M_2, interacting through the operating system OS, must respond to stimuli I_1 and I_2, for which the maximum rates of occurrence are given. Each stimulus I_1 must result in a reply O_1 within a given maximum delay time. The same holds for I_2–with a different delay.

Use the incrementality principle to design a test strategy for this system. Notice that the two modules could run on different processors or on the same processor, but they share access to OS. Furthermore, the "service" provided by M_1 might require some computation by M_2, and conversely.

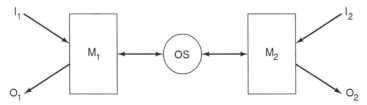

Figure 6.13   Two modules interacting through an operating system.

6.48   Notice the similarity between the syntax-driven testing criterion and the statement coverage criterion by simply considering syntactic productions instead of statements. In some sense, syntax-driven testing suffers from similar weaknesses as statement coverage. For instance, suppose that a compiler uses at most k temporary cells to evaluate arithmetic expressions. During the compilation, it keeps a counter of the number of cells used, and after using the kth cell, it starts again from the first cell, without checking whether the cell is still in use.

    a.   Assume that arithmetic expressions are described by the grammar of Example 6.7.

    b.   For several given values of k, give examples of expressions satisfying the syntax-directed criterion that fail to expose the error in the compiler.

    c.   Augment the testing criterion by using similar approaches to the way the corresponding white-box criterion has been strengthened in Section 6.3.4.1, in order to allow the detection of erroneous overwriting of a cell and of other errors.

6.49   Build a program that generates test sentences for any given BNF satisfying the criterion of syntax-driven testing augmented according to point **c.** of Exercise 6.48.

6.50   The classic approach to testing a compiler is to supply the compiler itself–written in the source language–as the test set. Does this approach satisfy the criterion of syntax-driven testing?

6.51   (For readers with some familiarity with formal language theory and/or compiler construction.) Notice that the syntax-driven testing criterion applies to a test domain D consisting of syntactically correct sentences. A compiler, however, should also be tested on incorrect sentences. Try to extend the criterion in order to achieve some completeness even in the compilation of incorrect programs.

6.52   (For readers with some familiarity with formal language theory and/or compiler construction.)It is well known that classical BNF defines programming languages only partially. For instance, the Pascal rule that variable identifiers can be used only if previously declared and type compatibility rules cannot be expressed by means of the BNF notation. Augment the criterion of syntax-driven testing in such a way that both correct and incorrect sentences with respect to such non-BNF rules may be considered possible test cases. Notice that, in practice, such rules are given informally. The reader may refer to the specialized literature to find sample formalizations of these and other aspects of programming language definitions.

6.53   Try to use the cause-effect graph technique, to give a Boolean-function definition of a program that computes the square root of its input value. Why can't you do this?

6.54 By following the same philosophy we used to reduce the size of the test set for cause-effect graphs, design a criterion that reduces the size of test sets derived by the multiple condition coverage criterion given in Exercise 6.7.

6.55 Systematic test strategies are certainly useful. They should, however, not dissuade us from applying our intuition and empirical knowledge to a problem. Consider the problem of finding *the* plane in a three-dimensional space in which three given points lie. This can be formally specified as follows:

- For any given three triples $<x_1, y_1, z_1>$, $<x_2, y_2, z_2>$, and $<x_3, y_3, z_3>$, find values a, b, c, and d that satisfy the equations
- $a*x_1 + b*y_1 + c*z_1 = d$
- $a*x_2 + b*y_2 + c*z_2 = d$
- $a*x_3 + b*y_3 + c*z_3 = d$

Which data are most appropriate to check a program implementing this specification?

6.56 Consider a lock-managing system that services sequences of lock (f_i), unlock (f_j) requests, where f_i and f_j are file names issued by several users. Clearly, testing such a system should involve submitting several sequences of lock-unlock requests from different users, both acceptable and unacceptable, to check appropriate reactions of the system. For instance, the system should accept the sequence

lock (f_1)	issued by user a
lock (f_2)	issued by user b
unlock (f_1)	issued by user a
lock (f_1)	issued by user b
unlock (f_2)	issued by user b
unlock (f_1)	issued by user b

but, the sequence

lock (f_1)	issued by user a
lock (f_2)	issued by user b
lock (f_1)	issued by user b
unlock (f_1)	issued by user a
unlock (f_2)	issued by user b
unlock (f_1)	issued by user b

should cause a rejection by the system at the third line.

Figure 6.14 gives a formal definition of acceptable sequences for any file f_j, under the simplifying hypothesis that there are only two users. (As a side exercise, you could generalize the definition to the case of any number of files and users by using Petri nets augmented with predicates and actions.)

Use the net of Figure 6.14 to derive test sequences–whether accepted or not–for the system. (For instance, one can derive the second sequence above by explicitly looking for the firing of a transition that is not enabled in a given PN marking.) Use your intuition and experience on locking policies to rule out some irrelevant sequences from the specified ones in order to limit the amount of testing.

6.57 Researchers and practitioners have proposed several "mixed testing strategies" intended to combine the advantages of the various techniques discussed in this chapter. Propose your own combination, perhaps also using some kind of random testing at selected points. You may find some suggestions in the specialized literature referenced in the bibliographic notes.

6.58 List some of the problems that could result from adding debugging statements to code. Discuss possible solutions to these problems. Design an appropriate interface for the assert routine suggested in Section 6.6.

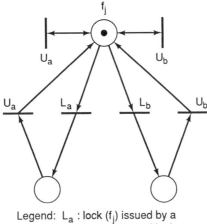

Legend: L_a : lock (f_j) issued by a
L_b : lock (f_j) issued by b
U_a : unlock (f_j) issued by a
U_b : unlock (f_j) issued by b

Figure 6.14   A Petri net description of the locking policy of the generic file f_j with two users.

6.59 Design testing criteria for the following graph-oriented problems. In some cases, you may decide to use a formal specification of the problem to gain better insight into it.

    a. Stating whether a directed graph is connected.
    b. Finding the number of connected components of an undirected graph.
    c. Finding maximal cliques in an undirected and in a directed graph. (A clique of a graph G is a complete subgraph of G; a maximal clique is a clique with the largest number of nodes.)
    d. Finding a path, if any, joining any pair of nodes in a graph (whether directed or not).

6.60 Design a test set for a spell-checker. Then run it on a word processor having a spell-checker, and report on possible inadequacies with respect to your requirements.

6.61 Give proof rules for statements not covered in Chapter 6, such as **for** loops and **case**.

6.62 Prove the correctness of the sorting program fragment proposed in Exercise 6.45.

6.63 Design testing criteria for the problem of finding the intersection of two convex polygons. The polygons are given as sequences of points in the integer Cartesian plane. The program must also be able to check whether the given polygons are convex or not. Take into account the fact that, even if the vertices have integer coordinates, their intersections may not have integer coordinates.

6.64 Design testing criteria for the problem of formatting a text according to the following rules:

The text is a sequence of characters. The special character '\' is used only for specifying commands. \lbreak is the "line break" command; the traditional RETURN, however, may also be used. Commands may be combined with braces { and } to indicate the scope of the application of the command. For example, {\b ...text...} says to turn the ...text... into boldface. The command for italicizing text is \i. Other formatting commands may be defined by the reader. Formatting commands can be nested. Beginnings and ends must match. Furthermore, two consecutive identical commands negate one another. As an example of the application of these rules, the text

> yesterday {\b I was {\i in NY {\b but it was} {\i raining}} a lot}

should be printed as

> yesterday **I was** *in NY but it was* **raining a lot**

The program must detect and signal formatting errors.

You should do a complete and detailed formalization of the specification before designing any tests.

6.65 Suppose you have a huge data base with several millions of records. An error causes a failure whenever the first record of the data base is accessed. Discuss how reliable the data base appears to its users.

6.66 Design an integration testing strategy for the module hierarchy of Figure 5.42(b).

6.67 Write a correct version of the merge algorithm of Example 6.12, and then prove it correct.

6.68 Consider symbolic execution in the general case of an augmented Petri net (with token values, predicates, and actions), where a place can hold more than one token. Explain why path conditions associated with firing sequences do not necessarily enable a unique firing sequence and why the same firing sequence could be enabled by different path conditions.

6.69 Give assertions to help in debugging the programs of Exercise 6.4.

6.70 Discuss the differences between worst case and average case performance evaluation by means of testing. How can we be sure that the real worst case has actually been observed?

6.71 Code Euclid's algorithm given in Example 6.5 in Pascal and C. Then compute the quantities η, η_1, η_2, N, N_1, and N_2 for each program. Also, evaluate McCabe's cyclomatic number for the programs.

6.72 Show that thanks to the fact that operands and operators tend to alternate in programs (e.g., a+ b * c), the following relation on the length of a program holds:

$$N \leq \eta \cdot \eta_1{}^{\eta_1} \cdot \eta_2{}^{\eta_2}$$

6.73 Critically assess the definition of program level in Halstead's theory.

6.74 Suppose you derive the control flow graph for a program P in order to evaluate its cyclomatic complexity. Is the value you obtain affected by the transformation described in Figure 6.2?

6.75 While a compiler's functional specification may be easily provided by the official definition of the source language, some other aspects of the compiler are not so easy to specify. For example, how would you specify the requirements for the optimization part of a compiler? How do you specify what code is optimized? Is it possible for a compiler to produce *optimal* code in the mathematical sense of the word?

6.76 How do you test an *optimizing* compiler? How do you distinguish between a normal compiler and an optimizing compiler? Define a plan for testing an optimizing compiler for Ada.

HINTS AND SKETCHY SOLUTIONS

6.7   If the testing criteria are formulated as

Let $\{D_i\}$ be a finite partitioning of D: then a test set must contain at least one element from each D_i.

then C_1 is a finer criterion of C_2 if $\{D_{1,i}\}$ is a finer partitioning of $\{D_{2,j}\}$.

6.11 Inputs to a programs may have a rich structure that can be defined by a BNF grammar. For example, consider a program that uses as input a business form with several (possibly repeated) fields and several options. One can use the input's BNF as a driver for generation of test sets.

6.12 Certain combinations of inputs may generate an ERROR action.

6.17 Top-down integration may anticipate the detection of errors occurring in the early phases of design. The availability of high-level modules, integrated with suitable stubs, may be used as an early prototype of the whole system, perhaps to be demonstrated to the end user.

Top-down testing usually requires testing a subsystem without I/O operations. (In general, these are in lower levels of the hierarchy.) This decreases both the reliability of the testing results (many errors are I/O dependent) and the efficiency of the testing activity, which requires ad hoc procedures for the input of test cases. Observation and evaluation of test results are easier with bottom-up integration.

6.18 Policy 1: The error is certainly discovered. In fact, even assuming that initially control is given to the consumer, the task will run until the buffer has been emptied. At that point, control will be given to the producer, which will execute four consecutive writes to the buffer (due to the error). This will result in a failure.

Policy 2: Execution is similar to that in policy 1, but starts immediately with the producer.

Policy 3: The failure does not occur, since, whenever there is an item in the buffer and the producer reaches a synchronization point, control is given to the consumer, which empties the buffer. Thus, even a buffer of length 1 would work properly.

6.19 It is crucial to consider the *times of occurrence* of input events, i.e., when the items are supplied to the producer. Thus, it is reasonable to submit stimuli to the system whose frequency is related to the execution speed of the several processes–e.g., a sequence of stimuli at a rate that is double the execution time of the two processes, a sequence at a greater speed, and a sequence at a lower speed. For each sequence, it should be verified whether some data are lost, that is, whether the sequence of data read by the consumer is the same as the sequence of data input to the system.

6.25 Part **a.**

Use as part of the invariant $I : x = z^{j-1}$ **and** $y \geq j - 1$. The first clause of I formalizes the intuitive notion that, at each loop iteration, x stores the $(j - 1)$th power of z, j being the loop counter. The second clause is used to ensure that $y = j - 1$ at loop exit.

Part **b.**

Suggested invariant: the greatest common divisor of x and y is equal to the greatest common divisor of $input_1$ and $input_2$. See Exercise 6.25 for the formal definition of "greatest common divisor."

Warning: In order to avoid tricky situations, use different identifiers for quantified variables (i.e., variables subject to the **exists** and **for all** operators) and program variables.

6.33 Let p be the probability that, during restarting, the initialization failure occurs. Let $\{p_i\}$ be the probabilities of occurrence of all failures that result in system restart (including switching off the system by the operator). Then the probability of occurrence of the initialization failure is

$$P = \Sigma_i \, p_i \cdot p = p \cdot \Sigma_i p_i$$

6.34 We view an array reference as similar to a function call, i.e., it should be considered an operator applied to a list of operands. The pair (,) is an operator as well, and the comma too. In statements of the type a := b, where a and b are arrays, a and b should be considered operands.

6.47 First, provide sequences of I_1 stimuli, with no signals of type I_2. Then the opposite should be tried. Finally, try with more complex sequences interleaving both types of stimuli.

6.51 You may use a "negative" grammar generating the complement of the language. You should integrate systematic approaches to the problem (deterministic context-free languages are closed with respect to the complement operation) with common sense and insight. In fact, the compiler should not only detect errors, but also provide as much guidance as possible to help in correcting them. This is a typical requirement that is almost impossible to formalize completely. All programmers have probably had the experience that a good compiler behaves quite predictably on correct programs and on programs containing "simple" errors, but becomes less and less predictable as it encounters more numerous and more intricate coding errors.

6.54 Let a condition C be of the type c_1 **or** c_2 ... **or** c_n. Instead of trying all possible combinations of input values that make c_i's true and false, just try the case where they are all false and n cases where just one is true. Repeat similarly for **and** conditions.

6.55 Some elementary knowledge of Cartesian geometry suggests the following choice:

a. three points not on the same straight line.

b. three points on the same line.

None of the systematic techniques discussed in this section, however, would have led to this choice.

6.56 We know that unlock operations preceding lock operations will never be issued. Furthermore, even in the case where the user does so by mistake, they are unlikely to cause trouble. Thus, we can limit–or even avoid completely–the testing of the system with unlock operations corresponding to the firing of transitions U_a, U_b, with tokens coming from place f_j. But note that an unlock by b when a has the lock should be tested.

6.57 As an example of a mixed testing strategy, you may proceed as follows. Choose a technique that leads to the definition of classes $\{D_i\}$ of the input domain D. Try, by hand, to find an element for each class. Also, try an element for each boundary between different classes. Then, try to achieve more completeness by randomly generating a given number of elements for different classes. (The number of elements to be generated may vary from class to class according to the relevance of the class.)

Writing a random generator for each class can be very hard in some cases. (A "perfect" tool of this type would imply the decidability of the emptiness problem for the class.) Thus, for those cases in which you are unable to randomly generate elements of a given class, you may proceed as follows: randomly generate elements within D; then decide whether the element generated is in the considered class D_i. (This will be decidable in *most* cases.) The failure to generate an element of D_i after a while may suggest a more careful analysis of D_i's properties, whether or not you were able to find some of its elements by hand.

The above procedure should be applied to at least one white-box technique and one black-box technique.

6.58   The debugging code itself may contain errors and need to be verified–e.g., an uninitialized variable may be printed. The new code might also change the behavior of the program– e.g., by causing variables to be allocated to different addresses.

6.68   With reference to the Petri net of Figure 6.11, the path condition

M_1.ok_parity **and not** M_2.ok_parity **and** M_3.ok_parity

enables both the firing sequence

<message_reception, send_ack$_2$, message_reception, send_nack,
      message_reception, send_ack$_3$>

and the firing sequence

<message_reception, message_reception, send_ack$_2$, send_nack, message_reception,
      send_ack$_3$>

The firing sequence

<message_reception, message_reception, send_ack$_2$, send_nack, message_reception,
      send_ack$_3$>

is enabled also by the path condition

(**not** M_1.ok_parity **and** M_2.ok_parity **and** M_3.ok_parity).

6.70   Worst case analysis is an example of verification of qualities that cannot be done safely on a purely experimental basis. In principle, the only way to achieve results that are absolutely certain is through exhaustive testing. Again, however, some preliminary analysis, to be performed as rigorously as possible, can drive the selection of test cases that are most likely to produce worst case performance. For instance, a simple inspection of the sorting algorithm given in Exercise 6.45 suggests reverse-ordered sequences as test cases to obtain worst case performance. Once again, we have integrated–more or less formal–inspection with experimental evaluation.

6.72   The number of different strings of length $k_1 + k_2$ consisting of alternating symbols belonging to A_1 of size k_1 and A_2 of size k_2, respectively, is

$$k_1^{k_1} \cdot k_2^{k_2}$$

6.73   Is it always true that smaller volume means more abstraction?

6.75   Let N be the number of records in the data base. In general, if n record accesses are performed during the day, and the probability of access is uniformly distributed, the probability of having a failure during a day is $1 - (1 - 1/N)^n$, which could be considered acceptable if N is large and n is not too large (e.g., for N = 10M and n = 10K, it is still less than 10^{-3}). If some user accesses the data base in a nonuniform way, however, then that particular user will find it unreliable! This happens, for example, if a user needs to access a specific record very often and the failure occurs when that record is accessed.

BIBLIOGRAPHIC NOTES

The special issues of the *Communications of the ACM* on *Software Testing* (CACM [1988]) and of *IEEE Software* on *Software Verification and Validation* (Software

[1989b]) provide overviews of the field of verification. For the basic terminology, refer to Adrion et al. [1975] and the Standard IEEE [1989]. The issue of verification versus validation is addressed by Boehm [1984b]. Kemmerer [1985] contains an excellent discussion of why specifications should be tested; it also shows how to do this in the context of formal specifications based on logic.

The field of testing is presented by Myers [1979] (who introduces cause-effect graphs and covers code inspections and walk-throughs), Beizer [1983], Hetzel [1984], and Howden [1987]. Good surveys, classifications, and definitions are also given by Chandrasekaran and Radicchi (eds.) [1981], White [1987], DeMillo et al. [1987], and the seminal paper by Goodenough and Gerhart [1975]. We noticed, however, that the testing terminology is not always used in the literature in a consistent way. For instance, Goodenough and Gerhart [1975] define a test as being *successful* if the program being tested executes the test successfully. Myers [1979] and others define it in exactly the opposite way: a test is successful if it causes the program to fail. The differences in the two viewpoints is in whether the notion of success is associated with the program succeeding or the test succeeding in discovering an error. Also, Hetzel [1984] and others define a *test case* to be a set of values belonging to the input domain, whereas others define it to be a single value.

Dijkstra's famous sentence on testing being useful to prove the presence, and not the absence, of errors is from Dahl et al. [1972].

Much theoretical and experimental research has addressed the issues of evaluating, comparing, and integrating different testing criteria. Within the rich literature on this topic, let us mention Basili and Selby [1987] (who include also code inspection techniques in their comparison), Duran and Ntafos [1984] (who suggest that random testing has its own advantages), Ntafos [1988] (who compares white-box techniques), and Clarke et al. [1989] (who suggest a systematic approach for the selection of paths in the control flow graph of a program). Zeil [1989] introduces *perturbation testing*, a method that focuses on faults in arithmetic expressions, and describes a method of generating test data.

An important technique is the so-called *mutation analysis*, which may be used to evaluate the thoroughness of a test set T supplied to a given program P. The basic idea is that if T is not able to reveal some difference between P and a suitable variation P' of P, called a *mutant*, then it is unlikely that T can provide evidence of P's correctness. A tutorial presentation of mutation analysis is given by Budd in Chandrasekaran and Radicchi (eds.) [1981].

Jalote [1989] provides a method that can be used both to verify the completeness of specifications of abstract data types (testing specifications) given in an algebraic language and to automatically derive test cases for its implementation in a black-box way. Bouge et al. [1986] also describe the generation of test cases from algebraic specifications. A syntax-driven technique for automatically generating test cases for a compiler is given by Celentano et al. [1980].

The problem of testing concurrent and real-time systems has not yet been investigated thoroughly. The problem is presented by Brinch Hansen [1978]. Interesting approaches are suggested by Tai [1986], with particular reference to the issue of testing repeatability.

Choppy and Kaplan [1990] propose a technique for testing a large system of modules that integrates the execution of implemented and partially specified modules, as is suggested in Example 6.10.

The notion of program scaffolding to support debugging is addressed by Bentley [1985]. Brindle and Taylor [1989] address the problem of debugging concurrent Ada programs. A survey of concurrent debugging techniques is given by McDowell and Helmbold [1989].

Informal analysis techniques are described by Fagan [1976 and 1986]; Basili and Selby [1987] evaluate them experimentally.

Formal verification methods obviously require formal specifications. Thus, it is not surprising that the same pioneering papers by McCarthy [1963], Floyd [1967], and Hoare [1969], that laid the foundations of a formal definition of semantics also addressed the issue of formal correctness analysis. Formal correctness analysis is introduced by Manna [1974] and Mandrioli and Ghezzi [1987], among others.

The extension of correctness proof methods to concurrent systems has been pioneered by Hoare [1972] and pursued by Owicky and Gries [1976], Lamport[1979 and 1989], and Pnueli [1981] (who uses temporal logic), among others. The issue of correctness of real-time software is discussed by Haase [1981], Fuggetta et al. [1989], and Liu and Shyamasundar [1990].

In this book, we have focused attention on correctness proofs based on logic style specification languages. Other methods associated with different specification and implementation languages are also available. Among these, we mention Burstall's structural induction (Burstall [1974]), which originated proof techniques based on the inductive analysis of programs.

Although formal methods are still far from wide application in the industrial world, early significant examples of their application to real cases are reported in Good (ed.) [1977] and Walker et al. [1980]. Crispin [1987] reports on the application of VDM to industrial projects. Bjorner and Druffel [1990] summarize the most recent industrial experiences with formal methods. More on this will be said in Chapter 9.

The "cleanroom" approach to software development has been proposed by Mills et al. [1987b]. The approach is named by analogy with semiconductor production, where defects are prevented by manufacturing in an ultraclean atmosphere. The cleanroom approach is based on error prevention, rather than error correction. In particular, modules are formally specified and mathematically proved correct; testing of modules is abolished. Testing is done only at the integration level, by supplying test data that reflect expected usage patterns and using a reliability model to decide when the system has been tested adequately. Preliminary practical experience with the approach within IBM has been quite encouraging, according to Selby et al. [1987].

The practical usefulness of formal methods of software verification is a controversial topic. Formal methods are often improperly contrasted with testing, whereas we have claimed that the two approaches are complementary. One can get an idea of the intensity of the debate from DeMillo et al. [1979], Fetzer [1988], and the correspondence on Fetzer's paper in the *ACM Forum* (see Ashenhurst [1989]).

Young and Taylor [1988 and 1989] propose a taxonomy for evaluating and possibly integrating different verification techniques, including testing, the static analysis of programs, correctness proofs, and symbolic interpretation.

An introduction to symbolic execution and to its applications to software verification is provided by Clarke and Richardson in Chandrasekaran and Radicchi [1981]. Ghezzi et al. [1989] show how symbolic interpretation can be extended to the verification of concurrent systems through a suitable extension of Petri nets.

Complexity analysis is treated in depth in many texts on algorithm design. A classic text is Aho et al. [1974]. For a discussion of performance evaluation, the reader can refer to Ferrari [1978] and Smith [1989].

A complete treatment of software reliability based on the application of statistical methods is presented by Musa et al. [1987]. Several contributions are also contained in Bittanti [1988]. In particular, the paper by Bittanti et al. provides an overview of the theoretical foundations for the application of statistical models, upon which we have based our discussion. A novel approach supporting recalibration of the chosen model is described in Brocklehurst et al. [1990] .

Knuth [1974] provides an assessment of programming styles with and without GOTO statements and concludes that, in general, the absence of GOTO statements does not unequivocally determine the quality of code.

A general view of several kinds of software metrics, their relations, and their application can be found in Basili [1980], Conte et al. [1986] and Frewin et al. [1985]. The special issue of *IEEE Transactions on Software Engineering* edited by Iyer (TSE [1990]) contains several papers addressing the problem of experimentally validating several subjective software qualities.

Software science is defined by Halstead [1977]. McCabe [1976, 1983, and 1989] presents a measure of complexity and its application to the development of testing strategies. Among the many papers providing critical evaluations, experimental validations, combinations, and variations of different software metrics, we mention Hamer and Frewin [1982] and Shen et al. (who provide a critical evaluation of Halstead's theory), Albrecht and Gaffney [1983], Basili and Hutchens [1983], Basili et al. [1983], Coulter [1983], Curtis et al. [1979], Henry and Kafura [1981], and Kearney et al. [1986]. The special issue of *IEEE Software* [1990b] provides a view of the current state of the art.

The role of measurements in the tailoring of a development support environment is discussed by Basili et al. [1986] and Basili and Rombach [1988]; Basili and Caldiera [1988] suggest how software metrics can be applied to enhance and measure software reusability. Metrics are also applied to software maintainability in Harrison et al. [1982], Kafura and Reddy [1987], and Gibson and Senn [1989].

Chapter 7

The Software Production Process

There are many steps and activities involved in building a software product. We studied software design in Chapter 4, software specification in Chapter 5, and software verification in Chapter 6. How should these activities be organized in relation to each other? The order in which we perform them defines a life cycle for the software product. More generally, the process we follow to build, deliver, and evolve the software product, from the inception of an idea all the way to the delivery and final retirement of the system, is called a *software production process*.

Production and manufacturing processes are studied extensively in any discipline whose goal is to produce products. The goal of production processes is to make production reliable, predictable, and efficient. A well-defined production process, as used, for example, in automobile production, has many benefits, including supporting automation and the use of standard components and processes.

By defining a model of the software production process, we can reap some of the benefits of standardized processes. But we must also keep two distinguishing characteristics of software in mind. First, software production is largely an intellectual activity, not easily amenable to automation. And second, software is characterized by high instability: requirements change constantly, and, as a consequence, the products themselves must be evolvable.

How, then, should we organize a software production process that will enable us to produce high-quality software products reliably, predictably, and efficiently? In this chapter, we examine different models that attempt to capture this process, also called the "software life cycle." Such models are based on the recognition that software, like any other industrial product, has a life cycle that spans from its initial conception to its retirement, and that that life cycle must be anticipated and controlled in order to achieve the desired qualities in the product. We will also study how these processes can be more or less automated, or at least made predictable, by the use of standards and methodologies. In our examination, we will see that blanket prescriptions for the "best methodology for software productivity" do not exist. We will examine some development methodologies critically and assess their usefulness in the software process.

In short, while the previous chapters have focused on the software *product*, this chapter focuses on the software development *process*. We will postpone all management issues to the next chapter, which deals also with the economic aspects of producing software.

In this chapter, Section 7.1 deals with software production process models. After analyzing the traditional waterfall model, other models are presented which try to overcome the weaknesses of the traditional model. In particular, we show that the waterfall model works well when requirements are understood well and are not expected to change much but the model is rigid and lacks flexibility. Sections 7.2.1 and 7.2.2 then examine two case studies of software projects.

Section 7.3 deals with organizing the software production process. In Section 7.3.1, we review two important methodologies that are widely adopted in the software industry: Structured Analysis/Structured Design, and Jackson's System Development. We discuss the merits and the weaknesses of these methods and–more generally–we question the feasibility of completely general and prescriptive methodologies. Section 7.3.2 deals with the important organizational issue of how to manage all the artifacts produced in the process, an issue known as "configuration management." Finally, we discuss the need for software standards in Section 7.3.3.

7.1 SOFTWARE PRODUCTION PROCESS MODELS

As discussed in Chapter 1, in the early days of computing, software development was mainly a single-person task. The problem to be solved–very often of a mathematical nature–was well understood, and there was no distinction between the programmer and the end user of the application. The end user–very often a scientist or an engineer–developed the application as a support to his or her own activity. The application, by today's standards, was rather simple. Thus, software development consisted only of coding in some low-level language.

The model used in these early days may be called *the code-and-fix model*. Basically, this appellation denotes a development process that is neither precisely formulated nor carefully controlled; rather, software production consists of the iteration of two steps: (1) write code and (2) fix it to eliminate errors, enhance existing functionality, or add new features. The code-and-fix model has been the source of many difficulties and deficiencies. In particular, after a sequence of changes, the code structure becomes so messy that subsequent fixes become harder to apply and the results become less reliable. These problems, however, were mitigated by the fact that applications were rather simple and both the application and the software were well understood by the engineer.

As hardware capacity grew, the desire to apply computers in more and more application domains, such as business administration, led to software being used in less and less understood environments. A sharp separation arose between software developers and end users. End users with little or no technical background in science and mathematics, such as sales agents and personnel administrators, could not be expected to develop their own applications, due both to the intrinsic complexity of the application's design and implementation and to the users' lack of technical background required to master the complexity of computer systems.

In today's environment, software is developed not for personal use, but for people with little or no background in computers. Sometimes, software is developed in response to a request from a specific customer; other times, it is developed for the general market. Both of these situations add new dimensions to the software that were not present in the previous age. Now software is a product that must be marketed, sold, and installed on different machines at different sites. Users must be trained in its use and must be assisted when something unexpected happens.

Thus, economic, as well as organizational and psychological, issues become important. In addition, demand has increased for much higher levels of quality in applications. For example, reliability requirements have become more stringent. One reason is that end users are not as tolerant of system failures as are system designers. Another reason is that computer-based systems are increasingly applied in areas such as banking operations and plant control, where system failures may have severe consequences.

Another sharp difference from the previous age is that software development has become a group activity. Group work requires carefully thought-out organizational structures and standard practices, in order to make it possible to predict and control developments.

The code-and-fix process model was inadequate to deal with the new software age. First, the increased size of the systems being developed made it difficult to manage their complexity in an unstructured way. This problem was exacerbated by the turnover of software personnel working on projects. Adding new people to an ongoing project was extremely difficult because of the poor (or total lack of) documentation available to guide them in the task of understanding the application properly. Fixing code was difficult because no anticipation of change was taken into account before the start of coding. Similarly, it was difficult to remove errors that required major restructuring of the existing code. These problems underscored the need for a *design phase* prior to coding.

The second reason behind the inadequacy of the code-and-fix model was the frequent discovery, after development of the system, that the software did not match the user's expectations. So the product either was rejected or had to be redeveloped to achieve the desired goals. Almost inevitably, software development became a sort of never-ending activity. As a result, the development process was unpredictable and uncontrollable, and products were completed over schedule and over budget and did not meet quality expectations. Consequently, it was realized that a more detailed and careful analysis of the requirements was necessary before design and coding could start.

The failure of the code-and-fix model may be attributed to a general phenomenon that was observed in Chapter 2: the fact that software is malleable does not imply that any required behavior is achievable, especially when we try to change a piece of code written by someone else. Thus, the apparent ease of change that characterizes software as opposed to other kinds of products is misleading and is a constant source of misconceptions and unrealistic expectations.

As mentioned in Chapter 1, the failure of the code-and-fix process model led to the recognition of the so-called software crisis and, in turn, to the birth of software engineering as a discipline. In particular, the recognition of a lack of methods in the software production process led to the concept of the software life cycle and to structured models for describing it in a precise way in order to make the process predictable and controllable.

Boehm [1988] states that the goals of structured process models are to

determine the *order of stages* involved in software development and evolution, and to establish the *transition criteria* for progressing from one stage to the next. These include completion criteria for the current stage plus choice criteria and entrance criteria for the next stage. Thus a process model addresses the following software project questions:

a. What shall we do next?

b. How long shall we continue to do it?

According to this viewpoint, process models have a twofold effect: on the one hand, they provide guidance to software engineers on the order in which the various technical activities should be carried out within a project; on the other hand, they provide a framework for managing development and maintenance, in that they enable us to estimate resources, define intermediate milestones, monitor progress, etc.

Sections 7.1.1 through 7.1.4 discuss several software production process models in detail; Section 7.1.5 contains a general evaluation of these models.

7.1.1 Waterfall Model

The waterfall model was popularized in the 1970s and permeates most current software engineering textbooks and standard industrial practices. Its first appearance in the literature dates back to the late 1950s, as the result of experience gained in the development of a large air-defense software system called SAGE (Semi-Automated Ground Environment).

The waterfall model, illustrated in Figure 7.1, is a slight variant of the one presented in Chapter 1. As the figure shows, the process is structured as a cascade of phases, where the output of one phase constitutes the input to the next one. Each phase, in turn, is structured as a set of activities that might be executed by different people concurrently. The phases shown in the figure are the following:

- feasibility study
- requirements analysis and specification
- design and specification
- coding and module testing
- integration and system testing

- delivery
- maintenance

There are many variants of the waterfall model, depending on the organization that uses the model and the specific project; the one we describe here is a representative example. Even though the variants differ in the number and nature of their stages, the underlying philosophy is the same, so that the comments we give here apply to all of them.

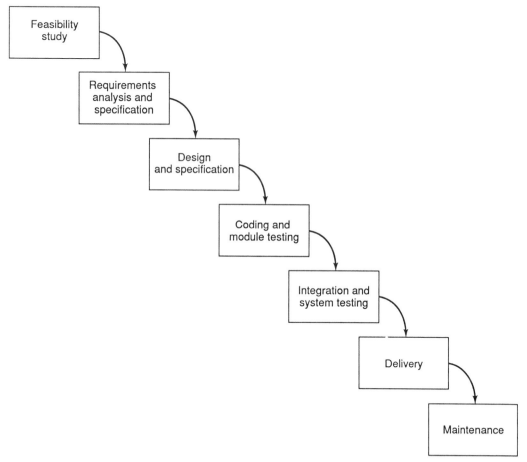

Figure 7.1   The waterfall model.

The choice of a waterfall model may be based on the criticality and complexity of the application. Simple and well understood applications are less demanding in terms of the formal structure of the process by which they are produced; larger and more critical applications may require decomposition of the process into finer grains in order to achieve better control and ensure more rigorous development steps. As another example of the need to vary the waterfall model, consider the development of an application that is expected to be used by nonspecialist end users, as opposed to expert users. In this case, the process should accommodate a phase during which special training material is designed and developed to become part of the product and also a delivery phase that might include training for the user. By contrasts, for the expert users, the training phase may not exist in practice; it is sufficient to provide precise technical manuals. Other details and questions could be answered on the phone by a special customer service.

Another factor that may affect the structure of the production process is the different roles that the customer and the developer may play. If we rule out the simple case of the software developer who develops software for personal use, we may observe the following categories:

1. A software house develops customized software in response to a specific request from a customer, who belongs to a different organization.
2. A software development group develops customized software for other groups within the same company.
3. A software house develops a generalized application for the marketplace.

As an example of how the software production process may be affected, the nature of the feasibility study phase may be different in the three cases. It is crucial in the third case, since it requires estimating the potential market for the application and identifying the features that make it appealing to potential customers. The application must not be offered on the market too early or too late. In the second case, the feasibility phase may consist of an evaluation of the trade-offs between buying an existing solution (if there is any), developing a solution entirely within the development group, or commissioning (part of) the project to external developers. Again, in the first case, the alternative between making or buying has already been analyzed by the customer, who decided that the software house should develop the new system. In all three cases, it is necessary to estimate the resources needed to accomplish the development task. In the second case, however, there is less pressure on the developers, who may take their time analyzing the problem before committing themselves to a certain cost. In fact, in general, this case is characterized by a less risky development process than the first case, which, in turn, is likely to be less risky than the third situation.

Despite all these differences, all waterfall processes look alike and share the same underlying philosophy: they prescribe a sequential, linear flow among phases that may be more or less precisely identified with those described in Figure 7.1.

Organizations that adopt a waterfall model define standards on the way the outputs (*deliverables*) of each stage must be produced. Often, they also prescribe *methods* to be followed in order to produce the desired outputs. These methods are organized in a coherent framework that constitutes the organization's *software development methodology*. The precise definition of the deliverables is important because it gives an unambiguous way of measuring the progress of the project: it is easy to check whether a certain deliverable is delivered exactly on the date when it was expected. If the structure of the deliverable is standardized, one can check not only the delivery date, but also the internal quality of the deliverable in terms of adherence to the specified standard. Even more significant control is possible if the method to be followed for producing the deliverable is also prescribed, since one can check whether the result was produced according to the method.

Sections 7.1.1.1 through 7.1.1.6 discuss the major phases of the waterfall life cycle illustrated in Figure 7.1. As we will see, the life cycle allows software engineers to structure most of the activities to be accomplished during software production as individual steps within individual phases. There are, however, other activities that may be performed independently throughout the life cycle; these will be discussed in Section 7.1.1.7.

7.1.1.1 Feasibility study

As we already have mentioned, the contents of the feasibility study phase are highly dependent on the type of software developer and the application at hand. The purpose of this phase is to produce a *feasibility study document* that evaluates the costs and benefits of the proposed application. To do so, it is first necessary to analyze the problem, at least at a global level. Obviously, the more we understand the problem, the better we can identify alternative solutions, their costs, and their potential benefits to the user. Therefore, ideally, one should perform as much analysis of the problem as is needed to do a well-founded feasibility study. Unfortunately, this is often too ideal for practice. The feasibility study is usually done within limited time bounds and under pressure. Often, its result is an offer to the potential customer. Since we cannot be sure that the offer will be accepted, economic reasons prevent us from investing too many resources into analyzing the problem.

On the basis of the definition of the problem during the preliminary analysis, we proceed to identify alternative solutions. For each suggested solution, we analyze costs and delivery dates. Thus, what the feasibility study phase does is a sort of simulation of the future development process through which it is possible to derive information that helps decide whether development is worthwhile and, if so, which development process should be followed. As we observed, however, we incur the risk of constraining the future development process too early, when the available information is still fuzzy.

In sum, the feasibility study tries to anticipate future scenarios of software development. Its result is a document that should contain at least the following items:

1. a definition of the problem.
2. alternative solutions and their expected benefits.
3. required resources, costs, and delivery dates in each proposed alternative solution.

7.1.1.2 Requirements analysis and specification

The purpose of a requirements analysis is to identify the qualities required of the application, in terms of functionality, performance, ease of use, portability, and so on. The list of software qualities presented in Chapter 2 can serve as a checklist when requirements are specified. The specifier must state *what* qualities the application must exhibit, not *how* such qualities are achieved by design and implementation. For example, one should define what functions the software must provide, without stating how a certain module structure or an algorithm may help in this respect. The reason is that requirements should not unduly constrain the software engineer in the design and implementation activity: the engineer should have the freedom–and the responsibility–to select the modular structure best suited to the task and any other choice related to the implementation of the software.

The result of this phase is a *requirements specification document*, which documents what the analysis has produced. The purpose of this document is twofold: on the one hand, it must be analyzed and confirmed by the customer in order to verify whether it captures all of the customer's expectations; on the other hand, it is used by the software engineers to develop a solution that meets the requirements.

The requirements specification document must meet all the specification qualities discussed in Section 5.2. Because many individuals must communicate with each other through it, the document must be *understandable*, *precise*, *complete*, *consistent*, and *unambiguous*. Also, it must be easily *modifiable*, since we know that it must evolve in order to accommodate the evolutionary nature of large systems. These properties were discussed in Chapter 5, especially with reference to functional specifications. We examined several techniques for expressing and documenting system requirements.

As we have observed, these characteristics of a specification are rather difficult to define and achieve independently of their context. For example, "precise" may mean rigorous or even formal for the software engineer. Yet, formal specifications may be unreadable for the end user. A way to reconcile the needs of both the customers and the developers may be to transliterate formal specifications into a more palatable form expressed in natural language. One may even go further in this direction and complement the requirements specification document with a preliminary version of the *user manual*. The user manual describes precisely how the user will eventually interact with the system. Such a description can be useful in assessing the results of requirements analysis.

Another deliverable of the requirements analysis phase is the definition of the *system test plan*. In fact, during system testing, the system is expected to be tested against its requirements. Therefore, the way this will eventually be done may be agreed upon with the customer at this stage and documented along with the requirements specification document.

As can be seen from the previous paragraphs, the requirements analysis phase has multiple goals. In order to master these goals, as well as the complexity of the application, the software engineer must be able to apply the set of principles that we discussed in Chapter 3. The crucial issues here are separation of concerns, abstraction, and modularization. The application must be understood and then described at different levels of abstraction, from its overall aspects down to any necessary details. The application must be partitioned into parts that are separately analyzable. It should be possible to view, understand, and describe the application from different viewpoints. This last feature is very important in requirements analysis, because it allows engineers to analyze and represent the entire system by means of only a few properties.

As opposed to usual application of modularity which may be called *vertical modularity*–wherein each module hides lower level design decisions–this kind of *horizontal modularity* structures the system as a collection of views at the same level of abstraction. A typical way to use horizontal modularity is to separate functional requirements into three views: a model of data that are operated upon by the application, a model of the functions performed, and a model of how control structures govern the execution of such functions. In terms of notation, this may be done by using, say, ER diagrams to define the relations among the data, data flow diagrams to define functions, and Petri nets to define control, as we suggested in Section 5.7.

The way requirements are actually specified is usually subject to standardized procedures in software organizations. Standards may prescribe the form and structure of the requirements specification document, the use of specific analysis methods and notations (e.g., data flow diagrams), and the kind of reviews and approvals that the document should undergo.

A possible checklist of the contents of the requirements specification document that might guide in its production is the following:

1. *Functional requirements.* These describe what the product does by using informal, semiformal, formal notations, or a suitable mixture. Chapter 5 illustrated various kinds of notations and discussed pros and cons of the different approaches.

2. *Non-functional requirements.* These may be classified into the following categories: reliability (availability, integrity, security, safety, etc.), accuracy of results, performance, human-computer interface issues, operating constraints, physical constraints, portability issues, and others.

3. *Requirements on the development and maintenance process.* These include quality control procedures–in particular, system test procedure–priorities of the required functions, likely changes to the system maintenance procedures, and other requirements.

7.1.1.3 Design and specification

As discussed in Chapter 4, design involves decomposing the system into modules. The result is a *design specification document,* which contains a description of the software architecture: what each module is intended to do and the relationships among modules. The decomposition process may proceed iteratively and/or may be described through levels of abstraction. Each component identified at some step may be decomposed into subcomponents. Some organizations try to freeze this inherently iterative process into a predefined number of levels. In particular, it is customary to distinguish between *preliminary* (or *high-level*) *design* and *detailed design,* but the meaning of these terms–i.e., the exact difference between the two–varies considerably from case to case. For some, preliminary design is intended to describe the modular structure in terms of relations (such as USES, IS_COMPOSED_OF, and INHERITS_FROM), whereas detailed design deals with specifying module interfaces (both syntactically and semantically). Others use the terms to imply a distinction between a logical decomposition (high-level design) and a physical decomposition of the program into programming language units. Still others refer to module decomposition as preliminary design and detailed design as defining the main data structures and algorithms for each module.

The exact format of the design specification document is usually defined as part of companywide standards. The standards may also indicate suggested design methods and practices, along with notations that should be used to document the design. Such notations are similar to TDN or GDN (see Chapter 4). Other notations will be illustrated in the analysis of a sample of available methodologies in Section 7.3.1.

7.1.1.4 Coding and module testing

Coding and module testing is the phase in which we actually write programs using a programming language. It was the only recognized development phase in early development processes, but it is just one of several phases in a waterfall process. The output of this phase is an implemented and tested collection of modules.

Coding can be subject to companywide standards, which may define the entire layout of programs, such as the headers for comments in every unit, naming conventions for variables and subprograms, the maximum number of lines in each component, and other aspects that the company deems worthy of standardization.

Module testing is also often subject to company standards, including a precise definition of a test plan, the definition of testing criteria to be followed (e.g., black-box versus white-box, or a mixture of the two), the definition of completion criteria (when to stop testing), and the management of test cases. Debugging is a related activity performed in this phase.

Module testing is the main quality control activity that is carried out in this phase. Other such activities may include code inspections to check adherence to coding standards and, more generally, to check for a disciplined programming style, as well as checking of software qualities other than functional correctness (e.g., performance), although this is often better done at a later stage.coding

7.1.1.5 Integration and system testing

Integration amounts to assembling the application from the set of components that were developed and tested separately. This phase is not always recognized as being separate from coding. In fact, incremental developments may progressively integrate and test components as they are developed (see Section 6.3.5). Although the two stages may be integrated, they differ conceptually in the scale of the problems that they try to address: the former deals with programming in the small, the latter with programming in the large.

Recall from Section 6.3.5 that integration testing involves testing collections of modules as they are integrated, with each individual module having been tested separately previously. Often, this is done not in a single shot (big-bang testing), but incrementally on progressively larger sets of modules, from small subsystems until the entire system is built.

At the final stage, the development organization performs system testing on the running application. Once the application has undergone system testing, it may be put through "actual" use within the development organization. The purpose of this step is to test the system under realistic conditions, but with understanding and forgiving users. This kind of testing is called *alpha testing*.

Internal standards may be adopted both on the way integration is to be performed, such as top down or bottom up, and on how to design test data and document the testing activity.

7.1.1.6 Delivery and maintenance

The delivery of software is often done in two stages. In the first stage, the application is distributed among a selected group of customers prior to its official release. The purpose of this procedure is to perform a kind of controlled experiment to determine, on the basis of feedback from users, whether any changes are necessary prior to the official release. This kind of system testing done by selected customers is called *beta testing*. In the second stage, the product is distributed to the customers.

We defined maintenance as the set of activities that are performed after the system is delivered to the customer. Basically, maintenance consists of correcting any remaining errors in the system (corrective maintenance), adapting the application to changes in the environment (adaptive maintenance), and improving, changing, or adding features and qualities to the application (perfective maintenance). Recall that the cost of maintenance is often more than 60% of the total cost of software and that about 20% of maintenance costs may be attributed to each of corrective and adaptive maintenance, while over 50% is attributable to perfective maintenance. Based on this breakdown, we observed that *evolution* is probably a better term than maintenance, although the latter is used more widely.

Another type of breakdown of maintenance costs was described by Lientz and Swanson [1980] as a result of a survey of over 400 software developers. The analysis showed that about 42% of costs were attributed to changes in user requirements, about 17% were due to changes in data formats, 12% to emergency fixes, 9% to routine debugging, 6% to hardware changes, 5% to improvements in documentation, 4% to improvements in efficiency, and the rest to other sources.

In general, we can draw the following conclusions regarding maintenance:

- Requirements analysis is a serious source of problems, especially in applications directed to end users, both because requirements are difficult to capture and because they change over time.
- Many errors are not removed until after the system is delivered. This is a serious problem because the later the errors are found, the more expensive it is to remove them. It is certainly preferable and cheaper to remove a requirements error during analysis than after the system is delivered, possibly in the many copies that need to be repaired.
- Change is an intrinsic property of software, but it is difficult to incorporate in our products.

Exercise

7.1 Requirements errors may be viewed by customers as errors that need to be repaired by the
software producer before the application is formally accepted. They may be viewed by
software engineers as incorrectly stated requirements that were accepted by the customer
when the requirements specification document was issued and reviewed. Since the
customer did not object to the specification at that point, the software engineers reject the
arguments of the customer, holding that if the customer wants the application changed, the
customer should pay for it. What is your opinion? How can the problem be solved or
alleviated?

7.1.1.7 Other activities

The waterfall model provides a phased view of the software life cycle. Some activities,
however, are ongoing and span the entire life cycle. Among these activities are
documentation, verification, and management.

Documentation is intrinsic to the waterfall model, since most deliverables of the
various phases are in fact documents. In other words, the waterfall model does not view
documentation as an afterthought of development–at least in principle. Indeed, the
waterfall process may be called *document driven*: documentation is the expected output
of the activities performed in the various stages of the process. Based on the output, a
transition to the next phase may be permitted or denied. As mentioned earlier, the
companywide standards that accompany the waterfall model usually specify the form in
which documentation must be provided.

Verification is also an independent activity of the waterfall life cycle. Even though
we singled out two specific phases where verification is performed (module testing and
system testing), appropriate verification is done at every stage on various kinds of
activities and following suitable standard procedures. In most cases, verification is
performed as a process of quality control by means of reviews, walk-throughs, and
inspections. Its goal is to monitor the quality of the application during the development
process–not only *a posteriori*, after the application is implemented. The discovery and
removal of errors should be anticipated as early as possible in order to avoid delivery of
defective systems.

As we already have said, some authors distinguish between validation–an
assessment of how the product we are building responds to the needs of the customer–
and verification–an assessment of the internal correctness of the process (e.g., how a
software architecture is correct with respect to the stated requirements). This distinction
is motivated by the fact that requirements might not capture exactly what the customer
wishes, so that a verified system might still be unacceptable.

Finally, *management* is a fundamental activity that shapes and monitors the entire
development and maintenance process. There are three main aspects that fall under
management. The first is the *tailoring of the process* (see also Section 7.1.5). In fact, the
life cycle model adopted by a software organization should not be so rigid that it must be
applied identically from product to product. More often, it gives an ideal–almost generic–
model of a process that needs to be tailored to the specific project. For example, some

verification procedures might be needed for some critical products, but might be too costly for simpler, in-house, applications.

The second main aspect of management is the definition of policies: how the deliverables of the process are stored, accessed, and modified; how the different versions of the system are built; and what the necessary authorizations are for checking in and out software components in a product data base. This is usually called *configuration management* (see Sections 7.3.2 and 9.3.9).

Finally, management has to deal with all resources that affect the software production process–in particular, *human resources*. This aspect is covered in Chapter 8.

Exercise

7.2   In which phase(s) of the waterfall life cycle would you require tailoring of the process and configuration management policy definitions?

7.1.1.8 A waterfall life cycle case study

In this section, we briefly illustrate the military standard MIL-STD-2167 as a case study of a waterfall software life cycle. This standard contains requirements for the development and acquisition of mission-critical computer systems. Quoting from the standard, "it establishes a uniform software development process which is applicable throughout the system life cycle." The standard is intended to be applicable to a wide variety of cases, with the exception of simple ones, i.e., "small applications which perform a fixed function which is not expected to change for the life of the system."

In what follows, we will briefly summarize the main characteristics of the standard. But the document that describes the standard is available publicly, and we urge the reader to read it as an example of a standardized waterfall process model. Reading the original document will give a deeper understanding of the evaluation of the waterfall model that will be presented in Sections 7.1.1.9 and 7.1.2 through 7.1.5.

MIL-STD-2167 views software development as a phase in the more general system life cycle. The four phases of the system life cycle are:

a.1   concept exploration

a.2   demonstration and validation

a.3   full scale development

a.4   production and deployment

According to MIL-STD-2167:

"The concept exploration phase is the initial planning period when the technical, strategic, and economic bases are established through comprehensive studies, experimental development, and concept evaluation. This initial planning may be directed toward refining proposed solutions or developing alternative concepts to satisfy a required operational capability....

"The demonstration and validation phase is the period when major system characteristics are refined through studies, system engineering, development of preliminary equipment and prototype computer software, and test and evaluation. The objective is to validate the choice of alternatives and to provide the basis for determining whether or not to proceed into the next phase....

"The full scale development phase is the period when the system, equipment, computer software, facilities, personnel subsystems, training, and the principal equipment and software items necessary for support are designed, fabricated, tested, and evaluated. It includes one or more iterations of the software development cycle. The intended outputs are a system which closely approximates the production item, the documentation necessary to enter the system's production and development phase, and the test results that demonstrate that the system to be produced will meet the stated requirements. During this phase the requirements for additional software items embedded in or associated with the equipment items may be identified. These requirements may encompass firmware, test equipment, environment simulation, mission support, development support, and many other kinds of software....

"The production and deployment phase is a combination of two overlapping periods. The production period is from production approval until the last system item is delivered and accepted. The objective is to efficiently produce and deliver effective and supported systems to the user(s). The deployment period commences with delivery of the first operational system item and terminates when the last system items are removed from the operational inventory....

"The software development cycle may span more than one system life cycle phase, or may occur in any one phase. For example, mission simulation software may undergo one iteration of the software development cycle during the concept exploration, while mission application software may undergo many iterations of the software development cycle during the demonstration and validation, full scale development, and production and deployment phases."

The software development cycle consists of six phases:

b.1 software requirements analysis

b.2 preliminary design

b.3 detailed design

b.4 coding and module testing

b.5 computer software component integration and testing

b.6 computer software configuration item testing

These phases map naturally to the stages of the generic waterfall process model illustrated previously. Some comments are necessary, however, on phases b.5 and b.6. Delivered software is designated a *computer software configuration item* (CSCI) by MIL-STD-2167; thus, phase b.6 corresponds to system testing in the previous classification. According to the standard, a CSCI consists of one or more *computer software components* (CSCs), which are logical entities composed of one or more *units*.[1] Units are the smallest logical entities; it is they that are implemented in code. Thus, phase b.5 corresponds to what we called integration testing.

An important aspect of MIL-STD-2167 is that, for each phase of the software life cycle, the standard gives a detailed specification of (a) the activities to be carried out in the phase, (b) the products to be delivered, (c) the reviews to be performed for monitoring, and (d) the structure of the developer's software and associated documentation, as well as the procedures for archiving and accessing the software and its documentation.

7.1.1.9 A critical evaluation of the waterfall model

The waterfall model has played an important role because it has imposed much-needed discipline on the software development process, thus overcoming unstructured code-and-fix processes. The model has made two fundamental contributions to our understanding of software processes, namely, (1) that the software development process should be subject to discipline, planning, and management, and (2) that implementing the product should be postponed until after the objectives of doing so are well understood.

Because it is an ideal model, the waterfall model can only be approximated in practice. We can characterize it as linear, rigid, and monolithic, as explained next.

The waterfall model is based on the assumption that software development may proceed linearly from analysis down to coding. In practice, this cannot happen, and one should account for disciplined forms of feedback loops. Actually, the purpose of alpha and beta testing is exactly to provide feedback to earlier stages.

To allow explicit and disciplined feedback, a common life cycle model, shown in Figure 7.2, confines the feedback loops to the immediately preceding stages, in order to minimize the amount of rework involved in unconstrained repetition of previous phases. The underlying rationale, however, is that one should strive for linearity of the life cycle, in order to keep the process predictable and easy to monitor. Plans are based on the assumption of linearity, and any deviation from the linear progression through successive stages is discouraged, as it represents a deviation from the original plan and therefore requires replanning.

Another underlying assumption of the waterfall model is phase rigidity–i.e., that the results of each phase are frozen before proceeding to the next phase. As a consequence, the model assumes that requirements and design specifications may be frozen at an early stage of development, when our knowledge of the application area and experience in how to deal with it are still rather preliminary and subject to change. This assumption does not recognize the need for customer-developer interaction to evolve the requirements throughout the life cycle.

Finally, the waterfall model is monolithic in the sense that all planning is oriented to a single delivery date. All analysis is performed before all design and implementation are done. delivery may occur much later, after analysis has been performed. If we make mistakes during analysis, and these mistakes are not caught by reviews, we are only able

---

[1] Actually we are diverging slightly from MIL-STD-2167, which distinguishes between top-level CSCs and low-level CSCs, where the latter may recursively contain low-level CSC as well as units.

to identify the errors after delivery of the system to the user. But this occurs after much time and effort have been spent, without any possibility of having more immediate forms of feedback. Moreover, since the development process may be long for complex applications–perhaps years–the application may be delivered when the user's needs have changed, and this will require immediate rework on the application.

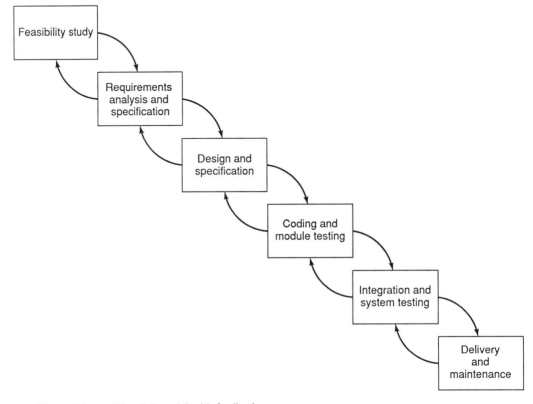

Figure 7.2   Waterfall model with feedback.

To summarize, the waterfall model has introduced much discipline into the software development process, but this discipline is accomplished through rigidity. This rigidity, in turn, introduces new problems into the process, especially when the software is being developed for poorly understood requirements. Among the problems associated with the rigidity of the model are the following:

• It is difficult to estimate resources accurately when only limited information is available. The waterfall model often forces cost estimation and project planning to occur after only a limited amount of analysis has been performed.

• Requirements specification results in a written document that describes the requirements. But no matter how precise the description is, it is very difficult for the user to anticipate whether the final system that will be constructed according to the specifications will eventually meet his or her expectations. No matter how readable the textual and graphical description is, it will always be an inanimate document as opposed to the active tool that will eventually be delivered. The real feedback will always be given after the real system is delivered. Moreover, the customer might approve even very imprecise and incomplete requirements specifications, which turn out not to be a rigorous enough starting point for development. In short, the verification of the requirements specification document performed by the customer is not very effective, and basing future developments on it may cause serious problems.

- The user often does not know the exact requirements of the application. In some cases, the user cannot even know. For example, what were the requirements for a spreadsheet before the first one was ever developed and delivered to users? Thus, the assumption that all requirements should be frozen before any development starts is unrealistic.

- The waterfall model does not stress the need for anticipating changes. Quite the opposite, the underlying philosophy is that we should strive for linearity by freezing as much as we can in the early stages. Unfortunately, real life shows that changes occur more frequently than expected. But since changes are not anticipated by the model, accommodating them is hard, costly, and unreliable.

- The model enforces standards that are heavily based on the production of certain documents at certain specific times. In fact, we characterized the process as document driven. This emphasis leads to a somewhat bureaucratic style of work, where many forms are required to be filled out and approved and the software engineer is inclined to pay more attention to the syntax imposed by the standard than to its semantics. Thus, it may happen that fairly elaborate specifications incorporating a variety of diagrams and tables are written for poorly understood user interfaces and functions.

We can indeed trace the reasons for the high maintenance costs of many of today's software systems to the characteristics of the waterfall model. In particular, the difficulty of producing complete and correct requirements specifications results in greater maintenance later. In fact, much of maintenance amounts to eliminating requirements errors, e.g., introducing into the system exactly those functions that the user wants, but that were disregarded or misunderstood in the first place during requirements analysis and specification.

Moreover, since the system that is eventually delivered may not match the user's expectations, maintenance must start immediately. But this poses some serious contractual problems. Who is responsible for the additional costs incurred during maintenance? As we discussed in Exercise 7.1, do we consider such maintenance as repair of errors (and thus payable by the developer) or as meeting new requirements (billable to the customer)? In theory, one should be able to find a precise answer to this question in the requirements specification document.

These points underscore the reasons for high maintenance costs. Software evolution is vital, but it is neither anticipated nor planned. Thus, it is always done under pressure and within a limited budget. In an attempt to minimize the maintenance effort, changes are viewed as "code fixes" and are not documented appropriately. Thus, the implementation soon diverges from the requirements and the design specification.

Of course, not all software is required to evolve. Sometimes, the requirements are well defined from the very beginning and undergo only minor changes, if any. As an example, take the case of a compiler for a given programming language. Unless the language itself is being defined and progressively refined, requirements are frozen when the project starts: the syntax and semantics of the language are known, the target language is also known, and the number and nature of optimizations (if any) are also easy to specify and may be known in advance. In such a case, there are no obstacles in principle to adopting a prespecified and rigid model such as the waterfall process model.

The requirements for a large number of applications, however, are less stable and not perfectly known *a priori*. Even in cases where initial requirements are clear (e.g., in the case of a process control system where the environment is well known), one should not forget that changes are likely to occur in the future–for example, due to changes in the environment in which the application is embedded or due to changes in technology. Even in the compiler example, one might first deliver a compiler that does a limited number of optimizations and then produce new releases, each providing more and more optimizations. The practical effectiveness of some optimizations may actually be measured only by observing the actual use of the language (See Case Study C at the end of the book). Or one might decide to embed the compiler in a programming environment that provides a progressively richer set of facilities (e.g. a syntax-directed editor, debugger, static analyzer, incremental compiler).

The situation, however, is more serious in the case of interactive end-user applications. Most software systems of this kind are dynamic entities that are required to change over time as they acquire more users. To constrain the development of this kind of software in a rigid and monolithic process may be unnatural and counterproductive: evolution here cannot be kept separate from software development and is an intrinsic part of it.

These deficiencies of the respected and widely adopted waterfall model have led to alternative software production process models, illustrated in Sections 7.1.2. through 7.1.4.

7.1.2 Evolutionary Model

It has been observed that the software engineer should be ready to accept the fact that failures in the first version of an application inevitably lead to the need for redoing the application. "Do it twice" is a principle advocated by Brooks [1975]. According to this approach, the first version of a product is viewed as a trial whose main purpose is to assess the feasibility of the product and to verify the requirements. Then the product is thrown away, and the real development starts on more solid foundations provided by firmly established requirements. Using common terminology, the first version may be viewed as a *throwaway prototype* of the application. In fact, the initial version or prototype is used only temporarily, until it provides enough feedback to the software engineer on what the exact requirements are. The second version is then developed following a waterfall process model. This technique is only a partial solution to the problems discussed in the previous section. In particular, it does not eliminate the time gap between the definition of requirements and final delivery of the application. Nor does it stress the need for anticipating changes.

The need for flexible and nonmonolithic approaches–also called *evolutionary* or *incremental approaches*–has been widely acknowledged in the literature. A rigid and monolithic approach completely details all aspects of a stage of development before proceeding to the next stage; nothing is working or delivered until the very end of the development cycle. By contrast, an incremental approach consists of a stepwise development, where parts of some stages are postponed in order to produce some useful set of functions earlier in the development of the project.

Boehm [1988] defines the *evolutionary process model* as a "model whose stages consist of expanding increments of an operational software product, with the direction of evolution being determined by operational experience." Increments may be delivered to the customer as they are developed; this is called *evolutionary*, or *incremental, delivery*.

Although incremental delivery is not implied by an evolutionary model, it adds to the value of the model by getting early user feedback. Obviously, if increments are to be delivered to the customer, they should consist not only of code and internal project documentation, but also of user-oriented documentation. In other words, we may define a *delivered increment* to be a self-contained functional unit of software that performs some useful purpose for the customer, along with all supporting material (requirements and design specifications, test plans and test cases, a user manual, and training material).

The development strategy behind an evolutionary process model may be stated in the following simple form (see Gilb [1988]):

1. *Deliver* something to the real user.
2. *Measure* the added value to the user in all critical dimensions.
3. *Adjust* both the design and the objectives based on observed realities.

At first sight, an evolutionary process may resemble the old code-and-fix unstructured process. We must, therefore, be careful to retain the discipline introduced by the waterfall model.

The definitions we gave of an evolutionary process are general enough to accommodate a number of specific models. Here, we review the most important ones.

The minimal departure from the waterfall model in the direction of an evolutionary process is represented by what might be called an *incremental implementation* model. The idea here is that the waterfall process model is followed down to the design of the whole application; implementation, however, is done incrementally. During requirements analysis and design, special care is placed on the identification of useful subsets of the system that might be delivered to the user and on the definition of interfaces that will later allow new subsystems to be added smoothly. This leads to a plan where different parts are implemented, tested, and delivered according to different priorities and at different times. Thus, instead of a single two-step cascade of code-and-test and integration-and-test stages in which the application is developed as a monolith, we have a sequence of code-and-test and integration-and-test stages for the various increments.

We may accommodate a limited amount of incrementality even in a strict waterfall process, such as the one shown in Figure 7.1. In fact, as we observed in Section 7.1.1.4, integration may be kept tied to coding in an incremental scheme in which components are progressively integrated and tested as they are developed–for example, following a top-down or a bottom-up approach.

Incremental implementation provides only a partial solution to the problems inherent in the waterfall process model. For example, the earliest point at which we can provide the first increment may still be too late. Also, the results of the requirements analysis are still subject to being invalidated later.

The incremental approach may be extended to all stages of the life cycle in order to achieve finer granularity in the process. We will call this most general approach an *incremental development and delivery model*. Here, we start with a step that covers system objectives, architecture, and planning. The development begins by analyzing an increment at the requirements level; each increment is then separately designed, coded and tested, integrated, and delivered. In other words, the waterfall model is still followed, but for each separate increment; the overall process model is thus a sequence of miniwaterfall processes. Increments are developed one after the other after feedback is received from the customer. In fact, as users actually use the delivered parts, they start to understand better what they actually need. This leads to changes in the requirements for further increments and revisions of the original plan. Viewed from the developer, since each increment is simpler than the whole system, it is easier to predict the resources needed to accomplish the development task within acceptable accuracy bounds.

One way to characterize this kind of evolutionary model is to say that maintenance disappears as a stage of the life cycle–or, paradoxically, that the life cycle becomes all maintenance. In a waterfall model, change–which is discouraged during the development stages–manifests itself *a posteriori* in the form of maintenance. Since the process does not anticipate change, it is expensive to accommodate such change later. In the incremental development and delivery model, by contrast, change may be taken into account easily. In fact, it is so easy, that discipline and careful planning are required to prevent useless iteration and never-ending developments, as in the case of the early code-and-fix model.

Prototyping is an evolutionary principle for structuring the life cycle. We have already mentioned the throwaway prototype that follows the do-it-twice rule. We also mentioned the concept of an *evolutionary prototype*. In this case, the prototype is progressively transformed into the final application. An example is a software system in which some parts are deliberately missing and substituted for by a stub. The stub may be viewed as a prototype of the real components it simulates. For example, if the stub stands for a function, it may be implemented by suitable interaction with the user, who receives input parameters and is asked to provide results, as we saw in Section 6.3.5.2. If interfaces have been designed properly, future development of the real component to replace the prototype will not require any change in the overall structure of the system; i.e., the evolution from the prototype to the final system will occur smoothly. In the testing example, the purpose of the prototype is to permit some early testing of functions that would otherwise have to be postponed until after development of the whole (sub)system.

More frequently, prototyping is viewed as a tool in the process of understanding the user's requirements. For example, it is well known that user interfaces are a most critical aspect of interactive end-user applications. Thus, before developing the software that implements the required functionality of an interactive application, the software engineer might wish to define and test possible ways of interacting with the application by showing the user how interaction will actually occur in the final application. This may result in several prototypes, that do nothing more than display panels on the computer screen and activate dummy functions when specific services are requested by the user through interaction with the application. Different prototypes might differ in the layout of panels, in the sequences of possible operations, and so on. Some of these will be throwaway prototypes, but one may be chosen to be evolutionary. In fact, the tool used by the software engineer as a prototype of user interfaces may be able to generate the run-time actions that are needed to support input and output in the final application. Once the user has selected the preferred prototype, the task left to the software engineer consists of designing the modules that accomplish what is requested by the various functions that are to be activated as a consequence of interaction. Thus, the prototype gradually evolves into the final system.

This example reveals an important point: prototyping–and, more generally, evolutionary techniques–may require specific supporting tools. For example, interactive user interfaces are possible because the software engineer can use an appropriate tool for rapid development of these interfaces, such as any of the tools provided by modern user interface management systems and fourth-generation languages. These points will be discussed further in Chapter 9.

Exercise

7.3   Suppose you are developing a system composed of four modules A, B, C, and D, where A USES B, A USES C, C USES D, E USES D, F USES C, and B USES D. Define some possible incremental implementation strategies.

7.1.3 Transformation Model

The transformation model is rooted deeply in theoretical work on formal specifications. The idea here is that software development may be viewed as a sequence of steps that gradually transform a specification into an implementation. First, informal requirements are analyzed and functions are specified formally, possibly in an incremental way. Then, the development process takes this formal description and transforms it into a more detailed, less abstract formal description. As we proceed, the description becomes executable by some abstract processor. If we can achieve early executability in the transformation process, then the executable description may be viewed as an evolutionary prototype that is obtained as a by-product of the transformation process. Further transformations, however, are still necessary to make execution as efficient as specified in the requirements.

Transformations may be performed manually by the software engineer. In this circumstance, the formal nature of the derivation may provide a form of mathematical check that one step is a correct transformation of the previous. It is also possible, however, that the support system performs transformations automatically, possibly under the software engineer's direction. Examples of this are automatic transformation from a recursive to a nonrecursive implementation and other kinds of source-to-source program optimization.

An ideal transformation-based process model is illustrated in Figure 7.3. The process consists of two main stages: *requirements analysis* and *optimization*. requirements analysis provides formal requirements, which are fed into the optimization process that does the performance tuning, until we reach a satisfactory, optimized result. The transformation process is controlled by the software engineer and may take advantage of the availability of reusable components. Reusable components may take the form of modules to be included in the applications, perhaps after minor modifications, or even derivation steps to be replayed. As the figure shows, new reusable components may be developed during the process and stored in the library.

Before being transformed, specifications are verified against the user's expectations to check whether they capture the real requirements. In the ideal scenario of Figure 7.3, verification of requirements is done in a variety of ways, such as proving formal properties or executing the software.

As shown in the figure, the transformation-based life cycle is supported by a suitable computer-aided software development environment. The environment provides tools for verifying requirements, handling reusable components, performing optimizations (according to some existing catalogue and/or following directives from the software engineer), and storing the history of the development of the software. The last is an important feature for supporting future requests for changes: any redevelopment will start from the appropriate point in the history of the previous development, in order to accommodate changes in a reliable way and keep the documentation consistent.

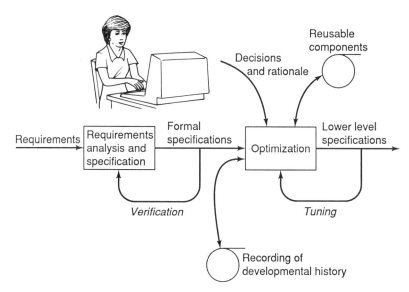

Figure 7.3   The transformation model.

The ability of the transformation-based model to support program evolution contrasts with the common practice based on conventional waterfall process models. As we observed, in a waterfall model, experience has shown that since changes are not anticipated, they are often treated as emergency repairs: they are performed under strong pressure from the customers and management and within strict time constraints. As a consequence, programmers tend to make changes only by modifying the code, without propagating the effects of those changes to changes of the specifications. Thus, specification and implementation gradually diverge, making future changes to the application even more difficult to perform. Updating the affected requirements and design specifications is also difficult because these are usually textually documented, and changes are difficult to make and trace back.

The situation is quite different in the transformation-based approach. Since the history of the development of the software–along with the rationale of every transformation step–is recorded by the support environment, the programmer may be forced to forgo changing the code directly, and instead start retransforming from the appropriate intermediate step of the history. This is exactly the approach we advocated in Section 4.1.2, which deals with program families: conceptually, each change produces a new family member.

Unfortunately, at present, the transformation approach is not a practical paradigm for software production process models. It is still a research-oriented approach, and only experimental environments are available to support it. It may become practical when research scales up from small programs to the development of large and complex systems.

The transformation approach has been studied for small programs as a dual method for proving program correctness. Program correctness proofs represent an *analytic*, mathematically based approach: they provide a formal framework for analyzing program correctness *a posteriori*, after the program is developed. Transformations, instead, are a *constructive*, mathematically based approach. Given a program P, and its specification in terms of pre- and postconditions Pre and Post, program correctness proofs describe how to verify the truth of {Pre} P {Post}. The transformation approach, by contrast, tries to derive a program P that is guaranteed to be correct *a priori*, given a specification pair <Pre, Post>.

The transformation process, of course, cannot be made entirely mechanical and requires skill and creativity from the programmer. The latter, however, is constrained to operate within well-defined formal boundaries, so that his or her confidence in the design process is greatly enhanced, and complexity is dominated and kept under control. In addition, the program is derived hand in hand with its correctness proof, so that the result is guaranteed to be correct.

In order to scale up the transformation approach to handle the development of real-life software systems, some researchers argue that some of the techniques developed in artificial intelligence should be incorporated into the support environment. The environment, they maintain, should interact with the software engineer via a suitable *automated assistant*. The assistant mediates and supports all activities of the software process, as directed by the software engineer. Such assistance involves recording the derivation steps and their rationale, carrying out decisions made by the software engineer, producing the information necessary to make those decisions, suggesting strategies, and so on. The assistant should operate on the basis of knowledge of software processes and application domains. Some successes have already occurred in this area with moderate-sized applications for restricted application domains. The application of artificial intelligence to software engineering is currently an active research area.

Exercise

7.4   Discuss why one can say that the transformation-based approach as described in Figure 7.3 favors the reusability of software processes.

7.1.4 Spiral Model

The goal of the spiral model of the software production process is to provide a framework for designing such processes, guided by the risk levels in the project at hand. As opposed to the previously presented models, the spiral model may be viewed as a *metamodel*, because it can accommodate any process development model. By using it as a reference, one may choose the most appropriate development model (e.g., evolutionary versus waterfall). The guiding principle behind such choice is the level of risk; accordingly, the spiral model provides a view of the production process that supports risk management.

Let us present a few definitions. *Risks* are potentially adverse circumstances that may impair the development process and the quality of products. Boehm [1989] defines *risk management* as a "discipline whose objectives are to identify, address, and eliminate software risk items before they become either threats to successful software operation or a major source of expensive software rework." The spiral model focuses on identifying and eliminating high-risk problems by careful process design, rather than treating both trivial and severe problems uniformly. Software risk management will be discussed further in Chapter 8.

The main characteristic of the spiral model is that it is cyclic and not linear like the waterfall model (see Figure 7.4). Each cycle of the spiral consists of four stages, and each stage is represented by one quadrant of the Cartesian diagram. The radius of the spiral represents the cost accumulated so far in the process; the angular dimension represents the progress in the process.

Stage 1 identifies the objectives of the portion of the product under consideration, in terms of qualities to achieve. Furthermore, it identifies alternatives–such as whether to buy, design, or reuse any of the software–and the constraints on the application of the alternatives. The alternatives are then evaluated in stage 2 and potential risk areas are identified and dealt with. Risk assessment may require different kinds of activities to be planned, such as prototyping or simulation. Stage 3 consists of developing and verifying the next level product; again, the strategy followed by the process is dictated by risk analysis.

If the requirements for the application are understood reasonably well, a conventional waterfall process model may be chosen, which leads to a simple one-turn spiral. In less understood end-user applications, however, the next step may be evolutionary in nature; i.e., several spiral turns may be required in order to achieve the desired results. It can also accommodate any mixture of the previously discussed models, with the appropriate mix chosen so as to minimize the risks involved in development.

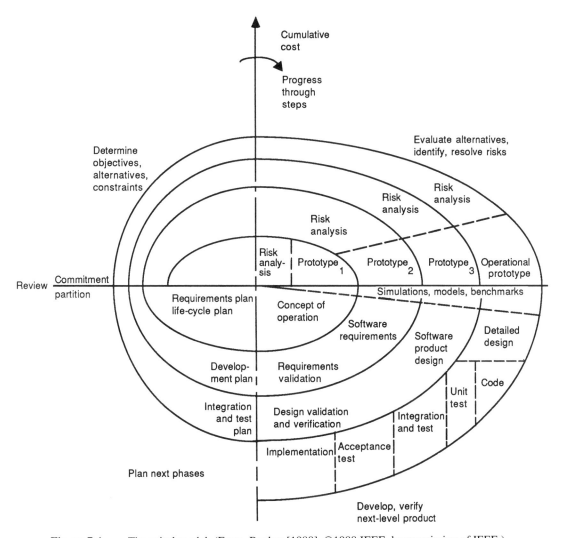

Figure 7.4   The spiral model. (From Boehm [1988], ©1988 IEEE, by permission of IEEE.)

Finally, stage 4 consists of reviewing the results of the stages traversed so far and planning for the next iteration of the spiral, if any.

The spiral model allows us to restate the issue of robustness versus correctness, discussed in Chapter 2, in a new framework. After one cycle of the spiral, unstated requirements are checked as part of the robustness of the application. As we realize that they should have been specified as requirements, they become part of the specification of the next cycle, if any. Consequently, after each iteration through the cycles, robustness approximates correctness more closely.

7.1.5 An Assessment of Process Models

Our description of software process models has followed the actual historical evolution of these models, from the unstructured code-and-fix model to the waterfall model to evolutionary models to transformation-based models. The driving force behind this evolution was the recognition of weaknesses in the extant models and the desire to devise the most effective process to achieve the qualities required for the application at hand.

The code-and fix model can actually be considered no model at all. It consists of following the inspiration and the needs of each particular moment, without carefully thinking and planning out the entire process beforehand. The code-and-fix model, the waterfall model falls into the other extreme: it is rigid, prespecified, nonadaptive, and monolithic. In its practical application, it is usually driven by documentation that measures the progress of the process. Generally, this documentation is voluminous, but totally passive, making changes difficult to apply as the application enters the maintenance stage and causing the documentation to diverge from the implementation.

If the waterfall life cycle is *documentation driven*, we can characterize evolutionary approaches as *increment driven*. In fact, progress through the evolutionary process is marked by the development and possible delivery of increments. The transformation-based approach, instead, can be called *specification driven*, as the development process occurs through iterative refinement of formal specifications. Finally, as we saw, the spiral model is a metamodel that may be called *risk driven*.

So far, there has been little detailed comparison of the various models. Some initial experiments led by Boehm explored the productivity of a waterfall-based life cycle compared with that of an evolutionary life cycle based on prototyping and the use of fourth-generation languages in the area of interactive end-user applications. The results showed that the waterfall approach addressed product and process control risks better, whereas the prototyping approach addressed user interfaces better. The prototyping approach also avoided the risks of spending much time on not-so-important aspects and helped to concentrate attention on the relevant issues and risks. In addition, both projects had roughly equivalent productivity in terms of their rates of delivered source instructions. They also had comparable performance, but the evolutionary process had 40% less development time and resulted in a product with roughly 40% less source instructions. The waterfall-based process had less problems in debugging and integration, due to more thought-out design. More on this point will be said in the bibliographic notes.

Even though comparative studies of the various models are still preliminary and do not support decision making in a quantitative fashion, there is a consensus that in most cases a strictly sequential, monolithic waterfall model should be replaced by a more flexible approach that incorporates some features of evolutionary models. Because evolutionary models come in various forms, achieving different degrees of incrementality, the process is more easily adaptable throughout its phases. The higher the level of incrementality, the closer the interaction becomes between software engineers and end users. As interaction becomes stronger, software development really becomes cooperative work, in which different cultures and conflicting goals must be reconciled.

The involvement of the end user in the software development process has become a major factor characterizing the evolution of software engineering in recent years. The availability of higher level languages and tools encouraged a more explorative style of work than that permitted by the waterfall life cycle. Today, the end user may become one of the partners of the process and even a principal driving force behind it. Tools for end-user computing–such as spreadsheets and data bases–are increasingly available to support small individual business applications, so that in certain application domains the distinction between software developers and users disappears, as was the case in the early years of computing.

Software engineers can now concentrate on complex, long-lived applications with high reliability and longevity constraints. For example, the architecture of a complex information system will be designed and implemented under the software engineer's responsibility, whereas a simpler, temporary, individual application will be more directly developed by the end user. The issue of end-user computing will probably have a significant impact on future developments in software engineering.

The evolution of process models may be observed from yet another viewpoint. The dominant aim of the waterfall model is directed towards the cost-effective development of a single application. No emphasis is placed on processes that span a family of products, let alone on building tools and libraries for general use. Cost effectiveness is measured on a short-term scale: the time to develop the application at hand. Very often, the development method adopted is top down–from the problem down to its solution. The method is based on functional decomposition and uses a conventional programming language (e.g., C, FORTRAN, COBOL, or Pascal) for implementation.

Another culture that has emerged more recently emphasizes the production of higher quality products that satisfy their expected users, possibly through the adoption of evolutionary approaches. In this culture, product quality comes first and process quality is in some sense ancillary to it.[1] This culture also emphasizes the production of tools and libraries, through which specific applications are constructed fast, reliably, and economically. The cost effectiveness of this approach is measured on a medium to long-term time scale: it is based on investments that progressively enrich the set of available tools and components.

As a new application is required, first the library is searched to determine whether something is available for reuse. If the search is successful, the application is constructed by assembling existing components. It may happen that these components only allow the development of a prototype, which is refined later to produce the final product. If so, new components are evolved from existing ones, and the new components may become part of the library.

To sum up our discussion of process models, we emphasize once again that the lessons learned from the past show that no unique, perfect, and ready-to-use process model exists that can be adopted once and for all and used in all organizations, for all

---

[1]Quoting an authoritative Japanese software engineer, the vice president of NEC Corporation's C&C Software Development Group, "When quality is pursued, productivity follows" (Fujino [1990]).

kinds of products or product families. Drawbacks have been discovered in models that did not stress the need for disciplined development, as well as in prescriptive models that were supposed to be applied in a rigid and purely mechanical way. Also, the emphasis on designing processes just for developing a single application, without long-term investments in tools and libraries, is shortsighted and will result in reduced productivity in the long term.

It is impossible, however, to reconcile all these conflicting requirements in a new, universal, blanket process model that will replace the old waterfall life cycle. The way different factors should be weighted is highly variable, and the software engineer should apply expert knowledge to define the most appropriate model for any specific situation. Actually, the first step of any software process should always consist of selecting or designing the appropriate model to be followed in the succeeding steps.

7.2 CASE STUDIES

In this section, we discuss two case studies of software projects that illustrate two quite different situations which resulted in different development approaches. The first study exemplifies a complex system with stringent reliability and efficiency requirements whose expected functions were perfectly understood and frozen when the project started. The second exemplifies a system in which interaction with the end user was the major critical issue and the requirements were largely unknown when the project started and evolved progressively during development.

7.2.1 Telephone Switching System

A company had developed one of the first digital switches in the world and had already sold many systems making use of the switches. This initial success had caused a demand for both more features and more powerful switches. The company was ready to invest in a major release to satisfy these demands.

Switching systems are among the most complex embedded, real-time software systems and offer many challenging software engineering problems. Their major characteristics are the following:

- They complex functional specifications.
- There is a need to interface to a large input-output system with tens of thousands of lines and to process thousands of calls in parallel, with response times of well under 1 second.
- They provide uninterrupted service in the presence of intermittent or permanent hardware and software faults.
- There is a need for a large number of instances of the system with individual variations.
- There is a need to support on-line modification and enhancement over a lifetime of 20 or more years.

The particular development we study here followed the classic waterfall model primarily because the problem was well defined and the company had much experience with the existing system. Based on this experience, the people involved felt confident about the accuracy of their estimates.

7.2.1.1 The existing system

The existing system was primarily the creation of a single (electrical) engineer. It had been written in assembly language for an Intel 8080. The engineer was thoroughly familiar with switching systems, and when microprocessors were introduced, he recognized their potential in telephony. Until that time, special-purpose devices were used for telephone switching. Over several months, the engineer had programmed the major parts of the system to demonstrate the feasibility of his approach. At the time, two other engineers joined him to complete and polish the system.

When first shipped, the system consisted of approximately 50,000 lines of assembly code. By the time a major release was being planned, the system was being "maintained" by a group of approximately 30 software engineers. The original three engineers were still with the company, and they were the main sources of information about the design of the system.

7.2.1.2 Switching systems in general

A telephone switching system is responsible for establishing and maintaining connections among telephone lines. There are different classes of systems. The system we are discussing here was a "subscriber" switch. Such a switch is installed in a community and is responsible for connections to and from the actual telephone users in that community. If a call is made from the community to a telephone number in another community that is not served by the same switch, the switch contacts a higher level switch that is responsible for connecting subscriber switches. There are five classes of switches, with the subscriber switch at level 1. The telecommunications network in the world is connected according to a hierarchy. Level 5 switches connect across country boundaries.

The software for a switching system has very stringent real-time, reliability, and fault-tolerance requirements. Because the telephone system is a utility, some of the reliability requirements are even legal requirements. These systems use redundant hardware to achieve fault tolerance. Run-time diagnostics attempt to detect failures and automatically configure replacements for failing devices; messages are then sent to the operator to effect the replacement Such systems are required to work even in the event of major disasters such as earthquakes, and, in general, they do.

7.2.1.3 The structure of the system

The structure of the switching system at issue is shown in Figure 7.5. The subsystems and their functions are as follows:

- *The executive.* This subsystem is the switching system's "operating system." It provides processing, memory, and time management facilities. It performs all the low-level machine operations such as interrupt processing. The executive allows the system to be used by the different subsystems simultaneously.

- *Call processing*. This subsystem performs the main telephone-switching operations: it supports the placing of a telephone call by detecting the lines going on and off, and the numbers being dialed, providing the appropriate dial tones, and connecting to the appropriate lines. Strict real-time requirements are specified for the operation of this function. For example, the shortest and longest times allowed between two consecutive numbers dialed are specified. Different actions must be performed based on the time elapsed between dialed numbers. In general, the response to each particular subscriber action must be limited strictly. For example, if a telephone goes "off hook," this must be detected–through an interrupt–and a dial tone must be generated. The duration of the interrupt-processing code determines how many off-hook signals can be detected simultaneously and, eventually, how many calls can be processed simultaneously. Thus, adding even a single instruction to the interrupt code could change the system's performance. The actual speech path connections are maintained by hardware. Hence, the call-processing software is responsible only for detecting changes in the line signals and establishing the speech paths. Once a path is established, the next action required by the software is only after termination of the call is detected. The operations of the call-processing subsystem can be specified precisely by a finite state machine.

- *Administration*. This subsystem maintains information on subscribers. It is basically a data base that contains information about the numbers supported by the system, the services supported at each number, and which lines can be used to connect to each number. It contains facilities for updating the data base either on line or at regular intervals. It also maintains statistics about traffic patterns in the system.

- *Fault processing*. This subsystem detects malfunctions in the systems and performs the steps necessary to recover from them. For example, it may cause a processor or a memory card to be switched out of service and a replacement to be put into use. Some of the fault-processing function may be performed in hardware.

- *Diagnostics*. This subsystem performs diagnostic operations to locate malfunctioning components and perhaps determine their cause. It may be run manually by technicians, or may be automatically invoked by the fault-processing subsystem, or may be run at regular intervals.

The software is, of course, part of a larger system that consists of the processor, hardware devices such as dial-tone generators, and the telephone and trunk lines controlled by the switch. This whole collection must fit in as a node in the country's telephone network.

7.2.1.4 The new release

The software development department was already structured according to the structure of the system: there were five groups, each responsible for one of the subsystems. In addition, there was an integration and testing group that performed system testing and released the software. Each group had between four and seven members.

A switch can be characterized by how many lines can be connected to it (i.e., how many subscribers it has), how many calls per hour it can process, and how many calls it can process at a given time. The system under discussion here was capable of handling 10,000 calls per hour. The requirement for the new release was that the system handle 20,000 calls per hour.

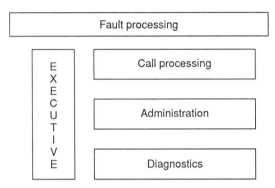

Figure 7.5   Subsystems of a telephone switching software system.

Although the evolution of the new release was not deliberately planned to follow a systematic life cycle, in practice it can be described as having followed a waterfall life cycle quite closely. There was a trivial requirements study phase, specifying the required increase in the capacity of the switch. The three original engineers then did a preliminary feasibility study and design of the system. Not surprisingly, they concluded that the initial system structure had to be maintained. They produced a set of high-level requirements for changes to be made to each existing subsystem. Their thorough familiarity with the existing system made this step possible.

The changes were not confined to the software. For example, the new design required adding more memory to the system. Because the processor was not able to address more than 64K, this required building a special hardware device to allow switching among memory banks. This, in turn, of course necessitated changes in the executive subsystem to support what was essentially a primitive form of virtual memory. The addition of memory banks also required substantial changes to the diagnostics and fault-processing subsystems.

The requirements for each subsystem were then given to the appropriate groups. The design team had built a simulator of the hardware, including the memory banks, during their feasibility study. This simulator was used by each group to test their individual subsystems modularly before the actual hardware became available. Once the hardware became available, people still used the simulator for their initial testing because it was much easier to use. Eventually, when all the subsystems were ready, they were given to the integration and testing group, which integrated them and performed extensive functionality and reliability tests. Many defects were found, but they were all local to individual subsystems. Since no major design errors were discovered, the development cycle was fairly linear, requiring iteration only to repair inconsistencies in interfaces between modules. After several months, the system was released and was quite successful in the field.

7.2.1.5 An analysis

The software development for the switching system described in the previous section is fairly typical of a large class of software engineering projects. In many organizations, the major development task is to produce the next release of an existing software system. It is easier to follow the waterfall model for the new release of an existing system because the application area and the requirements are relatively well understood. This removes the usual difficulties involved in performing requirements analysis for a new system. Also, the design phase does not suffer from as much uncertainty because the current design of the system and its limitations are known. It is therefore less likely that the requirements and design phases will have to be repeated, resulting in a linear development cycle exemplified by the waterfall model. In some sense, the previous version of the system behaves like a prototype of the new release.

In this case study, the major difficulties were due to the fact that the implementation language was assembly language. The original reason for using assembly language was the nonexistence of any high-level languages at the time. When high-level languages became available, the reason the engineers gave for not using them was the overriding need for efficiency! As a matter of fact, the early compilers for the processor did not generate efficient code but, the real reason for not using the high-level languages was probably resistance to change. The use of assembly language caused significant technical difficulties. For example, because "clever" pointer arithmetic was used to access the different entries in the subscriber-information data base, increasing the number of allowable entries or increasing the size of each entry sometimes required major modifications.

The major factor that made the project successful was probably the presence of the original designers of the system. The designers had all the details of the system and all the timings of the different code paths in their heads. Any changes to critical pieces of code were checked first by these "gurus." This continuity also contributed to the linearity of the development cycle, because most defects were detected by the original designers' reviews. Finally, the system was probably also helped along by having to meet very strict reliability requirements. Not only was the initial system, which was the starting point for the new release, reliable, but every engineer knew that reliability was a primary requirement and–due mainly to regulatory requirements–that the system would not be released before demonstrating the required reliability.

7.2.1.6 Footnote

While the release just described was successful, we hasten to add that problems inherent in the system–the unmanageability of large assembly language programs and the lack of any formal or, in any case, adequate specification and documentation–eventually made it impossible for the system to evolve. One study of the feasibility of redoubling the capacity of the system showed that it could not be done. The only solution was to adopt a new, more powerful processor, but this meant rewriting the software completely, which was not possible in the time frame required to meet the market needs. After searching for solutions, such as automatic translation of the software into the assembly language of the new processor, or "decompiling" into a high-level language, it was decided to abandon enhancing the system. By law, the currently installed systems must be maintained for 20 years, but no new versions of the system with any new functionality will be released.

Exercise

7.5 It is possible to plan for the retirement of a system during the planning stages of the system. Discuss how such a plan would have applied to the above case study. What kinds of information would be included in the plan? What would be the benefits of such a plan?

7.2.2 Budget Control System

Every company has a budget control activity, devoted to monitoring its financial transactions and ensuring their correspondence with original plans. In general, these transactions and plans are embedded in the company's annual budget. In this section, we present a case study describing the construction and the evolution of a system that supports budget control for a small, high-tech company in the consulting and software development business. The description is given in the style of a report on an imaginary software process taking place in an imaginary company where the tool was developed for internal use only. The process, however, is a true account from the real world. We will see that the history of this system development process fits quite well into an evolutionary model.

In this case study, Section 7.2.2.1 presents the problem and its peculiarities with respect to more conventional problems in business administration, and Sections 7.2.2.2 through 7.2.2.4 present the evolution of the system from a first, rough prototype to a final–but still evolving–system that is integrated with the company's information system. All versions of the system were used in the company–i.e., the initial prototypes were not just throwaway prototypes, but were used as intermediate products.

7.2.2.1 The problem and its peculiarities

The main goal of budget control is understanding whether the activities performed by the company are proceeding according to the original budget and forecasts, so that appropriate decisions can be taken early if this is not the case. This control activity is clearly related to other administrative activities such as payroll processing, income and expense monitoring, inventory tracking, and tax payment. It is also clear, however, that budget control is not just a mechanical activity and cannot be based exclusively on administrative data. The reasons for this are twofold.

First, the information that is relevant to budget control comprises not only objective data–such as time and material costs, prices, and number of items sold–but also more subjective estimates such as "work in progress," i.e., an estimate of the value of what was produced so far by the development process while it is still ongoing. It is always difficult to make accurate estimates in the case of software, as we will see in Chapter 8. In the case of work in progress, this difficulty may be appreciated by comparing the software industry with traditional industries such as the automobile or hi-fi industry, where manufacturing proceeds in a precise, standardized, and often automatic way, so that the status of production may be identified precisely and even measured quantitatively at any point. The company under consideration in this case study had even more difficulties because of its peculiarities. In fact, both the development of new and innovative market products and the consulting activity–consisting mainly of feasibility studies and early R&D prototypes–made it difficult to estimate production costs, end-product prices, and the work in progress. Thus, the traditional expertise of professionals skilled in budget control for engineering manufacturing–such as the manufacture of cars or electronics parts–was not applicable to company in question, whose processes were less formalized and much more flexible.

Second, budget control needs some data that are not usually found in the administrative data base. Even when the information is available in the data base, its logical organization may be peculiar. This was exactly what happened in this case study.

As an example, consider personnel costs. In the company we are considering, as far as administrative procedures were concerned, employees were kept separate from external consultants, since different payment procedures were applied. Also, the total cost of an employee was partitioned into net salary, tax withheld, possible health insurance, social security contribution, etc. From the point of view of budget control, however, these distinctions are not relevant: the total cost of a worker is all that matters. On the other hand, budget control needs to know how much time a person spends on various projects, in order to determine which projects are doing well and which are in trouble; but this information is irrelevant to conventional administrative procedures. As a result, the information stored in the existing administrative data base of the company was not very useful for budget control.

7.2.2.2 The first, semiautomated system

When the company realized the need for a well-organized and reliable budget control procedure, the difficulties related to the above peculiarities soon became apparent. The company realized that the problem was not just choosing a budget control system among those available on the market–assuming one could be found; rather, the problem really was to understand exactly what budget control was all about and to develop a mechanized solution hand in hand with the incremental understanding of the problem. Thus, the company decided to form a team composed of a software engineer (with some background in business administration) and an administrative manager, whose joint job was to organize budget control and design an automated system to support the activity.

Initially, the team focused attention on understanding the nature of the problem. This soon confirmed that the existing administrative information system was not suitable for the intended task. In fact, the information system was a standard one that was rather inflexible with respect to the changes and enrichments that were needed for the new application. On the other hand, it was shortly realized that most of the difficulties of the problem were not in the amount of data to be managed–the company consisted of about 30 people and just a few ongoing projects–but in the unusual nature of the activities of the company, in the lack of standard production rules, in a fairly hectic re-scheduling and rebudgeting of most activities, in personnel turnover, etc. It was therefore clear that a precise statement of the requirements for budget control automation could be reached only after some experience and trial and error. Thus, a major decision was to apply an evolutionary approach to the development of such a system and to concentrate attention initially more on organizational than on technical aspects, even at the risk of throwing away the first few prototypes.

The first prototype consisted mainly of internal organizational procedures, definition of logical relations among different pieces of information, and a very limited amount of automatic computation performed through simple productivity tools. Its main features were the following:

- All pieces of information that were relevant to budget control were listed and classified. Their relations and sources were defined. It was made clear which were likely to change and what the expected changes were. Examples of expected changes were in the classification of items: initially, a rough distinction between administrative, production, and distribution expenses was satisfactory, but later, managers would probably ask to distinguish between, say, telephone versus travel expenses. It was also necessary to account for different levels of aggregation of items–for example, travel costs for each project or per project type, or travel costs for the whole company. Other changes were anticipated in the kind of queries supported by the system. Besides standard queries such as "What is the difference between the estimated and actual revenue of a project?" "What are the total expenses of a given project?" and "How much do we pay for travel?" many unpredictable questions could be raised. Again, the decision was that a first prototype would supply only answers to a fixed and predefined set of questions, but later versions would allow a richer and more flexible set of queries.

- A set of procedures for data collection was defined. Attention was focused on the organizational and logical aspects of the required information, not on its physical format. For instance, every person, whether an employee or an external consultant, was requested to fill out a monthly form stating the time spent on each project and possible expenses, charging them to a given project or activity.[1] Since the first prototype was not supposed to be integrated with the administrative information system, it was decided that data already existing in that system should be duplicated and supplied independently to the budget control system. This decision made it possible to ignore the differences in data formats, even at the expense of manual conversion. (Actually, it turned out that no single item could be copied trivially from one system to the other.)

At this point, data aggregation was quickly and roughly implemented by a spreadsheet. In the first instantiation, the spreadsheet performed just sums and

---

[1]Although this procedure is applied widely, it caused organizational problems in this small company, since most people worked on several activities in a fairly unstructured way. On the one hand, this lack of structure was a major reason for asking people to fill in such a form; on the other, people who did not fill out the form on a daily basis had problems reconstructing it at the end of the month.

comparisons, splitting results into major categories. Also, data were manually input into the spreadsheet. Thus, the "budget control data base" was just a collection of paper forms, processed through a spreadsheet that produced a report of the type shown in Figure 7.6.

month: **March**

  project 1:   CASE-study

income (= a + b - c)	**40,000**
(a) *invoices*	20,000
(b) *work in progress at the end of the month*	30,000
(c) *work in progress at the end of previous month*	10,000
expenses	**25,000**
man power in software development	10,000
man power in administrative work	5,000
hardware *	500
...	...
earnings	**15,000**

  project 2:   MODULA-2 Compiler

                            :
                            :

Total income	**150,000**
Total expenses	**120,000**
Net earnings	**30,000**

*This means the hardware depreciation cost attributed to the project for the given time period.

Figure 7.6   A spreadsheet report of an oversimplified budget control.

Clearly, such a procedure involved much manual work. But it was feasible because the amount of data was not so large. In fact, its initial use required much more work in checking the procedure than in data processing. Not only subjective estimates had to be verified and fixed, but even objective data acquisition required much attention because of the tight time synchronization requirements. For instance, on the 31st day of a month, a clerk could ship an invoice for the delivery of a product, but a different clerk could record the removal of the same item from inventory on the first day of the following month. This would generate an inconsistency that needed to be reconciled. Thus, the flexibility and simplicity of a spreadsheet overwhelmed its computational deficiencies. In many cases, the spreadsheet was rearranged "online" to supply answers to specific questions from the managers.

In sum, for the first prototype, two months were required to understand the major problems of the and take organizational decisions, and half a day to set up the first spreadsheet. Furthermore, in the first three to four months of operation of the software, it was nearly impossible to distinguish between the time needed to perform budget control and the time required to understand the problems of such control and design solutions that would yield better support tools. The development process thus proceeded hand in hand with a deeper understanding of the problem. The spreadsheet used in the fourth month was much richer than the first one. In particular, thanks to using a hierarchical spreadsheet, it was possible to achieve different levels of data aggregation, e.g., by project, by area (a section of the company devoted to similar projects), and by cost category.

7.2.2.3 A more complete version

Once the procedures–and risks–related to budget control were better understood, more attention was paid to the automation of the process. The company decided to develop a new family of prototypes, but to keep the budget control procedure as a stand-alone system, even at the cost of duplication and possible inconsistency of data. A real data base was used for storing all information related to budget control. A fourth-generation environment was chosen for its flexibility (many changes in data formats and classification were still anticipated), high-level querying facilities, and support for simple computations.

7.2.2.4 Towards an integrated system

Eventually, it was decided to integrate the budget control system into the companywide information system. This meant, not that the budget control system's organization and specification were "frozen," but that they were sufficiently well understood and that the evolution of the system could now be better scheduled and controlled.

   At that point, two independent systems existed: the *administrative information system* (AIS)–a conventional system running on a minicomputer–and the *budget control prototype* (BCP), running in a fourth-generation environment on a personal computer. A first major decision was to use the AIS as a source of data for the BCP, but to avoid the opposite–at least via automatic procedures. The rationale of this decision was twofold: the desire not to affect the AIS, a fairly standard and hard-to-modify system; and the need to integrate AIS data with additional information needed by the BCP. Since efficiency of execution was not a critical aspect of the budget control system, partial reuse of the existing prototype was preferred over reimplementing the system for more efficient hardware and software utilization.

   In sum, the major steps in the evolution of the new version of the product were the following:

- Construction of a batch translator to translate all relevant data already existing in the AIS into the BCP format. The typical output of such a translator was an incomplete form that needed to be filled in during the budget control activity. For instance, all travel expenses were automatically reported from the AIS by the translator, but some information, such as the project to which they referred, had to be added in a later phase.

- Improvement of the existing data-base manipulation facilities. This was done in an incremental way, by simply adding new functions.

Exercise

7.6   Discuss the various prototypes developed in the budget control example as either throwaway or evolutionary prototypes.

7.3 ORGANIZING THE PROCESS

Organizing the software process is a critical activity that takes in the management of
people to the management of all products produced during the life cycle. It also involves
the definition of appropriate methods and their combination within methodologies.
According to Webster's New World Dictionary (1977), a *method* is defined as a way of
doing anything, especially in an orderly way; a *methodology* is defined as a system of
methods. As we already observed, methodologies have frequently been packaged by
software organizations into companywide *standards*, in order to make software processes
more predictable and reusable. The management of human resources is discussed in the
next chapter. Here, we deal with product management, methodologies, and standards. In
particular, Section 7.3.1 deals with software methodologies, Section 7.3.2 deals with
product management, and Section 7.3.3 deals with standards.

7.3.1 Software Methodologies

In this section, we illustrate two widely known methodologies that have found
acceptance among software professionals: Structured Analysis/Structured Design
(SA/SD) and Jackson's System Development (JSD). Each is representative of state-of-
the-art industrial practices and is supported by tools that help develop software according
to the methodology. Each aims at complete coverage of the software development
process, by providing guidance from the analysis phase down to implementation.

The idea of a methodology that guides programmers in their work in all phases of
software development is appealing: it increases people's confidence in what they are
doing, it teaches inexperienced people how to solve problems in a systematic way, and it
encourages a uniform, standard approach to problem solving.

The main drawback of existing methodologies is that they lack solid formal
foundations. Most of the advice they provide in their formal steps may only be justified
in terms of good, solid common sense; other advice is at best questionable. In addition, if
one scratches the surface of where the methods appear to be applicable as simple recipes,
one can see that their application is far from mechanical and requires much personal
judgment. This is not bad *per se*, but it may turn out that more effort goes into trying to
understand how to apply the methodology rather than into how to solve the problem!
Another drawback of these methodologies when they are imposed as standards is that
they tend to reduce the intellectual responsibility of people, rather than enhance it. This,
however, is a general comment that may be applied to standards and thus will be taken up
in Section 7.3.3.

On the positive side, empirical evidence suggests that methodologies such as SA/SD and JSD are successful in specific application areas, especially business applications of small to moderate size.

7.3.1.1 Structured Analysis/Structured Design

Structured Analysis/Structured Design (SA/SD) is a methodology that has evolved through the contribution of several individuals over a number of years. In this section, we provide the main ideas of the methodology.

SA/SD suggests the use of three major conceptual tools for constructing system models in the requirements analysis phase: *data flow diagrams* (*DFDs*), a *data dictionary* (*DD*), and *structured English* (*SE*). Data flow diagrams were already illustrated in Chapter 5; their main components are shown in Figure 7.7 as a reminder to the reader. A data dictionary is a centralized collection of definitions of all data flowing among functions and to or from data stores. Centralizing all definitions in the dictionary removes the danger of duplications and inconsistencies. Structured English is any highly constrained subset of natural language used to describe the data transformation performed by each elementary bubble–i.e., a bubble that is not refined in terms of another DFD. SE can obviously be replaced by any other semiformal algorithmic notation. Structured design–SD–will then follow the analysis phase.

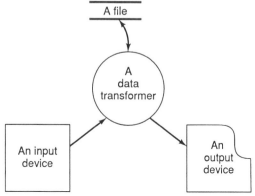

Figure 7.7   A sample DFD.

The above tools may provide system descriptions at various levels of abstraction that may be useful for documenting the results of analysis. First, DFDs may be used both to describe an existing environment in which the automatic procedure to be designed will eventually be embedded and to describe the logical structure of the application. For example, one may record the work flow in an office with the DFD fragment shown in Figure 7.8. The fragment shows that requests are received and registered by the office concerning, say, the purchase of material. If a special authorization is requested, it is handled by a specific person in the office; if special authorization is not requested (or if the authorization is given), the form is stored in a physical file and then processed by employees 4 through 6. The figure shows the manual operations currently in the system and is the basis for automating them according to SA/SD.

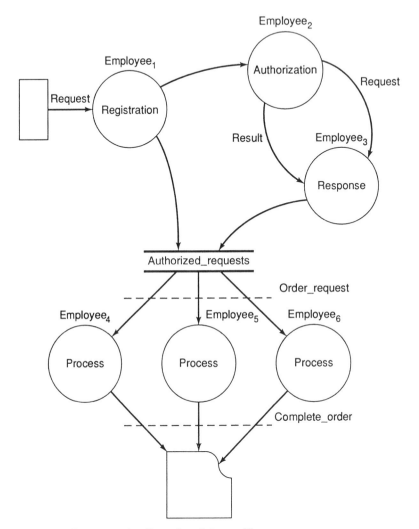

Figure 7.8   DFD representing flow of work in an office.

Another possibility offered by data flow diagrams to describe systems at different levels of abstraction consists of allowing the details of any bubble to be given by a diagram. For example, the DFD of Figure 7.8 might be the result of providing the details the description of a bubble that is called "Office XXX" in some higher level diagram that shows the flow of information among offices within a company. Actually, SA/SD suggests that decomposition be done until we reach the point where each transformation is sufficiently simple that we may detail its behavior in terms of SE.

SA/SD uses the DFD as a specification of the behavior–i.e., the functional requirements–of the application. The design–i.e., the decomposition of the system into modules,–is based directly on the DFD and is documented using *structured diagrams* (*SD*s). For example, Figure 7.9. illustrates the behavior of an automated application that will eventually be substituted for employees 4 through 6. The job of design is to convert this DFD into an appropriate hierarchy of modules represented as an SD.

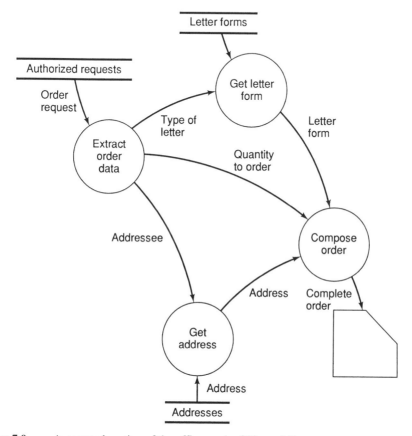

Figure 7.9   Automated portion of the office work of Figure 7.8.

An SD is a DAG-like structure in which nodes represent modules. Each module represents a functional abstraction, to be implemented later by a subprogram. Thus, in Figure 7.10, if modules M_1, M_2, and M_3 are subordinate to module M, then M calls M_1, M_2, and M_3.

The process from which an SD is derived from a DFD should aim for structures of modules with good coupling and cohesion. For example, one should avoid pathological connections such as the following:

* a jump inside a subordinate module instead of a call to that module;

- • a reference from a module to private data of another module instead of passing data to the second module via parameters.

SDs may be made more expressive by decorating them with additional notations, as shown in Figure 7.11. The figure illustrates which parameters flow between modules: M passes B to M_1 and receives A back; M also receives C from M_2. The figure also illustrates the control patterns governing the calls of subordinate modules: M either calls M_1 or repeatedly calls M_2. Selection is represented by the diamond symbol, and looping is represented by the circular arrow that groups the modules whose execution is iterated.

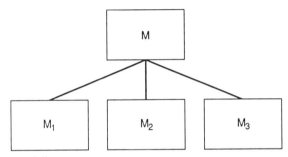

Figure 7.10   Structured diagram

DFDs are transformed into SDs manually, but the methodology provides some guidelines to follow. For example, one may arrange the decomposition illustrated in Figure 7.10 in such a way that M_1 acts like an abstract input module, M_3 acts like an abstract output module, and M_2 acts like a transformation module. This is illustrated by the decorated SD shown in Figure 7.12. The figure also shows that in order to provide the abstract input to M, M_1 requests lower level input from $M_{1,1}$ and for transformation of such input from $M_{1,2}$. A similar decomposition might occur for M_2 and M_3.

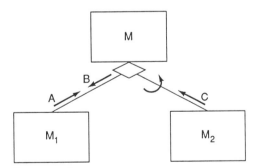

Figure 7.11   Decorated structure diagram.

A possible SD for the DFD of Figure 7.9 is shown in Figure 7.13. SA/SD calls such a decomposition *transform flow centered*. An alternative decomposition pattern, called *transaction flow centered*, is used to describe a module M that may call one of several subordinates, depending on the type of the incoming transaction request.

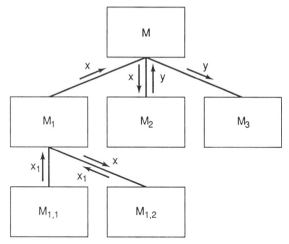

Figure 7.12   Typical structure of a decorated SD.

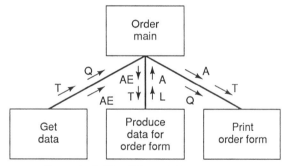

Figure 7.13   SD corresponding to the DFD of Figure 7.9. Legend: T = type of letter; Q = quantity; AE = addresses; L = letter form; A = address.

Exercise

7.7   What are the differences between SDs and GDN?

7.3.1.2 Jackson's System Development and Structured Programming

Jackson's System Development (JSD) has been an evolving methodology since its birth in 1983, and it still is. JSD has grown as a complete life cycle methodology on the foundations provided by Jackson Structured Programming (JSP), a popular design method adopted in many organizations for business data processing. The concise view of JSD/JSP we give here is not intended to be complete or to reflect the exact present stage of the methodology; rather, its purpose is to give an idea of the concepts on which the methodology is based.

While SA/SD bases system modelling on DFDs, JSD suggests a technique that represents a mixture of descriptive approaches based on object-oriented design and functional decomposition. Both approaches address all aspects of software development, from analysis to implementation. As we will see shortly, however, JSD is a more mechanical methodology, especially in its JSP component.

According to JSD, software development proceeds through a sequence of three stages: the modelling stage, the network stage, and the implementation stage. In the *modelling stage*, the real world is analyzed and represented in terms of *actions* (or *events*) that may affect *entities*, which model objects in the real world. An entity is composed of actions which model events that occur in its history. For example, the entity FORM may be composed of the actions GET, to get a form, FILL_IN, to fill the necessary data into the form, and CHECK_IN, to return the filled-in form.

All actions that characterize an entity are ordered in time; this ordering provides a process view of the entity, which is described by a *process structure diagram* (*PSD*). For example, the entity FORM may be described by the PSD of Figure 7.14(a), where the left-to-right placement of actions denotes the time sequence of the actions. In the diagram, A represents FORM, B denotes the action GET, C denotes the action FILL_IN, and D denotes the action CHECK_IN. The ordering represents the fact that first we must GET a form, then we FILL_IN the form, and finally we CHECK_IN the form. In general, PSDs are annotated trees that can describe different orderings of actions–for example, selection (Figure 7.14(b)) and iteration (Figure 7.14(c)).

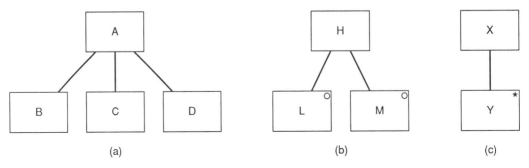

(a)   (b)   (c)

Figure 7.14   Process structure diagrams. (a) Sequence. (b) Selection. (c) Iteration.
(The symbol "*" in a corner of a box stands for iteration of the
corresponding function; the symbol "o" stands for selection.)

In the *network stage*, each entity is modelled as a process, and the entire system is a network of interconnected and communicating processes, described by a *system specification network* (*SSN*). The graphical appearance of SSNs is illustrated in Figures 7.15(a) and 7.15(b). Figure 7.15(a) illustrates the case where the processes P and Q are interconnected by the *data stream* R. A data stream is a FIFO queue of messages; if the queue is empty, then Q waits until P generates a message.

Another form of process connection is provided by *state vectors* (Figure 7.15(b)), whereby one process may inspect the state of (i.e., data owned by) another process. The figure shows the case where process Q inspects P's state vector. By inspecting the state vector, a process may access the history of another process, which is recorded in the form of data.

In the *implementation stage*, the network of processes is transformed into an implementation. That is, the concurrent network of processes is transformed into a sequential system, that is executable by a conventional machine. This transformation is necessary only if the system is implemented in a traditional programming language, such as COBOL. To effect the transformation, JSD introduces a technique called *process inversion*. Basically, process inversion transforms a pair of communicating sequential processes into a hierarchical structure whereby a program invokes a subprogram. More precisely, observe that the case illustrated in Figure 7.15(a) may be made sequential according to one of the following schemes:

- P runs, produces an information item to be consumed by Q, and then transfers control to Q. Q completes its job and then reactivates P;

- Q runs until it needs a datum produced by P. It then transfers control to P, asking for the datum, and resumes execution upon receipt.

At this stage, the JSD specifications are nearly complete, so that one may easily implement them using any programming language. To facilitate this final step, further details may be added to PSDs in order to show where some physical operations–such as opening or closing files, initializing counters, and updating relevant variables–actually occur. Since this step is exactly the same as a step in the JSP methodology, we explain it shortly in an example of JSP.

(a)   (b)

Figure 7.15   System specification networks.
                   (a) Connection by data structure. **(b)** Connection by state vector.

JSD supersedes JSP by covering the entire life cycle from requirements analysis to programming, whereas JSP is limited to the programming phase. Another difference between JSD and JSP is that JSP is based on the assumption that the program structure may fall directly out of the modelling of input and output data. By contrast, JSD models the program structure directly from analysis of the problem specification. Within the JSD methodology, however, it is possible to develop parts of a system using JSP, especially subsystems in which the process structure is influenced greatly by the structure of the data. Based on this comment, and also on the fact that JSP has found wide acceptance among practitioners, we briefly explain the principles of JSP.

According to JSP, one should model a problem by specifying relations among the input and output data using tree-structured diagrams described in the same notation as is used for PSD. Figure 7.16 shows a typical example of the input and output files for an inventory problem. The input file is a sequence of transfer orders, which may be either a receipt or a delivery, grouped by item code; the output is a summary report, where the net transfer is reported for each item.

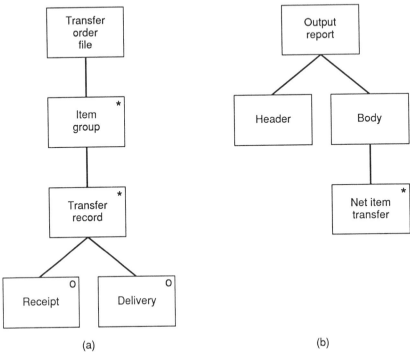

Figure 7.16   Input and output processing for an inventory problem.
(**a**) Input structure. (**b**) Output structure.

In order to derive a program that transforms the input file into the output file, JSP suggests that we identify the correspondence between the nodes of the diagrams. This correspondence is shown in Figure 7.17 by means of the zigzag connections. As a result of these, it is fairly obvious to derive a structure for the required program (see Figure 7.18(a)). Note, however, that it is not always so trivial to establish the correspondence between the input and output data structures and, hence, to derive the program structure. JSP, however, provides guidance with specific techniques to solve most practical problems arising in common data-processing situations.

In order to translate the abstract program structure of Figure 7.18(a) into the desired program, one may proceed by listing all the operations that are needed by the application and then associating them with the program structure by annotating the corresponding diagram. For the example of Figure 7.16, the operations are listed in Figure 7.18(b) and the annotated diagram is shown in Figure 7.18(c). A trivial transformation may translate the annotated diagram into pseudocode or even a programming language.

Exercise

7.8   Write a Pascal-like program corresponding to the decorated tree of Figure 7.18(c).

7.3.2 Configuration Management

When software is being developed, several individuals interact and cooperate towards a common goal. These individuals produce several products, some of which are strictly personal items, such as intermediate versions of modules or test data used during debugging, and others of which become, in one way or another, part of the final products. Very often the goal of production is not to produce a single product, but to generate a collection of products, e.g., module interface specifications or delivered source-code modules. Finally, products undergo many changes in their maintenance phase. There may be hundreds or thousands of components in a collection. How do we keep all this under control, in order to avoid its being lost in an unstructured collection of files, both in the computer and in the drawers of our desks? This is where the need for configuration management arises.

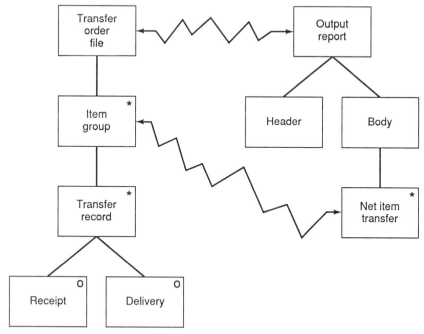

Figure 7.17   Matching of input and output structures.

A *configuration* of a product refers not only to the product's constituent components, but also to specific versions of the components. Configuration management is the discipline of *coordinating software development and controlling the change and evolution of software products and components*. It is an old discipline that has traditionally been studied in the context of systems manufacturing. Its application to software, however, is relatively new; in addition, software has special features that make it different from traditional manufacturing. Software adds complexity to configuration management because it is malleable; thus, changes are easy to make and, in fact, occur more frequently than in other kinds of products. Conversely, configuration management is amenable to increasing automation, since all items may be stored on media that are accessible by the computer.

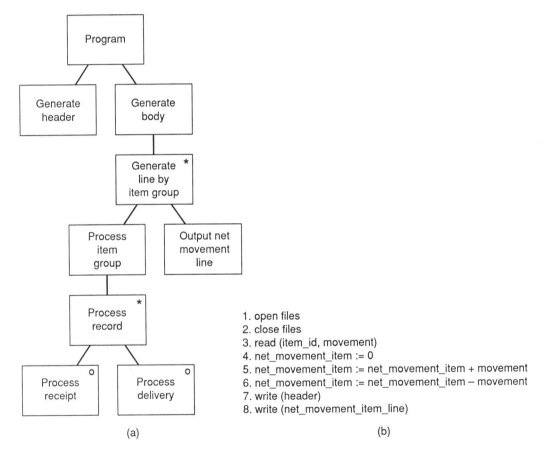

Figure 7.18   Deriving a program according to JSP. (**a**) Program structure.
(**b**) Program operations.

Let us examine more closely some of the issues that are addressed by software configuration management. One class of problems has to do with multiple accesses to a common repository of components. Suppose that one of the software engineers of a team has developed a module (say, M) and put it in a centralized data base of components for use by other members of the team. For example, M implements some services that are needed by other subsystems, and it might be convenient to use M for developing and testing those subsystems. Suppose also that for some reason, a member of the team picks up M from the data base and modifies it. Finally, suppose that the modification introduces an error and that other members of the team are not notified of the change. Then when they use M later, their executions will probably fail. To their surprise, the system might crash even in the case where no modification was made to their modules and to the input data. They simply do not know that a change occurred in M!

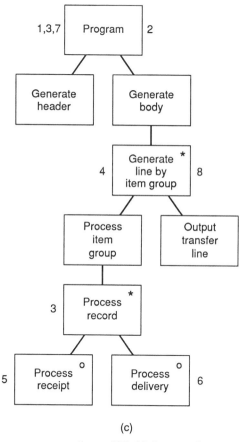

(c)

Figure 7.18   Deriving a program according to JSP. **(c)** Annotated program structure.

Another instance of the same problem occurs if two members of the team simultaneously check out the same component and modify it independently. After one checks the component back into the data base, there is no guarantee that the same component will be obtained through a later checkout. In fact, the changes made by one member of the team may be overwritten by another member of the team: only the latest checked-in copy will be kept.

The above problems are due to *sharing of components*. The simple and natural way to prevent these problems is to give a private copy of M to each of M's potential users. But the difficulty is that each private copy will eventually diverge into a different component.

Exercise

7.9   Explain the above problems of component sharing by drawing the analogy with shared variables accessed by different tasks in a concurrent programming language like Ada. How do we prevent these problems in an Ada program?

A second class of problems has to do with *handling product families*. The term "product family" is used instead of "program family" to stress the fact that configuration management deals not just with programs, but also with documentation, test data, user manuals, etc. Problems arise because, as a consequence of changes, a component may exist in several versions. Or if a product undergoes a series of releases. Each member of the product family may consist of different versions of components. Figure 7.19 illustrates this point: components are grouped together, and different subscripts are used to indicate the various versions of the same component. Three members of the product family F are also indicated.

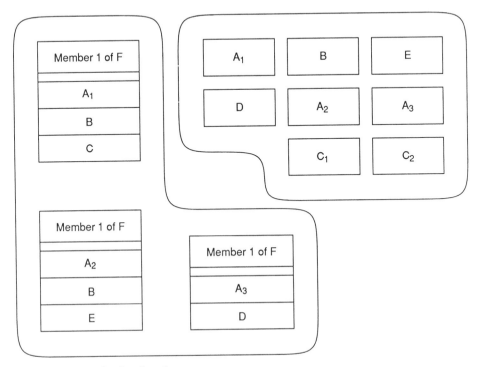

Figure 7.19   A family of products.

Even though different members of a product family are indicated by listing the names and versions of components, they are not necessarily stored and kept in this way. An alternative solution might be to have each family member include a copy of all the components. Whatever solution is adopted, however, special care must be taken to keep the state of families consistent as a change occurs in one or more components that may belong to one or more family members.

In order to proceed in our discussion of configuration management, we need to refine the concept of a version of a component that we have used so far. First, observe that we may formally define the concept by introducing the relation IS_VERSION_OF among components. IS_VERSION_OF may then be further refined by introducing the two relations IS_REVISION_OF and IS_VARIANT_OF.

According to standard terminology in the field, IS_REVISION_OF defines the concept of a component C_i being a *revision* of another component C_j. This means that C_i is obtained by changing a copy of C_j. The version of the component we obtain through revision supersedes the previous version; thus, revisions are created in a linear order. There are many reasons one may wish to create a revision of a component, and this might be reflected by further specializing the relation IS_REVISION_OF. For example, one might wish to specify that one version is the correction of another, or that it has been obtained by replacing an internal stub with an actual subprogram.

Another specialization of IS_VERSION_OF is the relation IS_VARIANT_OF. This relation holds if two components are indistinguishable under some given abstraction. For example, they might be two implementations of the same specification. Another example is an application whose different variants permit access to different I/O devices (a line printer vs. a laser printer, etc.). Obviously, variants do not supersede the original component, and thus they are not organized as a linear succession.

In order to handle all products that are generated during the software process, it is necessary to establish projectwide configuration management policies. A typical case may consist of using a *project base line* in conjunction with a private work space for each member of the development team. The project base line is a central repository that serves as a shared data base associated with the project. For example, when programmers are developing their own modules, they use their own private work space for storing intermediate versions. The policy followed to manage the private work space is left to the individual programmer. When a module is released to the rest of the team, however, it becomes public and must be stored in the base line.

Management of the base line is critical, and therefore, suitable policies must be defined. Such policies may be enforced by tools for configuration management. For example, we may specify that revisions should follow a check-out/manipulate/check-in policy. The check-out policy might lock the component, which then becomes inaccessible to other members of the team until a check-in is done to insert a modified version in the base line.

It is important that the base line be kept in a consistent state. This is especially critical because many of the components in the baseline are actually related to one another. We use the term *derived version* to capture this fact. For example, an object code component is a derived version of a source code component. Similarly, a source code module might be viewed as a derived version of its specification. Note that in the first case, the generation of a derived version from the source component may occur automatically, whereas in the second case human intervention is required. In general, however, care must be taken to ensure that a modification in one component leaves the system in a consistent state with respect to derived versions. Here, too, such policies may be automatically enforced by tools, as we will see in Chapter 9. For example, the tool might ensure that if an object code is used and its corresponding source code was changed, the compiler is automatically invoked to keep the system in a consistent operational state.

Exercises

7.10   Provide a detailed description of the two methods for handling product families discussed in Section 7.3.2. Discuss the pros and cons of the methods.

7.11   Characterize IS_VERSION_OF as a mathematical relation. Is it symmetric? Transitive? What about IS_REVISION_OF? Does it define a hierarchy? Why? Why not?

7.3.3 Software Standards

There is no doubt that we need software standards in order to achieve acceptable levels of quality in both software products and processes. Standards may be imposed internally or externally. In the first case, the software organization itself decides to adopt standards in order to achieve certain expected benefits. In the latter instances, the standard may be mandated to contractors by the customer. For example, for military contractors involved in software development, the standard document is MIL-STD 2167, discussed in Section 7.1.1.8.

The main benefit of standards is that they enforce a uniform behavior within an organization. This facilitates communication among people, stabilizes the production process, and makes it easier to add new people to ongoing projects. From the point of view of customers, the fact that contractors adhere to certain standards means that it is easier to assess the progress and quality of results. Even more important, this reduces the strict dependency of customers on specific contractors: switching contractors is easier if the contractors all follow the same standards.

One must be careful, however, in the enforcement of standards. If a standard is too prescriptive and covers even minor details, then it tends to frustrate progress by constraining creativity within narrow boundaries. In such a case, people tend to adhere to the standard on the surface, but behave sloppily in substance.

Problems are even more serious when we try to standardize things that we do not understand completely. The comment applies also to life cycle methodologies, such as SA/SD or JSD. If we view these as general guidelines and sample approaches to the methodical development of software, then they may be useful. Imposing them dogmatically on designers as *the* approach for all applications, however, is counterproductive.

As we have already observed in other cases, it is difficult to define standards that reconcile all the conflicting goals that exist in a project. The following principles, however, should guide the definition of standards:

- Make a clear distinction between mandatory and recommended practices, and then keep the former to a minimum and apply them only to aspects of the system that are understood perfectly. It is discouraging to be forced to follow a standard that is poorly understood.

- View standards as a means of improving the professional responsibility of people, not as a substitute for it. Software engineers should decide which additional standards are worth adopting in any specific case.

7.4 CONCLUDING REMARKS

The software production process is the set of all activities that must be accomplished in order to produce a software product. As such, it is a glue that amalgamates both technical and managerial issues. Technical issues are those that deal with accomplishing single activities within the process, such as designing the software architecture or deriving test cases for a module. Managerial issues are those that deal with the handling of resources.

In this chapter, we discussed various approaches to organizing the software development process. Based on the characteristics of the different approaches, the software engineer should be able to tailor the most appropriate life cycle model to the application under consideration.

We also discussed the need for methodologies that guide software development, and we gave two examples taken from current industrial practice. Finally, we addressed the issue of standards. We concluded that we should not hope for a fixed, standardized set of methods to be followed in any practical case. Methodologies and standards cannot replace the need for creativity or the intellectual responsibility of software engineers.

Learning from the various life cycle models presented here and from the principles and methods illustrated in the previous chapters, and taking inspiration from existing methodologies (where applicable), the software engineer must be able to define the most appropriate process model and choose an effective blend of methods.

FURTHER EXERCISES

7.12 Discuss the waterfall model in light of the principle of separation of concerns.

7.13 MIL-STD-2167 does not list maintenance as a stage of the life cycle. Read the manual and explain why.

7.14 Read and critically evaluate MIL-STD-2167. In particular, discuss the rationale, the pros, and the cons of the standard partitioning in terms of CSCIs, CSCs, and units.

7.15 For the process model represented in Figure 7.2, critically evaluate the loop from maintenance to integration and system testing and, possibly, to coding and unit testing.

7.16 Discuss evolutionary models in the light of the principles illustrated in Chapter 3.

7.17 If the USES relation is a hierarchy, then incremental implementation is possible. Prove or disprove the truth of this statement

7.18 Refer to some examples and exercises in Chapter 4, where we gave an initial design and then discussed possible changes. Classify the initial designs as either throwaway or evolutionary prototypes.

7.19 Discuss how the transformation-based approach may improve the qualities of software products listed in Chapter 2.

7.20 For the case study of Section 7.2.2, point out the differences that could occur in the case of a large company, as opposed to the small one in the study. How would you change the approach?

7.21 How would you design the process of developing a product for budget control to be sold on the market? Would you try to obtain a unique product suitable for any company, or a family of different products for different kinds of companies? How can the target company affect the application?

7.22 Discuss how Case Study A (at the back of the book) could have been approached following the case study of Section 7.2.2.

7.23 Discuss why and how the development of a compiler for a standard programming language may fall in the same category as the case study of Section 7.2.1.

7.24 Why is it desirable that the SD is a DAG instead of a tree?

7.25 Follow SA/SD to model a hotel reception desk. The desk deals with incoming reservations, check-in, and check-out. Feel free to deal with all possible details in the operations of the desk. Derive a hierarchical DFD and a first-cut SD.

7.26 Sketch the elevator problem of Section 5.5.3.1 using JSD.

7.27 Consider the process inversion step of JSD. Explain why the units in the sequential implementation are actually coroutines.

7.28 Refer to the activities performed during maintenance, and propose further specializations of IS_REVISION_OF and IS_VARIANT_OF.

7.29 Characterize IS_VARIANT_OF as a mathematical relation.

7.30 A module is a variant of another module under a given abstraction. Revise the definition of relation IS_VARIANT_OF so that you may formally take into account the abstraction under which one is a variant of the other.

7.31 The software development group of a computer company is involved in producing successive versions of the system software, which consists of the operating system, compilers, data bases, and other utilities. To control the management of many source modules, the group adopts a procedure in which a directory, called *public*, contains the sources and executables for all the modules used in the currently released product. Another directory, called *new*, contains the sources and executables for the next release of the software, which is being worked on by the organization. When a new component, e.g., a new compiler or a new editor, is developed and is ready for use by other people in the development organization, the developer moves it into the directory *new*. Do you see any difficulties with this approach? Are there any advantages to allowing more than one *new* directory? Is it better to have rel_1, rel_2,..., rel_N?

7.32 Formally define the concept of a derived version in terms of a mathematical relation. Describe how to determine the components that are affected by a modification of a given component.

HINTS AND SKETCHY SOLUTIONS

7.5   Include information about the capacity limits of the system, such as that no more than 100,000 subscribers can be supported. Such a plan would warn of the approaching end of the life of the system. One would then have more time to react.

7.20 If the processes involved in the company and their control procedures are fairly well understood from the beginning (which is more likely to occur in a large company than in a small one), then one could immediately design suitable procedures for data processing, going closer to a waterfall model. If the same level of uncertainty as in the case study occurs, however, it would probably be wiser to follow an incremental approach. For instance, one could single out a small and significant subsection of the company and produce early prototypes to be applied to it more or less in the same way as in the case study. Only after some experience with early prototypes could one move to the design of a full system for the whole company.

7.31 Consider the integration problems faced when, for example, the new release of the compiler requires a new feature in the operating system and the operating system needs to be compiled with the new compiler. Which one is moved into *new* first?

7.32 Use the transitive closure of the relation.

BIBLIOGRAPHIC NOTES

Bennington [1956] and Royce [1970] are among the early proponents of the concept of the software life cycle. They were influenced by the SAGE project, where development was done in successive stages: an operational plan, operational specifications, coding specifications, coding, parameter testing, assembly testing, shakedown, and system evolution.

The main issues of software engineering, including the process issue, were established by Boehm [1976]. According to Brooks [1975], the first implementation of every real-life system will always have weaknesses; thus, we should be always plan to throw it away and do every system twice!

An excellent source on various paradigms of software processes can be found in the guide to the literature and annotated bibliography by Agresti [1986]. A clear picture emerges of both the conventional, waterfall-based paradigm and the newer approaches. Different life cycle models are compared by Davis et al. [1988], who present a method of comparing various process models based on an appealing graphical representation. Graham [1989] provides a thorough review of process models, with emphasis on flexible models.

The issue of how human factors affect the life cycle is addressed by Mantei and Teorey [1988]. A report on a field study of the software design process on large development projects is given by Curtis et al. [1988]; the study is based on a behavioral process.

The evolution of large systems has been studied by Belady and Lehman [1979] and Lehman and Belady [1985], who derived the following rules:

i.   **Law of continuing change.** A system undergoes continuing change, until it becomes economical to replace it by a new or a restructured version;

ii. **Law of increasing entropy.** The entropy of a system increases with time, unless special care is taken to maintain or reduce it;

iii. **Law of statistically smooth growth.** Attributes that measure the growth of a system are self-regulating and statistically smooth.

Parnas and Clements [1986] provide convincing arguments to show that the waterfall model is an idealized, purely theoretical, process and that we will never see a software project which proceeds according to its tenets. No such project can proceed in that way, due to human fallibility; indeed it *should* not proceed in that way, in order to be adaptable to changing requirements. The products of a software project are documentation that we ideally should produce as the process progresses. After stating these criticisms, however, Parnas and Clements propose that we *fake* the real process by producing documents *as if* we were proceeding in the ideal way. The documentation produced in a way that reflects the ideal and purely rational waterfall-based process helps in understanding the system, no matter what process was actually followed to produce the system. Parnas and Clements observed, however, that some information on the actual production process deserves proper documentation, too: "We make a policy of recording all of the design alternatives that we considered and rejected. For each, we explain why it was considered and why it was finally rejected. Months, weeks, or even hours later, when we wonder why we did what we did, we can find out. Years from now, the maintainer will have many of the same questions and will find his answers in our documents."

Different organizations adopt different models at different stages of their maturity. Humphrey [1989] illustrates a model for classifying software organizations according to the software model they adopt.

The issue of reengineering existing applications to make them maintainable is addressed in the papers in the special issue on maintenance, reverse engineering, and design recovery of *IEEE Software* [1990a].

A critical view of the conventional life cycle model is presented by McCracken and Jackson [1982], who advocate evolutionary prototyping. Gilb [1988] discusses software development in the light of a highly flexible life cycle model. Basili and Turner [1975] provide an early report on an evolutionary approach and its success. The benefits of incremental development are discussed by Wong [1984], while Alavi [1984] contrasts a prototyping-based life cycle with a conventional one. Throwaway prototyping is discussed by Gomaa and Scott [1981]. Boehm et al. [1984] performed an experiment to compare the relative benefits of software development based on prototyping and on specifications. According to Swartout and Balzer [1982], one of the reasons that the rigid waterfall model fails is that it does not recognizes that specification and implementation are inevitably intertwined.

The spiral model is due to Boehm [1988]; the model is motivated by concepts of software costs and risk analysis, discussed by Boehm and Papaccio [1988b] and [Boehm 1989], respectively.

The transformation-based process model has been advocated by Balzer [1981], Cheatham et al. [1981], Kant and Barstow [1981], Balzer et al. [1983], and Bauer et al. [1989]. Knowledge-based approaches in software engineering are presented in the special issue of *IEEE Transactions on Software Engineering* edited by Mostow (TSE [1985]), Goldberg [1986], Rich and Waters [1988], and by some contributions in the special issue of *IEEE Software* [1990a].

Formal approaches to program derivation were pioneered by Dijkstra [1976]; see also Gries [1976], Gries [1978], Linger et al. [1979], and Mills et al. [1987a]. A formal approach to the transformational derivation of software is described in Bauer et al. [1989]; this approach is based on a wide-spectrum language. Partsch and Steinbruggen [1983] provide an excellent review of program transformation systems.

Mills et al. [1987b] discuss the so-called cleanroom software development approach, based on formal verification (and no testing) at the unit level and statistical testing at the system level. The emphasis of the approach is on the prevention, rather than the removal, of errors. Selby et al. [1987] provide an empirical evaluation of the approach.

A formal approach to software development based on VDM is described by Bjorner and Jones [1982], Jones [1986a and 1986b]. The Larch methodology also covers the derivation of programs from their formal specification (see Guttag et al. [1985a and 1985b] and Guttag and Horning [1986a and 1986b]).

Osterweil [1987] introduces the concept of process programming: just like programs, software processes should be described formally, so that one can reason formally about them. The issue of defining the appropriate life cycle and factory models to support both application development and software enhancement and reuse is addressed by Basili and Rombach [1988] and Basili and Caldiera [1988].

The series of workshops on software processes sponsored by ACM SIGSOFT describes ongoing research in the area; the fourth of the series is edited by Tully [1988].

A comparison of software methodologies is described by Bergland [1981]. SA/SD has been advocated by several authors. In particular, DeMarco [1978] illustrates Structured Analysis, while Yourdon and Constantine [1979] and Myers [1978] illustrate Structured Design. The methodology has been extended by Ward and Mellor [1985] and Hatley and Pirbhai [1987] to cover the issues of real-time systems.

The Jackson methodology–JSD–is presented by Jackson [1983]; Jackson [1975] describes JSP, the earlier methodology addressing the programming phase of software development.

SADT, presented by Ross [1977], and SREM, presented by Alford [1977], are two other well-known methodologies. The former is a structured analysis and design methodology; the latter is a process-based methodology for real-time applications.

The general theme of configuration management along with a description of support tools, is addressed by Babich [1986] and Tichy [1989].

There are many originators of software standards, including the IEEE [1989] and the U.S. Department of Defense, which issued the well-known MIL-STD-2167 (DOD [1984]). Other organizations, such as NATO, the ESA (European Space Agency), and even industrial companies, have their own standards, although these are for internal use only.

Chapter 8

Management of
Software Engineering

Chapters 4 through 6 have dealt with the product of software engineering and techniques for producing quality products. Chapter 7 discussed the process of software engineering and how to organize it. This chapter deals with the management of software engineering.

There are many software engineers involved in the development of a software product. Their work must be coordinated and managed. It is a traditional engineering practice to define a project around the product to be developed and have a project manager responsible for the project. Large projects may be composed of several subprojects, each of which may be divided into further subprojects, if necessary. The primary job of the project manager is to ensure that the project is completed within budget and on schedule.

The project manager has many tasks. First comes planning: understanding and–following the principle of rigor–documenting the goals and developing a schedule, budget, and other resource requirements. Then comes acquisition of resources–e.g., space, computing resources, materials, and human resources. We will concentrate on the primary resource used in software engineering: the human resource. Human resource acquisition is called *staffing* and involves recruiting, hiring, training, rewarding, retaining, and directing project members. Next comes execution–putting the plan into action. Finally, there is monitoring the progress of the project and taking necessary actions to handle both foreseen and unforeseen deviations from the plan. The basic challenge facing the project manager is to make decisions on how best to use limited resources to achieve a set of interdependent and sometimes conflicting goals. A commonly stated summary of the project manager's task is "*plan the work and work the plan.*"

Management decisions have a strong impact on the technical aspects of software engineering. For example, if a software engineer's performance is measured in terms of how many lines of code are produced, the engineer is discouraged from reusing existing code written by others. If an unrealistically aggressive schedule is imposed on the engineers, they are encouraged to take shortcuts that usually affect the quality of the product and reduce its maintainability. A slack schedule, on the other hand, encourages the engineers either to make grandiose decisions or not to proceed carefully enough because they depend on having extra time later. Such a schedule could thus reduce design time and increase debugging time.

The manager faces many decisions that involve complicated trade-offs. What is the benefit of investing in modern software engineering tools? Will investing in such tools shorten the development time and, if so, what is the value of the time saved? How much will the addition of a particular feature cost in terms of development time, and how much benefit will it produce? What will be the impact on the development schedule if every engineer is given a state-of-the-art workstation? Is it possible to shorten the time of the initial delivery of the system at the cost of increased future maintenance? By what factor will maintenance costs increase? What are the costs and benefits of incremental delivery, and which features should be delivered first? If a particular feature is not tested yet, what is the benefit of delivering the product without that feature? What are the trade-offs involved in developing a particular module in-house or modifying a commercially available module? Should an existing software system be modified further, or should an entirely new system be developed from scratch? In an industrial discipline, such questions must be answered quantitatively. Without a clear cost model for the economic impact of these decisions, there is no good way for a manager and an organization to choose among alternative strategies. The current state of practice in software engineering is to make judgments, check against expert opinions, try to achieve consensus, and, if possible, calibrate against the data on previous similar projects within the same organization.

To help in resolving software engineering management problems, the last decade has seen a rise in quantitative approaches to software cost estimation, cost modelling, and cost analysis. Many models have been developed, some of which are even available commercially, that allow the manager to design cost and schedule estimates for a project and do a sensitivity analysis based on various criteria. Such models are far from perfect; the best that can be said about them is that they are accurate to within 20%, 80% of the time. Even so, they are useful and can complement the manager's judgment and intuition. In this chapter, we study the underlying ideas of these approaches and examine some representative models.

The principles outlined in Chapter 3 apply to the management, as well as to technical aspects, of software engineering. For example, the principle of modularity is the underlying motivation for assigning the responsibility for different tasks to different engineers or even groups. By setting up one group to do design, another to develop code, and another to do testing, we are applying modularization to the responsibilities and organization of the project. Hierarchical management organizations apply the principle of abstraction to allow each management level to cope with its own level of abstraction.

Much of project planning and scheduling involves estimation–of the complexity of the product, the productivity of individual engineers, the availability of people and other resources, etc. Estimation is always accompanied by the risk of being wrong. Small errors in estimation can usually be tolerated and should not affect the success of a project. Large deviations from the estimates, however, can cause the total failure of a project. Since risk and estimation always go hand in hand, the job of the project manager is to organize a project to minimize risk initially and, when deviations from the original estimates do occur, whether small or large, to detect them and take corrective action. This subject will be discussed in Section 8.5 under the topic of risk management.

Following a general discussion of the functions of management in the next section, Sections 8.2 through 8.4 will respectively cover the specific management functions of planning, control, and organization. Section 8.5 will cover the topic of risk management as applied to software engineering management. Finally, Section 8.6 will summarize the chapter and also contain some general and concluding remarks on the topic of software engineering management.

8.1 MANAGEMENT FUNCTIONS

Management can be defined informally as the art of getting work done through other people. But a more classic definition that allows a systematic study of the subject is the following from Koontz [1980]:

> The creation and maintenance of an internal environment in an enterprise where individuals, working together in groups, can perform efficiently and effectively toward the attainment of group goals.

Thus, the main job of management is to enable a group of people to work towards a common goal. Management is not an exact science, and the many activities involved in it may be classified according to many different schemes. It is standard, however, to consider management as consisting of the following five interrelated activities, the goal of which is to achieve effective group work:

- **Planning**. A manager must decide what objectives are to be achieved, what resources are required to achieve the objectives, how and when the resources are to be acquired, and how the goals are to be achieved. Planning basically involves determining the flow of information, people, and products within the organization.

- **Organizing**. Organizing involves the establishment of clear lines of authority and responsibility for groups of activities that achieve the goals of the enterprise. Organizing is necessary at the level of a small group, such as a five-person team of software engineers, all the way up to a large corporation composed of several independent divisions. The choice of the organizational structure affects the efficiency of the enterprise. Clearly, the best organizational structure can be devised only when the goals of the enterprise are clear, and this depends on effective planning.

- **Staffing**. Staffing deals with hiring personnel for the positions that are identified by the organizational structure. It involves defining requirements for personnel; recruiting (identifying, interviewing, and selecting candidates); compensating, developing, and promoting employees.

- **Directing**. Directing involves leading subordinates. The goal of directing is to guide the subordinates to understand and identify with the organizational structure and the goals of the enterprise. This understanding must be continuously refined by effective and exemplary leadership. Setting examples is especially important in software engineering, where measures of good engineering are lacking. The best training for a beginning engineer is to work alongside a good engineer.

- **Controlling**. Controlling consists of measuring and correcting activities to ensure that goals are achieved. Controlling requires the measurement of performance against plans and taking corrective action when deviations occur.

These general functions of management apply to any management activity, whether in a software engineering organization, an automobile manufacturing plant, or a boy scout group. They also apply at the various levels of an organization, from the first-level manager directing a few engineers to the president of a company directing several vice presidents. A detailed discussion of management principles and techniques is clearly beyond the scope of this book. We have already touched on the subject of organizing the process in Chapter 7. Our discussions of software qualities and objectives in Chapter 2 can form the basis for applying proper planning activities in software engineering. In this chapter, we will concentrate on the planning and control of software engineering; we will touch on the other management functions only when the nature of software requires that general management considerations be modified before they can be applied to software engineering.

8.2 PROJECT PLANNING

The first component of software engineering project management is effective planning of the development of the software. The first step in planning a project is to define and document the assumptions, goals, and constraints of the project. A project needs a clear statement of goals to guide the engineers in their daily decision making. Many engineers on typical projects spend many hours discussing alternatives that are known clearly to the project manager, but have not been documented or disseminated properly. As an extreme example, if the project is forced to develop software in assembly language because of an explicit requirement from the customer, this requirement must be stated clearly and made known to all the engineers. If it is not universally known and accepted, inevitably the engineers will periodically argue the merits of high-level languages and perhaps–in the interest of progress, as they see it–even decide to do some of their work in a high-level language. The goal of the project planning stage is to identify all the external requirements for and constraints on the project.

Once the external constraints have been identified, the project manager must come up with a plan for how best to meet the requirements within the given constraints. One of the questions at this stage is what process model will serve the project best. We have discussed the various alternatives in Chapter 7. Another critical decision is to determine the resources required for the project. The resources include the number and skill level of the people, the amount of computing resources (e.g. workstations, personal computers, and data-base software).[1] Unlike traditional engineering disciplines, where one has to budget for material, the "raw material" used in software is mainly the engineer's brain power. Thus, the cost of a software project is directly proportional to the number of engineers needed for the project. The problem of predicting how many engineers and other resources are needed for a given software project is known as *software cost estimation*.

Forecasting how many engineers will be needed is a difficult problem that is intimately tied to the problem of how to estimate the productivity of software engineers. There are two parts to the forecasting problem: estimating the difficulty of the task and estimating how much of the task each engineer can solve. Clearly, to estimate the difficulty of the task, one must know what the task is–that is, what the requirements are. But, as we have seen in previous chapters, it is often difficult to specify the software requirements completely *a priori*. It was precisely such difficulties that motivated us to look at the evolutionary process as an alternative to the traditional waterfall model.

Incomplete and imprecise requirements hinder accurate cost estimation. The clearer and more complete the requirements are, the easier it is to determine the resources required. But even when the requirements are clear, estimating the number of engineers needed is a formidable task with inherent difficulties. The best approach is to develop the resource requirements incrementally, revising current estimates as more information becomes available. We have seen that an appropriate adaptation of the spiral model allows one to start with an estimate in the early planning stages and revise the estimate for the remaining tasks at the conclusion of each iteration of the particular phase of the life cycle.

How long it will take a software engineer to accomplish a given task is primarily a function of the complexity of the problem, the engineer's ability, the design of the software, and the tools that are available. For example, adding an undo facility to an editor may require adding a new module or a complete redesign, depending on the current design of the editor. Similarly, writing a front-end parser for a system may be a simple task for an engineer who is familiar with parsing technology, but an extremely difficult task for an engineer who is unaware of, and thus tries to reinvent, the parsing technology. Finally, writing a compiler with compiler development tools is a lot easier than writing it without them.

Unlike other engineering disciplines, software is design intensive as opposed to manufacturing intensive. This means that how long software development will take depends on the intellectual ability of the engineers, or worse yet, on a nonlinear combination of the intellectual abilities of all the engineers.

---

[1] In a more general setting, resources include such things as space and utilities. We concentrate only on software-related issues here. Keep in mind, however, that even the choice of space–e. g. private offices versus shared work areas–has a significant impact on software productivity.

We have already observed that management decisions have a strong impact on the technical aspects of a project. We can see another example of this in the interplay between management planning and the entire software life cycle. For example, the choice of an evolutionary process model will impose a different kind of resource planning from a waterfall model. While an evolutionary model allows the manager to do resource planning incrementally as more information becomes available, it also requires more flexibility from the manager. Similarly, an incremental model will affect the resource loading for the different phases of the project, such as design and testing, because the phases are iterated incrementally. In general, there is a strong interplay between management functions and the technical aspects of a software engineering project.

8.2.1 Software Productivity

One of the basic requirements of management in any engineering discipline is to measure the productivity of the people and processes involved in production. The measurements obtained are used during the planning phase of a project as the basis for estimating resource requirements; they also form the basis for evaluating the performance of individuals, processes, and tools, the benefits of automation, etc. The ability to quantify the impact of various factors on productivity is important if we want to evaluate the many claims made for various "productivity improvement" tools. Indeed, there is an economic need for continued improvements in productivity. Of course, we can be sure that we are making improvements only if we can measure productivity quantitatively. Unfortunately, few, if any, claims made about tools that improve software productivity are based on quantitative measurements.

8.2.1.1 Productivity metrics

We clearly need a metric for measuring software productivity. In manufacturing-dominated disciplines such as automobile or television production, there are simple and obvious metrics to use. For instance, a new manufacturing process that doubles the number of television sets produced per day has doubled the productivity of the factory. By taking into account the costs of the new process, we can determine whether adopting the new process was cost effective.

The situation is not so simple in a design-dominated discipline like software engineering. To begin with, there is the problem that software does not scale up. For example, the typical productivity figure reported for professional software engineers is a few tens of lines of code per day. If we compare this number with the productivity exhibited on a student project, even beginning students appear to be much more productive than professionals if we simply extrapolate from what they produce on a simple homework project.

There are, however, several obvious reasons why a professional's productivity appears to be less than a student's. First, students work longer hours, especially when a project is due. Second, professionals don't spend the majority of their time in strictly engineering activities: up to half their time may be taken up by meetings, administrative matters, communication with team members, etc. One study showed that up to 40% of a typical workweek is spent on nontechnical work. This implies that the larger a programming team becomes, the lower the individual productivity figures will be. Third, the professional has to meet more quality requirements than the student: reliability, maintainability, performance, etc. Fourth, the inherent complexity of the application affects the programmer's productivity. For example, experience has shown that programmers developing application programs produce as much as three times as many lines per day as programmers working on systems programs.

An ideal productivity metric measures not lines of code but the amount of *functionality* produced per unit time. The problem, however, is that we have no good way of quantifying the concept of functionality. For example, how can we relate the functionality offered by a payroll system to that offered by an air-traffic monitoring system? We need to either find a measure that somehow takes into account the inherent complexities of the different application areas or develop metrics that are specialized to different application areas. One such metric, developed for information systems, is called *function points* and is described in the next subsection.

Because of the difficulty of quantifying functionality, the search for a productivity metric has for the most part concentrated on the most tangible product of software engineering: the actual code produced by the engineer. Various metrics based on code size have been developed. These will be discussed below, following our discussion of function points.

Existing metrics, however, are quite controversial, and one must be careful in adopting and using them. This remark holds both for the metrics of product quality that we presented in Section 6.7.3 and for the metrics of productivity that we illustrate next. Thus, managers should not use their results as objective measures of the ability or the productivity of a software engineer: inappropriate use of such measures may have large, damaging effects by rewarding poor design and programming practices and demoralizing good engineers.

Function points

Function points attempt to quantify the functionality of a software system. The goal is to arrive at a single number that completely characterizes the system and correlates with observed programmer productivity figures. Actually, the function point characterizes the complexity of the software system and thus can be used to forecast how long it will take to develop the system and how many people will be needed to do it.

The function point method was derived empirically, and the limited amount of experimentation to date shows that it applies well in business applications, e.g., information systems. For example, using the function point as a productivity metric, it has been possible to quantify improvements in productivity due to such factors as the use of structured programming and high-level languages. We can measure programmer productivity in terms of the number of function points produced per unit time.

According to the function point method, five items determine the complexity of an application and the function point of a given software is the weighted sum of these five items. The weights for these items have been derived empirically and validated by observation on many projects. The items and their weights are shown in Table 8.1.

The number of inputs and outputs count the distinct number of items that the user provides to the system and the system provides to user, respectively. In counting the number of outputs, a group of items such as a screen or a file counts as one item–that is, the individual items in the group are not counted separately. The number of inquiries is the number of distinct interactive queries made by the user that require specific action by the system. Files are any group of related information that are maintained by the application on behalf of the user or for organizing the application. This item reveals the bias of the method towards business data processing. Finally, the number of interfaces is the number of external interfaces to other systems, e.g., the number of files to be read or written to disk or transmitted or received from other systems. Therefore, if the application reads a file that is produced by another application, the file is counted twice, once as input and once as an interface. If a file is maintained by two different applications, it is counted as an interface for each application. The focus of function point analysis is to measure the complexity of an application based only on the function the application is supposed to provide to users. Therefore, any temporary files produced by the application are not counted in the measure; only those files that are visible or required by the user are so counted.

Item	Weight
Number of inputs	4
Number of outputs	5
Number of inquiries	4
Number of files	10
Number of interfaces	7

Table 8.1   Function point items and weights.

Once we have a metric, we can use it in many ways. For example, we can compute the productivity of an engineer or a team per month by dividing the function point for an existing software by the number of months it took to develop the software. Or we can divide the amount of money spent to produce the software by the function point to compute how much each function point costs. Or again, we can measure the error rate per function point by dividing the number of errors found by the function point. These function point-related numbers can be recorded and used as bases for future planning or interproject comparisons. If the function point is an accurate description of product complexity, the numbers should be similar across different projects.

In an interesting experiment, function points were used to measure the relative power of different languages by computing the number of source lines required to code a function point in these languages. The numbers range from 324 for assembler language to 150 for C, 91 for Pascal, 71 for Ada, 32 for APL, 21 for Smalltalk, and 6 for "spreadsheet languages." This experiment is both an indication of the utility of function points and a kind of validation of the idea, because the results match our intuitive judgment about the power of the languages.

There are obvious weaknesses in the function point metric, but they do not seem to be insurmountable. For example, it is unlikely that a single weight number is sufficient for all cases. For instance, in counting the number of inputs, some inputs probably require complicated processing and others very simple processing. The same holds for other items. Indeed, a solution to this problem has been to provide a range of weights for each item, basing the particular weight used on a subjective determination of whether the required processing is simple, average, or complex.

Despite these problems, function points are a promising approach that requires further experimentation, validation, and extension to other application areas. For example, the items needed to be measured in a real-time system are probably different from those given above. But the basic idea of finding a small number of items that can be used to characterize the complexity of software is valid. Research can find the items of interest for each application area.

Exercises

8.1   Compute the function point FP for a payroll program that reads a file of employees and a file of information for the current month and prints checks for all the employees. The program is capable of handling an interactive command to print an individually requested check immediately.

8.2   Assume that the previous payroll program is expected to read a file containing information about all the checks that have been printed. This file is supposed to be printed and also used by the program the next time it is run, to produce a report that compares payroll expenses of the current month with those of the previous month. Compute the function point for this program. Justify the difference between the function points of this program and those of the previous payroll program by considering how the complexity of the program is affected by adding the requirement of interfacing with another application (in this case, itself).

Code size

Since software engineers are supposed to produce software, the most tangible product of software engineering is the running software that they deliver to their clients. This has led many people to use the size of the software as a measure of productivity. Of course, the size of the software is not necessarily an indication of how much effort went into producing it, and a programmer that produces twice as many statements as another is not necessarily twice as productive. In general, the size of code is not a measure of any quality: a program that is twice as big as another is not necessarily twice as good in any sense. Nevertheless, the most commonly used metrics to measure productivity are based on code size, for example, in terms of number of source lines produced per unit time.

Of course, a code size metric has to be qualified immediately by considering the same issues we did with the software science metric in Chapter 6: Should we count comment lines? Should we count programming language "statements" or simply the number of line feeds? How many times should we count the lines in a file that is "included" several times? And should we count declarations or just executable statements? By choosing answers to these questions, we arrive at a particular productivity metric based on code size.

Two of the most common code size metrics are DSI (delivered source instructions), in which only lines of code delivered to the customer are counted, and NCSS (non-commented source statements), in which comment lines are not counted. We will use the generic unit, KLOC (thousands of lines of code), when we do not want to distinguish between the specific metrics.

Lines of code have been used as a productivity metric in many organizations. The acceptance of this metric is due to the ease of measuring it and probably also due to the fact that using any metric is better than using nothing at all. But at the same time, we must be cognizant of the many problems associated with the measure. At the heart of the problem is that there is no semantic content to code size; rather, it is merely a function of the form of software. The following observations show some of the deficiencies inherent in the metric.

Consider two programmers faced with the task of programming a module that needs a sort operation internally. One programmer writes his own sort routine, and the other uses her time to find out how to use an existing sort routine in the system library. Even though both accomplish the same task, the use of the library routine is generally a better idea for many reasons: over the life of the software, the library routine has less chances of containing errors and is better tested; it allows the programmer to concentrate on the real problems she is trying to solve and perhaps gain better insight into the application rather than code a sorting routine, etc. Yet, the size metric penalizes the use of the library routine because it recognizes the other programmer as more productive! In general, the size-based metric has the unfortunate effect of equating software reuse with lower productivity.

Consider also a programmer who one day discovers a clever abstraction that allows her to replace many special cases in the code she has been developing and replace several specialized procedures with a single general procedure. On this day when she has probably increased the reliability of her software, she can be charged with negative productivity because she has reduced the size of the software. If productivity is measured only in terms of lines of code, she is personally better off not making the improvement in the code.

When using lines of code as a productivity metric, it is important to know what lines are being counted in order to be able to make accurate comparisons between individuals, projects, or organizations. For example, an organization may produce many software tools to support the development of a particular project. These tools may become useful to many other projects in the organization, but are not delivered to the customer as part of the product. Should these programs be counted in the measurements? A commonly adopted convention is to count only the lines of code that are delivered to the customer. To emphasize this decision, the models that use the convention refer to the measure as KDSI–thousands of delivered source instructions.

Using DSI as a measure does not mean that producing internal tools is a worthless activity. In any engineering activity, investments in tools and a support infrastructure are needed to improve productivity. The DSI measure focuses on the objective of the engineering organization and separates the effort involved in building internal tools from that involved in building the product itself. In other engineering disciplines, too, productivity is measured in terms of the final product, not the intermediate "mock-ups."

Another point to consider when comparing the productivity figures reported by different organizations is whether the reported figures include the effect of cancelled projects. For various reasons, many projects are cancelled in organizations before they produce and deliver a product. Whether the lines of code of these cancelled projects are counted in the overall productivity of the organization has a material effect on the productivity figure. Such cancellations also have a secondary impact on the motivational attitude of engineers in the organization and thus affect overall productivity. Whatever criteria are used for measurement, comparison of figures is possible only if the criteria are applied consistently. Since there are no standard metrics, the use and interpretation of available productivity data in the literature must be examined with care.

Another important phenomenon that helps in understanding the problems inherent in using lines of code as a software productivity metric is due to the nature of software evolution. The software evolves according to what can be called "the urban renewal principle" in software maintenance. When a new feature is to be added to the software or an old one enhanced, the engineer tends to spend as little time as possible in understanding what is currently in the software; instead, he or she spends most of the time adding new code to perform the new function. The engineer avoids removing any code that he or she does not understand, even if the code appears to be useless. This behavior causes the code size to grow but portions of the code to be rendered useless, a situation contributing to "code decay," which is, not entirely facetiously, analogous to urban decay. Eventually, a brave engineer on some future maintenance assignment will undertake to apply "urban renewal" and remove or replace all the decayed code. At this point, the code size will shrink, possibly substantially. Has the engineer suddenly reduced the productivity of the entire organization, or is it that the previous engineers were falsely inflating the productivity figures?

Finally, lines of code are tied to line-oriented languages and are inherently incapable of dealing with the emerging visual languages in which the programmer uses diagrams or screen panels rather than statements.

Exercises

8.3   List the benefits and disadvantages of using library routines rather than writing your own code.

8.4   Define a size-based productivity metric that does not penalize the use of library routines.

8.2.1.2 Factors affecting productivity

Regardless of what metric we use for productivity, even if we simply have an intuitive notion, there are factors that affect engineering productivity. One of the important effects of a productivity metric is that it allows the benefits of the various factors to be quantified. By identifying the major contributors to productivity, organizations can determine quantitatively whether they can afford to change their practices, that is, whether the improvements in productivity are worth the expenses. For example, will changing to a new programming language, or adopting a new development process, or hiring an efficiency expert, or giving the engineers a private office, or allowing them to work at home increase productivity sufficiently to justify the expenses?

In one study that used lines of code as a metric, it was found that the single most important factor affecting productivity was the capability of the personnel; half as important, but second on the list, was the complexity of the product, followed by required reliability and timing constraints (i.e., as in real-time software). The least important items on the list were schedule constraints and language experience. The effects of these various factors on productivity are reflected in the "cost driver functions" used in cost estimation models, such as the COCOMO model which we will see later.

Many managers believe that an aggressive schedule motivates the engineers to do a better, faster job. However, experiments have shown that unrealistically aggressive schedules not only cause the engineers to compromise on intangible quality aspects, but also cause schedule delays. A surprising finding was that in a controlled experiment, the subjects who had no schedule at all finished their project first, beating out both the group that had an aggressive schedule and the one that had a relaxed schedule. It has been shown that engineers, in general, are good at achieving the one tangible goal that they have been given: if the primary goal is to finish according to a given time schedule, they usually will–but at the cost of other goals such as clarity of documentation and structure.

A specific example of the effect of overly aggressive scheduling can be seen when design reviews are scheduled far too early in the development cycle. While the manager may want to motivate the engineers to do the job in a shorter time, such premature design reviews force the designer to document only issues that are well understood and deny the reviewers an opportunity to provide useful feedback.

In one project at Hewlett-Packard Company, it was found that a group located at a remote location–namely, a rented house in a small mountainside resort community– showed productivity figures that were considerably higher than the average numbers for the corporation. The original management fears about leaving the engineers to work by themselves away from the guidance of the "headquarters" turned out to be ill founded. Several explanations have been given for this surprising result. Some have to do with the Hawthorne effect (named after the British psychologist Hawthorne who noted the phenomenon that there is an improvement in the performance of subjects of an experiment, caused simply by the fact that the subjects know that they are being observed, and thus somehow treated as special), others with the fact that the engineers had a much shorter commuting time to work, and still others–perhaps the most important–with the fact that the engineers were isolated from the "distractions" provided by the many meetings that they had to attend at their usual place of work. Of course, some of these meetings are meant to inform employees about the company and keep the engineers involved with the company. However, the trade-off between keeping engineers involved and motivated about the company as a whole and keeping them focused and productive on a particular project is a complicated one. Making such choices between short- and long-term goals is the manager's job and requires careful thought and deliberation.

In addition to the above tangible factors, there are many intangible factors that affect productivity and reduce the credibility of the published numbers. Examples of these intangible factors are personnel turnover, cancelled projects, reorganizations, and restructuring of systems for better quality.

8.2.2 People And Productivity

Because software engineering is predominantly an intellectual activity, the most important ingredient for producing high-quality software efficiently is people. As we mentioned in the last section, experimental evidence shows that the most determinative factor of productivity is the capability of the engineers. Despite the intuitive appeal of this notion and strong supporting empirical evidence, however, many managers and organizations consistently behave as if they did not believe it. Considering the great difference in software engineering competence between the best and the worst engineers, and the critical importance of engineering competence in attaining high software productivity, the costs of hiring, retaining, and motivating the best engineers can be justified on economic grounds.

Yet, a common misconception held by managers, as evidenced in their staffing, planning, and scheduling practices, is that *software engineers are interchangeable*–that is, that one software engineer is as productive as another. In fact, experiments have revealed a large variability in productivity between the best, the average, and the worst engineers. The worst engineers even reduce the productivity of the team.

Apart from engineering capability, however, because of the strong amount of interaction required among team members, the personalities of the members also should be taken into account. Some engineers function better on centrally controlled teams, while others are better suited for teams with decentralized control. In short, engineers are simply not interchangeable, due to underlying reasons that have to do with both technical ability and personality.

Another common management practice that fails to recognize the importance of people in the software engineering process is that managers often staff a project with the best *available* people rather than attempt to find the best people *per se*. Considering the strong impact of personnel capability on software costs, this is a foolish thing to do. In effect, by assigning ill-prepared engineers to a project, the manager is committing the organization to a training period for these engineers. Since this commitment is unintentional and the training haphazard, there is a strong risk that the training will be ineffective and the project unsuccessful or at least late. The way to solve the problem of finding appropriate people must be faced deliberately: one must schedule the training period as a required task and train the people appropriately, hire outside consultants, and control the project closely, perhaps by scheduling frequent incremental deliveries. The point is to recognize the utter importance of key personnel to an intellectual project such as software engineering.

8.2.3 Cost Estimation

Cost estimation is part of the planning stage of any engineering activity. The difference in cost estimation between software engineering and other disciplines is that in software engineering the primary cost is for people. In other engineering disciplines, the cost of materials–chips, bricks, or aluminum, depending on the activity–is a major component of the cost that must be estimated. In software engineering, to estimate the cost, we only have to estimate how many engineers are needed.

Software cost estimation has two uses in software project management. First, during the planning stage, one needs to decide how many engineers are needed for the project and develop a schedule. Second, in monitoring the project's progress, one needs to assess whether the project is progressing according to schedule and take corrective action if necessary. In monitoring progress, the manager needs to ascertain how much work has already been accomplished and how much is left to do. Both of these tasks require a metric for measuring "software work accomplishment."

Group	Factor
Size Attributes	Source instructions
	Object instructions
	Number of routines
	Number of data items
	Number of output formats
	Documentation
	Number of personnel
Program attributes	Type
	Complexity
	Language
	Reuse
	Required reliability
	Display requirements
Computer attributes	Time constraint
	Storage constraint
	Hardware configuration
	Concurrent h/w development
	Interfacing equipment, s/w
Personnel attributes	Personnel capability
	Personnel continuity
	Hardware experience
	Application experience
	Language experience
Project attributes	Tools and techniques
	Customer interface
	Requirements definition
	Requirements volatility
	Schedule
	Security
	Computer access
	Travel/rehosting/multi-site
	Support software maturity

Table 8.2   Factors used in cost estimation models. (Adapted from Table II of Boehm [1984a], ©1984 IEEE, by permission of IEEE.)

In Section 6.7.3, we discussed Halstead's software science as a method of measuring the complexity of a program. Halstead's metric is applied to an existing piece of software and can be used to compare such things as the complexity of two different programs or the relative benefits of two programming languages. By allowing us to compare the inherent complexity of two programs, the software science metric can also be used to measure the productivity of the two programmers who produced those programs. But in the planning stages of a project, we do not have the program and therefore cannot use Halstead's metric to measure its inherent complexity. Metrics like Halstead's are called

Feature	Mode		
	Organic	Semidetached	Embedded
Organizational understanding of product objectives	Thorough	Considerable	General
Experience in working with related software systems	Extensive	Considerable	Moderate
Need for software conformance with pre-established requirements	Basic	Considerable	Full
Need for software conformance with external interface specifications	Basic	Considerable	Full
Concurrent development of associated new hardware and operational procedures	Some	Moderate	Extensive
Need for innovative data processing architectures, algorithms	Minimal	Some	Considerable
Premium on early completion	Low	Medium	High
Product size range	<50 KDSI	<300 KDSI	All sizes
EXAMPLES	Batch data reduction	Most transaction processing systems	Large, complex transaction processing systems
	Scientific models	New OS, DBMS	Ambitious, very large OS
	Business models	Ambitious, inventory, production control	Avionics
	Familiar OS, compiler	Simple command-control	Ambitious command-control

Table 8.3   COCOMO Software development modes. (From Boehm [1984a], ©1984 IEEE, reprinted by permission of IEEE.)

structural metrics, because they depend on the structure of the software. Instead, we need a *predictive* method to estimate the complexity of software before it has been developed, based on available information, such as the requirements. As we have seen, function points are an example of this class of metrics.

8.2.3.1 Predictive models of software cost

While lines of code are not an ideal metric of productivity, they do seem like an appropriate metric for the total life cycle costs of software. That is, the size of an existing piece of software is a good measure of how hard it is to understand and modify that software during its maintenance phase. Furthermore, if we could predict how large a software system was going to be before developing it, that size could be used as a basis for determining how much effort would be required, how many engineers would be needed, and how long it would take to develop the software. That is, the size of the software can help us infer not just the initial development cost, but also the costs associated with the later stages of the life cycle.

The majority of software cost estimation methods thus start by predicting the size of the software and using that as input for deriving the total effort required, the required effort during each phase of the life cycle, personnel requirements, etc. The size estimate drives the entire estimation process. Inferring this initial estimate and assessing its reliability can be considerably simpler if the organization maintains a data base of information about past projects.

We can also base the initial estimate on an analytical technique such as function point analysis. We first compute the function point for the desired software and then divide it by the number FP/LOC for the project's programming language to arrive at a size estimate.

Development Mode	Nominal effort	Schedule
Organic	$(PM)_{NOM}=3.2(KDSI)^{1.05}$	$TDEV=2.5(PM_{DEV}))^{0.38}$
Semidetached	$(PM)_{NOM}=3.0(KDSI)^{1.12}$	$TDEV=2.5(PM_{DEV}))^{0.35}$
Embedded	$(PM)_{NOM}=2.8(KDSI)^{1.20}$	$TDEV=2.5(PM_{DEV}))^{0.32}$

Table 8.4   COCOMO Nominal effort and schedule equations. (From Boehm [1984a], ©1984 IEEE, reprinted by permission of IEEE.)

Besides basing the estimation of effort on code size, most cost estimation models share certain other concepts. The purpose of a software cost model is to predict the total development effort required to produce a given piece of software in terms of the number of engineers and length of time it will take to develop the software. The general formula used to arrive at the *nominal* development effort is

$$PM_{initial} = c \cdot KLOC^k$$

That is, the nominal number of programmer-months is derived on the basis of the number of lines of code. The constants c and k are given by the model. The exponent k is greater than 1, causing the estimated effort to grow nonlinearly with the code size. To take into account the many variables that can affect the productivity of the project, so-called cost drivers are used to scale this initial estimate of effort. For example, if modern programming practices are being used, the estimate is scaled downward; if there are real-time reliability requirements, the estimate is scaled upward. The particular cost-driver items are determined and validated empirically. In general, the cost drivers can be classified as being attributes of the following items:

- *Product.* For example, reliability requirements or inherent complexity.
- *Computer.* For example, are there execution time or storage constraints?
- *Personnel.* For example, are the personnel experienced in the application area or the programming language being used?
- *Project.* For example, are sophisticated software tools being used?

Cost Drivers	Ratings					
	Very low	Low	Nominal	High	Very High	Extra High
Product attributes						
Required software reliability	.75	.88	1.00	1.15	1.40	
Data base size		.94	1.00	1.08	1.16	
Product complexity	.70	.85	1.00	1.15	1.30	1.65
Computer attributes						
Execution time constraints			1.00	1.11	1.30	1.66
Main storage constraints			1.00	1.06	1.21	1.56
Virtual machine volatility*		.87	1.00	1.15	1.30	
Computer turnaround time		.87	1.00	1.07	1.15	
Personnel attributes						
Analyst capability	1.46	1.19	1.00	.86	.71	
Applications experience	1.29	1.13	1.00	.91	.82	
Programmer capability	1.42	1.17	1.00	.86	.70	
Virtual machine experience*	1.21	1.10	1.00	.90		
Programming language experience	1.14	1.07	1.00	.95		
Project attributes						
Use of modern programming practices	1.24	1.10	1.00	.91	.82	
Use of software tools	1.24	1.10	1.00	.91	.83	
Required development schedule	1.23	1.08	1.00	1.04	1.10	

*For a given software product, the underlying virtual machine is the complex of hardware and software (OS, DBMS, etc.) it calls on to accomplish its tasks.

Table 8.5   Effort multipliers used by the COCOMO intermediate model. (From Boehm [1984a], ©1984 IEEE, reprinted by permission of IEEE.)

The particular attributes in each class differ from model to model. For example, some models use object code for the size estimate, others use source code, and some both object code and source code. Personnel attributes that can be considered include the capability and continuity (lack of turnover) of the personnel. Table 8.2 shows the set of factors considered by different models, classified into five different groups of attributes. Size is separated into its own group because of its importance and the different ways in which it is treated in the different models.

The basic steps for arriving at the cost of a proposed software system are the following:

1. Estimate the software's eventual size, and use it in the model's formula to arrive at an initial estimate of effort;
2. Revise the estimate by using the cost driver or other scaling factors given by the model;
3. Apply the model's tools to the estimate derived in step 2 to determine the total effort, activity distribution, etc.

The best known model for cost estimation today is the Constructive Cost Model, known by its acronym, COCOMO. COCOMO is actually three different models of increasing complexity and level of detail. We next give an overview of the intermediate COCOMO model and the steps and details involved in the use of such a model.

COCOMO

The following fleshes out how the general estimation steps described above apply in the case of COCOMO:

1. The code size estimate is based on delivered source instructions, KDSI. The initial (nominal) development effort is based on the project's development "mode." COCOMO categorizes the software being developed according to three modes: *organic*, *semidetached*, and *embedded*. Table 8.3 shows how to determine which mode each project falls in. The estimator arrives at the development mode by deciding which entries in the table best characterize the project's features as listed in column 1. The heading on the column that best matches the project is the development mode for the project. For example, flight control software for a new fighter airplane falls into the embedded class, and a standard payroll application falls into the organic class. Study the table carefully to see the effect of the various features on the mode and, therefore, on the development effort.

    Each development mode has an associated formula for determining the nominal development effort based on the estimated code size. The formulas are shown in Table 8.4. Tables 8.3 and 8.4 together can be considered a quantitative summary of a considerable amount of experimental data collected by Boehm over the years.

2. The estimator determines the effort multiplier for the particular project, based on cost-driver attributes. COCOMO uses 15 cost-driver attributes to scale the nominal development effort. These attributes are a subset of the general factors listed in Table 8.2 and are given in Table 8.5, along with the multiplier used for each, based on rating the driver for the particular project.

    There is a guideline for determining how to rate each attribute for the project at hand. The rating ranges from very low to extra high. The multipliers are multiplied together and with the nominal effort derived in step 1 to arrive at the estimate of total effort for the project.

Table 8.5 contains a wealth of information. For example, the range of the multipliers for each factor shows the impact of that factor and how much control the manager has over the factor. As an example, the range of analyst capability shows that the difference between using an analyst of very high capability and one of very low capability is a factor of two in the cost estimate. The product attributes, in general, are fixed by the inherent complexity of the product and are not within the control of the manager.

3.   Given the estimate of the total effort in step 2, COCOMO allows the derivation of various other important numbers and analyses. For example, Table 8.4 shows the formulas, again based on the development mode, for deriving a recommended length for the project schedule, based on the estimate of the total effort for the project.

The COCOMO model allows sensitivity analyses based on changing the parameters. For example, one can model the change in development time as a function of relaxing the reliability constraints or improving the software development environment. Or one can analyze the cost and impact of unstable hardware on a project's software schedule.

Software cost estimation models such as COCOMO are required for an engineering approach to software management. Without such models, one has only judgment to rely on, which makes decisions hard to trust and justify. Worse, one can never be sure whether improvements are being made to the software. While current models still lack a full scientific justification, they can be used and validated against an organization's project data base.

A software development organization should maintain a project data base which stores information about the progress of projects. Such a data base can be used in many ways: to validate a particular cost estimation model against past projects; to calibrate cost-driver or scaling factors for a model, based on an organization's particular environment; as a basis for arriving at an initial size estimate; or to calibrate estimates of effort that are derived from a model.

With the current state of the art of cost estimation modelling, it is not wise to have complete and blind trust in the results of the models, but a project manager would be equally unwise to ignore the value of such tools for a software development organization as a whole. They can be used to complement expert judgment and intuition.

Exercises

8.5   Suppose that you are faced with developing a system that you expect to have about 100,000 lines of source instructions. Compute the nominal effort and the development time for each of the three development modes, i.e. organic, semidetached, and embedded.

8.6   You are the manager of a new project charged with developing a 100,000-line embedded system. You have a choice of hiring from two pools of engineers: highly capable programmers with very little experience in the programming language being used, or programmers of low quality but a lot of experience with the programming language. What is the impact of hiring all your engineers from one or the other group?

8.3 PROJECT CONTROL

As we said before, the purpose of controlling a project is to monitor the progress of the activities against the plans, to ensure that the goals are being approached and, eventually, achieved. Another aspect of control is to detect, as soon as possible, when deviations from the plan are occurring so that corrective action may be taken. In software engineering, as in any design-dominated discipline, it is especially important to plan realistically–even conservatively–so as to minimize the need for corrective action. For example, while in a manufacturing-dominated discipline it may be justifiable to hire the minimum number of workers necessary and add more employees if production falls below the required level, it has been observed in software engineering that adding people to a project that is late can delay the project even further. This underscores the importance of not only planning, but also controlling, in software engineering. The sooner deviations from the plan are detected, the more it is possible to cope with them.

8.3.1 Work Breakdown Structures

Most project control techniques are based on breaking down the goal of the project into several intermediate goals. Each intermediate goal can in turn be broken down further. This process can be repeated until each goal is small enough to be well understood. We can then plan for each goal individually–its resource requirements, assignment of responsibility, scheduling, etc.

A semiformal way of breaking down the goal is called the *work breakdown structure* (*WBS*). In this technique, one builds a tree whose root is labelled by the major activity of the project such as "build a compiler." Each node of the tree can be broken down into smaller components that are designated the children of the node. This "work breakdown" can be repeated until each leaf node in the tree is small enough to allow the manager to estimate its size, difficulty, and resource requirements. Figure 8.1 shows the work breakdown structure for a simple compiler development project.

The goal of a work breakdown structure is to identify all the activities that a project must undertake. The tasks can be broken down into as fine a level of detail as is desired or necessary. For example, we might have shown the substructure of a node labelled "design" as consisting of the three different activities of designing the scanner, parser, and code generator. The structure can be used as a basis for estimating the amount of resources necessary for the project as a whole by estimating the resources required for each leaf node.

The work breakdown structure is a simple tool that gives the manager a framework for breaking down large tasks into more manageable pieces. Once these manageable pieces have been identified, they can be used as units of work assignment. The structure can be refined and extended easily by labelling the nodes with appropriate information, such as the planned length of the activity, the name of the person responsible for the activity, and the starting and ending date of the activity. In this way, the structure can summarize the project plans.

The work breakdown structure can also be an input into the scheduling process, as we will see in the following subsections. In breaking down the work, we are trying to decide *which* tasks need to be done. In scheduling, we decide the *order* in which to do these tasks. Each work item in the work breakdown structure is associated with an *activity* to perform that item. A schedule tries to order the activities to ensure their timely completion.

Two general scheduling techniques are Gantt charts and PERT charts. We will present these in the next two subsections.

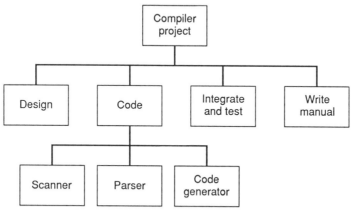

Figure 8.1   Work breakdown structure for a compiler project.

8.3.2 Gantt Charts

Gantt charts (developed by Henry L. Gantt) are a project control technique that can be used for several purposes, including scheduling, budgeting, and resource planning. A Gantt chart is a bar chart, with each bar representing an activity. The bars are drawn against a time line. The length of each bar is proportional to the length of time planned for the activity.

Let us draw a Gantt chart for the tasks identified in the WBS of Figure 8.1. We estimate the number of days required for each of the six tasks as follows: initial design, 45; scanner, 20; parser, 60; code generator, 180; integration and testing, 90; and writing the manual, 90. Using these estimates, we can draw the Gantt chart of Figure 8.2 for the compiler project.

A Gantt chart helps in scheduling the activities of a project, but it does not help in identifying them. One can begin with the activities identified in the work breakdown structure, as we did for the compiler example. During the scheduling activity, and also during implementation of the project, new activities may be identified that were not envisioned during the initial planning. The manager must then go back and revise the breakdown structure and the schedules to deal with these new activities.

The Gantt chart in the figure is actually an enhanced version of standard Gantt charts. The white part of the bar shows the length of time each task is estimated to take. The gray part shows the "slack" time, that is, the latest time by which a task must be finished. One way to view the slack time is that, if necessary, we can slide the white area over the gray area without forcing the start of the next activity to be delayed. For example, we have the freedom to delay the start of building the scanner to as late as

October 17, 1994 and still have it finished in time to avoid delaying the integration and testing activity. The chart shows clearly that the results of the scanner and parser tasks can be used only after the code generator task is completed (in the integration and testing task). A bar that is all white, such as that representing the code generator task, has no slack and must be started and completed on the scheduled dates if the schedule is to be maintained. From the figure, we can see that the three tasks, "design," "code generator," and "integration and testing" have no slack. It is these tasks, then, that determine the total length of time the project is expected to take.

This example shows that the Gantt chart can be used for resource allocation and staff planning. For example, from Figure 8.2, we can conclude that the same engineer can be assigned to do the scanner and the parser while another engineer is working on the code generator. Even so, the first engineer will have some slack time that we may plan to use to help the second engineer or to get a head start on the integration and testing activity.

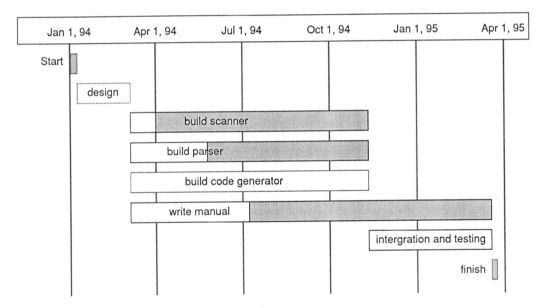

Figure 8.2   Gantt chart for a simple compiler project.

Gantt charts can take different forms depending on their intended use. They are best for resource scheduling. For example, if we are trying to schedule the activities of six engineers, we might use a Gantt chart in which each bar represents one of the engineers. In such a chart, the engineers are our resources and the chart shows the *resource loading* during the project. It can help, for example, in scheduling vacation time, or in ensuring that the right number of engineers will be available during each desired period. Figure 8.3 shows an example. We could label appropriate sections of the bars to show how much time we expect each engineer to spend on each activity (e.g., design and building the scanner).

Gantt charts are useful for resource planning and scheduling. While they show the tasks and their durations clearly, however, they do not show intertask dependencies plainly. PERT charts, the subject of the next section, show task dependencies directly.

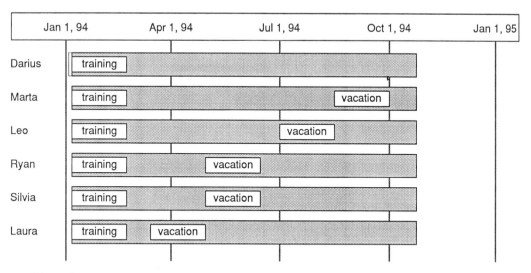

Figure 8.3   Gantt chart for scheduling six engineers.

8.3.3 PERT Charts

A PERT (Program Evaluation and Review Technique) chart is a network of boxes (or circles) and arrows. There are different variations of PERT charts. Some use the boxes to represent activities, and some use the arrows to do so. We will use the first approach here. Each box thus represents an activity. The arrows are used to show the dependencies of activities on one another. The activity at the head of an arrow cannot start until the activity at the tail of the arrow is finished. Just as with the nodes in the work breakdown structure, the boxes in a PERT chart can be decorated with starting and ending dates for activities; the arrows help in computing the earliest possible starting dates for the boxes at their heads. Some boxes can be designated as *milestones*. A milestone is an activity whose completion signals an important accomplishment in the life of the project. On the other hand, failure to make a milestone signals trouble to the manager and requires an explicit action to deal with the deviation from the schedule.

As with Gantt charts, to build a PERT chart for a project, one must first list all the activities required for completion of the project and estimate how long each will take. Then one must determine the dependence of the activities on each other. The PERT chart gives a graphical representation of this information. Clearly, the technique does not help in deciding which activities are necessary or how long each will take, but it does force the manager to take the necessary planning steps to answer these questions.

Figure 8.4 shows a PERT chart for the previous compiler project. The information from the work breakdown structure of Figure 8.1 is used to decide what boxes we need. The arrows show the new information that was not available in the work breakdown structure. The chart shows clearly that the project consists of the activities of initial design, building a scanner, building a parser, building a code generator, integrating and testing these, and writing a manual. Recall that the previous estimates for these six tasks were, respectively, 45, 20, 60, 180, 90, and 90 days.

The figure assumes that the project will start on January 1, 1994 (shown underlined). Taking holidays into account (January 1 and 2 are holidays in 1994), the design work will start on January 3, 1994. Since the design activity is estimated to take 45 days, any activity that follows the design may start on March 7, 1994 at the earliest.The dependency arrows help us compute these earliest start dates based on our estimates of the duration of each activity. These dates are shown in the figure. We could also compute the earliest finish dates or latest start dates or latest finish dates, depending on the kind of analysis we want to perform.

The chart shows that the path through the project that consists of the "design," "build code generator," and "integration and testing" activities is the *critical path* for the project. Any delay in any activity in this path will cause a delay in the entire project. The manager will clearly want to monitor the activities on the critical path much more closely than the other activities.

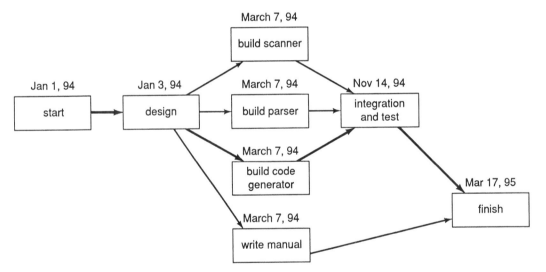

Figure 8.4   PERT chart for a simple compiler project. Activities on the critical path are shown in bold.

Some of the advantages of PERT are as follows:

- It forces the manager to plan.
- It shows the interrelationships among the tasks in the project and, in particular, clearly identifies the critical path of the project, thus helping to focus on it. For example, in the figure, the code generator is clearly the most critical activity in terms of the schedule. The critical path is shown by a dark solid line. We may decide to build a separate subproject for this activity alone, or put our best

people on the project, or monitor the critical activity very closely. The fact that the PERT chart has exposed the critical path allows us the opportunity to consider alternative approaches to cope with a potential problem.

- It exposes all possible parallelism in the activities and thus helps in allocating resources.
- It allows scheduling and simulation of alternative schedules.
- It enables the manager to monitor and control the project.

Despite these advantages, PERT is just a tool, and its use does not automatically guarantee the success of the project. The manager has much latitude in how PERT is used. For example, the granularity of the activities used is completely up to the manager. In the compiler example, we could have included such activities as hiring people, purchasing equipment, and securing office space, or we could have added activities such as coding, reviewing, and testing for each activity shown. The accuracy of the estimates of the length of time taken by the activities is also an important factor in how well the PERT chart can help in the scheduling activity.

Many variations of PERT charts are possible. For example, we could be interested in the earliest time in which an event can be accomplished or the latest time in which it can be accomplished. In the model presented, there is only one resource associated with each activity, that of time. We can also incorporate other resources, such as personnel requirements or computer time, to help with budgeting for the project.

For a big project, a PERT chart may contain hundreds of nodes and span many pages. The availability of computer support is essential for managing large PERT networks. Many such tools are available for most computers. They support both the initial preparation of the network and the continuous updating of the chart during the project. These tools make it possible to experiment with different scheduling options in order to create different critical paths.

Gantt charts can be derived automatically from PERT charts. Each kind of chart has its own place in the manager's toolbox of control techniques. The Gantt chart helps in planning the utilization of resources, while the PERT chart is better for monitoring the timely progress of activities. If rescheduling becomes necessary–for example, because of a missed milestone, we may want to go back and draw new Gantt charts for replanning the utilization of resources. Again, since revisions of these charts are often necessary, computer support is essential.

Exercises

8.7   In the PERT variation where activities are associated with arrows, boxes represent the completion of the activities. For example, instead of "build scanner," which is an activity, a box would say "scanner coded," which is an event. Draw a PERT chart with this new convention for the previous compiler example.

8.8   For the PERT chart of Figure 8.4, decorate the boxes with the following dates that are of interest in different scheduling situations: *earliest start time, earliest finish time, latest allowable start time, latest allowable finish time*.

8.3.4 Dealing With Deviations From the Plan

Gantt and PERT charts are useful for scheduling the activities and resources of a project. They are also useful for monitoring the progress of the project in contrast with the planned schedule and detecting deviations from it. As each activity is completed, it can be noted in the schedule chart by marking the associated boxes and arrows or bars. Any late completions are easily noticed. Of course, if a delay is associated with a milestone, this is a more serious problem and requires some action on the part of the manager. In addition to checking the chart when activities are completed, the manager should consult the chart at frequent intervals during the project to evaluate the status of the project.

No matter how deviations from the schedule are detected, the manager must decide on how to handle them. In activities where production is limited by raw human labor, it is usually easy to try to get back on schedule by adding people or increasing overtime for existing people. In software engineering and other design activities, however, it is not labor, but intellectual power, that is in short supply. It is much more difficult, therefore, to deal with deviations from the schedule.

The choices of the software engineering manager are rather limited, but there are some options that must be considered carefully. While it is important to recognize that merely adding engineers is not going to help meet the schedule, it is as important to recognize that the right engineering talent *can* help. Thus, temporarily reassigning senior engineers to a part of the project that is suffering or hiring expert troubleshooting consultants are viable options.

Another option is to examine the requirements and remove the ones that are not absolutely necessary. Sometimes, the requirements are "goldplated," i.e., there is too much attempt to provide a shiny veneer that does not add to the substance of the product. Cutting out unnecessary requirements is called *requirements scrubbing*. The success of such a recovery action is directly related to the incrementality principle described in Chapter 3. Even if we are not planning incremental delivery of the product, it is important to design a product that may be divided into subsets. Furthermore, it is important that development proceed incrementally in the order of importance of the requirements. It will not be helpful if we decide that we can scrub some requirements in order to recover from a slip in the schedule but those requirements have already been implemented. Thus, the incrementality principle must be adhered to not only during requirements analysis but also during project planning, scheduling, and implementation.

It is possible that, once all options for recovering from a slip in the schedule have been considered, no appropriate solution is found. At this point, the best thing to do is to admit the incorrectness of the original plans and schedules and revise the schedule based on the new knowledge about the difficulties of the tasks, the capabilities of the engineers, and the availability of the resources. The manager must view a schedule as a best attempt to predict the development cycle. That is, it is merely a prediction. While it is important to attempt to produce the most accurate prediction possible, it is also important to realize the risks involved with predictions and be prepared to revise the plans if necessary. Clearly, the larger the consequences of a slip in the schedule are, the more important it is to plan and schedule carefully. For example, if a slip will delay the introduction of a product that has been scheduled for months and invitations have already been sent out to newspaper reporters and security analysts to attend the formal introduction, almost any attempt to recover from such a slip can be justified. In less dramatic cases, accepting a delay may be the right course of action to take.

8.4 ORGANIZATION

The organizing function of management deals with devising roles for individuals and assigning responsibility for accomplishing the project goals. Organization is basically motivated by the need for cooperation when the goals are not achievable by a single human being in a reasonable amount of time. The aim of an organizational structure is to facilitate cooperation towards a common goal. An organizational structure is necessary at any level of an enterprise, whether it is to coordinate the efforts of a group of vice presidents who report to the president of the corporation or to orchestrate the interactions among programmers who report to a common project manager.

Management theorists and practitioners have studied the effects of different organizational structures on the productivity and effectiveness of groups. Because the goal of organization is to encourage cooperation, and because cooperation depends substantially on human characteristics, many general organizational rules apply to any endeavor, whether it deals with software production or automobile production.

The nature of software, however, as we discussed in Chapters 1 and 2, distinguishes it from other human artifacts to the extent that it also influences the effectiveness of different organizational structures when used in software development. In this section, we discuss how the unique characteristics of software can guide us in the choice of the appropriate organizational structure and how the right organization can help in achieving software qualities.

The task of organizing can be viewed as building a team: given a group of people and a common goal, what is the best role for each individual, and how should responsibilities be divided? Analogies with sports teams are illuminating. A basketball team consists of five players on the floor who are playing the game and another perhaps five players who are substitutes. Each player knows his role. There is one ball, and at any one time, only one player can have it. All other players must know their responsibilities and what to expect from the player with the ball. On well-organized teams, the patterns of cooperation and their effects are clearly visible. In poorly organized teams or teams with novice players, the lack of patterns of cooperation is just as clearly visible: when one player has the ball, the other four scream to be passed the ball. The player with the ball, of course, shoots the ball instead of passing it to anyone! We observe a similar phenomenon in Case Study A towards the back of the book.

Some of the considerations that affect the choice of an organization are similar to the factors that are used in cost estimation models that we have seen earlier. For example, what constitutes an appropriate organization for a project depends on the length of the project. Is it a long-term project or a short, one-shot project? If it is a long-term project, it is important to ensure job satisfaction for individuals, leading to high morale and thus reducing turnover. Sometimes, the best composition for a team is a mix of junior and senior engineers. This allows the junior engineers to do the less challenging tasks and learn from the senior engineers, who are busy doing the more challenging tasks and overseeing the progress of the junior engineers.

Because of the nature of large software systems, changing requirements, and the difficulties of software specification, it has been observed that adding people to a project late in the development cycle leads to further delays in the schedule. Thus, the issue of personnel turnover is a serious one that must be minimized. On a short-term project, personnel turnover is not as important an issue. On a long-term project, it is important to enable junior personnel to develop their skills and gain more responsibility as senior personnel move on to other responsibilities. The trade-offs involved in organizing for a short-term or a long-term project are similar to those involved in organizing a basketball team to win a single game, to be a winner over a single season, or to be a consistent winner over many years.

Another issue affecting the appropriate project organization is the nature of the task and how much communication the different team members need to have among themselves. For example, in a well-defined task such as a payroll system in which modules and their interfaces have been specified clearly, there is not much need for project members to communicate among each other, and excessive communication will probably lead to a delay in accomplishing their individual tasks. On the other hand, in a project where the task is not clearly understood, communication among team members is beneficial and can lead to a better solution. Strictly hierarchical organizations minimize and discourage communication among team members; more democratic organizations encourage it.

One of the general considerations in team organization is the appropriate size for the team. On the one hand, a small team leads to a more cohesive design, less overhead, more unity, and higher morale. On the other hand, some tasks are too complex to be solved by a small team. Since we cannot control the size or the complexity of the tasks we have to solve, we need to match the size and organization of the team to the problem. Too few people cannot solve an inherently large problem, but assigning an inherently small problem to a large team also leads to problems such as too much overhead, overambitious solutions, and solutions that are too costly.

The direct relationship between program complexity and team size, as we saw in Section 8.2.3.1, is formalized by the COCOMO model, where, given the estimate of software size, we can derive the required number of engineers from a formula. How should these engineers be subdivided into teams? In general, a small team suffers less overhead and therefore has more productivity per member. We can summarize the considerations of team size as follows: a team should be large enough, but not too large and small enough, but not too small. For programming teams, experimental evidence has shown that the optimal size is between three and eight, depending on the task. If more than eight people are needed, one can introduce extra, hierarchical levels of management to keep the span of control of each manager to a manageable size.

The size of a team involved in software development is influenced by the characteristics of the software. If a group of modules exhibits high coupling (as described in Chapter 3), assigning the modules to different people will require too much interaction among the programmers. Thus, an appropriate design must be accompanied by an appropriate assignment of tasks to individuals and an appropriate team organization that makes that assignment possible. Rather than dogmatically dictating a team organization, one must have a flexible approach and choose the organization based on the design of the system. Of course, the design must be produced by a team in the first place, and a good way to approach the task of building the team is incrementally: start with a small team that produces a first set of the requirements and design, form a larger team and produce a first implementation and then use the results produced by the team to decide whether an iteration of the whole cycle is required (as in the spiral model), with a possible need for a team reorganization.

Unfortunately, while reorganizing a team might in theory be the best way to accomplish a task, it is disruptive of people's routines and in conflict with human beings' need for security and inertia. When, why, and how to reorganize a team requires judgment on the part of the manager and cannot be based solely on the design of the software system. As always, the manager must weigh many factors, including the need to complete the project on schedule, to meet budget constraints, to produce a product that meets quality requirements–such as maintainability, which will reduce the project's overall life cycle costs–to keep the engineers motivated and satisfied for future projects, and to allow engineers to exercise their individuality where desirable and to conform to team standards when necessary.

As in any engineering discipline, software engineering requires not only the application of systematic techniques to routine aspects of the software but also invention and ingenuity when standard techniques are not adequate. Balancing these requirements is one of the most difficult aspects of software engineering management. Clearly, ingenuity and invention cannot be scheduled, but practical software development requires schedules and cost forecasts. Depending on the task, therefore, the organization must allow individual creativity while "legislating" team standards when necessary.

We can categorize software development team organizations according to where decision-making control lies. A team can have centralized control, where a recognized leader is responsible for and authorized to produce a design and resolve all technical issues. Alternatively, a team organization can be based on distributing decision-making control and emphasizing group consensus. Both of these types of organization, as well as combinations of the two, have been used in practice successfully. The following subsections discuss the two kinds of organization in more detail.

8.4.1 Centralized-Control Team Organization

Centralized-control team organization is a standard management technique in well understood disciplines. In this mode of organization, several workers report to a supervisor who directly controls their tasks and is responsible for their performance. Centralized control is based on a hierarchical organizational structure in which several supervisors report to a "second-level" manager and so on up the chain to the president of the enterprise. In general, centralized control works well with tasks that are simple enough that the one person responsible for control of the project can grasp the problem and its solution.

One way to centralize the control of a software development team is through a *chief programmer team*. In this kind of organization, one engineer, known as the chief programmer, is responsible for the design and all the technical details of the project. The chief programmer reports to a peer project manager who is responsible for the administrative aspects of the project. Other members of the team are a software librarian and other programmers who report to the chief programmer and are added to the team on a temporary basis when needed. Specialists may be used by the team as consultants when the need arises. The need for programmers and consultants, as well as what tasks they perform, is determined by the chief programmer, who initiates and controls all decisions. The software library maintained by the librarian is the central repository for all the software, documentation, and decisions made by the team. Figure 8.5 is a graphical representation of patterns of control and communication supported by this kind of organization.

Chief programmer team organization has been likened to a surgical team performing an operation. During an operation, one person must be clearly in control, and all other people involved must be in total support of the "chief" surgeon; there is no place or time for individual creativity or group consensus. This analogy highlights the strengths of the chief programmer team organization, as well as its weaknesses. The chief programmer team organization works well when the task is well understood, is within the intellectual grasp of one individual, and is such that the importance of finishing the project outweighs other factors (such as team morale, personnel development, and life cycle costs).

On the negative side, a chief programmer team has a "single point of failure." Since all communication must go through, and all decisions must be made by, the chief programmer, the chief programmer may become overloaded or, indeed, saturated. The success of the chief programmer team clearly depends on the skill and ability of the chief programmer and the size and complexity of the problem. The choice of chief programmer is the most important determinant of success of the chief programmer team. On the other hand, since there is a great variability in people's abilities–as much as a 10-to-1 ratio in productivity–a chief programmer position may be the best way to use the rare highly productive engineers.

8.4.2 Decentralized-Control Team Organization

In a decentralized-control team organization, decisions are made by consensus and all work is considered group work. Team members review each other's work and are responsible as a group for what every member produces. Figure 8.6 shows the patterns of control and communication among team members in a decentralized-control organization. The ringlike management structure is intended to show the lack of a hierarchy and that all team members are at the same level.

Such a "democratic" organization leads to higher morale and job satisfaction and, therefore, to less turnover. The engineers feel more ownership of the project and responsibility for the problem, leading to higher quality in their work. A decentralized-control organization is more suited for long-term projects because the amount of intragroup communication that it encourages leads to a longer development time, presumably accompanied by lower life cycle costs. The proponents of this kind of team organization claim that it is more appropriate for less understood and more complicated problems because a group can invent better solutions than a single individual. Such an organization is based on a technique referred to as "egoless programming" because it encourages programmers to share and review one another's work.

On the negative side, decentralized-control team organization is not appropriate for large teams, where the communication overhead can overwhelm all the engineers, reducing individual productivity. It also runs the risk of establishing a group that is forever in futile search of a perfect solution to please everyone.

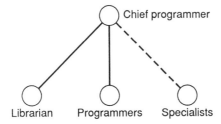

Figure 8.5   Patterns of control and communication in a chief programmer team.

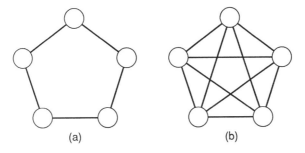

Figure 8.6   A decentralized-control team.
(**a**) Management structure. (**b**) Patterns of communication.

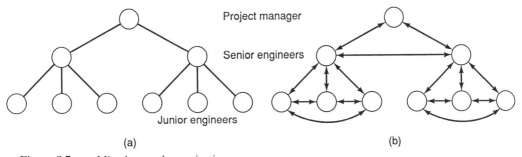

Figure 8.7   Mixed-control organizations.
(**a**) Management structure. (**b**) Patterns of communication.

8.4.3 Mixed-Control Team Organization

A mixed-control team organization attempts to combine the benefits of centralized and decentralized control, while minimizing or avoiding their disadvantages. Rather than treating all members the same, as in a decentralized organization, or treating a single individual as the chief, as in a centralized organization, the mixed organization distinguishes the engineers into senior and junior engineers. Each senior engineer leads a group of junior engineers. The senior engineers, in turn, report to a project manager.

Control is vested in the project manager and senior programmers, while communication is decentralized among each set of individuals, peers, and their immediate supervisors. The patterns of control and communication in mixed-control organizations are shown in Figure 8.7.

A mixed-mode organization tries to limit communication to within a small group that is most likely to benefit from it. It also tries to realize the benefits of group decision making by vesting authority in a group of senior programmers. The mixed-control organization is an example of the use of a hierarchy to master the complexity of software development as well as organizational structure.

8.4.4 An Assessment of Team Organizations

In the previous subsections, we have presented different ways of organizing software development teams. Each kind of organization discussed in the previous three subsections has its proponents and detractors. Each also has its appropriate place.

Experimental assessment of different organizational structures is difficult. It is clearly impractical to run large software development projects using two different types of organization, just for the purpose of comparing the effectiveness of the two structures. While cost estimation models can be assessed on the basis of how well they predict actual software costs, an organizational structure cannot be assessed so easily, because one cannot compare the results achieved with those one *would have* achieved with a different organization.

Experiments have been run to measure the effects of such things as team size and task complexity on the effectiveness of development teams. In the choice of team organization, however, it appears that we must be content with the following general considerations:

- Just as no life cycle model is appropriate for all projects, no team organization is appropriate for all tasks.

- Decentralized control is best when communication among engineers is necessary for achieving a good solution.

- Centralized control is best when speed of development is the most important goal and the problem is well understood.

- An appropriate organization tries to limit the amount of communication to what is necessary for achieving project goals–no more and no less.

- An appropriate organization may have to take into account goals other than speed of development. Among these other important goals are: lower life cycle costs, reduced personnel turnover, repeatability of the process, development of junior engineers into senior engineers, and widespread dissemination of specialized knowledge and expertise among personnel.

8.5 RISK MANAGEMENT

An engineering project is expected to produce a reliable product, within a limited time, using limited resources. Any project, however, runs the risk of not producing the desired product, overspending its allotted resource budget, or overrunning its allotted time. Risk accompanies any human activity.

Risk analysis and control is a topic of management theory. Several standard techniques exist for identifying project risks, assessing their impact, and monitoring and controlling them. Knowledge of these techniques allows a project manager to apply them when necessary to increase the chances of success of a project.

We have already seen, in previous chapters, many examples of software development problems that can be viewed from a risk analysis point of view. For example, we have discussed the difficulties of specifying product requirements completely. Given these difficulties, a project runs the risk of producing the wrong product or having the requirements change during development. An effective approach for reducing this risk is prototyping or incremental delivery. A different type of approach to handling the risk of late changes in the requirements is to produce a modular design so that such changes can be accommodated by actual changes to the software. Of these approaches, prototyping tries to minimize changes in the requirements, while modular design tries to minimize the *impact* of changes in the requirements. Choosing between the two alternatives, or deciding to use both, should involve a conscious and systematic analysis of the possible risks, their likelihood, and their impact.

An extreme example of poor risk management is given in Case Study A at the back of the book, where we see that improper management of the project indeed caused the entire company to face the risk of bankruptcy. That project was characterized by a total lack of attention to risk management issues, even though it would have been easy to identify plausible risks and their impact early on and make contingency plans for dealing with them.

At different levels of an organization, different levels of risk can be tolerated. For example, a project manager at the beginning of his career may not want to tolerate any delay in the schedule (to minimize risk to his personal career), while his supervisor might be more concerned with the reliability of the product. A project manager might not be able to tolerate the risk of running over budget by more than 10%, while a higher level manager who is more aware of the value of early time to market, and therefore more concerned with the time taken by the project might be willing to overspend the budget by much more if the product can be produced sooner. To complicate matters even more, different people have different tolerances of risk based on their personal nature, as can be evidenced by observing people at a gambling casino.

Exercise

8.9   Study Case Study A at the back of book. List three major risks associated with the project described there, and propose a technique for managing each risk.

8.5.1 Typical Management Risks in Software Engineering

By examining the difficulties that arise in software engineering, we can identify typical areas of risk that a software engineering project manager must address. We have already discussed the example of changes in requirements. Another important risk is in not having the right people working on the project. Since there is great variability among the abilities of software engineers, it makes a big difference whether a project is staffed with capable or mediocre engineers. If key positions in a project are staffed with inappropriate people, the project runs the risk of delaying deliveries, or producing poor-quality products, or both.

RISK ITEMS	RISK MANAGEMENT TECHNIQUES
1. Personnel shortfalls	- Staffing with top talent; job matching; team-building; key-personnel agreements; cross-training; pre-scheduling key people
2. Unrealistic schedules and budgets	- Detailed multisource cost & schedule estimation; design to cost; incremental development; software reuse; requirements scrubbing
3. Developing the wrong software functions	- Organization analysis; mission analysis; ops-concept formulation; user surveys; prototyping; early users's manuals
4. Developing the wrong user interface	- Prototyping; scenarios; task analysis; user characterization (functionality, style, workload)
5. Gold plating	- Requirements scrubbing; prototyping; cost-benefit analysis; design to cost
6. Continuing stream of requirements changes	- High change threshold; information hiding; incremental development (defer changes to later increments)
7. Shortfalls in externally furnished components	- Benchmarking; inspections; reference checking; compatibility analysis
8. Shortfalls in externally performed tasks	- Reference checking; pre-award audits; award-fee contracts; competitive design or prototyping; teambuilding
9. Real-time performance shortfalls	- Simulation; benchmarking; modeling; prototyping; instrumentation; tuning
10. Straining computer science capabilities	- Technical analysis; cost-benefit analysis; prototyping; reference checking

Table 8.6   Common risk items in software engineering management and techniques for managing them. (From Boehm [1989], reprinted by permission of the author.)

Schedule overrun risks can be reduced by limiting dependencies among tasks. For example, if many tasks cannot be started until a given task is completed, a delay in that one task can delay the entire project. Imagine a computer system project where hardware and software are being developed concurrently. If all software development is scheduled to start after the hardware is completed, any delay in completion of the hardware translates directly into a delay in the entire project. A way to control this schedule risk is to produce a simulation version of the hardware so that software development can be carried on even if the hardware is delayed. This was done in Case Study C at the back of the book.

PERT charts can help a manager identify schedule bottlenecks immediately–even mechanically: a node with many outgoing arcs is a sign of trouble, and the manager should try to reschedule activities to avoid it. Such a node should be rescheduled especially if it happens to be on the critical path. One way to reschedule the activity is to break it up into smaller activities, such that the arrows going into the original node are distributed among the new (smaller) nodes. Another schedule risk that can be spotted from a PERT chart is a node with many ingoing arcs. This type of node depends on too many activities and often acts as a synchronization point. While such a node may sometimes be necessary, heavy interdependencies should be avoided in general.

Table 8.6, from Boehm [1989], can be used as a checklist of common risks and their typical solutions in software engineering management. Examining the risk items in column 1 of the table, we can see that they overlap the items that are used in software cost estimation models. If a factor has a high multiplier in cost estimation, it represents a risk that must be managed carefully.

8.6 CONCLUDING REMARKS

This chapter has presented a concise overview of software engineering management, based on the standard management practice of dividing the management function into planning, organizing, staffing, directing, and controlling. We have discussed the important aspects of software that require special management attention.

While we have only talked about management in the large, that is, management of a group of engineers that must cooperate to produce a common product, many techniques we have discussed can and should be used by the individual engineer as well, that is, in the small. Indeed, each engineer must carefully plan, monitor, and execute the plan for his or her own work. Staffing and directing are the only two management functions that do not apply in the small. In particular, a carefully derived work breakdown structure and PERT chart can help individual engineers on nontrivial activities.

While we have discussed the difficulties in measuring software productivity, we have also stated the importance of defining and collecting such metrics. A software engineering organization must define and adopt metrics, collect measurements on existing projects, and validate the metrics in order to be able to apply management principles to guide the planning, decision making, and monitoring of future projects. In the absence of metrics, there is no way to measure whether progress is being made and, if so, at what rate.

In addition to the technical aspects of management that we have discussed, the manager is involved in resolving conflicts among competing goals. For example:

- In assigning tasks to people, should the experienced engineer be assigned to do all the difficult jobs and get them done fast, or should he or she work with less experienced engineers to have them trained for the future?

- Large software systems exhibit what have been called progressive and antiregressive components in their evolution. A software is evolving progressively when features are being added and functionality is increasing. But after adding to the software for a long time, its structure becomes so difficult to deal with, that an effort must be undertaken to restructure it to make it possible to make further additions later. Reengineering, which does not add any functionality, is an antiregressive component of software because its goal is to stop the software from regressing beyond hope. The decision that the manager must make is when it is time to undertake antiregressive activities. In its logical extreme, this decision amounts to whether a software system must be retired and a new one developed.

- A common conflict is known as *the mythical man-month conflict.* In some disciplines, people and time are interchangeable, that is, the same task can be accomplished by two people in half the time that it takes a single person. In software engineering, as we have seen, adding more people increases the overhead of communication on each engineer, preventing a linear increase in productivity with any additional people. In fact, after a certain point in the project, and beyond a certain number of people, adding more people to the project can delay the project rather than speed it up. The difficult task of the manager is to determine when those limits have been reached. The cost estimation models that we have discussed are the beginning of a foundation for allowing such decisions to be made quantitatively.

- Will the approaches that worked on one project work on another project? One of the painfully observed phenomena in software engineering is that many techniques do not scale up; that is, a method that works on smaller projects does not necessarily work on larger projects. Our emphasis throughout the earlier chapters on in-the-small versus in-the-large approaches in, for example, testing or design, was in fact motivated by this inability to scale up in software engineering. A corollary of this observation is that it is not in general possible to derive precise scheduling information from a throwaway prototype. For example, if the prototype demonstrates a tenth of the functionality of the final product, the product will *not* take ten times the development time that the prototype took. The COCOMO equations reflect this phenomenon.

- Should engineers be encouraged to reuse existing software in order to reduce schedule time? While software reuse reduces coding time, it may cause difficulties in other phases of the life cycle. If the modules that are reused do not supply the exact interfaces suitable to the design and functionality of the product, they cause the engineer to go through extra effort just to match the interface, and, worse, they lessen the evolvability of the product. These problems point out the immaturity of software reuse technology, rather than an inherent flaw in the idea of software reuse. Whatever the reasons, however, the manager is left with a difficult set of compromises to consider.

Finally, we must recognize that there are no panaceas to software engineering problems. For example, using the latest process–an incremental, prototype-oriented, life cycle model–or the latest technology–an advanced tool for configuration management–or the latest methodology–object-oriented analysis and design–will not solve all software production problems. In truth, software engineering is a difficult intellectual activity, and there are no easy solutions to difficult problems. Using the right process, the right technology, the right methodology, and the right tools will certainly help to control the complexities of software engineering, but it will not eliminate them altogether. In practice, because software engineering is such a difficult task at times, and because costs are rising rapidly, managers tend to grasp at any solution that comes along which promises to solve their very real problems.

Panaceas do not exist, however, and a manager is best advised to accept the difficulties of the job and carefully evaluate the impact of any newly offered proposed panaceas.

FURTHER EXERCISES

8.10 Compare software science measures and function points as measures of complexity. Which do you think is more useful as a predictor of how much a particular software's development will cost?

8.11 Consider an application that produces a certain report on a daily, weekly, and monthly basis. Because the focus of function point analysis is to measure the complexity of an application based on the function it is supposed to provide to users, each report is counted as one because it provides a distinct function to the user. Discuss the pros and cons of counting these reports as three instead of one.

8.12 Discuss a possible rationale for including, and one for not including, the cancelled projects in an organization's productivity measure.

8.13 Discuss possible rationale for including and not including in an organization's productivity measure, the tools developed in support of a project but not included in the delivered product.

8.14 Discuss the problem of using the lines-of-code productivity metric (DSI) by comparing a programmer who quickly develops a module full of subtle defects that will be discovered after system delivery with a programmer who develops a module much more slowly but without the subtle defects. Discuss possible solutions to this problem.

8.15 Some experimental evidence suggests that the initial size estimate for a project affects the nature and results of the project. Consider two different managers charged with developing the same application. One estimates that the size of the application will be 50,000 lines, while the other estimates that it will be 100,000 lines. Discuss how these estimates affect the project throughout its life cycle.

8.16 Change the WBS of Figure 8.1 to show some subactivities under "design." Modify the Gantt chart of Figure 8.3 and the PERT chart of Figure 8.4 to reflect the change in the WBS.

8.17 Establishing a chief programmer team is one way of organizing a centralized-control software development team. Describe other ways of organizing a centralized control team.

8.18 Argue for or against the following statements:

- A decentralized organization is better than a centralized organization for ill-understood problems.
- For a decentralized organization, a design where modules have high coupling is more suited than one where modules have low coupling.
- A decentralized organization requires a longer development schedule than a centralized organization.

8.19 Suppose you are charged with organizing a team to develop a telephone switching system that runs on a new processor. (Refer to the case study of Section 7.2.1 for the details of a switching system.) Describe a team organization that you would adopt, and justify your choices.

8.20 Refer to the case study of the budget-control system of Section 7.2.2. Describe how you would organize a chief programmer team to produce the system. Describe how you would organize an egoless team to produce the system. Which organization do you think is more appropriate for this kind of system?

8.21 State the rules for deriving a Gantt chart from a PERT chart, and vice versa. How complete are your rules? As a project, develop a program to do the conversions.

8.22 Observe that the goal of both Petri nets and PERT charts is to show parallelism and synchronization among activities. State the rules for converting a Petri net to a PERT chart, and vice versa. How complete are your rules? As a project, develop a program to do the conversion.

8.23 Go back to the case study of Section 7.2.1. Discuss the major risks that were associated with the project and how they were (or could have been) managed.

8.24 Go back to the case study of Section 7.2.2. Discuss the major risks that were associated with the project and how they were (or could have been) managed.

HINTS AND SKETCHY SOLUTIONS

8.4 Find a way to include a count for the library routines that are used.

8.8 Consider these questions: What if the engineers only produce tools and no product? What if they produce only the product and no tools? What if they produce tools that others can use? What is the behavior that should be rewarded?

8.10 Consider what the input to each measure is.

8.15 How many people will be hired? What happens towards the end when one manager discovers that there is a lot more work left to be done, while the other might discover that he or she is ahead of schedule?

BIBLIOGRAPHIC NOTES

Koontz et al. [1980] is a standard textbook on management. Buckle [1977] is a concise, readable overview of issues involved in software management. Boehm [1981] is a classic text on understanding and controlling software costs. In a classic book, *The Mythical Man-Month*, Brooks [1975] provides many insightful observations on the development process of large software systems, including the empirical law that adding people to a project that is late delays the project further. Gilb [1988] discusses software management, with a strong emphasis on the incremental development and delivery approach. DeMarco

[1982] is another good book on software management. Reifer [1986] is a tutorial on of software management. Boehm [1989] introduces the subject of software risk management and contains many relevant papers.

The influence of human factors in software development is discussed by Weinberg [1971] and Weinberg and Schulman [1974]. The latter is an often-cited source of the study that programmers can achieve the primary objective set for them at the cost of short-changing secondary goals.

Capers Jones [1986] contains a long list of factors and cogent analyses of the different approaches to modelling programming productivity. Curtis et al. [1988] reports on a field study to analyze the factors that affect productivity. "Since large software systems are still generated by humans rather than machines," the authors claim, "their creation must be analyzed as a *behavioral* process." The paper shows that different factors affect software at different layers of the organization. For example, at an individual level, intellectual and technical competence affects the design of the software whereas at the team level, social processes dominate. Kearney et al. [1986] critically evaluate the role of complexity metrics within an organization. The impact of measurement on management and on the structure of the environment is addressed by Basili and Rombach [1988] and Basili and Caldiera [1988].

Grady and Caswell [1987] report on the history and results of a companywide effort to establish a metrics program at Hewlett-Packard. The "urban decay" analogy is due to M. Mackey of Hewlett-Packard Labs (personal communication). The observation that there are progressive and regressive components of software development is due to Belady and Lehman [1979].

Albrecht et al. [1983] introduces function points (see also Behrens [1983]). Low and Jeffrey [1990] compare function points and lines of code and conclude that function points provide a more accurate estimate of project size.

Section 8.2.3.1 is based on Boehm [1984a], which is an introductory overview of the field of software engineering economics and an update of the state of the art since Boehm's text was published in 1981. Boehm [1984a] also observes that cost models are far from perfect; they are accurate to within 20%, 80% of the time.

Our discussion of team organizations follows Mantei [1981], which contains a discussion and an evaluation of different team structures in software development. Baker [1982] discusses chief programmer teams.

Abdel-Hamid [1989] and Abdel-Hamid and Madnick [1989] discuss a dynamic model with feedback loops for software project management. The model integrates technical and managerial aspects of software engineering. Practical experience with COCOMO is also illustrated. Abdel-Hamid [1990] discusses how scheduling decisions affect software development costs.

For a presentation of PERT, the reader may refer to Wiest and Levy [1977].

Chapter 9

Software Engineering Tools
and Environments

In the previous chapters, we have discussed many approaches and principles aimed at building high-quality software by means of an effective development process. In this chapter, we discuss various tools and environments for the support of this endeavor.

An *environment* refers to a collection of related tools. The tools and environments we discuss all aim at automating some of the activities that are involved in software engineering. The generic term for this field of study is *computer aided software engineering (CASE)*.

Sometimes, tools are strictly necessary to support a given activity. Other times, they simply help in making some jobs easier or more efficient. For example, programming languages and their compilers or interpreters are indispensable for executing programs; without them, software would not even exist. On the other hand, even if one can write specifications manually with paper and pencil, a simple word processor to edit the specifications is a useful tool that may increase the productivity and reliability of the whole production process.

Section 9.1 begins the chapter with a historical account of software engineering tools. This will help to understand the present state of the art in a field that is evolving in a rapid and tumultuous way. Section 9.2 classifies tools according to several viewpoints. Section 9.3 presents the main categories of tools. Because of their major impact on the design techniques discussed in Chapter 4, programming languages are analyzed separately in Section 9.4. Section 9.5 presents a sampler of tools that are currently available commercially and more or less widely used in industrial environments. Finally, Section 9.6 outlines an ideal scenario for a software engineering environment.

9.1 HISTORICAL EVOLUTION OF TOOLS AND ENVIRONMENTS

We have already observed that, in the early years of computing, constructing software was essentially a matter of programming. Thus, the programming language was the major tool used by software developers. Associated with it were other tools used to facilitate programming, chiefly, the compiler or the assembler (depending on the programming language).

When the *compiler* was the only tool, the result of coding consisted mainly of punched cards. Later, with the advent of third-generation computer systems with time-shared, interactive terminals and on-line disk storage, interactive *editors* supported a much easier way of creating and manipulating programs. The major breakthrough introduced by these tools was the capability of correcting errors on line; previously, even a simple typing error required deletion of the current card, repunching a new one, and resubmission of the entire card deck. On-line storage of programs allowed several versions of the same program to be stored into files, thus giving rise to the possibility of computer-supported configuration management, because all software was directly under computer control.

A major improvement in program editing has been obtained quite recently by recognizing that programs are not just pure text: they have a structure, defined by the syntax of the language. This recognition led to *syntax-directed editors*, which are especially helpful to novice programmers, because they enforce syntactic correctness as the program is being edited. Now, programs may be created by expanding predefined templates in accordance with the grammar of a language, and any program manipulation constrains the portions of programs that may be legally replaced by others to those that match the same syntactic template.

Another area that is receiving increasing attention is *program verification and debugging*. Symbolic debuggers, which aid in analyzing program execution states in terms of source code identifiers, are probably the most widely used tools in this area. Advanced testing support tools, such as test case generators and data and control-flow analyzers–and even tools for verifying formal program correctness–are now becoming available.

Modularization has always been recognized as vital in the construction of large systems, even when the techniques to exploit it were not well understood. Early examples of the construction of modular software were the integration of mathematical routines into scientific applications and the linking of assembly language routines to object code compiled from (possibly different) high-level languages. The *linker* is the tool that makes this combination possible.

The more complex the programming activity became, the more tools were developed to support it and the more sophisticated those tools became. The need for the *integration of tools* arose naturally, the better to cope with the activity of software construction, which is in itself an integrated set of several subactivities. This led to the notion of an *integrated project support environment (IPSE)*, as a collection of tools and related methods with which the software engineer interacts during the entire life cycle of a product and across several products.

Integration may be viewed as an *internal* quality of the environment, meaning that different tools or tool fragments cooperate easily. This may mean, for example, that no complex format conversions are needed from the output of tool 1 to the input of tool 2, if tool 1 and tool 2 are used in sequence.

Integration may also be viewed as an *external* quality that may be appreciated by the environment's users. For example, consider the debugging activity. First, one needs a debugger to monitor program execution and to locate errors. Once the errors have been located, they must be removed by editing, recompiling, and relinking the program. If the different activities–debugging, editing, compiling, and linking–are supported by separate, nonintegrated tools, the programmer has to quit the debugger before invoking the editor; then, after correction, recompilation, and relinking, debugging resumes from scratch. The process is painful when repeated several times. By contrast, if the tools are integrated and can run concurrently–perhaps even in a multi-window setting–the editor can be invoked from the debugger, which, based on the kind and amount of editing, can cause the minimum amount of recompilation to take place. In such an integrated environment, switching from inspection of the execution state to program editing and back could be done quite naturally and effectively.

Integration of the environment, however, should be done with discipline: the ease of editing the program directly from the debugger should not be a substitute for careful analysis and planning of the required changes.

Until the middle of 1980s, effective environments for the production of industrial software were available only for the lower level phases of the life cycle. Almost no support was provided for higher level phases. Only general-purpose editing facilities were available to produce documentation. Before the advent of interactive graphic tools, no automated support was provided for graphical design notations. Instead, drawing masks were used with paper and pencil for drawing diagrams such as HIPO charts.[1]

As more attention was devoted to the higher level phases of the life cycle, more suitable methods, notations, models, and languages were developed to support those phases. Accordingly, the need for associated tools arose. Tools of this class appeared on the market in the late 1980s. Although these tools are not yet as well established as, say, programming languages are, they promise to gain acceptance in the coming years.

At present, tools are available to support some of the methods and techniques presented in this text. Some of them are widely–or at least increasingly–used. (A sample will be presented in Section 9.3.) Others are still under evaluation or are in transition from academic to industrial use. Complete and integrated environments that support the whole life cycle are not yet a reality in everyday work. Much debate goes on about the roles such environments should fulfill. Section 9.6 will discuss the important trends in this area.

---

[1]HIPO (hierarchy-process-input-output) charts were developed by IBM as design representation schemes.

9.2 CLASSIFICATION OF SOFTWARE TOOLS
AND ENVIRONMENTS

Software tools can be classified from several standpoints, such as the level of formality they enforce, the life cycle phase to which they are devoted, and the interface they provide to the user. In this section, we present several criteria for classifying and evaluating software tools.

Interaction medium

The user can interact with computer tools in several ways. In this context, the user corresponds to the software engineer. Still, the goal of making the use of the computer as friendly and intuitive as possible is relevant and helps the software engineer feel at ease while using the environment, thereby reducing the chance of error.

The evolution of computer technology has allowed human-computer interfaces to become increasingly more friendly. Initially, human-computer interaction was mainly textual. Later, the availability of low-cost graphics terminals and the introduction of pointing devices, such as the mouse, made it possible to provide graphical interfaces. In turn, these became supportive of notations with a higher expressive power than the corresponding textual notations. Recent technologies, such as multimedia interfaces and hypertext, have the potential of making human-computer interaction even more sophisticated and productive. These new technologies are expected to have an impact on the structure of the tools that support cooperative group work during the entire life cycle.

When we talk about human-computer interfaces here, the emphasis is on the way users interact with tools: we are dealing with the *external*–i.e., syntactic–appearance of the interactive language, not its semantics. Also, our discussion is not limited to any particular class of language: one should try to provide a friendly external notation for any language, be it a specification language or a programming language. Although external notations do not add to the conceptual power of languages, they are important in practice because they may favor the adoption of such languages, by making notations more palatable to the expected users of the language. They may also reduce errors in the use of the language.

For instance, consider TDN and GDN, the two design notations introduced in Chapter 4. These are two different external representations of the same design language. But GDN may be easier to read and understand, especially if a tool is available to support browsing through a GDN document in a stepwise fashion, according to the hierarchy defined by the IS_COMPONENT_OF relation. For example, interacting with the tool, one might explode a high-level module in terms of its components, by clicking on the mouse when pointing to the module; or one might examine the text that gives the details of an exported resource by popping up a message box as a consequence of clicking on an arrow.

Exercise

9.1   Based on your experience with modern interfaces for personal computers or workstations, specify the requirements of the interface for a hypothetical tool supporting design specification using TDN or GDN. Then proceed to the design of the software architecture.

Level of formality

Software development involves the production of several documents. Each document is written in some language whose syntax and semantics can be defined in a more or less formal way. In principle, suitable processors can be associated with any language. The functionality they may provide, however, is highly dependent on the level of formality of the language. Typically, a compiler–i.e., a translation algorithm–can be built only for a language whose syntax and semantics are defined formally, while an editor can be built for any language. Similarly, one may build a specialized graphical editor for data flow diagrams, thanks to the fact that their composition rules (their syntax) are defined precisely. On the other hand, we already have observed that data flow diagrams lack a precise semantics; thus, we cannot build an interpreter for executing them. Or, more precisely, if we build an interpreter for data flow diagrams, we would implicitly define a semantics for them.

Exercise

9.2   Give some possible execution rules for DFDs.

Dependency on phase of life cycle

Most software tools only help in some specific activity that is limited to a certain phase of the software life cycle. We can, therefore, classify tools on the basis of the phase they are intended to support. For example, there are tools for writing requirements specifications, tools for specifying module interfaces, tools for editing code, and tools for debugging. We have also seen the importance of an environment that integrates tools, so that it can support a natural and smooth transition through the software development phases, according to the model that is selected for the software life cycle. As we said before, these tools are called integrated project support environments.

Dependency on application or method

In previous chapters, we stressed the concept that the application area affects the relevance of several software qualities, the selection of appropriate design techniques and methods, and, more generally, the choice of life cycle model. For instance, SA/SD was conceived mainly for conventional data-processing applications; for these applications, the friendliness of user interfaces is an important quality, because their expected end users have little or no computer background. As other examples, LOTOS[1] was introduced for specifying communication protocols, while Petri nets are particularly useful for specifying control aspects of concurrent and real-time systems; in both application areas, reliability is a key quality, and hence, so is formality of the specifications.

Some methods have their own associated, specifically designed, tools and thus affect the features provided by the tools. For example, stepwise refinement is best supported by syntax-directed editors. In fact, at some derivation point of the refinement process, the screen might display a partially derived program, as in Figure 9.1(a). At some later point, after a few refinement steps, the screen might display the program in Figure 9.1(b).

```
read (a, b, c);                    read (a, b, c);
d := b ** 2 - 4 * a * c;           d := b ** 2 - 4 * a * c;
if d ≥ 0 then                      if d ≥ 0 then
   <stat>;                            --roots are real
else                                  s := sqrt (d);
   <stat>;                            root1 := (s - b) / 2 * a;
endif ;                               root2 := (-s - b) / 2 * a;
<stat>;                            else
                                      --roots are complex
                                      <stat>;
                                   endif ;
                                   <stat>;


         (a)                                (b)
```

Figure 9.1   Stepwise derivation of a program via a syntax-directed editor.
(a) Initial program. (b) Program after some refinement steps.

Most software development methods can be made more effective by the availability of appropriate supporting tools. One should, however, not count on tools alone. Tools may enhance a method, but are not a substitute for it: by themselves, they do not provide any magic solution. One may even say that tools can be useless or even dangerous without sound underlying methods.

Software qualities do not improve just by using tools to draw bubbles and arrows, without attention to their meaning and purpose within the methodology. For instance, SA/SD has been used for a long time without supporting tools. The availability of such tools now makes the application of SA/SD easier. If we draw diagrams without following the spirit of the underlying method, we may generate confusion in a reader who knows about the method and expects our diagrams to conform to it. Similarly, a design support

---

[1]See bibliographic notes of Chapter 5.

tool based on GDN will not improve a poor design based on inappropriate choices of what is made visible through a module interface and what is hidden by the implementation.

Degree of standardization

In Chapter 7, we debated the controversial issue of standardizing software construction methods and tools. On the one hand, standardizing an item–say, a life cycle method or a tool–enhances its applicability; on the other hand, it freezes its evolution.

The more a method or a language is standardized, the more software producers are willing to invest in developing support for it. The stability of a method or language guarantees the longevity of its support tools, and this, in turn, guarantees the return on investments.

Using a standardized tool or method also guarantees a supply of people who are familiar with it and the portability of their knowledge from one project to the next. This is what happens, for example, if we base a development effort on an industrywide operating system or development methodology. Using a proprietary operating system reduces the supply of candidates and adds overhead for training.

In practice, standardization is a matter of degree. Most developers add extensions to a base-level standard.

Exercises

9.3   Discuss the pros and cons of early standardization in the case of programming languages.

9.4   Document the initial development and the evolution of the UNIX operating system, and discuss this history as a case study in standardization.

Language dependency

Some tools are associated with a particular language, and others are language independent. The former class is called *monolingual*, the latter *polylingual*. For instance, a conventional text editor or a word processor can be used as an editor for any programming or specification language, but there are specialized syntax-directed editors for, say, Pascal, and there are graphical editors for Petri nets or DFDs.

Compilers are a typical example of monolingual tools. On the other hand, an operating system like UNIX, which provides a large variety of tools in support of software development, may be viewed as a polylingual facility, since it supports program development in different programming languages. Similarly, conventional linkers are polylingual, since they support the linking of object modules derived from the compilation of programs written in different source languages. There are, however, linkers that are specialized to particular programming languages such as Ada, or Modula-2. The Smalltalk environment is a good example of a monolingual environment.

Static versus dynamic tools

Some tools neither perform nor require execution of the object they operate on, be it a program or a specification document. They are applied to such an object to create it, modify it, verify its consistency with respect to some rule, or even measure some static properties, such as length, or detect the presence of certain constructs. We call these tools *static*. For example, the parser of a programming language, which checks the syntactic correctness of a program, is a static tool. Also, a type checker for a typed language is a tool that evaluates whether the variables appearing in a program are manipulated consistently with their declared type. In Section 9.3.7, we will discuss this point further.

A tool that requires execution of the object is called *dynamic*. For example, an Ada interpreter or a Petri net simulator are dynamic tools.

Exercise

9.5   Imagine a tool that helps the programmer build correctness proofs. Is this a static or a dynamic tool? What about a symbolic interpreter?

Development tools versus end-product components

Some tools support the development of end products, but do not become part of them: once the product is complete, nothing of the tools remains in the application that is released. Other tools are kits of software components that can be included in–and become a part of–the end product. These components are usually provided as a run-time support library. The former category includes such tools as project management tools, software specification simulators, test case generators, and debuggers. Examples of the latter category are window managers, which provide run-time libraries to support the human-computer interaction, libraries of mathematical routines to be linked to an application, and a set of macros for the development of specialized spreadsheets.

Exercise

9.6   Discuss compilers and interpreters as development tools versus end-product components. Why is an interpreter useful as a development tool? Why is it more convenient to release a compiled version of an application?

9.3 REPRESENTATIVE TOOLS

In this section, we review the most important software production tools. Where appropriate, we analyze a tool with respect to the classification discussed in Section 9.2. Because of their key role in the programming environment, we examine programming languages separately in Section 9.4, where we address their special impact on, and strong connection with, the principles and methods discussed in Chapters 4, 5, and 6.

9.3.1 Editors

Since software is ultimately a more or less complex collection of documents–requirements specifications, module architecture descriptions, programs, etc.–editors are a fundamental software development tool.

With respect to the classification of the previous section, we can place editors in different categories:

- They can be either textual or graphical.

- They can follow a formal syntax, or they can be used for writing informal text or drawing free-form pictures. For instance, a general-purpose graphical editor such as Apple's MacDraw could be used to produce any kind of diagrams, including formal diagrams such as DFDs or Petri nets, but cannot perform any check on their syntactic correctness (say, an incorrect Petri net arc connecting two transitions). Similarly, we may use a word processor to write programs in any programming language, but the tool cannot help in finding missing keywords, ill formed expressions, undeclared variables, etc. In order to perform such checks, one should use tools that are sensitive to the syntax–and, possibly, the semantics–of the language.

- They can be either monolingual (e.g., an Ada syntax-directed editor) or polylingual (e.g., a generic syntax-directed editor that is driven by the specific syntax of a programming language). A conventional word processor is intrinsically polylingual.

   The Emacs editor discussed later in this chapter is capable of operating in different modes. A mode may be driven by the syntax tables of a particular language, allowing simple checks and standard indentation to be performed by the editor.

- They may be used not only to produce, but also to correct or update, documents. Thus, editors should be flexible (e.g., able to be run interactively or in batch) and easy to integrate with other tools. We have already discussed an example in which an editor was integrated with a debugger, in order to support program correction during debugging.

   As another example, consider the integration of a textual and a graphical editor. In fact, even in a graphical editor, there are parts that are more conveniently handled as text–for example, in the case of GDN, the header of an exported subprogram through a module interface, or a comment describing a module. In addition, if the GDN and TDN notations are both provided, it should be possible to enter (or modify) a description using one of these notations, and view the resulting design under the other notation.

9.3.2 Linkers

Linkers are tools that are used to combine mutually referencing object-code fragments into a larger system. Thus, they can be both monolingual (when they are language specific) or polylingual (when they can accept modules written in different languages).

Basically, a linker binds names appearing in a module to external names exported by other modules. In the case of language-specific linkers, this may also imply some kind of intermodule type checking, depending on the nature of the language. A polylingual linker may perform only binding resolution, leaving all language-specific activities to other tools.

The concept of a linker has broader applicability than just to programming languages. Typically, if one deals with a modular specification language, a linker for that language would be able to perform checking and binding across various specification modules. For example, for the design illustrated in Figure 4.10, a language-specific linker for TDN/GDN ought to be able to check interfaces according to the USES and IS_COMPONENT_OF relations.

Exercise

9.7   Give a list of functions that should be supported by a language-specific linker for TDN.

9.3.3 Interpreters

An interpreter executes actions specified in a formal notation–its input code. At one extreme, an interpreter is the hardware that executes machine code. As we mentioned in Chapter 5, however, it is possible to interpret even specifications, if they are written in a formal language. In this case, the interpreter behaves as a simulator or a prototype of the end product and can help detect mistakes in the specifications even in the early stages of the software process.

We already have observed that requirements specification often occurs incrementally, hand in hand with the analysis of the application domain. Even in such cases, it would be useful to check the requirements by suitable execution of an incompletely specified system. For example, initially one might decide to specify only the sequence of screen panels through which the end user will interact with the system, leaving out the exact specification of the functions that will be invoked in response to the user input. This decision might be dictated by the fact that, in the application under development, user interfaces are the most critical factor affecting the requirements. Thus, we would decide to check with the end user whether the interaction style we intend to provide corresponds to his or her expectations, before starting any development. This implies that the interpreter of the specifications should be able to generate screen panels and should allow us to display sequences of screen panels in order to demonstrate the interactive sessions with the application. The interpreter should tolerate the incompleteness of specifications–e.g., when no functions are provided in response to the various commands that might be entered in the fields of the screen panels. In essence, the interpreter operates like a *partial prototype*, allowing experimentation with the look and feel of the end product.

In other cases, the results of interpreting the requirements is more properly called *requirements animation*: what we provide on the screen is a view of the dynamic evolution of the model, which corresponds to the physical behavior of the specified system. For example, one might easily animate a finite state machine that is used to model the evolution of a state-changing dynamic system. If the state-changing system is a plant controlled by a computer, and a finite state machine–displayed on the terminal– describes the states entered by the plant as a consequence of commands issued by the computer, we may achieve animation by blinking the states of the finite state machine as the corresponding state of the plant is entered. The control signals may be simulated by pressing any key on the terminal, for example.

Usually, interpreters operate on actual input values. It is possible, however, to design *symbolic interpreters*, which operate on symbolic input values. As we observed in Section 6.5, a symbolic execution corresponds to a whole class of executions on input data. Thus, a symbolic interpreter can be a useful verification tool and can be used as an intermediate step in the derivation of test data that cause execution to follow certain paths.

Exercise

9.8   Give the requirements of a tool for supporting the execution of DFDs, based on the rules you gave in Exercise 9.2. The tool might provide facilities to animate specifications. You may then proceed to design and implement the tool.

9.3.4 Code Generators

The software construction process is a sequence of steps that transform a given problem description called a *specification* into another description called an *implementation*. In general, the latter description is more formal, more detailed, and lower level than the former; it is also more efficiently executable. The transformation process eventually end in machine-executable code. As mentioned in the previous section, even intermediate steps may be executable. The reason we decide to proceed through additional transformation steps is that interpreters of intermediate are, in general, slower than the interpreter of the final product (which is the computer itself).

Derivation steps may require creativity and may be supported by tools to varying degrees. A simple and fully automatic step is the translation from source code into object code. This is performed by one of the oldest and best known software tools, namely, the compiler. Other derivation steps–for example, the decomposition of modules according to the IS_COMPOSED_OF hierarchy–can be supported by tools only partially. The transformation may be recorded, and even controlled, by a suitable tool, but the choice of which lower level modules to use to implement a given higher level module is the designer's responsibility and cannot be automated fully.

With reference to the transformation-based life cycle model illustrated in Chapter 7 (see Figure 7.3), the optimizer tool is essentially a translator supporting the stepwise transformation of specifications into an implementation. As we discussed, the optimizer is only partially automated. The clerical job of recording the transformation steps is automated in order to support later modifications. We also envisioned the case where the optimizer plays the role of an intelligent assistant. The difficult and critical steps, however, cannot be automated; thus, even in this case, most of the creative tasks are the software engineer's responsibility.

Moving from a formal specification of a module to an implementation may also be viewed as a transformation that involves creative activities such as designing data structures or algorithms. Again, the clerical parts of such a transformation can be supported by automatic tools. For instance, in Section 5.7.2.1, we saw that the structure of a Larch specification may be automatically mapped into partial Pascal code, leaving the creative part of the transformation to the designer.

Examples of generalized code generators are provided by several so-called *fourth-generation* tools, which automatically generate COBOL code from a higher level language (a *fourth-generation language–4GL*). Often, such systems are centered around a data-base system. Screen panels for human-computer interaction may automatically be generated for inserting or manipulating data in the data base and for querying the data-base. Also, reports may be automatically generated from the data-base definition. In this case, the user can choose among several options to define the report formats. For instance, given a data base of employees, a report on all employees that match certain selection criteria can automatically be generated by specifying simple declarative options, with no need for defining and coding report generation algorithms.

9.3.5 Debuggers

Debuggers may be viewed as a kind of interpreter. In fact, they execute a program with the purpose of helping to localize and fix errors, by applying the principles described in Chapter 6. Modern debuggers give the user the following major capabilities:

- to inspect the execution state in a symbolic way. (Here, "symbolic" means "referring to symbolic identifiers of program objects," not that the debugger is a symbolic interpreter.)
- to select the execution mode, such as initiating step-by-step execution or setting breakpoints symbolically.
- to select the portion of the execution state and the execution points to inspect without manually modifying the source code. This not only makes debugging simpler, but also avoids the risk of introducing foreign code that one may forget to remove after debugging.
- to check intermediate assertions, as discussed in Section 6.6.

A debugger can also be used for other reasons than just locating and removing defects from a program. A good symbolic debugger can be used to observe the dynamic behavior of a program. By *animating* the program this way, a debugger can be a useful aid in understanding programs written by another programmer, thus supporting program modification and reengineering.

Exercise

9.9   Based on your experience (and frustrations) with existing debuggers, specify the requirements for an ideal debugger for your favorite programming language.

9.3.6 Tools Used in Software Testing

testing may be supported by tools in several ways. Following are the main categories of such tools:

Tools supporting documentation of testing. These tools support the bookkeeping of test cases, by providing forms for test case definition, storage, and retrieval. A typical example of a form describing a test-case, as provided by a documentation tool, is illustrated in Figure 9.2.

A documentation tool of this type supports testing not only during initial development, but also during maintenance and in regression testing (see Section 6.3.6).

Project Name:	Date of test:
Tested function:	
Tested module:	
Test case description:	
Description of results:	
Comments:	

Figure 9.2   A sample description form for test cases.

Tools supporting test-case derivation. In Chapter 6, we examined several techniques for building test cases. Such techniques can be made more effective by supporting tools, although we know that these tools cannot provide completely mechanical solutions. The main prerequisite for tools that generate test cases is the availability of a formal description. Thus, white-box techniques can be naturally implemented in a (semi)automatic way, since they apply to programs–formal descriptions of algorithms. To apply white-box techniques, we may first use a symbolic interpreter to derive path conditions and then synthesize a set of test values that satisfy those conditions and guarantee traversal of the desired paths. In the case of black-box testing, test cases can be automatically derived only if formal specifications are available.

Tools of this type are still in an early, experimental stage in industry, and few test case generators are available commercially. On the other hand, tools are available to aid software engineers in deriving test cases from informal specifications. In this case, the engineer follows the structure of the specification document and is helped in the editing of test cases which reflect that structure. For example, there are tools that allow the engineer to mark up the specification document to isolate individual functions that must be provided by the application. For each marked-up function, the tool presents the engineer with a form to be filled in, of the kind illustrated in Figure 9.2. The "tested function" field of the form may be automatically filled in by the tool with a reference to the page of the specification document where the function is specified.

Tools supporting an evaluation of the testing activity. These include tools that provide various kinds of metrics, such as the number of statements executed, the percentage of paths covered in the control flow graph, and reliability and software science measures. For example, one can decide that system testing is sufficiently complete when a certain reliability level is reached according to Musa's model.

Tools supporting testing of other software qualities. testing may be used to evaluate qualities such as performance. *Performance monitors* help keep track of, and verify, execution time, usage of main memory, and other performance-related parameters.

Exercise

9.10   Given any path condition, can you write an algorithm to synthesize test data that would satisfy the condition? Why? Why not?

9.3.7 Static Analyzers

We have seen in Chapter 6 that program analysis can be considered a verification technique that complements testing. Similarly, dynamic verification tools such as interpreters and debuggers, as well as other testing support tools, can be complemented by tools that are devoted to certifying some desired properties without executing the program. Clearly, the features offered by such tools depend highly on the type of property under consideration. For example, one might desire a deadlock detection tool, to help in designing deadlock-free concurrent systems, or a tool for timing analysis, to prove that a critical real-time system always responds to certain input stimuli within a specified time constraint. For many important properties, tools with industrial applicability are still unavailable. A particularly relevant and practical case, however, is given by flow-based tools.

Several important properties of programs can be classified as *flow properties*, i.e., properties of the variation of some relevant entities–in particular, *data* and *control*– during program execution. Thus, tools for flow analysis are static tools that characterize certain dynamic properties of the flow of data and control.

Data and control flow analyzers can help in the discovery of errors. For instance, data flow analysis can reveal the use of uninitialized variables and control flow analysis can determine whether there are any unreachable statements in the program. Such properties, however, are undecidable in the general case. Thus, the associated tools may fail to give absolutely precise answers. For example, a data flow analyzer could report some variable as potentially uninitialized, even if no execution of the program will ever reference the variable before initializing it first.

An oversimplified data flow tool for detecting uninitialized variables could work as follows:

1.   Every variable is set to "undefined."
2.   The program code is scanned. When a read instruction referring to variable x is found, variable x is set to "defined." An assignment to variable x also causes x to become defined. A reference to an undefined variable in an expression is signalled as a potential error.

Of course, there are cases where some variable may be either defined or undefined, depending on program execution (due to the use of conditional statements). Thus, a static analyzer for such an undecidable property can only state weaker properties, such as the *possibility* that some variable is uninitialized when referenced during execution. For instance, in the program fragment

```
begin
            read (x);
            if x > 0 then
                    read (y);
            end if;
            z := y;
            x := x - w;
             .
             .
             .
end;
```

it is easy to see that x is always initialized. The assignment x := x - w is certainly an error, however, because it will execute with w uninitialized. On the other hand, y may or may not be uninitialized when z := y is executed.

In a similar manner, flow analysis may reveal the presence of unreachable statements (unreachable edges in the control flow graph). This is not an error in itself, but certainly shows that the program is coded in a sloppy fashion. Moreover, it is often the symptom of the presence of an error. In the case of concurrent programming, flow analyzers can help detect the risk of deadlocks and other synchronization anomalies.

An interesting use of data flow analysis is to build specialized analyzers for particular applications. For example, in some secure applications, one should prove that no data are transferred from certain modules to other modules. To do this job, rather than use program verification, we can use data flow analysis. In this connection, one may think of a tool that allows the user to define a particular flow property of interest and automatically generates an analyzer that checks for the presence of that property.

Flow analyzers can also support program transformation, whether automatic or not. For instance, many techniques for code optimization are based on data flow analysis. We refer the reader to the specialized literature in the bibliographic notes.

Exercise

9.11 Consider the following program fragment. Is it erroneous or not? Why? Why is it unlikely that an automatic data flow-based tool can provide the exact answer to this question?

```
read (x);
if x > 0 then
        read (z);
else
        read (y);
end if;
if x > 0 then
        w := z;
else
        w := y;
end if;
```

9.3.8 User-Interface Management Tools

The recent evolution of technology has improved the friendliness of human-computer interaction greatly. This is particularly relevant when the end user has little or no technical background, but it is also appreciated by engineers. Thus, the design of good user interfaces has increasingly become an integral part of the development of software products.

Most modern user interfaces are built from a set of common concepts that have become fairly standard. Here we list some of them briefly; the reader will probably already be familiar with many of them.

Windows. A window is a virtual screen, in the sense that it provides an interface to the user for an independent activity. Several windows can be active on the screen at the same time, supporting the so-called *desktop metaphor*, i.e., the use of the screen in a manner similar to the way a traditional desk is used, with many documents in use simultaneously. Although windows may usually be overlapping, as are papers on our desks, the effectiveness of the metaphor depends on the number and size of the windows that may be shown on the screen; these factors, in turn, depend on the technology employed. In general, the larger the screen is and the higher its resolution, the better the desktop metaphor is supported. Figure 9.3 shows how a screen may look with two active windows.

Windows can be managed by the user quite naturally with the aid of a mouse. They can be dragged into different screen positions, their size can be modified, and their contents can be scrolled in order to display different portions of a document. Scrolling is performed through the use of *scroll bars*. For example, a scroll bar at the bottom of the window is used for horizontal scrolling, while a scroll bar at the right is used for vertical scrolling (see Figure 9.3).

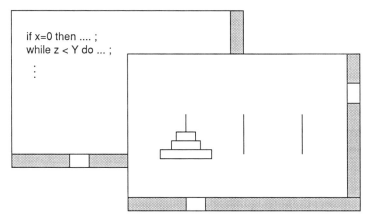

Figure 9.3   Two partially overlapping windows containing different documents (a program and a figure).

🍎	File	Edit	Format	**Font**	Document	Utilities
				Chicago		
				Courier		
				Geneva		
				Helvetica		
				New York		
				Symbol		
				Times		
				Venice		

Figure 9.4   A pull-down menu.

Icons. Icons are the graphical representation of particular objects (a document, an application, a command, etc.). By operating visually on an icon, using a mouse, the user obtains the same effect as typing a command–e.g., opening a document or running an application–with much less mnemonic effort. As a typical example, deleting a file on the Macintosh personal computer is performed by dragging the icon that represents the file into an icon that represents a trash can.

Menus. Menus have been in use for a long time as a technique for improving the ease of use of applications. Instead of requiring the user to remember a long list of commands or to consult manuals in order to use an application, the list of available commands is made visible on some portion of the screen. (This explains the "menus" metaphor.) In some cases, the execution of a command needs the specification of some options.

For instance, in a word processor, a command FONT allows the user to choose a font for symbols. After selecting the FONT option of the menu, the user may select a specific font through a *pop-up menu*, i.e., a menu that pops up once the option has been selected to display a list of available choices, or a *pull-down* menus, i.e., a menu that is opened by dragging down a selection with the aid of the mouse. Figure 9.4 shows the pull-down menu of the Microsoft Word word processor after the command FONT has been selected. By moving the mouse along the menu, one can make the appropriate selection.

Dialog boxes. In much the same spirit as menus, dialog boxes (see Figure 9.5) allow the user to specify a command and its options with no mnemonic effort and almost no need for consulting manuals. They are often used in combination with menus. For instance, the box of Figure 9.5 is an approximation of what appears on the screen after selecting the option Print from the menu File in Microsoft Word.

The "dialog" between the user and the system occurs as the user goes through the fields that specify a command (in this case, the type of printer, the number of copies, etc.). Some of these fields are automatically initialized with a default value. For example, Number of copies is set to 1 when the box appears on the screen, but the user may change its value. Some other fields represent Boolean options. For example, the option Print back to front is represented by a Boolean box in the figure. The value in the box may be changed by the user, for example, by clicking on it with the mouse. Other fields have the shape of *push buttons*. For example, OK, Cancel, and Help are push buttons that are manipulated by clicking on them with the mouse. OK is the default option, since it is highlighted; it causes the document to be printed. Cancel is used to cancel the print command. Help is used to ask for on-line directions.

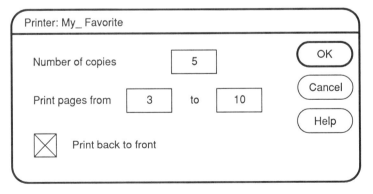

Figure 9.5   A dialog box.

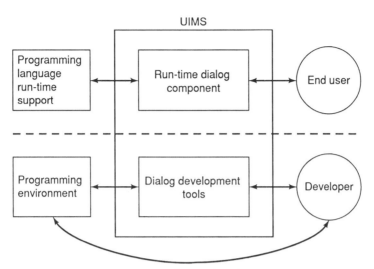

Figure 9.6   The two-component structure of a user interface management system.

Diagrams. Diagrams are graphical presentations of collections of data. Typical examples are bar charts and pie charts. Diagrams are often produced by productivity tools, such as spreadsheets, to provide a visual presentation of data.

The spread of standard user interfaces built from a common set of abstractions has spurred the development of tools that support the definition and implementation of such interfaces for different applications. For instance, some support tools for 4GLs provide primitives such as define_dialog_box, define_menu, etc. The definition of a dialog box is accomplished quite naturally in two phases. First, its logical contents are defined, i.e., the fields and types of the items represented in the box. Then, its graphical layout is defined, perhaps with the aid of a mouse.

Tools of this type are called *user interface management systems* (*UIMSs*). A UIMS provides a set of basic abstractions (icons, menus, scroll bars, etc.) that may be used to customize a variety of interfaces. It also provides a library of run-time routines to be linked to the developed application in order to support input and output. Thus, a UIMS falls both under the category of development tools and under the category of end-product components. This view is summarized graphically in Figure 9.6.

The run-time component of the UIMS manages the bindings between internal data structures of an application and the external view(s) of the application (see Figure 9.7). The internal structure of the data is the one that is manipulated by the application, while the external structure is the one that is visualized on the screen for human-computer interaction. In the example shown in the figure, the dialog component stores the values of the fields of the record entered through the dialog-box into the corresponding nodes of the portion of the tree data structure that represents the record internally.

Also, consider the important case of a window-based human-computer interaction system. We saw that each window acts as the interface of a single activity, so that one can simulate different terminals on the same screen. One virtual terminal can be devoted to editing a program, another can be used to draw pictures, yet another can be used for electronic mail, etc. In this case, the dialog development component of the UIMS is used to define the graphical shape of each window, while the run-time component provides the user with an interface to the programming language editor in one window, an interface to a graphical editor in another window, etc.

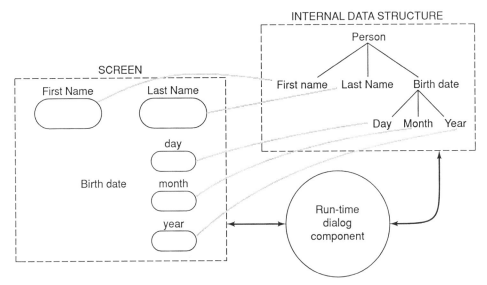

Figure 9.7   The run-time structure of a UIMS.

9.3.9 Configuration Management Tools

We have seen that software construction involves many activities and the production of many types of artifacts. According to Section 7.3.2, an important task of configuration management deals with coordinating the activities of different individuals and teams involved in software production. Furthermore, since software evolves over time, most of these documents evolve, too. And many of the documents have to exist in several versions. For instance, after performing some code optimization, we keep the original program until we have verified that the new version works, or we may maintain different versions of a manual, one for each type of machine that supports the application. Thus, configuration management also deals with controlling the change and evolution of software artifacts.

Configuration management tools should provide the following functions:

- The capability of controlling access to libraries of components, e.g., preventing two members of a software team for checking out the same component for modification at the same time.

- The capability of defining, storing, and retrieving variants and revisions of a program.
- The capability of keeping a system in a consistent state by automatically generating derived versions upon modification of some components.

These functions are integrated together with the services offered by the software engineering data base (see Section 9.3.11). We briefly discuss here how they are supported within the UNIX environment.

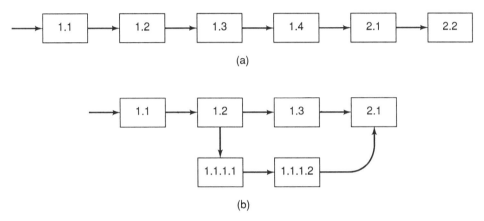

(a)

(b)

Figure 9.8   Versions in SCCS. **(a)** A sequence of revisions.
(b) A fork (variant) and a later join.

Source code control system (SCCS). SCCS is a tool whose purpose is to control and manage different versions of text files. The tool provides an efficient way of storing versions that minimizes the amount of occupied disk space. Basically, if a module is present in three versions–say, MOD 1.1, MOD 1.2, and MOD 1.3–then SCCS stores the original module–MOD 1.1–together with the changes needed to transform MOD 1.1 into MOD 1.2 and MOD 1.2 into MOD 1.3. Such modifications are called *deltas*. When a delta is constructed, SCCS asks the engineer for a description of the new version. This provides a way of informally recording the change history of a software component.

One of the facilities provided by SCCS deals with access control. In particular, SCCS allows a way to restrict the set of individuals that may create new versions–i.e., give delta commands. It also provides facilities for checking components in and out. When a component is checked out, SCCS applies all deltas. If the component is transferred to a private directory for possible change, SCCS locks it so that other engineers are prevented from performing simultaneous updates.

SCCS supports a numbering scheme for versions based on major and minor version numbers. *Revisions* are denoted by numbers in ascending order, e.g., 1.1, 1.2, 1.3, 1.4, 2.1, and 2.2 (see Figure 9.8(a)). The idea is that the minor number–the one appearing to the right of the point–is increased when changes are minor; the major number is increased for major modifications. It is also possible to create *variants* of a component, by creating a *fork* in the development history (see Figure 9.8(b)). When a fork is created, a new development stream is created, which may proceed through a sequence of autonomous revisions. At a later point, if one wishes to combine two parallel revisions into one new version–say, 2.1–this must be done manually in SCCS. RCS is another version control system under UNIX that provides, among other things, a feature to merge two development streams automatically.

Since SCCS and RCS work with any ordinary text file, they may be used not just with source programs, but also for documents, test cases, etc.

make. make is a tool that helps keep a system in a consistent state after modifications. In general, there are mutual dependencies among the components that constitute a configuration; for example, an object-code module depends on its corresponding source-code module. Once dependencies are specified, invoking make will cause the generation of new versions of any components that depend on components that have been changed.

The following make program says that the object code of system sys depends on the object code of modules mod1 and mod2 (line #1); specifically, it is obtained by linking the object codes of mod1 and mod2 (line #2). In addition, the object code of mod1 depends on its corresponding source-code module and the include file incl (line #3); it is obtained by compiling the source (line #4). A similar case holds for module mod2 (lines #5, and #6). (For those unfamiliar with UNIX, ld is the invocation of the linker, cc stands for the invocation of the C compiler, .c is a file suffix denoting C program modules, .o is the suffix for object modules and .h is the suffix for include, or *header*, files.)

```
#1.     sys : mod1.o  mod2.o
#2.         ld mod1.o  mod2.o  -o sys
#3.     mod1.o : mod1.c  incl.h
#4.         cc -c mod1.c
#5.     mod2.o : mod2.c  incl.h
#6.         cc -c mod2.c
```

Lines 1, 3, and 5 are *dependency* lines. Each dependency line specifies a *target* object that depends on a set of *source* objects (from which the target is built). Each such line in a make file is followed by a set of commands. When invoked, make checks each dependency specification and builds a dependency tree with the target (here sys) as its root. If a target depends on a source that is newer than it–e.g., a depends on b and b is newer than a–then the commands associated with the dependency line are executed, presumably to rebuild the target object from the recently modified source objects. The dependency tree is used to determine the minimum number of commands that have to be executed, as well as their order.

make uses time stamps (modification times) associated with files to evaluate dependencies. For example, if the time stamp associated with the object code of mod1 has an associated modification date that is older than the date associated with the include file incl.h, then the invocation of make will cause mod1 to be recompiled and relinked to mod2.o.

Exercise

9.12 Discuss the pros and cons of storing the complete text of the most recent version of a module along with deltas to enable the construction of the previous versions. The issues you should consider, among others, are efficiency (disk space and access time) and reliability (the possibility of recovery if a file gets damaged).

9.3.10 Management Tools

Management issues grow more critical as the complexity of a project increases. Thus, the usefulness of management tools becomes more relevant in large, multi-person projects.

As we have observed, most management principles and techniques are quite general and are not specific to software. A few such principles and techniques, however, such as cost estimation techniques, are heavily dependent on software. Accordingly, management activities may be supported by a variety of tools, some devoted to management in general, others specific to software development projects.

General management support facilities include scheduling and control tools based on PERT diagrams and Gantt charts.[1] Among the features typically offered by such tools is the capability of interacting both textually and graphically. For example, the duration of an activity and its precedence relations with other activities may initially be given textually, then may be visualized graphically, and finally may be updated by direct manipulation of a diagram on the screen. The tool may calculate the starting and ending dates for activities, may balance resource loading, may verify that a resource is not assigned beyond its maximum availability, etc.

Among software-related management facilities are cost estimation tools based on the estimation techniques presented in Chapter 8, such as the COCOMO model and function-point-based models. In the case of cost estimation, some tools allow the equation underlying the estimation method to be adapted to the specific organization, depending on historical data collected in that organization. Tools supporting source-code metrics can also provide useful information to managers.

Exercise

9.13 Design and implement (a subset of) the COCOMO model presented in Section 8.2.3.1 using an available spreadsheet. Illustrate how you can use the tool you implement as a decision support system for a manager. For example, show how the manager is assisted by the tool in deciding whether it is better to invest in hiring skilled engineers or in the adoption of modern software tools.

---

[1]The charts shown in Chapter 8 were produced with MacProject, a project scheduling tool for the Macintosh.

9.3.11 Software Engineering Infrastructures

In Section 9.1, we anticipated the need for integrated project support environments, i.e., an integrated collection of tools supporting all phases of the software production process. This requires that all artifacts produced in the process be collected in a *repository* to be accessed by different tools and saved for later use. Such a repository, together with the operations needed to manage it, constitutes the heart of the environment.

In principle, the repository is just a data base that stores data such as specifications, module interfaces and implementations, and test cases. Traditional data-base models, however, are inadequate for managing data with the complex and heterogeneous structure exhibited by software artifacts. For instance, consider the well-known relational model of a data base, where, essentially, each record is a tuple of elements. Then consider the information that represents a program, where by "program," we mean (1) the source program, which can be viewed as pure text in its internal representation–say, a parse tree–and which may be saved to facilitate incremental changes, and (2) the object code.

The source code could be considered either as a unique, huge record or as a sequence of small-grain elements, e.g., single characters. In the first case, navigation within the program, say, to retrieve all modules called by a given module would not be supported by data-base primitives. Also, it would be impossible to retrieve programs on the basis of their contents (e.g., all programs that do not contain I/O statements). Data-base primitives would only be able to retrieve the entire program, and navigation within it would be supported by *ad hoc* tools that might access its internals. At the other extreme, if one stores information at a very low level of granularity–say, single characters–the system would be extremely inefficient. In both cases, the representation would be quite unnatural, and logical links between, say, source statements and the parse tree would be quite hard to represent. Also, if we decide to save the parse tree, we could store each node of the tree as a record–or tuple–in the data base, but then traversing the tree according to its logical structure–e.g., top down or bottom up–would be quite inefficient. Even more complexity is added if we consider that the objects belonging to a software engineering environment include planning documents, specification documents, etc., many of which are written in quite different languages and formats.

The services provided by the infrastructure that we have discussed so far correspond to what is often called the *software engineering data base*. In fact, this data base includes such facilities as data (document) retrieval, updating, and composition. It should support the management of baselines, including access control to the stored components by different individuals. It should also support "browsing" through the repository, following the many relations that exist among different items. For instance, one could look for all modules that are used by a given module, for one or more implementations of a given interface of a given module, for all programmers that have been working on some subsystem, or for cost estimates related to the development of a library.

As an improvement in functionality, the infrastructure may provide some deductive capability to exploit nontrivial logical links between different items. For instance, suppose you are given a library of modules, each described by a formal interface specification and its implementation. Further, suppose you are building an application for which you identify a subproblem that you suspect has a solution already in the library.

Ideally, you should be able to search the library by providing the system with a formal specification of the model you want.

At present, however, deductive software engineering data bases of this type are more a dream than reality. The problems are studied both in the software engineering data-base area and in artificial intelligence research, namely, in such issues as semantic networks, automatic inference, and hypertexts. Artificial intelligence researchers are trying to devise effective higher-level "browsing" techniques through a network of complex and heterogeneous artifacts. Here, we cannot go deeper into these controversial issues, but refer the reader to the more specialized and advanced literature in the bibliographic notes.

Other services provided by the infrastructure may be viewed as functions at the level of the operating system, such as the following:

- Support for the concurrent execution of several related activities, possibly through a window system. The previous example of integration between debugging and editing suggests an application of such a feature.
- Support for the distribution of data and activities on different nodes of a distributed architecture. A typical architecture for an environment is in fact a set of workstations connected through a (local) network. Each node is the personal workstation of an engineer, and the infrastructure ensures the cooperation of individual nodes. Among other things, the system must provide mechanisms to support distributed transactions on the network.

Exercise

9.14 A tool like make in the UNIX environment may be viewed as a deductive facility. Given a declarative description of derived versions, the tool keeps the system in a consistent state after modifications. Critically evaluate and justify this statement.

9.4 THE ROLE OF THE PROGRAMMING LANGUAGE IN THE ENVIRONMENT

Although implementation of a system or algorithm in a programming language is not the most critical phase in software design, it certainly is the one that makes software executable. Thus, programming languages play a central role in the development environment. Not only do they contribute to program documentation and modifiability, but they can make programs checkable statically, thus contributing to their reliability.

Furthermore, modern programming languages are much more than simple coding tools: they increasingly invade the realm that is traditionally recognized as design by providing constructs that help in structuring complex systems. Consequently, the features they offer may either support, or bias, or even resist good design techniques.

Certainly, the history of programming languages cannot be read separately from that of software engineering. In this section, we review the main features of programming languages in the light of design principles and techniques. With respect to the classification of Section 9.2, programming languages are:

- a *formal* tool. In fact, their syntax and semantics are defined rigorously,[1] and this provides the basis for their execution.

- a *life cycle specific* tool. In fact, they are typically devoted to the implementation phase, although we will see that some languages may be used– at least partially–in the design and even in the specification phase of the life cycle.

- a *monolingual* tool, by definition. The capability of including modules written in different languages in the executable code may be supported by the available polylingual environment.

- a *development* tool.

In this section, we review some important concepts of programming languages. More comprehensive material is referenced in the bibliographic notes.

9.4.1 Procedural Versus Nonprocedural Languages

We already have seen an instance of the above classification in the case of specification languages and models, when we contrasted descriptive and operational approaches. We can classify programming languages in the same way. When referring to programming languages, we use the more traditional terms *procedural* (or *imperative*) and *nonprocedural*, instead of *operational* and *descriptive*, respectively.

Most traditional and widely used programming languages–such as FORTRAN, COBOL, Pascal, C, Modula-2, and Ada–are procedural in nature. They are also called *von Neumann languages* because they reflect an underlying von Neumann computer architecture. A von Neumann architecture is based on a modifiable repository of data and instructions (the main memory). Data are fetched sequentially from memory and are elaborated, and results are copied back into the memory. Thus, execution of an instruction causes a change in the state of the machine. Likewise, von Neumann languages describe computations by changes in state. States are represented by the values of variables, which, in turn, are abstractions of memory cells. The computational power in procedural languages is achieved mainly through iteration of elementary assignment statements, through which one can define the desired evolution of states.

By contrast, nonprocedural languages are based on a purely mathematical notion of variables that stand for a set of values. Programs describe functions or relations on such variables. In turn, nonprocedural languages can be classified into *functional* and *logic languages*. Functional languages like LISP, Scheme, and ML are based on the formalism of recursive functions, whereas logic languages like PROLOG are based on mathematical logic, as introduced in Chapter 5. Since predicates define relations among their arguments, logic languages are based on relations rather than functions.

---

[1]In most practical cases, the semantics is defined not formally, but implicitly by the implementation.

Without going into a deep discussion of the differences among these two classes of languages, we consider their essential aspects in the following example.

Example 9.1

Let us consider a classical example: Euclid's algorithm to compute the greatest common divisor of two positive integers. We will provide a description in both functional and logic style (The code in an operational style was given in Example 6.5.) To do this, we will use a self-explanatory syntax, without adopting any existing programming language. Figure 9.9(a) describes Euclid's algorithm in a functional style; Figure 9.9(b) describes its logic-style counterpart.

The program in Figure 9.9(a) defines the *function* GCD of variables x, y in a recursive way. The program in Figure 9.9(b) states a *relation* GCD among x, y, and z that holds if and only if z is the greatest common divisor of x and y. Both the functional and the logic description retain the rationale of Euclid's algorithm although they use a different notation from traditional ALGOL-like languages. In both cases, x, y, and z denote not memory cells, but mathematical variables.

$$\begin{aligned}
\text{GCD } (x,y) \equiv \textbf{if } x = y \textbf{ then} \\
x \\
\textbf{else if } \ x > y \textbf{ then} \\
\text{GCD } (x - y, y) \\
\textbf{else} \\
\text{GCD } (x, y - x) \\
\textbf{end if} \\
\textbf{end if}
\end{aligned}$$

(a)

$$\begin{aligned}
\text{GCD } (x, y, z) \equiv ((x = y) \ \textbf{implies } \ (z = x) \ \textbf{and} \\
(x > y) \ \textbf{implies } \ \text{GCD } (x - y, y, z) \textbf{and} \\
(y > x) \ \textbf{implies } \ \text{GCD } (x, y - x, z))
\end{aligned}$$

(b)

Figure 9.9   Euclid's algorithm in nonprocedural languages.
(a) In a functional style. (b) In a logic style.

The functional description shows how the result can be obtained on the basis of the function's arguments. The logic description just states a relation among variables. In some sense, it is more "symmetric" with respect to the variables involved: it does not distinguish between input–the arguments–and output–the results, but simply relates them in a predicate. Consequently, if we write GCD (9, 6, z), the only solution that makes the predicate true is z = 3. We could, however, also write GCD (4, 5, 3), which evaluates to false, or GCD (15, 35, 5), which evaluates to true, or even GCD (9, y, 3), which is satisfied by the infinite sequence y = 3, 6, 12, 15, 21,... In practice, however, existing interpreters of logic languages provide only an approximation to the above purely logical behavior, by restricting the kind of predicates they can handle.   ∎

A distinctive feature of logic languages is that they can often be used both as a specification and as a programming tool. As an example, we give a logic version of the sorting algorithm by straight insertion in Figure 9.10(a). In order to sort a sequence of n elements, the algorithm sorts a sequence of n - 1 elements (the original sequence except for the first element) and then inserts the first element in the appropriate position.

We assume that sequences are characterized by the operators Length, yielding the length of the sequence; First, yielding the first element of the sequence; Rest, yielding the sequence without the first element; and Cat, yielding a sequence obtained by concatenating an element with a sequence. **nil** is the empty sequence. The predicate Sort is defined in terms of the predicate Insert, which inserts an element into an ordered sequence.

$$\text{Sort (a, b)} \equiv \text{Length (a)} = 0 \textbf{ implies } b = a \textbf{ and}$$
$$\text{Length (a)} \geq 1 \textbf{ implies } (\textbf{exists } s (\text{Sort (Rest (a), s)} \textbf{ and}$$
$$\text{Insert(First(a), s, b)))}$$
$$\text{Insert (x, y, z)} \equiv \text{Length (y)} = 0 \textbf{ implies } z = \text{Cat(x, \textbf{nil})} \textbf{ and}$$
$$\text{Length (y)} \geq 0 \textbf{ implies}$$
$$(x > \text{First (y)} \textbf{ implies } \textbf{exists } w (\text{Insert (x, Rest (y), w)}$$
$$\textbf{and } z = \text{Cat (First (y), w))} \textbf{ and}$$
$$x \leq \text{First (y)} \textbf{ implies } z = \text{Cat (x, y))}$$

(a)

$$\text{Sort (a, b)} \equiv \text{Permutation (a, b)} \textbf{ and } \text{Sorted (b)}$$
$$\text{Sorted (x)} \equiv 1 \leq i < n \textbf{ implies } x (i) \leq x (i+1)$$
$$\text{Permutation (x, y)} \equiv ...$$

(b)

Figure 9.10   Two logic programs for sorting an array.
(a) An "operational" definition of insertion sort in a logical notation.
(b) A "nonprocedural" definition of insertion sort in a logical notation.

The description in Figure 9.10(a) has a strong operational flavor. This flavor is even more apparent if one compares the algorithm with the description given in Figure 9.10(b), which is closer to a descriptive specification for sorting (see also Section 5.3). The figure thus shows that one can use a nonprocedural language both in an "operational" style and in a "declarative" style.[1]

[1] One can also use a procedural language declaratively–although perhaps less naturally–if the language provides recursion.

In summary, procedural and nonprocedural languages support different programming styles or *paradigms*. The paradigms supported by nonprocedural languages are more abstract and mathematically based. Functional languages are based on the mathematical concepts of functions. Logic languages support a declarative approach. If one writes logic programs in a purely declarative fashion, without thinking algorithmically, the language becomes similar to a specification language.

Since different paradigms have their own merits, it may be useful to use more than one when appropriate, possibly for different parts of the same application. This may be done by using the facilities provided by the environment to link together parts written in different languages. Alternatively, some newer languages integrate the various paradigms in a unique framework. These languages are called *multiparadigm* languages.

Exercise

9.15   Complete the definition of the predicate Permutation in Figure 9.10(b).

9.4.2 Features for Programming In The Small

Programming in the small is the activity of programming single algorithms to solve specific problems that are likely to be subproblems of a more complex system. This kind of programming may be accomplished by using hardware-level instructions (load, jump, etc.) directly, but it is well known that the resulting programs are hard to read and, therefore, to maintain and verify. Conventional higher level languages provide many classical features, such as data structuring, arithmetic expressions, and structured control mechanisms.

The main difference between procedural and nonprocedural languages from the standpoint of controlling the flow of execution is that procedural languages are intrinsically based on iteration, whereas nonprocedural languages are intrinsically based on recursion. In practice, however, both control mechanisms are often available in both language categories. For example, a conventional language like Pascal provides recursive procedures, whereas a functional language like LISP imports a form of imperative iteration via the DO function.

Most modern programming languages are provided with a *type structure*. This feature is quite relevant both for programming in the small and for programming in the large. In the small, typing helps to prevent and detect errors, thanks to the consistency imposed between declarations and the use of variables. There is a wide consensus that *strong typing*–i.e., the ability to perform checks on the correct use of variables with respect to their type before run time–helps produce reliable programs. Perhaps surprisingly, however, most languages do not fully achieve strong typing.

Traditionally, procedural languages provide a richer type structure than do nonprocedural languages. Nonprocedural languages like LISP and PROLOG are even untyped and do not support checking prior to execution. Typing, however, has gained acceptance, and some newer functional languages, like ML, are strongly typed.

Typing mechanisms reach their full generality when they allow users to define abstract data types. When they do, however, they are features for programming in the large since abstract data types are a special kind of a module, as we saw in Chapter 4. This issue is taken up in the next section.

9.4.3 Programming Languages And Modularity

Almost all practical programming languages provide features to decompose large programs into smaller components. Even when the language does not provide specific modularization constructs, often the implementation offers *ad hoc* features that enable software developers to put together separately developed parts to form a more complex system. This is exactly what happened originally in the case of Pascal, when the language did not provide a standard notion of modules and separate compilation. (These became part of the standard only at a later point.)

As we saw in Chapter 4, modularization amounts to much more than breaking up lines of code into small pieces (e.g., 50 lines or one page). Next, we review the modularization features of some representative languages and discuss how they may support modular design.

9.4.3.1 Modularization of C programs

A C program consists of a number of data and function definitions. One of the functions must be named main; it is the function that is invoked at the start of program execution. The closest notion to a module in C is a program file. Any variables or functions declared in one file are visible only in that file, but they may be imported explicitly by other files. A special preprocessor command allows one file to "include" another file. For example, one might have a file that contains all the common data types and variables; this file can be included by all other files in the program, or selectively by any file that needs it. A file that contains only declarations is called a *header* file. By convention, the name of such a file ends in ".h", while the name of a normal C file ends in ".c".

The same modularization approach is used to integrate the use of libraries into the language. Each library is known both by the object code for the routines it supports and by a header file that contains the declarations for the supported routines. For example, the C standard input-output library has two components: the object code to be linked into programs and a header file called stdio.h that contains the declarations for all the functions that the library supports (e.g., printf and scanf). Any program that wants to use the library must include the corresponding header file so that the compiler can check for the validity of the calls in the program.

A C module may easily be used to build an abstract object (see Section 4.2.4.1). As an example, a program that uses a stack of floating-point numbers (such as the one in Example 4.8) may be structured as follows. First, we have a file, stack.c, which defines the operations allowed on a stack:

```
#include <stdio.h>
#define STACKSIZE 100
int stackp = 0
```

```
float val [STACKSIZE]
void push (float) {
.
.
.
}
float pop () {
.
.
.
}
```

The file stack.h will "export" the operations supported by the stack abstract object that we have constructed in stack.c. In this case, the header file is quite simple:

```
void push (int);
float pop ();
```

The C language supports program modularization based on files and a set of conventions. The language, however, does not enforce the conventions. For example, file stack.c above declares a variable stackp which it intends to use as a stack pointer. Any other module (i.e., file) can gain direct access to this variable simply by declaring it as an external variable. That is, any file that contains the declaration

```
extern stackp;
```

can manipulate the variable directly.

9.4.3.2 Block-structured languages

Block-structured languages are procedural languages in which a program is defined as a tree of units (or blocks). A unit is a procedure, a function, or a simple **begin-end** block. Block structure is often explained as a support for design by stepwise refinement. In fact, when an operation A is refined and two operational abstractions–say, B and C– are identified as needed in order to perform A's service, one may define a unit A with two locally nested units B and C to be invoked within A. This process leads naturally to a unique, monolithic program, i.e., a unique physical module, confirming what we observed in Chapter 4: that stepwise refinement is a programming-in-the-small method, and so is block structure.

Block structure is not an adequate mechanism for structuring large systems. Units cannot restrict the visibility of their internals; rather, all internally nested units automatically inherit the right to access all declarations appearing in outer units. Furthermore, if two units–say, procedures P_1 and P_2–need to access a common unit–say, procedure P_3–then P_3 must be declared in a suitable outer block, so that it becomes visible to both P_1 and P_2. This requirement ends up placing P_3, a lower level abstraction, at a higher level than expected.

Actually, most existing block structured-languages implicitly recognize the fact that block structure is not a true modularization mechanism, but just a structuring-in-the-small feature. Consequently, they allow the definition of external modules that may be developed and compiled separately, along with a precise definition of what each module imports and exports.

9.4.3.3 Packages and other modern modularization mechanisms

Modern procedural languages provide mechanisms that fit the principles illustrated in Chapter 4 much better than block structure does. Actually, the notation we introduced in Chapter 4 is fairly close to the *package* construct of Ada and the *module* construct of Modula-2.

Ada packages (and Modula-2 modules) may be nested within the block structure, as may any declaration; thus, they may be used as structures in the small. But they achieve their real justification as modularization mechanisms for structuring in the large. They allow module interfaces to be specified separately from their implementations. Furthermore, client modules only need to know the interfaces of the modules they use– i.e., the lists of exported services; implementation details are kept hidden and inaccessible. In both Ada and Modula-2, the USES structure is directly specified in module interfaces; neither language directly provides IS_COMPOSED_OF, although its effect can be achieved indirectly.

Although packages (and modules) are quite general modularization mechanisms, they can be used to describe abstract objects and abstract data types. Abstract objects are implemented as modules that hide a data structure in the implementation part and export the relevant operations through their interface. Abstract data types are supported by both languages in a similar way: (**limited**) **private** types in Ada and opaque types in Modula-2. In both cases, only the name of an exported type is made visible outside the module; the details of its structure are hidden in the implementation. Both constructs, however, are subject to some limitations (see Exercise 9.16). Ada also supports generic abstract data types.

Both languages allow modules to be compiled separately, but impose suitable restrictions on the order of compilation. For instance, if module M_1 uses module M_2, the interface of M_2–though not necessarily its implementation–must be compiled before compiling M_1. When a module's interface is compiled, its exported resources are kept in a compilation library, so that client modules may be type-checked for the correct use of other modules when they are compiled. This design is often called a *separate*–but *not independent*–compilation scheme; it combines the benefits of separate development and static intermodule checking.

Exercises

9.16 Consider the Ada programming language. Although its details are not externally visible, a **private** type exported by an abstract data type module must be fully described in the **private** section of the package interface. Why? For similar reasons, opaque Modula-2 types are not detailed in the interface, but data of such types are restricted to be accessible via pointers. Why? Give a critical evaluation, and contrast the choices made by the two languages.

9.17 Describe how abstract object modules may be implemented in Ada. As an example, sketch the interface and body of a module that implements a symbol table (see Example 4.2).

9.4.4 Object-Oriented Programming Languages

Object-oriented design techniques, as described in Section 4.3, are supported by several languages in different ways. All object-oriented languages have been more or less directly inspired by Simula 67, the first language to introduce the concepts of an instantiatable information-hiding module (called a **class**) and the hierarchical module organization through inheritance. These two concepts are usually recognized as characteristic of an object-oriented language. Apart from them, however, existing object-oriented languages have little in common with one another, making it impossible to provide a unique and rigorous characterization of object orientation.

One way to consider object orientation is to view it as a structuring-in-the-large scheme that can in principle be superimposed on any language or paradigm. Indeed, there are examples of object-oriented functional languages and object-oriented logic languages, but the majority of existing object-oriented languages are procedural. Object orientation adds to each of these languages the flavor of another paradigm. The object-oriented paradigm enforces a uniform view of software as a collection of abstract data-type modules organized in hierarchies of USES, IS_COMPOSED_OF, and INHERITS_FROM.

To present the important issues concretely, we use a small case study based on the object-oriented language Eiffel, leaving analysis of other languages of the family to the interested reader. One reason for the choice of Eiffel is that it supports the design principles we illustrated in Chapter 4. We will present only those features of Eiffel that are relevant to our concerns.

9.4.4.1 Language case study: the programming language Eiffel

In Eiffel, software is modularized on the basis of data. Classes implement abstract data types: they hide an internal data structure and provide access operations that are visible to clients. Apart from simple, built-in types (integer, real, character, and Boolean), all other types are defined by classes. Objects are obtained by instantiating a class. Classes are the only kind of module available in Eiffel; following the terminology of Chapter 4, this means that the only available abstraction is the abstract data-type module.

The underlying spirit of the language is that the designer should pay as much effort as possible to the identification of useful classes that may be developed, kept in a module library, and later reused. Thus, the library may be viewed as a warehouse of ready-made components, and–through the reuse of abstractions–Eiffel may be viewed as an extensible language.

Objects are created dynamically, by means of the create operation; they are accessible via variables that behave as pointers to objects. For example, an instance (object) empl of class Employee may be created by writing empl.create. The create operation is built in: it allocates an instance of the class and initializes its data fields with a default value. If the programmer so desires, a different create operation may also be provided to initialize instances differently from the default case. Objects that are created remain allocated until they become inaccessible, i.e., until no variable refers to them. Inaccessible objects are deallocated automatically by a run-time "garbage collector."

Eiffel classes can be generic–i.e., parametric with respect to a type. They may be organized according to the INHERITS_FROM hierarchy, and inheritance can be *multiple*. As we saw in Chapter 4–for example, Figure 4.14–inheritance may be used to *extend* a module, by adding new features (local data and/or procedures) to a class. Objects of the heir class may thus have some more private data slots and operations than do objects of their parent class. In the design of the heir class, the internals of the parent class are visible. It is thus possible for the heir to access the hidden data and procedures encapsulated by the parent. (Client modules are not allowed to access such secrets.)

An heir class is also allowed to redefine the services provided by its parent module. For reasons that will be clarified shortly, redefinition is required to preserve the semantics of the redefined operation. For example, we cannot redefine operation PUT_FIRST–which inserts an element in the first position of a list–as an operation that inserts an element in the last position.

The notion of preserving the semantics through redefinition is a hard one to enforce. Eiffel does this in part via syntactic restrictions on the header of the redefined subprograms and in part via semantic restrictions based on an embedded specification language. Briefly, the specification language allows subprograms defined in a class to be given a precondition and a postcondition. The precondition is a constraint on the clients' use of the operation; the postcondition is a statement of the desired effect of the operation that must be enforced by the operation's implementation, assuming that the precondition holds upon invocation.

Let pre_P and $post_P$ respectively be the pre- and postcondition of an operation defined in the parent module, and let pre_H and $post_H$ respectively be the pre- and postcondition of the corresponding redefined subprogram in the heir module. Then the semantics-preservation rule may be stated as

$$pre_P \textbf{ implies } pre_H$$
$$post_H \textbf{ implies } post_P$$

This means that (1) all possible invocations of the original operation are still valid for the redefined operation and (2) the resulting state after invocation of the redefined operation still satisfies the assertion stated by the parent module.

Exercise

9.18 Discuss how the Eiffel notion of preservation of semantics may be verified. State precise assumptions on the features you allow in the assertion language (e.g., full first-order predicate calculus).

With inheritance, the heir also has the capability to change the features that it exports from its parent. The rationale here is that the designer of the heir class has access to the internals of the parent class and thus may decide to modify the visibility rules of the parent class through definition of an heir module (This is exactly the same rationale by which Eiffel allows heirs to access the secrets of their parents.). For example, let $S_P = \{s_1, s_2,..., s_N\}$ be the set of services defined by a module P, and let E_P be a subset of S_P

denoting the exported features. An heir module is free to keep some elements of E_P (possibly redefined) as hidden secrets; also, some (possibly redefined) elements of $S_P - E_P$ may be exported by the heir module.

An important aspect of Eiffel is that it allows variables to refer at run time to objects of different types. Thus, when we write an instruction of the type obj.op to execute operation op on the object referred to (pointed at) by obj, we do not know statically exactly what the type of obj really will be (i.e., what class the object pointed at by obj is an instance of) when the instruction will be executed. This feature is called *polymorphism*. Since we do not know statically the class of the object, we must perform the binding between the object and its class at run time; this form of binding is called *dynamic binding*.

Intuitively, polymorphism provides flexibility, but may be a source of reduced reliability: if we do not know the class (i.e., the type) of an object statically, how can we enjoy the benefits of static type checking? Nevertheless, Eiffel has chosen to try to reconcile polymorphism and dynamic binding with static checking. To accomplish this, Eiffel constrains polymorphism by controlling it through inheritance.

If p refers to an instance of class P and h refers to an instance of P's heir class H, then Eiffel allows one to perform the assignment

   p := h

after which p refers to the same object referred to by h. Once this assignment is made, dynamic binding ensures that the effect of a statement like

   p.op

results in the execution of operation op as defined by class H, i.e., the class of the object that is currently bound to p. Because of the restrictions imposed on redefinitions of operations in heir modules, Eiffel can type-check the previous statement statically, ensuring that operation op is never applied to an object that cannot execute it.

As we mentioned, Eiffel supports multiple inheritance. The language also provides renaming facilities, in order to avoid name clashes among resources imported from several parent classes.

Exercises

9.19   Eiffel forbids the assignment of a reference to a class to a reference to one of its heir classes. In the previous example, h := p would be invalid. Justify this restriction in the light of static checking and dynamic binding.

9.20   Consider the class hierarchy illustrated in Figure 4.14. Let e be a pointer currently bound to an object of class EMPLOYEE; similarly, let t and a be two pointers currently bound to instances of classes TECHNICAL_STAFF and ADMINISTRATIVE_STAFF, respectively. What are the valid assignments between the three pointers in Eiffel? Why?

Example 9.2

To illustrate the spirit of the language further, we present an Eiffel class Employee corresponding to the TDN example shown in Figure 4.14. We also present a subclass, Administrative_Staff. We modify the example of Figure 4.14 by exporting only the operations first_name, last_name, age, salary, where, and assign; we also export an operation create, discussed below.

```
class Employee
export first_name, last_name, age, where
--feature create is exported by default
feature
        first_name: string;
        last_name : string;
        age: integer;
        where: Site;
        --class Employee is a client of class Site
        create (f, l: string, s: Site) is
        require not company.exists (f, l)
        --it requires that no employees with the same first
        --name and last name exist.  This precondition must be
        --guaranteed by client modules; otherwise, a run-time exception
        -- occurs (and is handled in a manner that is not described). If
        --the exception is not raised, we create an employee whose
        --first name and last name are f and l, respectively, and we
        --assign the employee to Site s
        do
            first_name := f;
            last_name := l;
            s.assign (first_name, last_name);
        end
end Employee

class Administrative_Staff
export  first_name, last_name, where, do_this
--note that here we assume that age is not visible to clients
--also, we assume that a new operation do_this is provided by the
--subclass
inherit Employee
feature
procedure do_this (f: folder)
  .
  .
  .
end do_this;
  .
  .
  .
end Administrative_staff
```

The foregoing code should be self-explanatory; where necessary, we have inserted a few comments. As we already have observed, routines encapsulated in a class do not mention in their statements the object they operate upon; implicitly, such an object is the current object. For instance, if we write

> empl.create(f,l)   (empl is an object of class Employee)

the instruction

> first_name := f

assigns the value of f to the field first_name of the current object referred to by empl.

Note that the routine create encapsulated in the module Employee replaces the built-in procedure with the same name. The built-in routine would just allocate an instance and initialize the fields to the default values (the empty string for first_name and last_name, zero for age, and the null reference to the field where, denoting the fact that the employee is not assigned to any site). The programmer-defined routine create assigns an employee a first and last name, a unique identifier, and an initial salary. (Thus, the routine corresponds to the operation HIRE in Figure 4.14.)

Finally, no USES clause is required in Eiffel, since all classes are considered global and their interfaces are globally visible.   ∎

9.4.5 Programming Languages And the Handling of Anomalies

We have seen in Section 4.4 that anomalous situations may occur during execution, even if much care was applied in the design of a program. Anomalies must be handled carefully, possibly by applying separation of concerns and incrementality, e.g., one can first deal with normal execution, and then consider exceptional cases. It is, however, still quite controversial whether and, if so, how techniques to cope with exceptions (*exception-handling* features) should be embedded in a programming language. In fact, only some modern procedural programming languages–Ada and Eiffel are two examples–exhibit such features. In the past, the most notable case was PL/1.

In general, the main objections to embedding exception-handling features in programming languages have to do both with methodology–what is a clean design structure for exception handling?–and with semantic definition and efficient implementation of the programming language. Even the design principles illustrated in Section 4.4 are not accepted universally.

The exception-handling mechanism of a programming language provides the following capabilities:

- **Declaration of exceptions,** to declare a possible anomalous situation and give it an identifier. Moreover a set of built-in exceptions usually exists, such as Division_By_0 and Memory_Overflow.
- **Raising of exceptions**, to signal the actual occurrence of the anomalous condition. Such an occurrence is implicitly signalled in the case of built-in exceptions; for instance, Division_By_0 is automatically signalled by the

hardware. User-defined exceptions must be raised explicitly, by executing the statement RAISE <exception_identifier>.

- **Handling of, and recovery from, exceptions**. Once an exception has been signalled, an appropriate action must be executed in response to it. Quite possibly, the action may result in a recovery from the exception, say, by locally putting the system in a consistent state in such a way that normal execution may be resumed. In this case, the client does not even realize that an exception has occurred. If locally-initiated recovery is impossible, however, the exception may be propagated to another module–perhaps a higher level module in some abstraction hierarchy–notifying that module of the failure of the current operation, so that appropriate recovery may be taken at the higher level. Or, the higher level module may, in turn, propagate the exception further up the chain of modules.

  The choice of propagation strategy is one of the important semantic issues that faces the language designer in defining exception handling. Often, propagation follows the currently active USES chain: control is first transferred to the client, then to the client's client, and so on. In the worst case, the whole program aborts because of an unrecoverable exception that was propagated all the way up to the main control routine. (Even this is better than continuing execution in an inconsistent state.)

As we have observed, languages that provide exception handling do not adopt the same schemes; rather, they differ more or less sharply in many semantic aspects. As in the case of object-oriented languages, instead of providing a complete comparative review, we present here a small case study based on the Ada programming language and leave the study of other languages to the interested reader.

9.4.5.1 Language case study: exception handling in Ada

In Ada, built-in exceptions are raised by the underlying abstract machine that executes a program; user-defined exceptions are raised explicitly, e.g.,

```
raise ANOMALY_1;
```

Exception handlers can be attached to a subprogram body, a package body, or a block, after the keyword **exception**, as in the following:

```
begin
      .
      .
      .
exception
        when ANOMALY_1 => . . .;
        when ANOMALY_2 => . . .;
              .
              .
end;
```

If the unit that raises the exception provides a handler for it, control is transferred to the handler, the handler is executed, and then the unit terminates. If the currently executing unit does not provide a handler, the exception is propagated. For example, if the currently executing unit is a subprogram, the subprogram returns and the exception is reraised at the point the subprogram was called.

Ada makes it straightforward to implement an organized system shutdown as a consequence of an unrecoverable error. To shut down a system, the handler associated with the unit that raises the exception would clean up its local state (e.g., close all open files and reset the values of some variables), then transfer control to its caller, which, in turn, would clean up its own state, and so on.

It is also possible to repair errors in Ada, so that the caller is not notified of an exception in the callee. Error repair may be done by implementing appropriate actions in the **exception when** clause that is activated when an exception is raised. This is done differently in the Eiffel language, where one can perform a **retry** action in the course of exception handling. The **retry** tries to execute the subprogram that raised the exception, after performing suitable repair actions that modify the state of the unit.

How does Ada support–or enforce–a disciplined way of designing robust software that responds to adverse events? In Section 4.4, we proposed a method of doing this that was based on the principle that either a module performs its services as stated in the module's interface, or it signals an anomalous behavior to its client. In the latter case, it means that the module was unable to repair the error, and it so notifies the client.

Although this disciplined approach may be implemented in Ada, the language does not enforce it. For example, the language allows a module in which the **exception when** clause does nothing and lets the module return quietly to its client without recovering from the error and without propagating the exception, but just ignoring it!

Existing exception-handling features in languages such as PL/I, CLU, Ada, and Eiffel differ widely, pointing the fact that there are currently no universally accepted methods of exception handling.

9.4.6 Programming Languages And Concurrency

Traditionally, concurrency is not supported by the programming language; rather, it is provided by the operating system or even by directly accessing the underlying machine (via interrupts). Language-supported concurrent programming features, however, would have many benefits. Such features not only would support the construction of traditional concurrent systems–such as control systems and operating systems–but also would speed up even many sequential algorithms by exploiting the facilities for parallel computing that are now supplied by many hardware architectures. Many different constructs have been defined in the literature for concurrent programming. Again, however, there is little consensus as to what such constructs should be like; consequently, we are yet a long way from standardization.

A low-level feature provided by a few languages is the *coroutine* construct of SIMULA 67 and Modula-2. This construct introduces a kind of "pseudoconcurrency" on a conventional sequential machine. Coroutines run one at a time, so that there are no concurrently executed units. One can, however, simulate concurrency by *interleaving* the execution of coroutines. For instance, coroutine C1 runs up to a given point of its code, where it transfers control to coroutine C2. Then C2 transfers control to C3, which, in turn, runs for a while until it goes back to C1, which *resumes* execution from the state wherein it transferred control to C2, and so on.

```
task CHAR_BUFFER is
--This is the interface
        entry PUT (ITEM:in CHAR);
        entry GET (ITEM:out CHAR);
end ;

task body BUFFER_HANDLER is
--these are initializing declarations
        N: constant INTEGER := 100;
        CONTENTS: array (1. .N) of CHAR;
        IN, OUT: INTEGERrange 1. .N := 1;
        TOT: INTEGERrange 0. .N := 0;
begin
    loop
        select
        when TOT < N =>
            accept PUT (ITEM: in CHAR) do
                    CONTENTS (IN) := ITEM;
            end ;
            IN := (IN mod N) + 1;
            TOT := TOT + 1;
        or
        when TOT > 0 =>
            accept GET (ITEM:out CHAR) do
                    ITEM := CONTENTS (OUT);
            end ;
            OUT := (OUT mod N) +1;
            TOT := TOT - 1;
        end select ;
    end loop ;
end BUFFER_HANDLER;
```

Figure 9.11   A guardian task in Ada.

Most modern languages that support concurrency use a *process* as the basic unit of concurrent execution. A process may be executed asynchronously with respect to other processes; the decision whether logical concurrency is simulated by sharing a unique physical processor according to some policy or whether physical parallelism is achieved by allocating different processes to different processors is a matter left to the implementation. Referring to the concepts illustrated in Section 4.6, in some languages, such as Concurrent Pascal, processes synchronize with each other through passive objects (monitors); in other languages, such as Ada, cooperation among processes is regulated through active processes that act as guardians of resources.

Concurrency has also been introduced in nonprocedural languages; for example, Parlog86 is a concurrent logic language based on PROLOG.

9.4.6.1 Language case study: concurrency in Ada

In this section, we provide a brief case study based on the Ada programming language. This case study complements the discussion we started in Section 4.6.1.2 concerning the module CHAR_BUFFER.

The task CHAR_BUFFER is described by its *interface*–i.e., the information that other tasks need to know in order to communicate with it–and its *implementation*. The two parts are shown in Figure 9.11. The interface of the task BUFFER_HANDLER specifies GET and PUT as *entries*. Entries may be called by other tasks in much the same way as procedures are called. Unlike procedures, however, entry calls are executed only when the task owning the entry is ready to accept the call by executing the corresponding **accept** statement. As we observed in Section 4.6.1.2, at this point the two tasks perform a rendezvous. If the calling task issues the call before the task that owns the entry executes the corresponding **accept**, the calling task is suspended until the rendezvous occurs. Similarly, a task is suspended if it executes an **accept** statement before the corresponding call is issued.

A task may accept entry calls from more than one task; consequently, each entry is associated with a queue of suspended tasks. The queue is handled in a first-in, first-out order. The **accept** statement is similar to a procedure: the statements between the **do**...**end** keywords specify the action to be performed upon rendezvous. After the statements are executed, the caller and the callee proceed concurrently.

In the example in Section 4.6.1.2 (see Figure 4.22), **accept** statements are enclosed within a **select** statement, which specifies several alternatives, separated by **or**, that can be chosen in a nondeterministic way. That is, the first **accept** statement may be chosen when TOT < N (i.e., when the buffer is not full), and the second may be chosen when TOT > 0 (i.e., when the buffer is not empty). When 0 < TOT <N, either operation is applicable; thus, the language leaves the choice nondeterministic.

To support the implementation of real-time systems, Ada provides features to deal with time explicitly. The main construct of this type is the *timed entry call*, through which a calling task may wait for the occurrence of a rendezvous for only a limited amount of time, thus realizing the concept of a *time-out*. For instance, the following fragment allows a process to suspend execution, waiting to write into a buffer, for up to 200 milliseconds; after this time, an alternative action is chosen:

```
select
        BUFFER_HANDLER.APPEND (X);
or
        delay 0.2;
        DO_SOMETHING_ELSE;
end select;
```

We observed earlier that language constructs for concurrency and real-time are not yet standardized. One of the reasons for this is that there are still subtle problems that arise when we try to define the semantics of such constructs formally. Another reason is that it is difficult to achieve efficient implementations of those constructs in a generally portable way.

9.4.7 Programming Languages And Verification

In general, good design techniques–and languages that support them–may improve software qualities. In particular, programming languages can favor the production of correct programs by supporting powerful static checks. They can also improve verifiability by providing simple control structures and suitable modularization primitives that make reasoning about the behavior of programs simple, local, and incremental.

A few languages allow the programmer to add assertions to programs along the lines suggested in Sections 5.6.2, 6.4.2, and 6.6. This facility allows a specification language (an assertion language) to be integrated with the programming language; if tools are available to deal with assertions, we can then assess the correct behavior of the program with respect to the stated predicates.

As we have observed, there are two ways to use assertions: *proving* the correctness of the program with respect to the assertions and *monitoring* the assertions at run time to detect whether they are violated. In the first case, a tool must be available to verify the program's correctness; the tool would be interactive and would support verification along the lines illustrated in Section 6.4.2. In the second case, assertions are turned into predicates that are checked at run time.

A few tools are available to aid in proving the correctness of programs; in most cases, however, the programming language and its assertion language were not defined jointly. Rather, the assertion language is an *ad hoc* language based on first-order predicate calculus that is used to instrument the program under analysis; the instrumented program is then fed into the interactive tool to verify its correctness. Gypsy is a notable example of a language with an integrated environment that supports program correctness proofs.

In Eiffel, too, the assertions are integrated with programming language constructs. As we saw in Section 9.4.4.1, one can associate pre- and postconditions with the operations exported by a class. It is also possible to associate invariants with the class, i.e., predicates that are intended to hold before and after any operation that is performed on class instances. In addition, it is possible to insert intermediate assertions and loop invariants in the code. All these assertions must, of course, obey the syntax of the assertion language–a highly restricted subset of first-order predicate calculus.

The standard Eiffel environment does not provide any specific tool for verifying program correctness, but it does provide a way of turning assertions into run-time checks, as a compiler option. At run time, any violation of an assertion is handled by the exception-handling mechanism defined by the language. When the designer feels confident that the module does not violate the stated assertions, modules may be compiled with the run-time check option off. In such case, the assertions remain in the source code for documentation purposes.

Exercise

9.21 Disabling run-time checks after the testing phase, when the program is delivered to the customer, is like sailing in open sea without a life jacket, after a period of training with the life-jacket on in a small bay, in ideal weather conditions. This analogy is based on a remark made by Hoare [1973]. Comment briefly on this analogy.

9.4.8 Programming Languages And Software Design

An appropriate programming language can support or even enforce good design techniques, but one can write bad programs using a good language, as well as good programs using a poor language (though, with more difficulty). Thus, the unavailability of the "ideal" programming language is not a valid excuse for a poor design structure or a sloppy programming style.

Here are a few examples of disciplined programming practices that may be applied to languages that do not support them directly:

- If one uses a block-structured language that does not provide external modules, such as certain versions of Pascal, one can still develop outer level procedures as if they were separate modules, although they cannot be compiled separately. If such procedures access global variables, one may complement their headers with comments that explicitly state which global variables are read and/or written by the procedure.

    Also, one can still design information-hiding modules, even though they are not physically visible as such through language-defined constructs and even though the language cannot enforce protection of hidden secrets. For example, in order to implement an abstract object, one may use comments to bracket a set of procedures that represent access operations and use a comment to denote the hidden internal data structure. A similar solution may be adopted to document abstract data types.

- In FORTRAN or C, and in general, one may insert comments in subprogram headers to document the underlying USES relation.

- Program assertions can be quite useful, even when they are just treated as comments in the program. They can help a human reader in analyzing the program, and they can be (manually) turned into test cases.

- Even in an unstructured, low-level language, one may use comments and indentation to illustrate the conventions that were followed in structuring a program, since these conventions might not be clear from the code. For example, comments may be used to document an assembly language loop; or they may specify what the type of an operand should be in an untyped language.

Obviously, the benefits of these approaches will be far less than could be obtained by using languages that directly support the desired features. Even worse, there are cases where such an approach can be rather hard, if not impossible, to implement. An example is the use of sophisticated object-oriented design techniques such as inheritance, polymorphism, and dynamic binding in non-object-oriented languages.

9.5 A SAMPLER OF TOOLS AND ENVIRONMENTS

In this section, we present a few case studies of industrially available and more or less widely used tools and environments. Our choices are of different kinds and are strongly subjective. Our goal is not to provide a comprehensive review of the state of the art of available tools and environments–that would deserve an entire book by itself, and our analysis would quickly become outdated, due to the rapid evolution of the field. Nor is our aim to present a selection of the "best" state-of-the-art representatives. Rather, we seek to give the reader a flavor of what is currently available, following different viewpoints and evaluation criteria.

We start in Section 9.5.1 by presenting a system that is centered around the requirements specification and design phases of the life cycle and that supports a well-established, traditional methodology. Section 9.5.2 reviews the most typical features of UNIX, which may be viewed as an environment focused on the implementation phase of the life cycle. We then present, in Section 9.5.3, two rich environments, centered around a specific programming language, that are particularly suitable to exploratory, prototype-based software development. Finally, in Section 9.5.4, we illustrate an example of an infrastructure that is defined to support the design of integrated environments.

9.5.1 Teamwork

Teamwork is an integrated set of tools that support the higher phases of the software development process: requirements specification and design. It is mainly based on the SA/SD methodology. As it has evolved, it has actually become a *family* of environments devoted to different classes of applications, mainly traditional data processing and real-time applications.

Since Teamwork is based on SA/SD, its core features deal with DFDs (see Section 7.3.1.1) DFDs may be created by means of an interactive graphical editor that performs some automatic consistency checks against the "syntax" of DFDs. Specifically, the editor verifies that no arrows are left dangling, that all objects–bubbles, data stores, arrows, etc.–are properly identified, that every bubble has at least one incoming and one outgoing arrow, and other properties. Since the tool may be used incrementally, it allows intermediate versions of a document to be incomplete. For instance, one can write a first version of a DFD without completely defining the identifiers of all objects. In such cases, the system simply warns the user of the inconsistency.

Teamwork supports stepwise refinement, which is a fundamental method associated with the SA/SD methodology. In particular, any DFD process–represented by a bubble–can be refined by a more detailed DFD, as we suggested in Section 5.5.1 (see Figures 5.4 and 5.5). The system checks for consistency of refinements, in the sense that all data flows coming into and going out of the original bubble must be input and output arrows of the refined DFD.

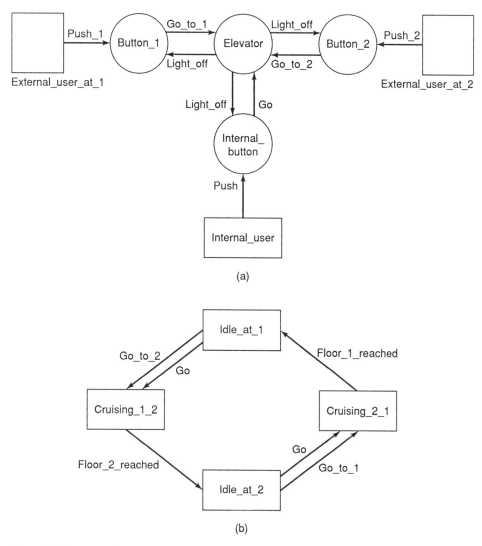

(a)

(b)

Figure 9.12   An elevator system with two floors, one elevator, external buttons at each floor, and internal button within the elevator. **(a)** DFD. **(b)** FSM.

In its version specialized for real-time applications, called Teamwork/RT, the environment provides the following enrichments:[1]

- It extends DFDs via control flows, as suggested in Section 5.5.1.
- It allows the actions executed by a process to be specified by means of finite state machines (FSMs). For instance, suppose one needs to specify an elevator

---

[1] We take some minor liberties in the description of the tool.

system consisting of just one elevator and two floors. Then one may use the DFD of Figure 9.12(a) to describe the elements upon which the system is based. Or, alternatively, one may specify how the "elevator process" evolves by providing the FSM of Figure 9.12(b). Both figures are self-explanatory.)

Because of the lack of semantic rigor of its underlying DFD model, Teamwork is unable to support any deep semantic analysis of specifications, such as execution. This is a major drawback of semiformal models, as we pointed out in Chapter 5.

A specialized version of Teamwork for information systems, Teamwork/IM, supports ER modelling. Other specialized tools are available to support the design phase of the life cycle and the transition to coding through several members of the Teamwork family. In particular, Teamwork/SD supports a structured design methodology (see Section 7.3.1.1) and Teamwork/ADA is a design and coding tool for Ada.

Teamwork offers a modern user interface. Besides supporting graphical, interactive editing, it supports the use of multiple windows, allowing the user to handle more than one diagram on the screen at the same time, e.g., a context diagram and its refinement. Textual and graphical information are integrated by allowing them to coexist in a unique diagram–say, a DFD with textual identifiers and comments–and by handling them separately in different windows. Commands are given through pop-up menus.

Teamwork's infrastructure consists of a fairly classical data dictionary called Teamwork/ACCESS, in which all objects that comprise a system–DFDs, FSMs, decision tables, specifications of data flows, etc.–are stored automatically as they are defined. The dictionary supports simple functions, such as consistency checks (e.g., making sure there are no duplicate definitions) and automatic report generation (e.g., which processes access a given data store). No sophisticated functions of the type suggested in Section 9.3.11 are provided. Also, a fairly classical configuration manager supports the management of different versions of the documents.

Exercise

9.22   Try to expand the elevator example of Figure 9.12 to several floors and several elevators. Discuss the difficulties you encounter, and outline how they may be mitigated.

9.5.2 The UNIX Environment

The UNIX operating system, born in the late 1960s, has grown to contain an increasingly rich and widely used collection of software development tools. The initial system was a small kernel that provided a basic set of mechanisms. The simplicity of the system and its widespread acceptance have resulted in the development of a large number of interrelated tools that now comprise the UNIX environment.

We have already discussed SCCS, RCS, and make as examples of tools that support software evolution. Besides these, UNIX supports several program development tools, including several interactive (e.g., ed, vi, and emacs) and batch-oriented editors (e.g., sed and awk). Interactive editors are useful for the initial creation of, or small changes to, documents, while batch editors are better suited for bulk changes to documents.

Software development in C is supported at various levels: editors for initial program creation and later modification; lint, a static analysis tool that reads a collection of C program files and reports on any anomalies that it finds (e.g., parameter mismatches); cflow, a tool that produces the control flow structure of a C program; cb (C beautifier), a "pretty-printer" for C; ctags, a tool for making and using a cross-reference listing of symbols used in a collection of C programs; the aforementioned make, SCCS, and RCS; and, of course, the usual compiler, linker, and debugger.

UNIX has a very simple–but surprisingly successful–notion for supporting the integration of tools: by convention, each tool reads its input from a standard input device and writes its output to a standard output device. The input-output devices may be assigned dynamically before a program is run. A built-in mechanism, called a *pipe*, can be used to combine several programs together by connecting the output of one program to the input of another. UNIX does not support any notion of a common, integrated store through which different tools may communicate. Files and pipes are the only mechanisms used for this purpose.

9.5.2.1 Emacs

Emacs is an advanced screen-oriented editor that is widely available on UNIX and personal computer systems. We discuss it here because it is an interesting example of how an extensible, customizable system can be integrated into a software environment.

In addition to providing basic editing features, Emacs allows its commands to be redefined or customized. For instance, the single command "justify text" or "indent text" is dependent on the current *mode*. The user can define new modes, which may be dependent on a number of parameters–for example, a specific programming language such as C or LISP, or a particular text formatter such as troff or tex. Using the mode definition facility, one can customize Emacs to act as a kind of syntax-directed editor for different programming languages or, in general, for particular document formats. We have previously discussed text editors as general tools that can be used to create documents of various types, e.g., programs, specifications, and manuals. The customizability of emacs allows it to be tailored for use in the different phases of software development, for instance, to enforce standard structures for documents.

Emacs also allows different facilities to be called up from within the editor. For example, the user can run a spell-checker on the buffer being edited, or sort the contents of the buffer, or produce "tag lists" to be used for cross-referencing documents. One can call up a window in which the operating system shell is run. The contents of the buffer associated with this window (the commands and their results) are editable, like the contents of any other buffer. In this way, Emacs is able to integrate itself with other tools in the environment. Besides this, Emacs is able to integrate several separate tools as described below.

Any given operating system command may be run from the editor. This feature is used in an interesting way to make the editor an integral part of a software development environment. A command can be issued to run the make utility for rebuilding the product

that the user is currently editing. After warning the user about saving all the buffers that
have been modified, make is run. If any errors are found during compilation, the source
file is automatically brought up in a new window, with the cursor pointing to the line that
contains the first compilation error. There is a command for moving on to the next error.
In this way, the user can systematically inspect and correct all errors before running
make again.

Emacs has a LISP-like language that can be used to define new commands. This
programming language power allows very sophisticated commands to be defined.

9.5.2.2 The X Window System

At the time UNIX was developed, the user-interface technology was based on the
use of "dumb" terminals connected to a minicomputer. The technological advances of the
last decade have changed this basic configuration: users are increasingly using bit-
mapped displays on workstations connected over networks, running applications on
remote machines. The X Window System is a recent addition to the UNIX set of tools
which tries to address the challenges posed by this new environment: How does an
application writer write a portable application that can use the variety of display monitors
that are available, and how can the application run in a network environment?

X is a network-transparent window system that can be used to build user interfaces.
A user is assumed to be using a display on a workstation, but perhaps running an
application on a different machine. An application is composed of two components: a
front end that interacts with the user–the user interface itself–and a back end that
performs the core functions of the application. The X Window System allows the two
components to run on different machines and still communicate with each other.

The user interface is built using facilities provided by X (e.g., windows). User
interactions with the interface component are communicated to the back end, if
necessary, through the *X server*. An X server runs on the machine with the display (and
thus the user interface). Any communication between the application and the user goes
through the X server. The application, which does not need to know whether the user is
on the same machine or not, sends all its output to the X server and receives its input
from the X server. The X server maintains the (textual and graphical) interaction with the
user.

The X model of interaction with the user, of course, imposes a certain structure on
the application. For example, X provides basic mechanisms for creating windows,
initializing them, requesting input from them, and sending output to them. In fact, the
fundamental part of X is the definition of the syntax and semantics of a protocol that
applications and servers can use to communicate with each other.

Just as the UNIX system is a basic system that provides an infrastructure on top of
which different tools can be built, X provides the infrastructure on top of which useful
tools can be built for the support of user interfaces. In particular, UIMS and user-
interface tool kits may be built on top of the basic facilities and protocol provided by X.

We can think of the user interface of an application as having two components: the
interaction with the user which is internal to the application (for example, typing text into
a text editor); and the interaction that is external to the application (for example, moving
the application window or changing its size). The external interaction is built into some

window systems. X, on the other hand, does not define an external user interface at all. Instead, it provides the protocol for building different styles of interactions rather than prescribing a particular interface. The idea is that higher level libraries or tool kits can be built on top of X to provide application-level abstractions for building user interfaces. These tool kits, among which are the X Toolkit, or Xt, and the tool kit InterViews, can favor particular styles of interface and interaction.

The *X Toolkit* consists of two components: a set of user-interface components, called *widgets*, and a layer on top of X windows called Intrinsics. The Intrinsics layer can support different widget sets. A particular widget set is the X Widget Set and some typical widgets are buttons, scroll bars, and arrows. The Intrinsics layer allows for creating, destroying, and managing widgets. The communication between the X server and the application are based on an *event* model. The application registers its interest in certain events and asks the server to call particular functions when these events occur. Most X applications are endless loops, waiting on events. Events may occur as direct or indirect results of user actions (e.g., pushing a mouse button or typing text). An event may tell the application that the window has just been exposed and the application needs to provide the data necessary to refresh the window.

Using the X Toolkit imposes a certain structure on the application, characterized, in general, by the following sequence of events:

1.   Connect to the X server and initialize the Intrinsics layer.
2.   Create the necessary widgets.
3.   Register the (application-defined) event handlers that respond to widget events.
4.   Create the windows needed by the widgets.
5.   Enter the event loop.

Every time the X server detects an event, such as the pressing of a mouse button or a keystroke, for which the application has registered a handler, it calls the application to handle the event.

InterViews is another tool kit built as a layer above the window system. Completely separating the application from the window system, Interviews uses the mechanisms of the window system to provide higher level user-interface abstractions to the application. Two kinds of abstractions are provided: basic components and composition mechanisms. The latter are used to combine the former. Examples of basic components are messages, menus and buttons. Examples of composition mechanisms are a *box*, which tiles its components in a non-overlapping fashion, a *tray*, which allows overlapping components, and a *deck*, which stacks its components so that only one is visible at any given time. For example, a dialog box may be composed of a message and several push buttons, composed in a box. The relationship between UNIX, X Windows, InterViews, and the application is shown diagrammed in Figure 9.13.

Similar in spirit to InterViews is the *Motif* widget set from the Open Software Foundation. This widget set supports *primitive* widgets, such as buttons and arrows, and *container* widgets, such as row-column, bulletin board, and form widgets, that can contain child widgets. Motif comes with a style guide to help application developers write applications that comply with a standard look and feel. Motif is a proposed industry standard.

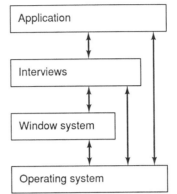

Figure 9.13   Relation between the operating system, the window system, InterViews, and the application.

9.5.3 Language-Centered Environments: Smalltalk80 And KEE

The idea of embedding a programming language in a complete environment that supports software development in that language originated with LISP environments. In this section, we give an account of modern language-centered environments by illustrating some features of the Smalltalk80 and KEE environments.

Both the Smalltalk80 and the KEE environment assume a workstation with a bit-mapped graphical screen and a mouse. The screen is dynamically partitioned into windows, in which the programmer can see everything he or she is working on. At any time, the programmer may switch from one activity to another by pointing to the objects that are operated upon, with little or no structure imposed by the environment.

In the Smalltalk80 environment, the object-oriented paradigm is supported not only by the programming language, but also by the interaction style with the environment. Basic concepts, such as an object, class, method (i.e., a procedure exported by a class), and message (i.e., a procedure call) are applied uniformly. The same syntax is used uniformly to send a message to an object created by the programmer (e.g., a table) and to invoke a tool provided by the environment.

Software structuring and modification are supported by the inheritance mechanism, which in Smalltalk80 provides almost no constraints on the programmer. The language is highly dynamic and does not provide static checking. An error is detected at run time if a message is sent to an object and neither the object's class nor its ancestor classes provide a corresponding method.

Inheritance, as we saw, is a powerful mechanism that supports software reuse. The Smalltalk80 environment supports inheritance and software reuse with a tool, called the *browser*, which allows programmers to search and inspect existing classes and add new classes to the system. After a class is created and modified, it can be tested by generating an instance of it and sending it a message. Facilities are available to inspect the data that are stored internally by an object. When an error is encountered, a debugger allows the user to change the state of an inspected object and then resume program execution.

The freedom provided by the Smalltalk80 programmer's interface can be used to adopt an undisciplined programming style. Several practical experiments, however, have shown that the flexibility of the inheritance supports a kind of exploratory development style that can provide support for rapid prototyping of new applications.

The KEE environment shares a number of similarities with Smalltalk80, especially in the kind of flexible interactions it supports. It is a popular and powerful knowledge-based environment born out of artificial intelligence in the recent past. The primary goal of the language is to support knowledge-based expert systems; it has, however, been used also as a prototyping language in software engineering applications.

KEE integrates functional (it is based on LISP), rule-based, and object-oriented paradigms. The *rule-based paradigm* allows one to represent knowledge through rules, i.e., in the form

if <premises> **then** <consequences>

The object-oriented paradigm of KEE derives from so-called *frames*. A frame is a structured–i.e., record-like–representation of an object or a class of objects. Frames can be organized in hierarchies through inheritance. Procedures may be attached to frames in two ways: as *methods* and as *active values*. A method is a LISP function that is part of the frame, like the routines encapsulated in an Eiffel class or Smalltalk80 methods. A method is explicitly invoked by the users of the frame. By contrast, an active value behaves like a demon that is activated asynchronously, as a consequence of some value changes. Active values resemble exception handlers in more traditional languages.

As in the case of Smalltalk80, the linguistic facilities of KEE are embedded in a rich and high-level environment that makes the development of applications–especially prototypes–very productive.

9.5.4 PCTE

Portable Common Tool Environment, or PCTE, is a public interface for software development tools. PCTE is not considered a software development environment in itself; rather, it is an infrastructure upon which software tools can be implemented and installed to provide an integrated environment. The underlying motivation is that once such a layer is available and widely adopted, software vendors will be encouraged to design and market tools, since tools conforming to the standard PCTE interface will be able to run on a large variety of systems (all systems on which PCTE will be available). Thus, ultimately, a richer choice of environments will be available to support software engineers, and this will improve the quality of software processes and products.

The services provided by PCTE largely correspond to those provided by an operating system like UNIX. Since UNIX has proven to be a popular host environment for supporting software development, PCTE has patterned itself after UNIX in many respects. In particular, it inherits from UNIX the style of running, synchronizing, and managing processes. PCTE also provides a UIMS to be used by tool writers to create and manipulate user interfaces.

PCTE departs most sharply from UNIX in its data management facilities. Data management in PCTE is supported by the *Object Management System* (OMS), which represents a major evolution of the UNIX file system. The OMS data model is based on the entity-relationship model, in which both entities and relationships have attributes. Thus, for example, one may define the entities Software_Engineer and Project and the relation Assigned_to to record the association of software engineers with projects. Software engineers have attributes, such as their first name, last name, status (consultant vs. employee), and salary. Projects have attributes such as their project name, expected duration, and contractual and budgetary information. An example of an attribute for the relation Assigned_to is the percentage of total working time the software engineer is assigned to a specific project. OMS provides features to access information by navigating along objects (i.e., instances of entities). For instance, for each software engineer, we may access budgetary information regarding the project the engineer works on for the maximum amount of time.

Entities may be organized in PCTE into a simple inheritance hierarchy. For example, instead of adopting the previous categorization, we may decide to classify software engineers into two categories. A software engineer would be characterized just by his or her first and last name; an employee would be characterized also by monthly salary, whereas a consultant would be characterized by hourly pay. Now, in general, if entity E_2 inherits attributes from entity E_1, all instances of E_2 have the attributes defined for E_1 and possibly other attributes. They also inherit the ability of being the source or destination of relations defined for the parent entity. Thus, employed engineers would be characterized by first and last name and salary; also, they might be the source of the relation Assigned_to, and they could be used to retrieve information on projects to which an employed engineer is currently assigned.

The preferred underlying architecture of the PCTE environment is a local network of single-user workstations, each equipped with a high-resolution graphical display; some nodes of the network night behave as servers. PCTE provides features for transparent use of the network. When OMS primitives are used to access and manage data, the user is not aware of the physical location of the data. Rather, the user has a logical view of the data and ignores the way the data are distributed around the network. Similarly, when two processes interact, they can ignore the physical location wherein they run.

9.6 AN IDEAL SCENARIO FOR THE FUTURE

Among the many fashionable acronyms for software products today, the prefix CA stands for "computer aided"–for example, CAD (computer-aided design) and CAM (computer-aided manufacturing). In this regard, it is rather surprising that CASE (computer-aided software engineering) is presently less CA than other, more traditional fields of engineering. In fact, software engineers have succeeded in automating a wide range of engineering processes, but have not been as successful in automating their own processes. As we observed, for a long time the only tool available for software design was the programming language.

The present scenario of CASE tools and environments is richer than a few years ago, but it is still unsatisfactory: the fashionable term "CASE" is more the statement of a vision than reality. Consequently, we expect that in the coming years, more development will help make CASE more of a reality. In this section, we extrapolate from the present state of the art to an ideal future scenario for CASE.

The following list presents the main features of an ideal scenario for CASE, in light of the classification provided in Section 9.2:

- *All phases* of the software process should be computer assisted, in an *integrated* way. This means that all of the tools for managing, specifying, programming, verifying, etc., software should belong to the same environment, and their interaction should be supported through an appropriate infrastructure. The software engineer should interact with the facility through an automated assistant, which not only should carry out all clerical activities involved in the process, but also should have enough knowledge of the process and deductive power to provide more "intelligent" support, e.g., as outlined in Section 9.3.11.

  An example of state-of-the-art integration–and of its limits–was discussed earlier in the case of Emacs, make, and compilers.

- *Formality* should be supported–not imposed–at every level of the software production process. Also, the appropriate *level of formality* should be decided by the user of the CASE environment, i.e., the software designer.

- *Incrementality* should be supported in all phases of the software production process (planning, requirements analysis and specification, design, testing, etc.). Formality should also be achieved incrementally. This requirement has a strong impact on the tools of the environment: tools should be able to accept partially specified objects and on-line modifications, incrementally checking their consistency and tolerating the remaining incompleteness.

  For instance, imagine you are specifying a system by means of a tool that supports augmented Petri nets which allow tokens to carry values, as we have seen in Section 5.5.3. Building the PN incrementally may mean that, initially, when attention is focused on the control aspects of the system, tokens are left "anonymous." Then, other features–say, the type and the value of messages described by some tokens–are gradually specified. At each step in the development of the model, the tool should accept a description, even if incomplete; furthermore, the tool should be able to interpret the net at each stage, by firing sequences of transitions and displaying the result on the screen.

  This incremental development requires the tool to be able to manage not only nets in which tokens are anonymous, but also the case of typed and valued tokens. The tool should also be able to handle the case where, at some intermediate step, some tokens are still anonymous while others are partially specified. For example, it might interact with the user to decide what the effect of the firing is; or it could allow the user to suspend the interpretation, switch to editing the net, provide the missing information, and then switch back to the interpretation.

- The infrastructure should allow the environment to be *open ended*; i.e., the environment should not be a fixed collection of tools, but rather, it should be easy to enrich the environment progressively by incorporating new tools into it over time. The benefits of integration and open-endedness cannot be overemphasized. As an example, integrating tools that measure program complexity parameters (see Section 6.7.3) with cost estimation and planning tools would allow automatic tuning of parameters based on the measures.

The merits of open-endedness have been demonstrated by a few cases in the past, say, UNIX and Emacs. By providing facilities that make it easy to aggregate new tools (e.g., pipes and redirection), UNIX proved that the programming environment can be progressively enriched by software engineers. UNIX, however, also shows the shortcomings of not basing open-endedness on a centralized infrastructure: tools cooperate directly, by accessing their (low-level) output data, with no notion of a central repository that keeps the data that are exchanged among tools. Thus, the tools interact with each other at a very low level.

- *Modularization* should be supported as a major mechanism for structuring complex objects, not only in the design phase, but throughout the production process. In fact, we have emphasized that not only designs, but also specifications, verification, and so on, should be given a modular structure. Also, the principle of *separation of concerns* should be supported by the environment by allowing the engineer to focus attention on a single issue at a time whenever possible.

  For instance, many modern word processors provide different views of the same document according to the particular topic of interest. Thus, one can see just the outline of the document, or a single section, or the first lines of any paragraph, etc. The same philosophy must be applied to the browsing of all software documents.

  An example is the capability of exploding a bubble of a DFD into a lower level DFD. This capability should be viewed not only as a feature to support stepwise design, but–perhaps more importantly–also as a structured way of reviewing the specification *a posteriori*. In the review process, one may separate the concerns pertaining to the global view of the interaction among functions from those pertaining to the detailed view of each individual function.

- The environment should be based on a set of sound *methods*. Tools themselves are of little use if the user does not have a sound understanding of the underlying methods. Thus, attention should be paid to associated educational and training material before any tool is introduced.

  Managers should take this point very seriously: the introduction of a software development environment should be planned and monitored carefully, taking into account the time and money that are needed to educate people on the underlying methods of the environment and to train people on the proper use of the tools. Too often, the managers of a company expect a dramatic increase in productivity and other software qualities just from the purchase of a new tool.

- The environment should be *user friendly* and provide a *natural* human-computer interaction. More precisely, the environment should fit the user's needs and expectations (see also Section 2.2.3), as well as the characteristics of the application. Both of these requirements are rather subjective, and both apply to the whole life cycle, but are more relevant to the earlier phases.

Clearly, user-interface management systems play a major role in the achievement of these goals, especially user friendliness. The issue of naturalness with respect to the application raises the alternative of having several specialized environments for different classes of applications, as against having a single general-purpose environment. Both alternatives exist in the present state of the art. Using the terminology we introduced in Section 9.2.6, the alternative is often between a polylingual environment and several monolingual environments.

For instance, SA/SD is strongly biased toward conventional data-processing applications; therefore, tools supporting SA/SD in a strict sense may be used naturally only in this application area. The method has been extended to cope with embedded, real-time applications; thus, a tool like Teamwork may be viewed as a general-purpose environment that actually corresponds to a family of products with strong similarities to one another, but wherein each product is targeted to one or more different application areas.

Will technology evolve towards of a unique, monolingual environment, defined and frozen once and for all? Or will it evolve towards separate, specialized monolingual environments? Or will it proceed towards a single flexible, polylingual environment? These questions are reminiscent of the never-ending debate that takes place in the area of programming languages: Are we moving towards "the" final programming language, which might absorb features from different paradigms–imperative, functional, logic, etc.– into an integrated framework? Or are we keeping different paradigms separate in smaller and cleaner languages? Or are we moving towards a more dynamic kind of integration that will allow programs to be written by combining parts written in different languages? Opinions on these points are often very strong, but highly subjective, and there is little consensus as to what will happen in the future.

Our viewpoint is that the environment must support different languages and paradigms. The need to switch from one style to another for different applications, and also for different parts of the same application, is especially strong in the early phases of the software production process. For example, we observed in Sections 5.7 and 7.1.1.2 that it may be natural to state functional requirements using DFDs, conceptual relationships among data using ER diagrams, and control aspects using finite state machines or Petri nets. If separate tools are used for specification of the data and control aspects, integration must be handled manually.

We also argue that the different styles and languages should not be combined and frozen into a single language. One reason is that we still do not know what is actually needed; more, however, is becoming known as research and experimentation progress. Second, a single language may be too complex for users to master and for the environment to support.

Following this view, the environment must be an integrated, but highly evolutionary and open-ended facility. The facility may be tailored to match the needs of the application at hand and, perhaps, even the personal tastes of the developers. It should be possible to integrate new tools and perhaps adapt or modify existing ones. Consider, for example, the case where different specification formalisms are progressively integrated. Integration should apply not only to the syntax of the formalisms, but also to their semantics.

In this type of an environment, one can recognize two logical classes of users: the *environment administrator*, who can manipulate the environment by adding or modifying functions, and the *environment user*, who interacts with the environment in developing an application. This type of open, highly flexible environment may be called *eclectic*.

Tools, however, should be based on methods; otherwise, they provide no help in the production of high-quality software. Certain methods may be organized into a coherent set–a methodology–to cover a large portion, or even all, of the software process. Thus, around individual tools, the environment may provide services that enforce the use of tools according to given methodologies. Figure 9.14 provides an intuitive global view of such a scheme, by showing the following points:

- The infrastructure is the heart of the environment: all connections among different components take place through it.
- Individual tools constitute a layer that uses the services provided by the infrastructure.
- Methods and methodologies–the external layers of the structure–provide guidance on the use of tools. They enforce a predefined strategy of using the tools according to the principles that underlie the method or the methodology.

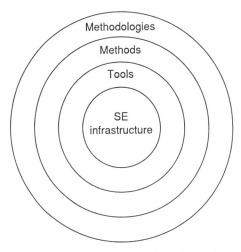

Figure 9.14   An ideal logical view of a software engineering environment

Finally, the environment must support group work: designers do not work in isolation, nor can they interact only through the data base. Much critical activity in the software production process is of a "social type" (brainstorming sessions, walk-throughs, code inspections, etc.) not presently supported by the available commercial technology.

Since distributed applications are now becoming available, support for this kind of cooperative group work will probably appear. For instance, future workstations, with their window systems, connected on a network can support the realization of an "electronic, distributed blackboard" where all participants in the meeting can contribute in much the same way as in a brainstorming meeting using a conventional blackboard.

9.7 CONCLUDING REMARKS

In this chapter, we have analyzed the structure of the environments that support software production processes. As we have observed, automated support for software production is still unsatisfactory, and therefore, we expect this area to advance rapidly in the coming years. Because of the present highly unstable and rapidly evolving nature of software engineering environments, we did not survey the area exhaustively; rather, we stressed the principles that should enable the reader to understand, classify, compare, and analyze the various approaches critically.

The historical developments, the classification of tools and environments, and the sampler of available technology that we have covered in this chapter give a broad perspective on the state of the art in the area and its potentials, enabling the reader to understand the various approaches, evaluate their merits and limitations, and choose among the available options.

Once again, we emphasize that tools and environments must be based on principles and methods. They are not substitutes for a sound knowledge of foundations, but can support and enhance software engineers' skills. Software engineers should be equipped with sufficient critical judgment to be able to discriminate among the tools that indeed help improve the quality of software processes and products, and those that are not relevant to that end. In particular, they should be able to understand how tools can be used and what the expected benefits really are. This is especially important because there is an increasing tendency in the market to oversell products and present useful tools as panaceas. But we should remember that there are not now, nor are there going to be, any panaceas.

FURTHER EXERCISES

9.23 Discuss a class library in an object-oriented environment as a development or end-product tool. Refer to specific languages in your evaluation (e.g., Eiffel and Smalltalk80).

9.24 Detail the functions of a language-specific linker for Larch.

9.25 Design and implement a code generator for an extension of a programming language of your choice (e.g., Pascal, C, Modula-2, or Ada). The extension provides a high-level feature to retrieve records from tables. The records to be retrieved are specified declaratively by giving a predicate on their fields, such as field(1) > field(3) **and** field(2) $\leq$ 0.

Complete the specification as you wish in order to fill in the missing details.

9.26 Classify a tool that supports Halstead's metrics as either static or dynamic. How about language independence?

9.27 In Section 9.3.11, we discussed different ways of storing a source program. Discuss the pros and cons of these two ways. Also, discuss another technique, consisting of storing each line as a separate record. What are the benefits? What are the drawbacks?

9.28 Given the specification of a module to be implemented and a library of pairs <module_specification, module_implementation>, specify exactly what kind of logical deductions the infrastructure should be able to perform. Can this be done in a completely mechanical fashion?

9.29 Discuss the pros and cons of not having the definition of (separately developed) modules in a language, but instead relying on an implementation to provide it.

9.30 Study and describe modules and separate compilation in the present Pascal ISO standard.

9.31 Explain how you can express IS_COMPOSED_OF in Ada.

9.32 Consider the separate compilation facilities of a language like C or FORTRAN. Such languages do not place any restriction on the order of module compilations. Such a scheme is called separate and independent. What are the pros and cons of this scheme compared to Ada or Modula-2?

9.33 Discuss the differences in the graph that describes the INHERITS_FROM relation in the two cases of simple inheritance and multiple inheritance.

9.34 Discuss the semantic differences between subroutines and coroutines.

9.35 Discuss how you could implement (simple) inheritance, polymorphism, and dynamic binding in Ada. Feel free to assume restrictions on such features, if necessary.

9.36 Give the requirements of a tool that supports the execution of finite state machines. The tool must provide facilities to animate specifications. Provide a detailed design of the tool.

9.37 Give the requirements for a tool that supports the evaluation of the testing activity.

HINTS AND SKETCHY SOLUTIONS

9.2 You may assume that the data that flow between any two bubbles are typed. Then you must define the language used to specify the function of each bubble and the way bubbles synchronize their access to the data that are produced and consumed.

9.3 The answer to this question depends on how innovative the language is–although according to Hoare [1973], the job of the language designer is consolidation, not innovation. Wide experimentation with the language is needed anyway before the language may be frozen. This means that compilers must be available and that people must use them. Otherwise, a premature standard either makes the language useless or does not prevent its later evolution or the spread of dialects.

9.5 A tool for proving formal correctness is static. A symbolic interpreter is dynamic, although several possible executions are "collapsed" into a single symbolic one. According to some authors, however, this categorization is questionable.

9.6 An interpreted application is often more efficient and supports software evolution more readily. If the compiled version is released, the presence of the interpreter at run time is not needed. Also, the compiled version provides more protection, since it cannot be easily read or modified by the user.

9.11 The tool should be able to handle a condition under which variables are either defined or undefined. Furthermore, it should have enough theorem-proving power to state whether such conditions are true, satisfiable, or false.

9.12 In order to retrieve a component, all deltas must be applied. If the original file is lost, all versions are lost, too. Thus, backups are critical here.

9.27 The notion of a line of code is rather elusive for block-structured languages, so that logical links between source code and a parse tree can hardly be expressed in terms of line numbers.

9.31 Use the **separate** mechanism.

BIBLIOGRAPHIC NOTES

Dart et al. [1987] provide a taxonomy of software development environments, while Osterweil [1981] is an interesting historical reference. The special issue of *IEEE Software* [1990c] provides a view of existing software tools. Tahvanainen and Smolander [1990] provide a rich annotated bibliography. Norman and Nunamaker [1989] provide an assessment of the impact of CASE tools on software engineering productivity.

Whereas most software engineering tools are fairly new and evolving rapidly, programming language compilers and interpreters are based on well-established theory and techniques and are described in many books. Aho et al. [1986] is a standard text on compilers that can also be used as a reference for flow analysis. Olender and Osterweil [1990] present a language for specifying the constraints to be checked by a data flow analyzer. The language then supports automatic generation of the analyzer.

If we rule out compilers as a special case of code generators, a sampler of tools that support the derivation of code from higher level specifications is given by Lewis in the aforementioned special issue of *IEEE Software* [1990c]. Martin and Leben [1986] give a comprehensive view of fourth-generation languages. Misra and Jalics [1988] and Verner and Tate [1988] provide a critical evaluation of fourth-generation languages and tools.

Surveys of testing support tools are given by DeMillo et al. [1987] and in the aforementioned special issue of *IEEE Software* [1990c]. Osterweil, in Chandrasekaran and Radicchi [1981], describes both a technique for program verification that integrates testing and analysis strategies and a tool that supports the technique. Kemmerer and Eckmann [1985] describe UNISEX, a symbolic interpreter for Pascal supporting program verification.

Gypsy is a language that is designed to be provable and that is supported by an environment wherein correctness is proved mathematically. Gypsy is described by Good [1977] and Good et al. [1979].

For performance monitors, the reader may refer to Ferrari and Minetti (eds.) [1981].

Dittrich [1989] surveys some problems and approaches to software engineering data bases. Clemm and Osterweil [1990] describe a persistent object store called Odin, used as the infrastructure for the integration of tools into an environment.

Problems, principles, and tools to build user interfaces are described by Coutaz [1985], Schneiderman [1987], Myers [1988], Hartson and Hiix [1989], Young et al. [1988], Linton et al. [1989], and the special issue of *IEEE Software* on user interfaces

(Software [1989a]). For some psychological and ergonomic aspects of human-computer interaction, which have not been discussed in this text, refer to Rubinstein and Hersh [1984], Guindon [1988].

Tichy [1989] and Babich [1986] give a tutorial presentation of configuration management. Tichy [1985] describes the design of RCS. Horwitz et al. [1989] discuss how consistency among versions is verified on a semantic basis, rather than through simple text comparison. The tool make is described by Feldman [1979].

Products that support Gantt and PERT scheduling, as well as software cost estimation, exist, and their user manuals can be consulted for specific machines.

Ghezzi and Jazayeri [1987] give a comprehensive view of programming languages. For Ada, refer to the manual by AJPO [1983] or to Booch [1987a and 1987b], which discuss good software engineering practices for Ada developments. Eiffel is presented by Meyer [1988]. Abelson et al. [1985] illustrate the functional approach to programming, through the language Scheme, a dialect of LISP. ML, a strongly typed functional language, is presented by Wilkstrom [1987]. Clocksin and Mellish [1984] is an introduction to logic programming with PROLOG. Parlog86 is a concurrent extension of PROLOG discussed by Ringwood [1988].

Some typical artificial intelligence programming environments are INTERLISP, presented by Teitelman and Masinter [1981], Loops, presented by Stefik et al. [1983], and KEE, presented by Filman [1988]. Stefik et al. [1986] discuss some issues revolving around a multiparadigm environment. Smalltalk80 and its interactive programming environment are described by Goldberg and Robson [1983].

Many tools for software specification, besides Teamwork, are now commercially available. Among these, Software Through Pictures provides interesting features for prototyping user interfaces; the tool has an open architecture that lets users extend and customize their work environment (see the special issue of *IEEE Software* [1990c]). Statemate, presented by Harel et al. [1990], is a specification support tool for real-time applications that is based on finite state machines. RdP by Verilog (*Catalogue des produits*, Sept. 1989) is a specification support tool based on Petri nets.

The real-time version of Teamwork is based on the extension of the SA/SD methodology proposed by Ward and Mellor [1985]. Software Through Pictures also extends SA/SD for real-time systems; it is based on the notation presented by Hatley and Pirbhai [1987].

Kernighan and Pike [1984] and Schmitt [1989] describe the UNIX and OS/2 environments, respectively. Scheifler et al. [1988], Young [1989], and Stallman [1984] are references for the X Window system, the Xt tool kit, and Emacs, respectively. Boudier et al. [1988] and Thomas [1989] describe PCTE's main features. The "Stoneman" document (DOD [1980]) defined the requirements for Ada programming support environments (known as APSEs); Oberndorf [1988] describes the interface set (CAIS) for an APSE.

Complete software engineering environments satisfying the requirements outlined in Section 9.6 are still more a vision than reality. Much literature, however, is available with suggestions, criteria, and proposals for their construction including Balzer et al. [1983], Stenning [1987], the special section of *IEEE Transactions on Software Engineering* on environment architectures edited by Penedo and Riddle (TSE [1987]), the special issue of

IEEE Computer edited by Henderson and Notkin (Computer [1987]). Taylor et al. [1988] describe a current research effort.

Simon [1986] and Tichy [1987] argue about the role of artificial intelligence in software engineering. Smith et al. and other contributions in the special issue of *IEEE Transactions on Software Engineering* edited by Mostow (TSE [1985]) and Goldberg [1986] deal with AI-based environments.

Conklin [1987] surveys hypertext; Bigelow [1988] discusses its role in computer-aided software engineering.

The issue of eclectic environments is discussed by Ghezzi and Mandrioli [1987] and Sanden [1989b].

Chapter 10

Epilogue

Our society is growing increasingly dependent on software for its critical functions–from health to defense, from industry to education. Software provides the glue for many services and devices on which we now rely: banking services, home security devices, air-traffic control, airplane navigation, etc. As software is being used to provide more functions, our need for larger and more complex software grows. This growth of society's reliance on software both promises exciting opportunities for the software engineering community and, at the same time, places responsibility on the community to find better ways of meeting society's expectations. To meet these expectations, we must be able to produce reliable software at a reasonable cost and within a reasonable time schedule. That is exactly the goal of software engineering.

Throughout this book, we have maintained that the best way to meet software requirements is to apply traditional engineering principles. We started by presenting a set of software qualities (Chapter 2), followed by a set of engineering principles (Chapter 3). In succeeding chapters, we showed how these principles can be applied methodically in different software engineering activities, including software design, specification, verification, and management.

In this chapter, we conclude the book by looking to the future of software engineering–where we think the field is headed and where the best payoffs will occur. We will then examine societal and ethical issues that are being raised by the increasing use of software in critical applications. Finally, we offer some concluding remarks. As usual, the last section of the chapter contains references to further reading material.

10.1 THE FUTURE

It is common to hear about the "software crisis." But not all software engineering projects are examples of bad management and engineering. There have been many successes in the field, some quite spectacular. Without such major successes, software would not have become the pervasive component of our society that it is. Indeed, it is these successes that have caused the explosive demand for software in increasingly demanding tasks, leading to unrealistic expectations and the inevitable failures in trying to meet those expectations.

The rapid rise in demand for software, combined with the effort required to maintain existing software, has created a large and rising backlog of software applications that need to be written. This is a tremendous problem that is blocking the progress of many companies, as well as society at large: new products cannot be introduced and new services cannot be provided because the software that is needed cannot be written quickly enough. This serious situation causes organizations and managers within those organizations to be constantly looking for solutions and even panaceas. But the previous chapters demonstrate that software engineering is a difficult intellectual activity that defies cure-all types of solutions.

Successful software engineering requires the application of engineering principles guided by informed management. The principles must themselves be rooted in sound theory. While it is tempting to search for miracles and panaceas, it is unlikely that they will appear. The best course of action is to stick to age-old engineering principles. There simply are no "silver bullets."

But all is not lost. Software engineering is a young discipline, and steady progress is being made. There are a number of areas that promise to increase software productivity, as well as to help the field mature into a real engineering discipline. In the rest of this section, we attempt to predict where such progress is necessary and likely.

We have emphasized throughout the book that mathematical, rigorous approaches must be combined with experimentation and empirical approaches. For example, program verification and software prototyping must be used in complementary ways. Standard models and notations, which make both specification and prototyping possible, are prevalent in mature engineering disciplines. They will have to become so also in software engineering.

Specialization is another sign of a mature engineering profession. Civil engineers, for example, specialize, some in bridges, some in residential houses, and others in hotels, restaurants, or hospitals. Years of specialized experience allow a bridge designer to develop the judgment and intuition that help him or her to design increasingly sophisticated bridges. One would not ask an engineer with experience in building apartment complexes to build an important bridge. In the software field, unfortunately, having written a "hello world" program, a beginning programmer earns the title of programmer and may be asked to program any kind of application. Software engineers will have to specialize in different application domains. We are already seeing some level of specialization–for example, in real-time or data-base systems. Specialization will aid in developing common models, notations, and abstractions specific to the different domains. The common abstractions can, in turn, lead to common software components.

Specialization, however, should be built on top of wide-spectrum educational foundations. Such foundations should equip the software engineer with the necessary mathematical maturity and with the ability to understand and speak the technical language of other fields where software applications will ultimately be embedded.

An important area in which we must see progress is software reusability. The best way to deal with the software backlog is to *avoid* writing new software. If we could build software by combining preexisting proven parts, we could reduce the time needed to build and verify new software. But there is much work to be done before reusable software components become commonly used by software engineers in the same way that electronic parts are used by electronics engineers.

There are many difficulties, as we have seen, in determining which components should be standard, how to specify the standard components, how to build them, how to classify and retrieve them from catalogues, etc. If there were standard designs for software products–such as the standard designs for houses, for example–then there would be hope in designing reusable software components. Standard designs, however, will probably only come about after software specializations occur in different fields. We are already seeing some example of this: in the telecommunications industry, software engineers specialize in switching system software and standard architectures are used for switching systems.

Some of the difficulty involved in reusing software is specific to in-the-small software issues. In software engineering, the building blocks we use are essentially programming language instructions, which are atomic units. Anything larger is crafted over and over by software engineers for every new application. Simple data structures, such as lists and stacks, and functions for accessing them are recreated many times over because the technology does not exist yet for reusing anything more than programming language instructions. This is almost akin to an architect redesigning new bricks for each new building. While on some occasions new kinds of bricks may have to be designed, there are many standard bricks that fit almost all situations. The software engineering field will have to find ways to invent and use the necessary "software bricks."

Reusability is sometimes more easily achieved with larger pieces of software. One successful example of software reusability is with user-interface management systems. These systems are built on the basis of a standard design for applications, in which the interface component is well isolated from the rest of the system. As we mentioned earlier, a standard application design is a prerequisite for the discovery and use of standard components.

Another example of software reusability is the use of a data-base system as a component in other applications. The success here can also be attributed to a standard application design that takes advantage of a component for data storage and retrieval. But the success is also due to the application designers' knowledge of the existence, of the interface, and of the function of the data-base management systems. The well-defined functionality of such systems allows the application designers to tailor the design of their application to take advantage of, and accept the restrictions of, a data-base system as a subcomponent. The software engineering field as a whole, and software engineers in their everyday practice, will have to build on these successes in order to create a true engineering profession.

In general, software reusability needs to be generalized to apply to all software artifacts and not just lines of code. That is, we need to be able to reuse knowledge, requirements, architecture, design, code, and tests. In the current state of practice of software engineering, each application requires invention of new knowledge, new requirements, new architecture, etc., and the best that is done is that some lines of code may be reused from previous work.

Again, the reuse of previous knowledge and designs is standard practice in established engineering disciplines such as civil and mechanical engineering. A prerequisite of this reuse is the ability to codify (i.e., specify) existing knowledge. Once such knowledge can be codified, it is provided in handbooks that are consulted by practicing engineers to avoid rederiving knowledge. In a sense, software engineering will be considered to have achieved the status of a true engineering discipline only after we have such handbooks that software engineers can use in their daily work.

10.2 ETHICS AND SOCIAL RESPONSIBILITY

In this book, we have discussed the technical aspects of software engineering. We have presented principles and methods for producing reliable software. But the growing dependence of society on software also places a tremendous social responsibility on the shoulders of software engineers and their managers. When the software is being used to monitor the health of patients, control nuclear power plants, apply the brakes in an automobile, transfer billions of dollars in an instant, launch missiles, or navigate an airplane, it is not simply good engineering to build reliable software; it is also the engineer's ethical responsibility to do so.

There are many reports of software defects that have cost lives or tremendous business losses. One such defect–discovered, fortunately, before the software was put into use–would have caused a fighter airplane to flip each time it crossed the equator. Another software defect was responsible for administering large doses of radiation that caused the deaths of several patients. And a rather famous defect caused the usually extremely reliable telephone lines to become unavailable for many hours. While not all program defects are as dramatic or as well publicized, all must be treated seriously: even a seemingly innocuous defect in an electronic game can cause serious stress for a young (or old!) user.

Finally, just as computers and their software have opened up new opportunities for increasing productivity and services, they have also opened up new opportunities for criminal fraud and sabotage. They have provided another way to steal without leaving fingerprints and shut down, or otherwise sabotage, businesses without being physically present. While these problems have not been invented by software engineering, and their solutions are not the sole responsibility of software engineers, we are responsible for minimizing, if not eliminating, the new problems that software creates. In particular, it is within the purview of software engineering to build software that resists, as much as possible, unauthorized use, so-called viruses, and serious damage.

In summary, program defects are not merely inconvenient "bugs" or interesting technical puzzles to be captured, but potentially serious business- or life-threatening errors. Building reliable software is a technical objective of the software engineer, but it also has ethical and social implications that must guide the actions of a serious professional. In this light, "hacking," i.e., inserting "playful" bugs into programs, creating viruses, writing quick and dirty code just to meet a schedule or a market window, shipping defective software, and even shipping software that works but does not meet the agreed-upon specifications is unethical.

10.3 CONCLUDING REMARKS

We have presented many details and principles of software engineering in this book. Successful software engineering requires the integration and use of principles, tools, and methodologies. It requires an understanding of theory and the use of intuition and judgment that is developed only through practice. Textbook knowledge is not enough and does not make one a good software engineer. But practical experience alone, without the textbook knowledge, is not enough either. Both are required. This book provides the necessary textbook knowledge. The application of this knowledge in practice can help make you a successful software engineer.

BIBLIOGRAPHIC NOTES

Brooks [1988] is a thoughtful piece that argues that there are no "silver bullets." Parnas [1985] provides insightful comments on the inherent difficulties of software and addresses the ethical issues raised by mission-critical applications.

Neumann [1989] provides an impressive list of documented risks to the public due to defective software; the list is continuously updated by Neumann's column ("Risks to the Public") in *ACM Software Engineering Notes*.

Denning [1989] is the editor of a special issue of the *Communications of the ACM* that contains a controversial essay by Dijkstra and rebuttals by other prominent educators on the subject of how to teach software engineering. Dijkstra argues for absolute formality. Our viewpoint in this text is that a sound engineering approach must build on formal foundations, but should also integrate empirical knowledge.

CACM [1989] contains several papers dealing with the social responsibility of computing professionals. The papers deal with the use of computers in law and the military and in support of the disabled.

Miles [1984] examines the landmark Apple vs. Franklin case that established some of the bases of computer software copyright laws.

The report issued by the Computer Science and Technology Board of the National Research Council of the U.S.A. (CTSB) [1989] contains a research agenda for software engineering.

Having finished this book, you can now follow the current state of the art in several journals. The most important ones for software engineering are the journals of *IEEE Transactions on Software Engineering*, *IEEE Software*, *ACM Transactions on Software Engineering and Methodology*, *Communications of the ACM*, *Software–Practice and Experience*, and *Journal of Systems and Software*. The newsletter *Software Engineering Notes* of the Special Interest Group on Software Engineering of the ACM also contains much useful information.

Case Studies

Software engineering principles provide a firm foundation upon which to build software systems. Throughout this book, we have presented principles and techniques for a disciplined approach to software engineering. In order to motivate the need for such a systematic approach, the case studies here offer a close look at the current state of practice of software engineering and the problems faced every day by software engineers.

These are case studies of real software engineering projects. We will review the progress of the projects from inception to delivery of the product. We will show what can go wrong in such projects. We will also show that the success or failure of a project depends heavily on technical skills or mistakes, as well as on nontechnical ones, in inseparable ways.

We will purposefully emphasize the mistakes that were made in order to highlight the important issues that are often ignored in a software project. The key point is that the people involved in each project were educated and experienced software engineers. Yet, they repeated the well-known mistakes of many projects that went before them. These projects are fairly typical of current industry practices.

As you read through these case studies, contrast the events described with the principles presented in the book. In what ways were the principles followed and in what ways were they not? Were the reasons for success or failure technical or nontechnical?

A. CASE STUDY 1: AUTOMATING A LAW OFFICE

A few years ago, the leaders of a software company realized that law offices such as title companies were poorly automated. At most, these offices used general-purpose word processors and, possibly, some package for computing invoices or the payroll.

The company felt that an integrated office automation tool, including sophisticated and specialized word-processing features, could lead to more efficiency in law offices. For example, legal documents could be prepared much more efficiently with such a tool because they typically follow some standard composition rules. Many sales agreements could be expressed approximately in the following terms:

- Write the standard header of the document (e.g., "This document pertains to the sale of a residence").
- Write the relevant data about the seller. (The typist should have to type only the data necessary to identify the person; all remaining data should be retrieved automatically from the appropriate data base.)
- If the seller is married, the data about the spouse should also be included. This action should be done automatically as well.
- The same procedure must be followed for the buyer.
- Then a standard schema of the document should follow. However, some particular data (e.g., dates and payments) should be typed explicitly, some data should be filled in automatically from files, and some data (e.g., taxes) should be computed automatically on the basis of other data.

The analysis of rules of this type, combined with the fact that the company had a strong experience in sophisticated word-processing tools and with the facts that potential customers were generally wealthy and no strong competitors existed yet in the market, convinced the leaders of the company that developing a tool for automating law offices could be good business.

Thus, the company's first decision was to contact a sample of potential customers to see whether they would be interested in such a product and which features would be desirable. At first, the executives of the firm contacted a few personal acquaintances. Next, they contacted the members of a professional committee on the use of computers in law offices. In both cases, the reaction was enthusiastic, and this led directly to the decision to go ahead with the project.

Thus far, the company's behavior seems quite natural, but it contains a first, serious, mistake: we will see later that the selected sample of potential customers was biased. In both cases of contact, the people were already familiar with and fairly supportive of the benefits of automation. There was no evidence, however, that this attitude was representative of the whole profession.

Here we see a first example of the interaction between technical and nontechnical knowledge in the feasibility study of software projects. This early analysis of the potential market for the software product was conducted nonscientifically for probably two kinds of reasons. On the one hand, market analysis techniques have difficulty dealing with ill-defined markets: it is difficult or even impossible to plan a software product on the basis of the same considerations one uses when examining a project to build a new car or a new washing machine model. In this case, the planned software product was intended to create a new market and required analysis of an as-yet nonexistent market.

On the other hand, the marketing analysis was performed by "pure software engineers" who had little or no background in the marketing field, but who exhibited a "pioneering" attitude. This attitude overwhelmed the engineering attitude: innovative software was considered to be the result of a stroke of genius–maybe even luck–more than that of a structured, tedious, job.

While innovation and pioneering have their places, they cannot form the basis of a discipline and certainly not the basis of a product development schedule.

A.1 Economic And Financial Planning

Economic and financial planning is another area in which strong interaction between engineering and nonengineering skills is needed in the early planning of a product. Economic and financial planning requires both the ability to forecast future sales–which is influenced by the price at which the product can be sold and by the number of items sold–and the ability to estimate development costs.

The same market analysis difficulties we discussed before make it difficult to forecast the revenue expected of a new product. The difficulty with estimating software development costs is that software cannot be developed faster by simply adding more people to the project. This distinguishes software from most other engineering products. While the same phenomenon holds during the design phase of any product, what sets software apart is that the "design phase" for software is not a relatively short period at the beginning of development, but seems to go on throughout the entire development process. The person making the cost estimates–who is usually not an engineer–must understand this phenomenon.

In this case study, the economic analysis, as well as the market analysis, was flawed dramatically. Since the difficulties of making estimates in both areas are well known, the major error–a very common error–was the lack of risk analysis. No precautions were taken to control what was known to be a critical activity.

When it became apparent that all original estimates were terribly wrong, nobody suggested a plan of action of a type that said, "Well, guys, we missed the first deadlines; we are going to spend much more money than originally planned. So let's rethink the whole plan, and examine more carefully if we can still afford to do the project." Instead, only "day by day" actions were undertaken, both from a technical and from a financial point of view. The result was that in a short time, the company was in serious financial trouble. (At the beginning, it was claimed that "we are going to finance this product from net income; thus, in the worst case, we are only risking our earnings!")

Again, this management mistake is a very common one. It is naturally explained by the fact that short-term decisions overwhelm long-term planning. Too often, the damages of this psychological attitude become apparent when it is too late to recover from them.

A.2 Technical Planning And Management

At the start of the project, it would have been wise to write clear and precise documents stating the requirements for the new product. These documents should have been based on a careful and organized interaction with potential users, paying close attention to choosing a representative sample of the user population.

One might argue that it would have been difficult, or even impossible, to write such documents, since the desirable features of the system were not clear in the first place. A possible solution to this problem would have been to put a limited effort into the development of a system that would act as a prototype. The prototype system would then help assess the most critical issues and derive firm requirements by observing users' reactions when using the system. Unfortunately, the designers did not even realize that a problem existed, and therefore, they did not even consciously choose between the first alternative–specifying requirements carefully–and the second–developing a fast, exploratory prototype.

Similarly, careful planning of resource allocation should have started, both from the point of view of work assignment to designers and programmers and from the point of view of physical resource management (e.g., hardware acquisition and office space). But instead, just the opposite happened. An amusing but dangerous "game" started between the designers and the very few representative clients. In this case, of course, the designers included the company leaders, since they were technical people and they had originated the idea of the product in the first place.

In fact, everybody was excited with the innovative and challenging features of the product, but nobody paid much attention to fairly obvious but critical details. For instance, a true programming language was designed to allow the sophisticated user to define his or her own document composition rules. Very sophisticated–and expensive–word-processing facilities were included without measuring their cost effectiveness. (They were just "nice to have.")

For a long time, nobody paid attention to the definition of suitable user interfaces to facilitate the interaction of nontechnical people–a lawyer or a secretary–with the system. Similarly, sophisticated features for the automatic computation of invoices on the basis of input data (people time, service value, travel expenses, etc.). were designed, but no attention was paid to standard office operations such as the filing of large numbers of documents (e.g., records of automobile sales–in some offices, several hundreds of such documents are produced every day).

From a management point of view, all of the designers of the system were attracted by the most interesting features of the new product, so that a lot of work was done in the early phases to find and to compare clever solutions to marginal problems, and no structure was arranged for the design team. Later, someone observed that the design team looked like a soccer team composed of beginning players: everybody was playing close to where the ball was!

From a technical viewpoint, many typical mistakes were made:

- No analysis was performed to determine whether all the product features were needed by all users, or whether it would be better to restructure the functionality of the product based on different classes of users. More generally, no effort was put into determining which qualities of the product were most critical for its success. For instance, in the choice of the hardware and of the development software (the operating system, programming language, etc.), little or no attention was paid to their evolution, and no effort was made to prepare for possible changes to them.

- No "design for change" was done, i.e., no design decision was influenced by any analysis of which parts of the product were likely to change during the product's lifetime (e.g., how might possible changes in the law affect product requirements?).
- Strong pressure was applied to have some (*any*) code running as early as possible.
- No precautions were taken to minimize damages due to personnel turnover.

What is perhaps worth pointing out is that everybody in the company was, of course, aware of such classical mistakes in software engineering. This awareness notwithstanding, the mistakes were made. This remark shows that knowing the difficulties is not enough: it is also necessary to have the technical and organizational ability and willingness to face them, even at the cost of doing something that does not appear immediately attractive and productive.

A.3 Project Monitoring

After a while (about six months after the start of development), some mistakes became apparent, both from a technical and from a management point of view. For instance, the lack of a clear definition of the product's functionality caused some initial misunderstandings between the potential users–the ones with whom the early contacts had been established–and the designers. It was realized that some features that had been neglected at the beginning were actually quite important.

Also, getting in touch with other potential users showed that not all of them needed the same features. Thus, a modular architecture would have been preferable, even from the user point of view, allowing the product to be customized for different classes of users, just as the same "skeleton" of a car can be sold with different types of engines, with different optional features, etc., or the same personal computer can be sold with many optional features–e.g., a color monitor or a floating-point coprocessor.

Finally, it became apparent that the original cost estimates were off by an order of magnitude. This invalidated the initial economic and financial plans.

The reaction to this situation was even worse than the problem itself: the impact of the mistakes–both technical and nontechnical–was again underestimated. In general, the attitude was of the following type: "OK, we made a few mistakes, but now we are almost done. So let's put in a little more effort, and we will complete the product soon and will start earning money." That is, no critical and careful analysis of the mistakes was made, nor was a serious replanning and redesign of the whole project attempted. There was only a generic claim of an intuitive confidence in being close to the end.

The consequences of this attitude were disastrous. Under the pressure of "being almost done and close to delivering the product," the design focused more and more on the very end product–i.e., *machine code*. Classical "patches" on object code were made wildly, no systematic error and correction logs were kept, and communication among designers occurred almost exclusively orally in an attempt to save time.

The same attitude prevailed on the managerial and financial front: since "we are almost done," "we just need a little more financing and can accept almost any terms."

A.4 Initial delivery

It was decided that income could be generated as soon as the company started delivering the first versions of the product or as soon as new contracts could be signed. In turn, the customers would be good references for the product, resulting in an opportunity both to improve the product and to increase the sales of the product.

This decision, too, turned out to be a big mistake. In fact, a new dimension was added to the already critical technical and management problems. Since the rule was "sign the contract anyway," while the product was not clearly defined and was only partially developed, early customers had many problems with the product. This caused a lot of internal problems also, because it was not clear whether some activity fell under product development or user assistance; nor was it clear who had to do what. After a while, it was realized that almost everybody on the product team had performed some marketing, some development, some user assistance, some hardware acquisition, etc., according to an unpredictable flow of events.

A.5 Partial Recovery

Eventually, it was realized that the naive way the firm was managing the project was leading to disaster. Thus, a real effort was made, first to define responsibilities clearly (who was responsible for the design, who was responsible for the distribution, etc.)[1], and second, to achieve a clear picture of the state of the product, of its weaknesses, of the effort required to fix them, etc. This was done even at the expense of slowing down the project, increasing costs, and reducing sales. Thus, people had to resist an initial feeling that the restructuring of the project was impeding "real" progress.

After a while, however, the improvements became apparent, so that, eventually, the product really existed and full documentation was available. The company actually started to ship the product and earn money from it, although far less than expected initially, mainly because the delayed introduction of the product caused it to enter a more competitive market than anticipated.

---

[1]These roles, of course, existed even before, but they were merely nominal, so that, in practice, everybody was responsible for everything (and nobody was responsible for anything).

B. CASE STUDY 2: BUILDING A FAMILY OF COMPILERS

As a contrast with the previous case study, we now review a software engineering project that was a modest success.

B.1 Initial Product Planning

The project was conducted in a medium-sized computer company. The goal of the project was to produce a new family of compilers (for C, FORTRAN, and Pascal) for the company's line of computers. There were several reasons why the project was undertaken:

- The existing compilers were showing their age: they had too many defects that were too hard to fix, and more defects were being reported than could be fixed by the engineers. The current compilers were written when the company was started, under strict time pressures. This showed in the quality of the code and the quantity and quality of its documentation. This was the reason that the compilers were so hard to repair. It seemed that the compilers had outlived their useful time, and the best thing to do with them was to retire them.

- There were three different compilers, one each for the three languages C, FORTRAN, and Pascal. Thus, any code generation or optimization essentially had to be applied three different times, and the same defect was reported three different times, once for each language. The technology of compiler writing now was advanced enough that it was possible to write a family of compilers that shared many parts and specialized only in their treatment of language-specific aspects. In particular, the plan called for different parsers for different languages, but a code generator and, as important, a code optimizer to be shared by all the compilers.

- The main attraction of the company's computer was its high performance. But competitors were now introducing new computers with essentially the same hardware performance but much better compilers. The only way for the company to compete in the performance area was to have the compilers generate much better code. (A new processor was being designed, but it was not expected to be available for several years). Unfortunately, the current compiler design and code did not allow easy optimization extensions, and the cost of doing three different optimizers seemed prohibitive.

The combination of all these reasons led the company to the decision that a new family of compilers was needed.

B.2 Economic And Financial Planning

There were no specific economic and financial forecasts. In well-established companies, a major product development is preceded by a study of *return on investment* (ROI), to determine whether the product will produce sufficient profit. In this case, however, the decision to proceed with the development of the compilers was essentially dictated by technical considerations and absolute need.

The only consideration given to economics was a rough calculation of how many people the project would require. Even that analysis was mostly based on how many people were already part of the compiler team, rather than the magnitude of the work to be undertaken.

B.3 Technical Planning And Management

Early investigation revealed that several software vendors sold compilers that could be used as starting points. Since the company produced a proprietary processor, they would have to write a new code generator (or modify an existing one). There was no reason, however, to rewrite parsers for C, Pascal, or FORTRAN if they could be bought at a reasonable price. The value that the company was going to add to the product was not in parsing technology, but in code generation and optimization.

After studying several vendors and their products, one was chosen on the strength of the design of its compilers. The winning compiler satisfied all the requirements: it was constructed from a language-specific parser (C, Pascal, FORTRAN, and others), which translated the source code into a canonic "intermediate code"; an optimizer, which translated from the intermediate code to the same intermediate code; and a code generator, which translated from the intermediate code to assembly language. The code generator and optimizer were shared by all compilers for a given machine. The intermediate language was general enough to handle languages that the company was planning to offer later (such as Ada). Finally, and most importantly, the vendor's compilers for existing machines generated very efficient code (benchmarked against other compilers), and the structure of the optimizer allowed the addition of more optimizations.

There was no specific technical or management plan for the project. Since the company was already maintaining a set of compilers, it had a general plan that once the new compilers arrived from the vendor, three engineers would spend "enough" of their time to write a new code generator and optimizer. It was vaguely expected that this would take about a year. There was a great reliance on the competence and help of the software vendor. Estimates of time and effort were simply requested from the vendor. This method of software cost estimation is called "expert judgment": simply ask an expert. It is probably the most commonly practiced method of software cost estimation.

B.4 Early Development Phases

The requirements and specifications for the project were comparatively easy to produce, as is usual for a compiler project for a standard language. There were some issues that had to be resolved, such as which versions of the languages to accept (for example, there was a FORTRAN standard, but several popular supersets of the standard), and what compiler speed or code quality was required, but these issues were easily resolved by using the existing set of compilers as a minimum base: the new compilers had to be compatible with the existing ones in terms of *functionality* and had to exceed the existing ones in terms of *quality*. Quality was defined roughly to include the amount of code optimization, the speed of the compiler, the extent of extensions accepted for the standard languages, and the amount of support for source-level debugging (the original compilers did not support this).

Once the software became available from the vendor, three engineers were assigned to the project. The senior member of the three was sent to the vendor for one week of training on the software. There was not much external documentation on the software: the code was the only source of any information on the software design, assumptions, algorithms, etc. Therefore, the personal training of the engineer was a kind of "oral documentation"on the software.

Once the engineer returned from his training session, the engineers started working on understanding the existing software and designing their extensions to the "skeleton" code generator that they had also bought from the vendor. Again relying on the expertise of the vendor, the engineers decided that the design of the code generator skeleton was sufficient, and they did not have to do any major design themselves. They proceeded on to the coding phase.

B.5 Project Monitoring

For a variety of reasons, the project was not monitored very closely or carefully. First, the engineers assigned to the project were already responsible for maintaining the existing compilers. The problems with these compilers always took priority over work on the new compilers, which were not scheduled for release until "sometime later." While the engineers were supposed to spend half of their time on the existing compilers and half on the new ones, in practice, the problems with the existing compilers always took precedence and, thus, more of the engineers' time. Second, six months after the vendor software arrived, the project manager decided to leave the company. The second-level manager was assigned as acting manager of the group while a search was initiated for a new manager. The acting manager was, of course, too busy to monitor the compiler project too closely (or at all!). His time was spent looking for a new manager, as well as looking after other groups under his control.

B.6 Project Reexamination, Revival, And Goal Setting

Eighteen months after the arrival of the software, 12 months after the departure of the project manager, a new manager was found and hired. The last words of the acting manager before handing over responsibility of the project to the new manager were that the project was in excellent shape and that the release of the new compilers was imminent. What the new manager found, however, was different: there was no explicit schedule, there was no explicit assignment of responsibility to people, there was no explicit definition of quality requirements, and there was no effort toward producing manuals. These factors led to the engineers not having a focused goal, in terms of either time or product.

The new manager had two points in his favor: he was well versed in software engineering, and, more importantly, he did not feel any personal responsibility for the project's already being late. He could thus draw up a schedule and resource requirements based on his best judgment: making the current problems in the project visible to company management did not reflect adversely on his abilities as a manager.

The project also had several points in its favor. The most important was that the senior engineer was a very competent software engineer. Second, the base software was indeed well designed, well constructed, and extensible. The extensions made by the engineers all had contributed toward the final goal, and none of them had to be removed.

The first job of the new manager was to quantify the status of the project: how much work was already done, how much work was left to be done, and how much time and effort would be required to get it done. As a first attempt at estimating the work, the size of the compilers, in terms of number of lines, was measured against the vendor's compilers for other, similar machines. The sizes turned out to be roughly the same. This raised a vague hope that maybe not much more new code was left to be written.

At the time, the engineers had been working on their part of the code, slowly polishing what each was responsible for. For example, one had spent weeks trying to generate the best possible code for Pascal **for** loops. Yet, there was no overall feeling of how much each part that they were working on was contributing to the whole project.

The next step in assessing the current state of the project was to identify a standard test suite for Pascal compilers. The test suite would serve several purposes: first, it would show management (i.e. document) how far the compiler project still had to go; second, it would give the engineers an objective goal; and third, it would establish a basis for regression testing.

Unfortunately, on the first try, of the 350 test cases, the compiler passed fewer than 10! Though this was discouraging to the whole team, a little reflection and examination of the test results made it clear that the situation was not so bad. Indeed, the situation was a clear example of the difficulty of measuring how much software work is left to do. In this case, a few simple defects in the basic code generation scheme were responsible for all the failures. Fixing those defects, which took less than a day, helped the reputation of the compiler team tremendously: now, the compiler passed over 100 tests successfully! Disabling the optimizer allowed the compiler to pass another 50 tests. Regardless of how many tests the compiler was still failing–over 200–the foundations were now laid for a way to measure progress. Thus, while the publicly available test suite was initially viewed with skepticism by most of the team as a toy test suite, it now became a challenging goal to be conquered.

The manager informed company executives that the compilers were not even close to being released. The "toy" test suite was proof enough: no matter how much management was interested in shipping the product, it was not interested in shipping a product that clearly did not work. The manager also started working on establishing an agreement between the different departments in the company–marketing, customer service, documentation, and engineering–as to the minimum product that would be shipped. The marketing department was asked to identify 10 beta sites. More importantly, it was asked to locate two existing customers who had the largest applications and had had trouble with the company's first set of compilers. All parties agreed that unless these two customers were happy with the compilers, the compilers would not be released. This agreement established a common goal for the compiler team that was visible to, and understandable by, the whole company.

Once this major agreement had been reached–essentially establishing the major project *requirements*–it was possible to make a project plan and schedule various activities. Some activities were external to the compiler team and some were internal. An effort was started to write manuals for the products. The marketing department started producing promotional material (using "carefully tested products" as a marketing slogan).

Internal to the team, the project was able to identify some major milestones: passing the standard Pascal test suite completely, self-compilation (being able to compile the compiler family with the Pascal compiler being written), successfully compiling major in-house applications (e.g., editors and simulators), successfully compiling the operating system, successfully compiling typical customer applications (in all three languages), and successfully compiling the two agreed-upon major customer applications. These milestones all assessed functional requirements. Other acceptance milestones were also established. Common industry performance benchmarks were selected to measure the quality of the compilers' code optimization. The minimal goal was established that the code produced by the new compilers had to execute at least 20% faster than the old compilers. Another goal was that the compilation speed had to be no worse than that of the old compilers.

A monthly progress report was established to keep the company management and the team informed of the state of the project.

B.7 Assignment of Responsibility

It was clear that the abilities of the team members were not uniform and that the team members had not been assigned to the most appropriate tasks. For example, it appeared that if the senior engineer had been left alone, he would have been able to produce more than all three engineers combined! The situation called for a reassignment of responsibilities in such a way as to ensure rapid progress, take advantage of all the engineers' strengths, and keep all team members happy and motivated.

The senior engineer was made the lead architect responsible for the overall design and correctness of the software. One junior engineer was assigned to debug the symbolic debugging code under the close supervision of the manager. This was a challenge to the engineer, and the supervision was welcomed. The other junior engineer was assigned to assist the senior engineer and to be responsible for running the tests and summarizing the results. (For example, how many of the 200 test failures were due to the same defect?) Testing is usually not a glamorous activity among software engineers, but in this case, because of the important role that the test suite had played, it was perceived as very important (which it was!).

Finally, one of the company's largest customers, an overseas computer company, was asked to send two compiler testing experts to help in debugging the compilers. The customer was happy to provide this help because it gave the firm better visibility as to how the project was going and better assurance that it would get a more reliable product.

B.8 Steady Progress And Release of the Product

Clear goals, clear job assignments, good software design, competent engineering, and concerned supervision led to steady progress. Milestones were met in rapid succession.

The testing team was able to identify defects, narrow them down as much as possible, and pass them on to the code experts, who in most cases were able to fix them very quickly. The results of the test suites were routinely "advertising" the amount of progress being made. The new environment created a team out of what used to be individual engineers working on their own code. The team environment reinforced the individual motivations, and the progress reported by the test results added encouragement.

Eight months after the new manager had joined the project and the team had been reorganized, the compilers were released to the manufacturing department. No defect reports were received for two months after the release of the compilers (This was in sharp contrast to the experience with the old compilers, which could now be retired). The careful testing had definitely paid off.

B.9 Product Distribution

An interesting side remark about this case study involves the timing of the release of the product to customers. The manager had been pressed for a release date from the beginning. But he resisted committing the company to a release date until after the compilers had passed the first test suite completely. At that time, with some confidence, he gave a release date of October 15. By coincidence (and no doubt, with much luck), the compilers were indeed released to the manufacturing department on October 15. Yet the compilers were not released to customers until six weeks later, meaning that–because of year-end holidays–the customers did not receive the new compilers until January of the following year.

Much of the work needed in manufacturing–book-keeping, assignment of product numbers, inventory updating, etc.–could have been done in anticipation of the October 15 release, so that the product could have been distributed to customers in November. Yet, based on its experience with all previous estimates from the engineering department, the manufacturing department had all the confidence that the compilers would not be released to them on October 15. To them, a promise from engineering was sure to be broken!

The monetary effect of the engineering department's promise not being taken seriously was that back orders for the compilers were not filled as early as they could have been, delaying receipt of important revenue for close to two months. The delay in receiving the sizable revenue in fact made a big difference to the company.

B.10 Remarks

This case study reveals the following interesting points, which we have examined throughout the book: Let us examine some of them in detail:

Software reusability. Probably the most important factor that led to the success of the project–despite lax initial management–was the fact that the major part of the software and the major design for the rest of it were bought from a vendor who specialized in the product. Reusable parts are crucial to other engineering disciplines, and we have repeatedly emphasized the importance of software reusability. The case study shows that the reusability of both code and design is possible. While we have not mastered the art producing small reusable modules in software engineering, it is definitely possible and worthwhile–yet uncommon–to reuse large subsystems.

Key personnel. There is no doubt that the project would have failed without the lead engineer. In this case, the support of the other two engineers and the project manager allowed the lead engineer to concentrate on the key problems–in a sort of a chief programmer team style. Highly skilled, highly productive software engineers are rare and hard to replace. Cost estimation models and practical experience show that key personnel are a major determinant of project success or failure.

Cost estimation. If software engineering were truly an engineering discipline, the company's choice of whether to buy software or develop it in-house would have been made on the basis of a cost analysis. Indeed, even the code generator could have been developed through a contract to the compiler vendor, but for reasons that are not clear to us, it was not. It would have made a very good case study for a software engineering textbook to say that a cost estimation model (e.g., COCOMO) was used to decide whether to develop or buy software. Unfortunately, all these decisions were simply based on "expert judgment," with no supporting quantitative assessments. Even the estimate of October 15 for a release date–which turned out to be exact–was based on an intuitive analysis of test results and engineer competence, rather than a quantitative analysis of how much work was left to do.

Clear requirements. While the requirements were not specified formally in one document, the project was helped by having clear, if not documented, goals. The existing language standards formed precise functional requirements. Further, the company's market dictated that the execution speed of the generated code was the most important quality factor. It is interesting that not all compiler projects enjoy the same success. Many suffer from unclear requirements: which standard and which extensions are required, the trade-off between execution speed and usage of memory, how much optimization is desired, and the relative importance of optimizations versus the debuggability of code or program environment support may all be specified so vaguely that no clear decisions regarding them can be made. The project was also helped by the existence of a base software (the old compilers) against which progress could be measured.

Testing. In many projects, testing is an activity that is done after all the work is finished. In this project, testing had a key role–after project revitalization. The tests were used as a means of measuring and communicating the status of the project, as a motivating factor for the engineers, and as a planning tool for what to do next. Again, because the project was a compiler project, many standard test suites existed that could be used. Thus, the project team itself did not have to spend time inventing good test cases. As is common with many other engineering products, standard test suites can be used to certify software products. Of course, this can only be done for standard software products, such as compilers and operating systems, but it can also extend to file systems, sort routines, mathematical libraries, etc. A final point about the role of testing in this project is that enough time was allotted to correct the defects found during testing. That is, testing was performed not merely to prove that the software worked, but instead to find the defects that had to be fixed.

Visibility. Many projects suffer from a lack of visibility as to their status due to psychological and sociological factors, in addition to the technical factors that we have already discussed in relation to estimating the amount of software work that has been accomplished. Individual engineers may not want to admit to themselves or their supervisors that they are behind, or even ahead of schedule. Their supervisors may not want to admit to themselves or to their managers that they are behind schedule. (They would be thus jeopardizing their careers.) In turn, the top managers in the company may not want to hear that their projects are behind schedule, and they do not want to admit to the outside world that they are behind schedule. (They would be jeopardizing their company's competitiveness in the marketplace.) In general, the status of a project becomes visible only if the project has truly serious problems from which it may not be able to recover. In the project described above, the new manager had no personal credibility at stake, since he had not drawn up the original schedule and had not made any promises. His lack of personal accountability for the existing problems allowed him to be able to separate the concerns for his career from those for the schedule. He was able to assess the situation and make it known to all the people who were important in making business decisions based on the technical data. Further, the new visibility of the status of the project to top management was another motivating factor to team members. The standard test suite results served as an impartial, objective, and quantitative way of communicating the status of the project among technical and nontechnical people. The monthly status reports assured managers that progress was being made and gave the engineers a focused goal and motivated them to make progress towards that goal. The first run of the test results dashed all hopes of any miracles. The tendency to hope for miraculously getting back on schedule is common among software engineers because of the absence of objective measures in the discipline for measuring progress. This has led to the popular saying that, "the first 90 percent of the work is done in the first 10 percent of the time; it is the last 10 percent that takes the remaining 90 percent of the time!"

Life cycle. There certainly was no life cycle planning on the project and no clear life cycle apparent even in hindsight. This situation is probably typical of many medium-sized software projects.

Compromises among goals. Technical issues are one of many factors involved in making organizational decisions. In fact, the many departments in an organization have different, and sometimes conflicting, goals. For example, the marketing department wants to ship the product as soon as possible, the engineering department wants to delay shipment until the product is perfect, the finance department may want to choose the shipment date based on when it wants the revenue to show on the books, the manufacturing department wants to schedule the shipment of the product to balance the work over the different products, and the customer service department wants to ship a perfect product as soon as possible to resolve all the problems it keeps hearing about on the current product, but it wants to make sure that the product is perfect before it is shipped. Reaching a compromise among these goals is often a difficult management task. In this project, however, the test results were sufficient to convince all parties that the product was not ready for shipment. And the steady progress reported in the monthly status reports allowed the different parties to plan ahead and reach common decisions based on the data. In practice, it is often the lack of objective data that makes group decision making difficult. Psychological and sociological factors are involved here, too, such as the personal ambitions of the decision makers and the friendship or animosity among the different protagonists. But these are beyond the scope of this book.

C. CASE STUDY 3: INCREMENTAL DELIVERY

This brief case study shows the benefits of incrementality in refining requirements and in delivery of the product.

A computer manufacturer was building a new computer. The hardware people were busy designing and building the hardware. The software groups were busy designing and building the system software. For several reasons, the company had decided to use Pascal for all of its software development. A classic problem in these circumstances is to have a compiler ready as early as possible.

The weaknesses of Pascal for systems programming were well known at the time of the project, so it was clear that many extensions were going to be needed. The language group took a poll of all the software engineers on the project to see what extensions would be needed. Every language feature ever discovered was proposed by at least one person as an absolutely necessary feature! It was clear that the compiler, including all the extensions, could not be delivered by the time the other groups were ready to start coding.

The language group decided to use the principle of incrementality. First, they ranked the needed extensions. They scheduled three releases of the compiler: standard Pascal, Pascal with minimal extensions, and Pascal with all other extensions. The agreement was that after the minimal extensions were used for a while, a more informed decision could be made about what other extensions were actually required.

The extensions were first prototyped by implementing a preprocessor for an existing Pascal compiler. Although the preprocessor was slow and only ran on a VAX machine (which was not the target machine), it allowed the engineers to use the extensions and provide feedback on their usability.

Soon after the hardware was available, a Pascal compiler with minimal extensions was ready. This compiler allowed the engineers to start implementing their software (e.g. the operating system and a data base). It actually turned out that many people had early versions of their software developed and tested on the VAX version of the prototype. In many cases, all they had to do was recompile their code.

After six months of using the compiler with minimal extensions, another poll was taken to see whether any other extensions were needed. No other extensions were considered necessary by the users! One new extension (logical operations on integers) made the list nonetheless. This extension was meant to solve some of the efficiency problems with the code generated by the compiler. It is interesting that the original list of user requests did not include any efficiency-related extensions.

Once the language features were stabilized, there were several other compiler releases, each introducing a more sophisticated level of code optimization. Finally, an extension was added to allow bit-level operations, allowing some system code to look clearer and be more efficient.

The incremental delivery of the compiler allowed users to have access to useful functions, and it allowed the compiler developers to enhance the compiler on the basis of explicit and definitive user feedback.

CONCLUDING REMARKS

The preceding real-life experiences demonstrate several points. First, the stories are instances of a fairly large class of software projects and related problems. Second, they show that knowing, and even understanding, software development difficulties does not guarantee that mistakes will be avoided. This book has tried to provide principles and tools for the production of better software; the responsibility for making appropriate use of them, however, is up to the designer.

Third, the case studies show that software engineering, as well as any other engineering field, does not consist of a pure and systematic application of design techniques and tools in a more or less mechanical style, but requires the integration of the techniques and tools with knowledge of several other disciplines and several application areas. No amount of technical competence can replace the need for common sense and ingenuity in the construction of any engineering product. All these skills must be integrated with each other.

It is such integration that allows the software engineer to forecast software development, estimate the value of work in progress, etc. Evaluating the percent of the project completed requires technical knowledge and experience in software development, but it also requires the ability to evaluate the economic and financial impact of over- and underestimation.

References

Abdel-Hamid [1989]
>   T. K. Abdel-Hamid, "The dynamics of software project staffing: a systems dynamics based simulation approach", *IEEE Transactions on Software Engineering*, 16(2): 109-119, February 1989.

Abdel-Hamid [1990]
>   T. K. Abdel-Hamid, "Investigating the cost/schedule trade-off in software development", *IEEE Software*, 7(1): 97-105, January 1990.

Abdel-Hamid and Madnick [1989]
>   T. K. Abdel-Hamid and S. E. Madnick, "Lessons learned from modeling the dynamics of software development", *Communications of the ACM*, 32(12): 1426-1438, December 1989.

Abelson et al. [1985]
>   H. Abelson, G. J. Sussman, and J. Sussman, *Structure and Interpretation of Computer Programs*, The MIT Press, Cambridge, Mass., 1985.

ACM [1975]
>   *Proceedings of International Conference on Reliable Software*, (Los Angeles, 21-23 April 1975), published as *SIGPLAN Notices*, 10(6), June 1975.

Adrion et al. [1975]
>   R. W. Adrion, M. A. Branstad, and J. C. Cherniavsky, *Validation, Verification and Testing of Computer Software*, NBS Special Publication 5000-75, National Bureau of Standards, 1975.

Agresti [1986]
>   W. W. Agresti, "Guide to the literature and annotated bibliography", in W. W. Agresti, editor, *New Paradigms for Software Development*, IEEE Computer Society Press, 1986.

Aho et al. [1974]
>   A.V. Aho, J.E. Hopcroft, and J.D. Ullman, *The Design and Analysis of Computer Algorithms*, Addison-Wesley, Reading, Mass., 1974.

Aho et al. [1986]
> A. V. Aho, R. Sethi, and J.D. Ullman, *Compilers–Principles, Techniques, Tools*, Addison-Wesley, Reading, Mass., 1986.

Aho et al. [1988]
> A. V. Aho, B. W. Kernighan, and P. J. Weinberger, *The AWK Programming Language*, Addison-Wesley, Reading, Mass., 1988.

AjmoneMarsan et al. [1984]
> M. AjmoneMarsan, G. Balbo, and G. Conte, "A class of generalized stochastic Petri nets for the performance evaluation of multiprocessor systems", *ACM Transactions on Computer Systems*, 2(2): 93-122, 1984.

AJPO [1983]
> Ada Joint Program Office Military Standard, *Reference Manual for the Ada Programming Language*, MIL-STD-1815A, Washington, D.C., 1983.

Alagic and Arbib [1978]
> S. Alagic and M. A. Arbib, *The Design of Well-Structured and Correct Programs*, Springer-Verlag, Berlin-New York, 1978.

Alavi [1984]
> M. Alavi. "An assessment of the prototyping approach to information systems development", *Communications of the ACM*, 27(6): 556-563, June 1984.

Albrecht and Gaffney [1983]
> A. J. Albrecht and J. E. Gaffney, Jr., "Software function, source lines, and development effort prediction: a software science validation", *IEEE Transactions on Software Engineering*, 9(6): 639-647, November 1983.

Alford [1977]
> M. W. Alford, "A Requirements engineering methodology for real-time processing requirements", *IEEE Transactions on Software Engineering*, 3(1): 60-69, January 1977.

Ames et al. [1983]
> S. R. Ames, Jr, M. Gasser, and R. R. Schell, "Security kernel design and implementation: an introduction", *IEEE Computer*, 16(7): 14-22, July 1983.

Ashenhurst [1989]
> R. L. Ashenhurst, editor, Forum Letters, *Communications of the ACM*, 32(3): 287-290, March 1989.

Auernheimer and Kemmerer [1985]
> B. Auernheimer and R. A. Kemmerer, *ASLAN User's Manual*, Technical Report TR-CS-84-10, Department Computer Science, University of California at Santa Barbara, March 1985.

Auernheimer and Kemmerer [1986]
> B. Auernheimer and R. A. Kemmerer, "RT-ASLAN: a specification language for real-time systems", *IEEE Transactions on Software Engineering*, 12(9): 879-889, September 1986.

Babich [1986]
> W. A. Babich, *Software Configuration Management*, Addison-Wesley, Reading, Mass., 1986.

Baker [1972]

> F. T. Baker, "Chief programmer team management of production programming", *IBM Systems Journal*, 11(1): 57-73, 1972.

Balzer [1981]

> R. Balzer, "Transformational implementation: an example", *IEEE Transactions on Software Engineering*, 7(1): 3-14, January 1981.

Balzer et al. [1983]

> R. Balzer, T. E. Cheatham, Jr., and C. Green, "Software technology in the 1990s: using a new paradigm", *IEEE Computer,* 16(11): 39-45, November 1983.

Bartussek and Parnas [1978]

> W. Bartussek and D. L. Parnas, "Using assertions about traces to write abstract specifications for software modules", in G. Bracchi and P. C. Lockemann, editors, *Information Systems Methodology*, pages 211-236, Springer-Verlag, Berlin-New York, October 1978.

Basili [1980]

> V. R. Basili, *Tutorial on Models and Metrics for Software Engineering*, IEEE Computer Society Press, October 1980.

Basili and Caldiera [1988]

> V. R. Basili and G. Caldiera, "Reusing existing software", Technical Report Institute for Advanced Computer Science, Department of Computer Science, University of Maryland at College Park, *UMIACS-TR-88-72, CS-TR-2116*, October 1988.

Basili and Hutchens [1983]

> V. R. Basili and D. H. Hutchens, "An empirical study of a syntactic complexity family", *IEEE Transactions on Software Engineering*, 9(6): 664-672, November 1983.

Basili and Rombach [1988]

> V. R. Basili and H. D. Rombach, "The TAME project: towards improvement-oriented software environments", *IEEE Transactions on Software Engineering*, 14(6): 758-773, June 1988.

Basili and Selby [1987]

> V. R. Basili and R. W. Selby, "Comparing the effectiveness of software testing strategies", *IEEE Transactions on Software Engineering*, 13(12): 1278-1296, December 1987.

Basili and Turner [1975]

> V. R. Basili and A. J. Turner, "Iterative enhancement: a practical technique for software development", *IEEE Transactions on Software Engineering*, 1(4): 390-396, December 1975.

Basili et al. [1983]

> V. R. Basili, R. W. Selby, Jr., and T.-Y. Phillips, "Metric analysis and data validation across Fortran projects", *IEEE Transactions on Software Engineering*, 9(6): 652-663, November 1983.

Basili et al. [1986]
        V. R. Basili, R. W. Selby, and D. H. Hutchens, "Experimentation in software engineering", *IEEE Transactions on Software Engineering*, 12(7): 733-743, July 1986.

Bauer et al. [1989]
        F. L. Bauer, B. Moeller, M. Partsch, and P. Pepper, "Formal program construction by transformations: computer-aided, intuition-guided programming", *IEEE Transactions on Software Engineering*, 15(2): 165-180, February 1989.

Behrens [1983]
        C. A. Behrens, "Measuring the productivity of computer systems development activities with function points", *IEEE Transactions on Software Engineering*, 9(6): 648-652, November 1983.

Beizer [1983]
        B. Beizer, *Software Testing Techniques*, Van Nostrand Reinhold, New York, 1983.

Belady and Lehman [1979]
        L. A. Belady and M. M. Lehman, "Characteristics of large systems", in *Research Directions in Software Technology*, P. Wegner, editor, The MIT Press, Cambridge, Mass., 1979.

Bennington [1956]
        H. D. Bennington, "Production of large computer programs", *ONR Symposium on Advanced Programming Methods for Digital Computers*, June 1956.

Bentley [1985]
        J. L. Bentley, "Programming pearls: confessions of a coder", *Communications of the ACM*, 28(7): 671-679, July 1985.

Bentley [1986]
        J. L. Bentley, *Programming Pearls*, Addison-Wesley, Reading, Mass., 1986.

Bentley [1988]
        J. L. Bentley, *More Programming Pearls*, Addison-Wesley, Reading, Mass., 1988.

Bergland [1981]
        G. D. Bergland, "A guided tour of program design methodologies", *IEEE Computer*, 14(10): 13-37, October 1981.

Berry [1987]
        D. M. Berry, "Towards a formal basis for the formal development method and the InaJo specification language", *IEEE Transactions on Software Engineering*, 13(2): 184-201, February 1987.

Bidoit et al. [1985]
        M. Bidoit, B. Biebow, M-C. Gaudel, C. Gresse, and G. Guiho, "Exception handling: formal specification and systematic program construction", *IEEE Transactions on Software Engineering*, 11(3): 242-252, March 1985.

Bigelow [1988]
        J. Bigelow, "Hypertext and CASE", *IEEE Software*, 5(2): 23-27, March 1988.

Biggerstaff and Perlis [1989]
> T. Biggerstaff and A. J. Perlis, editors, *Software Reusability*, volumes 1-2, Addison-Wesley, Reading, Mass., 1989.

Bittanti [1988]
> S. Bittanti, editor, *Software Reliability Modelling and Identification*, Lecture Notes in Computer Science, vol. 341, Springer-Verlag, Berlin-New York, 1988.

Bjorner and Druffel [1990]
> D. Bjorner and L. Druffel, Position statement: ICSE-12 Workshop on Industrial Experience Using Formal Methods, *Proceedings 12th International Conference on Software Engineering*, Nice, 26-30 March 1990, IEEE Computer Society Press, pages 264-266, 1990.

Bjorner and Jones [1982]
> D. Bjorner and C. B. Jones, *Formal Specification and Software Development*, Prentice-Hall International, London, 1982.

Bjorner and Prehn [1983]
> D. Bjorner and S. Prehn, "Software engineering aspects of VDM, the Vienna Development Method", in *Theory and Practice of Software Technology*, D. Ferrari et al., editors, pages 85-134, North-Holland, Amsterdam, 1983.

Boehm [1976]
> B. W. Boehm, "Software engineering", *IEEE Transactions on Computers*, 25(12): 1226-1241, December 1976.

Boehm [1981]
> B. W. Boehm, *Software Engineering Economics*, Prentice-Hall, Englewood Cliffs, N.J., 1981.

Boehm [1984a]
> B. W. Boehm, "Software engineering economics", *IEEE Transactions on Software Engineering*, 10(1): 4-21, January 1984.

Boehm [1984b]
> B. W. Boehm, "Verifying and validating software requirements and design specifications", *IEEE Software*, 1(1): 75-88, January 1984.

Boehm [1988]
> B. W. Boehm, "A spiral model of software development and enhancement", *IEEE Computer*, 21(5): 61-72, May 1988.

Boehm [1989]
> B. W. Boehm, *Tutorial on Software Risk Management*, IEEE Computer Society Press, 1989.

Boehm and Papaccio [1988]
> B. W. Boehm and P. N. Papaccio, "Understanding and controlling software costs", *IEEE Transactions on Software Engineering*, 14(10): 1462-1477, October 1988.

Boehm et al. [1978]
> B. W. Boehm, J. R. Brown, H. Kaspar, M. Lipow, G. MacLeod, and M. J. Merritt, *Characteristics of Software Quality*, volume 1 of TRW Series on Software Technology, North-Holland, Amsterdam, 1978.

Boehm et al. [1984]
>   B. W. Boehm, T. E. Gray, and T. Seewaldt, "Prototyping vs. specifying: a multi-project experiment", *IEEE Transactions on Software Engineering*, 10(3): 133-145, May 1984.

Bolognesi and Brinksma [1987]
>   T. Bolognesi and E. Brinksma, "Introduction to the ISO specification language LOTOS", *Computer Networks*, 14(1): 25-59, 1987.

Booch [1986]
>   G. Booch, "Object-oriented development", *IEEE Transactions on Software Engineering*, 12(12): 211-221, December 1986.

Booch [1987a]
>   G. Booch, *Software Components with Ada–Structures, Tools, and Subsystems*, Benjamin/Cummings, Menlo Park, Calif., 1987.

Booch [1987b]
>   G. Booch, *Software engineering with Ada,* 2nd ed., Benjamin/Cummings, Menlo Park, Calif., 1987.

Boudier et al. [1988]
>   G. Boudier, F. Gallo, R. Minot, and I. Thomas, "An overview of PCTE and PCTE+", Proceedings of Software Development Environments (SDE3), Boston, November 28-30, 1988), published as *SIGPLAN Notices*, 24(2): 248-257, February 1989.

Bouge et al. [1986]
>   L. Bouge, N. Choquet, L. Fribourg, and M. C. Gaudel "Test sets generation from algebraic specifications using logic programming", *Journal of Systems and Software*, 343-360, November 1986.

BrinchHansen [1977]
>   P. Brinch Hansen, *The Architecture of Concurrent Programs*, Prentice-Hall, Englewood Cliffs, N.J., 1977.

BrinchHansen [1978]
>   P. Brinch Hansen, "Reproducible testing of monitors", *Software–Practice and Experience*, 8(6): 721-729, 1978.

Brindle and Taylor [1989]
>   A. Brindle and R. N. Taylor, "A debugger for Ada tasking", *IEEE Transactions on Software Engineering*, 15(3): 293-304, March 1989.

Britton et al. [1981]
>   K. H. Britton, R. A. Parker, and D. L. Parnas, "A procedure for designing abstract interfaces for device interface modules", *Proceedings 5th International Conference on Software Engineering*, San Diego, California, 9-12 March 1981, pages 195-204, IEEE Computer Society Press, 1981.

Brocklehurst et al. [1990]
>   S. Brocklehurst, P. Y. Chan, B. Littlewood, and J. Snell, "Recalibrating software reliability models", *IEEE Transactions on Software Engineering*, 16(4): 458-470, April 1990.

Brooks [1975]
>   F. P. Brooks, Jr. *The Mythical Man-Month: Essays on Software Engineering*, Addison-Wesley, Reading, Mass., 1975.

Brooks [1988]

F. P. Brooks, Jr., "No silver bullet: essence and accidents of software engineering", *IEEE Computer*, 20(4): 10-19, April 1987.

Browne [1980]

J. C. Browne, "The interaction of operating systems and software engineering", *Proceedings of IEEE*, 68(9): 1045-1049, September 1980.

Bruno and Marchetto [1986]

G. Bruno and G. Marchetto, "Process-translatable Petri nets for the rapid prototyping of process control systems", *IEEE Transactions on Software Engineering*, 12(2): 346-357, February 1986.

Buckle [1977]

J. K. Buckle, *Managing Software Projects*, Americal Elsevier, New York, 1977.

Buhr [1984]

R. J. A. Buhr, *System design with Ada,* Prentice-Hall, Englewood Cliffs, N.J., 1984.

Burstall [1974]

R. M. Burstall, Program proving as hand simulation with little induction, *Proceedings IFIP Congress*, pages 308-312, North Holland, Amsterdam, 1974.

Bustard et al. [1988]

D. Bustard, J. Elder, and J. Welsh, *Concurrent Program Structures*, Prentice-Hall International, Hemel Hempstead, 1988.

CACM [1988]

Special issue on Software Testing, published as *Communications of the ACM*, 31(6), June 1988.

CACM [1989]

Special section on Computing and Social Responsibility, published as *Communications of the ACM*, 32(8): 925-956, August 1989.

Capers Jones [1986]

T. C. Jones, *Programming Productivity*, McGraw-Hill, New York, 1986.

Celentano et al. [1980]

A. Celentano, S. Crespi-Reghizzi, P. L. DellaVigna, C. Ghezzi, G. Granata, F. Savoretti, "Compiler testing using a sentence generator", *Software–Practice and Experience*, 10: 897-918, 1980.

Chandrasekaran and Radicchi [1981]

B. Chandrasekaran and S. Radicchi, editors, *Computer Program Testing*, North-Holland, Amsterdam, 1981.

Chandy and Misra [1988]

K. M. Chandy and J. Misra, *Parallel Program Design: A Foundation*, Addison-Wesley, Reading, Mass., 1988.

Cheatham et al. [1981]

T. E. Cheatham, Jr., G. H. Holloway, and J. A. Townley, "Program refinement by transformation", *Proceedings 5th International Conference on Software Engineering*, San Diego, 9-12 March 1981, pages 430-437, IEEE Computer Society Press, 1981.

Chen [1976]

P. Chen, "The entity relationship model - towards a unified view of data", *ACM Transactions on Database Systems*, 1(1): 9-36, 1976.

Choppy and Kaplan [1990]

C. Choppy and S. Kaplan, "Mixing abstract and concrete modules: specification, development and prototyping", *Proceedings 12th International Conference on Software Engineering*, Nice, 26-30 March 1990, IEEE Computer Society Press, pages 173-84, 1990.

Clarke et al. [1989]

L. A. Clarke, A. Podgursky, D. J. Richardson, and S. J. Zeil., "A formal evaluation of data flow path selection criteria", *IEEE Transactions on Software Engineering*, 15(11): 1318-1332, November 1989.

Clemm and Osterweil [1990]

G. Clemm and L. Osterweil, "A mechanism for environment integration", *ACM Transactions on Programming Languages and System*s, 12(1): 1-25, January 1990.

Clocksin and Mellish [1984]

W. Clocksin and C. Mellish, *Programming in PROLOG*, 2nd ed., Springer-Verlag, Berlin-New York, 1984.

Cohen et al. [1986]

B. Cohen, W. T. Harwood, and M. I. Jackson, *The Specification of Complex Systems*, Addison-Wesley, Reading, Mass., 1986.

Computer [1987]

Special issue on Seamless Systems, published as *IEEE Computer*, 20(11), November 1987.

Computer [1989a]

Special Issue on Rapid Prototyping in Software Development, published as *IEEE Computer*, 22(5), May 1989.

Computer [1989b]

Special Issue on Scientific Visualization., published as *IEEE Computer*, 22(8), August 1989.

Conklin [1987]

J. Conklin, "Hypertext: an introduction and survey", *IEEE Computer*, 20(9): 17-42, September 1987.

Conte et al. [1986]

S. D. Conte, H. E. Dunsmore, and Y. E. Shen, *Software Engineering Metrics and Models*, Benjamin/Cummings, Menlo Park, Calif., 1986.

Coulter [1983]

N. S. Coulter, "Software science and cognitive psychology", *IEEE Transactions on Software Engineering*, 9(2): 166-171, March 1983.

Coutaz [1985]

J. Coutaz, "Abstractions for user interface design", *IEEE Computer*, 18(9): 21-34, September 1985.

Crispin [1987]
> R. J. Crispin, Experience using VDM in STC, *VDM-Europe Symposium 1987*, Brussels, pages 19-32, Springer-Verlag, Berlin-New York, March 1987.

CSTB [1989]
> Computer Science and Technology Board, National Research Council, *Scaling Up: A Research Agenda For Software Engineering*, National Academy Press, Washington, D.C., 1989.

Curtis et al. [1979]
> B. Curtis, P. Milliman, and S. B. Shepper "Third time charm: stronger prediction of programmer performance by software complexity metrics", *Proceedings 4th International Conference on Software Engineering*, Munich, 17-19 September 1979, pages 356-60, IEEE Computer Society Press, 1979.

Curtis et al [1988]
> B. Curtis, H. Krasner, and N. Iscoe, "A field study of the software design process for large systems", *Communications of the ACM*, 31(11): 1268-1287, November 1988.

Dahl et al. [1972]
> O. J. Dahl, E. W. Dijkstra, and C. A. R. Hoare, *Structured Programming*, Academic Press, New York, 1972.

Dart et al. [1987]
> S. A. Dart, R. L. Ellison, P. H. Feiler, and A. N. Habermann, "Software development environments", *IEEE Computer,* 20(11): 18-28, November 1987.

Davis [1988]
> A. M. Davis "A comparison of techniques for the specification of external system behavior", *Communications of the ACM*, 31(9): 1098-1115, September 1988.

Davis [1990]
> A. M. Davis, *Software Requirements: Analysis and Specification*, Prentice-Hall, Englewood Cliffs, NJ, 1990.

Davis et al. [1988]
> A. M. Davis, E. H. Bersoff, and E. R. Comer, "A strategy for comparing alternative software development life cycle models", *IEEE Transactions on Software Engineering*, 14(10): 1453-1461, October 1988.

DeMarco [1978]
> T. DeMarco, *Structured Analysis and System Specification*, Yourdon Press, New York, 1978.

DeMarco [1982]
> T. DeMarco, *Controlling Software Projects*, Yourdon Press, New York, 1982.

DeMillo et al. [1979]
> R. D. Millo, R. Lipton, and A. Perlis, "Social processes and proof of theorems and programs", *Communications of the ACM*, 22(5): 271-280, 1979.

DeMillo et al. [1987]
>R. A. DeMillo, M. W. McCracken, R. J. Martin, and J. F. Passafiume, *Software Testing and Evaluation*, Benjamin/Cummings, Menlo Park, Calif., 1987.

Denning [1989]
>P. J. Denning, editor, "A debate on teaching computing science", *Communications of the ACM*, 32(12): 1397-1414, December 1989.

DeRemer and Kron [1976]
>F. DeRemer and H. Kron, "Programming-in-the-large versus programming-in-the-small, *IEEE Transactions on Software Engineering*, 2(2): 80-86, June 1976.

Dijkstra [1968a]
>E. W. Dijkstra, "Cooperating sequential processes", in F. Genuys, editor, *Programming Languages*, pages 42-112, Academic Press, New York, 1968.

Dijkstra [1968b]
>E. W. Dijkstra "The structure of the THE multiprogramming system", *Communications of the ACM*, 11(5): 341-346, May 1968.

Dijkstra [1971]
>E. W. Dijkstra, "Hierachical ordering of sequential processes", *Acta Informatica*, 1(2): 115-138, 1971.

Dijkstra [1976]
>E. W. Dijkstra, *A Discipline of Programming*, Prentice-Hall, Englewood Cliffs, NJ, 1976.

Dijkstra [1989]
>E. W. Dijkstra, "On the cruelty of really teaching computing science", *Communications of the ACM*, 32(12): 1398-1404, December 1989.

Dittrich [1989]
>K. R. Dittrich, "Database technology for software engineering environments", Tutorial 5, *Tutorial Notes of 2nd European Software Engineering Conference*, Warwick, 11-15 September, 1989.

DOD [1980]
>United States Department of Defense, *Stoneman: Requirements for Ada Programming Support Environment*, February 1980.

DOD [1984]
>United States Department of Defense, MIL-STD-2167, March 1984.

Duran and Ntafos [1984]
>J. W. Duran and S. Ntafos, "An evaluation of random testing", *IEEE Transactions on Software Engineering*, 10(4): 438-444, July 1984..

Fagan [1976]
>M. E. Fagan, "Design and code inspections to reduce errors in program development", *IBM Systems Journal*, 15(3) : 182-211, 1976.

Fagan [1986]
>M. E. Fagan, "Advances in software inspection", *IEEE Transactions on Software Engineering*, 12(7): 744-751, July 1986.

Fairley [1985]
>R. Fairley, *Software Engineering Concepts*, McGraw-Hill, New York, 1985.

Feldman [1979]

S. I. Feldman, "Make–A program for maintaining computer programs", *Software–Practice and Experience,* 9: 255-265, 1979.

Ferrari [1978]

D. Ferrari, *Computer Systems Performance Evaluation*, Prentice-Hall, Englewood Cliffs, NJ, 1978.

Ferrari and Minetti [1981]

D. Ferrari and V. Minetti, editors, *Experimental Computer Performance and Evaluation*, North-Holland, Amsterdam, 1981.

Fetzer [1988]

J. H. Fetzer, "Program verification: the very idea", *Communications of the ACM,* 31(9): 1048-1063, September 1988.

Filman [1988]

R. E. Filman, "Reasoning with worlds and truth maintenance in a knowledge-based system shell", *Communications of the ACM*, 31(4): 382-401, April 1988.

Floyd [1967]

R. Floyd, "Assigning meanings to programs", *Symposium on Applied Mathematics*, volume 19 of Mathematical Aspects of Computer Science, pages 19-32, J. Schwartz, editor, American Mathematical Society, New York, 1967.

Freeman [1987a]

P. Freeman, *Software Perspectives: The System is the Message*, Addison-Wesley, Reading, Mass. 1987.

Freeman [1987b]

P. Freeman, *Tutorial on Resusable Software Engineering*, IEEE Computer Society Press, 1987.

Frewin et al. [1985]

E. Frewin, P. Hamer, B. Kitchenham, N. Ross, and L. Wook, "Quality measurement and modelling–state of the art report", *Technical Report REQUEST/STC ESPRIT*, July 1985.

Fuggetta et al. [1989]

A. Fuggetta, C. Ghezzi, and D. Mandrioli, "Some considerations on real-time behavior of programs", *IEEE Transactions on Software Engineering*, 15(3): 356-359, March 1989.

Fujno [1990]

K. Fujno, "Concepts of software factory engineering", presentation given at Italsiel Seminar on Industrial Perspectives of Software Engineering in the 90s., Torino, 2 April 1990.

Futatsugi et al. [1985]

K. Futatsugi, J. Goguen, J. Jouannaud, and J. Meseguer, "Principles of OBJ2", *Annual Symposium on Principles of Programming Languages, New Orleans*, pages 52-66, 1985.

Garzotto et al. [1987]

F. Garzotto, C. Ghezzi, D. Mandrioli, and A. Morzenti, "On the specification of real-time systems using logic programming", Proceedings 1st European

Software Engineering Conference, *Lecture Notes in Computer Science* vol. 289, Springer-Verlag, Berlin-New York, pages 180-190, 1987.

Gehani and McGettrick [1986]
N. Gehani and A. McGettrick, editors, *Software Specification Techniques*, Addison-Wesley, Reading, Mass., 1986.

Genrich [1987]
H. Genrich, "Predicate/transition nets", in *Advances in Petri Nets*, W. Reisig and G. Rozenberg, editors, Lecture Notes in Computer Science 254-255, Springer-Verlag, Berlin-New York, 1987.

Ghezzi and Jazayeri [1987]
C. Ghezzi and M. Jazayeri, *Programming Language Concepts*, 2nd ed., John Wiley and Sons, New York, 1987.

Ghezzi and Mandrioli [1987]
C. Ghezzi and D. Mandrioli, "On eclecticism in specifications: a case study centered around Petri nets, *Proceedings 4th International Workshop on Software Specification and Design*, Monterey, pages 216-225, 3-4 April 1987, IEEE Computer Society Press, 1987.

Ghezzi et al. [1989a]
C. Ghezzi, D. Mandrioli, S. Morasca, and M. Pezzè, "A general way to put time in Petri nets", *Proceedings 5th International Workshop on Software Specification and Design*, Pittsburgh, 19-20 May 1989, pages 60-67, IEEE Computer Society Press, 1989.

Ghezzi et al. [1989b]
C. Ghezzi, D. Mandrioli, S. Morasca, and M. Pezzè, "Symbolic execution of concurrent systems using Petri nets", *Computer Languages*, 14(4): 263-281, 1989.

Gibson and Senn [1989]
V. R. Gibson and J. A. Senn, "System structure and software maintenance performance", *Communications of the ACM*, 32(3): 347-358, March 1989.

Gilb [1988]
T. Gilb, *Principles of Software Engineering Management*, Addison-Wesley, Reading, Mass., 1988.

Goguen et al. [1978]
J. A. Goguen, J. W. Thatcher, E. G. Wagner "An initial algebra approach to the specification, correctness, and implementation of abstract data types", in *Current Trends in Programming Methodology*, vol. 4, R. T. Yeh, ed., pages 80-149, Prentice-Hall, Englewood Cliffs, NJ, 1978.

Goldberg and Robson [1983]
A. Goldberg and D. Robson, *Smalltalk-80: The Language and Its Implementation*, Addison-Wesley, Reading, Mass., 1983.

Goldberg [1986]
A. T. Goldberg, "Knowledge-based programming: a survey of program design and construction techniques", *IEEE Transactions on Software Engineering*, 12(7): 752-768, July 1986.

Gomaa and Scott [1981]

H. Gomaa and D. Scott, "Prototyping as a tool in the specification of user requirements", *Proceedings 5th International Conference on Software Engineering*, San Diego, 9-12 March 1981, pages 333-342, March 1981.

Good [1977]

D. Good, editor, Constructing verifiably reliable and secure communications processing systems, *Technical Report ICSCA-CMP-6*, University of Texas at Austin, January 1977.

Good et al. [1979]

D. Good, R. Cohen, and J. Keeton-Williams, "Principles of proving concurrent programs in Gypsy", *Proceedings of 6th Annual Symposium on Principles of Programming Languages*, pages 42-52, January 1979.

Goodenough and Gerhart [1975]

J. B. Goodenough and S. L. Gerhart, "Toward a theory of test data selection", *IEEE Transactions on Software Engineering*, 1(2): 156-73, June 1975.

Grady and Caswell [1987]

R. B. Grady and D. L. Caswell, *Software Metrics: Establishing a Company-wide Program*, Prentice-Hall, Englewood Cliffs, NJ, 1987.

Graham [1989]

D. R. Graham, "Incremental development: review of monolithic life-cycle development models", *Information and Software Technology*, 31(1): 7-20, 1989.

Gries [1976]

D. Gries, "An illustration of current ideas on the derivation of correctness proofs and correct programs", *IEEE Transactions on Software Engineering*, 2(4): 238-44, December 1976.

Gries [1981]

D. Gries, *The Science of Programming*, Springer-Verlag, Berlin-New York, 1981.

Guindon [1988]

R. Guindon, editor, *Cognitive Science and Its Application for Human-Computer Interaction*, Lawrence Erlbaum Associates, Hillsdale, N.J., 1988.

Guttag [1977]

J. Guttag, "Abstract data types and the development of data structures", *Communications of the ACM*, 20(6): 396-404, June 1977.

Guttag and Horning [1983]

J. V. Guttag and J. J. Horning, "An introduction to the Larch shared language", *Proceedings 9th IFIP World Computer Congress* (Paris), pages 809-814, North-Holland, Amsterdam, September 1983.

Guttag and Horning [1986a]

J. V. Guttag and J. J. Horning, "Report on the Larch Shared Language", *Science of Computer Programming*, 6(2): 103-134, March 1986.

Guttag and Horning [1986b]

J. V. Guttag and J. J. Horning, "A Larch shared language handbook", *Science of Computer Programming*, 6(2): 135-157, March 1986.

Guttag et al. [1985a]
     J. Guttag, J. Horning, and J. Wing, "The Larch family of specification
     languages", *IEEE Software*, 2(5): 24-36, September 1985.

Guttag et al. [1985b]
     J. V. Guttag, J. J. Horning, and J. M. Wing, "Larch in five easy pieces",
     Technical Report 5, Digital Systems Research Center, Palo Alto, CA, July
     1985.

Haase [1981]
     V. Haase, "Real-time behavior of programs", *IEEE Transactions on Software
     Engineering*, 7(5): 494-501, September 1981.

Halstead [1977]
     M. H. Halstead, *Elements of Software Science*, North-Holland, Amsterdam,
     1977.

Hamer and Frewin [1982]
     P. G. Hamer and G. D. Frewin, "M. H. Halstead's software science–a critical
     examination", *Proceedings 6th International Conference on Software
     Engineering*, Tokio, 13-16 September 1982, pages 197-205, IEEE Computer
     Society Press, September 1982.

Harel [1988]
     D. Harel, "On visual formalisms", *Communications of the ACM*, 31(5): 514-
     530, May 1988.

Harel et al. [1990]
     D. Harel, H. Lachover, A. Naamad, A. Pnueli, M. Politi, R. Sherman, A.
     Shtull-Trauring, and M. Trakhtenbrot, "STATEMATE: A working
     environment for the development of complex reactive systems", *IEEE
     Transactions on Software Engineering*, 16(4): 403-414, April 1990.

Harrison et al. [1982]
     W. Harrison, K. Magel, R. Kluczny, and A. DeKock, "Applying software
     complexity measures to program maintenance", *IEEE Computer*, 15(9): 65-
     79, September 1982.

Hartson and Hiix [1989]
     R. Hartson and D. Hiix, "Human-computer interface development: concepts
     and systems", *ACM Computing Surveys*, 21(1): 5-92, March 1989.

Hatley and Pirbhai [1987]
     D. Hatley and I. Pirbhai, *Strategies for Real-Time System Specifications*,
     Dorset House, New York, 1987.

Heninger [1980]
     K. L. Heninger, "Specifying software requirements for complex systems: new
     techniques and their application", *IEEE Transactions on Software
     Engineering*, 6(1): 2-13, January 1980.

Henry and Kafura [1981]
     S. Henry and D. Kafura, "Software structure metrics based on information
     flow", *IEEE Transactions on Software Engineering*, 7(5): 510-518,
     September 1981.

Hester et al. [1981]
>   S. D. Hester, D. L. Parnas, and D. F. Utter, "Usign documentation as a
>   software design medium", *Bell Systems Technical Journal*, 60(8): 1941-1977,
>   October 1981.

Hetzel [1984]
>   W. Hetzel, *The Complete Guide to Software Testing*, QED Information
>   Sciences, Wellesley, MA, 1984.

Hoare [1969]
>   C. A. R. Hoare, "An axiomatic basis for computer programming",
>   *Communications of the ACM*, 12(10): 576-580, October 1969.

Hoare [1972]
>   C. A. R. Hoare, "Towards a theory of parallel programming", in C. A. R.
>   Hoare and R. H. Perrott, editors, *Operating Systems Techniques*, Academic
>   Press, New York, 1972.

Hoare [1973]
>   C. A. R. Hoare, "Hints on programming language design", *Annual
>   Symposium on Principles of Programming Languages*, Boston, October 1973.

Hoare [1974]
>   C. A. R. Hoare, "Monitors: an operating system structuring concept",
>   *Communications of the ACM*, 17(10): 549-57, October 1974 (See also
>   Erratum, *Communications of the ACM*, 18(2): 95, February 1975.)

Hoare [1974]
>   C. A. R. Hoare, *Communicating Sequential Processes*, Prentice-Hall
>   International, Hemel Hampstead, 1985.

Hoffman [1989]
>   D. Hoffman, "Practical interface specification", *Software–Practice and
>   Experience*, 19(2): 127-148, February 1989.

Hoffman [1990]
>   D. Hoffman, "On criteria for module interfaces", *IEEE Transactions on
>   Software Engineering*, 16(5): 537-542, May 1990.

HOOD [1989]
>   European Space Agency, Noordwijk, The Netherlands, *HOOD Reference
>   Manual*, Issue 3.0, September 1989.

Horwitz et al. [1989]
>   S. Horwitz, J. Prins, and T. Reps, "Integrating noninterfering versions of
>   programs", *ACM Transactions on Programming Languages and Systems*,
>   11(3): 345-387, July 1989.

Howden [1987]
>   W. E. Howden, *Functional Program Testing*, McGraw-Hill, New York, 1987.

Humphrey [1989]
>   W. S. Humphrey, *Managing the Software Process*, Addison-Wesley,
>   Reading, Mass., 1989.

IEEE [1989]
>   *Software Engineering Standards*, 3rd ed., Institute of Electrical and
>   Electronics Engineers, Catalog No. 1001, 1989.

Jackson [1975]
> M. A. Jackson, *Principles of Program Design*, Academic Press, New York, 1975.

Jackson [1983]
> M. A. Jackson, *System Development*, Prentice-Hall International, London, 1983.

Jalote [1989]
> P. Jalote, "Testing the completeness of specifications", *IEEE Transactions on Software Engineering*, 15(5): 526-531, May 1989.

Jones [1986a]
> C. B. Jones, *Systematic Software Development Using VDM*, Prentice-Hall International, London, 1986.

Jones [1986b]
> C. B. Jones, Program specification and verification in VDM, *NATO Advanced Study Institute on Logic of Programming and Calculi of Discrete Design* (Marktoberdorf, West Germany), pages 149-84, Springer-Verlag, Berlin-New York, August 1986.

Kafura and Reddy [1987]
> D. Kafura and G. R. Reddy, "The use of software complexity metrics in software maintenance", *IEEE Transactions on Software Engineering*, 13(3): 335-343, March 1987.

Kant and Barstow [1981]
> E. Kant and D. R. Barstow, "The refinement paradigm: the interaction of coding and efficiency knowledge in program synthesis", *IEEE Transactions on Software Engineering*, 7(5): 458-471, September 1981.

Kearney et al. [1986]
> J. K. Kearney, R. L. Sedlmeyer, W. B. Thompson, M. A. Gray, and M. A. Adler, "Software complexity measurement", *Communications of the ACM*, 29(11): 1044-1050, November 1986.

Kemmerer [1985]
> R. A. Kemmerer, "Testing formal specifications to detect design errors", *IEEE Transactions on Software Engineering*, 11(1): 32-43, January 1985.

Kemmerer and Eckmann [1985]
> R. A. Kemmerer and S. T. Eckmann, "UNISEX: A UNIX based symbolic interpreter for Pascal", *Software–Practice and Experience*, 15(5): 439-458, May 1985.

Kernighan and Pike [1984]
> B. W. Kernighan and R. Pike, *The UNIX Programming Environment*, Prentice-Hall, Englewood Cliffs, N.J., 1984.

Knuth [1974]
> D. E. Knuth, "Structured programming with goto statements", *Computing Surveys*, 6(4): 261-301, December 1974.

Koontz et al. [1980]
> H. Koontz, C. O'Donnell, and H. Weihrich, *Management*, McGraw-Hill, New York, 1980.

Kroeger [1987]

> F. Kroeger, *Temporal Logics of Programs*, EATCS Monographs on Theoretical Computer Science, Springer-Verlag, New York-Berlin, 1987.

Lamb [1988]

> D. Lamb, *Software Engineering: Planning for Change*, Prentice-Hall, Englewood Cliffs, N.J., 1988.

Lamport [1979]

> L. Lamport, "A new approach to proving the correctness of multiprocess languages", *ACM Transactions on Programming Languages and Systems*, 1(1): 84-97, July 1979.

Lamport [1989]

> L. Lamport, "A simple approach to specifying concurrent systems" *Communications of the ACM*, 32(1): 32-45, January 1989.

Lehman and Belady [1985]

> M. M. Lehman and L. A. Belady, *Program Evolution*, Academic Press, New York, 1985.

Leveson [1986]

> N. G. Leveson, "Software safety: what, why, and how", *ACM Computing Surveys*, 18(2): 125-164, June 1986.

Lientz and Swanson [1980]

> B. P. Lientz and E. B. Swanson, *Software Maintenance Management*, Addison-Wesley, Reading, Mass., 1980.

Linger et al. [1979]

> R. C. Linger, H. D. Mills, and B. I. Witt, *Structured Programming: Theory and Practice,* Addison-Wesley, Reading, Mass., 1979.

Linton et al. [1989]

> M. A. Linton, J. M. Vlissides, and P. R. Calder, "Composing user interfaces with InterViews", *IEEE Computer*, 22(2): 8-22, February 1989.

Liskov [1988]

> B. Liskov, "Distributed programming in Argus", *Communications of the ACM*, 31(3): 300-312, March 1988.

Liskov and Guttag [1986]

> B. Liskov and J. Guttag, *Abstraction and Specification in Program Development*, The MIT Press, Cambridge, Mass., 1986.

Liskov and Zilles [1974]

> B. Liskov and S. N. Zilles, "Programming with abstract data types", *SIGPLAN Notices*, 9(4): 50-60, April 1974.

Liskov and Zilles [1975]

> B. Liskov and S. Zilles, "Specification techniques for data abstraction", in ACM [1975].

Liu and Shyamasundar [1990]

> L. Y. Liu and R. K. Shyamasundar, "Static analysis of real-time distributed systems", *IEEE Transactions on Software Engineering*, 16(4):373-388, April 1990.

Low and Jeffery [1990]
>   G. C. Low and R. Jeffery, "Function points in the estimation and evaluation of the software process", *IEEE Transactions on Software Engineering*, 16(1): 64-71 January 1990.

Luqi and Ketabchi [1988a]
>   Luqi and M. Ketabchi, "A computer aided prototyping system", *IEEE Software*, 22(3): 66-72, March 1988.

Luqi et al. [1988b]
>   Luqi, V. V. Berzins, and R. T. Yeh, "A prototyping language for real time software", *IEEE Transactions on Software Engineering*, 14(10): 1409-1423, October 1988.

Mandrioli and Ghezzi [1987]
>   D. Mandrioli and C. Ghezzi, *Theoretical Foundations of Computer Science*, John Wiley & Sons, New York, 1987.

Mandrioli et al. [1985]
>   D. Mandrioli, R. Zicari, C. Ghezzi, and F. Tisato, "Modeling the Ada task system by Petri Nets", *Computer Languages*, 10(1): 43-61, 1985.

Manna [1974]
>   Z. Manna, *Mathematical Theory of Computation*, McGraw-Hill, New York, 1974.

Manna and Waldinger [1985]
>   Z. Manna and R. Waldinger, *The Logical Basis for Computer Programming*, Addison-Wesley, Reading, Mass., 1985.

Mantei [1981]
>   M. Mantei, "The effect of programming team structures on programming tasks", *Communications of the ACM*, 24(3): 106-113, March 1981.

Mantei and Teorey [1988]
>   M. M. Mantei and T. J. Teorey, "Cost/benefit analysis for incorporating human factors in the software lifecycle", *Communications of the ACM*, 31(4): 428-439, April 1988.

Martin and Leben [1986]
>   J. Martin and J. Leben, *Fourth Generation Languages*, volume 2, Prentice-Hall, Englewood Cliffs, N.J., 1986.

McCabe [1976]
>   T. J. McCabe, "A complexity measure", *IEEE Transactions on Software Engineering*, 2(4): 308-320, December 1976.

McCabe [1983]
>   T. J. McCabe, *Tutorial on Structured Testing*, Catalog number EHO 200-6, IEEE Computer Society Press, 1983.

McCabe and Butler [1989]
>   T. J. McCabe and C. W. Butler, "Design complexity measurement and testing", *Communications of the ACM*, 32(12):1415-1425, December 1989.

McCarthy [1962]
>   J. McCarthy, "Towards a mathematical science of computation", *Proceeding of IFIP*, pages 21-28, 1962.

McCracken and Jackson [1982]

D. D. McCracken and M. A. Jackson, "Life-cycle concept considered harmful", *Software Engineering Notes*, pages 29-32, April 1982.

McDowell and Helmbold [1989]

C. E. McDowell and D. P. Helmbold, "Debugging concurrent programs", *ACM Computing Surveys*, 21(4): 593-622, December 1989.

McLean [1984]

J. McLean, "A formal method for the abstract specification of software", *Journal of the ACM*, 31(3): 600-27, July 1984.

McLean [1990]

J. McLean, "The specification and modeling of computer security", *IEEE Computer*, 23(1): 9-16, January 1990.

Merlin and Farber [1976]

P. Merlin and D. Farber, "Recoverability of Communication Protocols", *IEEE Transactions on Communications*, 24(9): 1036-1043, September 1976.

Meyer [1988]

B. Meyer, *Object-Oriented Software Construction*, Prentice-Hall International, Hemel Hempstead, 1988.

Miles [1984]

D. E. Miles, "Copyrighting computer software after Apple vs. Franklin", *IEEE Software*, 1(2): 84-87, April 1984.

Mills et al. [1987a]

H. D. Mills, V. R. Basili, J. D. Gannon, and R. G. Hamlet, *Principles of Computer Programming: A Mathematical Approach*, Allyn & Bacon, Boston, Mass., 1987.

Mills et al. [1987b]

H. D. Mills, M. Dyer, and R. Linger, "Cleanroom software engineering", *IEEE Software*, 4(5): 19-25, September 1987.

Milner [1980]

R. Milner, A *Calculus of Communicating Systems*, Lecture Notes in Computer Science, volume 92, Springer-Verlag, Berlin-New York, 1980.

Misra and Jalics [1988]

S. Misra and P. Jalics, "Third-generation versus fourth-generation software development", *IEEE Software*, 5(4): 8-14, July 1988.

Moriconi and Hare [1986]

M. Moriconi and D. F. Hare, "The PegaSys system: pictures as formal documentation of large programs", *ACM Transactions on Programming Languages and Systems*, 8(4): 524-456, October 1986.

Musa and Ackermann [1989]

J. D. Musa and A. F. Ackermann, "Quantifying software validation: when to stop testing?", *IEEE Software*, 6(3):19-27, May 1989.

Musa et al. [1987]

J. D. Musa, A. Iannino, and K. Okumoto, *Software Reliability: Measurement, Prediction, Application*, McGraw-Hill, New York, 1987.

Musser [1980]
     D. Musser, "Abstract data type specification in the AFFIRM system", *IEEE Transactions on Software Engineering*, 6(1): 24-32, January 1981.

Myers [1978]
     G. J. Myers, *Composite/Structured Design*, Van Nostrand Reinhold, New York, 1978.

Myers [1979]
     G. J. Myers, *The Art of Software Testing*, John Wiley & Sons, New York, 1979.

Myers [1988]
     B. A. Myers, "A taxonomy of window manager user interfaces", *IEEE Computer Graphics and Applications*, 8(5): 65-84, September 1988.

Nakagawa et al. [1988]
     A. T. Nakagawa, K. Futatsugi, S. Tomura, and T. Shimizu, "Algebraic specification of Macintosh's QuickDraw using OBJ2", *Proceedings 10th International Conference on Software Engineering*, Singapore, April 1988, pages 334-343, IEEE Computer Society Press, April 1988.

Naur et al. [1976]
     P. Naur, B. Randell, and J. Buxton, editors, *Software Engineering: Concepts & Techniques*, Petrocelli/Charter, New York, 1976.

Neumann [1989]
     P. G. Neumann, "RISKS: Cumulative index of Software Engineering Notes", *Software Engineering Notes*, 14(1): 22-26, January 1989.

Norman and Nunamaker [1989]
     R. J. Norman and J. F. Nunamaker, Jr., "CASE productivity perceptions of software engineering professionals", *Communications of the ACM*, 32(9):1102-1108, September 1989.

Ntafos [1988]
     S. C. Ntafos, "A comparison of some structural testing strategies", *IEEE Transactions on Software Engineering*, 14(6): 868-874, June 1988.

Oberndorf [1988]
     P. A. Oberndorf, "The common Ada programming support environment (APSE) interface set (CAIS)", *IEEE Transactions on Software Engineering*, 14(6):742-748, June 1988.

Olender and Osterweil [1990]
     K. M. Olender and L. J. Osterweil, "Cecil: a sequencing constraint language for automatic static analysis generation.", *IEEE Transactions on Software Engineering*, 16(3): 268-280, March 1990.

Osterweil [1981]
     L. J. Osterweil, "Software environment research: directions for the next five years", *IEEE Computer*, 14(4): 35-43, April 1981.

Osterweil [1987]
     L. Osterweil, "Software processes are software too", *Proceedings 9th International Conference on Software Engineering*, Monterey 30 March-2 April 1987, pages 2-13, IEEE Computer Society Press, 1987.

Ostroff [1989]
>   J. S. Ostroff, *Temporal Logic for Real-Time Systems*, John Wiley & Sons, New York, 1989.

Owicki and Gries [1976]
>   S. Owicki and D. Gries, "Verifying properties of parallel programs: an axiomatic approach", *Communications of the ACM*, 19(5): 279-284, May 1976.

Parnas [1972a]
>   D. L. Parnas, "A technique for software module specification with examples", *Communications of the ACM*, 15(5): 330-336, May 1972.

Parnas [1972b]
>   D. L. Parnas, "On the criteria to be used in decomposing systems into modules", *Communications of the ACM*, 15(12): 1053-8, December 1972.

Parnas [1974]
>   D. L. Parnas, "On a buzzword: hierarchical structure", *Proceedings IFIP Congress* (1974), Nort Holland, Amsterdam, 1974.

Parnas [1976]
>   D. L. Parnas, "On the design and development of program families", *IEEE Transactions on Software Engineering*, 2(2): 1-9, March 1976.

Parnas [1977]
>   D. L. Parnas, "The use of precise specifications in the development of software", *Proceedings IFIP* , Toronto, Canada August 1977, pages 861-7, B. Gilchrist, editor, North-Holland, Amsterdam, August 1977.

Parnas [1978]
>   D. L. Parnas, "Some software engineering principles", in *Structured Analysis and Design*, State of the Art Report.INFOTECH International, pages 237-247, 1978.

Parnas [1979]
>   D. L. Parnas, "Designing software for ease of extension and contraction", *IEEE Transactions on Software Engineering*, 5(2):128-138, March 1979.

Parnas [1985]
>   D. L. Parnas, "Software aspects of strategic defense systems", *Communications of the ACM*, 28(12): 1326-35, December 1985.

Parnas [1988]
>   D. L. Parnas, "Why engineers should not use artificial intelligence", *INFOR*, 26(4): 234-246, 1988.

Parnas and Clements [1986]
>   D. L. Parnas and P. C. Clements, "A rational design process: how and why to fake it", *IEEE Transactions on Software Engineering*, 12(2): 251-7, February 1986.

Parnas and Weiss [1987]
>   D. L. Parnas and D. M. Weiss, "Active design reviews: principles and practices", *Journal of Systems and Software*, 7(4): 259-65, December 1987.

Partsch and Steinbruggen [1983]
>   H. Partsch and R. Steinbruggen, "Program transformation systems", *ACM Computing Surveys*, 15(3): 199-236, 1983.

Peterson [1981]
>   J. L. Peterson, *Petri Net Theory and the Modeling of Systems*, Prentice-Hall, Englewood Cliffs, N.J., 1981.

Petri [1962]
>   C. A. Petri, *Kommunikationen Mit Automaten*, PhD thesis, University of Bonn, 1962, PhD dissertation. English translation: Technical Report RADC-TR-65-377, Vol. 1, Suppl 1, Applied Data Research, Princeton, N.J.

Pnueli [1981]
>   A. Pnueli, "The temporal semantics of computer programs", *Theoretical Computer Science* 13, 45-60, 1981.

Pressman [1987]
>   R. S. Pressman, *Software Engineering: A Practitioner's Approach*, McGraw-Hill, New York, 1987.

Pressman [1988]
>   R. S. Pressman, *Making Software Engineering Happen*, Prentice-Hall, Englewood Cliffs, Incorporated, 1988.

Prieto-Diaz and Neighbors [1986]
>   R. Prieto-Diaz and J. M. Neighbors, "Module interconnection languages", *Journal of Systems and Software*, 6: 307-334, 1986.

Reifer [1986]
>   D. J. Reifer, *Tutorial on Software Management*, IEEE Computer Society Press, 1986.

Reisig [1985]
>   W. Reisig, *Petri Nets: An Introduction*, Springer-Verlag, Berlin-New York, 1985.

Rich and Waters [1988]
>   C. Rich and R. C. Waters, "The programmer's apprentice: a research overview", *IEEE Computer*, 21(11): 10-25, November 1988.

Ringwood [1988]
>   G. A. Ringwood, "Parlog86 and the dining logicians", *Communications of the ACM*, 31(1): 10-25, January 1988.

Roman and Cox [1989]
>   G. C. Roman and K. C. Cox, "A declarative approach to visualizing concurrent computations", *IEEE Computer*, 22(10): 25-37, October 1989.

Ross [1977]
>   D. Ross, "Structured analysis (SA): a language for communicating ideas", *IEEE Transactions on Software Engineering*, 3(1): 16-34, January 1977.

Royce [1970]
>   W. W. Royce, Managing the development of large software systems: concepts and techniques, *Proceedings WesCon* , August 1970.

Rubinstein and Hersh [1984]
>   R. Rubinstein and H. Hersh, *The Human Factor: Designing Computer Systems for People*, Digital Press, Bedford, Mass., 1984.

Sanden [1989a]

B. Sanden, "Entity-Life modeling and structured analysis in real-time software design–a comparison", *Communications of the ACM*, 32(12): 1458-1466, December 1989.

Sanden [1989b]

B. Sanden, "The case for eclectic design in real-time software", *IEEE Transactions on Software Engineering*, 15(3): 360-362, March 1989.

Scheifler et al. [1988]

R. W. Scheifler, J. Gettys, and R. Newman, *X Window System-C Library and Protocol Reference*, Digital Press, Bedford, Mass.,1988.

Schmitt [1989]

D. A. Schmitt, *The OS/2 Programming Environment*, Prentice-Hall, Englewood Cliffs, N.J., 1989.

Schneiderman [1987]

B. Schneiderman, *Designing the User Interface*, Addison-Wesley, Reading, Mass., 1987.

Selby et al. [1987]

R. W. Selby, V. R. Basili, and F. T. Baker, "Cleanroom software development: an empirical evaluation", *IEEE Transactions on Software Engineering*, 13(9): 1027-1037, September 1987.

Shatz and Wang [1989]

S. M. Shatz and J.-P. Wang, *Tutorial on Distributed-Software Engineering*, IEEE Computer Society Press, 1989.

Shen et al. [1983]

V. Y. Shen, S. D. Conte, and H. E. Dunsmore, "Software science revisited: a critical analysis of the theory and its empirical support", *IEEE Transactions on Software Engineering*, 9(2): 155-165, March 1983.

Simon [1986]

H. A. Simon, "Whether software engineering needs to be artificially intelligent", *IEEE Transactions on Software Engineering*, 12(7): 726-732, July 1986.

Skillicorn and Glasgow [1989]

D. B. Skillicorn and J. I. Glasgow, "Real-time specifications using Lucid", *IEEE Transactions on Software Engineering*, 15(2): 221-229, February 1989.

Smith [1989]

C. Smith, *Performance Engineering of Software Systems*, Addison-Wesley, Reading, Mass., 1989.

Snyder [1986]

A. Snyder, "Encapsulation and inheritance in object-oriented programming languages", *Object-Oriented Programming Systems, Languages and Applications (OOPSLA) Conference* (November 1986), published also as *SIGPLAN Notices*, 21(11): 38-45, November 1986.

Software [1989a]

Special issue on User Interfaces, published as *IEEE Software*, 6(1), January 1989.

Software [1989b]
>   Special issue on Software Verification and Validation, published as *IEEE Software*, 6(3), May 1989.

Software [1990a]
>   Special issue on Maintenance, Reverse Engineering and Design Recovery, published as *IEEE Software*, 7(1), January 1990.

Software [1990b]
>   Special issue on Metrics, published as *IEEE Software*, 7(2), March 1990.

Software [1990c]
>   Special issue on Tools Fair (May 1990), published as *IEEE Software*, 7(3). May 1990.

Sommerville [1989]
>   I. Sommerville, *Software Engineering* (3rd ed.), Addison-Wesley, Reading, Mass., 1989.

Spector and Gifford [1986b]
>   A. Spector and D. Gifford, "A computer science perspective of bridge design", *Communications of the ACM*, 29(4): 268-283, April 1986.

Spivey [1989]
>   J. Spivey, *The Z Notation–A Reference Manual*, Prentice-Hall, Englewood Cliffs, N.J., 1989.

SPW [1988]
>   *Proceedings of the 4th International Software Process Workshop*, C. Tully, editor, Moretonhampstead, Devon, UK , May 1988, Published as SIGSOFT Software Engineering Notes, 14(4), IEEE Computer Science Press, June 1989.

Stallman [1984]
>   R. Stallman, "EMACS: the extensible, customizable, self-documenting display editor", in D. R. Barstow, H. E. Shrobe, and E. Sandewall, editors, *Interactive programming environments*, pages 300-25, McGraw-Hill, New York, 1984.

Stankovic [1988]
>   J. A. Stankovic, "Misconceptions about real-time computing: A serious problem for next-generation systems", *IEEE Computer*, 21(10): 10-19, October 1988.

Stefik et al. [1983]
>   M. Stefik, D. Bobrow, S. Mittal, and L. Conway, "Knowledge programming in Loops: report on an experimental course", *AI Magazine*, 4(3): 3-13, Fall 1983.

Stefik et al. [1986]
>   M. Stefik, D. Bobrow, and K. Kahn, "Integrating access-oriented programming into a multiparadigm environment.", *IEEE Software*, 3(1):10-18, January 1986.

Stenning [1987]
>   V. Stenning, "On the role of an environment", *Proceedings 9th International Conference on Software Engineering*, Monterey, 30 March-2 April 1987, pages 30-34, IEEE Computer Society Press, 1987.

Sunshine et al. [1982]
C. Sunshine, D. Thompson, R. Erickson, S. Gerhart, and D. Schwabe, "Specification and verification of communication protocols in AFFIRM using state transition models", *IEEE Transactions on Software Engineering*, 8(5): 460-489, July 1982.

Swartout and Balzer [1982]
W. Swartout and R. Balzer, "On the inevitable intertwining of specification and implementation", *Communications of the ACM*, 25(7): 438-440, July 1982.

Tahvanainen and Smolander [1990]
V.-P. Tahvanainen and K. Smolander, "An annotated CASE bibliography", *Software Engineering Notes*, 15(1): 79-92, January 1990.

Tai and Obaid [1986]
K. C. Tai and E. E. Obaid, "Reproducible testing of Ada task programs", *2nd IEEE Int. Conference on Ada Applications and Environments*, April 1986.

Tanenbaum [1987]
A. S. Tanenbaum, *Operating Systems: Design and Implementation*, Prentice-Hall, Englewood Cliffs, N.J., 1987.

Taylor et al. [1988]
R. N. Taylor, F. C. Belz, L. A. Clark, L. Osterweil, R. W. Selby, J. C. Wileden, A. L. Wolf, and M. Young, "Foundations for the Arcadia Environment Architecture", Proceedings of Software Development Environments (SDE3) Boston, November 28-30, 1988); published as *SIGPLAN Notices*, 24(2): 1-13, February 1989.

Teichrow and Hershey [1977]
D. Teichrow and E. Hershey III, "PSL/PSA: a computer aided technique for structured documentation and analysis of information processing systems", *IEEE Transactions on Software Engineering*, 3(1): 41-48, January 1977.

Teitelman and Masinter [1981]
W. Teitelman and L. Masinter, "The INTERLISP programming environment", *IEEE Computer*, 14(4): 25-33, April 1981.

Thomas [1989]
I. Thomas, "PCTE interfaces: supporting tools in software engineering environments", *IEEE Software*, 6(6):15-23, November 1989.

Tichy [1985]
W. F. Tichy, "RCS-a system for version control", *Software–Practice and Experience*, 15(7): 637-654, July 1985.

Tichy [1987]
W. F. Tichy, "What can software engineers learn from AI?", *IEEE Computer*, 20(11): 43-54, November 1987.

Tichy [1989]
W. F. Tichy, "Software configuration management", IEEE Computer Society Press, *Tutorial notes of 11th ICSE*, May 1989.

TSE [1985]
Special issue on Artifical Intelligence and Software Engineering, published as *IEEE Transactions on Software Engineering*, 11(11) 1985.

TSE [1988]
> Special issue on Software Engineering Environment Architectures, published as *IEEE Transactions on Software Engineering*, 14(6) June 1988.

TSE [1990]
> Special issue on Experimental Computer Science, published as *IEEE Transactions on Software Engineering*, 16(2), February 1990.

Ullman [1988]
> J. D. Ullman, *Principles of Database and Knowledge-Base Systems*, volumes 1 and 2, Computer Science Press, Rockville, MD, 1988.

Verner and Tate [1988]
> J. Verner and G. Tate, "Estimating size and effort in fourth generation development", *IEEE Software*, 5(4): 15-22, July 1988.

Walker et al. [1980]
> B. Walker, R. A. Kemmerer, and G. Popek, "Specification and verification of the UCLA Unix security kernel", *Communications of the ACM*, 23(2): 118-131, February 1980.

Ward and Mellor [1985]
> P. T. Ward and S. J. Mellor, *Structured Development for Real-Time Systems*, Yourdon Press, New York, 1985.

Wasserman et al. [1990]
> A. I. Wasserman, P. A. Pircher, and R. J. Muller, "The object-oriented structured design notation for software design representation", *IEEE Computer*, 23(3): 50-63, March 1990.

Wegner [1984]
> P. Wegner, "Capital-intensive software technology", *IEEE Software*, 1(3): 7-46, July 1984.

Wegner [1987]
> P. Wegner, "Dimensions of object-based language design", *Object-Oriented Programming Systems, Languages and Applications (OOPSLA) Conference*; published as *SIGPLAN Notices*, 22(12): 168-82, December 1987.

Weihl [1989]
> W. E. Weihl "Local atomicity properties: modular concurrency control for abstract data types", *ACM Transactions on Programming Languages and Systems*, 11(2): 249-282, April 1989.

Weinberg [1971]
> G. M. Weinberg, *The Psychology of Computer Programming*, Van Nostrand Reinhold, New York, 1971.

Weinberg and Schulmen [1974]
> G. M. Weinberg and E. L. Schulman, "Goals and performance in computer programming", *Human Factors*, 16(1): 70-77, 1974.

Whiddett [1987]
> D. Whiddett, *Concurrent Programming for Software Engineers*, Ellis Horwood, 1987.

White [1987]
> L. J. White, "Software testing and verification", in M. C. Yovits, editor, *Advances in computers*, pages 337-91, Academic Press, New York, 1987.

Wiest and Levy [1977]
> J. D. Wiest and F. K. Levy, *A Management Guide to PERT/CPM*, Prentice-Hall, Englewood Cliffs, N.J., 1977.

Wilkstrom [1987]
> A. Wilkstrom, *Functional Programming Using Standard ML*, Prentice-Hall International, Hemel Hempstead, 1987.

Wing and Nixon [1989]
> J. M. Wing and M. R. Nixon, "Extending Ina Jo with temporal logic", *IEEE Transactions on Software Engineering*, 15(2): 181-97, February 1989.

Wirth [1971]
> N. Wirth, "Program development by stepwise refinement", *Communications of the ACM*, 14(4): 221-227, April 1971.

Wirth [1977]
> N. Wirth, "Towards a discipline of real-time programming", *Communications of the ACM*, 20(8): 577-583, August 1977.

Wirth [1983]
> N. Wirth, *Programming in Modula-2*, 2nd edition, Springer-Verlag, Berlin-New York, 1983.

Wong [1984]
> C. Wong, "A successful software development", *IEEE Transactions on Software Engineering*, 10(6): 714-727, November 1984.

Yadav et al. [1988]
> S. B. Yadav, R. R. Bravocco, A. T. Chatfield, and T. M. Rajkumar, "Comparison of analysis techniques for inoformation requirement determination", *Communications of the ACM*, 31(9): 1090-1097, September 1988.

Yau and Tsai [1986]
> S. S. Yau and J. J. P. Tsai., "A survey of software design techniques", *IEEE Transactions on Software Engineering*, 12(6): 713-721, June 1986.

Young [1989]
> D. A. Young, *X Window Systems-Programming and Applications with Xt*, Prentice-Hall, Englewood Cliffs, N.J., 1989.

Young and Taylor [1988]
> M. Young and R. M. Taylor, "Combining static analysis with symbolic execution", *IEEE Transactions on Software Engineering*, 14(10): 1499-1511, October 1988.

Young and Taylor [1989]
> M. Young and R. N. Taylor, "Rethinking the taxonomy of fault detection techniques", *Proceedings 11th International Conference on Software Engineering*, Pisstburgh, 15-18 May 1989, pages 53-63, IEEE Computer Society Press, 1989.

Young et al. [1988]
> M. Young, R. N. Taylor, and D. B. Troup, "Software environment architectures and user interface facilities", *IEEE Transactions on Software Engineering*, 14(6): 697-708, June 1988.

Yourdon and Constantine[1979]
> E. Yourdon and L. Constantine, *Structured Design*, Prentice-Hall, Englewood Cliffs, N.J., 1979.

Zave [1982]
> P. Zave, "An operational approach to requirements specification for embedded systems", *IEEE Transactions on Software Engineering*, 18(3): 250-269, May 1982.

Zave [1984]
> P. Zave, "The operational versus the conventional approach to software development", *Communications of the ACM*, 27(2):104-118, February 1984.

Zave and Schell [1986]
> P. Zave and W. Schell, "Salient features of an executable specification language and its environment", *IEEE Transactions on Software Engineering*, 12(2): 312-325, February 1986.

Zeil [1989]
> S. J. Zeil., "Perturbation techniques for detecting domain errors", *IEEE Transactions on Software Engineering*, 15(6):737-746, June 1989.

Index